GOD
AND ISRAEL

GOD AND ISRAEL

THE CHOSEN PEOPLE, THE HOLY NATION, AND THE PROMISED LAND

John D. Garr, Ph.D.

God and Israel: The Chosen People, the Holy Nation, and the Promised Land
© 2016 by John D. Garr

Published by Golden Key Press
P.O. Box 421218, Atlanta, GA 30342
www.GoldenKeyPress.org

Design and typeset: Resolute Creative, Inc., Houston, TX
Printed in the United States of America

Unless otherwise indicated, Scripture quotations are from the New American Standard Bible.

ISBN: 978-1-940685-31-1
Kindle ISBN: 978-1-940685-33-5
ePub ISBN: 978-1-940685-32-8

1. The People of Israel. 2. The Nation of Israel. 3. The Land of Israel. 4. Christian-Jewish Relations. 5. Covenants. 6. Antisemitism. 7. Zionism. I. Garr, John D. II. God and Israel

Library of Congress Control Number: 2015913564
        BT93-93.6 2015
        Religion, Christianity, Judaism, History

DEFINITIONS AND ABBREVIATIONS

Word Definitions:

Definitions of English words are from www.Dictionary.com. Definitions of words in other languages are taken from either www.Dictionary.com. or www.WordReference.com.

Hebrew Word Definitions:

Unless otherwise noted, all Hebrew word definitions are from one of the following: Wilhelm Gesenius, *Hebrew and Chaldee Lexicon of the Old Testament* (Andover, MA: Flagg and Gould, 1824); Francis Brown, S.R. Driver, and Charles A. Briggs, *Hebrew and English Lexicon* (Peabody, MA: Hendrickson Publishers, 1996); Ludwig Koehler, Walter Baumgartner, and Johann Jakob Stramm, *Hebrew and Aramaic Lexicon of the Old Testament*, tr. M.E.J. Richardson (Leiden: Brill Academic, 1994); William Lee Holladay, *Hebrew and Aramaic Lexicon of the Old Testament* (Leiden, E.J. Brill, 1988); or R. Laird Harris, Gleason L. Archer, Jr., and Bruce K. Waltke, eds., *Theological Wordbook of the Old Testament* (Chicago: Moody Press, 1980).

Greek Word Definitions:

Unless otherwise noted, all Greek word definitions are from one of the following: Timothy Friberg, Barbara Friberg, and Neva Miller, *Analytical Lexicon of the Greek New Testament* (Grand Rapids, MI: Baker Books, 2000); Barclay M. Newman, *Greek-English Dictionary* (Reading, UK: United Bible Societies, 2006); Walter Bauer and Fredrick William Danker, *Greek-English Lexicon of the New Testament and Other Early Christian Literature* (Chicago: The University of Chicago Press, 2001); H. G. Lidell and Robert Scott, *Abridged Greek-English Lexicon* (New York: Oxford University Press, 1935); Joseph Thayer, *Thayer's Greek-English Lexicon of the New Testament* (Peabody, MA: Hendrickson Publishers, 1996); or Johan Lust, Erik Eynikel, and Katrin Hauspie, *A Greek-English Lexicon of the Septuagint* (Peabody, MA: Hendrickson Publishers, 2008).

Scripture Versions:
Unless otherwise noted, quotations of Scripture are taken from the New American Standard Bible (1995).

Scripture Version Abbreviations:
ABPE: Aramaic Bible in Plain English (2007)
AJWS: American Jewish World Service (2010)
BBE: The Bible in Basic English (1964)
CEV: Contemporary English Version (1991)
CJB: Complete Jewish Bible (1998)
DBT: Darby Bible Translation (1890)
Douay-Rheims Bible (1899)
ERV: English Revised Version (1894)
ESV: English Standard Version (2007)
HCSB: Holman Christian Standard Bible (2004)
ISV: International Standard Version (1998)
KJV: Authorized King James Version (1611)
NIV: New International Version (1984)
NASB: New American Standard Bible (1995)
NAU: New American Standard Version (Updated) (1995)
NJB: New Jerusalem Bible (1985)
NET: NET Bible (2005)
NKJV: New King James Version (1982)
NLT: New Living Translation (1996)
NRSV: New Revised Standard Version (1989)
JPS: Jewish Publication Society Version (1917)
TNK: *Tanakh*, JPS *Tanakh* (1985)
WBT: Webster's Bible Translation (1833)
WEB: World English Bible (1901)
WNT: Weymouth New Testament (1903)

*To our treasured friends, Zvi and Ditza Zachor,
Israeli Sabras who have generously shared
their generational heritage in the Holy Land
by extending gracious love to us and
to all people, Jew and Gentile alike,
including some of the most challenged
and vulnerable members of society.*

CONTENTS

INTRODUCTION

This volume represents insights that I have gained from more than fifty years of research, scriptural analysis, and meditation on God's historical and continuing relationship with Israel and the Jewish people. I have always been amazed that so many Christians who profess to love Jesus have been, and continue to be, either apathetic or downright antipathetic toward Israel and the Jews. It is simply unfathomable to me that those who, by their own self-definition as "Christians" seek to be "like Christ," could possibly not wish to identify themselves with the nation and land which Jesus called home and with the one people from whom he received his incarnational identity and with whom he identified throughout his lifetime. Moreover, it is also a mystery to me why Christians generally have no mental or emotional connection with Judaism when it was the religion that Jesus affirmed, practiced, and never denied! Christians must face the historical and theological reality: Jesus was a Jew, and his religion was Judaism—and he never changed his ethnicity or his religion.

Every Christian should have both strong feelings for and strong identification with Israel because, they have escaped the realm of darkness and have been translated into the kingdom of God's Son through their faith in Jesus.[1] Because they have experienced this profound transformation, they are "no longer excluded from citizenship in Israel," and they are no longer "foreigners to the covenants of promise."[2] Instead, they are "fellow citizens with God's people and members of his family."[3] If Christians are not excluded from citizenship in Israel and, indeed, share enfranchisement in the commonwealth of God's chosen nation, then it is only logical that they should have a strong sense of patriotism for the nation and of loyalty to the people whom they have joined as naturalized

---

[1] Colossians 1:13.
[2] Ephesians 2:12, NIV.
[3] Ephesians 2:19, NIV, CJB.

citizens and to the family tree into which they have been grafted.[4] From the Apostolic Scriptures, Christians understand that because of their faith in Jesus, they are "Abraham's children," and, as such, they are also spiritual heirs of the promises that God made to Abraham concerning his natural progeny.[5] To anyone who knows the story of Abraham, this understanding is beyond dispute, for God promised Abraham that "all the nations of the earth would be blessed" in and through him.[6] Since the promises of the Abrahamic covenant include peoplehood, nationhood, and land, Christians should be proud of their spiritual heritage that has included them in the "people of God" and has made them a "holy nation."[7] And, they should take pride in the people, the nation, and the land to whom Abraham's covenant first pertained and still pertains.

While some of the issues regarding the state of Israel and the land of Israel are complicated—even for Jews around the world and for Israeli citizens themselves—one thing is simple: the Jewish people have an inalienable right to their own nation with the power of self-determination, free from any outside coercion, whether it be political, economic, or religious. And this right of corporate sovereignty is legitimately expressed in the moral and legal prerogative that the Jewish people have to inhabit their own land—the land which their ancestors have called home for four thousand years—as a place where they can enjoy life and liberty in security and peace. These are simple rights that all Christians everywhere understand and seek to enjoy in whatever circumstance they find themselves. They should, therefore, be passionate to see the same rights achieved and maintained by the Jewish people.

Time for Restoration

The very fact that a volume such as this is needed to underscore for Christians the historical and theological connection that they have with the people, nation, and land of Israel is testimony to the fact that the church has been ripped from its moorings in the safe harbor of Hebraic truth and set adrift in a maelstrom of non-biblical, man-made teachings and practices. Likewise, the very fact that scholarly investigation and discourse about the historical connections between Christianity and Judaism exists in our time is testimony to the tragic historical loss of Christianity's Jewish connection. In fact, Christianity's greatest tragedy had been its effort, both conscious and subconscious, to divorce itself from the Jewish matrix from

---

[4] Romans 11:17.
[5] Galatians 3:29.
[6] Genesis 18:18.
[7] 1 Peter 2:9–10.

which it was born two millennia ago. The time has come for Christians to make extensive, even exhaustive, efforts to return to that matrix so that they can recover the missing link of their faith—its Jewish connection. Indeed, it is time for restoration of all things, a worldwide effort to bring the church back to its biblical—and, therefore, Hebraic—foundations. Christians desperately need to recover their lost legacy, the Jewish faith of Jesus and the apostles. This is the time for renewal of the Jewish roots of the Christian faith so that all Christians can reconnect personally with the Jewish Jesus and the Jewish faith which he extended to all humanity. As Edward Flannery so wisely and succinctly said, today's "over-Hellenized, over-Latinized Christian church needs a re-Judaization process in order to return it to its original ideal."[8]

This is also the day for "rapprochement between Jews and Christians, a time of mutual acceptance and even cooperation."[9] It is time for Christians around the world to come alongside the Jewish community as partners in biblical faith. The estranged siblings, Judaism and Christianity, should be reconciled to one another through mutual acceptance and affirmation. Since historical Christianity was largely responsible for the proto-schism that produced the ever-widening divide between church and synagogue, Christians should seize the moment and make bold initiatives for repentance and restitution, for renewal and restoration. These efforts should include both affirmation of the international Jewish community and support for the nation of the Jews, Israel.

Appreciation

I wish to express my thanks to a number of friends, colleagues, and advisers who have shared insights with me and have inspired me with their wisdom. Foremost among these are Dr. Marvin R. Wilson, Dwight A. Pryor (of blessed memory), Rev. Isaac Rottenberg (of blessed memory), Dr. Karl D. Coke, Dr. DeWayne Coxon, Dr. Richard Booker, Dr. Brad H. Young, and Dr. Jacques B. Doukhan. I wish to thank my Hebraic Heritage Christian College colleague Dr. Robert Bleakney for his careful and constructive critique of the manuscript of this book. I am also grateful for review and feedback from Dr. Victoria Sarvadi, Judy Grehan, and Kate Miller, not to speak of a number of other friends and colleagues who have read and

---

[8] Edward Flannery, quoted George Cornell, "The Church after Jesus Loses His Jewish Context," Fredericksburg, VA *Free Lance-Star*, Friday, March 28, 1975, p. 16.
[9] Harold Earl Quinley and Charles Young Glock, *Anti-Semitism in America* (New Brunswick, NJ: Transaction Publishers, 1983), p. 94.

commented on the manuscript. Finally, I am grateful for the questions, comments, and suggestions that I receive from friends and colleagues around the world as we together explore the Jewish roots of our Christian faith and seek to find ways in which we can lend loving support to the international Jewish community and the nation of Israel in what continue to be trying times.

A New Day

The encouraging news is that significant things are happening in the advancement of the vision for restoration and renewal in the Christian church. This is a grassroots movement that has no international leader, which is the way it should be. The internationality of the Hebraic roots movement is testimony not only to the synchronization of knowledge but also to the agency of the Holy Spirit who has released insight into the world and is nurturing that insight in the hearts and minds of even isolated believers in remote areas. This is truly a transdenominational, multiethnic work that is advancing a cause that has been long overdue. As with every movement, this one has its extremists; however, a solid core of balanced scholarship exists that is being used to give foundational insight into this work and to speak of its short-term and long-term benefits.

As you read this book, I pray that you will be invigorated with a new understanding of all the wide-ranging implications concerning Israel that are found in the Hebrew Scriptures, in Rabbinic Literature, and in the Apostolic Writings. If you are a Christian, I hope that you will gain a greater appreciation for the Chosen People alongside of whom you have come by being initiated into Christian faith. At the same time, I hope that you will receive new-found biblical value for the land and the Holy City where God placed his name and assigned his honor. If you are Jewish, I hope that you will recognize that solid support for Israel and the international Jewish community exists within the Christian church, especially among those who understand that their Christian faith is "from the Jews," as Jesus himself so graciously said.[10]

May God bless you and keep you in his grace, empowering you to "prosper and be in health even as your soul prospers."[11]

Shalom & Blessings!
John D. Garr, Ph.D.
Pesach, 2016

---

[10] John 4:22.
[11] 3 John 1:2.

PROLOGUE

Viewpoints on the people, the nation, and the land of Israel have long been diverse and, in many cases, bitterly contested. On the one hand, outright revulsion, loathing, contempt, and antipathy for Israel have characterized virtually all the antisemites of history, who have considered the people of Israel to be essentially a subhuman species, the nation of Israel to be a complete illegitimacy, and the land of Israel to be an utterly inconsequential piece of worthless real estate. Then, on the other hand, admiration, esteem, adoration, and even veneration for Israel have been representative of many who have championed the promises of Holy Scripture regarding the Jews, their nation, and their land, despite the fact that many romanticized views about Israel, particularly about the nation and the land,[1] have been based on constantly shifting eschatological scenarios.[2] In the middle ground between the extremes, those who have not known what to think about the Chosen People, their nation, and their land, or simply have not cared about either, have best been distinguished by bewilderment, confusion, and ambivalence.

Why does such tension and disputation about the people, the nation, and the land of Israel exist? Why does such vitriol exist on the one hand and such veneration on the other? Why has a tiny sliver of the world population—18

---

[1] H. G. Kippenberg, "Reading Religious Violence in Terms of Theories of Social Action," in *Control of Violence: Historical and International Perspectives on Violence in Modern Societies*, Wilhelm Heitmeyer, Heinz-Gerhard Haupt, and Stefan Malthaner, eds. (New York: Springer Science+Business Media, 2011), p. 155.

[2] Thomas S. Kidd, *American Christians and Islam: Evangelical Culture and Muslims from the Colonial Period to the Age of Terrorism* (Princeton, NJ: Princeton University Press, 2009), p. 93. Kidd says that non-dispensationalist theologians have lamented the fact that many eschatological views relate the "anti-Christ . . . to the political powers of the day." Kidd's observation that "as the news changed, so did the eschatological scenarios" has been all too true, as endless successions of world leaders have been assigned to specific roles in such scenarios, making some of them seem like true phantasmagorias. Sadly, when the dramas that such speculators have predicted have not come to pass, their creators have merely moved on to find another cast of characters to serve in their interests.

million today[3]—been so controversial for so long? Why does such a small nation of only 7.125 million people continue to be such a cause cèlébre—for some a pariah, for others a luminary?[4] Why has such a minuscule land mass of less than 11,000 square miles—a mere scintilla of the surface of Planet Earth[5]—continued to be a focal point of world controversy, century after century, decade after decade, year after year, day after day? Why, indeed, do the most ancient of historical observations about the people, the nation, and the land of Israel still echo in the unending news and commentary reported by today's print and electronic media? Amazingly, the same things that were spoken and written about Israel centuries ago will doubtlessly reverberate in tomorrow's headlines, breaking news bulletins and editorials!

The Delegitimization of Israel

For millennia, concerted efforts have been made to marginalize the Jews and to delegitimize their right to exist as a people or a nation—and in their own land. The very first record of an orchestrated attempt at the genocide of the Jewish people[6] focused on just such delegitimization: "There is a certain people, scattered and dispersed among the other peoples in all the provinces of your realm whose laws are different from those of any other people and who do not obey the king's laws; and it is not in Your Majesty's interest to tolerate them."[7] This was the advice of Haman, the prime minister of Persia, to his king, Xerxes. In expressing his personal animus for the Jews in that realm, however, Haman was actually demonstrating his hatred for the God of the Jews. The contempt that seethed in his heart and the political machinations that his anger produced have become hallmarks for countless anti-semites across the pages of history who have also sought to delegitimize and destroy the Jews. This people has been singled out for marginalization, persecution, violence, mayhem, and murder simply because they have been "different." And their primary difference from others has been manifest in their belief sys-

---

[3] All the Jewish people in the world today (18.4374 million) represent only .25877% of the global population (7.125 billion).

[4] The Jewish citizens of Israel (6 million) represent only .08421% of the world population. The total citizenship of Israel (8.59 million) comprises only .12056% of the world population (7.125 billion).

[5] The present land mass of Israel (10,750 square miles) is .043623% of the inhabitable land mass of the earth (24,642,757 square miles) or .018659% of the total land mass of the earth (57,308,738 square miles).

[6] It could be argued that Pharaoh's order for the murder of the Israelite male infants was the first attempt at Jewish genocide; however, Pharaoh's order was designed for population control, not genocide.

[7] Esther 3:8, TNK, emphasis added.

tem, for they have worshipped the one and only God, and they have refused to syncretize their faith with that of their neighbors or their conquerors.

The same dynamic that manifest itself in Xerxes' court also confronted the prophet Daniel as he encountered political intrigue that unfolded in the court of Darius the Mede: "The administrators and satraps tried to find grounds for charges against Daniel in his conduct of government affairs, but they were unable to do so . . . [for] he was neither corrupt nor negligent. Finally these men said, 'We will never find any basis for charges against this man Daniel unless it has something to do with the law of his God.'"[8] And so they proceeded to draft a plan that would discredit Daniel by attacking his God,[9] a plan in which they identified the uniqueness of the prophet's faith and devised means for discrediting it within their traditions.

At bottom, then, efforts to delegitimize Israel as a people, a nation, and a land are anchored, either consciously or subconsciously, in a desire to delegitimize the God of the Jews. Antisemitism—hatred of the Jews—is rooted in hatred of the God of the Jews. "Strictly speaking, anti-Semitism is not reducible to Jew hatred, although that is where it finds its most immediate and most venomous expression. Anti-Semitism is God hatred and human hatred."[10] Antisemitism, therefore, is an attempt at deicide. As David Patterson has said, "Killing the God of Abraham requires killing the children of Abraham."[11] This is why Pharaoh said, "It is not only against the Jews whom this war is directed. It is against their God Himself!"[12] Richard Rubenstein was right when he spoke of the reason for God-hatred in the pagan mind: "Had we but the power, we would murder God, for we will never cease to be tempted by Ivan Karamazov's demonic fantasy that if God were dead, all things would be permitted."[13] Immanuel Kant went so far as to suggest that "the euthanasia of Judaism [produces] the pure moral religion freed from all ancient statutory teachings,"[14] and thereby answers the Jewish Question.[15]

---

8 Daniel 6:4–5, NIV.

9 Daniel 6:7–24. The jealous satraps attacked Daniel's faithfulness to the hours of prayer in Jewish tradition.

10 David Patterson, *Anti-Semitism and Its Metaphysical Origins* (Cambridge, UK: Cambridge University Press, 2015), p. 24.

11 David Patterson, *Anti-Semitism*, p. 17.

12 *Midrash HaGadol* 14, in Moshe Weissman, ed., *The Midrash Says* (Brooklyn, NY: Bnay Yakov Publications, 1980), vol. 2, p. 121.

13 Richard L. Rubenstein, *After Auschwitz: History, Theology, and Contemporary Judaism* (Baltimore, MD: Johns Hopkins University Press, 1992), p. 23.

14 Immanuel Kant, *Grounding for the Metaphysics of Morals*, tr. James W. Ellington (Indianapolis, IN: Hackett, 1981), p. 30.

15 Steven B. Smith, *Spinoza, Liberalism, and the Question of Jewish Identity* (New Haven, CT: Yale University Press, 1997), p. 185.

This is why antisemitism differs from all other forms of hatred. Robert Wistrich identifies the core issue: "The sacral, quasi-metaphysical quality of anti-Semitism is singularly absent in other cases."[16] Thomas Torrance said it well: "The story of Israel reveals a people hated by other nations because Israel's life bore witness to divine prohibitions among the Gentiles."[17] The apostle Paul summed up this phenomenon when he said, "The mindset of the flesh is hostile toward God; for it does not subject itself to the law of God, for it is not even able to do so."[18] Whether it is humanist, secularist, or pagan, the heart of godless man despises God. And because it does, it also hates Israel—the one people, the one nation, and the one land that stands for and bears witness to the one and only true God. The absolute ethics that God demands in Scripture and through his Chosen People are an affront to the "freedom" and "self-actualization" of the postmodern humanist today just as they have been for the pagans and secularists of the past. Like it or not, Israel as a whole represents God, and the Scriptures of Israel still speak for God, even when the Jewish people may not faithfully follow the instructions of the Torah.

Despite the record and witness of history and the truth that the Hebrew Scriptures confirm, many scholars—among them Christians, Jews, Muslims, and secularists—openly question the historicity of the people, the nation, and the land of Israel.[19] Nothing about the Jews, it seems, can be accorded a modicum of legitimacy. Though stories about the "perfidious Jews" have long endured,[20] they have for centuries consistently been

---

[16] Robert Wistrich, *A Lethal Obsession: Anti-Semitism from Antiquity to the Global Jihad* (New York: Random House, 2010), p. 588.

[17] Thomas Forsyth Torrance, *The Mediation of Christ* (Grand Rapids, MI: Wm. B. Eerdmans Publishing Co., 1984), pp. 7ff.

[18] Romans 8:7.

[19] The effort to delegitimize the history of Israel as a people began with the Enlightenment and became a feature of eighteenth and nineteenth-century German scholarship, including Christian scholarship.

[20] For centuries, during the Good Friday services of the Western Church, prayer was offered for "the perfidious Jews." The Latin word *perfideles*, from which the term *perfidious* was derived, actually means "unfaithful" or "half-believers," as contrasted with the *fideles*, "believers." Eugene Fisher and Dennis McManus point out, however, that "the theological polemics of Christian teaching against Judaism gradually drew out of the Latin word *perfidii* its modern connotations of treachery," constantly reinforcing the notion that the Jewish people were inherently evil. See Eugene J. Fisher and Dennis D. McManus, "Good Friday Prayer for the Perfidious Jews," in *A Dictionary of Jewish-Christian Relations*, Edward Kessler and Neil Wenborn, eds. (Cambridge, UK: Cambridge University Press, 2005), p. 171. For expansive insight into the extremes to which the idea of the "Perfidious Jews" was taken in history, see Mary C. Boys, *Redeeming Our Sacred Story: The Death of Jesus and Relations between Jews and Christians* (Mahwah, NJ: Paulist Press, 2013).

denied definition as a "people." In the middle of the third century AD, Cyprian said, "Now the peoplehood of the Jews has been canceled; the destruction of Jerusalem was a judgement upon them; the gentiles rather than the Jews inherit the kingdom."[21] Susan Nowak observes that from that time, "the crime of the Jewish people is so great that it annuls, repeals, rescinds the very identity of the Jewish people: to be *Klal Yisrael*, the Chosen People of God, a light to the nations sent to bring all peoples to the Covenant. Without appeal, without reconsideration, the Jews are placed *outside the norms of human relationship.*"[22] As Harry Cargas has noted, this statement was "used to justify the intimidation and even slaughter of Jews for seventeen centuries."[23] When any people group can be viewed as virtually subhuman, it becomes only a matter of time before calls for its eradication are raised.

Though historical documentation confirms the existence of the Jewish nation,[24] the Jews are denied recognition as a historical nation, and their claim to nationhood today is considered by many to be illegitimate.[25] And although there is undeniable physical and historical evidence to support the Jewish right to a land,[26] the "Jewish state" in Palestine is considered an aberration, an anomaly[27] that emerged from the evil machinations of Jews who

---

[21] Cyprian, quoted in Franklin Littell, *The Crucifixion of the Jews* (Macon, GA: Mercer University Press, 1986), pp. 27–28. For further analysis, see Leonard P. Zakim, *Confronting Anti-semitism: A Practical Guide* (Hoboken, NJ: KTAV Publishing House, 2000), p. 97, and Padraic O'Hare, *The Enduring Covenant: The Education of Christians and the End of Antisemitism* (Valley Forge, PA: Trinity Press International, 1997), p. 20.

[22] See Susan Nowak, *Christianity's Original Sin: Anti-Judaism,* posted at www.holocaustroad.org., author's emphasis.

[23] Harry J. Cargas, *Holocaust Scholars Write to the Vatican* (Westport, CT: Greenwood Publishing Group, 1998), p. 6.

[24] An Egyptian stele from the thirteenth century BC reads, ". . . carried off is Askelon; seized upon is Gezer; Yanoam is made as that which does not exist; Israel is laid waste, his seed is not. . . ." Archaeological evidence, therefore, supports the fact that shortly after the biblical account of the Israelite conquest of the land of Canaan, "Israel" experienced an invasion by Egypt. See Naomi E. Pasachoff and Robert Pittman, *A Concise History of the Jewish People* (Lanham, MD: Rowman & Littlefield Publishers, 1995), p. 14.

[25] Alan M. Dershowitz, "Countering Challenges to Israel's Legitimacy," in *Israel's Rights as a Nation-State in International Diplomacy,* Alan Baker, ed. (Jerusalem, Israel: World Jewish Congress, 2011), pp. 159–167.

[26] Haim Hillel Ben-Sasson, *A History of the Jewish People* (Cambridge, MA: Harvard University Press, 1976), pp. 315–316. Also Rachel Hachlili, *Ancient Jewish Art and Archaeology in the Land of Israel* (Leiden, The Netherlands: E. J. Brill, 1988), p. 234–235; K. L. Noll, *Canaan and Israel in Antiquity: An Introduction* (New York: Sheffield Academic Press, 2001), p. 312; David Biale, *Power & Powerlessness in Jewish History* (New York: Schocken Books, 1986), p. 11; and Gordon K. Oeste, *Legitimacy, Illegitimacy, and the Right to Rule: Windows on Abimelech's Rise and Demise in Judges 9* (London, UK: T & T Clark International, 2011), pp. 215–217.

[27] Yehoshafat Harkabi, *Arab Attitudes to Israel* (Jerusalem, Israel: Keter Publishing House, 1972), p. 72. Harkabi notes that "Israel is only an anomaly and an aberration [that] is dubbed 'an artificial state' or 'an exceptional situation.'"

wished to escape their heritage as the forever-doomed wanderers of the earth[28] who deserved no sovereignty, no fixed dwelling place, no land of their own.[29] In history, therefore, the Jews were totally disenfranchised, judged unworthy of any of the basic human rights that all people require and deserve.

The Delegitimized People: Scholars, politicians, and pundits have often argued that the biblical stories of Abraham, Isaac, Jacob, Moses, David, and Solomon are nothing more than myths that were created by sages in Second-Temple Judea in order to establish at least a modicum of legitimacy to the Jewish claim to nationhood and to the land of Israel.[30] While the Jewish historian Shlomo Sand does not deny the right of modern Israelis "to live in a democratic, open, and inclusive state of Israel that belongs to all its citizens,"[31] he argues that there was no such thing as "a Jewish people scattered across the world," just as "five hundred years ago, there was no French people, no more than there was an Italian or Vietnamese people."[32] He even counters the argument of many scholars that the "Jewish people" actually came to exist in the second-century BC by saying that the Hasmonean Kingdom of that time "in no way amounted to a nation, and we can seriously question whether it can be defined as a people."[33] Sand joins a chorus of scholars who trumpet the claim that Jewish attribution of a centuries-old history to the people of

[28] Sam Harris, *The End of Faith: Religion, Terror, and the Future of Reason* (New York: W. W. Norton & Co., 2004), p. 97. Harris notes that based on Augustine's argument, the Jews were "doomed to wander the earth bearing witness to the truth of scripture and the salvation of the gentiles. The suffering and servitude of the Jews was proof that Christ had been the messiah after all."

[29] Sadly, in history, many of the Jews themselves came to believe that they were exiled from their land because of their sins. As Stephen Wylen says, "The nations had their own reasons for oppressing the Jews, but the Jews themselves agreed that they deserved no more than to be treated as homeless exiles." Stephen M. Wylen, *Settings of Silver: An Introduction to Judaism* (Mahwah, NJ: Paulist Press, 2000), p. 167.

[30] Baruch Kimmerling, *The Invention and Decline of Israeliness: State, Society, and the Military* (Berkeley, CA: The University of California Press, 2001); David Ohana, *The Origins of Israeli Mythology: Neither Canaanites Nor Crusaders* (Cambridge, UK: Cambridge University Press, 2012); Virginia Tilley, *The One-State Solution: A Breakthrough for Peace in the Israeli-Palestinian Deadlock* (Ann Arbor, MI: The University of Michigan Press, 2005); Raphael Patai and Jennifer Patai, *The Myth of the Jewish Race* (Detroit, MI: Wayne State University Press, 1975); Nachman Ben-Yehudi, *Masada Myth: Collective Memory and Mythmaking in Israel* (Madison, WI: The University of Wisconsin Press, 1995); and S. Daniel Breslauer, *The Seductiveness of Jewish Myth: Challenge or Response?* (Albany, NY: The State University of New York Press, 1997).

[31] Shlomo Sand, *The Invention of the Land of Israel: From Holy Land to Homeland*, tr. Jeremy Forman (London, UK: Verso Books, 2012), p.17.

[32] Sand, *The Invention of the Jewish People*, tr. Yale Lotan (London, UK: Verso Books, 2009) p. 316.

[33] Sand, *Invention of the Jewish People*, p. 317.

Israel is utterly illegitimate nonsense, a contrived effort to establish and maintain power in the Middle East.

The Delegitimized State: Other scholars have sought to delegitimize Jewish claims to recognition as a "Jewish state" based on their historical nationhood from the beginning of the unified Davidic Kingdom in the tenth century BC until the Roman diaspora after the Bar Kokhba revolt in the second century AD.[34] Niels Peter Lemche says, "The Israelite nation . . . is a highly ideological construct created by ancient scholars of Jewish tradition in order to legitimize their own religious community and its religio-political claims on land and religious exclusivity."[35] Sand agrees, maintaining that Zionist "historians" in the early twentieth century created the myth that "the people of Israel . . . became a nation issuing from the seed of Abraham" and that they did so because "Zionist colonization could certainly not have been undertaken without an ideological preparation that gave rise to the blossoming and crystallization of myths."[36] Sand, therefore, applauds the science of modern archaeology for debunking the historicity of an "Exodus from Egypt" and for proving that "the great, unified monarchy of David and Solomon never existed."[37]

Interestingly, scholars who had long endeavored to disprove biblical stories about the Israelite monarchy based on what they perceived as an absence of archaeological evidence for its existence recoiled in shock when Israeli archaeologists digging at Tel Dan near the northern border of Israel in 1993-94 uncovered a ninth-century BC stele inscribed with the Hebrew words בית דוד (*Beit David*). Since steles were tall stone monuments that were erected for commemorative purposes in the ancient world,[38] this discovery established unmistakable physical

---

[34] Keith Whitelam, *The Invention of Ancient Israel* (Abingdon, UK: Routledge, 1996); Gösta W. Ahlström, *History of Ancient Palestine* (Sheffield, UK: Sheffield Academic Press, 1993); Thomas L. Thompson, *Early History of the Israelite People* (Leiden, The Netherlands: Koninklijke Brill, 1992); Thomas L. Thompson, *The Mythic Past: Biblical Archaeology and the Myth of Israel* (New York: Basic Books, 1999); John Van Seters, *Prologue to History* (New Haven, CT: The Yale University Press, 1992); and Philip R. Davies, *In Search of Ancient Israel* (Sheffield, UK: Sheffield Academic Press,1992).

[35] Niels Peter Lemche, *The Israelites in History and Tradition* (Louisville, KY: Westminster John Knox Press, 1998), pp. 165–166.

[36] Sand, *Invention of the Jewish People,* p. 314.

[37] Sand, *Invention of the Jewish People,* p. 316. For details of this and other arguments against the historical revisionists, see Baruch Halpern, "Erasing History: The Minimalist Assault on Ancient Israel," in V. Phillips Long, ed., *Israel's Past in Present Research: Essays on Ancient Israelite Historiography* (Winona Lake, IN: Eisenbrauns, Inc., 1999), pp. 415–426.

[38] Steles were used in various parts of the ancient world to mark borders or for government proclamations. These monuments set aside space and established rules for conduct within territorial boundaries which they circumscribed. The word *stele* comes directly from the Greek word στήλη (*stéle*). Sometimes the Latin word *stela* is also used to describe these monuments.

evidence for the existence of a "House of David" in the ninth century BC. Immediately after this discovery, however, the coterie of minimalist[39] scholars who had boldly trumpeted their conclusion that the Davidic Kingdom never actually existed immediately launched themselves into extraordinary contortions in order to try to explain away this discovery. Some suggested that the stele was a forgery or that it had been "salted in the tell by some desperate biblical literalist."[40] A disquieted Philip R. Davies even resorted to the argument that the Hebrew letters forming David's name actually meant "uncle" or "kettle," instead of "David" so that the stele was a celebration of the "Kettle House"![41]

Apparently it is easier for some scholars to argue from the *absence* of archaeological evidence than it is to accept the *presence* of archaeological evidence! Fortunately for the science of biblical studies, the ranks of scholars who recognize and affirm archaeological support for biblical narratives regarding the people, the nation, and the land of Israel is growing,[42] despite the fact that their findings are not without controversy. As more and more of the land of Israel is subjected to archaeological excavation, ancient mysteries continue to be unearthed, and evidence mounts for the historical accuracy of biblical narratives concerning the lives of patriarchs, kings, and prophets.[43]

---

[39] Megan Bishop Moore and Brad E. Kelle, *Biblical History and Israel's Past: The Changing Study of the Bible and History* (Grand Rapids, MI: Wm. B. Eerdmans Publishing Co., 2011), p. 33. Biblical minimalism is a label given to a trend that was developed in the 1990s by scholars Niels Peter Lemche and Thomas L. Thompson from Denmark's Copenhagen University who made arguments on biblical history based on their view that the biblical record is not reliable evidence for what actually happened in ancient Israel and that it is very problematic to consider Israel for historical study. Other scholars who shared this perspective included Philip R. Davies and Keith Whitelam. See Thomas L. Thompson, *The Historicity of the Patriarchal Narratives* (London: T & T Clark, 2002) and John Van Seters, *Abraham in History and Tradition* (Brattleboro, VT: Echo Point Books & Media, 2014). For a comparison of mimimalism and maximalism, see Christopher D. Stanley, *The Hebrew Bible: A Comparative Approach* (Minneapolis, MN: Fortress Press, 2010), pp. 120–125.
[40] F. H. Creyer, "On the Recently Discovered 'House of David' Inscription," *Scandinavian Journal of the Old Testament* 8 (1994), pp. 14–15, referenced by Halpern in Long, p. 415.
[41] Philip R. Davies, "'House of David' Built on Sand," *Biblical Archaeology Review*, July/August, 1994.
[42] For more balanced perspectives on archaeology and biblical studies, see Megan Bishop Moore and Brad E. Kelle, *Biblical History and Israel's Past: The Changing Study of the Bible and History* (Grand Rapids, MI: Wm. B. Eerdmans Publishing Co., 2011); Israel Finkelstein and Amihai Mazar, *The Quest for the Historical Israel: Debating Archaeology and the History of Early Israel* (Atlanta, GA: The Society of Biblical Literature Press, 2007); and Neil Asher Silberman and Israel Finkelstein, *The Bible Unearthed: Archaeology's New Vision of Ancient Israel and the Origin of Its Sacred Texts* (New York: Touchstone Publications, 2001). Perhaps the most objective study of biblical archaeology is David M. Rohl, *Pharaohs and Kings: A Biblical Quest* (New York: Crown Publishers, 1995). Rohl's work is especially balanced and pragmatic, lacking ideological and theological agendas.
[43] James K. Hoffmeier, *Israel in Sinai: The Evidence for the Authenticity of the Wilderness Tradition* (New York: Oxford University Press, 2005); Israel Finkelstein and Neil Asher Silberman, *David and Solomon: In Search of the Bible's Sacred Kings and the Roots of the Western Tradition* (New York: Simon & Schuster, 2006); John H. Sailhamer, *Biblical Archaeology* (Grand Rapids, MI: Zondervan Publishing, 1998).

The Illegitimate Land: Numerous scholars have also questioned the validity of the Jewish claims to the land of Israel based on the historical entitlement to or control of the land by their ancestors.[44] The most strident of these are the producers or distributors of Arab propaganda who claim that the Jewish people have no right to any of the land of Israel because there is "no evidence" that their ancestors ever lived there. Unfortunately, there are many Christian scholars who have joined the ranks of the Arab propagandists either out of sympathy for the "plight" of the "Palestinian" people[45] or out of their own personal animus for the Jewish people in general and Zionists in particular. Others have simply followed the positions established by centuries of scholars who have smugly "proven" to their own satisfaction that the people described in the Hebrew Scriptures simply never existed and that the events chronicled therein never occurred. They argue that both the characters and the events recorded in the sacred texts were part of an elaborate myth created by later people in an effort to legitimize their claims to the land and the power associated with it.

Davies has taken the lead in some circles, arguing against the notion that "Israel was the natural or rightful owner of this piece of land."[46] He blames the "sad state of affairs" of the Jewish state in the land of "Palestine" on the influence of the Bible in the West where "inherited Christian culture supports the notion that the territory west of the Jordan is and has always been somehow essentially 'the land of Israel.'"[47] Davies laments the fact that "biblical scholarship inevitably focuses on the Israelite identity of a land that has actually been non-Jewish in terms of its indigenous population for the larger part of its recorded history."[48] Such Christian scholarship joins with and adds strength to the pervasive secularist view regarding the land of Israel, which maintains that any Jewish

---

[44] Uri Davis, *Apartheid Israel: Possibilities for the Struggle Within* (London, UK: Zed Books, 2003), p. 65. Davis takes arguments beyond the disputed "West Bank" by asserting that "Israeli claims to West Jerusalem, Safad or Jaffa, occupied in 1948–49, are as thoroughly invalid as Israeli claims to East Jerusalem, Hebron or Gaza, occupied in 1967." Davis believes that Jewish claim to any part of the land of Israel (Palestine) is illegitimate.

[45] Many Evangelical Christians have also been recently swayed by inaccurate portrayals of the "suffering" of Palestinian Christians under Israeli "oppression." David Brog, "The End of Evangelical Support for Israel?" *The Middle East Quarterly*, Spring 2014, Vol. 21: No. 2, posted at meforum.org. Also Stephen Sizer, *Christian Zionism: Road Map to Armageddon* (Downers Grove, IL: InterVarsity Press, 2004), p. 23.

[46] Philip R. Davies, "Minimalism, 'Ancient Israel,' and Anti-Semitism," in Diane Nunn Banks, *Writing the History of Israel* (London, UK: T & T Clark International, 2006), p. 217. Davies says that suggesting Israel's land ownership claim is "inflammatory" and has no present analog in departments of history.

[47] Davies in Banks, p. 217.

[48] Davies in Banks, p. 217.

claim to the historical existence and, therefore, authenticity of such a land is utterly supposititious and is worthy of general repudiation.[49]

Such pretensions and fabrications are patently false, for, despite all of the Gentile conquests, captivities, and diasporas, direct descendants of Abraham, Isaac, and Jacob have continued to live in the Promised Land in an unbroken chain from the time of Abraham to the present. Though nobles and aristocrats were taken into captivity and though invading armies imported and imposed their own citizens upon the land, still not all of the Israelites/Jews were ever removed. As Joan Peters says, "The Jewish presence in "The Holy Land" — at times tenuous — persisted through its bloody history. . . . Buried beneath the propaganda — which has it that Jews 'returned' to the Holy Land after two thousand years of separation, where they found crowds of 'indigenous Palestinian Arabs' — is the bald fact that the Jews are indigenous people on that land who never left, but who have continuously stayed on their 'Holy Land.'"[50] Israeli Prime Minister Benjamin Netanyahu said it well: "There is a Jewish people here, it has been here for close to 4,000 years; we recognize this people, we recognize their historic bond with this land and this city."[51]

Why All the Vitriol?

In the postmodern world, the odds have been stacked against the establishment of a legitimate people called Israel, a legitimate nation identified as Israel, and a legitimate land named Israel. A world that increasingly has no absolutes, no moral standards, and no ethics, a world that is driven solely by glorified self-interest and, ultimately, by utter selfishness has no place for a people, a nation, and a land that rests on absolutes and particularity, especially those granted by the only sovereign of the universe: the God of Scripture. "What makes the Jewish people such a controversial element in the history of the world?" asks

---

[49] A prime example of the secularist animus toward Israel was seen when mega-publisher HarperCollins created a "Middle East Atlas" in which the word *Israel* was purposefully omitted from a map of the Middle East while the words *Gaza* and *West Bank* were clearly identified. This was more than a Freudian slip. It was representative of the liberal secularist view that Israel should be "wiped off the map." Terrence McCoy, "HarperCollins Omits Israel from Maps for Mideast Schools, Citing 'Local Preferences,'" *The Washington Post*, January 2, 2015, posted at http://www.washingtonpost.com/news/morning-mix/wp/2015/01/02/harpercollins-omits-israel-from-maps-for-mideast-schools-citing-local-preferences/.

[50] Joan Peters, *From Time Immemorial: The Origins of the Arab-Jewish Conflict Over Palestine* (Michael Joseph Publishers, 1985), p. 83.

[51] Benjamin Netanyahu, quoted Jerome R. Verlin and Lee S. Bender, *Pressing Israel: Media Bias Exposed from A–Z* (Philadelphia, PA: Pavilion Press, 2012), p. 148.

Isaac Rottenberg. "Could it be that their very survival and presence in our midst remind us of the God of Israel, the Great Disturber of our pagan souls?" he rightly wonders, with an answer that is all too obvious.[52] What is the reason for this disruption in the pagan heart? "The God of Israel refuses to be absorbed into a pantheon of gods."[53] Jacob Neusner has it right: "Those who hate Israel hate God, [and] those who hate God hate Israel."[54] It is the God of Israel who demands a conclusion that the pagan heart cannot endure: "Choose this day whom you will serve, whether the gods your ancestors served in the region beyond the river or the gods of the Amorites in whose land you are living, but as for me and my household, we will serve the LORD."[55] As Neusner says, "The nations hate Israel because of their remaining loyal to the Torah."[56] David Patterson argues further that "the anti-Semitic determination to erase the People of the Book from the face of the planet is a determination to erase the Book itself; without the People there is no Book; and without the Book there is no People."[57] Without the book, there is also no condemnation of the perversity of the pagan heart!

Chaim Schloss takes the argument even further by saying that "the world's hatred of the Jews came down from Mount Sinai together with the Torah."[58] The people of Israel are hated—and their destruction is sought—because, in the words of Emmanuel Lévinas, the faith of the Jews "stems from the religion which modern political life supplants,"[59] the religion that David Patterson calls the religion "of creation and covenant, of revelation and redemption."[60] Because "the Torah determines the covenantal relation to the land," postmodernism seeks to obliterate "the voice of the Torah—and with the Torah, God and Israel as well," including the Torah's focus "on the

---

[52] Isaac C. Rottenberg, *Judaism, Christianity, Paganism: A Judeo-Christian Worldview and Its Cultural Implications* (Atlanta, GA: Hebraic Heritage Press, 2007), p. 101.
[53] Rottenberg, p. 101.
[54] Jacob Neusner, *The Theology of the Halakhah* (Leiden, The Netherlands: Koninklijke Brill NV, 2001), p. 243.
[55] Joshua 24:15.
[56] Jacob Neusner, *A Theological Commentary to the Midrash: Lamentations Rabbah* (Lanham, MD: University Press of America, 2011), pp. 120–121.
[57] David Patterson, *Anti-Semitism*, p. 200. "The Book referred to here is, of course, the Torah," says Patterson.
[58] Chaim Schloss, *2000 Years of Jewish History: From the Destruction of the Second Bais HaMikdash until the Twentieth Century* (Jerusalem, Israel: Feldheim Publishers, 2002), p. 254. Schloss appeals to a rabbinic *midrash* which suggests that the word *Sinai* is derived from the word *sinah*, which means "hatred." He maintains that "even if the Jews themselves try to forget their origins, Hashem sends the Gentiles to remind them of the truth" by means of outbreaks of antisemitism, the outright hatred and persecution of the Jewish people.
[59] Emmanuel Lévinas, *Difficult Freedom: Essays on Judaism*, tr. Sean Hand (Baltimore, MD: Johns Hopkins University Press, 1990), p. 12.
[60] David Patterson, *Anti-Semitism*, p. 101.

land itself."[61] Because of this underlying agenda of hatred for God, Torah, and Israel, "the Jewish presence in Israel far transcends any political agenda."[62] The Israelis' struggle for their very survival, therefore, is far more than a mere sociological problem, and it amounts to something more than a simple power struggle for control of a land mass.[63] When someone suggested that the logical solution to antisemitism in the world would be for the Jewish people to have their own nation, Derek Prince made this astute observation: "If the problem of anti-Semitism is primarily sociological, you are correct. The state of Israel will solve this problem. But if the primary cause of anti-Semitism is spiritual, then the existence of the State of Israel will bring the greatest onslaught of anti-Semitism that the world has ever seen."[64] The postmodern secularists' efforts toward the elimination of the nation and land of Israel, therefore, are merely visible symbols of their determination to eradicate the God of the Jews and his demands. It is part and parcel of a secularist agenda for deicide.

The Vindication of God and His People

For centuries after the destruction of the temple in AD 70, Israel—the people, the nation, and the land—hovered between life and death, often nearer to death than to life. The words of Josif Rabinovich poignantly encapsulate Israel's historical condition: "Nation of Israel! . . . In only one portion of your heart is it still possible to notice now and then a small throbbing, your limbs shudder, and the traits of your face attest that it is not yet possible to place you on the list of nations that have expired. Yes, you are still alive, the name *Israel* still flutters above you."[65] In spite of centuries of efforts to secure the utter destruction of the Jews through various forms of ethnic cleansing that reached its nadir in the Final Solution of the Nazi *Judenrein*[66] program, Israel has continued to exist as a people—indeed, *the* Chosen People. And finally, after centuries of unrelenting hatred, persecution, violence, mayhem, and murder against them individually and corporately, the Jews have come together against all odds as the people of Israel to form the nation

---

[61] David Patterson, *Anti-Semitism*, pp. 200–201.
[62] David Patterson, *Anti-Semitism*, p. 201.
[63] David Patterson, *Anti-Semitism*, p. 201.
[64] Derek Prince, quoted in Daniel C. Juster, "Anti-Semitism Again," in *Jewish Voice Today Magazine*, July/August/September 2015, p. 7.
[65] Josef Rabinovich, quoted in V. S. Soloviev, *Freedom, Faith, and Dogma: Essays by V. S. Soloviev on Christianity and Judaism* (Albany, NY: The State University of New York Press, 2008), p. 91.
[66] *Judenrein* is the German term for "clean of Jews." A similar word, *Judenfrei*, meant "free of Jews."

of Israel, and they have done so in the land of Israel! This was *the* miracle of the twentieth century. No other event could have approached comparison with what emerged from the utterly chaotic world of this the twentieth century. The resurrection of Israel had to be an act of God!

"Israel," in fact, cannot be fully considered without each of three elements: people, nation, and land. Israel is not one or the other; it is a continuum of all three.[67] It is impossible, therefore, to delegitimize one without, at the same time, delegitimizing the others. The legitimization of either the people of Israel, the nation of Israel, or the land of Israel is not, however, derived from any human institution. Though unrelenting efforts have been made in century after century to separate the people, the nation, and the land of Israel, all three are inexorably and indissolubly connected. As Aaron Klingerman has rightly argued, "the peculiar Book, the peculiar people, and the peculiar land must always be viewed together. What God has put together let no man, be he theologian or politician, put asunder."[68] The authentication of all three entities is derived solely from divine decree and is validated and made certain by the only eternally enduring reality that exists: divine faithfulness.

God himself established this truth in utterly explicit fashion when he declared: "I am YHWH, I change not; therefore, you, the descendants of Jacob, have not perished."[69] As a matter of fact, as Jon D. Levenson says, "Israel exists only because of God's choice, and apart from God, it has no existence at all."[70] It is for this reason that "Israel has no profane history, only a sacred history, a history of redemption, of backsliding and return, punishment and

---

[67] This is proven by the fact that from the time when the Roman Empire forcibly removed the Jewish people from their land and denied their nationhood, the corporate heart of the people—and, indeed, of every individual Jew—refused to accept the destruction of their nation and the expropriation of their land. The expectation of the full restoration of people, nation, and land continued to be central expressions of the *Amidah, the* prayer *par excellence* of every synagogue through the centuries. Three times each weekday since before the time of Jesus, Jews have prayed the fourteenth of the *Amidah's* eighteen benedictions, the *Bo'ne Yerushalayim B'rakhah* ("Builder of Jerusalem Blessing"), imploring God with these words: "Return in compassion to your city, Jerusalem, and rest within it as you have said. Rebuild it speedily, and in our days, a structure forever. And may you establish the throne of David within Jerusalem speedily. Blessed are you, LORD, the Builder of Jerusalem." And through century after century, this same prayer has been extended to God in synagogues around the world regardless as to where the forced dispersion of the Jewish people has taken them.

[68] Aaron Klingerman, quoted in Matthew Avery Sutton, *American Apocalypse: A History of Modern Evangelicalism* (Cambridge, MA: Harvard University Press, 2014), p. 302.

[69] Malachi 3:6.

[70] Jon D. Levenson, "The Universal Horizon of Biblical Particularism," in *Ethnicity and the Bible*, Mark G. Brett, ed. (Leiden, The Netherlands: E. J. Brill, 1996), p. 153.

restoration."[71] As William Klein rightly observes, "Israel exists as a people because of God's choice."[72] God, therefore, "proved his sovereign faithfulness to his people, preserving them in spite of their unfaithfulness."[73] Indeed, "It is by God's grace and faithfulness—not by race, language, culture or religion—that the Jews have continued to exist in the face of persecution and genocide."[74] As Karl Barth said, they cannot be "overlooked, or banished, or destroyed—for the grace of God upholds [them]."[75]

God's "covenantal faithfulness to Israel was eternal."[76] The perduration of Israel as people, nation, and land is not predicated on the evanescent musings or stratagems of Machiavellian tyrants and politicians. It is guaranteed by the God "who does not change like shifting shadows."[77] This God is the one whose "plans [were] formed long ago, with perfect faithfulness."[78] Israel's greatness, therefore, has always been viewed solely in the context "of the greatness of her God."[79] This is what God clearly predicted through the prophet Isaiah: "'No weapon that is formed against you will prosper; and every tongue that accuses you in judgment you will condemn. This is the heritage of the servants of the LORD, and their vindication is from me."[80] What was true in the ancient kingdoms of Babylon and Persia has continued to be true in the centuries since that time. God has always ensured that his Chosen People would survive even when it appeared that their enemies had them on the verge of annihilation. Despite every effort to destroy them, *Am Yisrael chai.*[81]

---

[71] Levenson, "The Universal Horizon," p. 153.

[72] William Klein, *The New Chosen People: A Corporate View of Election* (Eugene, OR: Wipf and Stock Publishers, 1990), p. 34.

[73] Klein, p. 34.

[74] Mark R. Lindsay, *Barth, Israel, and Jesus: Karl Barth's Theology of Israel* (Burlington, VT: Ashgate Publishing Co., 2007), p. 79.

[75] Karl Barth, *Church Dogmatics, III/3: The Creator and His Creature*, G. W. Bromley, ed. (London, UK: T & T Clark International, 2000), p. 220.

[76] Glenn Stanfield Holland, *Gods in the Desert: Religions of the Ancient Near East* (Lanham, MD: Rowman & Littlefield Publishers, 2009), p. 252.

[77] James 1:17, NIV.

[78] Isaiah 25:1.

[79] Horst Seebass, "בחר *bachar*," in C. J. Botterweck and H. Ringgren, eds., *Theological Dictionary of the Old Testament* (Grand Rapids, MI: Wm. B. Eerdmans Publishing Co., 1975), vol. 2, p. 84.

[80] Isaiah 54:17.

[81] *Am Yisrael chai* means, "The People of Israel live."

CHAPTER 1

THE CHOSEN PEOPLE

DIVINE ELECTION

Has there ever been—or can there ever be—such a thing as a "Chosen People"? Does God somehow relate to all human beings equally, or does he identify himself exclusively with one particular people group? Is God a universalist or a particularist? Does God's universal sovereignty preclude the possibility of his participation in a particularist engagement, or does particularity serve the purposes of his universality? The answer to all of these questions is quite simple—and at the same time, very Hebraic:[1] God is both a universalist and a particularist at the same time!

---

[1] This kind of answer is completely in context with Hebraic thinking, which is able to hold seemingly polarized issues in dynamic tension so that the truth of both can be recognized. See Marvin R. Wilson, *Exploring Our Hebraic Heritage: A Christian Theology of Roots and Renewal* (Grand Rapids, MI: Wm. B. Eerdmans Publishing Co., 2014), p. 5. In contrast, Aristotelian logic forced Greek thinking—and Christian theologies developed in the context of Greek thought—to postulate that there can only be one truth and that all other ideas that appear to be opposed or contradictory to that "one truth" must be destroyed. Richard Lim notes that the acceptance of controlled dissensus in the earliest church was gradually replaced by the Greek and Roman notion of simplicity which insisted that there could be only one truth and that dissensus had to be controlled through *homonoia*—a social idea that insisted on agreement with an utter lack of disputation. See Richard Lim, *Public Disputation, Power, and Social Order in Late Antiquity* (Berkeley, CA: The University of California Press, 1994), p. 20. Lim also observes that at the time at which the church crystallized into hierarchical structures, it sought to "domesticate the perceived threat of dissensus" by mobilizing "hierarchical forms of authority against a culture that validated individualistic claims and rational argumentation." At that same time, says Daniel Boyarin, rabbinic Judaism was gravitating in the opposite direction, moving from the amoraic dialectic that had led to conclusions on normative law as demonstrated in the Jerusalem Talmud to the rejection of the desire for "certain knowledge" which characterized the Babylonian Talmud. See Daniel Boyarin, *Border Lines: The Partition of Judaeo-Christianity* (Philadelphia, PA: The University of Pennsylvania Press, 2004), pp. 151–153. Much later, Thomas Aquinas even maintained that philosophy (scientific inquiry) and theology had to be reconciled into "one truth" on the basis of this same argument that "there can be only one truth." See Ted Byfield, *The Christians: Their First Two Thousand Years; A Glorious Disaster: A.D. 1100 to 1300: The Crusades: Blood, Valor, Iniquity, Reason, Faith* (Edmonton, Canada: Society to Explore and Record Christian History, 2003), vol. 7, p. 199.

The fact that God is a universalist is supported from the words of Holy Scripture.[2] At the same time, however, Scripture also makes it clear that God is a particularist.[3] God relates universally to every human being;[4] however, he also relates uniquely to the particular people whom he has chosen to be his agents for extending his dominion of justice and shalom to all humanity. While all human beings belong to God,[5] "Israel is God's special possession and becomes known as a holy people. . . . God's choice of Israel is associated with the land of Israel, which becomes a constitutive element of being a people of God: 'I will give to you and to your descendants after you the land of your sojournings, all the land of Canaan for an everlasting possession; and I will be their God.'"[6] Brian McClaren summarizes this truth well: "[T]he way God brings salvation to others is by giving it to some, recruiting them as agents of salvation to others. So he blesses the whole world by blessing one nation" and using that nation as his emissary to the world.[7] David Novak is correct, then, when he argues that "only God and God's Torah and God's people are unique (*echad*)."[8]

Divine Particularity

The fulfillment of divine universality through a plan to redeem and bless all of humanity was the reason for which God sovereignly engaged

[2] As humanity's creator, God relates universally to every human being in some dimension. As a matter of fact, the apostle Paul, agreeing with the Greek poet Menander, said, "We are also [God's] children" (Acts 17:28).
[3] God's relationship as the creator of all humanity does not preclude or limit his particularity, which is manifest in his sovereign power to choose individuals and groups of people for particular purposes of his own design.
[4] Because God is the creator—and, in essence, the father—of the entire human race, it is not his will for "any to perish but for all to come to repentance" (2 Peter 3:9), and he simply "desires everyone to be saved" (1 Timothy 2:4, NRS). He has made provision, therefore, to save of all humanity: "For God so loved the world that he gave his only begotten Son, that whoever believes in him shall not perish, but have eternal life" (John 3:16). Because God limited his own sovereignty in order to give free will to every human being, however, each individual must choose whether or not to accept God's provision. God's universality, therefore, does not require, or even imply, that all human beings must be redeemed from their fallen state. The teachings of universalism (which maintains that all human beings will be reconciled to God) and ultimate reconciliation (which teaches that even Satan and the fallen angels will be reconciled to God) are clearly false and cannot be supported by Holy Scripture. In fact, both teachings are opposed by the specific words of Jesus (Matthew 25:34, 31) and the prophet Daniel (Daniel 12:2).
[5] Deuteronomy 14:1–2.
[6] Genesis 17:8. Kessler, Edward. "Chosen People," in *A Dictionary of Jewish-Christian Relations*, Edward Kessler and Neil Wenborn, eds. (Cambridge, UK: Cambridge University Press, 2005), p. 83.
[7] Brian D. McLaren, *A New Kind of Christian: A Tale of Two Friends on a Spiritual Journey* (San Francisco, CA: John Wiley & Sons, 2001), p. 230.
[8] David Novak, *Talking with Christians: Musings of a Jewish Theologian* (Grand Rapids, MI: Wm. B. Eerdmans Publishing Co., 2005), p. 151.

in particularity by choosing one man, one family, and one nation to serve the interest of bringing his divine revelation to the whole of humanity. Richard Bauckham has rightfully concluded that "Jewish monotheism is characterized by its way of relating YHWH's particularity as Israel's God to his universality as Creator and sovereign Lord of all."[9] Gabriel Fackre has further explained this process, observing that "the particular bonding with Israel does not preclude the covenant of the Creator with all humankind before and concurrent with the Abrahamic-Mosaic stream."[10] The dynamics of the manner in which divine particularity serves divine universality were very well summarized by Fackre when he said that "the gift to and claim upon Israel are related to Israel's role as that of a 'light to the Gentiles,' a particularity within the universality of the divine working."[11] G. C. Berkhower explained this understanding by demonstrating that divine revelation in Scripture serves the purpose of illuminating "the relations between the universality and particularity of the divine activity" so that "its taking place is historically limited" and "cannot, and may not, be generalized."[12] Postmodern philosophers and theologians alike have challenged the possibility of divine particularity with arguments such as this: "God, if there is a God, wouldn't even dare to choose only one." This kind of thinking has produced sardonic epigrams like the following that was penned by the British journalist William Ewer:

> "How odd of God
> To choose the Jews!"[13]

The fact remains, however, that God, in a divine act of his absolute sovereignty, did elect from among all the peoples of the earth one man, one family, and one nation to be his Chosen People.

The biblical concept of election is, indeed, founded in the sovereignty of God; however, as Reuen Thomas has wisely observed, "election . . . does not refer to personal salvation. . . . It refers to a service, to a purpose, to a

---

9 Richard Bauckham, *Jesus and the God of Israel: God Crucified and Other Essays on the New Testament's Christology of Divine Identity* (Crownhill, UK: Authentic Media, 2008), p. 84.

10 Gabriel Fackre, *The Christian Story: Authority: Scripture in the Church for the World* (Grand Rapids, MI: Wm. B. Eerdmans Publishing Co., 1987), p. 202.

11 Fackre, p. 202.

12 G. C. Berkhouwer, *General Revelation: Studies in Dogmatics* (Grand Rapids, MI: Wm. B. Eerdmans Publishing Co., 1955), p. 310, author's emphasis.

13 This bit of doggerel was likely an attempt to hide British gentility's covert antisemitism behind a witty saying. Perhaps the most appropriate reply was Ogden Nash's retort: "It wasn't odd; the Jews chose God!"

mission."[14] Daniel Elazar has noted the nature of this divine activity: "God's universality is expressed in his statement that he judges other nations. . . . The political imagery is essential to the definition of God's role; He is not so much a savior of individuals [as he is] a governor of nations, peoples, and polities."[15] In order to accomplish his objective of bringing his sovereignty— and, therefore, his blessing—to all people, God has always sought and ordained the existence of a collective chosen people who, as his servant nation, would advance his causes in the earth. At the same time, he has also searched for individuals who would choose to have relationship with him. Jesus, himself, established this truth: "But the hour is coming, and now is, when the true worshipers will worship the Father in spirit and truth; for the Father is seeking such to worship him."[16] This understanding is anchored in Ezekiel's declaration: "[God] searched for a man among them who would build up the wall and stand in the gap before me for the land."[17]

The God of Scripture, therefore, is a relational being[18] who constantly searches for human beings whom he can engage as volunteers to fulfill his purposes and share his love by worshipping him in spiritual truth.[19] Leonard Allen and Danny Swick explain this truth succinctly: "Throughout the Old Testament, God is never conceived of as an object to be studied, scrutinized, or proved. Instead, He is the God of covenant, the One who makes promises to people and receives in return their faithfulness. . . . In other words, He is the God who is identified and known through his

---

[14] Reuen Thomas, *Divine Sovereignty* (Boston, MA: D. Lothrop & Company, 1885), p. 174. Paul made the dynamics of predestination clear in Romans 8:29 when he said that "the *ones* [God] foreknew, he also did predestinate to be conformed to the image of his Son" (emphasis added). The word which is translated "predestinate," προορίζω (*proorízo*), is found only twice in Scripture (Romans 8:29; Ephesians 1:5). In both cases, the emphasis is on the collective ("the *ones,*" [*pl.*]), not the individual. The plans, purposes, and programs of God are predetermined, foreordained, or predestinated; however, individuals choose of their own free will which role they will fulfill in God's predetermined and predestined plans. This understanding is settled in Hebraic thought wherein it is understood that human beings were granted the personal sovereignty to choose their own destiny by God's decision to limit his own universal sovereignty in order to accommodate human free will. This follows from the fact that if God is sovereign over all, he is also sovereign over his own sovereignty and can limit his sovereignty when and to whatever degree he sovereignly wills.

[15] Daniel J. Elazar, *Covenant & Polity in Biblical Israel: Biblical Foundations & Jewish Expressions* (Piscataway, NJ: Transaction Publishers, 1995), pp. 130–131.

[16] John 4:23.

[17] Ezekiel 22:30.

[18] For an extensive discussion of the relationality of God both within his own being and with regard to humanity, see John D. Garr, *God and Women: Woman in God's Image and Likeness* (Atlanta, GA: Golden Key Press, 2011), pp. 73–99, 223–241.

[19] John 4:23.

relationships."[20] The mystery of God's election of Israel is "that it concerns a natural human family. God could have chosen according to some spiritual criterion: election according to faith or according to moral excellence. Instead, God chose the seed of Abraham, Isaac, and Jacob, a human family neither better nor worse than others. As a result, Israel's election is a corporeal election, and the foundation of Judaism is nothing other than the family identity of the Jewish people."[21]

As Abraham Heschel said, therefore, history is not a record of man's search for God but of God's search for man.[22] Unfortunately, historical Christian thought has largely replaced the biblical idea of God's search for man with the concept of man's search for God. William Hordern argued that this Christian perspective has distorted God's purposes in salvation history: "Thus the uniqueness of the biblical religion, with God's search for man, was lost, and the Bible was seen as an interesting page in the ongoing search of man for God."[23] Heschel drew the only reasonable conclusion about Israel's divine election when he said, "There is no concept of a chosen God, but there is the idea of a chosen people. . . . We have not chosen God; He has chosen us."[24] It was clearly in the context of this principle that Jesus said to his disciples, "You did not choose me, but I chose you and appointed you."[25]

The Purpose for Divine Election

God's particularity in electing one man and his lineal descendants to be his "Chosen People" was not designed to restrict him to the status of a mere tribal deity. The Almighty chose Abraham uniquely in order to accomplish his universal purposes in the earth. He did not choose the patriarch in order to establish a race of superhuman beings or demigods or to create a class of people who would have exclusive access to him to the exclusion of all others. In fact, God chose

---

[20] C. Leonard Allen and Danny G. Swick, *Participating in God's Life* (Orange, CA: New Leaf Books, 2001), p. 151.

[21] R. Kendall Soulen, *The God of Israel and Christian Theology* (Minneapolis, MN: Augsburg Fortress Press, 1996), pp. 5–6.

[22] Abraham Joshua Heschel, *God in Search of Man: A Philosophy of Judaism* (New York: Farrar, Straus and Giroux, 1955), p. 425.

[23] William Hordern, *The Case for a New Reformation Theology* (London, UK: Westminster Press, 1959), quoted in Barry L. Callen, *Discerning the Divine: God in Christian Theology* (Louisville, KY: Westminster John Knox Press, 2004), p. 39.

[24] Heschel, *God in Search*, p. 425.

[25] John 15:16.

Abraham in order to produce through him a servant nation which could be used in order to effect God's greater design, the work of bringing salvation and redemption to the entire human race and fully restoring what had been lost in the Edenic rebellion of the corporate heads of the human race, Adam and Eve. "Of all the families of the earth God elected Abraham to 'father' a people who would become a servant nation . . . God promised to provide Abraham and his offspring with a land, worldwide fame, and the opportunity to be a tool He would use to impact the world."[26] The plan of God had been devised before all creation, and God was merely enlisting those who would choose to volunteer their services as his agents to fulfill that plan by redeeming unto himself a people for his name.[27]

God made his intentions clear when he issued this profound promise to Abraham: "I will bless those who bless you, and the one who curses you I will curse. And in you all the families of the earth will be blessed."[28] In another promissory declaration, God covenantally promised Abraham, "Through your offspring all nations on earth will be blessed, because you have obeyed me."[29] When God chose Abraham and his descendants after him, therefore, his action was designed to have much larger implications than the election of just one family: it was to impact all of humanity with the blessing that God would pour upon the patriarch's descendants. In the progeny of Abraham, God would create a servant nation that would extend the insight and understanding of his divine Word and the blessing of his eternal purposes to all the "families of the earth."[30]

It is God's desire, therefore, to save the nations of the world through the agency of his Chosen People, beginning with Abraham. This was the special lesson taught in the prophecy of Jonah where God sought to bring salvation to the archenemy of his people by using a Jewish prophet. Nineveh, the imperial city of the despised Assyrian Empire, therefore, became "a cipher for all foreign nations who have abused Israel but who nonetheless fall under the aegis of YHWH's governance. . . . The narrative of

---

[26] Eugene H. Merrill, *The World and the Word: An Introduction to the Old Testament*, Mark F. Rooker, and Michael A. Grisanti, eds. (Nashville, TN: B & H Publishing Group, 2001), p. 183.

[27] Revelation 13:8; 1 Peter 1:20; Ephesians 1:4.

[28] Genesis 12:3.

[29] Genesis 22:18, NIV.

[30] Norbert Lohfink, *The God of Israel and the Nations: Studies in Isaiah and the Psalms* (Collegeville, MN: Liturgical Press, 2000), p. 49. Also, H. Wayne House, *Israel: The Land and the People—An Evangelical Affirmation of God's Promises* (Grand Rapids, MI: Kregel Academic, 1998), p. 270.

Jonah . . . portrays YHWH as ready to rescue Nineveh, that is, to save it,"[31] says Walter Brueggemann. Despite the Jonah ambivalence, the Almighty brought repentance and salvation to Nineveh through the recalcitrant prophet, even if he had to subject him to life-threatening circumstances in order to effect his obedience to the divine command.

Divine particularity, therefore, was designed to serve the purpose of divine universality. Aaron Hughes wisely and succinctly maintains that Judaism is, therefore, "universally relevant precisely on account of its particularity," for "in its singularity, the universal is both encountered and sustained."[32] Lévinas is correct when he argues that "Jewish universalism has always revealed itself in its particularism," so that "Jews—because of and not despite their religious particularity—provide a lesson for all."[33] The vision of God's universality would never have been fulfilled in the earth if it had not been for his particularity, his sovereign election of a uniquely Chosen People to facilitate the unfolding of his plan for all humanity. Consequently, "it is Judaism's particularity that 'conditions universality.'"[34]

Divine Election and History

Despite every effort to delegitimize the Hebrews, Israelites, and Jews as a people, the fact remains that they have been and continue to be God's Chosen People. Even though "to the traditional anti-Semite, the Jew was the member neither of a 'race' nor of a transnational community, but the follower of a false religion, doomed to suffer and wander homeless as a lesson to mankind,"[35] God always recognized the inherent peoplehood of the Hebrews/Israelites/Jews—indeed, their peoplehood as his Chosen People. In fact, he made this very clear: "For the LORD's portion is his people; Jacob is the allotment of his inheritance."[36] The Almighty also confirmed his act of sovereignly choosing the descendants of Jacob to be uniquely his people: "You Israel, my servant, Jacob whom I have chosen, descendant of Abraham my friend, you whom I have taken from the ends

---

[31] Walter Brueggemann, *An Introduction to the Old Testament: The Canon and Christian Imagination* (Louisville, KY: Westminster John Knox Press, 2003), p. 232.

[32] Aaron W. Hughes, *Rethinking Jewish Philosophy: Beyond Particularism and Universalism* (New York: Oxford University Press, 2014), p. 46.

[33] Lévinas, *Difficult Freedom*, p. 164, quoted in Hughes, p. 46.

[34] Hughes, p. 46, referencing Emmanuel Lévinas, *In the Time of the Nations*, tr. Michael B. Smith (Bloomington, IN: The Indiana University Press, 1994), pp. 3–4.

[35] Richard Pipes, *Russia Under the Bolshevik Regime* (New York: Alfred A. Knopf, 1994), p. 254.

[36] Deuteronomy 32:9.

of the earth . . . and said unto you, 'You are my servant, *I have chosen you*.''[37] Even non-biblical scholars like Ram Ramakrishnan have confirmed this truth: "Unlike other ancient religions and cultures, Judaism is rooted in history, not in mythology."[38] And the history of Judaism is not that of a transcendent idea or a philosophy of religion, but of a real people, the Jews. Neil Silberman and Israel Finkelstein expand this idea succinctly: "Unlike other ancient Near Eastern mythologies, such as the Egyptian tales of Osiris, Isis, and Horus or the Mesopotamian Gilgamesh epic, the Bible is grounded firmly in earthly history. It is a divine drama played out before the eyes of humanity."[39]

God's particularity in relationship to his Chosen People is not, therefore, based on rationalism, philosophical categories, or metaphysics, but on history and experience. And the only history that is meaningful in the Hebraic culture is that of the continuity of the family. This principle is confirmed by the fact that the only word in the Hebrew language that even suggests a concept of history is תּוֹלְדוֹת (*toledot*), which means "generations" or "genealogy" and speaks directly to the birth of children and grandchildren.[40] The Chosen People idea is established, therefore, not in some mythological phantasmagoria, but in four thousand years of the transgenerational unfolding of unbroken Hebrew, Israelite, and Jewish history. "The God of the Bible is not a static Greek metaphysical being who is unchangeable and immutable; rather he is the God of history, the God of Abraham, Isaac, and Jacob, a God who reveals himself in historical and political events,"[41] Arthur Gish rightly says. The immutability of God is manifest not in Greek philosophical categories but in his covenant faithfulness, his unending commitment to fulfilling the terms of his callings, commissions, and commitments to his people.[42]

---

[37] Isaiah 41:8–9, emphasis added.

[38] Ram Ramakrishnan, *Many Paths, One Destination: Love, Peace, Compassion, Tolerance, and Understanding Through World Religions* (Tucson, AZ: Wheatmark Publishing Services, 2009), p. 91.

[39] Neil Asher Silberman and Israel Finkelstein, *The Bible Unearthed: Archaeology's New Vision of Ancient Israel and the Origin of Its Sacred Texts* (New York: Touchstone, 2001), p. 8.

[40] Genesis 5:1; 6:9; 10:1; 37:2.

[41] Arthur G. Gish, *The New Left and Christian Radicalism* (Grand Rapids, MI: Wm. B. Eerdmans Publishing Co., 1970), p. 80.

[42] Greek philosophers assigned to God the category of immutability, by which they meant that God could never change in any way, for if he were to change, they said, either before or after his change, he would not be perfect and, therefore, could not be God. The Hebrews understood God's immutability as being manifest, not in a category of philosophy, but in his unimpeachable commitment and faithfulness to his covenants. The unchangeableness of God, therefore, is directly related to the faithfulness that he invariably and without exception demonstrates toward his covenant people (Malachi 3:6).

Karl Barth also placed God's covenant with Abraham in the context of the historical unfolding of the Almighty's plan for the ages: "The covenant which God made with Abraham and his seed . . . was not an arbitrary invention of God and therefore something wholly new in history. It was simply the initial stage in the execution of the purpose God intended when he caused history to commence in and with creation and therefore in and with the beginning of time generally."[43] God's dealings with Abraham established the fact that history is linear and covenantal, not cyclical and causal.[44] Salvation history started somewhere (with creation) and has proceeded rectilinearly toward an end (with the Messianic Age and the *Olam Ha-Ba*),[45] and it is based on God's sovereign covenantal election of a people to be uniquely his. God's particularity, therefore, is established in the covenant that he initiated when he elected and established a Chosen People.

This history was set in motion with God's choice of Abraham as his servant and with the covenant with the patriarch that he made irrevocable by swearing to its authenticity upon the authority of his own name.[46] Since the personal name of God, YHWH, is a statement of his eternity ("I will be [there]"), the covenant that God made with Abraham was established in the unending existence of the Eternal, making this covenant thereby everlasting and irrevocable. This was the covenant in which God specifically decreed that "all of Abraham's descendants in perpetuity"[47] would be the legitimate heirs of the promise, the Chosen People. Abraham

---

[43] Karl Barth, *Church Dogmatics, III/2: The Doctrine of Creation* (London, UK: T & T Clark International, 2004), p. 476.

[44] Unlike Hebraic biblicism, Greek philosophy and various monist religions view history as being cyclical (endlessly repeating itself) and causal (with each event or action precipitating another event or action *ad infinitum*).

[45] Hans Ucko, *The People and the People of God: Minjung and Dalit Theology in Interaction* (Hamburg, Germany: Lit Verlag Münster, 2002), p. 18. Ucko says, "Salvation history is linear and begins in the dawn of creation and ends with the end of history. . . . For salvation history the people Israel is called to be the very people of salvation history." Jacob Neusner says, "Cyclical thinking is . . . alien to sages . . . because it presupposes an eternal return, an endless recapitulation of the pattern." Jacob Neusner, *Rabbinic Judaism: The Theological System* (Boston, MA: Brill Academic Publishers, 2002), p. 247.

[46] Hebrews 6:13. When Abraham offered Isaac in the *Akedah*, God said, "I have taken an oath by my name, says the LORD . . . that I will certainly give you my blessing . . . your offspring will be increased like the stars of heaven and the sand by the seaside . . . and in your offspring shall all the nations of the earth be blessed" (Genesis 22:16–18, BBE, ESV).

[47] Sarah J. Melcher, "Lacan, the Phallus, and the Construal of Intergenerational Kinship in Genesis–Numbers," in *Relating to the Text: Interdisciplinary and Form-Critical Insights on the Bible*, Timothy Sandoval and Carleen Mandolfo, eds. (New York: T & T Clark International, 2003), p. 199.

was the first Hebrew and, in effect, the first Israelite and Jew;[48] however, God's covenant was not solely with Abraham—it was also with his lineal descendants through Isaac and Jacob forever. God said unequivocally, "I will establish my covenant between me and you, and your offspring after you throughout their generations, for an everlasting covenant, to be God to you and your offspring after you."[49] The covenant was an irrevocable divine decree that could never expire, because it rested in the infinite immutability,[50] faithfulness, and immortality[51] of God himself.

The Transgenerational Covenant

Because of his immutability, God did not hesitate to reiterate the continuity of the Abrahamic covenant to the patriarch's son, Isaac: "I will establish the oath which I swore to your father Abraham,"[52] and, "I will increase your offspring for the sake of my servant Abraham."[53] The terms of the covenant that God had made with Abraham were specifically reiterated and reinforced in the promise to Isaac: 1) God's personal presence would be with Abraham's son ("I will be with you and bless you"[54]); 2) God would give numerous progeny to him ("I will multiply your descendants as many as the stars of heaven"[55]); 3) God's covenantal blessing would be both particular and universal ("By your descendants all the nations of the earth shall be blessed"[56]); and 4) Isaac and his descendants would have permanent title of the land of Canaan ("To you and to your descendants I will give all these lands"[57]). In fact, when God had spared Isaac's life in the *Akedah*, the binding of Abraham's son at Mt.

---

[48] Though the terms *Israelite* and *Jew* did not exist in Abraham's day, he is considered by the Jewish people to be the first Jew because it is from him that "all Jews trace their descent." See Naomi E. Pasachoff and Robert J. Littman, eds., *A Concise History of the Jewish People* (Lanham, MD: Rowman and Littlefield Publishers, 1995), p. 1. Shaye Cohen notes that all converts to Judaism, "even first-generation converts, have an Israelite father in Abraham." Shaye J. D. Cohen, *The Beginnings of Jewishness: Boundaries, Varieties, Uncertainties* (Berkeley, CA: The University of California Press, 1999), p. 328.

[49] Genesis 17:7, NRS.

[50] Malachi 3:6; James 1:17; Hebrews 13:8.

[51] 1 Timothy 6:16.

[52] Genesis 26:1–5.

[53] Genesis 26:24.

[54] Genesis 26:3.

[55] Genesis 26:4a.

[56] Genesis 26:4c.

[57] Genesis 26:3, 4b. Interestingly, the real estate clause of the Abrahamic covenant was reconfirmed to Isaac in two separate declarations delivered on two separate occasions. This reiteration of the covenant paralleled God's making repeated declarations of his covenant with Abraham.

Moriah that was transformed from a holocaust offering into a virtual resurrection, God had already made it clear that "the covenant He had made with Abraham could be fulfilled only through Isaac."[58]

In due time, the covenant that Isaac had inherited from God through his father was reiterated and reaffirmed with Isaac's son Jacob, Abraham's grandson. This occurred when Isaac transferred the inheritance of the Abrahamic covenant to Jacob by quoting God's fundamental promise of the reciprocal blessing and cursing aspects of the sovereign decree: "Cursed be those who curse you, and blessed be those who bless you."[59] Whereas this primogeniture blessing had at first been transferred unwittingly by Isaac to Jacob through the ruse of Rebekah and her son, Isaac's full blessing was willingly and willfully given to Jacob when Isaac spoke these words over his son: "May [God] give you the blessing of Abraham, to you and to your descendants with you."[60] In this text, the phrase translated *the blessing of Abraham,* בִּרְכַּת אַבְרָהָם (*birkhat Avraham*) is a *hapax legomenon*, appearing only once in the entire corpus of the Hebrew Scriptures. Similarly, the same phrase appears only once in the Apostolic Scriptures, when Paul declared that the "blessing of Abraham," ἡ εὐλογία τοῦ Ἀβραάμ (*he eulogía tou Abraám*), would come to the Gentiles.[61] It is clear, then, that when Isaac spoke these specific words of blessing over Jacob, he confirmed and recognized his younger son as "the true heir of the Abrahamic covenant."[62] The continuing line of the Chosen People as the unbroken fulfillment of God's promises to Abraham was to continue specifically through Jacob.

Accompanying this blessing was a summarization of the same details that were present in Abraham's blessing upon Isaac: 1) God would multiply Jacob's children ("God . . . multiply you that you may become a community of peoples"[63]); and 2) God would give him possession of the land ("That you may possess the land of your sojournings, which God

---

[58] J. Dwight Pentecost and Kenneth M. Durham, *Faith That Endures: A Practical Commentary on the Book of Hebrews* (Grand Rapids, MI: Kregel Publications, 1992), p. 186.
[59] Genesis 27:29.
[60] Genesis 28:4.
[61] Galatians 3:14. In this case, Paul quotes the Septuagint Greek translation of Genesis 28:4: τὴν εὐλογίαν Ἀβρααμ (*ten eulogían Abraam*). See Nahum M. Sarna, *Understanding Genesis* (New York: Schocken Books, 1970), p. 195, quoted in Chee-Chiew Lee, *The Blessing of Abraham, the Spirit, and Justification in Galatians: Their Relationship and Significance for Understanding Paul's Theology* (Eugene, OR: Wipf and Stock Publishers, 2013), p. 82, n. 92.
[62] Sarna, p. 82.
[63] Genesis 28:3b, NIV.

gave to Abraham"[64]). By this time, Isaac had apparently come to recognize God's hand at work in Jacob and Rebekah's deception, for "from his actions, it appears that he was totally comfortable with things as they were and therefore left them as they were."[65] In making this blessing, Isaac "blesses [Jacob] with the blessings of the Abrahamic covenant, and reaffirms his position as the birthright son."[66]

Shortly after this event, when Jacob journeyed toward Haran to find his bride, he paused to rest at Bethel. There, God reaffirmed the Abrahamic covenant with Jacob when he appeared to him, identifying himself as "the LORD, the God of your father Abraham and the God of Isaac."[67] Then, precisely the same promises that God had given first to Abraham and then to Isaac were announced to Jacob: 1) God's presence would be with him continually ("I am with you and will keep you wherever you go"[68]); 2) The Lord would multiply his progeny ("Your descendants will also be like the dust of the earth"[69]); 3) God's blessing on him would be both particular and universal ("In your descendants shall all the families of the earth be blessed"[70]); and 4) God would give him and his descendants the Promised Land ("The land on which you lie, I will give it to you and to your descendants.")[71]

Years later in the same place, God appeared again to bless Jacob and to reconfirm the Abrahamic covenant. In that case, God identified himself as *El Shaddai*. Then he reiterated his unconditional promise of numerous descendants and repeated the promise that he had made to Abraham and Isaac, reaffirming that Jacob's descendants would possess the land of Canaan.[72] It seemed that God wanted to make certain to Jacob—who by then was named Israel—that the covenant he had made with him and his lineal descendants was to be precisely the same as the covenant that he had made with his grandfather Abraham. Nothing from the original covenant had been removed or modified when God reiterated it to Jacob. God himself was bound to the terms of the covenant as he had originally

---

64 Genesis 28:4b.
65 Douglas T. Bentley, *Abraham's Seed and Covenant* (Springville, UT: Cedar Fort Publishing, 2003), p. 8.
66 Bentley, p. 8.
67 Genesis 28:13.
68 Genesis 28:15.
69 Genesis 28:14a.
70 Genesis 28:14b.
71 Genesis 28:13b.
72 Genesis 35:9–13.

delivered it to Abraham because he had specifically said that the covenant was to be with Abraham and his descendants after him.[73]

As Robert Chisholm has pointed out,[74] there are, indeed, simply amazing and striking parallels between the covenant that God made with Abraham in Genesis 17:1–8 and the reiteration of the covenant with Jacob in Genesis 35:9–13. These include the following: 1) God identified himself to both Abraham and Jacob as *El Shaddai*.[75] He changed both of the patriarchs' names: Abram to Abraham[76] and Jacob to Israel.[77] He promised both of the patriarchs numerous descendants, including kings.[78] Finally, God affirmed the real estate clause in his covenant with both Abraham and Jacob.[79] From this biblical account alone, what the Psalmist declared is obviously true: God "is ever mindful of his covenant, the promise he gave for a thousand generations, that he made with Abraham, swore to Isaac, and confirmed in a decree for Jacob; for Israel, as an eternal covenant."[80] As if to underscore the fact that he had made the same appearance and the same promises not only to Abraham and Jacob but also to Isaac, God reiterated the continuing nature of his actions when he said to Moses, "I appeared to Abraham, Isaac, and Jacob as *El Shaddai*."[81] It was the one and only God, *El Shaddai*, the "Almighty," the "all-powerful" Provider,[82] who established his covenant with Abraham and reconfirmed it with his lineal descendants.

---

[73] Genesis 17:7, 9, 19.

[74] Robert B. Chisholm, "Evidence from Genesis," in *A Case for Premillennialism: A New Consensus*, Donald K. Campbell and Jeffrey L. Townsend, eds. (Chicago, IL: Moody Publications, 1992), p. 52.

[75] Abraham: Genesis 17:1; Jacob: Genesis 35:11.

[76] Genesis 17:5.

[77] Genesis 35:10.

[78] Abraham: Genesis 17:2, 6; Jacob: Genesis 35:11.

[79] Abraham: Genesis 17:8; Jacob: Genesis 35:12.

[80] Psalm 105:8–10, TNK. Elliot N. Dorff, *To Do the Right and the Good: A Jewish Approach to Modern Social Ethics* (Philadelphia, PA: The Jewish Publication Society, 2002), p. 95.

[81] Exodus 6:3.

[82] The name *El Shaddai*, usually translated "The Almighty (God)," comes from the Hebrew word *shad*, which means "breast." The omnipotence of God, therefore, is manifest in his unlimited ability to provide whatever is needed. The first mention of *El Shaddai* in Scripture confirms this truth: "The arms of his hands were made strong by . . . *El Shaddai* (שַׁדַּי), who blesses you with . . . blessings of the breasts (שָׁדַיִם) and of the womb" (Genesis 49:25). *El Shaddai* is directly revealed as the one who blesses with the "blessings of the breasts." See John D. Garr, *God and Women: Woman in God's Image and Likeness* (Atlanta, GA: Golden Key Press, 2012), pp. 109–112; G. Campbell Morgan, quoted in Herbert Lockyer, *All the Divine Names and Titles in the Bible* (Grand Rapids, MI: Zondervan Publishing House, 1988), p. 14; and Lewis Sperry Chafer, *Systematic Theology* (Grand Rapids, MI: Kregel Publications, 1948), p. 56.

Reaffirmation of the Perpetual Covenant

God's particularist covenant with Abraham did not, however, die with Jacob. It continued unabated in the lineage of the ever-expanding extended family that came to be known as the "Children of Israel." Through the subsequent years, Abraham's progeny through his promised son Isaac remained God's Chosen People because of the Abrahamic covenant. As God had predicted to Abraham, it would be well over four hundred years before the benefits of his covenant would become reality. In the meantime, the family of Jacob would follow their father into Egypt,[83] where God had already made provision by means of the wisdom of the patriarch's son Joseph to save the Israelites and all the realm of Pharaoh from a seven-year famine and almost certain death. Shortly thereafter, however, a new king, "who did not know Joseph,"[84] ascended to the throne and began to inflict onerous bondage upon the Israelites by enslaving and abusing them. Finally, the outcry of the Children of Israel reached the ears of their God,[85] who then commissioned a prophet to secure their freedom.

This servant of God was Moses, who, from infancy into adult life, had lived in the power and privilege of Pharaoh's family, only to be banished to the desert when he was forty years old. After four decades of divine preparation, however, Moses returned as an octogenarian to Pharaoh's court with the fateful divine imperative of fiery words that God had spoken to him from the burning bush. This command echoed from Moses' lips into Pharaoh's ears: "Let my people go so that they may observe a festival to me in the wilderness."[86]

After God had vented his wrath upon both Pharaoh and the gods of Egypt by means of the ten plagues,[87] the ruler of the most powerful dominion in the

---

[83] Genesis 15:13: "Then the LORD said to Abram, 'Know for certain that your offspring will be sojourners in a land that is not theirs and will be servants there, and they will be afflicted for four hundred years. But I will also judge the nation whom they will serve, and afterward they will come out with many possessions.'"

[84] Exodus 1:8.

[85] Exodus 2:23.

[86] Exodus 5:1.

[87] When God introduced the last of the ten plagues, he specifically said that by doing so, he would "execute judgments against all the gods of Egypt" (Exodus 12:12). Moses also observed later that God "had executed judgment against [the Egyptians'] gods" (Numbers 33:4). See Robert B. Hughes and J. Carl Laney, *Tyndale Concise Bible Commentary* (Wheaton, IL: Tyndale House Publishers, 1990), pp. 34–36; Charles F. Aling, *Egypt and Bible History* (Grand Rapids, MI: Baker Books, 1981), pp. 103–110; and George A. F. Knight, *Theology as Narration* (Grand Rapids, MI: Wm. B. Eerdmans Publishing Co., 1976), pp. 94–153. For a comparison of the ten plagues and the Egyptian gods that they punished, see John D. Garr, *Passover: The Festival of Redemption* (Atlanta, GA: Golden Key Press, 2013), p. 85.

world finally bowed to the will of the God of Israel and released the Chosen People from their slavery. This people fully experienced what God had promised them: "I am the LORD, and I will bring you out from under the burdens of the Egyptians, I will deliver you from their bondage. I will also redeem you with an outstretched arm and with great judgments. Then I will take you for my people, and I will be to you a God."[88] A few days later, when they faced the dilemma of 250,000 of Pharaoh's soldiers in hot pursuit behind them and the impassable Red Sea[89] in front of them, the Chosen People heard another of God's commands through Moses: "Move on!"[90] Instead of cowering in fear, each Israelite demonstrated amazing faith in God's Word by initiating a march between the walled-up waters of the sea. When the last Israelite escaped Egypt, the strong east wind that had parted the sea abated, and the same waters through which the Israelites had just passed to freedom collapsed upon Pharaoh's pursuing armies, drowning all of them.

By passing through the waters of the sea that towered above their heads, the Israelites, in effect, experienced death, burial, and resurrection.[91] When they realized that they had escaped Pharaoh's slavery, however, this people did not disperse and go their separate ways, because they had become a corporate entity, a separate and separated ("holy"[92]) people. Their sacrifice of the Paschal lamb in each of their households and their immersion in the waters and mist of the Red Sea had produced a reborn people, chosen and separated unto God. While some seventy Israelites had entered the land of Egypt during the time of the famine,[93] only four centuries later, six hundred thousand men, together with women and children,[94] were ready to be delivered from the slavery into which they had been forced. The Chosen People were ready for the singular events that would fulfill their divine destiny. Moses later would explain to these Chosen People the

---

[88] Exodus 6:7.
[89] The "Red Sea" was actually called the "Reed Sea" (סוּף יַם—*Yam Suph*) in Scripture.
[90] Exodus 14:15.
[91] In 1 Corinthians 10:2, Paul called the Israelite experience at the Red Sea a "baptism." In doing so, he drew from one of the prominent Jewish traditions in his day wherein the people immersed themselves in the waters of *mikva'ot* (ceremonial ablution pools) in order to demonstrate a change in status in their lives. By that time, the Jewish people had come to understand immersion in the *mikveh* as being "born again." For a complete discussion of the Red Sea event and its implications, see John D. Garr, *Christian Fruit—Jewish Root: Theology of Hebraic Restoration* (Atlanta, GA: Golden Key Press, 2015), pp. 76–90.
[92] The Hebrew word translated "holy," קָדוֹשׁ (*kadosh*), means "separate" or "set apart." Anything that is "holy" has been distinguished from everything else; therefore, it is "set apart" or "separate."
[93] Genesis 46:27.
[94] Exodus 12:37.

nature and extent of this divine calling and election: "You are a holy people unto the LORD your God: of all the peoples on earth the LORD your God chose you to be his treasured people."[95]

Finally, the Israelites assembled in one mind and one accord at Mt. Sinai to experience the ultimate encounter with the living God. They saw the fire on the mountain, and they heard the thunderous voice of God delivering to them the Ten Words that summarized and encapsulated the essence of all of God's instruction to humanity. After these words had been written by the finger of God on tablets of stone, God reaffirmed his intentions: "Now then, if you obey me fully and keep my covenant, then out of all nations you will be my treasured possession."[96] Later, Moses restated God's designation of this people as the Chosen People: "The LORD will establish you as a holy people to himself . . . so all the peoples of the earth will see that you are called by the name of the LORD."[97] This promise, however, represented nothing more than a reaffirmation and an expansion of the original covenant that God had made with Abraham well over four centuries before that time. It was an asseveration of God's everlasting commitment to his Chosen People.

The Israelite status of being the people chosen by God from and above all the other people groups and nations of the world was continually reasserted and reinforced to generation after generation of the descendants of Abraham, Isaac, and Jacob. It remained through the time of the Judges and into the era of the Monarchy.[98] It was not abandoned or abrogated during the Babylonian captivity,[99] and it was asserted again and again before, during, and after the restoration of the temple and the city of Jerusalem in post-exilic Judaea.[100] It was still firmly established in Second

---

95 Deuteronomy 7:6a, JPS; 6b, TNK.

96 Exodus 19:5.

97 Deuteronomy 28:10.

98 1 Chronicles 16:13: "O seed of Israel his servant, sons of Jacob, his *chosen ones*! . . . Remember his covenant forever, the word which he commanded to a thousand generations" (emphasis added). Psalm 105:6–10: "O seed of Abraham, his servant, O sons of Jacob, *his chosen ones*! . . . He has remembered his covenant forever, the word which he commanded to a thousand generations. The covenant he made with Abraham, and his oath to Isaac. Then he confirmed it to Jacob for a statute, to Israel as an everlasting covenant" (emphasis added). Psalm 33:12: "Blessed is the nation whose God is the LORD, the people whom he has *chosen for his own inheritance*" (emphasis added).

99 Jeremiah 31:1: "At that time, declares the LORD, I will be the God of all the families of Israel, and they shall be *my people*" (emphasis added). Amos 9:14: "I will also restore the captivity of *my people Israel*, and they will rebuild the ruined cities and live in them" (emphasis added).

100 Isaiah 65:9; Nehemiah 1:9; Zephaniah 2:9; and Zechariah 8:8: "I will bring them back, and they will live in the midst of Jerusalem, and they shall be *my people*, and I will be their God in truth and righteousness" (emphasis added).

Temple Judaism and especially during the time of Jesus and the apostles. In fact, this is what the apostle Paul said of his fellow Israelites: "They *are* Israelites, and to them belong the adoption, the glory, the covenants, the giving of the Law, and worship, and the promises. To them belong the patriarchs, and from them is traced the human ancestry of the Messiah."[101] When the Greek of this Pauline passage is translated literally, the intent of the author is very clear. As Marvin Wilson points out, what is translated "to them belong" is actually "to them [Israel] *are* [Greek, *eisin*, present tense] the covenants."[102] At the time at which Paul was discussing the partial hardening of some in Israel[103] and the breaking off of unfaithful branches from God's family tree,[104] he still maintained that adoption as children of God, the covenants, and the promises still pertained to Israel, and he argued further that even the branches of the olive tree that had been removed because of unbelief could still be restored to faith by a divine act of God himself.[105]

In discussing this issue, Paul asked a rhetorical question that so many Christians over the centuries have answered incorrectly: "God has not rejected *his people*, has he?" The entire Christian church should have listened to the answer that the apostle gave to his own question: "May it never be! For I too am an Israelite, a descendant of Abraham."[106] While a host of Christian theologians and leaders has argued that God's covenant

---

[101] Romans 9:4–5, ESV, NIV, emphasis added. In this, the preamble of the central theme of the Book of Romans (chapters 9–11), the apostle gave no indication that God no longer considered the Jews to be his Chosen People. He did not say, "They *were* Israelites." He said, "They *are* Israelites." While most Christian scholars have projected the idea that Romans 9–11 is a "great parenthesis," an incongruous anomaly inserted by Paul for some unknown reason in the middle of his profound and powerful discourse on Justification by Faith, the reality is that these three chapters are the focus of the entire Book of Romans. Chris Tiegreen captures this truth succinctly: "Many observers see Romans 9–11 as the 'great parenthesis' in this monumental letter—a sidebar commentary that takes Paul away from his primary purpose in writing. Others see this section as the pinnacle of the letter, the climax of all Paul has been saying. It's not a parenthesis at all." Chris Tiegreen, *90 Days Thru the Bible: A Devotional Journey from Walk Thru the Bible* (Wheaton, IL: Tyndale House Publishers, 2012), p. 163. Walter Kaiser, Jr., echoes this truth: "Romans 9–11 is not a 'parenthesis' in Paul's argumentation . . . rather, it is intrinsic to his argument. . . Paul's whole argument about soteriology *must include, throughout the whole book of Romans*, the place of the Jew." Walter C. Kaiser, Jr., *Toward Rediscovering the Old Testament* (Grand Rapids, MI: Zondervan Publishing, 1987), p. 54, author's emphasis.
[102] Marvin R. Wilson, *Exploring Our Hebraic Heritage: A Christian Theology of Roots and Renewal* (Grand Rapids, MI: Wm. B. Eerdmans Publishing Co., 2014), p. 248.
[103] Romans 11:25.
[104] Romans 11:17.
[105] Romans 11:23.
[106] Romans 11:1, emphasis added.

with Israel ended when Jesus was crucified,[107] at least two decades after that event, Paul still maintained that the covenants and the promises continued to pertain to Israel as they had done in an unbroken chain from the time of Abraham. Quoting the divine words recorded by the prophet Jeremiah, the author of Hebrews also offered a similar answer, "This is the covenant that I will make with the house of Israel after those days, says the Lord: I will put my laws into their minds, and I will write them on their hearts, and I will be their God, and they shall be my people."[108] For these original Christians, the continuance of Israel and the Chosen People was never in doubt. Their final conclusion was the same as God's: "They shall be my people."[109]

Israel, then, "is not a people existing in its own right that God sought out among the other peoples and then blessed with special privileges," says Christoph Schönborn. "No, God himself is Israel's *Creator*. . . . It is *he* who made it *his* people."[110] God's continually reiterated declaration of the election of Israel as his Chosen People was summed up by the prophet Isaiah when he spoke this reassuring word of the Lord to Israel: "You are my witnesses, says the LORD, and my servant whom I have chosen . . . *my chosen people*, the people whom I formed for myself."[111] The Hebrew word that God used to describe the chosenness of the Israelites was בָּחִיר (*bachir*), which means "choice one," "chosen," or "elect of God." God said it himself: "[You are] עַמִּי בְּחִירִי—*Ami B'chiri* (My Chosen People)."[112] Could anyone ever doubt this truth when God himself proclaimed it without the slightest reservation, hesitation, or equivocation? "Israel" is God-defined as a "people"—indeed, as *the* People of God! And God himself made it clear that his designation of Israel as עַמִּי בְּחִירִי—*Ami B'chiri* is something that will never be removed. Regardless as to what anyone in any time may say, the Jews are God's Chosen People!

---

107 Peter Williams, *Israel and the Covenants in New Testament Times* (Dundee, UK: Paragon Publishing, 2012), p. 43.
108 Hebrews 8:10.
109 Exodus 19:5; Leviticus 26:12; Isaiah 41:8; Jeremiah 24:7; 31:1–4; 32:38; Ezekiel 37:21–27; Amos 3:1–2; 2 Corinthians 6:16.
110 Christoph Schönborn, *Loving the Church: Spiritual Exercises Preached in the Presence of Pope John Paul II* (San Francisco, CA: Ignatius Press, 1998), p. 91.
111 Isaiah 43:10–12, 20–21, TNK, emphasis added.
112 Isaiah 43:20.

CHAPTER 2

THE CHOSEN NATION

A DOMINION OF PRIESTS

Is it possible for one nation to be intrinsically "above" all the other nations in the world? Has there ever been such a thing as a "chosen nation," and is there such a thing in today's world? The answer is found in the promissory clauses of the command that God made to Abraham four millennia ago, "Go forth from your country and from your relatives and from your father's house to the land which I will show you. And I will make you a *great nation*, and I will bless you, and make your name great; and so you shall be a blessing."[1] The provisions that God made in this imperative were designed to replace everything that the patriarch would be required to surrender when he stepped out in his walk of faith to fulfill the terms of God's command. Abraham had already departed from Babylon when his father Terah left the nation of his birth with the intention of settling in Canaan. Now, he was leaving Assyria, the nation of which he had become a citizen when his family had settled there.[2] To replace Abraham's loss of his two national identities, God promised the patriarch that he would make his descendants a "great nation." Additionally, in leaving Haran, Abraham was surrendering his good name and his reputation, *Avram*, which meant "Exalted Father." In return, however, God would give his faithful friend a greater name and reputation,

---

[1] Genesis 12:1–2, emphasis added.

[2] Abraham had left his native land, Babylon, and the city of his birth, Ur of the Chaldeans, when his father Terah proposed to "go into the land of Canaan" (Genesis 11:31). The Terah family never reached their planned destination, however. Instead, they settled in Haran, Syria. It was in Haran that Abraham received his immortal *"Lech l'chah"* ("Go [for yourself]") commission. Abraham, therefore, was a Babylonian by birth and a Syrian by nationality. He gladly surrendered both national identities in order to become the first Hebrew when he crossed over the River Euphrates and entered the land of Canaan.

Avraham[3], which meant "Father of a Multitude," or "Father of Many Nations." Finally, Abraham was surrendering the real estate on which his family had settled. In return, God assured the patriarch that he would give him the "Promised Land," which was Canaan, his father's original intended destination.

In effect, the nationhood of the descendants of Abraham, Isaac, and Jacob has been a settled fact in Divine Law for 4,000 years because of the decree that God issued to Abraham at that time. From the very moment when God called Abraham and gave him the commission, "Go!" the very first thing that God promised him was "I will make you a great nation." The nationhood of Israel and the Jews, therefore, is not merely a recent creation through Machiavellian manipulation, nor is it an enactment of political expediency. It is a most ancient entitlement that far predates and transcends the claims of any other people group or political entity to the status of nationhood in what came to be called Syria-Palaestina (Palestine) by the Roman Empire. Abraham's lineal descendants have been God's "nation" for four millennia; they continue to be his "Chosen Nation" to this day; and they will remain his nation forever.

A Dominion Unique among All the Nations

The "nation" that would be birthed from the loins of Abraham was to be *sui generis*. There had never been anything like it, and there would never be anything like it until the end of time when the Messianic Kingdom would establish God's dominion over the entire earth. When God chose Abraham and his descendants after him, he was not looking for a military juggernaut that would conquer the world and dominate its people. He was looking for a kingdom of priests[4] that would bring his justice and peace to all the nations.[5] This "kingdom" was not to be like the pagan kingdoms that believed they were destined to rule because they saw themselves as superior to the rest of the human race and viewed their leaders as gods.

In the Abrahamic tradition, God's kingdom was not to be characterized by a ragtag, amorphous anarchy with every individual doing whatever was pleasing to himself, nor was it to be an autocracy dominated by

---

[3] When God finalized his covenant with Abram and Sarai, he added to both of their names one of the letters of his own personal name ה/ו/ה/י (YHWH), the name that he would use in his covenantal relationship with his Chosen People. As a result, אַבְרָם (*Avram*) became אַבְרָהָם (*Avraham*) and שָׂרַי (*Sarai*) became שָׂרָה (*Sarah*).

[4] Exodus 19:6.

[5] Genesis 18:19.

48

demigods, superheroes, or autocrats. It was to be a commonwealth directed by ordinary men and women who would be endowed with the extraordinary power of God's Spirit. In the end, the glory of God's nation would be focused not on its rulers but on the God who had constituted that nation, established it as a theonomy,[6] and empowered its leaders to execute divine justice tempered with divine mercy. The form of government that God had planned for his Chosen People had first been demonstrated in the Abrahamic family when the patriarch manifested divine justice by observing all of God's commandments some five centuries before they were codified at Mt. Sinai[7] and, at the same time, established himself as the example *par excellence* of divine mercy by demonstrating the divine quality of mutuality and deference throughout his life.[8] This complementary balance of justice and mercy that Abraham exemplified was described by the prophet Micah as the definition of what it means to "walk humbly with God,"[9] something that Abraham superbly manifested in obedience to God's commandment.[10]

The dominion that God was preparing to establish in the earth, therefore, was to be revolutionary, entirely different from those that had emerged from the hearts and minds of men. God had a better idea for governance, and he planned to prove its effectiveness as he brought his Chosen People together to form them into his chosen nation. God had summoned the descendants of Abraham, Isaac, and Jacob and had brought them from Egyptian slavery to Mt. Sinai for the express purpose of empowering them

---

[6] The nation of Israel was the first dominion that was governed by "the rule of law." God did not establish an absolute monarchy, a family dynasty that exercised autocratic power over the people. Instead, he established a theonomy, a nation governed by "rule of God's law"—in this case, God's divine instructions to humanity that were encapsulated in the Ten Commandments and in the instructions delineated under the overarching principles of those Ten Words. For details on the system of government that God designed for the nation of Israel, see John D. Garr, *The Church Dynamic: Hebraic Foundations for Christian Community* (Atlanta, GA: Golden Key Press, 2015).

[7] Genesis 26:5: "Abraham obeyed my voice and kept my charge, my commandments, my statutes, and my laws" (ESV).

[8] Abraham's deference was demonstrated in his willingness to cede to his nephew Lot what appeared to be the best part of the Promised Land in order to have peace (Genesis 13:6–12). It was again evidenced when the patriarch was promised the birth of Isaac, only to exclaim, "If only Ishmael might live under your blessing!" (Genesis 17:18, NIV). It was finally manifest when Abraham, who had been commissioned as prophetic intercessor for blessing to all nations of the earth, interceded for the earth's worst example of evil and ungodliness, Sodom and Gomorrah (Genesis 18:22–33).

[9] Micah 6:8.

[10] Genesis 17:1. God commanded Abraham, "Walk before me, and be blameless."

to celebrate a festival in which they would worship him.[11] When they were assembled at the mountain of God, it was not to form a military-industrial complex: it was to form a worshipping nation! God's nation would be unique in the world in that it would focus not on world domination through the exercise of raw and murderous power. Instead, it would exemplify the incredible *chesed* of YHWH, the God of love and mercy, by gently leading the earth into the blessings of his divine instructions.

God established the uniqueness of his divine call to Israel in these instructions to Moses: "These are the words you are to speak to the Israelites: You shall be to me a kingdom of priests and a holy nation."[12] The nationhood of Israel was to be completely focused on its servanthood and on its intercessory action as a royal priesthood. This was the determining factor that was destined to make Israel a "holy nation," a nation set apart to the service of God. Israel was to be a worshipping nation, and, like its father, Abraham, it was to be a prophetic intercessor for the redemption of all humanity through the gift of the Torah and the understanding of God's lovingkindness toward the human race. God was preparing to create a nation out of the virtual nothingness of the least significant people on earth. Here is what he said: "The LORD did not . . . choose you because you were more in number than any of the peoples, for you were the fewest of all peoples."[13] God would birth a nation of priests, and it would be a miracle!

At the point in time at which the people of Israel were finally assembled in one mind and one accord at the base of Sinai, the same question that God posed to the prophet Isaiah centuries later regarding a future embodiment of Israel could well have been asked: "Can a nation be born in a single day?"[14] The obvious and logical answer to this question would have been, *No!* But, the obvious answer was not the correct one. God was not looking for a logical answer, or even for an illogical answer, for that matter. In his infinite foreknowledge, he knew that there was a supralogical answer, one that would transcend human reasoning and tap into the infinite logic of God himself.[15] What God had planned for the Jewish nation was "not simply *super*natural; it [was] *contra*natural,"[16] in

---

[11] Exodus 9:1. God said, "Let my people go that they may celebrate a festival to me in the wilderness."
[12] Exodus 19:6.
[13] Deuteronomy 7:7.
[14] Isaiah 66:8.
[15] Isaiah 55:8–9.
[16] Jon D. Levenson, "The Universal Horizon of Biblical Particularism," in *Ethnicity and the Bible*, Mark G. Bret, ed. (Leiden, The Netherlands: E. J. Brill, 1996), p. 155.

that it defied all the known laws of nature and the norms of history. God was planning to do something that no one could reasonably have expected would—or could—happen. He was planning to do the impossible.

So, in one day, the very day of Pentecost (*Shavuot*), when the Israelites had assembled before the smoking, quaking mountain of God, the *people* of Israel was constituted as a "*holy nation*," a dominion that would be a "kingdom of priests." At that time, such a thing must have seemed utterly impossible. Even in their wildest dreams, could such a motley aggregation of pathetic, disenfranchised people have ever expected to be molded into a nation even in decades, much less in a single day? The answer was, yes, but only because God was the one who was birthing this nation![17] God said it himself: "You shall be to me a kingdom of priests and a holy nation."[18]

God had predicted this very event centuries earlier when he had said to Jacob, "I am God Almighty; be fruitful and multiply; a nation and a company of nations shall come from you, and kings shall come forth from you."[19] Later, when the patriarch of the Israelite people considered taking his family to Egypt in order to escape the time of famine, God again said, "I am God, the God of your father. Do not be afraid to go down to Egypt, for I will make you a great nation there."[20] And what God had promised he did. When Jacob obeyed God and took his family to Egypt, there were only 70 people in his family entourage.[21] By the time that the "children of Jacob (Israel)" left Egypt more than 400 years later, there were 600,000 men, plus women and children— an estimated 1.5 to 2 million people![22] The Chosen People had indeed become a great nation while they were in Egypt, just as God had predicted.

---

[17] YHWH was the God who both fathered the nation of Israel and mothered it by writhing in labor pains to bring it forth. This was Moses' conclusion regarding this nation of people when he described the failure of the people in the golden-calf incident: "You deserted the Rock who fathered you; you forgot the God who gave you birth" (Deuteronomy 32:18, NIV). In this case, the NIV has captured the essence of the Hebrew of this text, wherein God is viewed in both masculine and feminine terms as the creator of the nation of Israel. The Hebrew word translated "fathered you" is יְלָדְךָ (*yeladkah*), the verb of which means "to beget." The Hebrew word translated "gave you birth" is חֹלְלֶךָ (*cholelekah*), which means to "writhe in labor pains." The God of Scripture was not a male god who needed a female consort, a goddess. This God, who is genderless, was demonstrating to Israel in graphic, theomorphic terms that he was both the father and the mother to his chosen nation.

[18] Exodus 19:6. The designations *kingdom of priests* and *holy nation* continued to be applied by the apostles to the Christian church when it emerged within and as a part of the community of Israel (1 Peter 2:9; Revelation 1:6; 5:10).

[19] Genesis 35:11.

[20] Genesis 46:3.

[21] Genesis 46:27; Deuteronomy 10:22.

[22] Exodus 12:37.

The nuclear family of Jacob had expanded into an extended family and then into a nation that needed only to be formally incorporated by means of the ordination and establishment of a federal constitution—the Mosaic Covenant.[23] When Israel agreed to accept God's Torah, they collectively were constituted as the nation of God's own election, the Chosen Nation.

Israel, a Covenant Nation

A profound miracle occurred when God intervened through the hand of his servant Moses to deliver Abraham's descendants from Egyptian bondage. Events were set in motion that would further reify God's particularity and serve to unfold his universal vision for humanity. After the Israelites passed through the walled-up waters of the Red Sea and then watched as Pharaoh's armies drowned when those same waters came crashing down upon them, the Chosen People set out for the mountain of the Lord and an already prepared meeting with divine destiny. They had heard Moses speak of the divine presence that he had experienced when he heard tongues of fire speak directly to him from the burning bush.[24] Now, it was their opportunity to see, hear, and feel for themselves the fiery presence of the Eternal God on Mt. Sinai as the divine words of thunder echoed from that mountain.[25] They had been summoned by God's voice to come to his mountain and there to enter into a covenant that would make them God's nation of priests[26] and would transform them into the Holy One's community, the *kahal* or *ekklesía* of the Chosen People.[27]

In the march from the Red Sea to Sinai, the Israelites made the transition from a liberated but disorganized throng into a corporate assembly

---

[23] The giving of the Torah and Israel's acceptance of it was what constituted the Nation of Israel. Stephen Wylen says that "the Torah was the Constitution of the Jewish nation. . . . The Sanhedrin, the ancient high court of rabbis, served as Congress and Supreme Court of the Jewish nation." Stephen M. Wylen, *Settings of Silver: An Introduction to Judaism* (Mahwah, NJ: Paulist Press, 2000), p. 58. Interestingly, Mati Alon maintains that when Israel (Judah) was restored after the Babylonian captivity, "Ezra and Nehemiah established the Torah as the Constitution of the restored State." Mati Alon, *Holocaust and Redemption* (Victoria, Canada: Trafford Publishing, 2003), p. 55.

[24] Exodus 3:2.

[25] Psalm 68:8.

[26] Exodus 19:6.

[27] At Sinai, the Israelites were identified as the קָהָל—*kahal* ("community" or "congregation") of God. The word *kahal* is derived directly from the Hebrew word קוֹל—*kol*, which means "voice." The basis for Israel's being God's community, therefore, was the summons of God's voice that brought the Israelites to Sinai. It was the same summons that made the Christian church the ἐκκλησία—*ekklesia* ("called out ones"). Israel, therefore, was truly "the church in the wilderness," as Stephen said in Acts 7:38.

that could walk in unity and discipline. When the two million finally reached Sinai, the Hebrew text affirms that Israel (*plural*) camped (*singular*).[28] The disparate people, who included many non-Israelites, was finally in one accord and in one place anticipating the experience for which God had liberated them from Egyptian bondage.[29] They had overcome previous divisions among themselves, and they stood unified at the foot of Sinai. All they awaited then was the appearance of the God of Abraham, Isaac, and Jacob. And they would not be disappointed!

"Now Mount Sinai was all in smoke because the LORD descended upon it in fire; and its smoke ascended like the smoke of a furnace, and the whole mountain quaked violently."[30] God, their God, had appeared on the mountain in an utterly shocking display of divine power. Not only did he appear, but he also thundered to the Israelites these immortal words: "I am the LORD your God, who brought you out of the land of Egypt, out of the house of slavery."[31] Then, having confirmed his identity and his mission, God continued to outline the briefest possible synopsis of his own instructions for humanity: the Ten Commandments.[32] This was not, however, a simple statement of divine preferences posted on a bulletin board for Israel to consider. These were not the Ten Suggestions! They were fiery words of infallible and uncompromisable divine truth that the Israelites not only heard but also saw. As a matter of fact, the text literally says, "And all the people *saw* the voices and the flames, and the noise of the shofar, and the mountain smoking."[33]

How does one *see* voices, the sages asked? Apparently, God's voice emerged from the flames in the form of tongues of fire so that the people

---

[28] Exodus 19:2. Until this time, references to the Israelites' journeyings such as Numbers 23:3 had noted that Israel (*pl.*) had journeyed (*pl.*) and had camped (*pl.*), indicating that the group that left Egypt was more like a disorganized mob than a unified, organized nation. When the Israelites came to Sinai, however, as Exodus 19:2 notes, the situation was drastically different. The body politic was "in one mind and one accord," awaiting God's revelation of himself. Rashi interpreted this text to mean that Israel camped in a state of utter unity. See Chaim Miller, ed., *Chumash, with Rashi's Commentary: Exodus* (New York: Kol Menachem, 2005), p. 131. The language employed regarding Israel's unity clearly parallels what was noted about the earliest Christian believers who were described as being "in one mind and one accord" as they prepared for the day of Pentecost (Acts 1:14).
[29] This Israelite experience was replicated with the 120 believers in Acts 1:14.
[30] Exodus 19:18.
[31] Exodus 20:2.
[32] Exodus 20:2–17. In reality, the declaration, "I am the LORD your God, who brought you out of the land of Egypt, out of the house of slavery" was the first of the Ten Words (Commandments).
[33] Exodus 20:18.

could actually see the words that God spoke at the same time as they heard them![34] In the first century BC, the Jewish philosopher/theologian Philo of Alexandria described the phenomenon in this manner: "From the fire . . . there sounded . . . a voice, for the flame became articulate speech . . . so clearly were the words formed . . . that they seemed to see them rather than to hear them."[35] Rabbi Yohanan further explained that all the fiery words at Sinai were divided into seventy languages,[36] just as God had said to the prophet Jeremiah, "Is not my word like fire . . . and like a hammer that breaks a rock in pieces?"[37] This was done, the sages said, so that both Israel and all the nations of the earth could hear the Ten Commandments in their own languages.[38] In effect, every nation and ethnicity was given the opportunity to receive God's Torah.[39] Only Israel, however, responded positively to God's offer.

After Israel had heard all the terms of the covenant that God was offering to them, they unanimously answered with one voice, "All the words which the LORD has spoken we will do!"[40] Later, the people made this affirmation in a slightly different and a much more powerful manner which would have extraordinary consequences for them. This text quotes the Israelites as saying, כֹּל אֲשֶׁר־דִּבֶּר יהוה נַעֲשֶׂה וְנִשְׁמָע ("*Kol asher diber YHWH na'aseh v'nishma*"), which is literally translated this way:

---

[34] This action was not entirely unique, for God had spoken to Moses in flames of fire at the burning bush, and he appeared as "cloven tongues of fire" to the disciples of Jesus in the first Pentecost of the earliest church (Acts 2:3). J. I. Packer, *Keep in Step with the Spirit: Finding Fullness in Our Walk with God* (Grand Rapids, MI: Baker Books, 1984), p. 210.

[35] Philo, *De Decalogo* 33; *De Praemiis* 2. See Christopher Forbes, *Prophecy and Inspired Speech in Early Christianity and its Hellenistic Environment* (Tübingen, Germany: J.C.B. Mohr, Siebeck 1995), p. 167, n. 43.

[36] Babylonian Talmud, *Shabbat* 88b. In Jewish tradition, the nations have been numbered at seventy because Genesis 10 lists exactly seventy descendants of Noah's sons, Shem, Ham, and Japheth. In the case of each of these three, the Scripture reports that "these are the sons of Japheth [v. 5] . . . of Ham [v. 20] . . . of Shem [v. 31] . . . in their lands, each with his own *language*, by their families, in their *nations*" (emphasis added). The direct descendants of Noah were for "languages" and "nations."

[37] Jeremiah 23:29.

[38] Hebrews 12:26 says that when God spoke from Sinai, "His voice shook the earth." King David also said that even from the moment of creation, the heavens have declared "the glory of God" because "their voice goes out into all the earth" (Psalm 19:1–4). In Romans 10:18, Paul applied the Psalmist's description of the heavens to the words of God that were thundered to the Israelites at Sinai: "Their voice has gone out into all the earth, and their words to the ends of the world."

[39] The sages suggested that the Torah was given in the wilderness, in a public place (Mt. Sinai), so that it would be accessible to anyone—to all humanity. If God had intended his Torah to be proprietary, he would have given it in a temple that was exclusive to one people. See W. Gunther Plaut and David E. S. Stein, eds., *The Torah: A Modern Commentary* (New York: UJR Press, 2005), p. 485.

[40] Exodus 24:3.

"All that the LORD has said, we will do, and we will hear [understand]."[41] In effect, the people declared that they would simply do whatever God commanded them even before they could understand it. They would "carry out God's will before they had learned its demands."[42] These Israelites had learned this valuable lesson: many of God's ways are ineffable; they cannot be understood unless they are first done. Indeed, the understanding often comes through the doing! And this is the level of commitment that God required from his Chosen People. Because they loved him and would be joined to him in a covenant, they would do what he commanded them even if they did not understand it because their faith was exclusively in him.

And so it was that Israel became God's witness nation. Repeatedly—indeed, incessantly—the Israelites recited the greatest of the Torah Commandments,[43] the *Shema*: "Hear, O Israel, the LORD our God, the LORD is one,"[44] and every time those words of Scripture erupted from their hearts and lips, the Chosen People underscored and bore witness to the bedrock foundation of all biblical faith: the oneness and unity of God. In fact, as Frans Josef van Beeck has observed, "monotheistic faith in YHWH is the *articulus stantis et cadentis* of Israel's faith and self-awareness from the beginning."[45] John Franke says it well: "The Hebrew community that had been shaped by the promises contained in the Abrahamic covenant asserted unequivocally that there was only one God and that this God alone was to be the object of their loyalty and worship."[46] Since the birth of the Israelite nation at Sinai, millions of Jews around the world have continued the tradition of proclaiming this declaration

---

41 Exodus 24:7. This passage is usually translated, "We will do everything the LORD has said; we will obey"; however, the Hebrew text actually says, "We will do everything the LORD has said; and we will hear (וְנִשְׁמָע—*v'nishma*)." Since the Hebrew word שָׁמַע (*shema*), which usually means "to hear," can also mean "to understand," the sages have interpreted the inclusion of the word *shema* in the phrase *nishmah* of this text to mean that the Israelites agreed to observe God's instructions even before they understood them. Literally, they said, "We will do everything the LORD has said; and [then] we will hear [it] [or understand it]."

42 Plaut and Stein, eds., p. 499.

43 Jesus confirmed the established truth of Judaism that the *Shema* is the "first" and the "greatest" of all the commandments (Mark 12:29).

44 Deuteronomy 6:4.

45 Frans Josef van Beeck, *God Encountered: A Contemporary Catholic Systematic Theology Vol. Two/2: The Revelation of the Glory: Part II: One God, Creator of All That Is* (Collegeville, MN: The Liturgical Press, 1996), p. 96. The Latin phrase *articulus stantis et cadentis* means the article on which something stands and falls—in this case, the nation of Israel stands or falls on the foundation of ethical monotheism.

46 John R. Franke, *The Character of Theology: An Introduction to Its Nature, Task, and Purpose* (Grand Rapids, MI: Baker Academic, 2005), p. 47.

of monotheistic faith, and countless ones among them have not ceased to lift up these words even when they were experiencing martyrdom for their faith.[47]

God's continuing plan for Israel to be his witness nation by constantly affirming him to be the one and only God was encapsulated in the declaration that he made through the prophet Isaiah, "'You are my witnesses . . . my servant whom I have chosen, so that you may know and trust me and understand that I am the One. Before me no God was formed, nor will there be one after me. I, yes I, am the LORD, and apart from me there is no savior. . . . You are my witnesses,' says the LORD, 'that I am God.'"[48] The particularity of God's covenant with Israel was that they would make a universal acclamation of the exclusivity of his deity. According to Isaiah, the heart of Israel's witness to the nations was to be the same as it was in the days of Abraham—the testimony to the divine truth of monotheism: the Lord God is the one and only God.[49] This witness was unique to Abraham's understanding, and it was to be the uniqueness of the Israelites as well. Robert Erlewine confirms this truth: "The people of Israel, in all their particularity, are to serve as the exemplar, the witness, to the universal idea of the unique God. . . . The Jews are elected insofar as they symbolize the universal idea of the unique God, and their mission consists in bearing witness to it."[50] Hermann Cohen has argued that for this reason, "Israel is not simply a people among a plurality of peoples." Instead, "because of its calling to profess the unique God and also to accomplish the historical work of the universal recognition of the unique God, Israel itself is distinguished as a unique people."[51]

Isaiah was also exercised by the Spirit to speak of God's commission for Israel to be his witnessing nation: "I, the LORD . . . will make you to be a

[47] Ivan G. Marcus, *The Jewish Life Cycle: Rites of Passage from Biblical to Modern Times* (Seattle, WA: The University of Washington Press, 2004), p. 200.

[48] Isaiah 43:10, 12, ISV, NIV.

[49] For a comprehensive study of Israel's monotheism, see Robert Karl Gnuse, *No Other Gods: Emergent Monotheism in Israel* (Sheffield, UK: Sheffield Academic Press, 1997), and Richard Bauckham, "Biblical Theology and the Problems of Monotheism," in *Out of Egypt: Biblical Theology and Biblical Interpretation*, Craig Bartholomew, ed. (Carlisle, UK: Paternoster, 2004), pp. 187–232.

[50] Robert Erlewine, *Monotheism and Tolerance: Recovering a Religion of Reason* (Bloomington, IN: Indiana University Press, 2010), p. 152. Erlewine was speaking of the philosophy of Hermann Cohen.

[51] Hermann Cohen, *Religion of Reason: Out of the Sources of Judaism*, tr. Simon Kaplan (New York: Frederick Ungar Publishing Co., 1972), p. 105, quoted in "Evil and Suffering," in *The Jewish Philosophy Reader*, Daniel H. Frank, Oliver Leaman, and Charles H. Manekin, eds. (London, UK: Routledge, 2000), p. 494.

covenant for the people and a light for the Gentiles."[52] The prophet further confirmed God's promise to Abraham that through his descendants all the families and nations of the earth would be blessed. The divine particularity of Israel was to be extended as a covenantal light to the nations! The children of Abraham through Isaac and Jacob, therefore, made a covenant with God that transformed them into his holy nation,[53] a commonwealth chosen above all the rest of earth's inhabitants.[54] When this covenant was made, however, it merely supplemented and expanded the covenant that God had already made with Abraham more than four centuries earlier, for it could never replace or abrogate that covenant. Paul recognized and confirmed this truth: "The Torah, which was four hundred and thirty years later, cannot annul the [Abrahamic] covenant that was confirmed before by God in Messiah, that it should make the promise of no effect."[55] In the ongoing experience of the Israelites while they were encamped at Mount Sinai, God continued to outline details of the covenant—in effect, expanding or further delineating the covenant that he had made with their father Abraham. The Sinai covenant was not to be a *new* covenant. It was rather to be a *renewed* covenant, the Abrahamic covenant expanded and explicated.[56]

In the midst of all the spectacles that seemed threatening to human life—fire, earthquakes, supernatural shofar blasts, and the like—Moses and the children of Israel were actually enclosed in a haven of peace and tranquility with God. As Ray Vander Laan says, ". . . the Israelites can be thought of as not just standing

---

[52] Isaiah 42:6, NIV.

[53] Deuteronomy 10:15. See Sol Scharfstein, *The Five Books of Moses* (Jersey City, NJ: KTAV Publishing House, 2005), p. 172.

[54] Charles Leslie, *A Short and Easy Method with the Jews, Wherein the Certainty of the Christian Religion Is Demonstrated* (Spitalfields, England: 1812), p. 123. Leslie said, "Thus a nation or people taken into federal covenant with God, more peculiarly than any other nation upon the earth, may be called blessed above all the nations of the earth: and an holy people, in respect of the holiness of their laws, covenant, promises, &c. given to them by God."

[55] Galatians 3:17.

[56] The Sinai covenant created no new commandments, for God had said that "Abraham obeyed me and kept my charge, my commandments, my statutes and my laws" (Genesis 26:5). What the Torah did was to expand and further explicate the instructions that God had given Abraham and make them definitive and systematic. The renewal of the Abrahamic covenant by means of expansion at Sinai demonstrated the process that would be used when the same Abrahamic covenant, including its Sinai renewal, would again be renewed by expansion with the death and resurrection of the Messiah. The "new" covenant was not a revolutionary, neoteric covenant that had never existed or had never been considered before. It was what Jeremiah and the author of Hebrews declared it to be: "This is the covenant that I will make with the house of Israel after those days, says the LORD: 'I will put my laws into their minds, and I will write them on their hearts. And I will be their God, and they shall be my people'" (Jeremiah 31:31; Hebrews 8:10). The law was not to be changed; the place where it was written was to be changed—from inscription on tablets of stone at Sinai to impression on the hearts and minds of believers thereafter. God promised to Israel that writing the renewed covenant on heart and mind would be fulfilled among the Chosen People.

at the base of the mountain but standing under God's great *chuppah*[57] . . . covered with the canopy of his intimate, protective love."[58] They were in a wedding chamber as it were, drawn together in the intimacy of divine love. Just as in modern Jewish weddings, the terms of God's marriage covenant with Israel were read, as the Decalogue detailed God's expectations of his bride. Under the *chuppah* of the cloud of divine glory, Israel said a corporate "I do" and was joined with the God of the universe in a perpetual covenant that would never be abolished. God himself had made this unequivocal promise to Abraham: "I will keep my covenant between me and you, and your offspring after you throughout their generations. . . . It will continue between me and your offspring forever."[59] It was on the basis of this covenant that God himself assured Israel centuries later: "I am YHWH your God; therefore, you children of Jacob are not consumed."[60] No wonder Paul exclaimed regarding the inviolability of God's covenant with Israel: "The gifts and callings of God are irrevocable."[61] The God of Israel is forever faithful to keep his covenant with his Chosen People.

In the context of his covenant, God set before the Israelites life and death, blessings and curses, and he exhorted them to "choose life."[62] While death lurked at every corner, life reigned for those who would yield their lives to God's Word. The distance between death and life was simply the thickness of indelible ink on parchment. "Keep my commands," God said, "and you will live."[63] And, death was also readily at hand, for "the wages of sin is death."[64] Since Sinai, the options have been clear: life or death, blessing or curse. And God still implores everyone, as he did all the Israelites of that day: "Choose life," for it is not his will "that any should perish, but that all should receive eternal life."[65]

At Sinai, the people of Israel learned that "to choose to respond to the true God was to choose the truly human as well. Living out the requirements of the Torah among the nations would be their priestly witness."[66] In accepting

---

[57] The Hebrew word חוּפָּה (*chuppah*) means "canopy." The canopy under which bride and groom stand during a traditional Jewish wedding ceremony is a reminder of the canopy (cloud) under which Israel stood when they were married to God at Sinai.
[58] Ray Vander Laan, *With All Your Heart* (Grand Rapids, MI: Zondervan Publishing, 2010), p. 78–79.
[59] Genesis 17:7.
[60] Malachi 3:6.
[61] Romans 11:29.
[62] Deuteronomy 30:19.
[63] Proverbs 7:2.
[64] Romans 6:23.
[65] John 3:16.
[66] Vinoth Ramachandra, *Faiths in Conflict?: Christian Integrity in a Multicultural World* (Downers Grove, IL: InterVarsity Press, 2000), p. 96.

YHWH's instructions and thereby joining him in an expansion of the Abrahamic covenant, the nation of Israel came to be defined "not only by ethnicity and land, but supremely by the Law (Torah) given to them by God as a witness to his character."[67] Out of all the nations of the world, only in Israel did God work "in terms of a redemptive covenant, initiated and preserved by his grace."[68] In this way, the nation of Israel "experienced something unparalleled 'from the day God created man on the earth' and 'from one end of the heavens to the other,' a unique revelation of Yahweh and a unique experience of his redemptive power."[69] Israel was not satisfied with the ways of the world: it chose the ways of the Almighty instead.

Erlewine sums up the uniqueness of Israel's election as God's Chosen Nation in this manner: "The vocation of Israel secures its uniqueness, which is a special kind of particularity . . . Israel is distinguished as unique, as distinct from all other particular communities, insofar as it points beyond history to the unique God, which alone is the true condition for totality."[70] Here is how God defined the covenant of election: "You have singled out God today . . . and God on his part has singled you out today."[71] Elazar B. Azariah pointed out that this passage was fulfilled[72] when Israel made God "a unique object of praise" by saying, "Hear O Israel, the LORD our God, the LORD is the One and Only"[73] and when God made Israel "a unique object of praise in the world" by saying, "Who is like your people Israel, a unique nation on earth."[74] As Leyla Gurkan notes, "Although God knew Israel long before, it was only 'when the people stood before Mount Sinai and received the Torah' that 'they had become completely God's people.'"[75] Israel, therefore, is "God's people, whether cosmic or historical, for the sake of Torah."[76]

---

[67] Ramachandra, *Faiths*, p. 96.
[68] Vinoth Ramachandra, *The Recovery of Mission: Beyond the Pluralist Paradigm* (Grand Rapids, MI: Wm. B. Eerdmans Publishing Co., 1997), p. 231.
[69] Ramachandra, *The Recovery*, p. 231.
[70] Erlewine, p. 152.
[71] Deuteronomy 26:17–18.
[72] Elazar B. Azariah, quoted in Jacob ben Solomon ibn Habib, *Ein Yaakov, The Ethical and Inspirational Teachings of the Talmud*, Yaakov bin Chaviv, ed., Abraham Yaakov Finkel, tr. (New York: Jason Aronson, 1999), p. 335.
[73] Deuteronomy 6:4.
[74] 1 Chronicles 17:21.
[75] S. Leyla Gurkan, *The Jews as a Chosen People: Tradition and Transformation* (Abingdon, UK: Routledge, 2009), p. 40. Gurkan quotes first Exodus *Rabbah* 32:2, then Canticles *Rabbah* 42:1, along with *Pesikta* 12:23.
[76] Gurkan, p. 40.

At Sinai, the Israelites found the freedom that they and their ancestors had desperately sought during all the years of Egyptian bondage. They were truly free when they were joined to God and fully submitted to his Word and will. Israel was not free when the Israelites escaped the tyranny of Egypt. True freedom came when Israel the people became Israel the nation by choosing to accept the "perfect law of liberty,"[77] the Torah of YHWH, and agreeing to walk therein. It was the law of God that taught Israel "how to be truly free."[78] This was the divine law principle that Jesus summarized when he said, "You shall know the truth, and the truth will make you free."[79] For Israel, accepting the yoke of the Torah was receiving the gift of freedom. It transformed them from a people who were familial heirs of the Abrahamic promise into the socially structured Chosen Nation of God. In effect, what they had been as Abraham's family was ratified and confirmed by the giving of the Torah.

The Torah, therefore, "is intrinsic to the 'institution of Israel' conceived in terms of the covenant established and initiated by God in relation to the people of Israel," says Alan Torrance.[80] The terms of the covenant do not, therefore, denote "immediately accessible *regulae remotae* or abstract laws of nature conceived in Stoic or Aristotelian terms."[81] Instead, Israel's election is "unilaterally established by Yahweh and . . . is neither conditional nor contractual."[82] For this reason, the Ten Commandments begin with an unconditional declaration: "I am the LORD your God who brought you out of the land of Egypt." Everything else in the Decalogue and, indeed, in all of the Torah simply spells out "the *obligations* which flow from this covenantal commitment."[83] Torrance concludes that because the summation of God's instructions begins with God's unilateral commitment to Israel, "we have apodictic, unconditional obligations not to kill, not to commit adultery, not to steal, bear false witness, and so

---

[77] James 1:25. See Lewis R. Donelson, *From Hebrews to Revelation: A Theological Introduction* (Louisville, KY: Westminster John Knox Press, 2001), p. 46, and Patrick J. Hartin, *A Spirituality of Perfection: Faith in Action in the Letter of James* (Collegeville, MN: The Liturgical Press, 1999), pp. 81–82.

[78] Andrew Knowles, *The Bible Guide: An All-in-One Introduction to the Book of Books* (Oxford, UK: Lion Publishing, 2001), p. 43.

[79] John 8:32.

[80] Alan J. Torrance, "On Deriving 'Ought' from 'Is'," in *The Doctrine of God and Theological Ethics*, Michael C. Banner and Alan J Torrance, eds. (New York: T & T Clark, 2006), p. 181.

[81] Torrance, p. 181.

[82] Torrance, p. 181.

[83] Torrance, p. 181.

on," and Israel "is obliged to live out the faithfulness of Yahweh and to 'correspond' to his covenant faithfulness communally."[84]

The Davidic Kingdom

When Israel was joined to God in covenant, the first truly free nation in human history was born. This was a people whose divinely accorded free will had enabled them to choose to follow God's commandments and to walk in his ways all the days of their lives. Unlike human despots, God had not forced his will upon his people. They were asked to choose. When God brought the Israelites out of Egypt, however, at precisely that same time, he made further selection and designated a part of Israel to have an even more particularist relationship with him. "[God] rejected the clan of Joseph; and the tribe of Ephraim he did not choose. But he chose the tribe of Judah, the mountain of Zion, which he loves"[85] in order to accomplish his purposes. "When Israel went out of Egypt, the house of Jacob from a people of strange language, Judah became his sanctuary, and Israel his dominion."[86] Even before the land of Israel was settled, God's foreknowledge prompted him to choose Judah to become the tribe that would lead the entire people of Israel and save them from lapsing into idolatry and obviating the covenant. The tribe of Judah, then, became a uniquely Chosen People unto God—a nation within a nation, as it were. Judah was not exalted above the other tribes; however, its people were given a specific calling and assignment. Judah was the tribe to which God entrusted his sayings[87] because Judah, more than all of the other tribes of Israel, was zealous for the law and the Word of God.[88] It was in Judah, therefore, that God chose to place his capital city and his temple.

When the Hebrew Israelites Became "Jews"

As time progressed, particularly following the reigns of David and Solomon, the tribe of Judah, with the tribe of Benjamin and much of the

---

[84] Torrance, p. 181.

[85] Psalm 78:67-68.

[86] Psalm 114:1–2.

[87] 2 Chronicles 30:12; Romans 3:1–2.

[88] Isidore Singer, Cyrus Adler, et. al., eds., *The Jewish Encyclopedia* (New York: Funk and Wagnalls Company, 1906), vol. 7, p. 328. This text notes the declaration in Exodus *Rabbah* 24:1 that at the time of the Red Sea crossing, "the other tribes refused to enter the slimy bed of the sea until the tribe of Judah set them the example by plunging in." It also reports that "the people of Judah are said to have been versed in the Law."

tribe of Levi, became even more separated from the rest of Israel when the divided kingdom emerged. The northern tribes followed Jeroboam while Judah, Benjamin, and Levi followed Rehoboam, Solomon's son. God's wisdom in having chosen Judah above the others at the time of the Exodus was validated by the fact that Judah continued to maintain God's religious system while the majority of the northern tribes lapsed into idolatry and, as a result, experienced the first Israelite Diaspora when God sent the Assyrian armies to carry them into captivity. During this time, Judah remained faithful to God and continued to dwell in the land. Additionally, "numbers of all the tribes joined the kingdom of Judah on account of the idolatry introduced by the kings of Israel."[89] Scripture confirms this enlargement of the people Judah by the addition of the righteous from the ten northern tribes: "Out of all the tribes of Israel such as set their hearts to seek the LORD God of Israel came to Jerusalem, to sacrifice unto the LORD God of their fathers. So they strengthened the kingdom of Judah."[90] The increasing identification of the ten tribes with the tribe of Judah tended to minimize the fragmentation of the past and encouraged a unified approach to the fulfillment of God's word and will revealed in the Torah.

This scriptural declaration belies the arguments of many theologians and historians who have viewed the destruction of Israel as total, claiming "that the Israelites were all taken into captivity to some distant exile and that foreigners [were] brought in by the Assyrians to replace them." In reality, as Sherwin Wine notes, what occurred in Israel was much different: "While

---

[89] Ethelbert W. Bullinger, *Number in Scripture: Its Supernatural Design and Spiritual Significance* (Grand Rapids, MI: Kregel Publications, 1967), p. 80.

[90] 2 Chronicles 11:16–17. This passage of Scripture disproves the argument that the Ten Tribes of Israel were "lost." While it is true that large numbers of Israelites in the Northern Kingdom were carried into the Syrian captivity, it is also true that significant numbers, perhaps even a majority of the people, joined Judah in the Southern Kingdom or simply remained in the North. Later, following the Babylonian conquest of Judah, substantial numbers of the tribe of Judah were also dispersed among the nations. The exiles, therefore, were not restricted to the ten tribes, and those tribes were never "lost." This is clear from the fact that centuries later when Ezra returned to Jerusalem after the Babylonian captivity, he offered sacrifices that included "twelve bullocks *for all Israel*" (Ezra 8:35, emphasis added). As a matter of fact, some three decades after the resurrection and ascension of Jesus, his brother James addressed his epistle to "the *twelve* tribes scattered abroad" (James 1:1). Even in the twelfth century, Benjamin of Tudela wrote of a Jewish congregation in the mountains of Nishapur in eastern Persia, saying that they were descendants of the original exiles. Benjamin of Tudela noted in Phillip K. Hitti, *History of Syria, Including Lebanon and Palestine* (Piscataway, NJ: Gorgias Press, 2002), p. 197. It is obvious, then, that the ten tribes were not "lost" either before, during, or after the time of Jesus. They came to be included among numbers of "the Jews" in Judea where they immigrated from the Northern Kingdom, and they continued to be included among all "the Jews" in the Diaspora.

foreigners were deported to Israel and the upper class was deported to other parts of the Assyrian empire, most of the Israelites stayed in Israel."[91] When necessary, they availed themselves of the land of Judah, the nearest refuge from the Assyrians. "Hundreds of Israelite refugees fled south into Judah,"[92] says Wine. Consequently, "Judah was surprisingly strengthened and transformed by the destruction of Israel."[93] The stage was set for Israelites of all tribes to be identified with Judah and to follow Judah's leadership in maintaining their faithfulness to God.

It was during this time that the members of the tribe of Judah came to be known by the appellation יְהוּדִים (yehudim— "Jews"), which was derived from the word יְהוּדָה (Yehudah—"Judah"). The first scriptural record of the use of this term is found in 2 Kings 16:6. By the time that the Babylonian captivity had ended, however, the term Yehudi (Jew)[94] had become the commonly accepted name for the people of Judah as well as for the members of the other eleven tribes who had aligned themselves with Judah. Finally, the word Jew came to be synonymous with all of God's Chosen People, with members of the other tribes of Israel proudly calling themselves Jews.[95] All the Hebrews and all the Israelites, therefore, were eventually included under the title Jew, so that the term came to connote a nationality or an ethnicity. In fact, while the term race has sometimes been applied to the Jewish people, the terms nationality and ethnicity are more appropriate for describing them since, in the strictest sense of the meaning of this word, the Jewish people are not a race within themselves.[96]

As lineal descendants of the Hebrews or Israelites, the Jewish people are an ethnic group, even though they are understood and identified primarily in

---

[91] Sherwin T. Wine, A Provocative People: A Secular History of the Jews (Farmington Hills, MI: International Institute for Secular Humanistic Judaism, 2012), p. 99.

[92] Wine, p. 99.

[93] Wine, p. 98, n. 2.

[94] The English word Jew is derived from the Old French giu, which is taken from the Greek Ioudaios, which was a transliteration of Yehudim. The term Jew is, in effect, an Anglicized contraction of Yehudi.

[95] In Acts 19:14, one of the temple priests (of the tribe of Levi) was called a Jew. In Acts 19:34; Acts 21:39; and Acts 22:3, Paul, who was clearly from the tribe of Benjamin (Romans 11:1), was either described as a Jew or called himself a Jew.

[96] Michael B. Hart, "Jews and Race: An Introductory Essay," in Jews and Race: Writings on Identity and Difference, 1880-1940, Mitchell Bryan Hart, ed. (Boston, MA: Brandeis University Press, 2011), p. xiii. Hart quotes the well-known Israeli writer A. B. Yehoshua who says, "Jews are not a race and never viewed themselves as such." See A. B. Yehoshua, "Who Is a Jew?," in Contemplate 3 (2005–2006), p. 73. Also Christopher Hutton, Race and the Third Reich: Linguistics, Racial Anthropology, and Genetics in the Dialectic of Volk (Cambridge, UK: Polity Press, 2005), p. 54. Hutton notes, "The Jews are not a race in the sense of anthropological race (Systemrasse)."

respect to religion.[97] This is what has empowered the Jewish people to maintain their distinctiveness despite centuries of being involuntarily dispersed among the nations. Though they were forcibly evicted from the Promised Land, they still maintained their identity as the Israel of God, the nation of the Jews. Though they essentially became a nation in exile, the people of Israel still understood themselves as being a divinely elected nation that needed only to be returned to its rightful homeland and be reconstituted there as the commonwealth of Israel. Even with all the vicissitudes of history, the Jewish people have been and continue to be God's Chosen Nation, born at Mt. Sinai and born again in Jerusalem in 1948. From the day of its constitution at Sinai, Israel has continued to be the holy nation of priests[98] who are witnesses to the oneness and unity of God. This was, and continues to be, the uniqueness of Israel, what makes them a "peculiar treasure" to God, "above all people."[99]

John Phillips makes this succinct summation of the Chosen Nation of the Chosen People: "Israel is the only nation with which God has signed a treaty."[100] That treaty was the sovereign decree that God made to Abraham in which he promised nationhood to the patriarch's descendants, a promise that was fulfilled when as many as two million of those descendants assembled at Sinai, affirmed God's covenant, and were constituted as God's nation. For this reason alone, "Woe betide the nation that turns its hand against the Jews," for "under the terms of this [treaty], God has unconditionally guaranteed the survival and security of the Hebrew people"[101] and their nation, Israel! Indeed, the one and only God specifically identifies himself as "the God of Abraham, the God of Isaac, and the God of Jacob." He is the God of only one nation: *Yisrael.*

---

[97] Daniel J. Elazar, "Jewish Religious, Ethnic, and National Identities," in *National Variations in Jewish Identity: Implications for Jewish Education*, Steven M. Cohen and Gabriel Horenczyk, eds. (Albany, NY: The State University of New York Press, 1999), p. 43. Elazar notes that "Jews are an ethnic group" that is "sustained in some parts of the world by their religion and in other parts by family, language, other aspects of culture, concern for the Jewish state, and, in some cases, by Antisemitism."
[98] Exodus 19:6.
[99] Exodus 19:5.
[100] John Phillips, *The View from Mount Calvary: 24 Portraits of the Cross Throughout Scripture* (Grand Rapids, MI: Kregel Publications, 2006), pp. 59–60.
[101] Phillips, p. 60.

CHAPTER 3

THE PROMISED LAND

COVENANT REAL ESTATE

Do the Jewish people have a legitimate right to the land of Israel? The answer given to this question by most of the nations of the world is, no, absolutely not! The answer given by the only one who really matters, however, is, yes, absolutely yes! This is the answer that God has consistently given for millennia, still gives today, and will continue to give without fail in the future, for he never changes or forsakes his covenantal commitments. Since Hebrews, Israelites, and Jews have lived in Israel and have recognized this piece of real estate as their homeland for the 4,000 years since the time of Abraham, their rights to the land should be readily conceded and supported by the world community of nations.[1] Sadly, this has not been the case in virtually all of the history of this people and this land, and it is certainly not the case in today's world.

In reality, however, the legitimate title to the land of Israel can never be given to anyone by any individual, nation, or group of nations. The land is only God's to give, for the Almighty specifically says that this land belongs exclusively to him.[2] It is for this reason that he issued a perpetual commandment that this

---

[1] It is unlikely that Israelites lived in the land of Canaan during the four centuries in Egypt; however, even in the Babylonian exile, isolated Jews remained in the land of Judah. Likewise, after the Hadrian exile, some Jews remained connected with the land. Small numbers continued the tradition through the centuries until the time of restoration was undertaken in the nineteenth century and beyond.

[2] Jacob Neusner, *Scripture and the Generative Premises of the Halakhah: A Systematic Inquiry* (Binghamton, NY: Global Publications, 1999), vol. 3, p. 165. Neusner says, "The halakhah accords to Israel possession, but not ownership of the Land, which God alone retains. God asserts his ownership when Israel proposes to exercise its rights of usufruct: when the tenant takes his share of the crop, he must also hand over to the Landowner . . . the portion of the crop that is owing." God, therefore, ceded the land of Israel to the Israelites only as stewards of "his" land.

parcel of real estate was never to be sold: "The land, moreover, shall not be sold permanently, *for the land is mine.*"[3] Marvin Wilson sums up this truth well: "The Hebrew Scriptures stress repeatedly that God is the true owner of the land. More than twenty-five passages in Deuteronomy . . . emphasize that the land is a gift from the LORD. Israel was only to 'possess' or 'inherit' what rightly belonged to their Suzerain."[4] Perhaps this truth is best summarized in the words of the earliest known extant non-biblical Hebrew text in which the word *Jerusalem* appears: "Yahweh is the God of the whole earth. The mountains of Judah belong to him, to the God of Jerusalem."[5] In fact, both the people of Israel and the land of Israel belong exclusively to YHWH.[6] For this reason, the Almighty is jealous not only concerning his Chosen People[7] but also concerning his Chosen Land.[8] As a matter of fact, God is so passionate about the Holy Land that in Scripture he even personifies the "the land of Israel" and its "hills and mountains, ravines and valleys," and he speaks directly to them.[9] Perhaps this is why the word *land* (אֶרֶץ—*eretz* and אֲדָמָה—*adamah*) is the fourth most common substantive in the *Tanakh*, where it appears a total of 2504 times,[10] and is a far more dominant theme than the term *covenant*, which appears only 280 times in the Hebrew Scriptures as בְּרִית (*berith*) and only 33 times in Apostolic Scripture as διαθήκη (*diathéke*).

The question that begs to be asked is this: Why has so much controversy been generated over such a small piece of real estate? If ever there were a tempest in a teapot, this must be it! The answer, however, is all too obvious: the land of Israel is the Promised Land, the parcel of real estate that God gave to Abraham and his descendants. But more than that, the land of Israel is uniquely God's chosen dwelling place. King David recognized

---

[3] Leviticus 25:23, emphasis added.
[4] Marvin R. Wilson, *Our Father Abraham: Jewish Roots of the Christian Faith* (Grand Rapids, MI: Wm. B. Eerdmans Publishing Co.,1989), p. 260.
[5] This text that dates to the seventh century BC was discovered in Khirbet Beit Lei in 1961. Joseph Naveh, "Hebrew Graffiti from the First Temple Period," in *Israel Exploration Journal*, vol. 51, no.2, pp. 194–207. Also LaMar C. Berrett, *Discovering the World of the Bible* (Provo, UT: Grandin Book Co.,1996), p. 178.
[6] Yitzchak Ginsburgh, *Rectifying the State of Israel: A Political Platform Based on Kabbalah* (Cedarhurst, NY: Gal Einai Institute, 2003), p. 67.
[7] Exodus 34:14. See Dietmar Neufeld, *The Social Sciences and Biblical Translation* (Atlanta, GA: Society of Biblical Literature, 2008), p. 88.
[8] Joel 2:18: "The LORD will pity his people and jealously guard the honor of his land" (NLT).
[9] Ezekiel 36:6.
[10] Gerald McDermott, "Covenant, Mission, and Relating to the Other," in Robert W. Jenson and Eugene Korn, eds., *Covenant and Hope: Christian and Jewish Reflections* (Grand Rapids, MI: Wm. B. Eerdmans Publishing Co., 2012), p. 29.

this truth: "God is known in Judah; his name is great in Israel. His taber-nacle is in Salem; his dwelling place also is in Zion."[11] It also prompted the Psalmist to exult in song: "Sing praises to the LORD, who dwells in Zion; declare among the peoples his deeds."[12] The ancient poetry of twelfth-century Egyptian Karaite poet Moses ben Abraham Dar'i cap-tures the essence of Israel very well: "Out of all nations and people I have chosen Zion as my residence and you, Israel, as my servant."[13] Why would God not be jealous over the specific plot of ground that he chose to be his dwelling place? And why would the Almighty not defend his own honor and the honor of the people whom he has chosen to inhabit his land and to uphold the remembrance of his name in the earth?

In reality, Israel—and particularly its capital city, Jerusalem—is the place where God chose to place his name. As a matter of fact, long before King David established the capital of Israel in Jerusalem, Moses instructed the Israelites in this manner: "You shall seek the LORD at the place which the LORD your God will choose from all your tribes, to establish his name there for his dwelling."[14] Later, David received this solemn promise from God, "David my servant [will] have a lamp always before me in Jerusalem, the city where I have chosen for myself *to put my name*."[15] God himself also told Solomon: "I have consecrated this house which you have built by *putting my name there forever*, and my eyes and my heart will be there perpetually."[16] Nehemiah understood the promise that God had made to Moses; therefore, he prayed this prayer: "Remember the word which you commanded your servant Moses . . . I will bring [the Israelites] to the place where I have chosen to *cause my name to dwell*."[17]

It has been suggested that God was speaking more than figuratively when he declared his choice of Jerusalem as a place to affix his name. It is possible that God quite literally engraved his name in the geological structure on which the city rests. Aerial photographs and topographical maps of Jerusalem cer-tainly seem to support this contention. The two mountains on which the Holy

---

11 Psalm 76:2.
12 Psalm 9:11.
13 Joachim Yeshaya, *Poetry and Memory in Karaite Prayer: The Liturgical Poetry of the Karaite Poet Moses ben Abraham Dar'i* (Leiden, The Netherlands: Koninklijke Brill NV, 2014), p. 62, quoting from lines 15–20 of poem 11.
14 Deuteronomy 12:5.
15 1 Kings 15:4, emphasis added.
16 1 Kings 9:3, emphasis added.
17 Nehemiah 1:9, emphasis added.

City sits, Mount Zion and Mount Moriah, are circumscribed and intersected by three valleys, the Kidron Valley on the east, the Hinnom Valley on the west and south, and the Refaiim (or Tyropoeon) Valley that bifurcates the two mountains. When Jerusalem is viewed aerially from the south, these three valleys almost perfectly form the Hebrew letter שׁ (*shin*). This phenomenon is very significant considering the fact the Jewish people universally recognize the letter *shin* as a symbol for the divine name שַׁדַּי (*Shaddai*).[18] It is even said that the *dagesh* in the letter *shin* (the dot above the right arm that distinguishes the letter *shin* [שׁ] from the letter *sin* [שׂ]) is positioned at the site of the ancient temple.[19] It is reasonable to assume, therefore, that God meant exactly what he said when he declared, "I have chosen Jerusalem that *my name might be there*."[20]

As Hans Ucko has observed, "A particular geography is chosen for God's action in history that seems to eclipse God's dealings with people throughout time and places."[21] It is this small tract of land of which it is said, "the LORD has chosen Zion; he has desired it for his dwelling place: 'This is my resting place forever; here I will dwell, for I have desired it.'"[22] For the Israelites, it was a well-established, incontrovertible fact that God resides in Jerusalem: "Sing praises to the LORD, who dwells in Zion!"[23] Zechariah spoke on behalf of God, "Thus

---

[18] The letter *shin* (שׁ) is prominently displayed on virtually all the *mezuzot* that are attached to the doorposts and gates of Jewish homes and buildings. Some *mezuzot* even display the entire name *Shaddai* (שַׁדַּי). The Hebrew word מְזוּזָה (*mezuzah*) means "doorpost." Since God commanded the Israelites to "write my Torah on the doorposts of your house and on your gates" (Deuteronomy 11:20), the Jews took the divine instruction literally and inscribed parchment scrolls with the words of this commandment (Deuteronomy 11:13–21), along with the words of the *Shema* (Deuteronomy 6:4–9), inserted them in small boxes, and nailed them to the doorposts of their houses. To this day, the name *Shaddai* is also inscribed in Hebrew on the back of the scrolls. The *Zohar* suggests that the three Hebrew letters in the name שַׁדַּי (*Shaddai*), שׁ (*shin*), ד (*dalet*), and י (*yud*), can be viewed as an acronym for the phrase שׁוֹמֵר דַּלְתוֹת יִשְׂרָאֵל—*shomer daltot Yisrael* ("Guardian of the Doors of Israel"). See Ronald L. Eisenberg, *Jewish Traditions: A JPS Guide* (Philadelphia, PA: Jewish Publication Society, 2004), p. 581.

[19] Interestingly, Jewish tradition also suggests that the letter *shin* is displayed in the structure of the human heart. This is clearly visible in a ventral echocardiogram of the heart. The tissues that circumscribe and separate the left and right ventricles of the heart form the letter *shin*. This is thought to be a fulfillment of the *Shema* in which the Israelites were commanded to write God's commandments on their hearts (Deuteronomy 6:6). A good argument could be made that this is evidence that God wrote his word on the heart of the first human being in the Garden of Eden and has continued to do so with every human being who has lived on Planet Earth, just as Paul maintained in Romans 2:15.

[20] 2 Chronicles 6:6, emphasis added. See Karl D. Coke, "Jerusalem and the Letter *Shin*," *Restore!*, vol. 10, no. 4, p. 13.

[21] Hans Ucko, *The People and the People of God: Minjung and Dalit Theology in Interaction* (Hamburg, Germany: Lit Verlag Münster, 2002, p. 18.

[22] Psalm 132:13–14.

[23] Psalm 9:11.

says the LORD of hosts: I am exceedingly jealous for Zion . . . I will return to Zion, and dwell in the midst of Jerusalem. Jerusalem shall be called the City of Truth, the mountain of the LORD of hosts, the Holy Mountain."[24]

This is, doubtless, the reason Isaiah declared that "the Torah will go forth from Zion and the word of the LORD from Jerusalem."[25] It would have seemed far more logical for the prophet to have said, "The Torah goes forth from Sinai," for that is where the Torah was given to Moses and the Israelites. Why was Zion, not Sinai, in the prophet's mind? The only conclusion that may be drawn from this text is explained by David Patterson thus: "Because Zion is where the Torah is *lived*."[26] It is the living of Torah that constitutes the dynamic modeling that is far more powerful than verbose theological explanations and argumentation. The Torah was given at Sinai; however, it was fully lived in Israel as it issued forth from Mount Zion, the City of the Great King. The Torah lived is far more important than the Torah written or spoken. This is why "the Jewish return to history through their return to the Land of Israel is a return of Torah to history."[27] Emmanuel Lévinas has said, therefore, that the state of Israel, "in accordance with its pure essence, is possible only if penetrated by the divine word."[28] The covenant and its commandments are what make Israel the *Eretz HaKodesh*, the "Holy Land."[29] Indeed, "if the advent of the State of Israel has no metaphysical meaning—if the Land of Israel is not the Holy Land—then the revelation at Mount Sinai has no meaning."[30]

The Integral Land Covenant

It should have come as no surprise, then, that when God determined to make a particularist covenant in order to advance his universal will to bless all of humanity, a land clause was among the most prominent features of the decree and agreement. This covenant was made between God and Abraham, and it was made at God's behest, not at the patriarch's suggestion.[31] The

---

[24] Zechariah 8:2–3.
[25] Isaiah 2:3.
[26] David Patterson, *Anti-Semitism and Its Metaphysical Origins* (Cambridge, UK: Cambridge University Press, 2015), p. 101.
[27] David Patterson, *Anti-Semitism*, p. 201.
[28] Emmanuel Lévinas, "Zionisms," in Sean Hand, ed., *The Levinas Reader* (Oxford, UK: Basil Blackwell, 1989), p. 271.
[29] David Patterson, *Anti-Semitism*, p. 202.
[30] David Patterson, *Anti-Semitism*, p. 201.
[31] God formalized the covenant that he made with Abraham when he commanded the patriarch to make the sacrifice through which he would seal his covenant with the patriarch (Genesis 15:9).

Abrahamic covenant was not something that Abraham had sought, much less petitioned the Divine to achieve. It was God who set in motion the events that would precipitate the covenant when he commanded Abraham to go from his "country" and from his "family" to "a land" which God would "show him."[32] At that time, God made these promises to Abraham, "I will make you a great nation, and I will bless you, and make your name great; and so you shall be a blessing; I will bless those who bless you, and the one who curses you I will curse. And in you all the families of the earth will be blessed."[33] Then, without fail, in each instance where God subsequently decreed his covenant to Abraham, the land promise was a central stipulation. As a matter of fact, when the patriarch arrived in the land of Canaan and was met there by *El Shaddai* at Shechem, the first and only words that came out of the Almighty's mouth were these: "I will give this land to your descendants."[34] Then, the next time God appeared to Abraham, he said this: "Lift up your eyes and look from the place where you are, northward and southward and eastward and westward; for all the land which you see, I will give it to you and to your descendants forever."[35]

Later, when Abraham sought God's assurance that the divine promises which he had received would, indeed, be fulfilled, God "took him outside and said, 'Now look toward the heavens, and count the stars, if you are able to count them.' And he said to him, 'So shall your descendants be.'"[36] Immediately, "Abram believed the LORD, and he credited it to him as righteousness."[37] Without hesitation, God instantly replied, "I am the LORD who brought you out of Ur of the Chaldeans, *to give you this land to possess it.*"[38] Here, God clearly said that the reason for his bringing Abraham first out of Babylon and then out of Assyria was this: "I brought you out . . . to give you this land." When Abraham asked God, "How may I know that I will possess [the land]?" God gave instructions to the patriarch that set the stage for the final enactment of the Abrahamic covenant. The Almighty instructed Abraham to take several animals, cut them in half, and lay them out on the ground so that God could pass between them, thereby formalizing and finalizing the covenant.

---

[32] Genesis 12:1.
[33] Genesis 12:2–3.
[34] Genesis 12:7.
[35] Genesis 13:14–15.
[36] Genesis 15:4–5.
[37] Genesis 15:6, NIV.
[38] Genesis 15:7, emphasis added.

After Abraham followed God's instructions and all the ensuing drama unfolded, "On that day the LORD made a covenant with Abram." And these were the words of promise that God spoke to him: "To your descendants I have given this land, from the river of Egypt[39] to the great river, the Euphrates."[40] Interestingly enough, the terms stated in the covenant after it was made involved nothing more than "this land," just as it had in the first—and only words—that God spoke after Abraham crossed the Euphrates: "I will give this land to your descendants." God's intentions were clear from the beginning to the ending of his interaction with Abraham: the covenant of the Almighty was that the "Promised Land" would be given to the patriarch's descendants forever. Nothing could be clearer from the biblical accounts. The "land covenant" was central to all of God's promises to Abraham. Indeed, in the first and last affirmations of the Abrahamic covenant, the only words that God spoke were, "I will give this land to your descendants."

If the repeated emphasis on the land conveyance as the integral part of the declaration of God's promises to Abraham were not enough to confirm the ongoing indispensability of the land of Canaan to the Abrahamic covenant, God made the land promise central to his reiteration of the covenant to Abraham's son Isaac: "I will be with you and bless you, for *to you and your descendants I will give all these lands*, and I will establish the oath which I swore to your father Abraham."[41] It is important to note that God tied the land contract directly with the fulfillment of the oath which he swore to Abraham. While God also reiterated other promises, the first term of the blessing that he reconfirmed was permanent ownership of the land of Israel. Some scholars even argue that with this iteration of the Abrahamic covenant's land contract, "the land promise seems to extend beyond Canaan to the surrounding

---

[39] Scholars differ as to what is meant by the term *river of Egypt*. Some Jewish commentators and the Aramaic Targumim to Scripture identify it as either the Nile River or one of its easternmost branches. See Alexander Keith, *The Land of Israel According to the Covenant with Abraham* (Edinburgh, Scotland: William Whyte and Co., 1844), pp. 89–90. Keith notes that the Hebrew word translated "river" in this reference is *nehar*, which in Scripture is always connected with the Nile or its branches, rather than *nahal*, which is used to describe the Euphrates and other rivers in Scripture. Other scholars argue that the "river" was actually the Wadi El-Arish in northeastern Sinai (Numbers 34:5; Joshua 15:4; 2 Kings 8:65; Isaiah 27:12), which was often recognized as Canaan's westernmost border, just southwest from Hebron in the plain of Mamre of the wilderness of Paran, where Abraham lived when he received the promise. See Peter Enns, *Exodus* (Grand Rapids, MI: Zondervan Publishing Co., 2000), p. 479. For a good discussion of options for interpreting the meaning of the term *the river of Egypt*, see Diana Edelman, "The Nile in Biblical Memory," in *Thinking of Water in the Early Second Temple Period* (Berlin, Germany: Walter de Gruyter GmbH, 2014), p. 81.
[40] Genesis 15:18.
[41] Genesis 26:3, emphasis added.

regions, as is indicated by this text's use of the plural form כָּל־הָאֲרָצֹת הָאֵלֶּה (kol-haaretzot ha'eleh), "all these lands."[42] Doubtless, this statement confirms the expansion of God's first promise to Abraham: "I will give your descendants this land [Canaan],"[43] into his last: "To your descendants I have given this land, from the river of Egypt to the great river, the Euphrates."[44]

Finally, as if to underscore and make his intentions utterly unmistakable, God also reconfirmed the covenant to Abraham's grandson, Jacob by saying, "*The land I gave to Abraham and Isaac, I will give it to you, and I will give it to your descendants after you.*"[45] Finally, centuries after God had reaffirmed the land promise to Jacob, Moses repeated and made clear the terms of the covenant to the Chosen People by reiterating God's commitment to give them the Promised Land: "[The LORD] has remembered his covenant forever, the word which he commanded to a thousand generations. The covenant he made with Abraham, and his oath to Isaac. Then he confirmed it to Jacob for a statute, to Israel as an everlasting covenant, saying, '*To you I will give the land of Canaan as the portion of your inheritance.*'"[46] This declaration is so simple that the proverbial wayfaring man, though a fool,[47] could not mistake God's intentions: God "confirmed" the land contract "to Israel as an everlasting covenant." Later, through the prophet Isaiah, God further verified his intentions, and he did so in absolute terms: "I will bring forth offspring from Jacob and an heir of my mountains from Judah; even my chosen ones shall inherit it, and my servants will dwell there."[48] There could be no mistake as to God's purposes for the land of Israel: it belonged to Abraham's descendants.

---

[42] The Hebrew word הָאֵלֶּה (ha'eleh) in this sentence is plural absolute; therefore, the intention of its use cannot be misunderstood. Nahum M. Sarna, *Understanding Genesis* (New York: Schocken Books, 1970), p. 170; Chee-Chiew Lee, *The Blessing of Abraham, the Spirit, and Justification in Galatians: Their Relationship and Significance for Understanding Paul's Theology* (Eugene, OR: Wipf and Stock Publishers, 2013, p. 183, n. 82; and Gordon J. Wenham, "The Akedah: A Paradigm of Sacrifice," in *Pomegranates and Golden Bells: Studies in Biblical, Jewish, and Near Eastern Ritual, Law, and Literature in Honor of Jacob Milgrom*, David P. Wright, David Noel Freedman, and Avi Hurvitz, eds. (Winona Lake, IN: Eisenbrauns Publishers, 1995), p. 189.

[43] Genesis 12:7.

[44] Genesis 15:18. This promise continued to specify the "lands" included in the territory from the river of Egypt to the Euphrates: ". . . the land of the Kenites, Kenizzites, Kadmonites, Hittities, Perizzites, Rephaites, Amorites, Canaanites, Girgashites, and Jebusites" (Genesis 15:19–21, NIV). Clearly, "all these lands" included more than just the land of Canaan.

[45] Genesis 35:12, emphasis added.

[46] Psalm 105:6–11, emphasis added.

[47] Isaiah 35:8.

[48] Isaiah 65:9.

The land contract was so intrinsic to the Abrahamic covenant that it was repeated over and over again almost to the point of redundancy (at least from a human perspective). This continual repetition, however, was designed by God to focus particular attention upon one geographical space so that his Chosen People would never lose, or even neglect, the tangible reality that confirmed his covenant. The land from the river of Egypt to the River Euphrates was singled out specifically as the physical place that God would assign to Abraham and his descendants—and, again, the assignation would be "forever." It was as though God was choosing a set-apart—and, therefore, holy—land mass in which he would establish his sovereign nation and its capital city, the parcel of land where he would place his name.[49] H. M. Orlinsky was correct when he maintained that "were it not for the Land that God promised on oath to Abraham and to Isaac and to Jacob and to their heirs forever, there would be no covenant."[50]

When the Israelites claimed the territory that God had assigned them during the time of Joshua, they actually did not so much conquer the land as they did inherit it. Kenneth Hanna points out that Israel "was never to forget that they [had] not 'taken' the land. Rather, God [had] 'given' them the land of Canaan."[51] This was clear from the initial instruction that God gave to Joshua as the Israelites prepared to enter the Promised Land: "Be strong and courageous, for you shall give this people possession of the land which I swore to their fathers to give them."[52] When the Israelites possessed the Promised Land, therefore, they did not engage in "ethnic cleansing" and "genocide," as some have charged.[53] Instead, God himself prepared the way for them by expelling the inhabitants of the land because the probationary period of 400 years that he had allotted them for repentance from their utter depravity had expired.[54]

---

[49] 1 Kings 11:36; Ezra 6:12.

[50] H. M. Orlinsky, "The Biblical Concept of the Land of Israel," in *The Land of Israel: Jewish Perspectives*, L. A. Hoffman, ed. (Notre Dame, IN: Notre Dame University Press, 1986), p. 34.

[51] Kenneth G. Hanna, *From Moses to Malachi: Surveying the Old Testament* (Bloomington, IN: Lifeway Publishers, 2014), p. 109.

[52] Joshua 1:6.

[53] Jeff Astley, Leslie J. Francis, and Mandy Robbins, *Peace or Violence: The Ends of Religion and Education?* (South Glamorgan, UK: The University of Wales Press, 2007), p. 12. Also, Jack Miles, *God: A Biography* (New York: Knopf Doubleday Publishing Group, 1995), p. 117. British atheist Richard Dawkins says the Book of Joshua is a "text remarkable for the bloodthirsty massacres it records and the xenophobic relish with which it does so." Richard Dawkins, *The God Delusion* (Boston: Houghton Mifflin, 2006), p. 248. In many cases, such charges are designed to delegitimize the present-day claim of the Jewish people to the land of Israel because, if the accounts in the Torah are not myths, Israel's original possession of the land was illegitimate. See Nur Masalha, *The Bible and Zionism: Invented Traditions, Archaeology, and Post-Colonialism* (London, UK: Zed Books, 2007), pp. 24–26.

[54] Genesis 15:16.

By far, the most egregious of the Canaanite sins was their worship of Molech, a chthonic deity represented by a giant iron statue with a bull's head and a human body. Molech's thirst for human death was regularly slaked by an infanticidal horror wherein newborn children were delivered by their parents into the god's arms and from thence into the conflagration in his belly. It is for this reason that the conquest of Canaan is "portrayed as God's acting in judgment on a wicked and degraded society and culture,"[55] and the Israelites' actions against the Canaanites are "never placed in the category of oppression but of divine punishment operating through human agency."[56] What God was doing, therefore, was similar to what he had done in Abraham's day to Sodom and Gomorrah,[57] and his action was well deserved. The then-current inhabitants of Canaan were not indigenous to the land; therefore, God was simply exercising an unlawful detainer action by using the Israelites to evict those who would not accept his dominion in peace. Even in executing this judgment, however, the Torah required the Israelites to "offer it terms of peace" to each Canaanite community before they engaged in military action against them.[58] The Talmud suggests, therefore, that before the conquest of the Promised Land began, Joshua sent letters to the Canaanites, offering them three options: ". . . to make peace, to leave the land, or to wage war."[59] Israelite inheritance of the land, therefore, was carried out within the parameters of God's provision, instructions, and plans.[60]

By the end of Joshua's career, the words that God had spoken to Abraham, Isaac, Jacob, Moses, and himself had been completely and meticulously fulfilled: "Not one word of all the good words which the LORD your God spoke concerning you has failed."[61] Indeed, the Israelite settlement of the land of Canaan prompted yet another recapitulation of God's prophetic promise to Abraham, Isaac, and Jacob and the rightful claim to its fulfillment: "So the LORD gave Israel all the land he had sworn to give their forefathers, and they took possession of it and settled there."[62] Andrew

---

[55] Christopher J. H. Wright, *The God I Don't Understand: Reflections on Tough Questions of Faith* (Grand Rapids, MI: Zondervan Publishing, 2008), p. 64.
[56] Wright, p. 64.
[57] Genesis 19:24.
[58] Deuteronomy 20:10.
[59] Babylonian Talmud: *Shevi'it* 6:1, noted in Avi Sagi and Daniel Statman, *Religion and Morality* (Amsterdam, The Netherlands: Rodopi B.V., 1894), p. 163. Also, Marlin Jeschke, *Rethinking Holy Land: A Study in Salvation Geography* (Harrisonburg, VA: Herald Press, 2005), p. 47.
[60] Paul Copan and Matt Flannagan, *Did God Really Command Genocide? Coming to Terms with the Justice of God* (Grand Rapids, MI: Baker Books, 2014).
[61] Joshua 23:14.
[62] Joshua 21:43.

Hill and John Walton rightly observe, therefore, that "in Israel's perception of herself as the covenant people of God, nothing is more central than the land."[63] The Promised Land is the continuing confirmation of the divine election of the Chosen People.

As God designed it, one small piece of Middle-Eastern real estate would be the canvas on which he would paint the mural of his dealings with humanity from Abraham's day until the final advent of the Messianic kingdom. According to the land conveyance in the Abrahamic covenant, therefore, God is just as much a particularist when it comes to geography as he is when it comes to people. There is a Chosen People, and there is a Chosen Land. Just as God uses one people to bless all people, so he uses one land to demonstrate his will and his plan for the entire earth. Gregory Wall has stated this premise very succinctly: "Put simply, God's plan of salvation for the whole world is to come about in and through his election of Israel. This principle applies . . . not only to the people of Israel but to the land as well."[64] It is undeniable, therefore, that "Israel's ownership of the land by divine decree is strategic in the current debate over control of Palestine and the setting of its boundaries. Palestinians and other Arab states may press their claims to land rights, but Israel was given permanent ownership of the land through the Abrahamic covenant,"[65] and its deed to this real property was recorded on the pages of the Torah itself.

The promise to Abraham that his descendants would inherit the land that God had conveyed to them by divine oath and covenant was never described in nebulous, equivocal, or evanescent terms. It was never a grand statement that was to be interpreted figuratively. The Abrahamic covenant was a literal agreement in that God instructed Abraham to walk through the land which he and his descendants were to receive.[66] This is how literal God intended the fulfillment of the promise to be: "Arise, walk about the land through its length and breadth; for I will give it to you."[67] There would have been no reason for Abraham to "walk about the land" if God had intended for the promise to be interpreted spiritually. Even when the Israelites would be scattered into a worldwide diaspora, God specifically said,

---

[63] Andrew E. Hill and John H. Walton, *A Survey of the Old Testament Introduction* (Grand Rapids, MI: Zondervan Publishing, 1991), p. 230.

[64] Gregory Wall, "Man Is the Land," in *John Paul II and the Jewish People: A Jewish-Christian Dialogue*, David G. Dalin and Matthew Severing, eds. (Lanham, MD: Rowman & Littlefield Publishers, 2008), p. 145.

[65] Hanna, p. 109.

[66] Mal Couch, ed., *Dictionary of Premillennial Theology: A Practical Guide to the People, Viewpoints, and History of Prophetic Studies* (Grand Rapids, MI: Kregel Publications, 1996), p. 122.

[67] Genesis 13:17.

"The LORD your God will restore you . . . and will bring you *into the land which your fathers possessed.*"[68] If the land promises were not to be taken literally, then why would it be necessary for the people to make *aliyah* to the same land "which their fathers possessed"? Doubtless, this means that a literal people will return to a literal land, not a "spiritual" people to a figurative, spiritual, or heavenly land.[69]

The Land Covenant Never Abrogated

Diverse Christian theologians have assumed that Jesus' message of the universal messianic kingdom on earth superseded and even abrogated the land contract of the Abrahamic covenant. The truth is that God's expansion of the Abrahamic covenant to include Gentiles through faith in Jesus did not, *ipso facto*, invalidate either the Abrahamic covenant or its land contract. Apostolic arguments for Gentile inclusion did not imply Jewish exclusion; likewise, arguments for the inclusion of the entire world in the land contract of God's universal covenant did not imply any supersession or repeal of God's particularist covenant with the lineal descendants of Abraham, Isaac, and Jacob and his exclusive conveyance of the land of Israel to the people of Israel in perpetuity. As Robert Bleakney points out, "In Romans 3, Paul says that the covenant of circumcision is upheld 'in every way.' Surely the word *every* includes the full meaning of this covenant, which has a physical aspect manifest not only in the act of circumcision but also in the gift of land."[70]

Some have argued that the absence of support for the Jewish right to the land of Israel in the Apostolic Scriptures proves that God had revoked the land contract of the Abrahamic and Sinaitic covenants. In reality, the Jewish people's right to the land conveyed to them by God's unilateral covenant with Abraham was an unquestioned truth among Christians in pre-70 AD Israel. McDermott is right when he argues that "the relative silence about land in the New Testament does not mean that the New Testament authors believed that the Abrahamic promises concerning land had been abrogated."[71] In fact, for them, as for their fellow Jewish compatriots of the time, the land promises were a given. No one would even have thought of questioning their legitimacy and their perdurability.

Jesus knew precisely what he was saying in the Sermon on the Mount, therefore, when he declared, "Blessed are the meek, for they shall inherit the

---

[68] Deuteronomy 30:3–5, emphasis added.
[69] Couch, ed., *Dictionary*, p. 122.
[70] Robert W. Bleakney, personal communication.
[71] McDermott, p. 32.

land."[72] He was quoting directly from Psalm 37:11, 29: "the meek shall inherit the land, and delight themselves in abundant prosperity. The righteous shall inherit the land, and live in it forever."[73] The Hebrew word translated "land" is אֶרֶץ ('eretz). This is the term that is still used by Jews and Israelis to identify *Eretz Yisrael*, the land of Israel. Without a doubt, therefore, Jesus was referring to the same thing that David predicted: the meek will inherit the land of promise as part of the irrevocable Abrahamic covenant. Jesus was not referring to a nebulous inheritance of "the earth" in the eschatological *Olam Ha-Ba* (the World to Come). He was speaking directly to Israelite people—and to them alone—promising them that those who were meek like Moses[74] would inherit the Promised Land as a part of the Abrahamic covenant.[75] In a very real sense, the mission of Jesus involved restored emphases on the very foundations of the Abrahamic covenant, including its land provisions, and the extension of the divinely sovereign particularity of that covenant to the whole earth in fulfillment of God's promise to the patriarch that in him all the nations and families of humanity would be blessed. The implication of the land provisions of this covenant for the non-Jewish nations could not be abrogated or ignored. Michael Bird is right when he contends that the ministry of Jesus was focused on the restoration of Israel. As a "prophet of Jewish restoration eschatology," he says, Jesus invoked the view of "the salvation of Gentiles in relation to the Jewish story, and retells it in a powerful and provocative way through speech and symbol, thus connecting the salvation of the Gentiles to the restoration of Israel."[76]

The land-grant clauses of the Abrahamic covenant have always been as irrevocable as the spiritual promises guaranteed therein. Their irrevocability, however, was not completely unique to God's relationship with the Abrahamic family. Hal Harless points out that this understanding was inherent in all

---

[72] Matthew 5:5.
[73] Psalm 37:11, 29, NRSV.
[74] Numbers 12:3.
[75] Kenneth E. Bailey, *Jesus Through Middle Eastern Eyes: Cultural Studies in the Gospels* (Downers Grove, IL: InterVarsity Press, 2008), p. 72. Bailey says, "Jesus identified himself as a prophet and was identified by many. Any prophet of Israel who discusses 'the land' has one primary meaning in mind. He is referring to the Holy Land of Israel/Palestine." As Bailey notes, the Greek word that is translated "land" in NRSV and "earth" in other versions is γῆ (*ge* [*ghay*]) which in the Septuagint Greek translation of the Hebrew Scriptures is used to render the Hebrew word אֶרֶץ ('eretz) "over two thousand times." Obviously, in the Sermon on the Mount, Jesus was teaching the fulfillment of the land contract of the Abrahamic covenant.
[76] Michael F. Bird, *Jesus and the Origins of the Gentile Mission* (New York, T & T Clark International, 1988), p. 29.

cultures surrounding Canaan at that time: "The grant covenant in the ancient Near East was considered irrevocable."[77] Because of the land clause in the Abrahamic covenant, Israel is the "Holy Land," the land set apart unto God and his people. This is demonstrated in the fact that when Zechariah spoke of the eschatological time when "many nations [will] join themselves to the LORD," thereby fulfilling God's promise to bless all nations through Abraham's descendants, the prophet also, for the first time in Scripture, explicitly referred to Judah as the "Holy Land": "The LORD will possess Judah as his portion in the holy land (אַדְמַת הַקֹּדֶשׁ —*adamat hakodesh*)."[78] The land is holy because God who lives there is holy! God was the one who set the Promised Land apart from all other real estate on Planet Earth, and that action is what made it the "Holy Land." Similarly, the Chosen People who inhabit the "Holy Land" are a holy people because God dwells among them and because he has set them apart to his service and commissioned them to be his witnesses to the world by bearing his name and demonstrating his instructions to all the nations.

The Intrinsic Interconnectivity of People, Nation, and Land

The Promised Land that was so integral to the lives of the Hebrews/Israelites/Jews of antiquity has continued to remain central to the self-identity of their descendants throughout the many centuries that have ensued since that time. Much of this understanding has been the result of the Jewish view that "it is irrelevant whether the Jews are in the land or outside the land or whether anyone else may control it. The land of Israel belongs to the Jews by divine decree."[79] Harold Ockenga rightly argued that the "biblical view-point" settled the debate of whether the Jews or the Arabs had rights to the land of Israel: "God did not give it to the Arabs, but gave it to Israel."[80] The attachment to the

---

[77] Hal Harless, *How Firm a Foundation: The Dispensations in the Light of the Divine Covenants* (New York: Petr Lang Publishing, 2004), p. 116. Harless cites the incident in 1350 BC when Niqmepa, the son of Niqmaddu II of Ugarit, brought a border dispute to the attention of Mursili II, the son of Suppiluliuma I of Hatti. In this case, "Mursili referred to the grant covenant that his father had made to settle the issue." Then, in 1250 BC, as part of a treaty between Tudhaliya IV of Hatti and Kurunta of Tarhuntassa, the "great King was not able to overturn a grant covenant." Indeed, "in this treaty it was not even permitted for the recipient of the grant to relinquish it." Harless draws the following conclusion from the historically established tradition: "Thus, as a grant covenant, we would expect the Abrahamic covenant to remain inviolate and irrevocable." The land grant that was a part of the divine covenant was also irrevocable.

[78] Zechariah 2:11–12. See Wall, in *John Paul II*, p. 144.

[79] Mal Couch, ed., *A Bible Handbook to the Acts of the Apostles* (Grand Rapids, MI: Kregel Academic, 1999), p. 221.

[80] Harold Ockenga, quoted in Matthew Avery Sutton, *American Apocalypse: A History of Modern Evangelicalism* (Cambridge, MA: Harvard University Press, 2014), p. 302.

land of Israel still runs as deep in the corporate psyche of the international Jewish community as it did in antiquity. Without the vision for the restoration of the nation of Israel in the land of Israel, the Jewish Diaspora would likely have faded into oblivion. The disenfranchised people, however, refused to give up the holy dream, a dream that was destined to impact not only the Jewish people but also the entire world. The Jews knew that their dream was from God: "God has had a dream, and the task of Israel is to interpret that dream," Abraham Heschel explained.[81] "In the upbuilding of the land we are aware of responding to the Biblical Covenant, to an imperative that kept on speaking to us throughout the ages, and which never became obsolete or stale,"[82] he said.

Now, the dream that millions of Jews maintained through interminable years of untold anguish and suffering has become a tangible reality in the world. *Am Yisrael chai!* And not only do the People of Israel live, but also in a very real sense, the Nation of Israel lives, and the Land of Israel lives. The three Israels—people, nation, and land—are intrinsically interconnected. In fact, there are many Israelis who believe in *"shallot ha-golah*, the view that Jewish life is impossible anywhere but in Israel."[83] David Patterson said, "The Jews of the world need the Jewish state as much as they need the Sabbath in order to be who they are. For Jerusalem is to space what the Sabbath is to time."[84] The Jewish people and the land of Israel, therefore, are intrinsically interconnected and form a symbiotic relationship with each other, the importance of which cannot be overemphasized and should never be minimized.[85] In fact, "without an understanding of the intricate relationship between law, land, and people, Jewish history becomes all but incomprehensible,"[86] says Jerold Auerbach. What W. D. Davies called the "scandal of territorial particularity in Judaism" is essential to the self-identity of the Jewish people, for "the Land is so embedded in the heart of Judaism, the Torah, that—so its sources, worship, theology, and often its history attest—it is finally inseparable from it."[87]

---

[81] Abraham Joshua Heschel, quoted in Karen Armstrong, *Holy War: The Crusades and Their Impact on Today's World* (New York, Anchor Books, 1988), p. 277.

[82] Abraham Joshua Heschel, *Israel: An Echo of Eternity* (New York, Macmillan, 1967), p. 48.

[83] Jonathan Sacks, *Future Tense: Jews, Judaism, and Israel in the Twenty-first Century* (New York: Schocken Books, 2009), p. 46.

[84] David Patterson, *Anti-Semitism*, p. 248

[85] Anthony J. Kenny, *Catholics, Jews, and the State of Israel* (Mahwah, NJ: Paulist Press, 1993), p. 108.

[86] Jerold S. Auerbach, *Rabbis and Lawyers: The Journey from Torah to Constitution* (New Orleans, LA: Quid Pro Books, 1990), p. 5.

[87] William David Davies, *The Territorial Dimension of Judaism* (Berkeley, CA: The University of California Press, 1982), p. 125.

Now, after nearly two millennia of dispersion, persecution, and derision, the people of Israel live as the nation of Israel in the land of Israel. This indisputable truth belies the dominant historical "prejudicial discourse prevalent in European fin-de-siècle literature: the inability of the 'wandering Jew,' who lacked roots in a native soil, to generate an indigenous culture."[88] Just as the Sabbath as the sanctuary in time,[89] has kept the Jews more so than the Jews have kept the Sabbath,[90] so the vision for the restoration of the Land of Israel has guaranteed the Jewish people the restoration of a sanctuary in space,[91] the Promised Land. The land of Israel is still the Promised Land, the place that all the Jews of the earth can now call "home." No individual, organization, or government has a right to detract from what the Jewish people have accomplished. As Arthur Koestler has so poignantly said, "Now that the mission of the Wandering Jew is completed, he must discard the knapsack."[92]

As it was in antiquity, when the focal point of the Holy Land was the Holy City and the focal point of the Holy City was the Holy Temple, so it is today. In antiquity, "the land was concrete expression of God's promise . . . a pointer to the 'city with foundations, whose architect and builder is God.'"[93] Walter

---

[88] Emily Braun, "The Faces of Modigliani: Identity Politics under Fascism," in Voljtěch Jirat-Wasiutyński, *Modern Art and the Idea of the Mediterranean* (Toronto, Canada: The University of Toronto Press, 2007), p. 192.

[89] Abraham Joshua Heschel, *Between God and Man: An Interpretation of Judaism*, Fritz A. Rothschild, ed. (New York: Simon & Schuster, 1959), p. 222. Heschel said, "The Sabbath itself is a sanctuary which we build, a sanctuary in time." Then, he also declared, "The sanctity of time came first, the sanctity of man came second, and the sanctity of space last. Time was hallowed by God; space, the Tabernacle, was consecrated by Moses." See Abraham Joshua Heschel, *The Sabbath* (New York: Farrar, Straus and Giroux, 1951), p. 10.

[90] Ahad HaAm coined the famous aphorism: "More than Israel kept the Sabbath, the Sabbath has kept Israel." Ahad HaAm, *Hashiloah,* 1898, iii, 6, quoted in Sylvia Barack Fishman, *Jewish Life and American Culture* (Albany, NY: The State University of New York Press, 2000), p. 130.

[91] Daniel I. Block, *The Book of Ezekiel, Chapters 1–24* (Grand Rapids, MI: Wm. B. Eerdmans Publishing Co., 1997), pp. 349–350. Block says, ". . . the notion of the sanctuary, sacred space/place, was at the heart of Israel's spiritual self-consciousness. The temple served as a visible sign of Yahweh's presence among them and as a symbol of their status as the people of Yahweh." From the time of the destruction of the Second Temple in 70 AD, the expectation of the building of the "Third Temple," either before or after the coming of the Messiah, has been central to the Jewish faith. This expectation has perpetuated the ascending hierarchy of holiness espoused by the sages: 1) the land of Israel, 2) the cities of Israel, 3) the land inside the wall of Jerusalem, 4) the temple mount, 5) the rampart, 6) the court of the women, 7) the court of Israel, 8) the court of the priests, 9) the space between the porch and the altar, 10) the sanctuary, and 11) the Holy of Holies. See Mishnah, *Kelim* 1.6–9, quoted in Jorunn Økland, *Women in Their Place: Paul and the Corinthians Discourse of Gender and Sanctuary Space* (London, UK: T & T Clark International, 2004), p. 231.

[92] Arthur Koestler, "A Valedictory Message to the Jewish People (1949)," in *The Jew in the Modern World: A Documentary History*, Paul R. Mendes-Flohr, and Jehuda Reinharz, eds. (New York: Oxford University Press, 1980), p. 282.

[93] Vern S. Poythress, *The Shadow of Christ in the Law of Moses* (Phillipsburg, NJ: P & R Publishing, 1995), p. 106.

Brueggemann has, therefore, advanced the argument that "land is a central, if not *the central* theme of biblical faith."[94] After the passing of four thousand years, nothing has changed. Without the land clause, the Abrahamic covenant is as void of substance as it would have been four millennia ago. Brueggemann was right both when he said that "no matter how spiritualized, transcendentalized, or existentialized," the covenant may be to some, "it has its primary focus undeniably on land," and when he concluded that "the Abraham imagery apart from the land promise is an empty form."[95] In fact, the land clause was central to the covenant in every instance of God's reiteration of that covenant both to Abraham and his descendants. The land clause, therefore, cannot be stripped from the covenant without annulling the covenant in its entirety. The physicality and materiality of the covenant simply cannot be abrogated in favor of the exaltation of some higher spirituality.[96] If God could not or would not keep his oath regarding the land, there would be nothing to guarantee that he would maintain his commitment to any other part of his promise, oath, and covenant, and there would be no reason to believe that he would fulfill the terms of the Noahic covenant that he has made with all humanity[97] or the New Covenant through which he renewed the Abrahamic covenant and extended it to all humanity.[98]

Howard Schwartz discusses Jewish beliefs about the "divine role of the Land of Israel," saying that such claims are "not based on acquisition or military conquest." Instead, they are derived "from a decision of God, in which the Torah serves as the deed and proof." This is why, says he, that "exile is an unnatural state, and it is the obligation of the Jewish people to return and settle the Land of Israel."[99] Eliezer Schweid maintains that "we must not err, then, by thinking that the Jewish people's claim that it had a historic right to its land rested upon the fact that its forefathers had dwelt there in the distant past. It

---

94 Walter Brueggemann, *The Land: Place as Gift, Promise, and Challenge in Biblical Faith* (Minneapolis, MN: Augsburg Fortress Press, 2002), p. 3, author's emphasis.

95 Brueggemann, p. 170. See also J. H. Wright, *God's People in God's Land: Family, Land and Property in the Old Testament* (Carlisle, UK: Paternoster Press, 1997), p. 111.

96 Yon-Gyong Kwon rightly argues that "the promise of land given to Abraham cannot be equated with the gift of the Spirit." Yon-Gyong Kwon, *Eschatology in Galatians* (Tübingen, Germany: Mohr Siebeck, 2004), p. 107. Mal Couch also confirms that "We cannot spiritualize 'land' to mean heaven or some other Christian experience." Couch, ed., *Dictionary*, p. 29. Christian scholars who attempt to spiritualize the literal promises that God made to Abraham appear to be textual contortionists engaged in exegetical gymnastics!

97 Genesis 9:8–11.

98 Jeremiah 31:31–34; Hebrews 8:8–10.

99 Howard Schwartz, *Tree of Souls: The Mythology of Judaism* (New York: Oxford University Press, 2004), p. 409.

was based on their statement that the bond between this people in this land had never been disrupted."[100] The Jews are entitled to the land not simply because some of their ancestors lived there thousands of years ago but because the land of Israel has lived in their hearts through all of their generations since Abraham. The land has laid claim to them, and they have never ceased to lay claim to it.

The connection of the Jewish people with the land of Israel through the centuries of the Diaspora was continuing grounds for their rightful claim to the land. "Even if the people had perforce lived for generations in exile and its land had been conquered by others, it had never relinquished his desire and hope to return there and wrest it from foreign domination," says Schweid.[101] It is an undeniable historical fact that "the Jews have never accorded this foreign domination legitimacy, even though it had gone on for so long, and they had never considered exile a natural way of life for them. Their unending protest against the conquest of the land and their efforts to maintain a Jewish presence there confirmed that their right of possession has never been disrupted or replaced by legitimate possession by any other people. Thus, the national right of possession of the Jewish people was not nullified by the exile, and the foreign conquest created no rival right of possession."[102] Former Israeli Ambassador to the United Nations Abba Eban captured the essence of this important truth and fact of history that is essential to the understanding of the world as it considers that "Palestine never became the birthplace of any other nation. Every one of its conquerors has his original home elsewhere. Thus the idea of Palestine as the Jewish land had never been obscured or superseded."[103]

The Promised Land, therefore, is the Holy Land, made holy not only by the presence of God but also by the continuing sacrifice—even to the death of martyrdom—of Jews who loved both God and the land he had given to them and who never at any time ceded or surrendered title of the land to anyone. Israel remains—and forever will remain—the chosen dwelling place of YHWH and the rightful dwelling place of the Chosen People. The land between the River of Egypt and the Euphrates is the land of Israel, and it belongs in perpetuity to the people of Israel who received title to it from its eternal and present owner, God himself.

---

[100] Eliezer Schweid, *The Land of Israel: National Home or Land of Destiny* (Madison, NJ: Fairleigh Dickinson University Press, 1985), p. 193.

[101] Schweid, p. 193.

[102] Schweid, p. 193.

[103] Abba Solomon Eban, *Heritage: Civilization and the Jews* (New York: Simon & Schuster, 1984), p. 244.

CHAPTER 4

THE UNILATERAL COVENANT

Divine Faithfulness

The very first time that YHWH, the Eternal God, entered into a private and exclusive covenant with anyone[1] occurred when he chose Abraham, and he did so because he knew that the patriarch would do what he instructed him to do.[2] The covenant that God made with Abraham was unilateral, unconditional, and eternal because it was initiated entirely by God and was based solely on divine faithfulness, not on Abraham's performance. Though Abraham was not aware of it, God had chosen him to be the "servant of YHWH."[3] Dariusz Ivanski rightly observes that "this title may be considered the most concise summary of Abraham's life and of the unique relationship the patriarch enjoyed with God."[4] Generally speaking, this title "has to do with

---

[1] The first covenant mentioned in Scripture was the Noahic covenant (Genesis 6:18; 9:8–17). God entered into a covenant with Noah and his family—and, indeed, with all humanity—promising that he would never again destroy the earth or its inhabitants with water. This, however, was not an exclusive covenant that made Noah's family God's "Chosen People," constituted them as a nation, or gave to them a land. David VanDrunen maintains that the Noahic covenant "is a natural covenant" in which "God promises to restrain his wrath against the ground and against every living creature . . . and reestablishes regular cycles of days and seasons." VanDrunen further argues that the Noahic covenant is consequently distinguished from "the redemptive covenants of grace with Abraham, Israel, David, and the New Testament church." David VanDrunen, *Divine Covenants and Moral Order: A Biblical Theology of Natural Law* (Grand Rapids, MI: Wm. B. Eerdmans Publishing Co., 2014), p. 124.

[2] Genesis 18:19. God said, "I know [Abraham] . . . will command his children and his household after him to keep the way of the LORD by doing righteousness and justice, so that the LORD may bring upon Abraham what he has spoken about him." Though many versions (e.g., NAU, NIV, NRS) translate the first clause, "I have *chosen* [Abraham]," the KJV rendering, "I know [Abraham]," is more accurate because it translates the Hebrew phrase יְדַעְתִּיו (y'datiu) as "I know [or have known] him," in congruity with its root word יָדַע (yada'), which specifically means "to know" in the sense of "touching with the hand (יָד—yad)." This "knowing" implies intimacy as in Genesis 4:1: "Adam knew (יָדַע—yada') Eve his wife; and she conceived." God, therefore, had intimate knowledge of Abraham's commitment to justice, so he chose him to fulfill his mission.

[3] Genesis 26:24. Interestingly, Abraham was never called "God's servant" during his lifetime. This title was revealed to Isaac only after his father's death.

[4] Dariusz Ivanski, *The Dynamics of Job's Intercession* (Rome, Italy: Editrice Pontificio Instituto Biblico, 2006), p. 111.

Abraham's role as the protoplast of the Chosen Nation. He has been elected to this role without personal merits, but thanks to the free decision of God, who called him out of his native land and brought him to Canaan with the promise of numerous progeny."[5] When Abraham obeyed God's command, לֶךְ-לְךָ — *Lech l'chah* ("Go [for yourself]), "he accepted the call and the invitation to enter into a unique and intimate relationship with God."[6] Mal Couch encapsulates this truth well when he observes, "The Abrahamic covenant is a unilateral covenant, a divine covenant in which God alone pledges Himself to a course of action through Abraham and his seed, which cannot be reversed (else God would prove untrue) and cannot be annulled by the failure either of Abraham or his descendants, for the existence and continuance of the covenant depends not upon the fidelity of Abraham or his seed, but on God alone."[7] God was the one who established the parameters of the agreement. The covenant, therefore, depended — and still depends — solely on divine faithfulness. Since the covenant was not predicated on human performance, the land could never be taken from Abraham's descendants for non-performance. The Synod of the Evangelical Church of the Rhineland in Germany affirmed this premise in a 1980 statement in which it referred to the "signs of the faithfulness of God towards his people" that included "the continuing existence of the Jewish people," their "return to the land of promise," and "the foundation of the State of Israel."[8]

The covenant between God and Abraham brought about a startling transformation. Abraham, who was a Babylonian by birth and a Syrian by nationality,[9] became the father of another nation, the nation of faith in the Eternal God. As far as God was concerned, Abraham was transformed from an Assyrio-Babylonian into a chosen vessel to father a holy nation that would bear his name among the Gentiles. From the time that Abraham crossed over

---

[5] Ivanski, p. 111.

[6] Ivanski, p. 111.

[7] Mal Couch, ed., *Dictionary of Premillennial Theology: A Practical Guide to the People, Viewpoints, and History of Prophetic Studies* (Grand Rapids, MI: Kregel Publications, 1996), p. 27. Also, Terence E. Fretheim, *Abraham: Trials of Family and Faith* (Columbia, SC: The University of South Carolina Press, 2007), p. 38.

[8] See Bertold Klappert, "An Alternative for Christian Substitution Theology and Christology," in *Humanity at the Limit: The Impact of the Holocaust Experience on Jews and Christians*, Michael Alan Signer, ed. (Bloomington, IN: Indiana University Press, 2000), p. 89.

[9] Genesis 11:31. Interestingly, Abraham's descendants continued to be known as Syrians long after the time of his grandson Jacob and his great-grandson Joseph. God even instructed the post-Sinai Israelites to give this account of their patrimony: "My father was a Syrian, about to perish, and he went down to Egypt and sojourned there, few in number; and there he became a nation, great, mighty, and populous" (Deuteronomy 26:5).

the River Euphrates, he was called a "Hebrew" because he came to be defined by his act of "crossing over" from the land of his birth and the land of his naturalization into the Promised Land.[10] His leaving the land of Ur of the Chaldeans and later departing from his father's house in the land of Haran of Syria and his arriving, at last, in the land of Canaan constituted the acts of faith that prompted God to extend his promise and covenant to Abraham. By passing over (through) the waters of the River Euphrates he had been transformed from a common Gentile into a chosen Hebrew.[11] Indeed, after God made his covenant with Abraham, he became even more than a Hebrew—he became the first Jew, the father of all the faithful who would ever live.[12]

"Cutting" the Covenant

When Abraham inquired of the Lord, "How shall I know that I will inherit [this land]?"[13] God instructed him to make a sacrifice that would be the basis for the covenant that he would seal with Abraham.[14] The Hebrew word that is translated "covenant," בְּרִית (berit), literally means "to cut." This distinction is in keeping with traditional Hebrew thought wherein things are identified by function, not form, and are, therefore, verbal actions, not static substantives. Eugene Boring makes it clear that "in the Bible, the divine beryith is an event, not an ideal or principle. The covenant is a gracious act of God, taken at the divine initiative for the benefit of humanity."[15] As Terence Fretheim notes, "Covenant means a promise under oath, solemnly sworn, not an agreement or contract, and the making

---

[10] In Hebrew, the word עִבְרִי—ivri ("Hebrew") is derived from עֵבֶר (eber), which means "beyond" or "across" and, hence, "from the other side," but can be more particularly traced to the verbal stem עָבַר (avar), which means "to pass over." The term eber can also be traced to Eber, one of the descendants of Shem (Genesis 10:21).

[11] It could be said that at the Euphrates, Abraham experienced what Israel did some five centuries later at the Red Sea, a spiritual event that Paul described as a "baptism," an immersion in water somewhat similar to that which later proselytes to Judaism would experience when they immersed themselves in the waters of the mikveh and were transformed from Gentiles into Jews.

[12] Romans 4:16 says, "The promise comes by faith, so that it may be by grace and may be guaranteed to all Abraham's offspring—not only to those who are of the law but all those who have the faith of Abraham, who is the father of us all" (NIV, ESV). While the term Jew did not emerge until post-exilic times, Abraham was the father of the Jewish people and as such he has been recognized by them as being the first Jew.

[13] Genesis 15:8.

[14] Genesis 15:9.

[15] M. Eugene Boring, An Introduction to the New Testament: History, Literature, and Theology (Louisville, KY: Westminster John Knox Press, 2012), p. 2.

(literally, 'cutting') has reference to the rite with cut animals."[16] The covenant ("cutting") was confirmed or sealed with the shedding of blood.[17]

In Middle Eastern antiquity, covenants were said to be "cut" because such agreements were usually sealed by means of the physical act of sacrificing animals, cutting them in half, laying them out on the ground, and having the parties of the covenant walk between the pieces of the sacrifice, thereby saying, in essence, "May I be cut in pieces like these animals if I do not fulfill the terms of this covenant." In fact, as Marvin Wilson notes, the covenant ceremony involving slaughtered animals served "as a type of self-maledictory oath for the parties involved."[18] The implication of the malediction involved in the "cutting" of a covenant was made clear in the graphic words that God spoke to the prophet Jeremiah concerning those people in Judah who had violated God's covenant and in doing so had heaped upon themselves the judgment of the covenant that they had "cut" with God.[19] The cutting of covenants with God was, therefore, never a casual matter.

This graphic demonstration was certainly common and traditional in Chaldea, the land of Abraham's birth. C. F. Keil and Franz Delitzsch maintained, therefore, that "God condescended to follow the custom of the Chaldeans, that He might in the most solemn manner confirm His oath to Abram the Chaldean."[20] God wanted to make sure that Abraham could not mistake the inviolability and irrevocability of the royal decree through which he would cut his covenant with the patriarch. Employing the ancient custom, therefore, the Almighty gave Abraham this commandment: "Bring me a three year old heifer, and three year old female goat, and a three year old ram, and a turtledove, and a young pigeon." In response, Abraham "brought all these to

---

[16] Fretheim, p. 38.

[17] The Abrahamic covenant involved shed blood (Genesis 15:9–10) and was confirmed by the shed blood of circumcision (Genesis 17:10–13). The Mosaic covenant was confirmed with blood sprinkled on the Tabernacle, the Torah, and the people (Hebrews 9:19). The New Covenant was also sealed with blood (Hebrews 9:15).

[18] Marvin R. Wilson, *Exploring Our Hebraic Heritage: A Christian Theology of Roots and Renewal* (Grand Rapids, MI: Wm. B. Eerdmans Publishing Co., 2014), p. 99. See also Heerak Christian Kim, *Intricately Connected: Biblical Studies, Intertextuality, and Literary Genre* (Lanham, MD: University Press of America, 2008), pp. 20–22.

[19] Jeremiah 34:18–19. "I will give the men who have transgressed my covenant, who have not fulfilled the words of the covenant which they made before me, when they *cut the calf in two* and *passed between its parts*. . . . I will give them into the hand of their enemies . . . and their dead bodies shall be for meat unto the fowls of the heaven, and the beasts of the earth" (emphasis added).

[20] Carl Friedrich Keil and Franz Delitzsch, *The Pentateuch*, tr. James Martin (Edinburgh, Scotland: T & T Clark, 1864), vol. 1, p. 214.

him, cut them in two and arranged the halves opposite each other; the birds, however, he did not cut in half."[21]

Then, Abraham waited, and waited, and waited to see what God would do or what he would further command him to do. First, when vultures tried to steal the pieces of his sacrifice, Abraham drove them away. Second, a "deep sleep" came over the patriarch. Third, "terror and great darkness fell upon him." Finally, when the sun had set and the scene had been enveloped in night, "a smoking fire pot with a blazing torch appeared and passed between the pieces."[22] After reporting this series of events, the Scriptures immediately declared, "On that day the LORD cut (כָּרַת —karath) a covenant with Abram, saying, 'To your descendants I have given this land, from the River of Egypt to the great river, the river Euphrates."[23] In this instance, says Frank Cross, "Abraham was granted progeny and the land by divine decree, apparently unconditionally."[24]

No doubt, the waiting that Abraham experienced was a symbolic recapitulation of his life wherein it seemed that he would never realize the fulfillment of God's promise that a son would be given to him and his wife in their old age.[25] The vultures that Abraham constantly had to drive away from his sacrifice may have represented those people who viewed him as delusional. Perhaps he was often lulled into a deep sleep as he considered the seeming impossibility of his dream, a sleep that must have made him feel as good as dead.[26] Finally, he was terrorized by the darkness of the almost certain impending failure of all his hopes and expectations.

Suddenly, however, everything came into profoundly clear focus. God appeared in a physical theophany—a demonstration of fire, which was the most

---

[21] Genesis 15:11.
[22] Genesis 15:18.
[23] Genesis 15:19.
[24] Frank Moore Cross, *Canaanite Myth and Hebrew Epic: Essays in the History of the Religion of Israel* (Cambridge, MA: Harvard University Press, 1973), p. 273.
[25] Paul Williamson observes parallels and symbolism in this story: "The intrusion into the ritual by the birds of prey . . . constitutes a potential 'foreign threat' to Abraham. . . . If a parallel exists at all between the problem posed by Abraham's steward and that posed by the scavenging birds, it must surely be antithetical. Other, less problematic parallels can at any rate be drawn: in the first pericope (vv. 1-6) God's promise of personal blessing (great reward, v.1) is apparently jeopardized by Abraham's circumstances (childlessness, vv. 2–3). In the second pericope (vv. 7–21), God's promise of national blessing (great possessions, v. 14) is apparently jeopardized by Israel's circumstances (subjugation, v. 13). The latter threat is typified in the action of the birds of prey, and the removal of this threat is typified by Abraham's expulsion of these birds." Paul R. Williamson, *Abraham, Israel and the Nations: The Patriarchal Promise and Its Covenantal Development in Genesis* (Sheffield, UK: Sheffield Academic Press, 2000), pp. 131–132.
[26] Hebrews 11:12.

common metaphor used to describe God used in Scripture.[27] The smoking fire pot and the blazing torch of the Divine Presence must have been a spectacular and comforting sight for Abraham. When he saw it, he knew beyond any doubt that he was witnessing a tangible manifestation of the Almighty. "The Theophanic symbols passing between the pieces . . . bring to completion the entire ceremony . . . and thus function as the sign which Abraham had requested."[28] So, it is unlikely that the patriarch was surprised to hear the accompanying words of covenantal assurance, the confirmation of the covenant: "To your descendants have I given this land, from the river of Egypt to the great river, the River Euphrates . . ."[29] Then, the narrative continued: "On the same day the LORD cut a covenant with Abram." This covenant, however, was not something new. It was but "a sworn formalization of a prior promise given by God."[30]

Something far more significant was manifest in this narrative when "only Yahweh, depicted as 'a smoking fire pot with a blazing torch,' passed down the aisle between the divided slain animals, thereby taking on himself an oath of annihilation if he, Yahweh, should fail to perform all that he had promised."[31] Abraham was not invited or commanded by God to walk between the pieces of the sacrifice nor did he even attempt to do so, despite the requirement of the Chaldean tradition that both parties who were "cutting" a covenant walk between the pieces of the sacrifice. This could mean only one thing: the Abrahamic covenant was not a bilateral contract—it was a divine decree. "Like a will, the covenant [was] simply there by imposition of the one who made it,"[32] says Boring.

The Abrahamic covenant was, therefore, a unilateral covenant, not a bilateral agreement "that would have allowed either side to opt out of the arrangement should either side default."[33] Both Eugene Merrill[34] and Craig Blaising[35] are right, therefore, when they portray God's covenant with

---

[27] Peter Schäfer, *The Origins of Jewish Mysticism* (Tübingen, Germany: Mohr Siebeck, 2009), p. 80. Schäfer says that in the Bible, "fire imagery is the most common metaphor used to describe the figure of God."
[28] Williamson, p. 129.
[29] Genesis 15:18.
[30] Fretheim, p. 38, referencing Genesis 12:7; 13:14–17.
[31] Walter C. Kaiser, *The Old Testament Documents: Are They Reliable & Relevant?* (Downers Grove, IL: InterVarsity Press, 2001), p. 145.
[32] Boring, p. 3.
[33] Kaiser, *Old Testament Documents*, p. 145.
[34] Eugene H. Merrill, *Everlasting Dominion: A Theology of the Old Testament* (Nashville, TN: Broadman & Holman Publishers, 2006), p. 239
[35] Craig A. Blaising, "The Structure of Biblical Covenants: The Covenants Prior to Christ," *Progressive Dispensationalism,* Craig A. Blaising and Darrell L. Bock, eds. (Grand Rapids, MI: Baker Academic, 1993), pp. 133–134.

Abraham as a "royal grant," a unilateral and unconditional covenant rather than a bilateral or conditional agreement. Couch sums up the event this way: "Since Abram did not make (cut) the covenant, he cannot break the covenant."[36] It is reasonable to conclude, then, that "Yahweh's covenant with Abraham, with its promise to bless or curse, is unconditional. In it He commits only Himself, not Abraham or his descendants, to do anything."[37] God's covenant with Abraham, therefore, could be passed on unconditionally and intact to Isaac, Jacob, and the succeeding generations of their descendants. In fact, as Marvin Wilson observes, "the unilateral, unconditional character of the covenantal agreement assures Abraham and his posterity that God's relationship with his people is permanent. The covenant with Abraham is sealed in blood."[38] This covenant, therefore, had the force of an irrevocable last will and testament in that it bequeathed unconditional blessings upon its intended beneficiary. Because the Abrahamic covenant was eternal and irrevocable, therefore, it still stands secure solely because it rests on the immutability of the divine decree.

The Abrahamic covenant, therefore, is "unilateral, declared and sworn by God at God's own initiative. The promise grants the land (with specific boundaries) to Abraham's descendants."[39] At the time at which it was made, the transaction, including its real estate clause, was present reality, not a future gift. "Israel's possession of Canaan, its homeland, is thus viewed as a divine right, a unilateral land grant from the Deity."[40] In reality, "God's promises had been irrevocable before, but, given the divine participation in the rite, Abraham should now 'know' how deeply God has entered into this commitment,"[41] says Fretheim. John Feinberg declares that by "unilaterally passing through the bones and meat of the animal sacrifice," God ratified his covenant with Abraham in an "activity that was a unilateral and unconditional way to make a covenant."[42] This meant that "even if the one with whom the covenant is made makes no promise," God "unconditionally committed himself to fulfill the covenant."[43]

---

[36] Couch, ed., *Dictionary*, p. 31.

[37] Sandra Teplinsky, *Why Care about Israel?: How the Jewish Nation Is the Key to Unleashing God's Blessings in the 21st Century* (Grand Rapids, MI: Baker Publishing Group, 2004), p. 32.

[38] Wilson, *Exploring*, p. 99.

[39] Fretheim, p. 38.

[40] Stephen L. Harris and Robert L. Platzner, *The Old Testament: An Introduction to the Hebrew Bible* (New York: McGraw-Hill, 2003), p. 12.

[41] Fretheim, p. 38.

[42] John S. Feinberg, *"No One Like Him,"* in *The Doctrine of God* (Wheaton, IL: Crossway Books, 2001), p. 765.

[43] Feinberg, p. 765.

The Unilateral Covenant Is Irrevocable

Some scholars have argued that God's covenant with Abraham was always revocable and could be canceled for disobedience.[44] Boring, however, underscores an important principle about the Abrahamic covenant when he says that since the covenant is unilateral, it "cannot be nullified from the human side."[45] The people to whom the covenant is directed "can ignore it or refuse to live by the responsibilities to which it calls them";[46] however, "they cannot break it in the sense of revoking, annulling, or destroying it," for such action "could be done only by the covenant's Maker."[47] Steven McAvoy further explains this truth: "The Abrahamic covenant is a unilateral covenant, a divine covenant in which God alone pledges Himself to a course of action through Abraham and his seed, which cannot be reversed (else God would prove untrue) and cannot be annulled by the failure of either Abraham or his seed, for the existence and continuance of the covenant depends not upon the fidelity of Abraham or his seed, but on God alone."[48] While "the faithfulness of God calls for human response," it is not "conditional on it," for "even though human beings are unfaithful, God remains faithful."[49]

Human infidelity can never obviate divine fidelity.[50] As Charles Ryrie notes, "It is apparent that Abraham sinned during the years between the making of the covenant and its confirmation to Isaac; so if God had viewed the covenant as conditioned on obedience, He would have had to nullify it because Abraham had been disobedient."[51] Paul Enns goes a step further by

---

[44] Daniel Fuller, *Gospel and Law* (Grand Rapids, MI: Wm. B. Eerdmans Publishing Co., 1980), pp. 121–145.

[45] Boring, p. 3.

[46] Boring correctly observes that "this is the only sense in which human beings can 'break' God's covenant" (Boring, p. 3). The actual "breaking" of the Abrahamic covenant can be done only by God, and since he has made the covenant contingent upon his own faithfulness, no one, not even he, can break the covenant. For this reason alone, the "New Covenant," the renewed and expanded Abrahamic covenant, sealed in the blood of Jesus, is also irrevocable (Hebrews 8:8–12) because it rests on the divine premise that "Jesus Christ [is] the same yesterday, and today, and forever" (Hebrews 13:8). Likewise, the "New Covenant" that God will make with Israel is also irrevocable (Jeremiah 31:31).

[47] Boring, p. 3.

[48] Steven L. McAvoy, "Abrahamic Covenant," in Couch, ed., *Dictionary*, p. 27, and Steven L. McAvoy, quoted in Mal Couch, ed., *An Introduction to Classical Evangelical Hermeneutics: A Guide to the History and Practice of Biblical Interpretation* (Grand Rapids, MI: Kregel Publications, 2000), p. 142.

[49] Boring, p. 3.

[50] Paul made this premise clear: What if some were unfaithful? Will their unfaithfulness nullify God's faithfulness? May it never be!" (Romans 3:3). The same apostle concluded that "the gifts and the calling of God are irrevocable" (Romans 11:29).

[51] Charles C. Ryrie, *A Survey of Bible Doctrine* (Chicago, IL: Moody Publishers, 1972), p. 161. Ryrie references Genesis 12:10–20 in his argument.

explaining the transfer of the irrevocability of Abrahamic covenant to the patriarch's progeny: "The unconditional and eternal nature of the covenant is seen in that the covenant is reaffirmed to Isaac. . . . It is noteworthy that God reaffirmed these promises amid the sins of the patriarchs, which fact further emphasizes the unconditional nature of the Abrahamic covenant."[52]

Ryrie also correctly extends the unilateral—and, therefore, irrevocable—nature of the Abrahamic covenant to the patriarch's descendants: "The covenant was reaffirmed to Abraham's son, Isaac, and to Isaac's son Jacob. No conditions were attached in either instance, and the reaffirmation was made on the basis of the oath with which God made the covenant with Abraham originally."[53] Bruce Waltke uses this principle to confirm the fact that the covenants that extend and expand the Abrahamic covenant are equally valid, unilateral, and irrevocable: "The Abrahamic, Mosaic, and Davidic[54] covenants function as complements of one another in defining true Israel. Though unilateral, these covenants are as inseparable as the strands that make up a rope."[55] The original covenant is never abrogated or restricted in order to accommodate its renewal.

After God had confirmed his covenant with Abraham to bless his descendants, the Mosaic law could not be retroactively added as a condition for the fulfillment of the original covenant. "Since, at the Aqedah, God put himself under an unconditional, unilaterally binding oath to fulfill his covenant with Abraham, this would be nonsense," says Scott Hahn. "To suppose that God added conditions (the Mosaic law) to the Abrahamic covenant, long after it had been unilaterally sworn by God would imply that God acted illegally, reneging on a commitment in a way not tolerated even in human contracts."[56] This truth is also confirmed by Paul: "What I am saying is this:

---

[52] Paul P. Enns, *The Moody Handbook of Theology* (Chicago, IL: Moody Publications, 2014), p. 56.

[53] Ryrie, p. 161. Ryrie references Genesis 26:2–4; 28:13–25 in his discussion.

[54] God's oath to King David was this: "One of your descendants I will place on your throne" (Psalm 131:11, NIV). The apostle Peter declared that the reason for the resurrection of Jesus was to provide the means for fulfilling this "everlasting" Davidic covenant: "Because [David] was a prophet and knew that God had sworn to him with an oath to seat one of his descendants on his throne, he looked ahead and spoke of the resurrection of the Christ, that he was neither abandoned to hades, nor did his flesh suffer decay. This Jesus God raised up again, to which we are all witnesses" (Acts 2:31–32). Peter's argument was that Jesus experienced a bodily resurrection so that he could eventually sit as King Messiah on David's throne, thereby fulfilling the terms of God's "everlasting" covenant with David.

[55] Bruce K. Waltke, *The Dance Between God and Humanity: Reading the Bible Today As the People of God* (Grand Rapids, MI: Wm. B. Eerdmans Publishing Co., 2013), p. 379.

[56] Scott Hahn, *Kinship by Covenant: A Canonical Approach to the Fulfillment of God's Saving Promises* (New Haven, CT: Yale University Press, 2009), p. 262.

the Law, which came four hundred and thirty years later, does not invalidate a covenant previously ratified by God, so as to nullify the promise."[57]

Fretheim points out another significant aspect of the inviolability and irrevocability of the covenant. Though the covenant "is a promise that God will never nullify," still God—as he always does—provides for and respects the free will that he created in the human race so that the choice of who participates in the covenant and benefits from its terms is determined by the individual. "While the promise is an everlasting one, participation in its fulfillment . . . is not guaranteed to every person or generation."[58] The unconditional promises that God has made, therefore, "do not make faith irrelevant."[59] The apostle Paul made this premise clear: "What if some were unfaithful? Will their unfaithfulness nullify God's faithfulness? May it never be!"[60]

God explained the unconditionality of the covenants that he had made with Abraham and his descendants in this manner: "If [David's children] forsake my law and do not follow my statutes . . . I will punish their sin with the rod, their iniquity with flogging; but I will not take my love from him, nor will I ever betray my faithfulness. I will not violate my covenant or alter what my lips have uttered."[61] In Ezekiel 16:60-63, God even employs graphic sexual imagery to describe the vileness of Israel's violation of his covenant; however, he then concluded his caustic rebuke of sinful Israel with "depictions of unilateral grace."[62] As Preston Sprinkle notes, "The most shocking feature of this scathing review of Israel's moral atrocities, however, is that it ends *not* with God's judgment *nor* with Israel's repentance, but with God's unilateral forgiveness: 'Yet I will remember my covenant with you in the days of your youth, and I will establish you for an everlasting covenant.'"[63] John Walvoord accurately summed up the nature of the unilateral Abrahamic covenant as being contingent upon God's faithfulness, not human performance: "The

---

[57] Galatians 3:17.

[58] Fretheim, p. 38.

[59] Fretheim, p. 38, referring to Genesis 22:15–18; 26:5.

[60] Romans 3:3–4, NIV, NASB. The KJV gives a picturesque translation of the apostle's answer to his own rhetorical question: "God forbid!"

[61] Psalm 89:30–34.

[62] Preston M. Sprinkle, *Paul and Judaism Revisited: A Study of Divine and Human Agency in Salvation* (Downers Grove, IL: InterVarsity Press, 2013), pp. 61–62.

[63] Sprinkle, pp. 61–62, referencing Ezekiel 16:60–63. Nancy Bowen observes that the language that God employs in this passage is "graphic, even pornographic." God's intent, therefore, was to shock disobedient Israel so as to bring them to repentance. Nancy R. Bowen, *Abingdon Old Testament Commentaries: Ezekiel* (Nashville, TN: Abingdon Press, 2010), p. 139.

seed of Abraham have been disobedient in every moral category. Yet in spite of that disobedience they have fulfilled many of the promises of the covenant. The very principle of grace is that God blesses the unworthy."[64]

Apostolic Confirmation of Irrevocability

Jesus himself confirmed the irrevocability of the Abrahamic covenant and its expansion at Sinai. As a matter of fact, he emphatically affirmed that he had no intention of abrogating or repealing the covenant that he as the divine *Logos/Memra* had made with Israel: "Think not that I have come to destroy the law or the prophets," he declared. "I have not come to destroy but to fulfill. For until heaven and earth pass, not one *yud* or crown [of the text] will disappear from the Torah until all is fulfilled."[65] Paul also made no effort to abridge this agreement. In fact, he built upon and expanded the concept: "From the standpoint of God's choice, [the Jews] are loved for the sake of the patriarchs, for the gifts and the calling of God are irrevocable."[66] Because he knew that if God is nothing else, he is faithful, the apostle was able to affirm this eschatological eventuality: "All Israel will be saved, just as it is written, 'The deliverer will come from Zion, he will remove ungodliness from Jacob.'"[67]

Paul's contention was not, however, without scriptural support: "Arise, shine, for your light has come, and the glory of the LORD has risen upon you," the Lord God said to Isaiah, predicting the restoration of Israel. Then, he declared further that at that time, *"All your people will be righteous.* They will possess their land forever; for I will plant them there with my own hands in order to bring myself glory."[68] These words of divine promise immediately followed the prophetic word that Paul had quoted: "The Redeemer will come to Zion, and to those who turn from transgression in Jacob. . . . 'As for me, this is my covenant with them,' says the LORD: 'My Spirit which is upon you, and my words which I have put in your mouth shall not depart from your mouth, nor from the mouth of your offspring, nor from the mouth of your offspring's offspring,' says

---

64 John Walvoord, *The Millennial Kingdom: A Basic Text in Premillennial Theology* (Grand Rapids, MI: Zondervan Publishing, 1983), p. 153.

65 Matthew 5:17–18, author's translation. The so-called "jot" is actually the smallest of all the letters of the Hebrew *alephbet*, the yud (ˑ). The so-called "tittles" are the decorative pen strokes that the scribes added to the tops of some of the Hebrew letters when they copied the Torah text. The *alephbet* is from the first two letters of Hebrew, *aleph* and *beth*. This is the source of the Greek word *alphabet*, which is taken from the first two letters of Greek, *alpha* and *beta*.

66 Romans 11:28–29.

67 Romans 11:26.

68 Isaiah 60:1, 21, emphasis added.

the LORD, 'from now and forever.'"[69] Of this final accomplishment, Ryrie notes, "To be sure, some contingencies are involved in the *intermediate* fulfillments of aspects of the covenant, but the *ultimate* fulfillment is unconditioned. . . . [and] will be brought about by God, and Israel will then be converted and obedient under the reign of the Messiah."[70] God's unconditional and final word regarding the Chosen People is this: "They will possess the land forever."

The Abrahamic covenant, therefore, was unilateral, irrevocable, and eternal. It was not predicated on Abraham's performance or on the performance of his progeny. It was conditioned and established solely on the immutability and faithfulness of the one and only God who created the covenant and extended it to Abraham by divine decree. It was, indeed, a blessing from God in the form of divine *chesed* in which the unmerited favor of transcendent grace was extended to Abraham without definitive terms of human response to that decree. For the first time in human history a divine-human transaction was enacted and accepted entirely through faith with no thought given to human performance. Abraham became the progenitor of a faith people.

The unilateral nature of Abraham's experience with God was summed up, therefore, in this declaration: "Abraham believed God, and it was credited to him for righteousness."[71] It was not God's demand for—or even expectation of—Abraham's punctilious performance that endeared him to God. It was entirely and only his faith—*sola fide*. For this reason alone, Abraham is rightly called the father of the faithful[72]—indeed, "the father of us all."[73] Later, when God followed up on the "cutting" of the covenant, he reiterated the irrevocable and eternal details of his unilateral covenant: "I will establish my covenant between me and you and your descendants after you throughout their generations for an everlasting covenant, to be God to you and to your descendants after you. I will give to you and to your descendants after you, the land of your sojournings, all the land of Canaan, for an everlasting possession, and I will be their God."[74]

In subsequent interaction with Abraham, God instructed him to circumcise himself and all the males of his household. God did not, however, even hint, much less demand, that the patriarch engage in the act of self-circumcision as a precondition to the covenant. The unconditional, unilateral covenant had

---

[69] Isaiah 59:20–21.
[70] Ryrie, pp. 161–162.
[71] Galatians 3:6.
[72] Galatians 3:16–29; Romans 4:11.
[73] Romans 4:16.
[74] Genesis 17:7–8.

already been made. Circumcision was designed only to be the ongoing "sign of the covenant,"[75] a physical seal[76] or a "badge" as N. T. Wright has called it.[77] This commandment and its fulfillment demonstrated that Abraham had finally completely severed himself from his former culture and life in Ur of the Chaldeans, where circumcision was not customary. After circumcising himself, Abraham could "never return home to Ur and 'fit in' with that culture since the operation is not reversible."[78] This, too, was a free-will act taken by Abraham because of his faith, not because of some presumptuous idea that he could achieve or maintain status with God (righteousness) by an action that he had undertaken (works). It was, in effect, a reciprocation of God's unilateral action in establishing the covenant by divine decree. God's promise was "reciprocated by Abraham's acceptance of circumcision, the sign of the covenant."[79] As Joyce Baldwin has said, "The covenant sacrifice established that the covenant was an unconditional act of God in which Abram had no part to play, and to which he could make no contribution. Now his response is stipulated, albeit in one all-embracing command."[80]

The seal of circumcision was introduced by God as a continuing memorial of the covenant among the descendants of Abraham. Abraham's circumcision and that of his descendants "demonstrates unwavering faith in God by which one decisively renounces one's former life and enters the new life promised by God."[81] In effect, the blood sacrifice which God had used as a means of sealing his unilateral covenant with Abraham was transferred to the shedding of blood in the act of circumcision. As a matter of fact, as Tremper Longman notes, "circumcision is called the sign of the covenant, which indicates that it is like a brand.

---

[75] Genesis 17:11: "You shall be circumcised in the flesh of your foreskin, and it shall be the sign of the covenant between me and you."

[76] Romans 4:11.

[77] Nicholas Thomas Wright, *Paul for Everyone: Romans, Part One: Chapters 1–8* (Louisville, KY: Westminster John Knox Press, 2004), p. 69.

[78] Troy W. Martin, "Circumcision in Galatia and the Holiness of God's Ecclesiae," in *Holiness and Ecclesiology in the New Testament*, Kent Brower and Andy Johnson, eds. (Grand Rapids, MI: Wm. B. Eerdmans Publishing Co., 2007), p. 221. Martin references Andreas Blaschke, *Beschneidung: Zeugnisse der Bibel und verwandter Texte*, TANZ 28 (Tübingen, Germany: A. Francke Verlag, 1998), p. 89.

[79] Jonathan David Magonet, "Abraham and God," *Judaism* 33 (1984), p. 162.

[80] Joyce G. Baldwin, *The Message of Genesis 15–20* (Downers Grove, IL: IVP Academic, 1986), p. 62.

[81] Martin, in Brower and Johnson, eds., p. 222. It could also be said that the "circumcision of the heart" which Gentiles experience through baptism into the Messiah (Colossians 2:11–12)—when they become Abraham's descendants through faith and, therefore, also heirs of the promises (Galatians 3:29)—is likewise the act of renouncing one's former life and entering into God's promises, just as Abraham renounced his Babylonian heritage and entered into God's covenant.

Every time someone was circumcised, the brand of the Abrahamic covenant was presented, which made children of Abraham remember their duty to uphold their loyalty to Yahweh."[82]

The covenant of circumcision (בְּרִת מִילָה—*berit milah*) has weathered the course of time as a continuing witness to God's everlasting covenant with Abraham's descendants, the Hebrews/Israelites/Jews, as well as with those who have been circumcised with the circumcision made without human hands[83]—the circumcision of the heart[84]—by being baptized into the Messiah, immersed in his death[85] and resurrected with him in the newness of eternal life.[86] In one form or another, what might seem to postmodernists as a quaint, even superstitious practice has maintained its validity for four millennia as a confirmation of the fact that the one and only God has "cut" a covenant with his one and only Chosen People. Though that covenant has been expanded to include others with its originally intended recipients, it remains the same covenant, the one and only covenant on which all successive expressions of divine election rest. As Ryan Lister wisely notes, "The Abrahamic covenant is not one covenant among many, but is formative for the rest of the covenants to come."[87] Because the Abrahamic covenant was initiated solely by God and because it rests solely on God's faithfulness, it could never be abrogated or diminished. It could only be expanded and extended.[88] The divine oath, promise, and covenant to Abraham remains sacrosanct in the mind of the Almighty, for its unilaterality, as well as its irrevocability and its eternity, bespeaks the essence of his own character—the eternal and immutable faithfulness on which he has predicated his own very existence.[89]

---

82 Tremper Longman III, *Old Testament Essentials: Creation, Conquest, Exile, and Return* (Downers Grove, IL: InterVarsity Press, 2014), p. 39. Longman notes that circumcision made sense in the Abrahamic situation, "where the focus of attention is on the birth of an heir." The excision of the prepuce of the penis placed greater focus on the sanctity and the transgenerational transfer of the covenant and blessing and was a reminder that survival of the Chosen People was dependent entirely on faithfulness to God and his Word.

83 Colossians 2:11; Ephesians 2:11.

84 Deuteronomy 30:6; Jeremiah 4:4; Romans 2:29.

85 Galatians 3:27; Romans 6:3; Colossians 2:12.

86 Romans 6:4.

87 J. Ryan Lister, *The Presence of God: Its Place in the Storyline of Scripture and the Story of Our Lives* (Wheaton, IL: Crossway 2015), p. 101.

88 This is why the New Covenant is merely a renewal of the Abrahamic covenant and of the first expansion of that covenant, the Sinai Covenant, wherein its instructions are written on the hearts of believers (Hebrew 8:8–9), and the faith that brings salvation is generated by the Word of God (Romans 10:17).

89 Malachi 3:6.

CHAPTER 5

UNEQUIVOCAL PROMISES
COVENANT LUCIDITY

The legitimacy of Israel—the people, the nation, and the land—is based on God's unilateral covenant with Abraham. This sovereign decree was finalized after God summoned the patriarch from Haran of Assyria and instructed him to go to the land which he would reveal to him. In every instance of God's self-initiated relationship with Abraham, his intentions were clear. "The language was not allegorical or figurative. It was literal and unequivocal."[1] Abraham's response, like God's initiative, was also unequivocal: he obeyed God's instructions immediately and precisely and without ambivalence. The Abrahamic covenant, however, was not based on the patriarch's goodness: it rested solely on God's grace and faithfulness. The Scriptures "affirm unequivocally that the covenant initiates and depends on God's unilateral commitment to fulfill his promise."[2]

After Abraham crossed the River Euphrates and entered into the land of Canaan, he reached Shechem where God began to speak of the covenant that he would cut with his friend by declaring, "To your descendants I will give you this land."[3] Later, God gave greater definition to his promise by instructing Abraham to look as far as he could see to the north, south, east, and west, saying, "All the land which you see I will give it to you and to your descendants forever."[4] Finally, after Abraham had passed several tests that confirmed his character and proved that God's promises could be fulfilled in him, the Almighty cut the covenant and made this promise: "This

---

[1] Edward P. Meadors, *Creation, Sin, Covenant, and Salvation: A Primer for Biblical Theology* (Eugene, OR: Wipf and Stock Publishers, 2011), p. 61.
[2] Mary Sylvia Chinyere Nwachukwu, *Creation–Covenant Scheme and Justification by Faith: A Canonical Study of the God-Human Drama in the Pentateuch and the Letter to the Romans* (Rome, Italy: Gregorian University Press, 2002), p. 111.
[3] Genesis 12:7, emphasis added.
[4] Genesis 13:15, NASB, NIV, emphasis added.

is my covenant with you: You will be the father of a multitude of nations. . . . Your name shall be Abraham. . . . I will make you exceedingly fruitful. . . . I will establish my covenant between me and you and your descendants after you throughout their generations for an everlasting covenant to be God to you and to your descendants after you. . . . The whole land of Canaan . . . I will give as an everlasting possession to you and your descendants after you; and I will be their God."[5]

The terms of God's covenant with Abraham were unequivocally and explicitly declared in unmistakable and exclusive terms: "But my covenant will I establish with Isaac, whom Sarah shall bear unto you in the set time in the next year."[6] Not the slightest hint of divine equivocation was manifest in any of the affirmations of God's covenant with the patriarch and his descendants. There was no hesitation on God's part to make the divine decree. His pronouncement of the covenant and its promises was perfectly lucid. God said what he meant, and he meant what he said. The covenant and its promises were unequivocal, inviolable, and irrevocable.[7] In reality, the very "godness" of God would be contingent upon his faithfulness to fulfill the promises that he had made to Abraham.[8] If the Almighty were to fail to bring to pass the terms of his covenant, he would not—could not—be the God of truth and faithfulness, and he would not be the God of Holy Scripture.

A Divine Oath—the Apex of Certitude

God was so determined to underscore and certify his unequivocal commitment to Abraham that he actually undertook to swear an oath that would bind him forever, saying, "By myself I have sworn, declares the LORD, because you have done this thing and have not withheld your son, your only son, indeed I will greatly bless you and I will greatly multiply your descendants as the stars of the heavens and as the sand which is on the seashore; and your descendants shall possess the gate of their enemies."[9] The author of the Book of Hebrews discussed God's intentions succinctly: "For when God made his promise to Abraham, since he could swear by no greater, he swore

---

5 Genesis 17:4–8, emphasis added.
6 Genesis 17:21; 18:14.
7 Samuel Austin, *A View of the Economy of the Church of God* (Newburyport, England: Thomas & Whipple, 1807), p. 58.
8 Malachi 3:6.
9 Genesis 22:16–17.

by himself, saying, 'I will surely bless you and I will surely multiply you.'[10] The detailed promises of the divine oath are rendered more literally in this translation "Blessing, I will bless you, and multiplying, I will multiply you."[11] The Greek text of Hebrews 6:14 is clear: ἠὶ μὴν εὐλογῶν εὐλογήσω σε καὶ πληθύνων πληθυνῶ σε (*ei mun eulogon eulogéso se kai plethúnon plethuno se*). The Greek is also a literal translation of the Hebrew of Genesis 22:17, which is quoted verbatim in Hebrews 6:14: כִּי־בָרֵךְ אֲבָרֶכְךָ וְהַרְבָּה אַרְבֶּה (*ki-barek 'abarekeka v'harbah arbeh*). The accuracy of this rendering is confirmed by Delitzsch's Hebrew translation of the Greek text of Hebrews 6:14 as: וַיֹּאמַר כִּי־בָרֵךְ אֲבָרֶכְךָ וְהַרְבָּה אַרְבֶּה אֹתָךְ (*v'yomar ki-barek 'abarekeka v'harbah arbeh otak*).

The very language employed in this text is also unique, for this is the first and only time in the Book of Genesis where the infinitive absolute (בָרֵךְ אֲבָרֶכְךָ [*barek 'abarekeka*] and הַרְבָּה אַרְבֶּה [*harbah arbeh*]) is employed to record God's promise: "I will surely bless you" and "I will surely multiply you."[12] If there were any question as to the unequivocal nature of the divine promise, it was totally dispelled by God's use of this grammatical device in the text.[13] As Abraham Kuruvilla notes, "every element of the original promise is fortified here, ratcheted up a notch, *because of [Abraham's] obedience*. It is an enhancement of the earlier promise, especially solidified in Yahweh's unique swearing by himself."[14] The original Hebrew text of God's oath of the promise to Abraham, then, is important in that it employs an infinitive absolute and uses the powerful idiom of repetition of words, which, in the Hebrew text, always serves the purpose of emphasizing a statement or affirming its certainty. By

---

[10] Hebrews 6:14, KJV.

[11] The Greek of Hebrews 6:14 quotes from the Septuagint of Genesis 22:17: ἦ μὴν εὐλογῶν εὐλογήσω σε καὶ πληθύνων πληθυνῶ τὸ σπέρμα (*ei mun eulogon eulogéso se kai plethúnon plethuno to spérma*). The Hebrew text, its Septuagint rendering, and the quotation of the Greek in Hebrews 6:14 all repeat the word *bless* (כִּי־בָרֵךְ אֲבָרֶכְךָ; εὐλογῶν εὐλογήσω) and the word *multiply* (הַרְבָּה אַרְבֶּה; πληθύνων πληθυνῶ). In the Hebrew these words are repeated in order to create emphasis and to establish the absolute certainty of the statement. The English rendering *surely bless* and *surely multiply* (or *certainly bless* and *certainly multiply*) translates the Hebrew; however, it does not fully convey the nuance of meaning conveyed by the repetition of words which in the Hebrew text emphasize the unequivocal and absolute inviolability of the promise.

[12] Abraham Kuruvilla, *Genesis: A Theological Commentary for Preachers* (Eugene, OR: Wipf and Stock Publishers, 2014), p. 262.

[13] Another example of the use of the infinitive absolute to establish total certainty can be seen in Genesis 2:17 in God's declaration to Adam and Eve concerning the fruit of the tree of the knowledge of good and evil, "In the day you eat thereof, you shall surely die." The phrase *surely die* in Hebrew is מוֹת תָּמוּת (*mot tamut*), literally, "dying you shall die," which emphasizes and establishes the absolute certainty of death.

[14] Kuruvilla, p. 262, author's emphasis.

repeating the words *blessing* and *multiply* in this text, God asserted the absolute, unequivocal certainty that his promise would, without fail, be fulfilled both in Abraham and in his descendants after him.

What is more important than the absolute language of the Hebrew idiom of repetition, however, is the fact that God undertook to swear an oath to confirm further the irrevocability and the eternity of his unequivocal intentions. When God made his unilateral royal decree of covenant to Abraham and then confirmed it with an oath, he did something in the combination of those actions that he had never done before and would never do again. Kevin Conway confirms the fact that this incident was unique: "Abraham receives the benefit of God's sworn oath that the promises would indeed come to pass. This is the only time that God swears with formal oath language to any of the patriarchs."[15] Though this "oath is reiterated to the later patriarchs,"[16] the use of an oath to establish the absolute nature of a divine covenant was not repeated in the Hebrew Scriptures except in the Psalmist's description of God's promise regarding his own Son. First, regarding his priesthood, "The LORD has sworn, You are a priest forever after the order of Melchizedek."[17] Then regarding his lineal descent from David, "The LORD has sworn to David . . . Of the fruit of your body I will set [the Messiah] upon your throne."[18] If anything, this oath was simply a further reiteration of the oath of the Abrahamic covenant. Since Scripture concludes that "an oath for confirmation is . . . an end of all dispute,"[19] God's oath affirming his covenant with Abraham and his descendants should end all controversy as to the perdurability of the covenant and its eternal and irrevocable provisions for Abraham's descendants, including the promises of peoplehood and nationhood and the legal title to the Promised Land.

Additionally, as Gordon Wenham points out, "the reliability of God's oath is underlined by adding the phrase 'says the LORD' (נאם יהוה).[20] This phrase is found frequently in the prophets but only here and in Numbers 14:28 in the

---

[15] Kevin P. Conway, *The Promises of God: The Background of Paul's Exclusive Use of 'Epangelia' for the Divine Pledge* (Berlin, Germany: Walter de Gruyter GmbH, 2014), p. 82.

[16] Genesis 24:7; 26:3; 50:24; Exodus 13:5; Numbers 14:1; Deuteronomy 1:8, *et. al.*

[17] Psalm 110:4.

[18] Psalm 131:11.

[19] Hebrews 6:16.

[20] Gordon J. Wenham, "The Akedah: A Paradigm of Sacrifice," in *Pomegranates and Golden Bells: Studies in Biblical, Jewish, and Near Eastern Ritual, Law, and Literature in Honor of Jacob Milgrom*, David P. Wright, David Noel Freedman, and Avi Hurvitz, eds. (Winona Lake, IN: Eisenbrauns Publishers, 1995), p. 101.

Pentateuch."[21] It is this formula that "points above all to God's dependability, as the addition in Ezekiel 37:14 (similarly 35:8) shows, 'I have spoken and I shall carry it out.' The same is shown by the twenty-one passages where it underlines an oath of God."[22] Wenham suggests that through the addition of the confirmation *says the Lord*, "God's promises to the patriarchs have now become guarantees."[23] In reality, since "the oath God swore to Abraham was dependent on God alone," the only thing Abraham had to do was to "trust God and patiently endure."[24] Just as God will move all of heaven and earth to fulfill the oath he swore to King David that of the fruit of his loins according to the flesh he would raise up the Messiah to sit on David's throne,[25] so he will move all of heaven and earth to fulfill the oath that he swore to Abraham promising that he would bless the patriarch and his descendants and "give them this land."

In effect—to employ modern oath language—God swore "to tell the truth, the whole truth, and nothing but the truth" when he made his covenant with Abraham. Nothing was left to chance. Nothing was vague, obscure, or ambiguous. No wiggle room was left for nuanced exegetical interpolations that could somehow leave the terms of his covenant with Abraham—and with his descendants to this day—in doubt. No exegetical attorney could possibly parse words and phrases to extrapolate an inconsistency or loophole that would negate the covenant and the oath or neutralize their provisions. God made it impossible for the terms of the covenant to be diminished or abrogated. Not even God himself could do so. And one thing is certain: "It is impossible for God to lie."[26] Dwight Pentecost summed it up by saying that it was "impossible for God to make any clearer that what was promised to Abraham was given him without any conditions, to be fulfilled by the integrity of God alone."[27] Of his own initiative, God made an absolute, unequivocal, unilateral decree, an oath covenant that would be eternal and irrevocable.

---

21 Wenham, in Wright, *et. al.*, eds., p. 102.
22 H. Eising, *"Ne'um,"* in *Theologisches Wörterbuch zum Alten Testament*, G. J. Botterweck, H. J. Fabry, and H. Ringgren, eds. (Stuttgart, Germany: W. Kohlhammer, 1986), vol. V, pp. 119–123, quoted by Wenham in Wright, *et. al.*, eds., p. 102.
23 Wenham, in Wright, *et. al.*, eds., p. 102.
24 J. Dwight Pentecost, *Faith That Endures: A Practical Commentary on the Book of Hebrews* (Grand Rapids, MI: Kregel Publications, 1992), p. 113.
25 1 Kings 8:25; Acts 2:30.
26 Hebrews 6:18.
27 J. Dwight Pentecost, *Things to Come: A Study in Biblical Eschatology* (Grand Rapids, MI: Zondervan Publishing, 1984), p. 69.

God conveyed the whole truth to the one man in the Hebrew Scriptures who was specifically called "the friend of God."[28] *El Shaddai* gave the patriarch complete understanding of his intentions not only for him but also for his descendants "to a thousand generations." Jesus made it clear that God reveals all things to the ones whom he calls friends when he said to his disciples, "No longer do I call you slaves, for the slave does not know what his master is doing; but I have called you friends, *for all things that I have heard from my Father I have made known to you.*"[29] God's original "friend," Abraham, had all the truth confirmed to him through infallible signs. He heard from God the "truth [that] endures to all generations,"[30] the certitude of God's utter faithfulness to his promises and his attention to detail in the fulfillment of those promises.

Then, God did specifically what he had promised when he miraculously gave Abraham and Sarah a son in their old age—when Abraham was 100 and Sarah was 90—this despite fact that Abraham was "as good as dead"[31] and "Sarah's womb was dead."[32] God brought forth life from "dead" bodies as only he has the power to do. And if God could perform this miracle, could Abraham ever have had any doubt that God would bring to pass the totality of truth that he had sworn to him? Though the ultimate fulfillment of the Abrahamic covenant would not occur until long after Abraham had died,[33] the patriarch could, nevertheless, walk in faith, "staggering not at the promises."[34] He had absolute confidence that what God had promised would come to pass, even the parts of the covenant that God said would occur over four centuries after his death[35]—and, indeed, those parts of the promises that were fulfilled two millennia after his time when the Messiah was revealed.[36] Abraham had God's promise, and he had God's solemn oath. What could be more certain and absolute?

---

[28] 2 Chronicles 20:7; Isaiah 41:8; James 2:23.
[29] John 15:15, emphasis added.
[30] Psalm 100:5.
[31] Hebrews 11:12.
[32] Romans 4:19.
[33] Anthony Lyle, *Ancient History: A Revised Chronology* (Bloomington, IN: AuthorHouse, 2012), vol. 1, p. 191.
[34] Romans 4:20.
[35] Genesis 15:13.
[36] John 8:56: "Your father Abraham rejoiced to see my day, and he saw it and was glad." Also, Romans 9:7 and Galatians 3:16.

Continuing, Explicit Commitment

The terms of God's everlasting covenant were reiterated verbatim to Abraham's son and his grandson in what could only be seen as a demonstration of the continuing commitment that God had to the realization of his sovereign promises to the Chosen People. Despite human failure, God constantly confirmed his unwavering commitment to the fulfillment of his oath and the promises attendant thereto. The repetition of the covenant oath to Isaac and Jacob served to establish further the immutability of the God who had made the promises and to the immutability of the promises themselves. The terms under which the covenant was transferred transgenerationally were unmistakable. God confirmed explicitly to both Isaac and Jacob that he was faithful to fulfill all the stipulations of his oath to Abraham.

Finally, some four centuries later, the same God confirmed the same covenant to some two million descendants of Abraham, Isaac, and Jacob— the Israelites whom he had summoned out of Egypt and gathered at his holy mountain in the desert. The Abrahamic covenant was reiterated and expanded to include many bilateral commitments, promises that were contingent upon the Israelites obedience to the divine instructions. The foundation of the covenant, however, remained unilateral and irrevocable. "The conditioned blessings that grow out of the original covenant do not change the unconditional character of that covenant,"[37] Pentecost says. The apostle Paul made this abundantly clear: "The Law, which came four hundred and thirty years [after the Abrahamic covenant], does not invalidate a covenant previously ratified by God, so as to nullify the promise."[38]

In reality, as Alan Torrance contends, Israel was "elected, therefore, into a unique kind of 'promising game'—one that is unilaterally established by Yahweh and which is neither conditional nor contractual."[39] This was confirmed by the fact that "the 'ten commandments' begin . . . with a description, an unconditional declaration. The commands or laws which follow simply serve to spell out the *obligations* which flow from this covenantal commitment. 'I am the LORD your God who brought you out of the land of Egypt . . . *therefore* you shall have no other gods before me . . . You shall not murder, etc.'"[40] Without the

---

[37] Pentecost, *Things to Come*, p. 68.
[38] Galatians 3:17.
[39] Alan J. Torrance, "On Deriving 'Ought' from 'Is'," in Michael C. Banner and Alan J. Torrance, eds., *The Doctrine of God and Theological Ethics* (New York: T & T Clark, 2006), p. 181.
[40] Torrance, p. 181.

unilateral covenant commitment established first in the Abrahamic covenant and then in the divine self-description and further declaration of the first of the Ten Commandments, "I am the LORD your God, who brought you out of the land of Egypt,"[41] the "very grammar of the *torah* 'promising game' is lost and there are no ethically relevant natural laws or orders of creation!"[42]

The fact that "apodictic, unconditional obligations not to kill, not to commit adultery, not to steal, bear false witness, and so on" exist is "due to the fact that Yahweh has unilaterally established a covenantal, koinonial family that Israel is . . . obliged to live out the faithfulness of Yahweh and to 'correspond' to his covenant faithfulness communally."[43] At Sinai, therefore, God made yet another step in the rectilinear unfolding of his plan to fulfill his promise to Abraham that through him and his descendants all the nations of the earth would be blessed.[44] God made no attempt to conceal his will or his intentions. He made them specific and explicit as he revealed his Torah ("instructions") to his Chosen People.

A Particularist Covenant with Universal Blessings

Forty years after the Sinai covenant expanded the Abrahamic covenant, the divine agreement was again reaffirmed to the Israelites as they prepared to enter the Promised Land. During this reiteration of the expanded Abrahamic covenant, God commissioned his people to make the words of his commandments clear in the eyes of the nations,[45] so that they thereby would become the "light to lighten the nations and for salvation to the ends of the earth."[46] God made this commandment specific: "When you have crossed the Jordan into the land the LORD your God is giving you, set up some large stones and coat them with plaster. . . . You shall write on the stones all the words of this very law *most distinctly*."[47] Joshua fulfilled these divine instructions by erecting pillars at Gilgal, less than a mile from Jericho, on which the words of the Torah were inscribed. In having Israel erect pillars and write upon them "most distinctly" the words of the Torah, God "intended for all the surrounding nations to benefit

---

41 Exodus 20:2.
42 Torrance, p. 181.
43 Torrance, p. 181.
44 Genesis 12:2.
45 Deuteronomy 27:2–5; Joshua 8:30–32.
46 Isaiah 42:6.
47 Deuteronomy 27:2–3, emphasis added. See Michael David Coogan, Marc Zvi Brettler, Carol Ann Newsom, and Pheme Perkins, eds., *The New Oxford Annotated Bible* (New York: Oxford University Press, 2007), p. 228. Also Ovadiah Bertinoro, ed., *The Mishnah* (Brooklyn, NY: Mesorah Publications, 1979), p. 117.

from the instructions that were given to the Israelites, too. This radically advanced law was to be Israel's wisdom in the sight of the nations that surrounded them."[48] The Israelites would accomplish the divine plan by dynamic modeling in their own lives the instructions that God intended for all humanity.

The sages of Israel—particularly Rashi—have suggested that the term *most distinctly* means that the words of the Torah were written in large letters in the seventy languages of the world's seventy nations.[49] This was done, said the sages, in order to spread the Torah among the nations, thereby fulfilling the ultimate purpose for Israel's existence: to be the spiritual center of the world, God's illumination for the nations.[50] Israel's ultimate calling was this: "I will make you a light of the nations so that my salvation may reach the end of the earth."[51] The inclusion of non-Jews in the kingdom of God was, indeed, God's original purpose in his call to Israel. Geza Vermes confirms this calling by saying, "A pure and sanctified Israel was to draw the Gentiles to God. The manifestation of God's sovereignty over his own was to serve as a magnet to the rest."[52] In fact, God has positioned "the Jews before us even to-day in order to teach us something that we cannot learn in any other way," said Thomas Torrance.[53]

Whether Israel was faithful or wayward, still, that nation was—and remains—*the* material witness in the world that YHWH is God alone. "Israel's existence is so intertwined with God's being as God that Israel's continuance through time assumes—openly or tacitly—the character of a proof for God's existence,"[54] says George Hunsinger. Karl Barth powerfully and poignantly encapsulated this truth and its relevance to Christians— and, indeed, to all the Gentile world—in a sermon at Schlosskirche in Bonn, Germany, in 1933: "The Jew—in his so puzzlingly foreign and just

---

[48] Gary Strunk, *As He Is* (Ringgold, GA: Teach Services Publishing, 2012), p. 130.

[49] Louis Ginzburg, *The Legends of the Jews*, tr. Henrietta Szold (Charleston, SD: BiblioBazaar, 2007), vol. 1, p. 108.

[50] Eliezer Schweid, *The Land of Israel: National Home or Land of Destiny* (Cranbury, NJ: Associated University Presses, 1985), p. 56.

[51] Isaiah 49:6.

[52] Geza Vermes, *Jesus and the Word of Judaism* (London, UK: SCM Press, 1983), p. 35.

[53] Thomas F. Torrance, "Salvation Is of the Jews," *Evangelical Quarterly* 22 (1950), p. 164.

[54] George Hunsinger, *For the Sake of the World: Karl Barth and the Future of Ecclesial Theology* (Grand Rapids, MI: Wm. B. Eerdmans Publishing Co., 2004), p. 126. Hunsinger references Barth's statement: "The real thing itself is the one natural proof of God adduced by God in the existence of the Jewish nation amongst other nations. It is hardly seen by Anti-Semites and liberals, but here a part of world-history gives the most direct witness to the biblical witness of revelation, and therefore to the God who is attested in the Bible." Karl Barth, *Reformed Dogmatics, III/3: The Creator and His Creature*, G. W. Bromley, ed. (London, UK: T & T Clark International, 2000), p. 210. Also, David W. Torrance, *The Witness of the Jews to God* (Edinburgh, UK: Handsel Press, 1983, vol. 1, pp. 1–12.

so puzzlingly indestructible existence—is living proof in the midst of all the peoples (*Völkern*) of the world that God is free to choose whom he will and that he is under no obligation to choose us either. It is sheer grace if he chooses us. For it could well be that if we resist this strict proof of God's existence, that if we resist too passionately the Jews, we resist this God of free grace!"[55] Barth's words were clearly prophetic to the German nation and the German people, as subsequent history would incontrovertibly prove, and they remain equally prophetic to every Christian community—and, indeed, to the world—as the drama of restored Israel continues to unfold in a world of increasing tension and violence.

Israel's status as God's witness nation has surely secured and will continue to secure the fulfillment of God's covenant with Abraham in which he was specifically promised that through his lineal descendants "all the families of the earth" would be blessed.[56] Multiplied millions of human beings from every ethnicity under the sun have received and believed Abraham's monotheistic insight that became Israel's first and foundational truth: "Hear, O Israel, the LORD our God is God alone." They have done so because of the testimony that has issued forth from the lips of both Jews and Christians, adherents of the two great religions that emerged from the matrix of biblical and Second Temple Judaism, as they have fulfilled God's commission for them to be witnesses to him and his eternal truth.

Initially and eternally, then, God's words of covenant promise to Abraham's lineal descendants of peoplehood, nationhood, and land have always been and will always remain absolute, categorical, unambiguous, unequivocal, and apodictic. The covenant and its promises are undeniable and irrefutable, they are trustworthy and dependable, they are immutable and irrevocable, and they are perpetual and everlasting. Like all of God's holy Word, nothing can be added to it or taken from it,[57] and woe be unto anyone who has the audacity even to attempt to do so![58]

---

55 Karl Barth, quoted in Dean Garrett Stroud, ed., *Preaching in Hitler's Shadow: Sermons of Resistance in the Third Reich* (Grand Rapids, MI: Wm. B. Eerdmans Publishing Co., 2013), pp. 67–68.

56 Genesis 12:3; 28:14.

57 Deuteronomy 12:32: "Whatever I command you, you shall be careful to do; you shall not add to nor take away from it." Psalm 119:89: "Forever, O LORD, your word is settled in heaven." Proverbs 30:5: "The Word of God is flawless. . . . Do not add to his words, or he will reprove you, and you will be proved a liar" (NIV, NASB).

58 Revelation 22:18–19: "If anyone adds to these things, God will add to him the plagues which are written in this book; and if anyone takes away the words of the book of this prophecy, God will take away his part from the tree of life and from the holy city."

CHAPTER 6

ETERNAL AGREEMENT

THE IMMUTABLE, IRREVOCABLE COVENANT

God's covenant with Abraham—and hence with all of Abraham's descendants—was and remains an everlasting agreement. It is an open-ended contract that has no escape clauses, no "sundown" provisions. There were simply no "ifs," "ands," or "buts" in the sovereign decree of *El Shaddai's* unilateral election of Abraham and his descendants to be his Chosen People. Edward Kessler explains it this way: "According to the prophets, the covenant is so established on the divine side that it cannot be broken on the human side; the God of Israel is linked to the people of Israel in a covenant that is eternal and unbreakable."[1] This truth is established in the words of God himself: "I will not reject them, neither will I abhor them, to destroy them completely, and to break my covenant with them."[2] This is true because God chose the Israelite people not on the basis of their own merit,[3] but solely with regard to his own love.[4]

Holy Scripture, therefore, repeatedly describes the Abrahamic covenant as an "everlasting covenant." This is clear in the divine promise to Abraham himself: "I will establish my covenant between me and you and your descendants *throughout their generations* for an *everlasting covenant* to be God to you and to your descendants after you."[5] As long as the earth endures and the generations of the Hebrews/Israelites/Jews continue, God's covenant with his Chosen People will remain. In reality, however, the converse of this statement is also true: As long as God endures and his everlasting covenant endures, so the generations of the Chosen People will endure: "I am YHWH; therefore, you O

---

[1] Edward Kessler, "Chosen People," in *A Dictionary of Jewish-Christian Relations*, Edward Kessler and Neil Wenborn, eds. (Cambridge, UK: Cambridge University Press, 2005), p. 83.
[2] Leviticus 26:44–45.
[3] Exodus 32:9; Deuteronomy 9:6.
[4] Deuteronomy 4:37; 10:15; 23:5.
[5] Genesis 17:7, emphasis added.

children of Jacob have not perished."[6] God and Israel are inseparably joined together by the terms of the covenant to which God swore his commitment and faithfulness. Nothing that human beings can do can negate that connection. In truth, the expression *everlasting covenant* "qualifies the covenantal promises as a permanent institution, irrevocable for generations because its motivation lies in the purpose of God."[7]

The "everlasting covenant" with Abraham's descendants, the Jews, has been as enduring as the "everlasting covenant" that God made with the earth and all its inhabitants in the days of Noah: "I will remember the *everlasting covenant* between God and every living creature of all flesh that is upon the earth. . . . Never again shall the water become a flood to destroy all flesh."[8] Since the great deluge of Noah's day, the earth has never been universally flooded. God's covenant with the Jews has also been as enduring as the institution of the Sabbath: "Every sabbath day . . . it is an *everlasting covenant* for the Sons of Israel."[9] The Sabbath that was blessed in the days of creation will continue to be blessed everlastingly, and it will remain as a sign for the Chosen People forever.[10]

God reiterated the durability of the covenant that he had made with Abraham when he spoke to the patriarch about his son Isaac: "I will establish my covenant with him for an *everlasting covenant* for his descendants after him."[11] He further confirmed that same covenant with the Israelites by giving them his Torah: "The covenant which he made with Abraham, and his oath to Isaac, he also confirmed it to Jacob for a statute, to Israel for an *everlasting covenant*, saying, 'To you I will give the land of Canaan.'"[12] It should not be a cause for consternation, therefore, that, despite Israel's unfaithfulness, God continued to reiterate the faithfulness of his covenant: "I will make an *everlasting covenant* with you, according to

---

6 Malachi 3:6, NRS.

7 Mary Sylvia Chinyere Nwachukwu, *Creation-Covenant Scheme and Justification by Faith: A Canonical Study of the God-Human Drama in the Pentateuch and the Letter to the Romans* (Rome, Italy: Gregorian University Press, 2002), p. 111.

8 Genesis 9:15, emphasis added.

9 Leviticus 24:8.

10 Exodus 31:16–17: "The Israelites are to observe the Sabbath, celebrating it for the generations to come as a perpetual covenant. It will be a sign between me and the Israelites forever." (NIV, NASB). Also Deuteronomy 5:15: "You shall remember that you were a slave in the land of Egypt, and the LORD your God brought you out of there by a mighty hand and by an outstretched arm; therefore the LORD your God commanded you to observe the sabbath day." History has proven that Israel and the Sabbath are inseparable.

11 Genesis 17:19, emphasis added.

12 1 Chronicles 16:16–18, emphasis added. Cf. Psalm 105:9–11.

the faithful mercies shown to David";[13] "I will faithfully give them their recompense and make an *everlasting covenant* with them";[14] "I will make an *everlasting covenant* with them that I will not turn away from them, to do them good";[15] "I will remember my covenant with you in the days of your youth, and I will establish an *everlasting covenant* with you";[16] "I will make a covenant of peace with them; it will be an *everlasting covenant* with them."[17] In each instance when God spoke of an "everlasting covenant, as if to underscore the perdurability of his obligations, he connected his action with the eternal, irrevocable provisions of the Abrahamic covenant.

If there were any possibility that the "everlasting" Abrahamic covenant and its provisions for the lineal descendants of the patriarch could be suspended, annulled, or abrogated no one could be confident that the "New Covenant" would never fail or that God could not destroy it. The very same language that was used in Scripture to confirm the eternity of the New Covenant was also used to support the eternity of the Abrahamic covenant: "I will faithfully give them their recompense and make an *everlasting covenant* with them."[18] This was the covenant of which Jeremiah spoke: "Behold, the days are coming, declares the LORD, when I will make a new covenant with the house of Israel and with the house of Judah. . . . I will put my law within them and on their heart I will write it, and I will be their God, and they shall be my people."[19] This was the same covenant which God promised to Abraham, "I will make an *everlasting covenant* with them: I will never stop doing good to them, and I will inspire them to fear me, so that they will never turn away from me."[20] This "everlasting covenant" is the same one that the author of Hebrews described, "Behold the days are coming, says the LORD, when I will effect a new covenant with the house of Israel and with the house of Judah. . . . I will put my laws into their minds, and I will write them on their hearts, and I will be their God, and they shall be my people."[21] It is clear, then, that the New Covenant is nothing more than a renewal of God's covenant with Abraham. Because of their signification in the Hebrew

---

[13] Isaiah 55:3, emphasis added.
[14] Isaiah 61:8, emphasis added.
[15] Jeremiah 32:40, emphasis added.
[16] Ezekiel 16:60, emphasis added.
[17] Ezekiel 37:26, emphasis added.
[18] Isaiah 61:8, emphasis added.
[19] Jeremiah 31:33.
[20] Jeremiah 32:40, emphasis added.
[21] Hebrews 8:8, 10.

text as being בְּרִית עוֹלָם (*berit olam*), the Abrahamic covenant is an eternal covenant, and the New Covenant is everlasting as well.

How Long Is "Everlasting"?

The Hebrew word that most often designates "everlasting" in the text of Scripture is עוֹלָם (*'olam*),[22] which means "of long duration," "antiquity," "futurity," "forever,"[23] "everlasting,"[24] "perpetual,"[25] "permanent,"[26] "ancient,"[27] and "world."[28] Essentially, the word *'olam* means "for an unlimited amount of time" or time for which there is no specific end. Thus, in antiquity, a bondservant who had become a love-slave to his master could be said to have committed himself to serving him "forever" (*l'olam*).[29] In similar fashion, subjects could say of their sovereign, "O king, live forever,"[30] or, "May my lord live forever (*l'olam*)."[31] In some cases, the word *'olam* is combined with the term וָעֶד—*va'ed* ("as far as" or "forever") to mean "forever and ever."[32] In other instances, *'olam* is connected with the word עַד—*'ad* ("for all time"), as in the phrase מֵהָעוֹלָם וְעַד הָעוֹלָם (*me-ha'olam v'ad ha'olam*)[33] to mean "from the everlasting to the everlasting," or simply "from everlasting to everlasting."[34] The phrase *me-ha'olam v'ad ha'olam* demonstrates that time stretches backward into the past as well as forward into the future. It also designates the concept of eternity past and eternity future. Thorlief Boman points out, therefore, that "in the term *'olam* is contained a designation of time

---

22 The word *'olam* appears in Scripture 205 times.

23 Genesis 3:22.

24 Genesis 9:16.

25 In 37 instances, NASB translates *'olam* as "perpetual." In 19 instances KJV translates *'olam* as "perpetual."

26 In 11 instances, NASB translates *'olam* as "permanent."

27 In 16 instances, NASB translates *'olam* as "ancient." In 7 instances, KJV translates *'olam* as "ancient."

28 Psalm 73:12. When *'olam* is translated "world," it means "in this present age" or during this "lifetime." It does not mean "earth," as the English word *world* often does.

29 Exodus 21:6 says, "His master shall bore his ear through with an awl, and he shall be his slave forever [*le'olam*]" (ESV). The NIV captures the essence of the implied meaning of this statement with its rendering: "Then he will be his servant for life."

30 Daniel 3:9; 6:6, 21. When he addressed the kings of the realm, Daniel used the Aramaic word עֲלָם (*'alam*) in "O king, live forever (*'alam*)." In Daniel 7:18; 12:3, 7, the text used the Hebrew עוֹלָם (*'olam*).

31 1 Kings 1:31.

32 Exodus 15:18 declares that God is king "for ever and ever (*'olam va'ed*)."

33 The phrase *m'ha'olam v'ad ha'olam* is usually contracted in Scripture to *m'olam 'ad-'olam*, eliminating the definite article, *ha*.

34 Psalm 90:2; 103:17; Jeremiah 7:1; 25:56.

extending so far that it is lost to our sight and comprehension in darkness and invisibility. It is characteristic of the nature of this term that it can be used of hoary antiquity as well as of the unbounded future."[35] This fact, in itself, establishes the unique Hebrew connection between the past and the future and the Hebraic understanding that the future can be understood, discerned, or predicted only in the context of the past.

Because of the uses of 'olam in connection with situations in which time is clearly limited, some have suggested that the Hebrew Scriptures do not speak of endless time. To this assertion, Conrad von Orelli responds: "When Hebrew antiquity's ability to form the concept of boundless time is disputed, it is the result of a prejudice."[36] This prejudice—and, therefore, misunderstanding—flows from the effort to impose a Greek "either-or" mindset on the Hebrew "both-and" mindset.[37] The truth is that, when applied to God, such phrases as *meolam 'ad-'olam* cannot be considered to speak of a limited existence of God or of a God who is totally constrained by time. The Lord is God *"from everlasting to everlasting,"*[38] both in the sense that he exists from unlimited time in the past to unlimited time in the future and in the sense that he preexists and postexists time itself. Therefore, in the context of the Hebraic understanding of time, eternity transcends time.

Some scholars have argued that since the Hebrew word *olam* can mean "for a long time," the "everlasting" nature of the Abrahamic covenant simply meant that

---

[35] Thorlief Boman, *Hebrew Thought Compared with Greek*, tr. Jules L. Moreau (New York: W. W. Norton & Co., 1960), p. 151.

[36] Conrad von Orelli, *Die hebräischen Synonyma der Zeit und Ewigkeit genetisch und sprachvergleichend dargestellt* (Leipzig, Germany: 1871; republished Ithaca, NY: Cornell University Library, 2009), p. 72, quoted in Boman, p. 151.

[37] Whereas Greek philosophy posits the idea that only one truth can exist, Hebrew recognizes the fact that truth is often found in polar opposites, and it, therefore, insists on holding both positions in dynamic tension. This is true for the word 'olam, which means both "in the distant past" and "in the far-reaching future," as well as "eternity past" and "eternity future." The Hebraic understanding, therefore, is that the future can be predicted by observing the past and that eternity future will reflect the principles of eternity past.

[38] Psalm 90:2. By applying the phrase *from everlasting to everlasting* to the existence of God, the Psalmist understood that God existed before the universe was created and that he will continue to exist after its end or when "the elements will be destroyed with intense heat, and the earth and its works will be burned up" (2 Peter 3:10). Since, as its creator, God predated the universe and since God will continue to exist after the universe ceases to exist, God can be seen to exist outside (before, during, and after) time. This is clear from the fact that the "universe" is in reality a "tri-universe" composed entirely of energy/matter (which are interchangeable), space, and time. It is not part energy, part space, and part time; it is all energy, all space, and all time—and all contemporaneously so! Since God is not a part of the created universe (else the universe would be God, confirming the ideas of pantheism), he exists from eternity past to eternity future wholly unconstrained by time (except when he deals with the universe and its inhabitants who are bound by time as one of the elements of their existence).

it would last for a "long time," after which it would be terminated.[39] If this were the case, the argument could also be made that the New Covenant could be intended to last only for a "long time," after which it, too, could be terminated. This can be lexically demonstrated from the Greek word αἰώνιος (aiónios) which is consistently used to translate olam in the Septuagint translation of Scripture. Aiónios is the word that is used to describe the "everlasting covenant" in the doxology of the Book of Hebrews: "Now the God of peace, who brought up from the dead the great Shepherd of the sheep through the blood of the everlasting covenant (διαθήκης αἰωνίου—diathékes aioníou), even Jesus our Lord, equip you in every good thing to do his will, working in us that which is pleasing in his sight, through Jesus Christ, to whom be the glory forever and ever (αἰῶνας [τῶν αἰώνων]). Amen."[40] It is obvious, therefore, that if the New Covenant is everlasting in the sense that it endures "forever and ever," then the Abrahamic covenant must also endure "forever and ever," because it, too, is an "everlasting covenant" (בְּרִית עוֹלָם—berit olam and διαθήκη αἰώνιος—diathéke aiónios). As a matter of fact, the perdurability of the Abrahamic covenant is parallel with the nature of the "eternal life" that is promised to believers in the Messiah, for "eternal life" in Greek is αἰώνιος ζωή (aiónios zoé). This is the "everlasting life" that Jesus promised to the believer,[41] the unending life that God gave his only begotten Son to secure for all who believe in him.[42]

The "New Covenant" Is the Renewed Abrahamic Covenant

The lexical evidence connecting the New Covenant and the Abrahamic covenant further establishes the fact that the New Covenant is actually a "renewed covenant" more so than it is a complete novelty that had never been considered before. Steven McKenzie says, "Jeremiah's new covenant . . . is not a brand new covenant. It is better understood, like those in the Deuteronomistic

---

[39] Steve Gregg, *All You Want to Know About Hell: Three Christian Views of God's Final Solution to the Problem of Sin* (Nashville, TN: Thomas Nelson, 2013), p. 100. Gregg suggests that "*olam* is said to speak of that which extends beyond the horizon of sight, or the vanishing point. That which is described as *olam* is not necessarily everlasting, but its end cannot be seen from here." Also Donald Gowan, *Eschatology in the Old Testament* (New York: T & T Clark International, 1986), p. 77. Gowan argues that "the word *'olam* never can be proved to mean 'eternal,' that is timeless, but it is ordinarily understood to designate a very long time, in either the past or the future." Generally, efforts to explain (or explain away) the meaning of *'olam* are associated with discussions of life in the hereafter, especially as associated with eternal punishment.

[40] Hebrews 13:20–21, emphasis added.

[41] John 6:47.

[42] John 3:16.

History, as a renewed covenant."[43] This is clear from the fact that the Hebrew word translated "new" in Jeremiah's promise of the "new covenant," חָדָשׁ (chadash), can also mean "to renew."[44] As Wolfhart Pannenberg has said, "The eschatological new covenant means for Israel renewal of the old covenant relationship with its God."[45] Israel, therefore, is to be "the community of the renewed covenant."[46] John Hayes is right to assert that, with respect to Israel, Jeremiah's "new or renewed covenant is to be part of a great transformation of both the people and the land."[47] Likewise, the new gospel covenant[48] was designed neither to replace the Abrahamic covenant nor to render it inoperative. Instead, "the Abrahamic covenant was not superseded, but *confirmed*, by the introduction of Christianity."[49]

In fact, the New Covenant was the same that had been given to Abraham, and it rested on the same foundation as the Abrahamic covenant in that it was established by "grace through faith."[50] The laws ("instructions"[51]) of God were not, therefore, abrogated or repealed when the Messiah came. Both Christians and Jews have Jesus' word on this: "Think not that I have come to destroy the law or the prophets."[52] What changed was the place where the laws of God were inscribed—in this case, on the hearts and in the minds of believers.[53] "The blessing that every believer will experience throughout all of eternity," therefore, "is a

---

[43] Steven L. McKenzie, *Covenant* (St. Louis, MO: Chalice Press, 2000), p. 59.

[44] Unlike Greek and English, Hebrew does not have two separate words for "new" and "renew." The word חָדָשׁ (chadash) means both new and renew. For a detailed discussion of the Hebraic understanding that "new" in Scripture generally means "renewed," see Walter C. Kaiser, *The Christian and the Old Testament* (Pasadena, CA: William Carey Library, 1998), p. 218.

[45] Wolfhart Pannenberg, *Systematic Theology* (Grand Rapids, MI: Wm. B. Eerdmans Publishing Co., 1998), vol. 3, p. 473.

[46] Shemaryahu Talmon, "'The Dead Sea Scrolls' or 'The Community of the Renewed Covenant,'" in *The Echoes of Many Texts: Reflections on Jewish and Christian Traditions*, W. G. Dever and J. E. Wright, eds. (Atlanta, GA: Scholars Press, 1997), pp. 135–140.

[47] John Haralson Hayes, *Interpreting Ancient Israelite History, Prophecy, and Law*, Brad E. Kelle, ed. (Eugene, OR: Wipf and Stock Publishers, 2013), p. 279.

[48] Jeremiah's prophecy of the renewal of Abraham's covenant has two fulfillments: 1) to extend Messianic salvation to all humanity (Hebrews 8:8–13) and 2) to effect the restoration of Israel to God (Romans 11:26–29).

[49] Richard Cunningham Shimeall, *The Second Coming of Christ* (New York: Henry S. Goodspeed & Co., 1873), p. 88.

[50] Ephesians 2:8–9.

[51] The word *torah* is better translated as "instruction" than it is with the traditional word *law*. While the Torah contains laws and commandments, it is more a set of instructions from a wise Father than it is a code of laws and penalties. This can be seen from the fact that the word *torah* is derived from the word *yarah*, which, as an archery term, means to "shoot toward a target." It can also be seen from the relationship of *torah* to the Hebrew words *moreh* ("teacher") and *horeh* ("parent"), both of whom provide "instruction."

[52] Matthew 5:17.

[53] Hebrews 8:10; 10:16.

perpetual fulfillment of the Abrahamic covenant."[54] The New Covenant, then, affirms the full force of all of God's promises and commitments to Abraham and his lineal descendants throughout all their generations. Any Christian effort to usurp the eternal promises in the everlasting Abrahamic covenant and to co-opt them exclusively for themselves is reprehensible at best and downright larcenous at worst. Any Christian attempt to assert the repeal, abrogation, or destruction of God's promises to Abraham and his descendants is an outright rejection of the premise of divine immutability and faithfulness. Any Christian effort to displace the Jewish people from the promises of God or to assert that they were superseded by Christianity and Christians is clearly heretical and inimical to the teachings of Jesus and the apostles, and it must be rejected.

Perdurability and Irrevocability

In order to underscore the perdurability and irrevocability of his covenant with Abraham, God repeated its terms in significant detail in the three times in which he confirmed the agreement: first to Abraham,[55] then to Isaac,[56] and finally to Jacob.[57] Perhaps this is the reason that God personally chose to identify himself by saying, "I am the God of Abraham, the God of Isaac, and the God of Jacob."[58] The specificity of this statement underscores the fact that *El Shaddai* was the living God and that his covenant was renewed with each generation. God did not say, "I was the God of Abraham, the God of Isaac, and the God of Jacob," nor did he say, "I am the God of Abraham, Isaac, and Jacob." Jesus noted the repetition in the declaration: "I am the God of Abraham, the God of Isaac, and the God of Jacob," as evidence that God "is the God of the living, not the dead."[59] This statement is further evidence that God's callings endure from generation to generation.[60]

Here is what God said about his covenant promise to Abraham and its perdurability: "The Lord your God has *chosen you* out of all the peoples on the face of the earth to be his people, his treasured possession. . . . he is the faithful God,

---

[54] John MacArthur, *MacArthur New Testament Commentary: 2 Corinthians* (Chicago, IL: Moody Publishers, 2003), p. 88.
[55] Genesis 15:7–21; 17:1–21; 22:15–18.
[56] Genesis 26:1–6.
[57] Genesis 28:10–15.
[58] Exodus 3:6.
[59] Matthew 22:32. Jesus used the exactness and specificity of this statement to underscore truth about the resurrection, for God said, "I *am* the God of Abraham," not "I *was* the God of Abraham," thereby indicating that Abraham is still alive in some dimension and that he will be fully restored to life in the resurrection at the end of the age. Thus, "God is the God of the living."
[60] Romans 11:29.

keeping his covenant of love *to a thousand generations.*"[61] King David echoed this promise: "O seed of Israel his servant, Sons of Jacob, *his chosen ones*! . . . Remember his covenant forever, the word which he commanded *to a thousand generations.*"[62] The Psalmist then added further confirmation in this song of exultation: "O offspring of Abraham, his servant, children of Jacob, *his chosen ones*! . . . He has remembered his covenant forever, the word which he commanded *to a thousand generations.* . . . To you I will give the land of Canaan as your portion for an inheritance."[63] Scripture, therefore, confirms two things: 1) Abraham and his descendants were—and continue to be—transgenerationally "chosen of God," and 2) their election will endure unto a "thousand generations."

When God established his covenant with Abraham, it is clear that he considered a generation to be 120 years as he had since the time of Noah.[64] This is proven in what God said when he predicted to Abraham that his descendants would be "enslaved and oppressed [in Egypt] for four hundred years"[65] but that they would return and possess the land of Canaan in the "*fourth* generation."[66] God's covenant with Abraham and his progeny—the Hebrews, then the Israelites, and now the Jews—extends, therefore, to a minimum of 120,000 years! Since only four millennia have passed since that time, at least 116,000 years still remain on the terms of the contract. Even if one were to consider a generation to be only 40–60 years, God's promise that the Abrahamic covenant would remain in force for a thousand generations would mean that it would endure for 40,000–60,000 years.[67] In reality, however, the royally decreed covenant remains in force forever because it was—and continues to be—an "everlasting covenant," not bound either by generational or time-based constraints. The phrase *a thousand generations*, therefore, is merely a metaphor for everlastingness or eternity.

---

[61] Deuteronomy 7:6, 9, NIV, emphasis added.

[62] 1 Chronicles 16:13, emphasis added.

[63] Psalm 105:5–6, 9–11, ESV, emphasis added.

[64] Though in the antediluvian era, humans lived as long as 969 years, in Genesis 6:3, God said that in the postdiluvian era, the human lifespan (a generation) would be 120 years. This definition certainly extended to Abraham's day and beyond, for Abraham was 175 (Genesis 25:7), Sarah was 127 (Genesis 23:1), Isaac was 180 (Genesis 35:28), Jacob was 147 (Genesis 47:28), and Moses was 120 (Deuteronomy 34:7) when they died.

[65] Genesis 15:13.

[66] Genesis 15:16, emphasis added. In Galatians 3:16–17, Paul said that the Torah was given to Israel 430 years *after* the God made his promises to Abraham. If a generation were less than 120 years, this event would have occurred in the *fifth* or later generation. It did occur within the 480-year span of four 120-year generations.

[67] Based on the fact that the Israelites wandered in the wilderness for 40 years until after the "generation" of the rebellious ones who were over twenty years of age had died (Hebrews 3:17–19), some scholars view a biblical generation as being 40–60 years in duration. See Tremper Longman III, ed., *The Baker Illustrated Bible Dictionary* (Grand Rapids, MI: Baker Academic, 2013), p. 649. Longman notes that "the forty years may represent the upper limit of the expected length of an adult's life in the wilderness conditions, which would be sixty years."

It should be no cause for wonder, then, that the Apostolic Scriptures confirm the immutable and eternal nature of the Abrahamic covenant and its impact upon the patriarch's descendants generation after generation. "Because God wanted to make the unchanging nature of his purpose very clear to the heirs of what was promised, he confirmed it with an oath. God did this so that, by two unchangeable things in which it is impossible for God to lie, we who have fled to take hold of the hope set before us may be greatly encouraged."[68] This passage makes it clear that God actually doubled down on his covenant with Abraham and his descendants and the promises contained therein. He made the promise, and he swore by his own name that he could bring it to pass. Could anything be more enduring and irrevocable?

This is the reason for the repeated declaration in the Hebrew Scriptures that the Abrahamic covenant is everlasting. God deemed it important to affirm and reaffirm the eternity of his covenant with Abraham and its promises to the patriarch and his descendants after him. Any attempt by anyone to minimize, modify, or annul what God has done or to indicate that he might somehow abandon his covenant is patently absurd. Darrel Bock is right: "To argue that the promises to Israel have been exclusively transferred elsewhere in such a way that the original recipients are largely excluded from its benefits . . . is to destroy the model of God's faithfulness and enduring mercy that the story of God's relationship to Israel is designed to portray."[69] The preeminent lesson in all of God's dealings with Israel is not that the Almighty is judgmental and vindictive, but that he is eternally faithful and full of tender mercies. "For the LORD is good; his steadfast love endures forever, and his faithfulness continues through all generations."[70] God has never been looking for an escape clause in his covenant with Israel. His love for his Chosen People is infinite, and his mercy toward them is endless and everlasting. God's covenant with Abraham—and hence with the patriarch's lineal descendants, the Hebrews, Israelites, and Jews who succeeded him generationally—is a "forever" covenant that is immutable and irrevocable!

---

[68] Hebrews 6:16–17.

[69] Darrell L. Bock, "Covenants in Progressive Dispensationalism," in Three Central Issues in Contemporary Dispensationalism: A Comparison of Traditional and Progressive Views, Herbert W. Bateman, ed., (Grand Rapids, MI: Kregel Publications, 1999), p.173.

[70] Psalm 100:5, NIV, ESV.

CHAPTER 7

THE FOUNDING FAMILY

WELLSPRINGS OF FAITH

The first three generations of heirs to the unilateral, unequivocal, and eternal covenant that conveyed peoplehood, nationhood, and land to the Chosen People were the most important in the historical unfolding of God's promises. These were the generations through whom the Hebraic worldview, the mindset, and the ethos would be manifest in order to ensure that the terms of God's covenant would continue to be fulfilled from generation to generation through their subsequent descendants. In fact, these three generations of patriarchs were so important that when God introduced himself to Moses during the burning-bush incident some four hundred years later, he chose to identify himself as being "the God of Abraham, the God of Isaac, and the God of Jacob,"[1] listing the patriarchs separately and affirming his personal relationship with each of them successively. Instead of receiving an understanding of God through oral or written traditions, these three generations of patriarchs experienced for themselves the personal, face-to-face encounters with the Eternal God that fashioned their self-identity and their divine calling.

God was not "ashamed to be called the God [of Abraham, Isaac, and Jacob]."[2] Apparently, he considered it a badge of honor to associate himself with the three patriarchs of faith whom he had chosen and anointed to establish divine justice and mercy in the earth and to extend those godly qualities to the entire earth. God's own personally announced self-identity was so profound and enduring that it was still prominently and repeatedly used as a descriptive of the Almighty nearly two millennia later. This can be clearly seen from the words of Jesus, who said, "Have you

---

[1] Exodus 3:6.
[2] Hebrews 11:8–16.

not read what was spoken to you by God: 'I am the God of Abraham, and the God of Isaac, and the God of Jacob'?"[3] These three patriarchs and their coequal partners in faith, the matriarchs Sarah, Rebekah, and Rachel/Leah,[4] constituted the founding family of the Chosen People who would bear the name of Israel and practice the faith of YHWH that would eventually be termed Judaism, and they were the wellspring of faith from which the stream of Hebrew, Israelite, and Jewish peoplehood, nationhood, and physical territory would flow.

ABRAHAM AND SARAH
"As Good as Dead"

The life of Abraham set the example of faith *par excellence* for all of his subsequent descendants—the faith and faithfulness that made it possible for God's covenant promises to be fulfilled. This is the foundational principle that continued to make the application of the Abrahamic covenant possible throughout subsequent history and ensures that it will remain so in the future: "I know [Abraham] that he will command his children and his household after him, and they shall keep the way of the LORD, to do justice and judgment, so that the LORD may bring upon Abraham that which he has spoken of him."[5] God had intimate and convincing knowledge that the patriarch of the covenant people would faithfully transmit the understanding of monotheism and the justice and mercy of the Almighty to his descendants after him so that all the promises that the covenant entailed could and would be fulfilled.

---

[3] Matthew 22:32.

[4] Sarah, Rebekah, and Rachel/Leah were prime examples of God's specific designation for his final act in the Genesis creation narrative. When the Almighty announced his intention to create woman, he declared that he would make for Adam an עֵזֶר כְּנֶגְדּוֹ (*ezer kenegdo*), "a power equal to him." See David Freedman, "Woman, a Power Equal to Man," *Biblical Archaeological Review,* 09:01 (Jan/Feb 1983), p. 56. None of these matriarchs of the faith was inferior to or subordinated to her husband. In fact, all of them were powerful women in their own right with prophetic insight and faith that rivaled—and, in some cases, exceeded—that of their husbands. When Abraham feared for his life, Sarah was convinced that God would protect her from defilement first in the harem of Pharaoh and then in the harem of Abimelech (Genesis 20:2–14). Rebekah had such faith in the prophetic revelation that God gave when her twin sons were *in utero*, "Two nations are in your womb . . . the older shall serve the younger" (Genesis 25:23), that she orchestrated the transfer of the patriarchal primogeniture blessing to Jacob, even over Isaac's objections. When Rachel was barren, she believed God would give her children, and, true to her faith, she experienced the birth of Joseph, the heir to Jacob's spiritual heritage.

[5] Genesis 18:19, KJV.

Sometime before or during his transition from Babylon to Canaan, Abram—as he was called before God joined him in the covenant—began a walk of faith. He "believed God." And his faith was more than mere intellectual assent to a set of belief premises. It was faithfulness.[6] It was walking faith—faith demonstrated in acting immediately and unhesitatingly on God's instructions.[7] Abram was not a procrastinator. When God said something, he reacted immediately by doing what God commanded. God's wish was truly Abram's command![8] He was not starry-eyed, impulsive, or irrational. He was simply convinced that the one God whom he had come to know was not capricious and irrational like the gods of the heathen. *El Shaddai* was utterly faithful and totally trustworthy.[9]

Abram, therefore, simply moved systematically in the direction of divine instruction, never hesitating in doubt as to what God had said or

---

[6] Abraham's life demonstrates the difference between the Hebrew and Greek conceptions of faith. The word that is translated "have faith" in Job 39:12 is אָמַן (aman), the verbal root for emunah, which means "to confirm" or "to support." Aman is translated "believe" twenty-two times in the King James Version. Because of the fundamental meaning of aman, it is clear from the perspective of the Hebrew Scriptures that "faith" is actually "faithfulness," in the sense of "firmness, steadfastness, constancy, stability, reliability, and support." The Hebrew word אֱמוּנָה (emunah) means "faithfulness" or "stability." When the Hebrew word אֱמוּנָה (emunah) was translated into Greek, however, the word that was used was πίστις (pístis), which means "intellectual assent (to a premise)." Pístis was nuanced toward the mind so that when employed in a Greek sense rather than in a Hebrew sense it bespoke "faith" as "intellectual assent to a philosophical premise." David Dilling agrees with Martin Buber's view that when emunah became pístis, the "action of a whole person . . . involving the active aspect of fidelity and the receptive aspect of trust was reduced to an intellectualistic matter of accepting a set of propositions." Even the verbal expression of faith, "to believe," when translated into Greek becomes πιστεύω (pisteúo), means "to think to be true." The Greek emphasis on the mind was a product of its dualistic philosophy. The Hebrew emphasis on the whole person is a result of its holistic philosophy. It is easy to see how simple linguistic nuances have helped shape a Christian view of faith that differs considerably from that of Judaism.

[7] A prime example of Abraham's walk of faith was seen when God later commanded him to sacrifice his son Isaac. The Scripture says, "So Abraham rose *early in the morning* and saddled his donkey and took two of his young men with him and Isaac his son" (Genesis 22:3). Abraham's response to God's instructions was always immediate and without hesitation or reservation.

[8] The phrase *very early in the morning* is used repeatedly to describe Abraham's prompt reaction to God's instructions (Genesis 19:27; 21:14; 22:3). Whenever Abraham heard a clear word from God, he rose up "early in the morning" and proceeded immediately to do what God had said.

[9] Contrast Abraham's true perspective of God with that of David Hartman who has argued that Abraham's experience of God manifests a God in whom "we encounter a furious irrational Force Whose unpredictability makes it impossible for us to rely on His commitments to us" and whose actions toward the patriarch revealed "the basic unintelligibility and mystery of God's actions." See David Hartman, quoted in Ken Koltun-Fromm, *Moses Hess and Modern Jewish Identity* (Bloomington, IN: Indiana University Press, 2001), p. 62. Abraham was not up against an "irrational Force" of "basic unintelligibility." He was in relationship with a personal God whom he knew he could implicitly trust to bring to pass precisely what he had promised him even when what God proposed to do was suprarational—beyond the patriarch's finite capacity to understand, to "think to be true," or to add his own "intellectual assent." Abraham's faith was not a "thinking" faith; it was an "action" faith: it was faithfulness!

what he had meant. This was clearly demonstrated when God gave Abram a simple two-word command: לֶךְ לְךָ ("*Lech l'chah*"—"Go!"). Even though he did not know the daily details or even the ultimate objective of this command, Abram moved on with God. He would be satisfied with whatever God gave him; however, his expectation was that he would ultimately find a "city which has foundations, whose architect and builder is God."[10] It was for this reason that Abram has, therefore, been viewed in both Jewish and Christian tradition "as a man of faith: a faith so profound, so firm, so unclouded, that he can converse with the Creator of the universe as naturally as ordinary human beings talk to one another."[11]

Lech l'chah is an idiomatic alliteration which emphatically means "Go!" Translated literally, however, it means "Go for yourself," with this implication: "Summon from within yourself all of your inner resources and go."[12] The further details that God gave in this command were summed up in the sacred text this way: "Go forth from your country, and from your relatives and from your father's house, to the land which I will show you."[13] This was a divine summons that moved Abram and his wife Sarai from the comfort zone of family and citizenship in Haran of Assyria to the status of nomads, transient aliens, or strangers (גֵּרִים—*gerim*) in a land that was foreign to them. Throughout Abram's lifetime thereafter, the patriarch was never again to be a settled, landed citizen.[14] He and his family

---

10 Hebrews 11:10.

11 John D. Rayner, *An Understanding of Judaism* (Oxford, UK: Berghahn Books, 1997), p. 17. Rayner argues further that Abraham had perfect faith in God's justice that even when he negotiated with his Lord over the fate of Sodom and Gomorrah, "Abraham never doubts, as Judaism never doubts, that God is just." In effect, Abraham was simply fulfilling the role that God had assigned him as prophetic intercessor for blessing for all the nations of the earth (Genesis 12:3). Abraham reasoned that if God's promise was that in him "all the families of the earth" would be blessed, surely that must have also included the families of Sodom.

12 Shmuel Goldin, *Unlocking the Torah Text: Shmot* (Jerusalem, Israel: Gefen Publishing House, 2008), p. 14. Goldin notes that Rashi translated *Lech l'chah* as "Go for yourself," meaning "travel for your own benefit." Israel Drazin and Stanley Wagner maintain that Rashi took this interpretation even further with the midrashic idiom, "Go for your own pleasure and benefit because I will make of you a great nation there." See Israel Drazin and Stanley M. Wagner, *Onkelos on the Torah: Be-reshit* (Jerusalem, Israel, Gefen Publishing House, 2006), p. 65. David of Lelov gave an even more mystical translation to this text, rendering it as "Go to yourself," meaning that Abraham was to "journey to the root of his soul in the Holy Land." David of Lelov, quoted in Shlomo Ben Yitzhak Halevi, *A Doctor's Torah Thoughts from Singapore* (Raleigh, NC: Lulu Press, 2010), p. 13.

13 Genesis 12:1.

14 Even though he was promised all of Canaan, Abraham had no land that he could call his own. As a matter of fact, in order to have a place of interment of himself and his family members, he had to purchase a cave from Ephron (Genesis 23:8).

simply moved at God's command. They were, quite literally, nomads of faith,[15] prisoners of hope,[16] moving toward an uncertain—yet absolutely certain—future!

God's challenging and abrupt *Lech-l'chah* command to Abraham was followed immediately, however, by this promise: "I will make you a great nation, and I will bless you, and make your name great; and so you shall be a blessing; and I will bless those who bless you, and the one who curses you I will curse. And in you all the families of the earth will be blessed."[17] God revealed from the very inception of his action in Abram's life that the divine intention was beyond the scope of his own life and that of his immediate, lineal descendants. It was a plan to employ him and his progeny as agents for advancing the divine dominion until it covered the entire earth.

This is how the apostle Paul summarized the patriarch's chosen relationship with God: "Abraham believed God, and it was credited to him as righteousness."[18] Further, James agreed with Paul: "Abraham believed God, and it was reckoned to him as righteousness, and he was called the friend of God."[19] The incident which prompted the biblical declaration on which these words are based took place when Abram sought divine confirmation of the terms of the covenant. Then, in response to God's promises, "[Abraham] believed in the LORD, and [God] reckoned it to him as righteousness."[20] Because of the profound degree of his faith and faithfulness, Abraham has been called the "Father of Faith."[21] In fact, Paul also called him "the father of us all"[22]—that is, the father of all those—whether Jew or Gentile—to whom the righteousness of God has been imputed because of their faith in God. Standing resolutely on the promises of God without wavering in doubt or confusion made Abraham the epitome of faith: "steadfastness," "constancy," "reliability," and "faithfulness."

An Amazing Transformation

Though Abram was a Babylonian by birth and an Assyrian by nationality, he aspired to more. His family pedigree connected him back through

---

[15] Walter Kasper, *Transcending All Understanding: The Meaning of Christian Faith Today* (San Francisco, CA: Ignatius Press, 1989), p. 138.

[16] Zechariah 9:12.

[17] Genesis 12:2–3.

[18] Romans 4:3.

[19] James 2:23.

[20] Genesis 15:6.

[21] Jonathan Edwards, *A History of the Word of Redemption* (Worcester, MA: Thomas & Whipple, 1808), p. 58.

[22] Romans 4:16.

generations directly to Shem, Noah, Enoch, Seth, and Adam. He was part of a divinely unique people. Still, he knew that with God, there was much more. He determined to live his life as a servant of the God of heaven and earth, to walk with his God in faith and faithfulness, to lead his family in the ways of the Lord. When Abram set out to find that land of promise to which God was directing him, he experienced a life-changing event. The moment that he left Assyria by crossing over the River Euphrates, he experienced a forensic change in his status. He had been a Gentile,[23] but when he crossed over the Euphrates, he became the very first Hebrew. The word *Hebrew*, עִבְרִי (*ivri*), comes from two words, 1) *avar* (עָבַר), which means "to pass over," and 2) *'eber* (עֵבֶר), which means "beyond," "across," or "from the other side." In the act of crossing over the Euphrates in obedience to God's *Lech-l'chah* command, Abram was amazingly transformed. He was still an Assyrio-Babylonian, but he was at the same time translated into a kingdom that before that time had never existed, a kingdom whose architect and builder was God. Abram was, in fact, its first citizen! When he came out of the water of the Euphrates and made his first step in the Promised Land, he became a Hebrew![24]

A Distressing, Unrelenting Problem

There was, however, a serious problem in Abram's world of faith and faithfulness. After decades of marriage, he and his wife remained childless. For Abram, this had to be high irony[25] because in Hebrew, his name, *Avram*, meant "exalted father" or "the father is exalted."[26] Since in the ancient world infants were named according to qualities they were thought to possess or to what was expected of them, his parents apparently had envisioned great accomplishments for their son. Now, despite the fact that he bore the name *Exalted Father*, he and his beloved wife Sarai had reached old age without children.

---

23 Abram was an Assyrio-Babylonian, a Babylonian by birth and an Assyrian by nationality or naturalization. Deuteronomy 26:5 specifically identifies Abraham's grandson, Jacob, as an Aramean (Syrian).
24 The patriarch's experience in becoming the first Hebrew (or Jew) was similar to that of the Gentile proselytes of the first century AD who "became Jews" when they emerged from the waters of the *mikveh* immersion.
25 R. Loren Sandford, *The Prophetic Church: Wielding the Power to Change the World* (Grand Rapids, MI: Baker Publishing Group, 2009), p. 54. Sandford says that being named "Exalted Father," with no children "must have impacted Abram like some kind of bad joke."
26 Ronald Youngblood, *The Book of Genesis: An Introductory Commentary* (Grand Rapids, MI: Baker Book House, 1991), p. 169. Youngblood suggests that "'Abram' means 'exalted father,' a reference not to Abram himself but to God."

This situation continued to vex Abram. Even though he believed God and his promises, still he sought to create a logical solution to the dilemma. So he cried out to God, "Sovereign LORD, what can you give me since I remain childless and the one who will inherit my estate is Eliezer of Damascus? . . . You have given me no children; so a servant in my household will be my heir."[27] In his advanced age, Abraham was undertaking the task of setting his house in order and providing a fair and proper method for the distribution of his estate after his death. God immediately responded to this question, however, by declaring, "This man [Eliezer] will not be your heir, but one who will come forth from your own body, he shall be your heir."[28] Once again, without any empirical evidence, Abram took a giant leap of faith: "[He] believed the LORD, and it was credited to him as righteousness."[29] There was no reason for anyone to believe that a man who was nearing the century mark in age and whose wife was almost ninety years old could possibly expect the birth of a child; however, Abram, along with his wife, stood firm in faith, trusting God to provide what he had promised. Finally, God appeared to both of them, changed their names to Abraham and Sarah, and announced to them the timing of his covenant intentions.

Miracle of Life from Dead Bodies

Sarah was postmenopausal. Scripture declares that her "womb was dead."[30] Abraham, likewise, was said to be "as good as dead."[31] No wonder they both laughed when God promised them a son. "Abraham fell on his face and laughed, and said in his heart, 'Will a child be born to a man who is one hundred years old? And will Sarah, who is ninety years old, bear a child?'"[32] Likewise, "Sarah laughed to herself, saying, 'After I am worn out and my lord is old, will I now have this pleasure?'"[33] The essence of Sarah's reasoning is clear in the Hebrew of this text: "Now that I am withered, am I to have enjoyment—with my husband so old?"[34] Essentially, Sarah said to herself, "Can this old man bring me pleasure [the pleasure associated with

---

27 Genesis 15:2–3, NIV.
28 Genesis 15:4.
29 Genesis 15:6, NIV.
30 Romans 4:19.
31 Hebrews 11:12.
32 Genesis 17:17.
33 Genesis 18:12, NIV.
34 Genesis 18:12, TNK.

conception and childbirth]?" Sarah's laughter probably concealed some pain and irony as well, for she knew that if by some miracle she were to conceive, she would be destined to carry a fetus for nine months when she was ninety years old! While most of the commentary has focused on Sarah's laughter, it is ironic that Sarah "laughed to herself" while Abraham laughed convulsively, "falling on his face" in a good belly laugh.

So what was God's response to all this laughter? "Is anything too difficult for the LORD?" he asked Abraham. Then, the sovereign Lord cut through all the fog and unequivocally answered his own question, saying, "At the appointed time I will return to you, at this time next year, and Sarah will have a son."[35] Then, just as God had predicted, an infant son was born to an "as-good-as-dead" couple. Another irony emerged when the child was born, for he was named יִצְחָק (*Yitzhak*), which means "laughter" or "he laughs"—precisely the very thing that both Abraham and Sarah had done when God had confirmed his continuing promise to them and had assured them that together they would accomplish the impossible by producing a son in their old age.

God's intervention in Abraham and Sarah's lives should not have been entirely unexpected, however. When in the very beginning he created humanity, God had set in motion a system that would ensure the replication of his image and likeness in the earth through the process of human reproduction; however, he never limited himself to the biological process as he had instituted it. As Randall Garr notes, "When trouble occurs in the genealogical trajectory, God intervenes. He can override natural biology and secure progeny for an infertile couple."[36] In some situations, God simply "assumes personal responsibility for fulfilling his promises of 'likeness' and 'image'; his role is active, deliberate, agentive, and causal. But his involvement may be greater still."[37] This was clearly demonstrated in the circumstance of Abraham and Sarah: "Despite Sarai's infertility and the seemingly insuperable obstacle that it poses against realizing God's promises . . . God remedies the situation himself."[38]

With Abraham as good as dead and Sarah laughing at the very idea that she could possibly conceive, much less give birth to a child, there was certainly no indication that new life was on the horizon. It was simply not to be. But, God

---

[35] Genesis 18:14.
[36] W. Randall Garr, *In His Own Image and Likeness: Humanity, Divinity, and Monotheism* (Leiden, The Netherlands: Koninkijke Brill, 2003), p. 233.
[37] Randall Garr, p. 174.
[38] Randall Garr, p. 174.

—yes, God—had different plans, and his powers were far beyond the normal course of human anatomy and physiology. God had never been lacking in "power to realize his promises, even when the order of nature presented no prospect of their fulfillment, and the power of nature was insufficient to secure it.[39]" Because *El Shaddai*, the Almighty, had this power, he compelled "nature to do what is contrary to itself, and subdue[d] it to bow and minister to grace."[40] Abraham's faith did, indeed, become "resurrection faith: faith that God will bring life from the dead."[41] Jon Levenson rightly argues that because the Hebrew Scriptures often represented childlessness as being equivalent to death,[42] those who were childless and then miraculously gave birth experienced as if it were a kind of resurrection.[43] The new life that sprang forth from dead bodies was resurrection life!

The Impact of the Covenantal Name Change

When, once and for all, God made his covenant and its terms absolute, the covenant represented a merger[44] between God and Abram and Sarai.[45] This agreement was similar to what would have been contracted between parties of agreement in the Middle Eastern societies of that day. When terms of a covenant had been reached, an exchange of personal names or parts of names often took place so that, after the agreement, both parties shared each other's name.[46] Because God's covenant with Abram and Sarai was a unilateral sovereign decree to which Abram and Sarai made no contribution, only Abram and Sarai's names

[39] Carl Friedrich Keil and Franz Delitzsch, *The Pentateuch*, tr. James Martin (Edinburgh, UK: T & T Clark, 1864), vol. 1, p. 233.
[40] Franz Delitzsch, quoted in Revere Franklin Weidner, *Biblical Theology of the Old Testament* (Philadelphia, PA: H. B. Garner, 1886), p. 42.
[41] J. R. Daniel Kirk, *Unlocking Romans: Resurrection and the Justification of God* (Grand Rapids, MI: Wm. B. Eerdmans Publishing Co., 2008), p. 73.
[42] Proverbs 30:15 says that of the "four things that are insatiable," one is "a barren womb."
[43] Jon D. Levenson, *Resurrection and the Restoration of Israel: The Ultimate Victory of the God of Life* (New Haven, CT: Yale University Press, 2006), pp. 114–115.
[44] Michael Kaufman, *Love, Marriage, and Family in Jewish Law and Tradition* (Northvale, NJ: Jason Aronson, Inc., 1992), pp. 11, 100. Kaufman points out that in Judaism, the covenant of marriage is not a partnership as much as it is a merger.
[45] The Holy Spirit, the manifestation of God's presence, was active in both Abraham and Sarah, empowering the impossible to emerge. This was not, however, unusual, for Jewish thought suggests that in the exclusivity and sanctity of marriage, three, not two, are involved, for God is also present in the holy covenant and its expressions. God, therefore, is intimately involved with those with whom he makes covenant.
[46] This has been an enduring practice through the centuries in cultures around the world where the covenant of marriage still involves an exchange of names. In Western societies, the bride usually assumes the name of the groom; however, in some cases, both assume each other's name or a combination of both names.

were changed, by having a part of God's name added to their own. This name change would have profound significance for the fulfillment of God's purposes in both of their lives, for what they received included a very special part of God's own personal name. In what could be described as the "*heh* factor," God infused new life into the as-good-as-dead couple, preparing them for a miracle.

Abram's birth name was אַבְרָם (*Avram*), which meant "exalted father." Needless to say, he had failed to live up to the expectations of his parents who named him, for he was nearly 100 years old and had no children from his wife Sarai. Sarai's birth name was שָׂרַי (*Sarai*), which meant "princess" or "ruler" but, more specifically, "controlling woman."[47] Sarai was, indeed, a powerful woman who was certainly Abram's equal in every way. Like most women, she felt a need to be in control of the circumstances of family life.[48] When this God-designed instinct is administered in a balanced way, it is highly beneficial for the welfare of the family, including that of the husband and father. In the case of Sarai, however, the controlling instinct expanded to the point that she assumed the right to determine how the manifestation of God's promise that she would give birth to the promised son would be fulfilled. She chose surrogate motherhood and, in doing so, settled for Ishmael rather than waiting for Isaac. And that decision has continued to impact the world even to this day.

The personal name that God had chosen for himself and that he would later use in his covenantal relationship with his Chosen People was ה/ו/ה/י (YHWH).[49] Since this divine name is so sacred as to be ineffable, it is usually represented in Jewish writings as *Adonai* ("LORD') or *Ha-Shem* ("The Name").[50] While it is called by the Greek term *Tetragrammaton* because it is comprised of four letters, God's personal name is actually made up of three letters of the Hebrew *alephbet*, one of which is used twice. In ancient Hebrew, each of these letters appeared as a pictograph. The first letter of the divine name, the י (*yud*), is a picture of a

---

[47] James Strong, *Strong's Exhaustive Concordance to the Bible* (Peabody, MA: Hendrickson Publishers, 2007), p. 1588.

[48] This is a part of the nurturing nature that God built into woman at creation. For details of this subject see John D. Garr, *Coequal and Counterbalanced: God's Blueprint for Women and Men* (Atlanta, GA: Golden Key Press, 2012), and John D. Garr, *Feminine by Design: The God-Fashioned Woman* (Atlanta, GA: Golden Key Press, 2012).

[49] The letters of the ineffable divine name are separated here by slashes in order to avoid printing the name on a text that could be mishandled, damaged, or destroyed. It also protects against the misreading or mispronunciation of the Hebrew text of the name.

[50] In Judaism, the name YHWH is known as *Shem HaMeforash*, literally "the Ineffable Name." See Moses Maimonides, *Guide for the Perplexed*, tr. Michael Friedländer (London, England: George Routledge & Sons, 1919), p. 91. Also Deirdre Carabind, *The Unknown God* (Eugene, OR: Wipf and Stock Publishers, 1995), p. 86.

"hand." The second letter, the ה (*heh*), is a picture of an "open window." The third letter, the ו (*vav*), is a picture of a "nail."

When God finalized his covenant with Abram and Sarai, he added one of the letters of his name to both of their names so that אַבְרָם (*Avram*) became אַבְרָהָם (*Avraham*) and שָׂרַי (*Sarai*) became שָׂרָה (*Sarah*). The Hebrew letter that was added to both Abram and Sarai's names was the ה (*heh*), the breath sound, the letter that mystical Judaism says possesses great power in the spiritual realm.[51] The *heh* is unique in Hebrew in that "only the breath of air [and not the tongue] is used . . . in forming its sound."[52] This is thought to indicate that "God created the world without any effort," says Israel Drazin.[53] Since the letter *heh* is a sound of breath or breathing, its use in the name change for Abram and Sarai can also be viewed as representing the introduction of the Spirit, the breath of God, into their lives.[54] Yitzchak Ginsburgh notes that when God added the letter *heh* to Abram's name, he, in fact, "infused him with the power of procreation of the Jewish soul, G-d's 'image' on earth, the power of the Infinite."[55] Ginsburgh also points out that the phenomenon in which the sound of every letter of the Hebrew *alephbet* is onomatopoeic is most obvious with regard to the letter *heh*, "which expresses the astonishment of a new revelation."[56] When this occurred, an "exalted father" became the "father of many nations," and a "controlling woman" became the "princess of God."[57] But, more importantly, the natural processes and boundaries of human reproduction were radically altered so that together a man who was "as good as dead"[58] and a woman whose "womb was dead"[59] conceived a child and brought it to term. As a consequence, Ginsburgh says, "The name of the

---

[51] Yitzchak Ginsburgh, *The Alef-Beit: Jewish Thought Revealed through the Hebrew Letters* (Rechovot, Israel: Gal Einai Institute, 1990), p. 88.
[52] Israel Drazin, *Maimonides and the Biblical Prophets* (Jerusalem, Israel: Gefen Publishing House, 2009), p. 199.
[53] Drazin, p. 199.
[54] The connection between the "breath of God" and the "Spirit of God" is clear in Job 33:4: "The Spirit of God has made me; the breath of the Almighty gives me life."
[55] Ginsburgh, p. 88.
[56] Ginsburgh, p. 88.
[57] In Sarai's case, the *heh* actually replaced the *yud*, indicating that the "controlling element" (hand) was replaced by the "window" of the Spirit. Instead of trusting her own ability to control matters, she was then able to put her complete trust in God in order to achieve the outcome that she knew she could not physically produce.
[58] Hebrews 11:12.
[59] Romans 4:19.

child born to Abram and Sarai, Isaac, means 'laughter' and 'delight' due to the supernatural revelation of the Divine."[60] This is what happens when the Spirit of God enters into the process of nature and by its transformational power produces the supernatural—the miracle of life.[61]

If there ever was a demonstration of God's power, this was it. As Levenson says, "Both the birth of a child to an infertile couple and the resurrection of a dead person testify to the triumph of the wonder-working God. . . . Each is a humanly inexplicable reversal of the seemingly inevitable sequence of events whose last word is death. Each represents a victory of life over death."[62] When the norms of human reproduction were utterly deficient, God's hands were not tied. As in the days of creation in the beginning, he simply summoned into reality what did not exist—could not exist—and through the agency of two reproductively dead bodies produced the chosen life from which the Chosen People would issue! With the gloom of defeat lurking all around, laughter (יִצְחָק — Yitzhak, "he laughs")[63] sprang forth, setting in motion the unstoppable, undeniable, and dynamic fulfillment of God's promise to make Abraham's descendants increase until they would be as innumerable as the "stars of heaven and the sand that is on the seashore"![64] Could anything ever obviate the continuing manifestation of God's promises to Abraham when their initial fulfillment began with such an amazing encounter with the supernatural? The Lord of heaven who literally summoned life from reproductively dead bodies has lost none of his power in the four millennia since he worked that miracle.

God could not have conceived or advanced a more powerful example of his faithfulness to the terms of his covenant than the wonder that he produced in the lives of Abraham and Sarah by giving them the child through whom the promises of multitudes of descendants (the Chosen

---

[60] Ginsburgh, p. 88.
[61] Some Jewish scholars have suggested that the *heh* in Hebrew symbolizes "the power of procreation" and, in some way, "carried and conferred this power." See Mosheh Volfson, *Wellsprings of Faith: Perspectives on the Sources of Emunah* (Jerusalem, Israel: Feldheim Publishers, 2002), pp. 24–25. "Because Avraham received a new name, it became possible for him to receive a new power of procreation from Hashem," says Volfson.
[62] Jon D. Levenson, *The Death and Resurrection of the Beloved Son: The Transformation of Child Sacrifice in Judaism and Christianity* (New Haven, CT: Yale University Press, 1993), p. 125.
[63] Nahum Sarna suggest that it is even possible that the proper name *Yitzhak* could have meant, "May [God] laugh." See Nahum M. Sarna, "Isaac," in Cecil Roth, *et. al.*, eds., *The Encyclopedia Judaica* (Jerusalem, Israel: Keter Publishing House, 1994), vol. 9, p. 4.
[64] Genesis 22:17.

People), of nations (including the Chosen Nation), and land (the Promised Land) could be fulfilled. The miracle of the Abrahamic covenant confirmed once and for all that the covenant was a supernatural divine decree, an everlasting covenant that would never be thwarted or destroyed. Nothing—not the course of nature, not the unfolding of world events, not the evil machinations of tyrants or of any other person, event, or circumstance—could obviate or even occlude God's solemn, sovereign decree, his unilateral covenant to bless Abraham and his descendants forever through the terms of the irrevocable "everlasting covenant." The very initiation of the unfolding events of the covenantal promise was a miracle, and many more would follow.

Protecting the Promised Son and the Covenant Promises

The intense nurturing spirituality of a godly mother ensured that Isaac would be reared in the "discipline and instruction of the Lord."[65] Sarah had a gift for insight that went beyond what has often been called feminine intuition. It was Sarah's prophetic gift that revealed to her what was not apparent to others. In order to support this gift, God even instructed Abraham in this manner: "Listen to whatever Sarah tells you, because it is through Isaac that your offspring will be reckoned."[66] Because of the language of this divine instruction to Abraham, the sages were prompted to suggest that Sarah had even greater prophetic power than her husband did.[67] As a matter of fact, in rabbinic *midrashim*, Sarah is often called *Yiscah*, which means, "one who looks forth," a testimony to her ability to see the future by divine inspiration.[68] The sages believed that this name was "a reflection of [Sarah's] greatness as a prophet."[69] This matriarch of the faith of YHWH had deeply spiritual and prophetic insight!

When God said to Abraham, "Whatever Sarah says to you, do as she tells you,"[70] he was speaking of an emerging and potentially perilous domestic

---

[65] Ephesians 6:4.

[66] Genesis 21:12, NIV.

[67] Rivkah bat Meir, *Rivkah Meneket: A Manual of Wisdom and Piety for Jewish Women* (Philadelphia, PA: The Jewish Publication Society, 2008), p. 132. Meir refers to *Shemot Rabah* 1:1. Also, Jill Hammer, *Sisters at Sinai: New Tales of Biblical Women* (Philadelphia, PA: Jewish Publication Society, 2001), p. 252.

[68] Rashi maintains that Sarah was *Yiscah* mentioned in Genesis 11:29, the daughter of Abraham's deceased brother Haran. See Shera Aranoff Tuchman and Sandra E. Rapoport, *The Passions of the Matriarchs* (Jersey City, NJ: KTAV Publishing House, 2004), pp. 3–4.

[69] *Megillah* 14a.

[70] Genesis 21:12, ESV.

situation that had been fomenting in the relationship between Isaac and Ish-mael, Abraham's son of the Egyptian bondwoman Hagar. Being a man of jus-tice, deference, and mercy, Abraham felt great responsibility toward both of his sons. He knew, however, that Isaac was the child whom God had promised, while Ishmael was the product of human reasoning in search of an alternative that would logically solve what seemed like an impossible situation.

The evolving problem reached an explosive level when Sarah "saw the son of Hagar the Egyptian, whom she had borne to Abraham, mocking."[71] On a cur-sory reading of this text, the reported action would seem to have been innocent enough. In fact, the language of the text looks like a play on words in Hebrew, with the description of Ishmael's action, מְצַחֵק (mitzachek), etymologically par-allel with Isaac's name, יִצְחָק (Yitzhak). Ishmael was making fun (מְצַחֵק) of Isaac (יִצְחָק). Just beneath the surface, however, something far more sinister was lurking. Ishmael was following in his mother's footsteps, deriding Isaac in the same way in which Hagar had scorned Sarah after the birth of Ishmael and in the same way in which she was probably continuing to deprecate her.[72]

John Calvin may well have been right in his assessment that Ishmael's "epi-thet" was a "malignant expression of scorn, by which the forward youth manifest-ed his contempt for his infant brother" compared with the positive laughter which was divinely imposed upon Isaac.[73] At any rate, competition for Abraham's favor and, indeed, the birthright of Abraham's inheritance was in the works. Whatever the case, Sarah noticed what had happened, and she "knew then that Ishmael would be a bad influence upon Isaac" that could well "imperil Isaac's future as the second patriarch" of the Chosen People.[74] Sarah apparently had sensitivity to righteousness in areas where Abraham seemed to have a blind spot.[75]

---

[71] Genesis 21:9.

[72] Genesis 16:4.

[73] John Calvin, *Commentaries on the First Book of Moses Called Genesis,* tr. John King (Edinburgh, UK: The Edinburgh Printing Co., 1847), vol. 1, pp. 542–543. In this same commentary, Calvin also gave the following explanation: "Ishmael turns the blessing of God, from which such joy flowed, into ridicule. Therefore, as an impious mocker, he stands opposed to his brother Isaac. Both (so to speak) are the sons of laughter: but in a very different sense. Isaac brought laughter with him from his mother's womb. . . . He therefore so exhilarates his father's house, that joy breaks forth in thanksgiving; but Ishmael, with canine and profane laughter, attempts to destroy that holy joy of faith."

[74] Walter Orenstein, *Teach Me about God: The Meaning and Significance of the Name of God* (Lanham, MD: Jason Aronson Publishing 2005), p. 75.

[75] For example, Abraham employed the half-truth, "She is my sister," to cover up his true identity as Sarah's husband when he feared that both Pharaoh and Abimelech might assassinate him in order to add the beautiful Sarah to their harems (Genesis 20:2; Genesis 26:9). When Abraham was less than diligent to protect his wife's honor, God stepped in and did so himself—and with stunning results! Abraham's faith deficiency was compensated by Sarah's faithfulness.

Ishmael was mocking both Isaac and Sarah and, in doing so, he was actually mocking his own father Abraham.

Because of her great spiritual insight, Sarah reacted immediately to her intuition and initiated the action that ensured that the son of promise would not be further exposed to challenges against his patrimony in the midst of a divided house. Hagar and Ishmael were expelled from the household of Abraham. What on the surface may have looked like an act of jealous anger and retribution against Hagar and Ishmael was actually an effort by Sarah to preserve the integrity of the Chosen People through the son of promise. With the conflict removed, Abraham was free to focus all of his energies on Isaac, the heir through whom his lineage was to be established forever.

ISAAC
Continuing in the Faith and the Promise

As time passed, God presented the ultimate challenge to both Abraham and his son Isaac. In spite of all the imprecations of Scripture against the horrific pagan practice of child sacrifice and immolation,[76] God issued this shocking command to Abraham: "Take now your son, your only son, whom you love, Isaac, and go to the land of Moriah, and offer him there as a burnt offering on one of the mountains of which I will tell you."[77] How could this be? While it was true that "in the ancient Near East during Abraham's time, human sacrifice and sacrificing children to foreign gods were commonly practiced,"[78] could the God of the covenant really be directing Abraham to engage in the most hideous and heinous of pagan practices, or was this just a trial of faith for which there would be a simple solution? Abraham could not be certain, but he was certain that the God whom he knew and served would do justice and would show mercy, so he did not hesitate to undertake the ultimate trial of his faith, the *Akedah*.[79]

A Mountain of Life, A Valley of Death

Moriah, the place to which God was sending Abraham, was unique. This mountain was located on the site of what would become Jerusalem, specifically

---

[76] Leviticus 18:21; Deuteronomy 18:10; 2 Kings 21:6; Jeremiah 7:31.
[77] Genesis 22:2.
[78] Paul Copan, *How Do You Know You're Not Wrong? Responding to Objections that Leave Christians Speechless* (Grand Rapids, MI: Baker Books, 2005), p. 166.
[79] The *Akedah* is the "binding of Isaac," the event when Abraham proved his faith in God beyond any doubt.

on the mountain on which the temple would be constructed and even more particularly on the spot where all the sacrifices of YHWH's temple would be offered. This mountain, however, was very close to the precipitous Hinnom Valley that was just south and west of the holy mountain. Perhaps this is why God gave very specific instructions to Abraham about the place where the sacrifice of his son was to take place: "Sacrifice him there as a burnt offering on a mountain *I will show you.*"[80] Not just any location—mountain or otherwise—would be acceptable or appropriate for this momentous event. It had to be the exact place that God had chosen, the most sacrosanct spot on earth.[81]

Though it was very close to the summit of the sacred Mt. Moriah, the Hinnom Valley was a particularly detestable place because it was the site where many gods, including Baal and Molech, were worshipped in utterly gruesome displays of degrading revelry and merciless infanticide. The dominant cult of Molech featured a religion in which the people customarily brought their firstborn infants to the idol temple where the priests would crush their skulls on the knees of the iron image, place them in the hands of the monster, and then let them fall still alive into the fiery furnace that was burning in the god's belly. Because many apostate Israelites also participated in these horrific practices, the site was cursed and recognized by all the Hebrews and Israelites as a profoundly evil place.[82]

In one small tract of land, clearly within sight of each other, glaring images of life and death, of blessings and curses were manifest. *El Shaddai,* the "Most High God," was worshipped on Mt. Moriah with blessings for long life.[83] In the Hinnom Valley, immediately below the mountain, however, the worship of Molech was accompanied by the screams of innocent infants and the sobs of bereaved parents. In the deep, dark valley, death was in control. This was the stark contrast that Abraham and Isaac faced when they reached the end of their three-day journey into destiny: Moriah and Hinnom—Life and Death. Moriah was a temple; Hinnom, a refuse heap.[84] Both Abraham and Isaac could clearly

---

[80] Genesis 22:2, NIV, emphasis added.
[81] Deuteronomy 12:5; 2 Kings 21:4.
[82] Jeremiah 7:31; 19:2–6.
[83] Moriah was the place where Melchizedek (*Malki-Tzedek*—"my king of righteousness") led the worship of "God Most High" with rituals of bread and wine and of blessings both for God and for man (Genesis 14:18).
[84] Luke 12:5. Jesus said, "And I say to you, my friends, be not afraid of those killing the body . . . fear him who, after the killing, is having authority to cast to the gehenna; yes, I say to you, Fear ye him" (YLT). In virtually all English translations this and the ten other references that Jesus makes to "gehenna" are translated as "hell." The Greek word rendered "gehenna" in this translation is γέεννα (*geenna*), a transliteration of the Hebrew גֵּהִנֹּם (*Gehinnom*), which means "from the Hinnom."

see the contrast that Abraham Joshua Heschel described: "The need of Molech was the death of man," but "the need of the Lord is the life of man."[85] It was important, therefore, for Abraham and Isaac to get this right. Only in the right place would God's power and his provision be manifest.

Entering the Stage of Divine Destiny

God did not instruct Abraham to go to the place "where I will send you," for the Almighty would not risk a wrong turn by a father who might have been distraught by being confronted with the prospect of killing his only son. God commanded Abraham to go to the mountain *"I will show you."* Abraham and Isaac were not making this journey alone. God was walking with them and "showing" them the way to the right mountain! For Abraham, this task would not be a stab in the dark. He would be guided by the rays of revelation more powerful and far more accurate than those from any global positioning satellite! There would be no mistake. He would arrive faithfully at the very rock on the mountaintop where Melchizedek worshipped and where thousands of sacrifices would later be offered by his descendants after him in God's Holy Place.

Perhaps this is the reason why on the third day of the journey, when Abraham "raised his eyes and saw the place from a distance," he instructed his servants in this manner: "Stay here with the donkey, and I and the lad will go over there; and we will worship and return to you."[86] Abraham did not say, "I will return to you." He said with all boldness, "We will go, we will worship, and we will return to you." The Father of Nations knew in his heart of hearts that there had to be a simple answer to the dilemma! The God whom he served was a God of blessings and life, not a god of curses and death. This simple knowledge was the basis of the Jewish tradition which has asserted that "through his prophetic gifts, Abraham knew that he would not have to carry out the command to sacrifice Isaac."[87] Jon Levenson points out, however, that "the knowledge at issue here still involves a not inconsequential measure of faith—faith that the prophetic message is authentic and the God who authors it, reliable."[88]

---

[85] Abraham Joshua Heschel, *Man Is Not Alone: A Philosophy of Religion* (New York: Farrar, Straus and Giroux, 1951), p. 245.
[86] Genesis 22:4–5.
[87] Levenson, p. 130.
[88] Levenson, p. 130.

Both the sages of Israel and the apostles of the Jesus movement shared the view that Abraham knew God well enough to know that his God would not bereave him of his promised son, the father of the Chosen People. Whether he prophesied the continued life of Isaac into being, as Rashi suggested,[89] or whether he simply believed that God would resurrect Isaac from the dead, Abraham knew God, and he believed that his God would be for life and not for death. No wonder the author of the Christian book of Hebrews spoke of the nature of Abraham's faith in this manner: "By faith Abraham, when he was tested, offered Isaac as a sacrifice, and he who had received the promises was offering up his only begotten son; He who had embraced the promises was about to sacrifice his one and only son, it was he to whom it was said, 'In Isaac your descendants shall be called.' Abraham reasoned that God could even raise the dead, and so in a manner of speaking he did receive Isaac back from death."[90] Indeed, the very Hebrew name of the place of the *Akedah* had already established the hope of life, even of resurrection, long before Abraham and Isaac made their fateful trek up the slopes of God's mountain. YHWH would meet them at Moriah, which in Hebrew means "chosen by God," but would be called *YHWH Yireh* by Abraham, because "God sees" and "God provides."[91] Clearly then, in the place called Moriah, there was "a hint of salvation and deliverance."[92] As Gordon Wenham has observed, "Salvation is thus promised in the very decree that sounds like annihilation."[93]

Life and Death Condensed into One Moment of Time

The journey ended. Walking with God had brought Abraham and his son to the right place at the right time to do the right thing that would establish the foundation of faith and faithfulness on which the saga of the Chosen People would rest for all time. Abraham dutifully set about the task of preparing the burnt offering. He arranged the wood on top of the rock of sacrifice. When Isaac observed, "The fire and wood are here, but where is the lamb for the burnt offering?" Abraham replied, "God will

---

[89] Rashi, *Perush al Hatorah*. See Omri Boehm, *Binding of Isaac: A Religious Model of Disobedience* (New York: T & T Clark International, 2007), p. 45.
[90] Hebrews 11:17–18, NASB, 19, NIV.
[91] Genesis 22:14.
[92] Copan, p. 165.
[93] Gordon Wenham, *World Biblical Commentary: Genesis 16–50* (Nashville, TN: Word Publishing, 1994), vol. 2, p. 105.

provide himself the lamb for the burnt offering, my son."[94] Then Abraham bound Isaac hand and foot and laid him on top of the altar. The old man reached fearlessly for the sheathed dagger that he had brought with him. He raised the instrument of death on high and prepared to plunge it into the heart of the son he loved.

Immediately, the angel of the Lord stopped Abraham's plunging dagger in midair, and these amazing words of grace echoed from the lips of God in the pregnant air atop the divine mountain: "Abraham! Abraham! . . . Do not lay a hand on the boy. . . . Now I know that you fear God, because you have not withheld from me your son, your only son."[95] Then, when Abraham turned around to see what God was doing, "there in a thicket he saw a ram caught by its horns."[96] Instantly, the patriarch of faith understood what God's intentions had been all along, so he "took the ram and sacrificed it as a burnt offering instead of his son."[97]

It was finished. The drama ended, and the saga of the Chosen People began afresh—first on the sacred foundation of a father's faith and willingness to sacrifice the one who was most important in his life in order to obey God's command, then on the son's faith to do his father's bidding, and finally on the intervention of God to bring forth life out of the clutches of death. Abraham did not withhold from God his only son, the son whom God had miraculously given to him by overriding the natural laws of human reproductive biology in order to produce human life from virtually dead bodies. And God did not take Abraham's miracle child from him. Instead, the patriarch received his son back as though he had been resurrected from the dead. Now, for the second time, he had been given God's gift of life in the person of his most precious son, Isaac, the living miracle that confirmed the divine covenant.

The Greater Meaning of the *Akedah*

Over the centuries, sages and prophets came to understand that the profound miracle upon which the continuation of the saga of the Chosen People was founded was more than just an event of history. Instead, it had powerful spiritual overtones for all of the descendants of Abraham and Isaac. The

---

[94] Genesis 22:7–8, NIV.
[95] Genesis 22:11–12, NIV.
[96] Genesis 22:13, NIV.
[97] Genesis 22:13, NIV.

Akedah came to be recognized as a vicarious atonement, a sacrifice that God accepted substitutionally for the entire Chosen People throughout all their generations. As the great third-century Carthaginian Christian polemicist Tertullian declared, "Abraham whom his faith made obey the command of God offered his only, beloved son as sacrifice to God so that God in His part bestowed on him the favor of the redemption of his posterity."[98] This Christian observation had been confirmed in the texts of the *Targumim* which specifically attributed "Israel's deliverance to the efficacy of the *Akedah*."[99] God's blessings upon the Chosen People were founded upon the faithfulness of Abraham and Isaac to fulfill God's instructions and to receive God's provision.

This understanding of the *Akedah* as a vicarious atonement flows from the principle of *Zekhut Avot* ("Merits of the Fathers"), which Louis Berman says "overlaps the Christian concept of vicarious atonement."[100] Rabbinic sources "always viewed the willing sacrifice of Abraham, and especially Isaac's willingness to offer himself, as an act of vicarious atonement through the future history of their descendants, the nation of Israel."[101] In this way, "the righteousness of the patriarchs could be vicariously applied to their descendants in time of spiritual need."[102] This is why there is a strong connection between the *Akedah* and the High Holy Days of *Rosh Hashanah* and *Yom Kippur*, the most sacred season of the Jewish liturgical calendar. The repeated blowing of the shofar (ram's horn) on *Rosh Hashanah* harks back to the ram that was caught by his horns in the thorn bush and was there held at ready for the burnt offering after Abraham and Isaac had fully obeyed God and had done what he had required of them. Likewise, in the *Zikhronot* (Remembrance Prayers) of *Rosh Hashanah*, an appeal is made to God to remember the *Akedah*. Then on the second day of *Rosh Hashanah*, the entire story of Genesis 22 is read.[103] In this case, the "reading of the *Akedah* is intended to remind God of the merits that accrued to Abraham and Isaac as a result of this awesome sacrifice."[104]

---

[98] Tertullian, *Adversus Judaeos*, 10.

[99] Kenneth A. Mathews, *The New American Commentary: An Exegetical and Theological Exposition of Holy Scripture: Genesis 11:27–50:26* (Goshen, IN: Broadman & Holman Publishers, 2005), p. 301. Mathews notes the texts of *Targum* Canticles 1:13, *Targum* Esther 2, 5:1, and *Targum* 1 Chronicles 21:15 to support his assertion regarding the connection between Israel's salvation and the *Akedah*.

[100] Louis Arthur Berman, *The Akedah: The Binding of Isaac* (Northvale, NJ: Jason Aronson, Inc., 1997), p. 152.

[101] Tim F. LaHaye and Edward E. Hindson, eds., *The Popular Bible Prophecy Commentary: Understanding the Meaning of Every Prophetic Passage* (Eugene, OR: Harvest House Publishers, 2006), p. 19.

[102] LaHaye and Hindson, p. 19.

[103] Berman, p. 155.

[104] Nathan MacDonald, Mark W. Elliott, and Grant Macaskill, *Genesis and Christian Theology* (Grand Rapids, MI: Wm. B. Eerdmans Publishing Co., 2012), p. 53.

The idea of vicarious atonement that was embedded in the *Akedah* on very solid applications of divine principles became a foundation for the Christian understanding that the death of Jesus on the cross was also a vicarious atonement for the redemption of the entire world from the bondage of sin. Many scholars suggest that Paul's understanding of the atoning nature of Jesus' death owed at least some of its foundation to the Jewish interpretation of the *Akedah* as being expiatory.[105] Geza Vermes did not hesitate to draw this conclusion: "That the Pauline doctrine of Redemption is basically a Christian version of the Akedah calls for little demonstration."[106] It was certainly not difficult to see the parallels between the binding of Isaac to the altar on Moriah and the binding of Jesus to the cross on Calvary. The motifs of a loving father and only son involved in sacrifice to God are parallel in both events. The theme of resurrection is also parallel, though in different ways.[107] While there are significant differences between Jewish and Christian understandings of atonement, particularly of vicarious atonement, it is clear that both religions are solidly anchored in the idea that the faith of the fathers made possible acts of atonement that somehow and to some degree relate to the ongoing blessing of God upon their communities.[108]

A Foundation for the Unfolding Faith

The *Akedah* provides a secure foundation for the unfolding dynamic saga of life that has characterized the Chosen People from time immemorial. Through one event in one fleeting moment of time, the fate of the entire

---

[105] Hans-Joachim Schoeps, *Paul: The Theology of the Apostle in the Light of Religious History*, tr. H. Knight (Philadelphia, PA: Westminster Press, 1961), p. 148; Robert J. Daly, "The Soteriological Significance of the Sacrifice of Isaac," *Catholic Biblical Quarterly* 39 (1977), pp. 45–74; and Karin Hedner Zetterholm, *Jewish Interpretation of the Bible: Ancient and Contemporary* (Minneapolis, MN: Augsburg Fortress Press, 2012), pp. 107–108. Other scholars, however, question the *Akedah* as a background for Paul's teaching on vicarious atonement and substitutionary righteousness. See Hyam Maccoby, *Early Rabbinic Writings* (Cambridge, UK: Cambridge University Press, 1988), p. 149.

[106] Geza Vermes, "Redemption and Genesis xxii—The Binding of Isaac and the Sacrifice of Jesus," in *Scripture and Tradition in Judaism: Haggadic Studies* (Leiden, The Netherlands: Brill, 1983), pp. 193–227, especially p. 219.

[107] Jon Davies, *Death, Burial and Rebirth in the Religions of Antiquity* (New York: Routledge, 1999), p. 204. In a midrash recorded in *Pirkei de-Rav Eliezer 31*, Rabbi Judah taught that when Abraham's knife touched Isaac's throat, "his soul flew clean out of him." Then when the Lord said, "'Lay not thy hand upon the lad,' the lad's soul returned to his body." *Midrash Lekah Tob* drew on Isaiah 26:19, "Thy dew is the dew of light, and the earth shall bring to life the dead" (JPS), to say that God restored Isaac's soul "by means of the dewdrops for the Resurrection of the dead." See Larry Stephen Milner, *Hardness of Heart/Hardness of Life: The Stain of Human Infanticide* (Lanham, MD: University Press of America, 2000), p. 349.

[108] In Judaism, the *Akedah* and the *Zekhut Avot* undergird the faith and obedience of the Chosen People. Christianity, the undeserved death of the sinless Jesus provided propitiation for sin and atonement that is foundational to the faith of every believer (Hebrews 2:9–12; 4:13–14; Romans 3:25; 1 John 2:2; 4:10).

Chosen People hung in the balance. Which would it be, life or death? The answer was life, for God provided himself the ram as a substitutionary sacrifice. Life triumphed over death, and life reigned then and ever thereafter for the Chosen People. Because of the faith and faithfulness of father and son to engage the Eternal in the drama of sacrifice and redemption, God produced resurrection life from the dead so that *am Yisrael chai*, the people of Israel live. Just when death seemed imminent, God's hand intervened to maintain life and thereby demonstrate his unequivocal and eternal commitment to the lineage of blessing that he himself had chosen.

Subsequent to the *Akedah*, when Abraham had become a "very old man," the patriarch of faith understood that it was not in the best interest of the Chosen People for his son Isaac to marry one of the local Canaanite women. He made plans, therefore, to send his servant to his homeland[109] and to his own people to find a wife for Isaac.[110] When Abraham's servant arrived in Aram-naharaim, circumstances that God had orchestrated fell into place for him to meet Rebekah, a young woman of grace and beauty who was a part of the Abrahamic family and who reflected the Abrahamic ideals of justice, deference, and mercy. The test that Abraham's servant had devised in order to recognize the one whom God had ordained to be Isaac's wife was designed to measure her demonstration of the qualities that endeared Abraham to God: "Now may it be that the girl to whom I say, Please let down your jar so that I may drink, and who answers, Drink, and I will water your camels also, may she be the one whom you have appointed for your servant Isaac."[111] Rebekah passed the test and, with the approval of her family, she agreed to accompany Abraham's servant to Canaan to be married to Isaac. When they neared the Abraham family complex, she saw Isaac at a distance, veiled herself, and prepared to be joined to her beloved in marriage. Shortly thereafter, Isaac "brought [Rebekah] into his mother Sarah's tent . . . and she became his wife, and he loved her."[112] So began the next chapter in the drama of the patriarchs. Isaac had walked with God alongside his father for decades. Now it was his turn to take the lead in the walk of faith and faithfulness. With the perspicacious Rebekah at his side, he was prepared to walk in the blessing of his father.

---

[109] It is interesting and very pertinent that Abraham would not allow his son Isaac to leave the Promised Land. The patriarch knew that the covenant and blessing of the Almighty was connected with the land that had been promised to him and his descendants after him.

[110] Genesis 24:1–5.

[111] Genesis 24:14.

[112] Genesis 24:67.

JACOB
"The God Wrestler"

Eventually, when Isaac was sixty years old, Rebekah gave birth to twin sons, Esau and Jacob. Before their birth, Rebekah had wondered why the two fetuses continually struggled in her womb.[113] When she inquired of the Lord, she received this stunning answer: "Two nations are in your womb . . . one people shall be stronger than the other; and the older shall serve the younger."[114] Even before the birth of her two sons, Rebekah's prophetic vision gave her insight into what would occur decades later.[115] With this definitive prophetic word from God, she was prepared for a long and eventful journey of faith, and she was determined to ensure that God's specific and explicit words to her were fulfilled.

Esau was a "man's man," brash and powerful, a skillful hunter and outdoorsman. He was his father's favorite. On the other hand, Jacob was a simple, quiet man who preferred to stay at home among the tents of the family compound. He was his mother's choice. As could have been expected, the potential for conflict was great when two young men of such different temperaments and inclinations lived in the same household, both vying for the attention of their parents. The situation was only exacerbated when it became clear that Isaac loved Esau and Rebekah loved Jacob.[116] In these circumstances, family discord was almost inevitable.

A Matter of Birthright

The prophetic word that Rebekah had received from God was, however, authoritative and final: "The older [son] will serve the younger [son]." This was not the outcome that she had sought or preferred, for any mother would welcome peace in her household. The message was not, therefore, the product of her Rebekah's contrivance. But, how could this be? The right of

---

[113] What was occurring in Rebekah's womb was, however, more than a simple "struggle." The Hebrew text says that the fetuses "crushed one another" within her, using the phrase וַיִּתְרֹצֲצוּ (*v'yitrotsatsu*) a form of the verb רָצַץ (*ratsats*), which literally means "to crush" or "to oppress." It was as if the twins were engaged in a life-and-death battle *in utero* that was, no doubt, predictive of their future lives.
[114] Genesis 25:23.
[115] *Midrash Psalms* 105:4; *Genesis Rabbah* 67:9. See David J. Zucker and Moshe Reiss, *The Matriarchs of Genesis: Seven Women, Five Views* (Eugene, OR: Wipf and Stock Publishers, 2015), p. 150.
[116] Genesis 25:28.

primogenitor dictated that the oldest son of the household would receive the father's blessing and birthright, would inherit a double portion of the family estate,[117] and as a consequence would "rule over" the rest of the family. From the time of the twins' birth, therefore, the stage had been set by the customs of the land for Esau to dominate Jacob.

Like her mother-in-law Sarah, however, Rebekah was a strong prophetic voice, and she had no reservations about doing whatever was necessary to see that the word that God had given her would come to pass. Sarah had discerned that Abraham's firstborn, Ishmael, was completely unqualified — and, indeed, had not been chosen — to lead the Chosen People. Likewise, Rebekah understood from Esau's lifestyle that he was not the one who had been anointed to carry the Abrahamic vision into the next generation. So, Rebekah waited to see what God would do and how he would do it.

One day, Esau came from the open country to the family compound exhausted and famished. "Quick, let me have some of that red stew!" he demanded of Jacob.[118] Having been schooled by his mother in the spiritual details of what had been taking place since before he was born, Jacob replied, "First sell me your birthright."[119] Astonished at the request, Esau responded in exasperation: "Look, I am about to die [of starvation]. . . . What good is the birthright to me?" When Jacob insisted, "Swear to me first," Esau did so, and in the process finalized "the sale of his birthright to Jacob."[120] In this casual, almost flippant, act driven by appetite and emotion, Esau "despised his birthright,"[121] considering it to be of minor importance compared to the immediate demands of his hunger. Esau had certainly not followed the pattern of conduct that had driven the lives of both his father and his grandfather as they had walked with God. He was a man of the world, a man of passion and self-indulgence, and nothing could constrain him.

With the birthright sworn to him, Jacob had only to wait until the time was fulfilled for him to receive what he had purchased. Working in concert with his mother, Jacob prepared to receive the right-hand blessing from his father that would transfer the rights of leadership and property from father to son — in this case, to the younger son. Since Isaac was virtually blind by

---

[117] Deuteronomy 21:17 describes the tradition as it was later formalized among the Israelites with the giving of the Torah.
[118] Genesis 25:30, NIV.
[119] Genesis 25:31, NIV.
[120] Genesis 25:32–33, NIV.
[121] Genesis 25:34.

that time, Rebekah believed it was possible that he could be induced to bless Jacob while thinking that he was blessing Esau. She and Jacob prepared one of the meals that Esau had traditionally made for his father, and they brought the food to Isaac. Rebekah saw to it that Jacob was disguised to resemble Esau as nearly as possible, including covering his hands and arms with a goat's skin to simulate Esau's hairy anatomy. The results, however, were only partly successful, for a puzzled Isaac wondered to himself, "The voice is Jacob's, but the hands are Esau's." Finally, Isaac was convinced that it was indeed Esau who was before him, so he conveyed the blessing of primogeniture to Jacob, including the prayer that his brother would serve him.[122] What God had predicted at the birth of the brothers and what Rebekah had orchestrated on God's behalf finally came to pass.

When Jacob had scarcely removed himself from his father's presence, Esau rushed in from his hunting expedition. When he learned what had occurred, he was furious. His father was also crestfallen and angry. How could he have been so deceived? Though Esau pled with his father, "Don't you have even one blessing for me?" Isaac could only moan, "I made him lord over you. What can I possibly do for you, my son?"[123] From that moment on, Esau "held a grudge against Jacob because of the blessing his father had given him." Consequently, he said to himself, "The days of mourning for my father are near; then I will kill my brother Jacob."[124] On his mother's advice, however, Jacob fled to Haran, to his uncle Laban's family compound. This piece of wisdom provided "an inheritance for Israel—safety from internal conflict and self-destruction and a new posterity to continue the race."[125] The only comforting thought for Jacob, however, was his mother's assurance, "When your brother is no longer angry with you and forgets what you did to him, I'll send word for you to come back from there."[126] Jacob was separated from his parents, but he still had hope.

It is true that Jacob acquired Esau's birthright in the bargain of the millennium, exchanging a mere bowl of lentils for the rights to the family fortune. Because he had bought the birthright, he rightly deserved the

---

[122] Genesis 27:18–29, NIV.
[123] Genesis 27:34–37, NIV.
[124] Genesis 27:41, NIV.
[125] Ann W. Engar, "Old Testament Women as Tricksters," in *Mappings of the Biblical Terrain: The Bible as Text*, Vincent L. Tollers and John R. Maier, eds. (Cranbury, NJ: Associated University Presses, 1990), p. 146.
[126] Genesis 27:45, NIV.

blessing of primogeniture from his father even though he and his mother had found it necessary to engage in deception in order to ensure Isaac's cooperation in the actual transfer of the rights that he had duly purchased. On the surface, Jacob and his mother appeared to be acting fraudulently at best or engaging in theft at worst. How could a wife be so duplicitous with her own husband? How could a son deceive his father so treacherously? How could such a feud develop in God's chosen family?

The answer is that Rebekah had heard the word of the Lord even before her sons were born: "The older will serve the younger." Being a prophet, she did not doubt God's Word and merely stood on his promise. Jacob trusted his mother and her spiritual wisdom, so he acted accordingly, following her advice explicitly. This did not, however, diminish the scorn that was heaped upon the young man. "Heel-Grabber,"[127] "Leg-Puller,"[128] "Thief!"[129] "Deceiver,"[130] "Supplanter"[131]—Jacob had heard all these stinging epithets that were implied by his name and that had been confirmed by his actions. His mother, too, was seen as a conniving, deceitful woman whose ethical standards were at the least very flexible when it came to actions that helped achieve her expectations for her son. Still, both mother and son were only following and working out the divine instruction, "The older will serve the younger."

Success in a New Environment

Jacob's journey back to Haran released him into a different environment where he could thrive. Filled with fear and consternation, he experienced his first personal encounter with God when he overnighted at Bethel. There, in a vision, he saw a ladder stretching between heaven and earth with angels ascending and descending.[132] When he awoke, he knew that he had experienced a divine visitation, so he used the stone that had been his pillow to construct a

---

[127] Jacob (*Ya'akov*) can mean "heel-catcher," a name applied at his birth because he came from the birth canal grasping his brother Esau's heel.

[128] Jacob was a "grabber" or "leg-puller" because he had "grabbed" the heel and "pulled the leg" of his brother when they were being born.

[129] In Genesis 27:36, Esau said that Jacob "took" or stole his birthright.

[130] In Genesis 27:35–36, Isaac said to Esau, "Your brother came deceitfully and took your blessing," prompting Esau to reply, "Is he not rightly named Jacob?" making a clear allusion to the fact that the name *Jacob* implied that he was a "deceiver" and a "thief."

[131] Jacob can also mean "supplanter" because Jacob took the place that had been rightly reserved for Esau.

[132] Genesis 28:12.

pillar to remind him of God's blessing.[133] He called the place Bethel, the "house of God," and he promised to tithe all of his increase to the Lord.

When Jacob finally reached Haran, he saw right away that his life would change dramatically. First he met the love of his life, the darling Rachel. In an act of rash, romantic love, he promised to serve his uncle for seven years if Laban would give him Rachel's hand in marriage.[134] But, in Laban, Jacob had met his own match when it came to deception. He let down his guard in a moment of passion and, as a result, he awakened the next morning to discover that he was married to Leah, Rachel's sister. Not to be denied, however, Jacob promised another seven years of service to Laban in order to be joined also to his beloved.[135]

In this state of affairs, it was finally Jacob who won the contest of wills, manipulation, and business negotiation. He became wealthy because of his relationship with Laban in the land of Haran. By contrivance and deception, he had gained the transgenerational blessing through the laying on of hands of his father Isaac and, in doing so, he had supplanted his brother. He had also paid dearly for his subterfuge and bravado, accepting self-exile from his family and voluntary servitude in the house of his uncle. Life was good, however, and he had no complaints. Still, something was nagging at his heart. He knew that the Abrahamic covenant of which he was the rightful heir was not to be fulfilled in Haran. Indeed, God had specifically commanded his grandfather Abraham to leave that place and go to the land where he would send him. Jacob could not help himself: he was a Hebrew, one of those who had "crossed over" and had achieved a new forensic status before God as the Chosen People.

The chosen status was not, however, some amorphous thing that had no real substance. It was a status preconditioned on a name and a land. The name was Sons of Abraham; the land was Canaan, the systematic and continuous promise of God to Abraham and his descendants forever. For this reason, Jacob knew that he would have to leave Haran as his grandfather had done and journey to the land promised by God to the Chosen People. There was an unquenchable yearning in Jacob's heart to return to his own family, a yearning that was tempered with the fear of fraternal retribution that could mean his own death. But, he was driven, so on he went. The problem was that when he would reach that land, he would again encounter his brother Esau who had been intent upon

---

[133] Genesis 28:18.
[134] Genesis 29:18.
[135] Genesis 29:27–28.

killing him. So, Jacob faced the continuing challenge that had been established for all human beings: life or death, blessings or curses. Which would he receive?

An Unexpected Encounter

When Jacob reached the ford of the Brook Jabbok, he knew things would never be the same. He might well die at his brother's hand, but he had to pursue the inheritance that God had promised him. Being a thoughtful and calculating businessman, he made as many preparations for possible contingencies that might arise as he plunged into the unknown, unsure of his brother's intentions. He even sent his family and offerings from his fortune ahead of him in hopes that if Esau were still in an evil mood, he would accept the gestures and spare his life. Despite the circumstances, whether it was for life or for death, Jacob simply had to move forward. For Jacob, Jabbok was a place of surrender, a place for saying to God as Jesus did generations later, "Not my will, but your will be done."[136] Jacob was a third-generation participant in a divine vision that had consumed the lives of his father and grandfather. He had heard all the promises, seen all the struggles, and even shared in the dream at Bethel; however, he desperately needed first-hand evidence—a face-to-face encounter with God that would confirm the fact that he was far more than a supplanter, that he was, indeed, the one whom God had elected to lead the Chosen People.

Finally, at Jabbok, Jacob faced the same decision his grandfather Abraham had faced. He had to cross over, and crossing over was precisely what it meant to be a Hebrew. He had to leave comforts behind and take on a new and life-threatening challenge. But before he could journey on, he would have to engage in a night of agony, struggling within himself and against doubts and fears, grappling with himself and with God's direction for his life. Jacob engaged in the action that produced his new name and the name of all his descendants. He became a *God-wrestler*. The power of this event is expressed poignantly in the alliterative Hebrew of the narrative: God wrestled (יֵאָבֵק—*ye'abek*) with Jacob (יַעֲקֹב—*Ya'akov*) at Jabbok (יַבֹּק—*Yabbok*).

All night long, the struggle continued. Did Jacob wrestle with a man, with an angel, with God? Jacob was never told who his antagonist was. He had to decide. Jacob and God joined together to wrestle against Jacob. Jacob struggled with an unknown man.[137] Jacob grappled with an angel, the angel

---

[136] Luke 22:42.
[137] Genesis 32:24.

of the Lord.[138] And when it was all over, Jacob realized that his protagonist was actually God himself.[139] As morning began to dawn, Jacob threatened the one with whom he had locked horns: "I won't let you go until you bless me."[140] And, bless him God did; however, he did so with a significant provision: Jacob's hip was dislocated so that afterward he walked with a limp which served as a humbling device to help him keep everything in proper perspective and constantly remind him of his encounter with the Divine.

Finally, God gave Jacob a new name: *Yisrael*, meaning, "God-wrestler," "I contend with God," or "I prevail with God." The Hebrew word יִשְׂרָאֵל — *Yisrael* (Israel) is a combination of the verbal root לִשְׂרוֹת — *lisrot* ("struggle" or "wrestle") and אֵל — *El* (God). Taken together, the name simply means "God-wrestler."[141] God's new name for Jacob stuck, not only for Jacob but also for all of his progeny in generation after generation of God-wrestlers! It remained not only as the man's name but as the name of the people and the nation that came from him. They were all Yisraelites. The Chosen People were to be a God-wrestling people,[142] a God-prevailing people, a people who were not content with anything less than the blessing of God and the opportunity to serve, albeit often with the limitations of handicaps that have been sometimes similar to Jacob's dislocated hip.

Blessing Emerging in Covenant

When dawn came, Jacob's wrestling partner vanished into thin air. No longer present, God was still not absent, for the blessing and the name that he had left behind were powerful elements that would prevail not only in Jacob's life but also in the lives of his descendants for millennia to come. Jacob was utterly astounded when his mind grasped the full significance of his night of struggle. He had seen God face-to-face and had prevailed with him. And, he was still alive! Impossible? Yes! But it was true. As a memorial to this

---

138 Hosea 12:4.
139 Genesis 32:30.
140 Genesis 32:26.
141 Steven E. Steinbock, *Torah: The Growing Gift* (New York: Union for Reform Judaism Books, 1993), p. 45. Most Christians understand that the name *Israel* means "the Prince of God"; however, this is only a secondary meaning for the name. The primary meaning is "God-wrestler" or "God wrestles."
142 Michael Lodahl, *Claiming Abraham: Reading the Bible and the Qur'an Side by Side* (Grand Rapids, MI: Baker Books, 2010), p. 31. Lodahl notes what has long been believed by the Jewish people: "If Israel is a wrestler with God, then it is not surprising that rabbinic Judaism developed self-consciously as a wrestling with holy texts, and a wrestling with one another over how to interpret and live by those texts." Lodahl contrasts Judaism with Islam: "Israel means . . . 'God-wrestler.' Islam means 'submission.' Therein may lie great differences."

death-defying struggle and the profound new life that had emerged from the contest, Jacob named the place of the contest, "Peniel," meaning, "I have seen God face-to-face, and my life is preserved," or "I have encountered God, and I live." Perhaps the word *Peniel* was a synopsis of a simple, yet utterly suprarational truth: those who see God face-to-face[143] are the only ones who are truly alive! "Jacob had feared to see Esau's face, but instead saw God *face-to-face and lived.*"[144] Only then could he march forth with the total confidence that he needed in order to achieve the destiny that God had planned for him.

"Jacob's life is changed. Hereafter, physically he literally limps; and the post-Peniel Jacob is a much more subdued and cautious person,"[145] says David Zucker. The legacy of Jacob's experience of life emerging from the clutches of death continued on in the children of this *Yisrael*, this God-wrestler. "The community of Israel, as descendants of this god-wrestler, is depicted as a group that successfully strives with God and humans."[146] It is no wonder that "in the Bible, Israel is the chief name for God's people. By definition, to belong to God is to be a 'God-wrestler'!"[147] To be an Israelite is to be a contender with God to receive a blessing and to be a blessing.[148] The legacy of Jacob's experience of life emerging from the clutches of death continued on in the children of this *Yisrael*, this God-wrestler. "The community of Israel, as descendants of this god-wrestler, is depicted as a group that successfully strives with God and humans."[149] It is no wonder that "in the Bible, Israel is the chief name for God's people. By definition, to belong to God is to be a 'God-wrestler'!"[150] To be an Israelite is to be a contender with God to receive a blessing and to be a blessing. "Our birthright as Jews is to be God-wrestlers; that is who we are,"[151] says Ron Wolfson. "Wrestling, asking, wondering, searching is just what God wants us to do!" says Edward Feinstein.[152]

---

[143] Only six places in the *Tanakh* do we find God encountering humanity "face-to-face": Genesis 32:30; Exodus 24:9–11; 33:11; Deuteronomy 34:10; Judges 6:22; Ezekiel 20:35.

[144] Michael Coogan, Marc Zvi Brettler, Carol Ann Newsom, and Pheme Perkins, eds., *The New Oxford Annotated Bible* (New York: Oxford University Press, 2001), p. 57.

[145] David J. Zucker, *The Torah: An Introduction for Christians and Jews* (Mahwah, NJ: Paulist Press, 2005), p. 47.

[146] Coogan, p. 57.

[147] Ben Patterson, *Waiting: Finding Hope When God Seems Silent* (Downers Grove, IL: InterVarsity Press, 1989), p. 143.

[148] Zucker, p. 47.

[149] Coogan, p. 57.

[150] Ben Patterson, p. 143.

[151] Ron Wolfson, *Relational Judaism: Using the Power of Relationships to Transform the Jewish Community* (Woodstock, VT: Jewish Lights Publishing, 2013), p. 49.

[152] Edward Feinstein, *Tough Questions Jews Ask: A Young Adult's Guide to Building a Jewish Life* (Woodstock, VT: Jewish Lights Publishing, 2012), p. 4.

When Jews engage in acts of worship, they do so as "God wrestlers too, struggling to strengthen and deepen their spirituality through prayer and praying."[153]

Women of Struggle, Endurance, and Faith

The three patriarchs of the Chosen People, Abraham, Isaac, and Jacob, were matched by equally spiritual and insightful matriarchs, Sarah, Rebekah, and Rachel/Leah, all of whom are "revered as the mothers of the Jewish people."[154] Sarah's prophetic insight was legendary, perhaps so much that the sages even saw her name in the name *Israel* that is the proper appellative for the people, the nation, and the land of the Chosen People.[155] Against all odds, Sarah brought forth the son of promise as proof that God's covenantal commitment was certain. Rebekah was endued with an uncompromisable commitment to what her prophetic gift revealed to her, a commitment that ensured the transmission of the divine election to the third generation of the Chosen People.

While the inclusion of Leah in the family of Jacob was the result of deception on her father Laban's part—in an action in which the trickster was himself tricked—she was used along with Rachel in God's master plan for the rapid expansion of the Abrahamic family and its faith. Indeed, the blessing that was pronounced generations later when the Gentile Ruth became a convert to the Israelite faith was this: "May the LORD make the woman who is coming into your home [Ruth] like Rachel and Leah, both of whom built the house of Israel."[156] Jacob's twelve sons, the heads of the twelve tribes of Israel, were birthed by Rachel, Leah, and her concubines. Rachel had the faith to believe that she would be delivered from her childless state (as was Sarah before her) and that she would bear children to fulfill the promise. Her firstborn son, Joseph, became the heir of the spiritual legacy of Abraham, Isaac, and Jacob

---

[153] Roberta Louis Goodman, Sherry H. Blumberg, eds., *Teaching About God and Spirituality: A Resource for Jewish Settings* (Denver, CO: A.R.E. Publishing, 2002), p. 200.

[154] Phyllis G. Jestice, *Holy People of the World: A Cross-Cultural Encyclopedia* (Santa Barbara, CA: ABC-CLIO, Inc., 2004), vol. 1, p. 562.

[155] In the middle of the name that God gave to Jacob and his descendants, יִשְׂרָאֵל (Yisrael), is the name of the first matriarch of the chosen family, שָׂרַי (Sarai). Jacob Lauterbach notes, "The element 'sarah' is identical with a part of the name 'Israel,' and 'Sarah' and 'Sarai' are appropriate names for Israel's mother." See Jacob Zallel Lauterbach, "Sarah—In Rabbinical Literature," in *The Jewish Encyclopedia*, Isidore Singer, Cyrus Adler, et. al, eds. (New York: Funk and Wagnalls Co., 1907), vol. 11, p. 56.

[156] Ruth 4:11. It is interesting that the names of Sarah and Rebekah were not mentioned in the blessing concerning Ruth. Ultimately, the blessing pronounced over Jewish girls was codified as, "May God make you like Sarah, Rebekah, Rachel, and Leah," even though this form did not appear in the *Tanakh* as did the blessing spoken over Jewish boys, "May God make you like Ephraim and Manasseh" (Genesis 48:20).

and was mightily used of God to preserve the lives of his family and their future progeny by means of his deep prophetic insight. Leah, likewise, was a woman of faith. In fact, "the names Leah chose [for her sons] revealed her piety and sense of obligation to the Lord," says Herbert Lockyer.[157] It was from the lineage of Leah's son Judah that King David and the Messiah were born.

All of the matriarchs of the Hebrews, then, were women of great faith and faithfulness, qualities that paralleled their husbands. They, too, chose to believe God and to observe his commandments and instructions. In so doing, they contributed immeasurably to the worldview, mindset, and ethos that set the Chosen People apart from the rest of the people groups around them and made it possible for God's covenant of peoplehood, nationhood, and land could and would be fulfilled in due time and within the family that God had chosen.

RETURNING TO THE SOURCES
Principles of Living Faith for Israel Today

God himself gave this prophetic instruction to all the future Israelites, including those who are living today: "Look to the rock from which you were hewn. . . . Look to Abraham your father and to Sarah who gave birth to you in pain."[158] According to biblical tradition, in order to know how to live in the present and to move into the future, one must be able to look back. As a matter of fact, there is no reasonable means of navigating from the present into the future without a clear working knowledge of the past. As Emil Brunner has so eloquently observed, the future "is from the outset bound up with history. For it is in history that this self-communication and apprehension takes place. God's coming to us is the theme of revelation history and saving history. Only within this history can the eternity be known which God communicates."[159] Antje Jackelén rightly says, "Yahweh is the God of Israel's history who becomes the God of world history."[160] The prophets and sages of Israel, therefore, "had the task of telling the people the meaning of the particular time in which they lived

---

[157] Herbert Lockyer, *All the Women of the Bible* (Grand Rapids, MI: Zondervan Publishing Co. 1967), p. 83. Leah named her sons Reuben ("Behold a Son"), Simeon ("Hearing"), Levi ("Joined") Judah ("Praise"), Issachar ("Reward"), and Zebulun ("From the Dwelling Place"). Her daughter was named Dinah ("Revenged").
[158] Isaiah 51:1–2.
[159] Emil Brunner, *Dogmatics III: Christian Doctrine of the Church, Faith & the Consummation* (London, UK: James Clark & Co., 2002), p. 376.
[160] Antje Jackelén, *Time & Eternity: The Question of Time in Church, Science and Theology*, tr. Barbara Harshaw (West Conshohocken, PA: Templeton Foundation Press, 2005), p. 66.

in view of a new divine act which was about to take place,"[161] and they did so by reviewing the acts of God in the past. "The nature of the present time was felt to be determined either by the saving acts of God in the past . . . or by the saving fact of God in the future."[162]

This is why both the God of revelation and the revelation of God are essential to human beings. Without God and divine revelation, as Isaac Rottenberg has observed, "One may find divine power in the spirits that inhabit the universe . . . one may believe in a nameless numinous power, a nebulous *mysterium tremendum* . . . or . . . find God in one's own ego as part of the divine 'All.'"[163] The God of Scripture, however, "does not invite us to . . . philosophize about divine being, but rather to recognize God as *being there*, present as the Holy One in our midst, involved in historical existence."[164] Jürgen Moltmann wisely concluded that "the more the covenant is taken seriously as the revelation of God, the more profoundly one can understand the historicity of God and the history in God."[165] Without a clear and accurate perception of the past, understanding the present or the future is impossible. "For the Jews the one and only basis for the continuity of events was God. It was God who ordained the times . . . the events of history were acts of God, and their sequence depended upon the free will of God."[166] With this perspective in mind, the future is secure because it rests in the province of God who is utterly dependable.

Looking Back in Order to Look Forward

While most cultures occupied their time with trying to discern the future, the Hebraic culture was content to observe the past for lessons about how to live in the present while trusting the future to the God whose name means, "I will be there."[167] The only reliable information that is available to anyone is obtained by observing the past as one moves through the present into the future. Winston Churchill aptly said, "The longer you can look back, the farther you can look

[161] Albert Nolan, *Jesus Before Christianity* (Maryknoll, NY: Orbis Books, 1978), p. 91.

[162] Nolan, p. 91.

[163] Isaac C. Rottenberg, *Judaism, Christianity, Paganism: A Judeo-Christian Worldview and Its Cultural Implications* (Atlanta, GA: Hebraic Heritage Press, 2007), p. 160.

[164] Rottenberg, p. 160.

[165] Jürgen Moltmann, *The Crucified God,* tr. R. A. Wilson and John Bowden (New York: Harper & Row, 1974), p. 271.

[166] Nolan, p. 76.

[167] "I will be there" is one of the possible translations of אֶהְיֶה אֲשֶׁר אֶהְיֶה (*ehyeh asher ehyeh*) though it is usually rendered in most translations of Exodus 3:14 as "I AM THAT I AM" or "I AM WHO I AM."

forward."[168] Indeed, without the past, there is no future. This understanding is confirmed by Solomon's dictum, "There is nothing new under the sun,"[169] which was based on his observation that "whatever is has already been, and what will be has been done before; for God will seek to do again what has occurred in the past."[170] The divine principles on which God works never change, and divine immutability rests upon God's sovereign faithfulness.

This is why it was always important to the Israelite people and their nation to have leaders and seers who "understood the time, with knowledge of what Israel should do."[171] God saw to it that he had such servants at his disposal, for the axiom of revealed truth has always remained the same: "Surely the LORD God does nothing unless he reveals his secret counsel to his servants the prophets."[172] And the means for understanding God's design for the present and for the future was eloquently summed up in perhaps the most ancient of all treatises in the corpus of Holy Scripture: "Please inquire of past generations, and consider the things searched out by their fathers. (For we are only of yesterday) . . . Will they not teach you and tell you, and bring forth words from their minds?"[173]

True biblical understanding of humanity's destiny, therefore, "has its origin in paradise," and from that origin—and only in the context of that origin—"flows into the fullness of the *plêrôma* of the Kingdom, into the mystery of the final *apocatastasis*, the recapitulation of all things in heaven and earth in Christ."[174] James Barlow confirmed and expanded upon this important truth in this manner: "Without the concept of God as the Lord of history, the Jews would have had no sense of history at all and no inkling of a great and glorious destiny. Conversely, without this concept of history the God of the Jews would have been no different from the gods of other nations."[175] The absolute certainty and security of the

---

[168] Winston Churchill, quoted in Richard Langworth, *Churchill by Himself: The Definitive Collection of Quotations* (London, UK: Ebury Press, 2008), p. 576.
[169] Ecclesiastes 1:9.
[170] Ecclesiastes 3:15, NET.
[171] 1 Chronicles 12:32.
[172] Amos 3:7.
[173] Job 8:8–10. Many scholars agree that the Book of Job is perhaps the oldest manuscript that came to be included in the canon of Holy Scripture (even though the Book of Genesis describes events older than those in Job), and some suggest that it may be the oldest book in the world. See John Kitto, *The Pictorial Bible: Judges–Job* (London, England: W. and R. Chambers, 1855), p. 613, and Larry Witham, *The God Biographers: Our Changing Image of God from Job to the Present* (Lanham, MD: Rowman & Littlefield Publishers, 2010), p. 185. *The New Pilgrim Bible* suggests that it was probably written before 1500 BC, a fact that is underscored by its lack of mention of any of the laws of the Torah. See *The New Pilgrim Bible* (New York: Oxford University Press, 2003), p. 736.
[174] Paul Evdokimov, *Woman and the Salvation of the World,* tr. Anthony P. Gythiel (Crestwood, NY: St. Vladimir's Seminary Press, 1994), p. 38.
[175] James C. Barlow, *God and Eternity* (Indianapolis, IN: Dog Ear Publishing, 2008), p. 37.

future of the Chosen People—as a people, as a nation, and as a land—were determined irrevocably and eternally in the covenant that God made and reiterated to the patriarchs of the Hebrew/Israelite/Jewish faith community, Abraham, Isaac, and Jacob. The patriarchs and matriarchs of the Jewish people set the example of faith and faithfulness in hearing God's voice, believing what he said, and acting on their faith. Application of this mindset has continued unabated for decade after decade, century after century, millennium after millennium.

The sages established the doctrine of *Zekhut Avot* and *Zekhut Imahot*[176] in which they maintained that "God visits the virtues of the fathers upon the children for His name's sake and as a mark of grace; but it would appear, on the other hand, that the principle applies only when the children continue the piety of their parents. . . . If the covenant is still kept with descendants, though they be unworthy, this is the result of God's grace."[177] This concept is based on Torah declarations such as this: "The LORD! the LORD! a God compassionate and gracious, slow to anger, abounding in kindness and faithfulness, extending kindness unto the thousandth generation, forgiving iniquity, transgression, and sin."[178] The idea expressed in the concept of *Zekhut Avot* is that "if the children are also God-fearing, their reward is enhanced because of the added merit of their parents."[179] The Apostle Paul appealed to *Zekhut Avot* when he said that in terms of divine election, the Israelites who appeared to be enemies of the first-century Messianic community were actually "beloved for the sake of the fathers." This principle was foundational to the apostle's argument that because "the gifts and calling of God are irrevocable," it is certain that "all Israel will be saved."[180] He knew that Jeremiah

---

176 The Hebrew *Zekhut Avot* and *Zekhut Imahot* mean "Merit of the Patriarchs" and "Merit of the Matriarchs" respectively.

177 Isadore Singer, Cyrus Adler, *et. al.*, eds. *The Jewish Encyclopedia: A Descriptive Record of the History, Religion, Literature, and Customs of the Jewish People from the Earliest Times to the Present Day* (New York: Funk and Wagnalls Co., 1907), vol. 12, p. 441.

178 Exodus 34:6–7, TNK.

179 Abraham P. Bloch, *The Biblical and Historical Background of Jewish Customs and Ceremonies* (Jersey City, NJ: KTAV Publishing House, 1980), p. 253.

180 Romans 11:26–29. The apostle did not even hint that Israel's election had been terminated. Instead, he concluded that all Israel would be saved when the Redeemer of whom Isaiah 59:20 had prophesied would turn away ungodliness from Jacob (Romans 11:16). Paul was even more magnanimous than many of his fellow Pharisees who argued that those who "say there is no resurrection of the dead," those who "say the Torah is not from heaven," and "the Epicureans" will "have no share in the world to come" (Babylonian Talmud, *Sanhedrin* XI). Paul's argument here was also consistent and in context with Romans 9:27 where he quoted Isaiah 10:22: "Though the people of Israel are as numerous as the sand of the seashore, a remnant will return," confirming his belief in one of the forms of Remnant Theology that were then current in some sects of Judaism. See Mark Adam Elliott, *The Survivors of Israel: A Reconsideration of the Theology of Pre-Christian Judaism* (Grand Rapids, MI: Wm. B. Eerdmans Publishing Co., 2000), pp. 47–56.

was right when he exclaimed: "Because of the LORD's great love we are not con-sumed, for his compassions never fail. They are new every morning; great is your faithfulness."[181] Indeed, "God's faithfulness" extends "to all generations,"[182] and "his mercy is for those who fear him from generation to generation."[183]

The foundation of the Chosen People was laid on Abraham, Isaac, and Jacob. Each of the three patriarchs of the biblical faith encountered God in life-and-death faith struggles, and each of them prevailed through faith and faithfulness to their call. J. H. Hertz described the very nature of the Chosen People in this manner: "Israelites are champions of God, contenders for the divine, conquering by strength from above."[184] In surviving face-to-face en-counters with God, they experienced what every believer in the God of Israel can achieve. Gordon Wenham's comparison of Hebrew and non-Hebrew tra-ditions of piety is profoundly revealing: "In modern thought, piety is often associated with weakness, prudishness, effeminacy, passivity, social seclu-sion, and abandonment of the world. In the patriarchal narratives, however, piety is often associated with those, like Jacob, who are courageous, strong, possessing dogged persistence, and having physical and mental toughness."[185] This is why "all generations of Jews are taught—indeed, each individual Jew is taught—to struggle personally to know God 'face to face' (intimately) and to come closer to him through asking the most personal of questions."[186] *Yisrael* means, "he who wrestles with God"; however, in reality, it is "God who fights [wrestles] tirelessly and unceasingly on Israel's behalf."[187]

The genealogical connection of Israel to the founding fathers and mothers of their people and their nation is a connection with the very wellspring of their faith through which their faithfulness can constantly be reinforced by the terms of God's covenant faithfulness to them. By remaining faithful to the vi-sion of faith and justice to which their founding patriarchs and matriarchs were committed, they can achieve the fullness of what God has designed for them and promised to them. The eternal blessing that YHWH has spoken over the children of Israel is irrevocable. So it is written; so shall it be!

---

181 Lamentations 3:22–23.
182 Psalm 100:5; 119:90.
183 Luke 1:50, ESV.
184 J. H. Hertz, ed., *The Pentateuch and Haftorahs* (London: Soncino Press, 1975), p. 124.
185 See Gordon J. Wenham, *Story as Torah: Reading Old Testament Narrative Ethically* (Grand Rapids, MI: Baker Academic, 2000), p. 90, noted in Wilson, *Exploring*, p. 230.
186 Wilson, *Exploring*, p. 233.
187 LaHaye and Hindson, p. 21.

CHAPTER 8

ESTABLISHING A NATION

FROM SLAVERY IN EGYPT TO FREEDOM AT SINAI

Jacob and his family lived for years in the land of Canaan where they prospered and became a large nuclear and extended family unit. Jacob had twelve sons, who would become the progenitors of the twelve tribes of Israel. These *"b'nai Yisrael"* ("sons of Israel") were a unique group with diverse gifts and callings in God.[1] Despite their frequent failings, as a group they maintained the faith of Father Abraham. Led by the now fearless and utterly faithful Jacob-Israel, they marched confidently across the pages of sacred history as God prepared to fulfill, through them, the promises that he had made to Abraham regarding the creation of a Chosen People, a chosen nation, and the inheritance of the Promised Land. Following the course of history that God had planned for the Chosen People and had predicted to Abraham, Jacob led the chosen family into Egypt in order to ensure their survival during a time of widespread famine. God himself had prepared the way and guaranteed very early on the fulfillment of the much later dictum: *Am Yisrael chai!* In his foreknowledge, the Almighty had orchestrated the positioning of the heir to Jacob's spiritual heritage, the patriarch's son Joseph, as the prime minister of Egypt, second only in authority to Pharaoh himself.

From the Pit to the Palace

Joseph was the firstborn son of Rachel, the wife whom Jacob loved. Of all of Jacob's children, Joseph was his favorite. He was, therefore, born to privilege and developed his young life under the watchful eyes of a doting father and mother. Beyond that, Joseph was a very special, godly child, one who doubtless received the transfer of family spiritual authority from his

---

[1] Genesis 49:1–48.

father as the family developed. He was a young man of vision, one with whom God communicated unique insight through dreams and visions. In spite of the love and respect that Jacob's sons had for their father, jealousy arose in their hearts when they observed what they considered to be their brother's gratuitous antics. It certainly did not help that their father had made an "ornate robe" for Joseph and that he clearly loved him more than any of his brothers. Something was happening that far transcended mere illusions of grandeur in the hyperactive imagination of one young Israelite boy. God was at work! The stage was being set for events that would change the course of history and would bring salvation to the household of Jacob, the Israelite family.

In time, Joseph's brothers had had enough, so they plotted against Joseph, intending to kill him; however, they decided at the last minute to spare his life and, instead, to sell him into slavery to a band of Ishmaelites, who then eventually resold him in Egypt. In the process, Joseph was guided by God's hand from a pit in the wilderness to the palace of Pharaoh. In Egypt, God used Joseph's gift for insight into the meaning of dreams to bring him to the attention of the sovereign whose own dreams had troubled him. "God has shown Pharaoh what he is about to do,"[2] Joseph boldly declared when he was brought from an Egyptian prison to Pharaoh's palace. The young heir to Jacob's anointing and Abraham's promise detailed what the future held for the Egyptian dynasty: "Seven years of great abundance are coming throughout the land of Egypt, but seven years of famine will follow them. . . . [T]he famine will ravage the land."[3]

Then, the young Israelite who had been an inmate of Pharaoh's prison gave the sovereign this advice: "Now let Pharaoh look for a discerning and wise man and put him in charge of the land of Egypt." Then, Joseph outlined a plan for saving the land from the impending famine. Pharaoh's reaction was swift and sagacious: "Can we find anyone like [Joseph], one in whom is the spirit of God?"[4] He immediately elevated Joseph to the position of second in command in all of Egypt and commissioned him with full authority to execute his plan for the salvation of the land and its people. From this position of power and influence, Joseph was able to orchestrate the program that would save the lives of all the people in the Egyptian nation and its vassal states from almost certain starvation.

---

2 Genesis 41:28, NIV.
3 Genesis 41:30, NIV.
4 Genesis 41:38, NIV.

The real reason for Joseph's circuitous journey from the pit to the palace became very apparent to Joseph when his father sent his brothers to Egypt to purchase grain, all the while never suspecting that they were negotiating with the brother whom they had betrayed. God's amazing *chesed* was at work, however, for when they arrived in Egypt, Joseph knew precisely why they were there, and the picture of his own success came into perfect focus. God had positioned him in Egypt for the deliverance of his family. True, God would save perhaps millions of Egyptians and other even more pagan peoples in the process, but the real divine objective was Jacob, his eleven sons, and their families, a small total of only seventy Israelites.[5] Joseph finally understood what God had been doing in his life with the circuitous journey that had brought him to Pharaoh's palace. "You," he told his brothers, "meant evil against me, but God meant it for good in order to bring about this present result, to preserve many people alive."[6] This event fulfilled what God had predicted to Abraham, "Know for certain that your descendants will be strangers in a land that is not theirs."

From Slavery to Freedom

The deliverance of the Israelites from the famine, however, also set the stage for the fulfillment of the remainder of God's prediction to Abraham concerning his descendants: "They will be enslaved and oppressed four hundred years."[7] But, how could such a thing happen in a place where Joseph and his family were honored guests? The answer was simple: "A new king to whom Joseph meant nothing came to power in Egypt."[8] *Sic transit gloria mundi!*[9] The Israelites, who had been honored guests in the land, became an easy target to be exploited for slave labor. The pharaonic court feared the Israelites because of their growing numbers, so they forced them into slavery and placed them under harsh taskmasters, just as God had warned Abraham. In time, however, God heard the cries of the beleaguered Israelites and sent Moses to deliver them from their slavery. God had ordained that the deliverer whom he had chosen from among the Israelites would become the adopted son of Pharaoh's daughter and that he

---

[5] Deuteronomy 10:22.
[6] Genesis 50:20.
[7] Genesis 15:13.
[8] Exodus 1:8, NIV.
[9] The Latin dictum means, "Thus passes the glory of the world." As history so readily confirms, the whims of power—and those who wield it—are unpredictable and transient.

would be reared in Pharaoh's house in power and privilege. Again the hand of divine providence moved in mysterious ways just as it had in the life of Joseph.

Knowing that he was an Israelite, Moses could not countenance the abuse of his Israelite family, so he finally took matters into his own hand and killed one of the brutal taskmasters who was abusing one of his people. Now, the once proud prince of Egypt found himself fleeing to the backside of the desert and tending his father-in-law's sheep just managing to eke out a meager existence from day to day. He had come to his own personal proving ground. It had taken only one day for Moses to get out of Egypt, but it would take God forty years to get Egypt out of Moses! In the desert, God molded Moses into the vessel of honor that he had always desired and then released him into his divine destiny. Finally, when he was eighty, Moses heard God's voice calling to him from the burning bush, "Moses, Moses!" When he turned aside to investigate, he listened further to the divine, fiery voice commissioning him with the immortal words that resounded in the court of Pharaoh and have echoed across the corridors of time: "Tell Pharaoh, Let my people go!"[10]

When Moses obeyed the newly revealed YHWH's instructions, an unfolding drama pitted the God of Israel against the gods Egypt, the prophet of Israel against the Pharaoh of Egypt. It was a contest with an inevitable conclusion. After the last of ten plagues had been hurled forth against the gods of Egypt and against Pharaoh himself, the arrogant and vicious potentate was finally humbled to the point of relenting, submitting his ever-hardened heart to the will of God. The violence that Pharaoh had exacted eighty years earlier on the Israelites[11] was revisited upon the Egyptians when the firstborn of every household was destroyed by the hand of God himself.[12] The Israelites, however, escaped the plague by following God's instructions to the letter: killing a lamb at the threshold of the door of their houses and applying the lamb's blood to the doorposts and lintels so that the door was encircled with blood.[13] While the Egyptians wailed in a night of terror, the Israelites worshipped their God by eating the roasted lamb, the bitter herbs, and the *matzah*, the unleavened bread of haste.[14]

---

[10] Exodus 7:16.
[11] Exodus 1:22.
[12] Exodus 12:12, 23.
[13] Exodus 12:7.
[14] Exodus 12:8.

The next day after the Passover, the Israelites were bound for the Promised Land. Another miracle awaited them at the Red Sea, where, facing the dilemma of an impassable body of water before them and Pharaoh's armies behind them, they heard God's command, "Move on!" Immediately, they began to march through the sea that had been walled up by a strong east wind. Every single individual Israelite rose up in faith to walk with God through the swirling waters that threatened them with certain death and continued walking into the new life that awaited them on the other side of the sea. Pharaoh's entire army rushed after them only to drown in the same place where Israel had just crossed unharmed. The same walled-up waters that had retreated in order to clear a path to life and freedom for the Israelites suddenly rushed in upon the Egyptians and swallowed them up in death and destruction![15]

The People and the Birth of the Nation

Less than fifty days later, some two million Israelites gathered at the mountain of the Lord where they expected to meet with the same God who had spoken with Moses from the burning bush. The profound sight was far greater than their expectation, for Sinai was ablaze with the Divine Presence and was quaking with violent tremors. God himself descended on the mountain with a shocking demonstration that confirmed the identity with which they had known him: *El Shaddai* (the Almighty). Then, he proceeded to introduce himself to the Israelites by disclosing to them his personal name with this declaration: "I am YHWH your God, who brought you out of the land of Egypt, out of the house of slavery."[16]

Then the one who would be Israel's personal God outlined the terms of his covenant with his people in the fiery, concise words of the Ten Commandments.[17] These tongues of fire that issued forth from the

---

[15] If the critics who have sought to demythologize this biblical story just happen to be right in saying that the Israelites actually crossed a marshy expanse of land, then an even greater miracle than what is recorded in Scripture occurred, for an entire army, including the cavalry, drowned in less than six inches of water. As a point of fact, it is absolutely impossible to drown horses in six inches of water! See Glen A. Fritz, *The Lost Sea of the Exodus: A Modern Geographical Analysis*, Ph.D. Dissertation Texas State University, 2006, p. 61. Fritz reports the case of nineteenth-century Egyptologist Heinrich Brugsch who argued that the Israelites crossed on "a narrow sandbar lying between the Mediterranean Sea and Lake Sirbonis" and then ingeniously ascribed the destruction of the Egyptian army to "a great wave that took by surprise the Egyptian cavalry."

[16] Exodus 20:2.

[17] Exodus 20:2–17. In reality, the declaration, "I am the LORD your God, who brought you out of the land of Egypt, out of the house of slavery" was the first of the Ten Words (Commandments).

mouth of God were so dynamic that the Israelites not only heard the words but also saw them. The text literally says, "And all the people *saw* the voices and the flames."[18] Then, after Israel had heard all the terms of the covenant, they responded to God with one voice: "All that the LORD has said, we will do, and we will understand."[19] In effect, the people declared that they would simply do whatever God commanded them even before they were able to understand what he had said and why he had said it.

In that one day, the Day of *Shavuot* (Pentecost) at Mt. Sinai, God fulfilled his pre-Passover promise to the Israelite family: "I will take you for my people, and I will be your God."[20] When the Israelites agreed to accept God's instructions, their legitimacy as a people was fully established because they became the people of God. Indeed, God himself made the declaration of their legitimacy: "Be silent and listen, O Israel! This day you have become the people of the LORD your God."[21] God established forever the divine legitimacy of their peoplehood: "I will maintain my covenant with you. . . . I will walk among you, and will be your God, and you shall be my people."[22] In fact, he made the particularity of his election even more explicit: "You shall be my own possession among all of the peoples."[23] The peoplehood of Israel could never be delegitimized.

On the day of *Shavuot*, the Israelite people also became the Israelite nation, a nation born in one day as it were. This was a staggering event that the prophet Isaiah declared would again be repeated at the time when the dispersed of Israel would be regathered into their own land: "Can a nation be brought forth in a single day? For as soon as Zion travailed, she also brought forth her sons."[24] It was clear then—and it is clear now—that "at Sinai Israel as a nation became the Lord's people through an extension of the covenant made with Abraham and the patriarchs."[25] As David Dockery notes, "Israel was a 'holy nation,' that is, a nation set apart to be God's special people. . . . Israel became God's vassal,

---

18 Exodus 20:18.
19 Exodus 24:7.
20 Exodus 6:7.
21 Deuteronomy 27:9.
22 Leviticus 26:9, 12.
23 Exodus 19:5.
24 Isaiah 66:8.
25 Arthur F. Glasser, Charles E. Van Engen, Dean S. Gilland, and Shawn B. Redford, *Announcing the Kingdom: The Story of God's Mission in the Bible* (Grand Rapids, MI: Baker Academic, 2003), p. 80.

the mediator of His saving grace to all the nations of the earth."[26] Joel Green rightly adds, "Israel was God's 'priestly kingdom and holy nation' whose obedience to Torah mediated the blessings of God to the whole of God's world."[27] No wonder King David exclaimed, "And what one nation on the earth is like your people Israel, whom God went to redeem for himself as a people and to make a name for himself."[28]

Sadly, the wilderness journeyings of the Chosen People, as well as their lives for centuries after the Exodus, were replete with examples of human failure. The most monumental example occurred while they were encamped at Sinai and in the process of receiving all of God's Torah. The people began to doubt that Moses would ever return from the mountain, so they began to chart a course for escaping the desert and returning to Egypt. The Golden Calf incident that followed has always been the greatest element of shame in Israelite history.[29] Though God was angered enough to destroy the people and the nation that he had just created, he was moved by Moses' prayer, "Please forgive their sin—and if not, please blot me out from your book which you have written."[30] Even in the face of this most disappointing failure of God's new bride, Moses interceded for the nation of Israel, and their sins were atoned.

The people whom God had summoned out of Egypt and had joined to himself in a covenant of incontrovertible commitment often came up short on their pledges of faithfulness to him. Despite human failure, God has always been, and will always be, faithful. As Jacob Neusner has said, "God has a heavy stake in Israel's well-being. He relates to Israel perpetually. Israel is a unique nation on earth, consecrated and separate from the nations of the earth and from their abominations."[31] When God's Chosen People

---

[26] David S. Dockery, ed., *Holman Concise Bible Commentary* (Nashville, TN: B&H Publishing Group, 2010), p. 38.

[27] Joel B. Green, Jacqueline Lapsley, Rebekah Miles, and Allen Verhey, eds., *Dictionary of Scripture and Ethics* (Grand Rapids, MI: Baker Academic, 2011), p. 789.

[28] 2 Samuel 7:23.

[29] This great failure, however, was not unique in human history. Paul Van Buren points out that "no sooner was the covenant of Creation established than Adam and Eve ate what was forbidden. . . . No sooner was the covenant of Creation renewed after the flood than we are told of Noah's drunkenness and shame, and then the disobedience of the men of Babel." Paul M. Van Buren, *A Theology of the Jewish-Christian Reality: A Christian Theology of the People of Israel* (Lanham, MD: University Press of America, 1995), part 2, p. 73.

[30] Exodus 32:32. The prayer of Moses is strikingly parallel with one that Paul prayed: "I have prayed that I myself might be accursed and cut off from Christ if this could benefit the brothers who are my own flesh and blood" (Romans 9:3, NJB).

[31] Jacob Neusner, *A Theological Commentary to the Midrash, Vol. 9: Mekhilta Attributed to Rabbi Ishmael* (Lanham, MD: University Press of America, 2001), pp. 224–225, alluding to *Mekhilta R. Ishmael* 48:I.20–21; 42: II.1; 43:I.2.

carry out his will "the nations have no power over them; when Israel sins, the nations are empowered. Sin, specifically abandoning the teachings of the Torah, causes the enemy to come against Israel. When Israel lacks merit of religious duties, then the enemy comes."[32] The God of Scripture, however, is the unchanging one, the one who cannot lie[33] and who cannot fail.[34] Though he has threatened divorce[35] and even destruction upon his Chosen People,[36] he has never abandoned them, and he never will.

At Sinai, the family of Abraham finally achieved the status that God had promised to the patriarch more than four centuries before. The Chosen People were transformed into God's "holy nation." The Torah which they unanimously accepted as the nation's constitution was the document that set them apart from all other nations and peoples. One *midrash* says that even God himself proclaimed this truth: "If it were not for my Torah which you accepted, I should not recognize you, and I should not regard you more than any of the idolatrous nations of the world."[37] So it was that the Torah became "the legal basis for the nation and for the Israelites' everlasting obligation to their God,"[38] says Niels Lemche. The Abrahamic covenant was "structured into a covenant between God and one nation."[39] The fundamentals of what God had promised Abraham were formalized and codified, confirmed by God and ratified by his Chosen People. The people Israel became the nation Israel, the kingdom of priests that was ready to fulfill its destiny to be "the mediator of [God's] saving grace to all the nations of the earth."[40]

---

[32] Neusner, pp. 224–225.

[33] Numbers 23:19; Titus 1:2.

[34] Isaiah 55:11; Romans 9:6–13.

[35] Isaiah 50:1; Jeremiah 3:8; Hosea 2:2–6.

[36] Deuteronomy 9:13–14. In Exodus 32:14, God's actions in this regard are summed up this way: "So the LORD changed his mind about the harm which he said he would do to his people."

[37] Exodus *Rabbah*, "Ki Tissa" 47:3.

[38] Niels Peter Lemche, *Prelude to Israel's Past: Background and Beginnings of Israelite History and Identity* (Peabody, MA: Hendrickson Publishers, Inc., 1998), p. 46.

[39] Vincent Martin, *A House Divided: The Parting of the Ways between Synagogue and Church* (Mahwah, NJ: Paulist Press, 1995), p. 79.

[40] Dockery, ed., p. 48.

CHAPTER 9

INHERITING THE LAND

FULFILLING THE PROMISE

The first—and perhaps the most important—of the promises that were part of God's covenant with Abraham was this unequivocal commitment: "Unto your descendants I will give this land."[1] John Walvoord underscores this truth: "An integral part of the original Abrahamic covenant was the promise of everlasting possession of the land. Specific boundaries given to Abraham (Gen. 15:18–21) indicate the extent of the promise."[2] Peter Walker agrees: "The divine promise of the land (an integral part of the covenant with Abraham) was explicitly stated to be 'forever' (Gen. 17:7–8). This cannot be revoked—neither by the passage of time, nor by the dawning of a "new covenant," nor by the disobedience of the descendants of Abraham. The Israelites would eventually go into exile . . . but they were 'restored' to the land—precisely because the gift of the land was itself unconditional."[3]

The land promise is so integral to the Abrahamic faith covenant that on each occasion when God declared his promises, along with the covenant that made them inviolable and the oath that made them incontrovertible, he immediately reiterated the land clause as tangible evidence of the concrete reality of his unilateral decree to Abraham and his descendants. Abraham, Isaac, and Jacob continually used the promise of land as an identifier of the God who had made covenant with them: 1) Abraham: "The LORD God of heaven . . . who

---

[1] Genesis 12:7; 15:7; 24:7; 26:3; 27:8.
[2] John F. Walvoord, *The Millennial Kingdom: A Basic Text in Premillennial Theology* (Grand Rapids, MI: Zondervan Publishing Co., 1959), p. 186.
[3] Peter Walker, "Summarizing the Points of Dispute," in *The Land Cries Out: Theology of the Land in the Israeli-Palestinian Context*, Salim J. Munayer and Lisa Loden, eds. (Eugene, OR: Wipf and Stock Publishers, 2011), p. 3.

swore to me, saying, 'To your descendants will I give this land,' he will send his angel before you, and you will take a wife for my son"[4]; 2) Isaac: "The LORD appeared unto [Isaac] and said, 'Sojourn in this land . . . and to your descendants I will give all these lands, and will establish the oath which I swore to your father Abraham'"[5]; and 3) Jacob: "God said to [Jacob], 'I am God Almighty. . . . The land which I gave to Abraham and Isaac, I will give it to you, and I will give the land to your descendants after you.'"[6]

This patriarchal understanding remained consistent with the Israelites through the centuries before and after they inherited the land of Israel. Even after the Babylonian exile, the prophets continued to reiterate the same promise. Isaiah predicted, "Then all your people will be righteous; they will possess the land forever."[7] Ezekiel prophesied, "I will take you from the nations, gather you from all the lands, and bring you into your own land."[8] Zechariah declared: "The LORD will possess Judah as his portion in the holy land and will again choose Jerusalem."[9] Even in post-prophetic Israel, the expectation remained the same: "The LORD certified for Abraham with a solemn pledge that he would . . . give them an inheritance from sea to sea and from the river to the end of the earth."[10] Centuries later, when the apostle Paul recounted the dealings of God with Abraham and his descendants, he declared that the Lord had "distributed their land as an inheritance"[11] to them.

After Abraham proved his willingness to sacrifice his son Isaac, God began to explain the unfolding of the land promise as he spoke his solemn oath: "By myself I have sworn . . . I will indeed bless you. . . . And your descendants shall possess the gate of their enemies."[12] The inheritance was to be distributed to Abraham's descendants as a land grant that would be the material evidence of the covenant's sovereign decree. Hebrews/Israelites, therefore, would "possess" the land by conquering it. Their conquering, however, was not to be simply by military might. The nation of Israel was never intended to be a marauding military juggernaut. It was a "kingdom of priests."[13] The Israelite nation was not

---

4 Genesis 24:7.
5 Genesis 26:3.
6 Genesis 35:11–12.
7 Isaiah 60:21.
8 Ezekiel 36:24–26.
9 Zechariah 2:12.
10 Sirach 44:21, CEB.
11 Acts 13:19. Here Paul uses the Greek κατακληροδοτέω (kataklerodotéo), "to distribute as an inheritance."
12 Genesis 22:16–18.
13 Exodus 19:6.

designed to conquer and rule: it was designed to bless. The possession of the Promised Land, therefore, was to be solely by the power of God's spoken Word.

YHWH made this clear to Moses, "I will drive them out before you little by little, until you become faithful and take possession of the land."[14] Before Moses made his final descent from Mt. Sinai with the tablets of the Torah in his hands, the Exodus prophet concluded his prayer for Israel with this petition: "Remember Abraham, Isaac, and Israel, your servants whom you swore by yourself, and said to them, 'I will multiply your descendants as the stars of the heavens, and all this land of which I have spoken I will give to your descendants, and they shall inherit it forever.'"[15] Forty years later, God repeated the same promise to Joshua: "Every place that the sole of your foot shall tread upon, that have I given you, as I said unto Moses."[16] This declaration, too, was but a reiteration of the promise that God had made to Abraham some five centuries earlier: "The LORD will drive out all these nations from before you, and you will dispossess nations greater and mightier than you. Every place on which the sole of your foot treads shall be yours; your border will be from the wilderness to Lebanon, and from the river, the river Euphrates, as far as the western sea."[17]

Possessing the Land

God, the people of Israel, and the land of Israel, therefore, "are tied one to another in an indissoluble unity."[18] While pointing out this undeniable reality, however, Michael Wyschogrod speaks to another important truth about the people, the nation, and the land of Israel: "The election and the covenant at Sinai were to occur before the nation obtained possession of the land that first belonged to others. Israel was thus not born in its land but, entering upon it in its adulthood, it was to live in an adopted even if divinely assigned land."[19] The fact that Israel was a people and a nation before it inherited a land is an astonishing historical anomaly: "Nowhere else in the memory of peoples is entry into a land remembered. A people is born out of a soil which is its mother. The people does

---

[14] Exodus 23:30.
[15] Exodus 32:13.
[16] Joshua 1:3.
[17] Deuteronomy 11:23–24.
[18] Michael Wyschogrod, *Abraham's Promise* (Grand Rapids, MI: Wm. B. Eerdmans Publishing Co., 2004), p. 92.
[19] Wyschogrod, p. 92.

not pre-date the land. It is the land which pre-dates the people. The land gives birth to a language and a people."[20] Wyschogrod concludes, therefore, that the God of Israel is "not a God of the earth. He is the God of a people that is brought into being in the interval between residence in one land which it is commanded to leave and settlement in another which is still in the future."[21] It is this quality that has made it possible for Israel to maintain its corporate identity as a people—the Chosen People—and as a nation in exile, even when scattered across the world in century upon century of ongoing diasporas. It would also make it possible for the people and nation of Israel to reclaim their land when the time came for restoration in their return from exile, first from Babylon and then from dispersion to north, south, east, and west.[22] Yitshak Korn says that it is also this quality that makes it possible for the land of Israel to be a homeland not only "for those living in its geographical boundaries, but also the property of the entire Jewish people, the heart of the scattered Hebrew nation.[23]

The Israelites/Jews are the only people and nation that has not been birthed by a land. They emerged as a people from the faith of one man, Abraham. More than four hundred years later, they were birthed as a nation by a sovereign act of God when he declared them to be a holy nation at Sinai. Another forty years would pass before the nation would inherit the land that had been prepared for them and promised to their ancestors as an eternal possession. The connection of the Hebrews/Israelites/Jews with the land of Israel, however, is inescapable. Whether in the land or cast out of it, they have been its rightful owners for the four millennia since God made his oath/covenant with Abraham contingent upon the inheritance of the land mass called Israel.

The possession of the land, therefore, was the inevitable consequence of the covenant. Jacob Neusner confirms the importance of the actions through which the Israelites inherited the land of Israel by possessing it: "The conquest of the land and inheriting it are marks of the covenant. . . . Whether or not Israel knows or likes the fact, it nonetheless remains that Israel therefore has no choice but to accept God's will and fulfill the covenant."[24] The inevitable fulfillment of the land clause of the covenant was vouchsafed by the faithfulness of God. God

---

[20] Whschogrod, p. 93.

[21] Wyschogrod, p. 93.

[22] Isaiah 43:6.

[23] Yitshak Korn, *Jews at the Crossroads* (New Brunswick, NJ: Rosemont Publishing and Printing Corp., 1983), p. 79.

[24] Jacob Neusner, *The Classics of Judaism: A Textbook and Reader* (Louisville, KY: Westminster John Knox Press, 1995), pp. 157–158.

did not equivocate when he said, "I will establish my covenant between me and you and your descendants after you throughout their generations for an everlasting covenant, to be God to you and to your descendants after you. I will give to you and to your descendants after you, the land of your sojournings, all the land of Canaan, for an everlasting possession; and I will be their God."[25] It was simply impossible for Israel to benefit fully from God's covenant promise "to be God to you and your descendants" unless the people and the nation possessed "all the land of Canaan, for an everlasting possession." If the Israelites had been unwilling or unable to possess the land as God had promised and instructed them, they would not—could not—have been the "Chosen People," and YHWH would not—could not—have been their God.

When confronted with the reality of possessing the defining terms of the covenant, however, 83% of Israel's finest leaders[26] ignored God's specific transgenerational promises and his explicit instructions. After reconnoitering the land with a view toward possessing it, they concluded, "We cannot go up against the people, for they are too strong for us."[27] Their protestations even became very graphic: "We are like grasshoppers compared to the giants in the land." This dreadful report by ten of the twelve-man survey team resulted in a forty-year delay in the fulfillment of God's promise—and the death of the generation of Israelites who chose not to believe God's promise. The pessimists won the day and disaster ensued.

On the other hand, two members of the team gave this report: "We are well able to possess this land," and they urged their countrymen, "Let us go up at once to possess it." These two valiant leaders were not delusional: they were faith-filled and faithful! They understood the utter dependability of God's promises. So, Joshua and Caleb are remembered to this day for their optimism and faith. The rest of the spies, though their names are specifically detailed in the text of Scripture, remain unknown to virtually everyone. Perhaps Paul Harvey's dictum is true: "Every pessimist who ever lived has been buried in an unmarked grave."[28]

Finally, after forty years of wandering and waiting, the descendants of those doubting Israelites came to the shores of the Jordan River just north of the Dead Sea. This time, they moved forward in faith, and they

---

25 Genesis 17:7–8.
26 Ten of the twelve tribal leaders represented 83% of the team.
27 Numbers 13:31.
28 Paul Harvey, quoted by Mike Thomas, "Paul Harvey," in *Salon*, Sep 25, 2001.

accomplished what the vast majority of their ancestors had thought impossible. They possessed the land! This is what Scripture concluded when Joshua neared the end of his career as actualizer of God's land promise: "So the LORD gave Israel all the land he had sworn to give their forefathers, and they took possession of it and settled there."[29] Since the land belonged entirely to God, he simply evicted its former inhabitants when their idolatry and wickedness reached a full measure,[30] and he then installed new leaseholders in the land: the Israelites.[31] The divine timepiece seemed to advance slowly; however, it moved inexorably toward its predetermined end, and it produced what God had promised to Abraham and within the timeframe that he had predicted for its fulfillment. The stage was set at the beginning of the fourteenth century BC for the people of Israel to establish their newly formed nation in the land of promise to begin continual Israelite possession of the land for sixteen hundred years that was interrupted only by the Babylonian *galut*[32] (captivity) and that for no more than 70 years.[33] It was not until the Bar Kokhba rebellion against Roman rule in AD 135 that the Jews were expelled from the land by imperial decree, and the nearly two-millennia-long worldwide Diaspora ensued.

Retaining the Possession

Maintaining possession of the land of Israel was a continuing drama for the Israelites as neighboring tribes and enemies from afar sought to evict them from their inheritance or to dominate the people and their resources.

---

[29] Joshua 21:43.

[30] This was God's stated reason for not allowing Abraham himself to inherit the land (Genesis 15:16).

[31] This should have been a warning to the Israelites, for if God would remove the Canaanites for idolatry, he would certainly have his own people dispossessed of the land if they engaged in the same activities, just as he promised in Leviticus 18:24–30. The Lord actually confirmed this in graphic language, saying that he would "vomit [the Israelites] out of the land as he had vomited out the nations." Jacob Neusner sums up this truth well: "If Israel rebels or rejects the Torah, it will lose the land, just as the Canaanites did for their idolatry." Jacob Neusner, *A Theological Commentary to the Midrash: Sifre to Numbers and Sifre to Deuteronomy* (Lanham, MD: University Press of America, 2001), p. 147. The removal of unfaithful Israelites from the land, however, did not abrogate God's covenant with Abraham, nor did it revoke their leasehold on the land. In due time, the Lord orchestrated the return of his people to his land—the land that he had leased to them in perpetuity.

[32] The Hebrew word *galut* means "exile."

[33] Even in the Babylonian captivity in the late sixth century BC, not all of the people were evicted from the land. Its political, social, and economic leaders were forcibly removed and taken to Babylon; however, many of the common people continued to live in the land. While Jerusalem was completely destroyed, other parts of Judea continued to be inhabited during the *galut*. See Ephraim Stern, "The Babylonian Gap," *Biblical Archaeology Review* 26, Nov–Dec, 2000, p. 6. Similarly when the Northern Israelite kingdom was invaded by the Assyrian Empire during the eighth century BC, the ruling class was removed; however, significant members of the ten northern tribes simply migrated to the southern kingdom of Judah while others remained in the rural areas of the north (2 Chronicles 11:17).

This ongoing saga was chronicled in the book of Judges when Israel was without dynastic leadership. Periodically the Israelites would drift away from God's Torah into idolatrous practices, inviting God's judgment upon them. Then, when they cried out to God, he raised up deliverer after deliverer to rescue them and reestablish their freedoms. Then, in the days of Samuel, the last of the judges, Israel resorted to the establishment of a monarchy,[34] despite God's wishes to the contrary.[35] The monarchy was both a blessing and a curse to Israel, for when the kings were righteous, Israel prospered. When they were evil, the people suffered.

The monarchy consolidated the largely independent tribes into a centralized civil government which made provision for the defense of the nation far more efficient, and it made possible the expansion of the realm into its greatest geographical territory during the reign of Solomon. At the same time, however, the absolute power arrogated by some of the monarchs brought pain and sorrow to the people. This was especially true in the divided kingdom that followed Solomon's reign. A succession of evil and idolatrous leaders, interspersed with a few righteous kings who called for repentance and renewal in the land, precipitated God's anger and judgment that saw first the Northern Kingdom vanquished by the Assyrians in the eighth century BC and, later, the Southern Kingdom conquered by the Babylonians in the sixth century BC. Such regal arrogance finally led to the destruction of Jerusalem and the temple when God sent his "servant" Nebuchadnezzar with the armies of Babylon to exact judgment upon his nation.[36] Once again, however, the people of Judah turned back to God in repentance, prompting him to orchestrate their return to the land and to the task of rebuilding Jerusalem. The nation was restored in its land and to at least some semblance of control over the land for another six centuries.

---

[34] Deuteronomy 17:14–16. God recognized that the nation of Israel would desire to be "like all the other nations" and would want a king. He gave specific and detailed instructions as to who should be chosen when such an occasion would rise, and he listed requirements that were to be imposed upon anyone who would be king in Israel. The king could not amass to himself horses (military might), women, or gold, and he was required to write his own personal copy of the Torah. These requirements of the Torah, like virtually everything else that God commanded, were also ignored, much to the damage of the body politic of Israel and the personal wellbeing of its citizens. Ultimately, the failure of so many of Israel's kings to follow the specific instructions of the Almighty was what prompted God to bring the Babylonian captivity upon his people.

[35] 1 Samuel 8:7. When the people clamored for a king, God said to Samuel, "They have rejected me from being king over them."

[36] Jeremiah 27:6; 43:10.

The saga of the Israelite possession of the land of Israel reflects the ongoing challenge by syncretistic elements among the people that sought to conflate the faith of YHWH with that of their pagan neighbors or with downright idolatry. When the God of Scripture stated the ten greatest principles of the faith that he delivered to his Chosen People, however, at the very top of the list were these two declarations: "I am the LORD, your God" and "You shall have no other gods before me . . . you shall not make for yourself an idol. . . . You shall not bow down to them or worship them."[37] YHWH had never countenanced idolatry, and he would never do so. From the beginning of the Israelite inheritance of the land, God warned them "against performing the abominations of the nations that God dispossessed."[38] No matter what people lived in God's land, whether Israelite or Canaanite, when they engaged in the abomination of idolatry, the land would vomit them out,[39] because the land itself is "holy,"[40] consecrated to the Lord by the Creator himself.

Still, as he demonstrated over and over again, the God of Israel has committed his land to his people, and his position has never changed, nor will it change. Thus the history of the Hebrews/Israelites/Jews has continually been a record of God's search for man, not man's search for God.[41] The God of Israel is irrepressible: he never gives up! He has always looked—and he continues to look—for someone to "stand in the gap" before him "on behalf of the land."[42] In spite of all the vicissitudes of history, God's intentions regarding the land and its rightful inhabitants have never changed. It is important, therefore, that the history of God's Chosen People be recognized for what it is: the succession of generations of chosen vessels who accepted God's call and received the yoke of the Torah and of the kingdom of God. This is the history of the land of Israel as well. Despite the efforts of a wide array of historical revisionists to discount the history of the Jewish people, the Jewish nation, and the Jewish land as legend and myth contrived by scheming Jews in order to support their claims to uniqueness, the historicity of the people, nation, and land of Israel is undeniable. It rests in the immutable promises of the Almighty God.

---

[37] Deuteronomy 5:7–9.

[38] Deuteronomy 18:9–12. See Tikva Frymer-Kensky, *Studies in Bible and Feminist Criticism* (Philadelphia, PA: Jewish Publication Society, 2006), p. 342.

[39] Leviticus 18:25.

[40] Ezekiel 48:14; Zechariah 2:12.

[41] Abraham Joshua Heschel, *God in Search of Man: A Philosophy of Judaism* (New York: Farrar, Straus and Giroux, 1955), p. 191. Heschel said, "The incidents recorded in the Bible to the discerning eye are episodes of one great drama: the quest of God for man; His search for man, and man's flight from Him."

[42] Ezekiel 22:30.

CHAPTER 10

AN EXISTENTIAL THREAT

THE BIRTH OF ANTISEMITISM

Through the centuries the Hebrews/Israelites faced difficult challenges from Gentile nations that sought to enslave them, afflict them, and even destroy them. These random acts of violence and mayhem, however, were generally motivated by the perennial human lust for conquest, the desire for power and privilege. Additionally, the land that God gave to the Israelites was situated at the confluence of three continents as well as at the juncture of north-south and east-west trade routes. This made the land of Israel not only attractive to empire builders but also virtually essential for exercising military might, controlling commerce, and mitigating against the designs of others who would impinge upon such interests. These military powers were more focused on controlling the area represented by the nation of Israel and extracting taxes from the inhabitants than they were on annihilating the people.

In the fifth century BC, however, something insidious was brewing in the world's most powerful kingdom of the day that was to have continuing and enduring impact upon the people, nation, and land of Israel. The first recorded instance of an attempt to annihilate the Jewish people through systematic genocide emerged in the Persian Empire. Antisemitism,[1] the hatred of Jews as Jews, which includes all hostility, prejudice, and discrimination toward Jews, was born. And for twenty-five hundred years,

---

[1] The term *antisemitism* comes from the German word *antisemitisch*, which was coined in 1860 by the Austrian Jewish scholar Mortiz Steinschneider and used in the phrase *antisemitische Vorurteile* (antisemitic prejudices) to attack the French philosopher Ernest Renan and his postulation that "Semitic races" were inferior to "Aryan races." Alex Bein, *The Jewish Question: Biography of a World Problem* (Madison, NJ: Fairleigh Dickinson University Press, 1990), p. 594; and Avner Falk, *Anti-semitism: A History and Psychoanalysis of Contemporary Hatred* (Westport, CT: Greenwood Publishing Group, 2008), p. 21.

this unparalleled[2] sociopathic disease has infested and infected large portions of the non-Jewish world, wreaking havoc upon the Chosen People through intimidation, violence, mayhem, and murder.

The foundation for antisemitism[3] had actually been laid in Babylon when the satraps and administrators of that kingdom sought to remove the king's favorite advisor, the prophet Daniel. After a diligent and unproductive search for any evidence of malfeasance or unethical conduct on Daniel's part, they finally concluded, "We will never find any basis for charges against this man Daniel unless it has something to do with the law of his God."[4] Then, they began to establish a foundation for what would become an insidious and enduring phenomenon wherein the Chosen People would be targeted individually and collectively simply because of their faith. This was the root cause of antisemitism: making charges against the Jewish people because of "something to do with God's law."

It was not long after Daniel's experience that this idea was taken to extreme in another generation of the Medo-Persian Empire that had been established by Cyrus the Great.[5] In the fortress city of Shushan (Susa),[6] the capital city of this realm, Xerxes the Great[7] ruled over the vast domain that stretched from India to Ethiopia and into southern Europe. In the midst of the intrigue that unfolded in the royal court, a plot was developed which, if it had been successful, would have resulted in the complete genocide of the Chosen People and the termination of the Abrahamic

---

[2] Alice L. Eckardt and A. Roy Eckardt, *Long Night's Journey into Day: A Revised Retrospective on the Holocaust* (Detroit, MI: Wayne State University Press, 1982), p. 58. The Eckardts said, "The phenomenon of antisemitism is incomparable. There are no parallels to it. There simply is no historical analogue to antisemitism. . . . Whether we speak of space or of time, the two primordial dimensions of human existence, no prejudice comes anywhere near antisemitism. No prejudice can approach antisemitism for either geopolitical pervasiveness or temporal enduringness."

[3] Antisemitism is the term that specifically means hatred of the Jews. Since the Holocaust, many scholars have suggested the replacement of the nineteenth-century form *anti-Semitism* with the more modern *antisemitism*. Jewish philosopher and Holocaust scholar Emil Fackenheim has argued that "the spelling ought to be antisemitism without the hyphen, dispelling the notion that there is an entity 'Semitism' which 'anti-Semitism' opposes." Emil L. Fackenheim, "Post-Holocaust Anti-Jewishness, Jewish Identity and the Centrality of Israel," in *World Jewry and the State of Israel*, Moshe Davis, ed. (New York: Arno Press, 1977), p. 11, n. 2.

[4] Daniel 6:5, NIV.

[5] Xerxes I was actually the grandson of Cyrus through his daughter Atossa's marriage to Darius the Great.

[6] The term *Shushan* described both the city and the palace of Xerxes (Esther 9:12–15).

[7] In most translations of Scripture, Xerxes is called Ahasuerus, which is a Latinized form of the transliteration of the Hebrew *Akhashverosh*. Both Ahasuerus and Xerxes ultimately are transliterated or approximated forms of the Persian *Xsayarsa*.

covenant. At the same time, however, God was at work, orchestrating events so that the plot for evil would be exposed and foiled.

Xerxes was in a celebratory mood. So, he organized an ostentatious party to showcase his power and might and the beauty of his capital city in front of all his nobles and bureaucrats. "For a full 180 days he displayed the vast wealth of his kingdom and the splendor and glory of his majesty."[8] At the end of that time, he gave a seven-day banquet for all the people in Susa to see the sumptuous magnificence of his palace. Finally, on the seventh day, Xerxes commanded that his queen be brought before him so that everyone could see her beauty. When the orders were delivered to Vashti, however, she refused to appear.[9] The king was furious and after consulting with his advisors determined that in order to limit confusion throughout the realm, Vashti should be removed and replaced by another queen.[10]

A New Queen

After a long process, a new queen was indeed chosen. She was Hadassah ("Esther" in Persian), a young Jewish girl who was extraordinarily beautiful. As it turned out, Hadassah was also amazingly resourceful, socially adroit, and powerfully resolute. On the advice of Mordecai, her cousin and mentor, she kept her true identity as a Jewish maiden totally secret. Her emergence as queen of the Persian realm was the result of circumstances and events that were divinely orchestrated in preparation for what would be needed to ensure the survival of the Chosen People.

At this time, Persia dominated the entire Middle East and beyond; therefore, every Jew in the entire world lived in the Persian Empire. This created a unique situation in which every living Jew was vulnerable to decisions that issued forth from the Shushan palace and were then enforced by the strong, efficient, and merciless Persian military. The strategic placement of Esther as the queen of the realm and a favorite of Xerxes could not have been more important in this

---

[8] Esther 1:4, NIV.

[9] There are various interpretations as to why Vashti refused her husband's bidding. Some suggest that it was because she would have been paraded in the nude before the male nobles in the midst of a drunken orgy. See Mark Mangano, *The College Press NIV Commentary: Esther & Daniel* (Goshen, IN: College Press Publishing Co., 2001), p. 44. Some commentators have even suggested that she was to wear only her royal crown. See Walter A. Elwell and Philip W. Comfort, *Tyndale Bible Dictionary* (Wheaton, IL: Tyndale House Publishers, 2001), vol. 4, p. 800. Others argue that the requirement for nudity is an interpolation into the text of Esther that has no substance. See Howard D. Wilcox, *Divine Providence* (Bloomington, IN: Life Way Publishers, 2011), p. 84.

[10] The reason given for Vashti's deposal was that her refusal would foment the rebellion of women throughout the realm against their husbands.

circumstance. Then, Esther's position was strengthened even more when Mordecai discovered an assassination plot against Xerxes and encouraged Esther to expose it. Afterwards, both Esther and Mordecai were honored by the king.

A powerful and insidious evil, however, was lurking in the highest halls of the Persian government, for the realm's newly appointed prime minister was a man who suffered from severe egomania. He loved the pomposity and the perquisites of power. He relished seeing the people bowing themselves to the ground in his presence. Because the Jewish people were under strict orders not to bow to anyone except God,[11] Mordecai refused to bow before Haman when he passed by in all of his pomp and glory. This, in turn, infuriated the prime minister, who sought for a way in which he could avenge himself against Mordecai and assuage the pain that this impudent Jew had inflicted on his ego. He could not be satisfied, however, with simply killing Mordecai. So, he "looked for a way to destroy all Mordecai's people, the Jews, throughout the whole kingdom of Xerxes."[12]

A Damnable Conspiracy

Instead of dealing directly with Mordecai, Haman approached the king with these scurrilous words of slander: "There is a certain people dispersed among the peoples in the provinces of your kingdom who keep themselves separate. Their customs are different from those of all other people, and they do not obey the king's laws; it is not in the king's best interest to tolerate them."[13] Then, he petitioned the king for the enactment of a vicious edict for genocide of the Jews and pledged to remunerate the king for any loss of revenue that might result from his plan to eliminate them: "If it pleases the king, let a decree be issued to destroy them, and I will give ten thousand talents of silver to the king's administrators for the royal treasury."[14] To Haman, the lives of "all the Jews" in the Persian Empire were worth over $200 million in today's money.[15]

The declaration, "It is not in the king's best interest to tolerate [this] certain people," was the first and perhaps most succinct description of

---

[11] The commandment in Exodus 20:5 not to bow to other gods was extrapolated to include men. Obeisance was to be done to no one but God.

[12] Esther 3:6, NIV.

[13] Esther 3:7. Literally, the text says, "It is not worthwhile for the king to let them rest."

[14] Esther 3:8–9, NIV.

[15] Haman's intention was to contribute this sum to the royal treasury from the booty seized from the Jews during their slaughter. Interestingly, this sum was approximately 60% of the annual income of the Persian government at that time. See Michael D. Coogan, Marc Z. Brettler, Carol A. Newsom, and Pheme Perkins, eds., *The New Oxford Annotated Bible with Apocrypha: New Revised Standard Edition* (New York: Oxford University Press, 2010), p. 1417.

overt antisemitism ever set forth. Throughout their history, the Jewish people had been—and would continue to be—judged because "their customs [were] different from those of other people," for they had followed God's instructions to separate themselves from participation in the idolatry of other nations. More often than not, the Jewish people found themselves unable to "keep the king's laws." While they did their best to be loyal subjects of the realms in which they lived, still they were bound by the Torah to keep God's commandments,[16] even if it meant suffering persecution and martyrdom. Their time in Persia was no different.

Haman's appeal was so effective that Xerxes gave him his own signet ring, told him to keep his money, and ordered him to "do with the people as you please."[17] Immediately, the royal secretaries wrote the decree in Xerxes' name in the languages of every province and sealed them with the king's signet ring. Dispatches were sent by couriers to all the provinces of the Persian Empire with this order: "Kill and annihilate all the Jews—young and old, women and children—on . . . the thirteenth day of the twelfth month . . . and plunder their goods."[18] Haman's evil plot had the force of imperial law that was irrevocable. The prospect was simple: all the Jews in Persia—and, therefore, virtually all the Jews in the world—were going to be killed, effecting their complete genocide.

When Mordecai learned of the edict, he, like Jews throughout the realm, tore his clothes, put on sackcloth and ashes, and went about "wailing loudly and bitterly." In short order, he conveyed the information of Haman's plot on to Esther. The queen thought her hands were tied because unless she was summoned to appear before Xerxes, she could not do so without risking her own life in the process. Mordecai made this response to her excuse: "Do not think that because you are in the king's house you alone of all the Jews will escape. For if you remain silent at this time, relief and deliverance for the Jews will arise from another place, but you and your father's family will perish."[19] Then he addressed his cousin with these immortal words: "Who knows but that you have come to royal position for such a time as this?"[20]

---

16 Specific commandments that prompted, if not assured, Israelite separation from the idolatry of the Gentile world included the laws concerning circumcision, Sabbath, hair and dress, and dietary regulations.

17 Esther 3:11.

18 Esther 3:13, NIV.

19 Esther 4:13–14a, NIV.

20 Esther 4:14b, NIV.

Exposing the Plot

Esther immediately demonstrated her profound faith, asking Mordecai to request that all the Jews in Shushan fast and pray for her for three days and nights. Then she said, "I will go to the king, even though it is against the law. And if I perish, I perish."[21] As she had promised, on the third day, Esther put on her royal robes and, fearing the worst, cautiously entered the royal court. When Xerxes saw her, however, he was pleased, so he held out the golden scepter, sparing her life. "What is it, Queen Esther? What is your request? Even up to half of the kingdom, it will be given you," he said.[22] The ever-resourceful Esther had already devised a plan as to how she would approach the king in the context of the court intrigue wherein Haman appeared to have the upper hand. "If it pleases the king," she replied, "let the king, together with Haman, come today to a banquet I have prepared for him." The king agreed, and, in due course, with Haman in tow, she dutifully arrived at Esther's banquet, asking, "Now what is your petition?" The coy Esther replied, "Let the king and Haman come tomorrow" to another banquet, and "then I will answer the king's question."

The biblical text reports that Haman went out that day happy and in high spirits. "I'm the only person Queen Esther invited to accompany the king to the banquet she gave," he boasted. At the same time, however, he moaned to his wife, "All this gives me no satisfaction as long as I see that Jew Mordecai sitting at the king's gate."[23] The resourceful woman had a solution: "Have a pole set up, reaching to a height of seventy-five feet, and ask the king in the morning to have Mordecai impaled on it."[24] This suggestion delighted Haman, so he had the pole erected on which he just knew he would see Mordecai die the next day.

During the ensuing night, Xerxes could not sleep, so he ordered his servants to read to him from a book that chronicled the events of his reign. This book just happened to open to the records that detailed how Mordecai had exposed the assassination plot against the king. "What honor and recognition has Mordecai received for this?" the king inquired. "Nothing," his servants replied. At that moment, Haman just happened to enter the royal chambers, so the king summoned him and asked, "What should be done for the man the king delights to honor?" he asked. The prime minister, thinking that the king was speaking of him, replied, "Have them bring a royal robe the king has worn and a horse the

---

21 Esther 4:16, NIV.
22 Esther 5:3, NIV.
23 Esther 5:12–13, NIV.
24 Esther 6:14, NIV.

king has ridden, one with the royal crest placed on its head. . . . Let them robe the man . . . and lead him on the horse through the city streets, proclaiming before him: This is what is done for the man the king delights to honor!"

To Haman's utter shock and dismay, Xerxes immediately gave him this order: "Go at once. Get the robe and the horse and do just as you have suggested for Mordecai the Jew, who sits at the king's gate." Now filled with fear and consternation, Haman dutifully fulfilled his king's command and then rushed home only to hear his wife say ominously, "Since Mordecai, before whom your downfall has started, is of Jewish origin, you cannot stand against him—you will surely come to ruin!"[25] Before Haman could do a thing, however, the king's messengers arrived to escort him to the queen's banquet.

After the festivities began, Xerxes again asked Esther, "What is your request?" This time, the queen boldly replied, "If it pleases you, grant me my life—this is my petition. And spare my people—this is my request. For I and my people have been sold to be destroyed, killed, and annihilated."[26] Immediately, the shocked king asked his bride, "Who is . . . the man who has dared to do such a thing?" Unhesitatingly, Esther pointed out the enemy: "This vile Haman!" Upon hearing this news, the king was furious and went out into the palace garden to collect his thoughts. Realizing that the king would certainly decide his fate in a matter of minutes, Haman stayed behind to beg the queen for his life. When Xerxes returned, he found Haman falling on the couch where Esther was reclining and exclaimed, "Will he even molest the queen while she is with me in the house?" The king's judgment was immediate and final: "Impale Haman on the pole by his house," and the sentence was then carried out forthwith.

Antisemitism Avenged

That left one important bit of unfinished business. What could be done about the inalterable imperial decree that specified a date for the annihilation of all the Jews in the Persian Empire? As a counter-measure, Xerxes issued another decree giving the Jews in every city the right to assemble and protect themselves against anyone who would attack them. When this decree was published, there was great joy in Persia, especially among the Jews, and Mordecai was highly honored. Then, the text of

---

[25] Esther 6:13, NIV.
[26] Esther 7:4, NIV.

Scripture makes this startling declaration: "Many people of other nation-alities became Jews because fear of the Jews had seized them."[27] The text does not explain how this was accomplished, but it does note the turn of events. Finally, on the day appointed, when "the enemies of the Jews had hoped to overpower them, now the tables were turned and the Jews got the upper hand over those who hated them."[28] The victory of the Jews was complete. Genocide was averted. *Am Yisrael chai*!

Among the Jews, the next day was a time of such great rejoicing that a new festival celebrating that day was added to the calendar of Torah festivals outlined in Leviticus 23. This festival, called Purim,[29] thereafter became a prominent fixture in the lives of the Jews.[30] Each year there-after, Purim was a time to celebrate God's deliverance of the Jews from the certainty of death into abundant life—all because divine providence had positioned a young Jewish girl in the palace of the world's most powerful king and had emboldened her with faith to intercede for the deliverance of her people. Esther was, indeed, elevated by God's hand into royalty "for such a time as this," and she did not fail to accomplish her mission. The genocide of the entire Jewish people was averted, and antisemitism failed. This deep-seated pathology, however, continued to seethe beneath the surface and spread like wildfire to most of the soci-eties into which the Jewish people were eventually dispersed.

The chronicle of Esther and Mordecai and their brave actions to prevent the genocide of the Jews during the height of the Persian Empire is a lesson not only for Jews but also for all human beings of conscience. Christians especially should take a fresh look at interpreting the Book of Esther with a view toward its parallels with the Holocaust. Drawing on these parallels, Emil Fackenheim identifies the state of Israel as "a new Mordecai for a new age in the history of Judaism, guarding the Jewish remnant."[31] Moshe Aberbach says that "the story of Esther . . . gives the same cathartic message—that Jews can escape genocide" when "in some cases human intervention may be necessary, though the invisible

27 Esther 8:17.
28 Esther 9:1, NIV.
29 The Hebrew word *Purim* means "lots," a term which refers to the lottery that Haman used to choose the date for his planned massacre of the Jews. Jeffrey M. Cohen, *Prayer and Penitence: A Commentary on the High Holy Day Machzor* (Northvale, NJ: Jason Aronson, 1994), p. 136.
30 Esther 9:20–26.
31 Emil L. Fackenheim, *The Jewish Bible after the Holocaust: A Re-reading* (Bloomington, IN: Indiana University Press, 1991), p. 95.

hand of God is in the background."[32] Bruce Zuckerman and Zev Garber maintain that the Book of Esther serves as an example "in which human protagonists must face and overcome a genocidal threat to the future of the Jewish people posed by an irresponsible Gentile government."[33] On a more personal level, Deborah Prescott suggests poignantly that the Book of Esther may well "serve as a paradigm for Shoah autobiographies as a 'new Bible.'"[34]

The Many Guises of Haman: Shapeshifting Antisemitism

While Haman epitomized antisemitism as no other person in history except for Adolph Hitler, antisemitism has many guises. Indeed, it is almost like the reptilian shapeshifters of science fiction lore who could change their physical appearance at will. Antisemitism manifests itself in myriads of ways and to varying degrees; however, in any form, it is insidious. Dennis Prager and Joseph Telushkin rightly report that "hatred for the Jew has been humanity's greatest hatred. While hatred of other groups has always existed, no hatred has been as universal, as deep, or as permanent as antisemitism."[35] Although antisemitism has emerged from various situations and has had many manifestations, its underlying cause has always been the pagan heart's hatred of Israel's God, an antipathy which has been directed against the Jewish people because they represent God in the earth. This pathology seethes in the subconscious recesses of the Gentile mind and is ready to leap forth at any time and in any place, only to be excused by a plethora excuses for mistrusting and despising Jews. For this reason alone, Jews for thousands of years have held the opinion that antisemitism is "religious and particularist."[36]

Proof that the underlying cause of antisemitism is hatred for Jews as symbols of God can be found in the first record of antisemitism outside of Jewish literature. When Alexander the Great conquered Egypt, significant numbers of Greeks and Jews immigrated to Alexandria, bringing with them cultures far different from that of the indigenous Egyptian

---

[32] Moshe Aberbach, *Jewish Education and History: Continuity, Crisis and Change* (Abingdon, UK: Routledge, 2009), p. 80.
[33] Bruce Zuckerman and Zev Garber, *The Impact of the Holocaust in America* (West Lafayette, IN: Purdue University Press, 2008), p. 172.
[34] Deborah Lee Prescott, *Imagery from Genesis in Holocaust Memoirs: A Critical Study* (Jefferson, NC: McFarland & Company, Publishers, 2010), p. 25.
[35] Dennis Prager and Joseph Telushkin, *Why the Jews?: The Reason for Antisemitism* (New York: Simon and Schuster, 1983), p. 3.
[36] Prager and Telushkin, *Why the Jews?*, p. 56.

people. There was no sociological reason for the Egyptians to resent and hate the Jews more than the Greeks; however, they did. Why? Prager and Telushkin point out that "the Egyptians found the Jews' religious culture and traditions offensive," as was clearly the case with the Egyptian priest Manetho, who, "annoyed by the Jews' liturgy and Bible with its depictions of the Jews' exodus from Egypt, decided to rewrite that event, saying that the Jews had been expelled from Egypt because they were lepers."[37]

While these scholars offer various secular explanations for antisemitism, such as resentment of the "higher quality of Jewish life," their first and foremost reason for antisemitism is "hatred of Judaism and ethical monotheism, followed closely by 'the Chosen People idea.'"[38] What they point out is true: "[T]oday, Jew-hatred is generally attributed to factors having little to do with Jews and Judaism; rather, its causes are generally held to be economic, political . . . ethnic prejudice, and the psychopathology of hate—all of which dejudaize antisemitism."[39] At bottom, however, an insidious force of the evil inclination in the human heart resents and hates the Jewish people because they represent a God who is foreign to their thinking—or lack thereof. Prager and Telushkin ultimately argue that "the causes of antisemitism are neither ethnic nor racial nor rooted in economic envy or religious bigotry, but that antisemitism is a response to Jews and their way of life, based upon its very foundations—God, Torah, and Peoplehood."[40]

The words of Haman's diabolical indictment of the Jewish people in Persia must continue to echo across the corridors of time so people of conscience can immediately recognize the subtlety of the newest guise of antisemitism and make an unequivocal stand against it. Red lights must flash and sirens must scream whenever and wherever words like these are heard: "There is a certain people dispersed among the peoples in the provinces of your kingdom who keep themselves separate. Their customs are different from those of all other people, and they do not obey the king's laws; it is not in the king's best interest to tolerate them."[41] Increasingly, this kind of rhetoric is becoming postmodernity's indictment against those who stand on the authority of the Hebrew Scriptures, whether they be Jews or Christians.

---

[37] Prager and Telushkin, *Why the Jews?*, pp. 68–69.
[38] Prager and Telushkin, *Why the Jews?*, p. vi, Contents.
[39] Prager and Telushkin, *Why the Jews?*, p. 56.
[40] Prager and Telushkin, *Why the Jews?*, p. 8.
[41] Esther 3:7.

CHAPTER 11

VIOLENCE AND DIASPORA
History Run Amok

Through his servant King David, YHWH, the one God of Israel, issued this important command to the entire world: "Do not touch my anointed ones, and do my prophets no harm."[1] It was a virtual "hands-off" warning that would have resounding consequences for any people group that would dare to lay a finger on the Chosen People or harm the prophetic voices that God had stationed among them to ensure the perpetuation of his Torah.[2] The landscape of world history has been littered with the bleached bones of empires that refused to heed God's warning and proceeded to impose pain and suffering upon the Jewish people. Kingdoms that seemed invincible crumbled when they dared to shove their fingers into the pupil of God's eye! How so? "He who touches [Israel] touches the pupil of [God's] eye."[3] The Almighty gave this assurance to the prophet Zechariah when he used a graphic and unmistakable metaphor to elucidate his attitude toward and relationship with Israel and the Jewish people. This declaration made it clear that Israel has always been the "focal point" of God's vision. It also confirms the fact that God is hypersensitive when it comes to Israel. If there is one thing that will ensure immediate reaction from God, it is to lay a hand on the

---

[1] Psalm 105:15.
[2] Deuteronomy 32:10.
[3] Zechariah 2:8. This passage is usually translated "He who touches you touches the *apple* of his eye" (emphasis added). Zechariah, however, based his declaration on Deuteronomy 32:10, where the Hebrew word אִישׁוֹן (*'ishon*) means "middle" or "pupil of the eye." Zechariah's word, בָּבָה (*babah*), is the active participle of an unused Hebrew root that means to "hollow out," to be "dark," and hence to describe the "dark" portion of the eye—the pupil. Like *'ishon*, *babah* also literally means "pupil" rather than the fruit of the apple tree.

Jewish people.[4] God is umbrageous to any action, whether overt or covert, that is undertaken against his Chosen People.[5]

In point of fact, God specifically predicted that every nation that would be presumptuous enough to divide his land would be punished.[6] But the nations have consistently refused to hear the voice of a God whom they have considered to be no god at all. For the polytheistic societies of virtually the entire non-Jewish world, the invisible and singularly unique God of the Jews was a laughingstock. The minds of natural humans despise the idea that a god could exist whom they had not made in their own image.[7] For the pagan, a God like YHWH, who is invisible and makes demands upon humanity, could not possibly be a god and, therefore, could not be tolerated. Because the Jews refused to worship the gods that were revered by the citizens of those polytheistic nations, they were considered by them to be "atheists."[8] The appellative *atheist* ("without God") was hurled against the earliest Christians a well because they, like the Jewish community from which they emerged, worshiped the one God of the Jews who specifically forbade the worship of all im-

---

[4] The following is a poignant story that was told by Corrie ten Boom: "One day as Father and I were returning from our walk we found the Grote Markt cordoned off by a double ring of police and soldiers. A truck was parked in front of the fish mart; into the back were climbing men, women, and children, all wearing the yellow star. . . 'Father! Those poor people!' I cried. . . .'Those poor people,' Father echoed. But to my surprise I saw that he was looking at the soldiers now forming into ranks to march away. 'I pity the poor Germans, Corrie. They have touched the apple of God's eye.'" Corrie ten Boom, *The Hiding Place*, Elizabeth Sherrill and John Sherrill, eds. (Grand Rapids, MI: Baker Publishing Group, 1971), p. 69.

[5] Even when the Israelites were unfaithful and deserved the judgment that God brought upon them through the agency of other nations, he also brought commensurate judgment upon those nations if they were overly abusive of his people. In the days of Eli, when the Philistines abused the Israelites, they found their god Dagon lying in ruins in his own temple, prostrated before the Ark of the Covenant, and they were they all afflicted with hemorrhoids (1 Samuel 6). Isaiah 10:7-19 predicted the judgment that God would bring upon the Assyrians for being arrogant and abusive when he, unbeknownst to them, had commissioned them to punish Israel's sins.

[6] Joel 3:2.

[7] Romans 8:7.

[8] In the first century BC, Apollonius Molon, head of a school of rhetoric on the island of Rhodes, made the same accusation against Jews in general, calling them, "atheists and man-haters." See William F. McCants, *Founding Gods, Inventing Nations: Conquest and Culture Myths from Antiquity* (Princeton, NJ: Princeton University Press, 2012), p. 129. Dominique Barthélemy points to a report by Dio Cassius which said that the Roman Emperor Domitian condemned Christian leaders like Clement and Domitilla for being atheists. Dominique Barthélemy, *God and His Image: An Outline of Biblical Theology* (San Francisco, CA: Ignatius Press, 2007), p. 70. Roy Saltman notes that both "Jews and Christians were called atheists because they refused to sacrifice to the gods of the state." Roy G. Saltman, *Sacred Humanism Without Miracles: Responding to the New Atheists* (New York: Palgrave Macmillan, 2012), p. 13.

ages of false gods.[9] Beginning in Babylon, therefore, and continuing to the present day, significant percentages of the non-Jewish world have been infected with—if not dominated by—antisemitism and overt persecution of the Jewish people that has been focused on them simply because they have been the visible representatives of the invisible God who is "God alone."

The final and universal dispersion of the Jewish people in the second century, however, involved a politically driven hatred that was primarily focused on the Jews' fierce independence and their belief that their God-appointed status as the Chosen People conveyed to them independent sovereignty over the land of Israel. From the time when Imperial Rome rose to world domination just before the beginning of the Common Era, this empire would never countenance the expression of such anarchical ideas, for such could well have spread like wildfire throughout their far-flung dominion, causing both political and economic disaster for Rome itself. Rome was certain of its destiny to dominate the world. Its divine right was confirmed by the imperative recorded in the *Rhetorica ad Herennium*, which gave the Romans this command: "*Imperium orbis terrae*" ("Rule the whole earth").[10] Divine right to world dominance was ensconced in the Roman poet Virgil's recapitulation of Rome's destiny:

> *Tu regere imperio populos, Romane memento*
> *Hae tibi erunt artes, pacisque imponere morem,*
> *Parcere subiectis et debellare superbos.*[11]
>
> You, Roman, remember to rule the people with power.
> [These will be your arts] and to impose customs on peace,
> To spare the vanquished, and to crush the proud.

The Romans had come to believe that the gods had given the entire earth to them and that they were destined to rule over it. And rule Rome did, extending its power far and wide and bringing millions of

---

[9] In this case, the Christians and Jews refused to worship the Roman national gods, including the emperors who were considered by their subjects to be divine.
[10] *Rhetorica ad Herennium* 4.9.13. This first-century BC text was attributed to Cicero; however, its authorship is unknown. *Rhetorica ad Herennium* is still important today because it is used as a textbook on structure and rhetoric as yet another gift from Rome to the modern world. Noted in Doron Mendels, *The Rise and Fall of Jewish Nationalism* (Grand Rapids, MI: Wm. B. Eerdmans Publishing Co., 1992), p. 244.
[11] Virgil, *Aeneid*, VI., 851–853.

people under its crushing dominion. In such universal dominance, the Jewish claim of independence could obviously not be tolerated.

Rome brought the Holy Land under its hegemony in 63 BC when Pompey invaded Israel and besieged Jerusalem. Thus began the occupation that would eventually result in the complete exile of the Jews from their land. Within less than seventy years of its annexation of Palestine in AD 4,[12] Rome would utterly destroy Jerusalem and the temple and begin the dispersion of the Jewish people throughout the world. Always on guard against any perceived threat to its domination of its vassal states, imperial Rome would descend upon Judea and systematically destroy every vestige of even suspected Jewish rebellion. This campaign would bring massive loss of life to the Jewish people and threaten the existence of Judaism. Only the hand of God and the resourcefulness of Jewish sages prevented such a dreadful outcome from taking place then and there.

The Jews and Judaism were destined to survive what became one of history's most massive paradigm shifts, but it would not be easy, and it would be costly in terms of Jewish life and treasure. Refusing to bow to Roman domination would cost countless Jewish lives. Thousands would be executed by means of crucifixion, the most cruel and unusual instrument of capital punishment that was ever developed in human history.[13] In the process of these violent actions, the Jews would eventually be forced to cease their active efforts to convert the nations to the faith of Abraham. "Until the Hadrianic persecutions," says Shlomo Riskin, "Jews attempted to fulfill that mission." With Hadrian's onslaught against them, however, "the Jewish people were forced to leave history. Jews were exiled from the stage of historic actors, and perforce became insularly concerned with ethnic

---

[12] The term *Palestine* derives from the Roman designation of the entire Middle East as "Syria Palaestina." The terms *Palestine* and *Palestinian* were first used by the Roman government to refer exclusively to the land of Israel and to the Jewish people. While the name *Syria Palaestina* originally included Syria and Phoenicia, by the end of the second century AD, the Emperor Hadrian had narrowed it to a definition of Judea. The word *Palaestina* was actually derived from the term *Philistine*, as is evidenced from the Arabic word for Palestine, *Filastin*. Hadrian actually applied the term *Palestine* to Judea out of his personal animus and derision for the Jews, calling them, in effect, Philistines and Syrians (Israel's great continuing enemies) rather than Jews.

[13] Andreas J. Köstenberger, *John* (Grand Rapids, MI: Baker Academic, 2004), p. 531. The first-century BC Roman statesman Cicero described crucifixion as "the most cruel and horrifying death." Marcus Tullius Cicero, quoted in Michael Licona, *The Resurrection of Jesus: A New Historiographical Approach* (Downers Grove, IL: InterVarsity Press, 2010), p. 304. William Barclay points out that crucifixion was originated by the Persians as a means of elevating an evildoer's body above the "sacred" earth so as not to defile it. The Persian system was appropriated by the Carthaginians, from whom it was learned by the Romans. William Barclay, *The Gospel of John* (Edinburgh, UK: Saint Andrew Press, 1975), vol. 2, p. 250.

survival."[14] The Roman destruction of the Jewish nation, its dispersion of the Jewish people, and its nullification of the Jewish claim to the land of Israel represented perhaps one of the most cruel—and undeserved—ethnic cleansings in history.[15] The Jews, who were unequivocally the "people of God," came to be viewed as no people at all. Their nation was destroyed, its capital city razed to the ground. They were banished from their land. They would endure century after century of dispersion, degradation, and death; however, they would ever refuse to recant their faith. Who did these Jews think they were, anyway?

The final nail in the sarcophagus that Rome had made for any idea of Israelite independence was driven in AD 135 after Simon bar Kokhba declared the restoration of the state of Judea and then ruled over it as *Nasi* ("prince") for three years. In the process, Simon was proclaimed to be the Messiah by no less a luminary than the great Rabbi Akiva. As could have been expected, the Romans utterly crushed the rebellion, eventually killing both bar Kokhba and Akiva. Because of Bar Kokhba's defiance of Rome, virtually all of the Judean Jews were methodically hunted down and slaughtered, resulting in the virtual depopulation of Judea that some scholars have described as genocide.[16] Indeed, according to Cassius Dio, at least 580,000 Jewish civilians were massacred, and the rest of the population of Judea was sold into slavery.[17] After the smoke had cleared, the emperor Hadrian utterly destroyed the city of Jerusalem and then built directly over its ruins a completely new city, which he named *Aelia*

---

[14] Riskin, p. 127.

[15] Ethnic cleansing has been defined as the action that is undertaken "when one group forcibly removes another by violence or deportation." See Harry I. Chemotsky and Heidi H. Hobbs, *Crossing Borders: International Studies for the 21st Century* (Thousand Oaks, CA: SAGE Publications, Inc., 2016), p. 242.

[16] Samuel Totten, *Teaching about Genocide: Issues, Approaches and Resources* (Charlotte, NC: Information Age Publishing, Inc., 2004), p. 24. Also, Joan E. Taylor, *The Essenes, the Scrolls, and the Dead Sea* (New York: Oxford University Press, 2012), p. 243. Taylor observes that "the Bar Kokhba documents indicate that towns, villages, and ports where the Jews lived were busy with industry and activity. Afterwards there is an eerie silence, and the archaeological record testifies to little Jewish presence until the Byzantine era . . . . The crucial date for what can only be described as genocide, and the devastation of Jews and Judaism within central Judea, was 135 CE."

[17] Cassius Dio, *Historia* 69, 13. Also noted in Arnold James Rudin, *Christians & Jews Faith to Faith: Tragic History, Promising Present, Fragile Future* (Woodstock, VT: Jewish Lights Publishing, 2011), p. 60. Dio estimated that 50 fortified towns and 985 villages were razed to the ground during the time of Hadrian's invasion and destruction of Judea. Rudin claims that the 580,000 Jews who were killed represented "horrendous numbers not reached again until the Holocaust." He also reports the account in the Jerusalem Talmud (*Ta'anit* 4:5) which said that the Romans "went on killing until their horses were submerged in blood up to their nostrils." Also, Doron Mendels, *The Rise and Fall of Jewish Nationalism* (Grand Rapids, MI: Wm. B. Eerdmans Publishing Co., 1992), p. 388. Mendels says that "in the slave market at Hebron at the time a Jew was worth no more than a horse."

Capitolina[18] and dedicated to Jupiter Capitolinus. The virulently antisemitic emperor then forbade the Jews to enter their own capital city upon penalty of death.[19] In less that two centuries, then, the Roman perception of the Israelite threat to their hegemony over the entire Middle East precipitated the destruction of Jerusalem, Israel's capital city; the razing of the symbol of the Jewish religion; the Second Temple; and finally the systematic exile of the Jews from their God-given homeland and the emergence of a new characterization of Jewish peoplehood.[20]

An Increasingly Vulnerable Populace

After the Jewish people were forcibly exiled from their land following the Bar Kokhba rebellion, they became disenfranchised, nationless, and landless. Only in their dreams of the past and in their visions of the future did they have any connection with their native land. The extent of their dispersion separated them into small groups that had no means of common defense. They were also forcibly evicted from various trades and straitjacketed into roles that were easily stereotyped and caricatured.[21] Essentially, they became a people without a country. As a result, they rapidly lost everyday connection with their native tongue.[22] Forced to learn the languages of the Diaspora, they neglected Hebrew except for reciting it in the context of synagogal life whenever and wherever that was possible. Eventually, they came to believe that Hebrew was such a "holy" language that it should be used only in the synagogue and should no longer be used in everyday discourse. Bereft of land and language, they were scattered throughout the world where for centuries they continued to be completely at the mercy of the nations and people among

---

[18] The name *Aelia* was a form of Hadrian's nomen gentile, *Aelius*. The word *Capitolina* referred to Jupiter Capitolinus. As a further sacrilege, Hadrian also built a temple to Jupiter on the temple mount precisely on the site of the razed Jewish temple.

[19] Craig A. Evans, *Jesus and His Contemporaries: Comparative Studies* (Leiden, The Netherlands: E. J. Brill, 1995), p. 72. Hadrian also forbade the Jews to teach the Torah.

[20] Despite the fact that Jews who were believers in Jesus did not support Bar Kokhba's rebellion, they too were banned from Jerusalem in the aftermath of Hadrian's victory. Karen Armstrong, *Jerusalem: One City, Three Faiths* (New York: Random House, 2005), p. 170.

[21] Dean Phillip Bell, *Jews in the Early Modern World* (Lanham, MD: Rowman & Littlefield Publishers, 2008), p. 18. Also, Guido Bolaffi, *Dictionary of Race, Ethnicity, and Culture* (Thousand Oaks, CA: SAGE Publications, 2003), p. 16.

[22] Paul Azous, *In The Plains of the Wilderness* (Jerusalem, Israel: Mazo Publishers, 2006), p. 54. Azous notes that "as Jews became scattered among the nations they adopted either the vernacular of the land or created their own languages, such as Yiddish (a blend of German with Hebrew) or Ladino (a blend of Old Spanish with Hebrew and other languages)."

whom they were forced to live their lives. In some situations, those people were tolerant, even hospitable toward the Jews. In others, Judaeo-phobic and superstitious masses taunted them because of their strange customs and beliefs. The Jews, however, could never deny who they were as Jews, and even minimal manifestation of their historical self-identity often caused them problems.

For a short time after the Roman dispersion, the Diaspora Jews found a degree of mercy and tranquility. Rodney Stark confirms that the five centuries from AD 500–1000 were relatively tranquil times for the Jews with only one confirmed instance of Christian anti-Jewish violence occurring in 554 in Clermont, France, where many Jews were killed, and five hundred accepted forced baptism.[23] Léon Poliakov notes that, generally speaking, during this time, "kings, nobles, and bishops granted Jews a broad autonomy. . . . Talmudic scholarship flowered again on the banks of the Rhine and the Seine at the very period when it was falling into decay in Babylonia. . . . [The Jews] continued to mix freely with the Christian populations and to live on excellent terms with them."[24]

The duration of five centuries of Christian tolerance for the Jews of Europe was largely the result of a decree by Pope Gregory the Great in 590 AD in which he declared that Jews "should have no infringement of their rights" and in which he gave this injunction to the church: "We forbid to vilify the Jews. We allow them to . . . have full authority over their possessions."[25] This decree by one of history's most powerful popes certainly had an impact on the clergy and laity of the Western Church. For 500 years at least, the Jews of Europe were able to live in relative peace and tranquility. Unfortunately, as ensuing history would prove, many further papal pronouncements and ecclesiastical declarations regarding the Jews would have ulterior motivations, such

---

[23] Rodney Stark, *One True God: Historical Consequences of Monotheism* (Princeton, NJ: Princeton University Press, 2001), p. 135.

[24] Leon Poliakov, *The History of Anti-Semitism, Volume One: From the Time of Christ to the Court Jews*, tr. Richard Howard (Philadelphia, PA: The University of Pennsylvania Press, 2003), p. 35.

[25] Gregory I, quoted in Sam Waagenaar, *The Pope's Jews* (Chicago, IL: Open Court Pub. Co., 1974), p. 71. Twentieth-century Jewish historian Cecil Roth, editor-in-chief of the *Encyclopedia Judaica*, said, "of all the dynasties in Europe, the papacy not only refused to persecute the Jews . . . but through the ages popes were protectors of the Jews. . . .For this we Jews must have gratitude." Cecil Roth, quoted in David Goldstein, *Jewish Panorama* (Boston, MA: Catholic Campaigners for Christ, 1940), p. 200. Berel Wein also points out that because the Jews of Renaissance Italy were protected by the pope, there were no overt acts of violence against them as was commonly the case across the rest of Europe. Berel Wein, *Patterns in Jewish History: Insights into the Past, Present, and Future of the Eternal People* (Jerusalem, Israel: Koren Publishers, 2011), p. 15.

as promoting forced baptism and conversion to Christianity, and some would not bode well for the Jewish people.[26] For those Jews who had retreated into Europe in an effort to escape the onslaught of the Roman violence in Palestine living in relative peace, therefore, must have seemed odd, and they must have been wary that such a respite might not be allowed to continue.

Jews, Israel, and the Rise of Islam

During the seventh century AD, a new religion arose in the Middle East. Having been rejected by the Jews and the Christians when he sought inclusion among them, an Arabian merchant named Mohammed created his own religion. This new religion, which was called Islam, was subsequently spread across the Middle East and northern Africa on the edge of the sword. In 637 AD, the Islamic conquest overwhelmed the land of Palestine and forced the surrender of the city of Jerusalem. Any subsequent Arab argument for entitlement to the land of Palestine, therefore, was based on the vicious program of conquest initiated by Mohammed himself and pursued passionately by his followers. Before Islam's military conquest of Palestine, there had been no Muslims or Arabs in Jerusalem, Judea, or Samaria. The Muslim attachment to the land, therefore, has always been associated "with a violent attack on the Jews. It was the Muslims who took the land by force. It is they who established the rules of the game that no matter how long the Jews had lived on the land, no matter if they had been the majority for well more than a thousand years, that those Jews were still subject to be conquered."[27] It is of great importance, therefore, to note that, unlike Arab or Muslim claims to the land of Israel, the title of the Jewish people to the

---

[26] The papacy was largely responsible for the ongoing Medieval European demand that Jews were to wear distinctive clothing or an emblem or mark on their outer garments to distinguish themselves as Jews. Established by Pope Innocent III in the Fourth Lateran Council in 1215, this requirement came to be fulfilled in the yellow badge or the *Judenstern* ("Jews' star) in Germany, in the 3" x 6" yellow felt image of the Decalogue in thirteenth-century England, in full-length red robes in fourteenth century Rome, and in the cone-shaped hat (*Judenhut*) that was common during most of the Middle Ages. This papal-inspired practice eventuated in Hitler's yellow star decree in 1938. For further discussion, see Frank K. Flinn, *Encyclopedia of Catholicism* (New York: Facts On File, Inc., 2007), p. 37, and Harry J. Cargas, *Holocaust Scholars Write to the Vatican* (Westport, CT: Greenwood Press, 1998), p. 9. Similarly, it was Pope Paul IV who created the Roman Ghetto in 1555, forcing the Jews of Rome to live on the left bank of the Tiber in a walled slum, called "the menagerie of the Jews," where they endured almost unspeakably unsanitary conditions. This practice then became entrenched in Europe and made possible such horrors as the twentieth-century Warsaw Ghetto. For further analysis, see Avner Falk, *A Psychoanalytic History of the Jews* (Madison, NJ: Fairleigh Dickinson University Press, 1996), p. 519; Edward Kessler and Neil Wenborn, eds., *A Dictionary of Jewish-Christian Relations* (Cambridge, UK: Cambridge University Press, 2005), p. 166; and Judith R. Baskin, *The Cambridge Dictionary of Judaism and Jewish Culture* (Cambridge, UK: Cambridge University Press, 2001), p. 202.

[27] Lawrence J. Epstein, "The Moral Case of Zionism," in *Israel Opinion*, 04.17.14, p. 1.

land was not appropriated by force of armed conquest. It was by divine gift wherein God himself drove out the inhabitants from the land. Marvin Wilson is right when he asserts that "military conquest may not be used to prove a nation's right to a given land."[28] Something more—much more—is required.

Because of what at that time was their two-millennia-old entitlement to the land of Israel, significant numbers of the Jewish people remained in the land after the Muslim conquest, just as they had done after their ancestors' defeat at the hands of the Assyrians, the Babylonians, and the Romans. It is important to note that the original Muslim conquerors of Palestine did not seek to remove the Jews from the land, nor did they attempt to force them to convert to Islam. Instead, they preferred the monetary advantage of enforcing upon the Jews the Muslim *jizyah* (poll tax) and *kharaj* (land tax) and thereby "permitting" them to live as Jews and to practice Judaism.[29] In fact, it is ironic that, compared with what they experienced in the Christian nations of Medieval Europe, the Jewish people lived relatively well under Muslim rule, even though they were a suppressed and exploited minority.[30] Whereas in Europe, the stated goal of the rulers was to force Jews to convert to Christianity, in Muslim lands, Jews were only *encouraged* to convert to Islam.[31] Daniel Gavron points out that "in Mesopotamia, the Jews flourished under Islam. Although as non-Muslims they were in many ways second-class citizens, they were honored as the 'People of the Book.'"[32] In fact, because of this perspectiver, early Muslims did not regard the Jews as "nonbelievers, since they shared with them the belief in one God,"[33] though they could not be considered to be "true believers either, because they failed to acknowledge

---

[28] Marvin R. Wilson, *Our Father Abraham: Jewish Roots of the Christian Faith* (Grand Rapids, MI: Wm. B. Eerdmans Publishing Co., 1989), p. 266. Wilson rightfully warns of the dangers of "real estate theology" which even to this day can inflame passions and move people of every religious persuasion to acts that violate and preclude social justice.

[29] Falk, p. 376. Falk notes: "The early Muslim rulers regarded the non-Muslim 'aliens' in their realm as 'protected' people who had to show their submission by paying special taxes. . . . In exchange for paying the *jizyah* (head tax or poll tax) and *kharaj* (land tax), these aliens received *dhimma* (protection) of their Muslim rulers, were granted freedom of worship, and were allowed to organize themselves into religious communities." The collection of the *jizyah* and *kharaj* taxes was one of Islam's five precepts or "pillars." See Nissim Rejwan, *Israel's Place in the Middle East: A Pluralist Perspective* (Gainesville, FL: The University of Florida Press, 1998), p. 36.

[30] Benny Morris, *The Road to Jerusalem: Glubb Pasha, Palestine and the Jews* (London, UK: I.B. Tauris & Co, 2002) p. 28.

[31] Scott A. Merriman, *Religion and the Law in America: An Encyclopedia of Personal Belief and Public Policy* (Santa Barbara, CA: ABC–CLIO, Inc., 2007), p. 87.

[32] Daniel Gavron, *Holy Land Mosaic: Stories of Cooperation and Coexistence Between Israelis and Palestinians* (Lanham, MD: Rowman & Littlefield Publishers, 2008), p. 88.

[33] Rejwan, p. 36.

the mission of Muhammad and did not accept the Koran as divine revelation."[34] Many Jewish scholars excelled in Arabic literature and in science, particularly medicine, and Jewish leaders "played an important role in the consolidation of the Muslim civilization."[35] One of the greatest Talmudists in history, Moses Maimonides, lived much of his life in Tunisia and Egypt, where he became the personal physician of Saladin, the Sultan of Egypt and Syria, who cemented Muslim control of Jerusalem and Judea by seizing Palestine from the Crusaders.

Exploding Violence and Destruction

The tranquility that the Jewish people experienced during the second half of the first millennium AD was to be short lived, however, for danger and death were lurking on the horizon of the immediate future that would bring centuries of misery to them. Beginning with the turn of the second millennium of the Common Era, Jews found themselves forced to live in lands and among people who were increasingly inhospitable and antisemitic. The times were changing. Christians, who for centuries had expended their energies fighting one another and advancing the City of God,[36] would soon be blindsided by a whirling dervish of political and religious fervor: militant Islam. Shortly after the turn of the millennium, a group of Muslims that was led by Fatmid Caliph al-Hakim attacked Jerusalem and destroyed the Church of the Holy Sepulchre, the very basilica that Constantine, at his mother Helena's request, had erected to enshrine the site of the tomb in which Jesus was interred before his resurrection. When word of this desecration reached Europe, Christian passions became inflamed, and the church turned its fury upon those new infidels. Tragically, that could mean only one thing: trouble for the Jews.

Christians who had hurled polemics against Judaism for centuries began to inflict personal violence upon the Jews. From the eleventh to the fourteenth centuries, the Crusades resulted in the death of countless Jews as the Christian soldiers bent on destroying the Muslim infidels turned their anger against an even older rival, the Jews. A prime example occurred when the first Crusaders took Jerusalem in 1099 and promptly herded Jewish men, women, and children into the Great Synagogue, torched that house of worship, and then marched around the inferno with their crosses held high,[37] chanting the *a cappella* anthem,

---

[34] Rejwan, p. 36.
[35] Gavron, p. 88.
[36] Gerard O'Daly, *Augustine's City of God: A Reader's Guide* (New York: Oxford University Press, 1999), p. 9.
[37] David Rausch, *Legacy of Hatred: Why Christians Must Not Forget the Holocaust* (Grand Rapids, MI: Baker Publishing Group, 1990), p. 27.

"Christ, We Adore Thee," in order to drown out the screams of Jewish men, women, and children who were being immolated in the synagogue.[38]

During this time, the Jews, who were "the people of God," essentially became "no people." Pope Alexander II wrote to the bishops of Spain around 1060, "In the same manner Saint Gregory also admonished those [who] agitated for annihilating [the Jews], indicating that it is impious to wish to annihilate those who are protected by the mercy of God, so that, with homeland and liberty lost, in everlasting penitence, damned by the guilt of their ancestors for spilling the blood of the Savior, they live dispersed throughout the various areas of the world."[39] Later, during the Reformation, German Protestant scholars assigned the Jews to the *Unheilsgeschichte* (disaster or damnation history) that was contrasted with the *Heilsgeschichte* (salvation or redemption history) of God's acts in biblical history that continued in and through the church.[40] In fact, in order to personify the notion of the Jewish *Unheilsgeschichte*, one of Martin Luther's students, Paul von Eitzen, created the myth of Ahasverus,[41] the "eternal Jew" (or the "wandering Jew"), who, because he had scoffed at Jesus as the Lord carried his cross to Golgotha, had been condemned to wander the earth forever with no home and no opportunity to escape his suffering even through death.[42] This mythical character came to be identified with the entire Jewish population[43] which, from the earliest days of Christianity, was thought to be doomed to wander forever with no homeland and to be afflicted with terrible circumstances as a living witness to what happens to anyone who rejects Jesus.

This concept gained solid credibility in the church when Augustine, in his *Reply to Faustus the Manichean*, drew a parallel between Cain and the Jews, concluding that just as Cain was not to be killed for his crime of murdering Abel but was to be a fugitive and a vagabond and was to bear a "mark" that would distinguish him from the rest of humanity and protect him from being

---

[38] Dagobert David Runes, *The War against the Jew* (New York: Philosophical Library, 1968), p. 37. Also, Arthur Blech, *The Causes of Anti-Semitism: A Critique of the Bible* (Amherst, NY: Prometheus Books, 2006), p. 360; and Hillel Halkin, *Yehuda Halevi* (New York: Random House, 2010), p. 111.

[39] Alexander II, quoted in Robert Chazan, ed., *Church, State, and Jew in the Middle Ages* (New York: Behrman House, 1980), pp. 99–100.

[40] The Term *Heilgeschichte* was devised by German scholars to contrast with *Weltgeschichte* (world history) in order to point to "salvation history" as distinct from "universal history."

[41] Ahasverus is sometimes written as Ahasver.

[42] Richard Eldemann, "Ahasuerus, the Wandering Jew: Origin and Background," in *The Wandering Jew: Essays in the Interpretation of a Christian Legend*, G. Hasan-Roken and A. Dundes, eds., (Bloomington, IN: Indiana University Press, 1986), pp. 1–10.

[43] Paul Lawrence Rose, *Revolutionary Antisemitism in Germany from Kant to Wagner* (Princeton, NJ: Princeton University Press, 1990), pp. 23–43.

killed,[44] so the Jews should be distinguished but not executed for their crime of killing Jesus."[45] As Clark Williamson explains, Augustine believed that the Jews should "groan and tremble on the earth, witnessing to the fate of those who reject Christ." In so doing, "the 'wandering Jew' makes the strange witness of unbelief in dispersion from the land of promise."[46] Later, at the Fourth Lateran Council in 1215 AD, the church drew from Augustine's spurious Cain analogy to require the Jews to wear a "mark of separation."[47] Even as late as the 1930s when the Nazi Party was ascending to power, German bishop Michael von Faulhaber was still making the same argument: "After the death of Christ, Israel was dismissed from the service of Revelation . . . and from that time forth Ahasuerus wanders, forever restless, over the face of the earth."[48] This was the only "logical" reason that church theologians and leaders, with their rampant antisemitism, could give for the continuing anomaly of Jewish existence.

Pervasive Judaeophobia, Anti-Judaism, and Antisemitism

Across all of Christian Europe, then, the second millennium of the Common Era was a time of unrelenting violent attacks on Jews, featuring pillage, rape, and murder. Some of the tragic events were spontaneous; however, most were well-organized, government-sponsored, and church-endorsed efforts to exterminate the Jews from Christian kingdoms. Jews who had fled the Roman persecutions and settled across Europe where they had enjoyed a time of tranquility during the second half of the first millennium were subjected to systematic efforts to bring about their genocide for virtually all of the second millennium. While many popes and other church leaders urged the church to be merciful to the Jews,[49] more often

---

[44] Genesis 4:12–15. God cursed Cain, saying, "A fugitive and a vagabond you will be on the earth."

[45] Salo Wittmayer Baron, *Social and Religious History of the Jews* (New York: Columbia University Press, 1974), vol. 12, pp. 177–182.

[46] Clark M. Williamson, *A Guest in the House of Israel: Post-Holocaust Church Theology* (Louisville, KY: Westminster John Knox Press, 1993), pp. 115–116.

[47] See note 26, p. 186. Also, John Byron, *Cain and Abel in Text and Tradition: Jewish and Christian Interpretations of the First Sibling Rivalry* (Leiden, The Netherlands: Koninklijke Brill NV, 2011), pp. 239–244.

[48] Michael von Faulhaber, quoted in George Mosse, *Nazi Culture: A Documentary History* (New York: Random House, 1966), p. 239.

[49] The papal tradition of tolerance for and protection of the Jews is traceable to the sixth century AD with Gregory the Great; however, though other popes followed suit with official pronouncements of support for the Jews, delegated institutional leaders of the Western Church often condoned and were sometimes complicit in the atrocities that were perpetrated against the Jews by civil authorities. This ambivalence continued through the time of the Holocaust wherein Pope Piux XII never "made it explicit that it was a sin for a Catholic priest to cooperate in delivering Jews to the Nazis." Richard L. Rubenstein and John K. Roth, *Approaches to Auschwitz: The Holocaust and Its Legacy* (Louisville, KY: Westminster John Knox Press, 2003), p. 274.

than not church leaders were either silent in the face of atrocities against the Jews or they were active sponsors of and participants in those acts.[50] Richard Rubenstein may well be right when he says that "the more one studies the classical utterances of Christianity on Jews and Judaism while at the same time reviewing the terrible history of the Nazi period, the more one is prompted to ask whether there is something in the Christian philosophy of history, *when pushed to a metaphysical extreme*, that ends in the justification, of, if not the incitement to, the extermination of the Jews."[51]

The Christian church, which should have served under the humility of the cross, instead turned the cross into a sword and used it to inflict unimaginable suffering on countless Jewish men, women, and children. The movement that was designed by Jesus to be an instrument of life became the foremost mechanism of death for Jewish people. The details of the complicity of Christian church leaders and civil authorities in the ongoing Jewish suffering can never be eradicated from history or from the corporate memory of the Jewish people. Christianity itself has been forever disfigured by this evil, and contemporary Christians can only repent in sackcloth and ashes for the "sins of the fathers" and vow in their hearts that they will never allow the same atrocities to be repeated. Eternal vigilance is essential, for, as Daniel Goldhagen says, antisemitism and the "antisemite's eliminationist" plans are "the devil that never dies."[52]

The only way to avoid repeating history is to study it and learn from it, for as George Santayana said, "Those who cannot remember the past are condemned to repeat it."[53] It is vital, therefore, for every Christian to undertake a personal study of readily available historical research in order to know personally the extent of Christian-sponsored violence against the Jewish people. One of the best texts that would aid such a review is *Codex Judaica: Chronological Index of Jewish History, Covering 5,764 Years*, Máttis Kantor's exhaustive listing of the suffering and loss of life that the Jewish people have experienced

---

[50] Mordecai Paldiel, *Churches and the Holocaust, Unholy Teaching, Good Samaritans, and Reconciliation* (Jersey City, NJ: KTAV Publishing House, 2006), pp. 26–23.

[51] Richard L. Rubenstein, "The Dean and the Chosen People," in *Wrestling with God: Jewish Theological Responses during and after the Holocaust,* Steven T. Katz, Shlomo Biderman, and Gershon Greenberg, eds. (New York: Oxford University Press, 2007), p. 410, author's emphasis. Rubenstein concludes this observation by saying, "Though there is an infinitude of pain in the exploration of this question, neither the Christian nor the Jew can avoid it."

[52] Daniel Jonah Goldhagen, *The Devil that Never Dies: The Rise and Threat of Global Antisemitism* (New York: Little, Brown and Co., 2013), p. 142.

[53] George Santayana, *Reason in Common Sense, Vol. 1: The Life of Reason* (Mineola, NY: Dover Publications, 1980). p. 221.

through history, with hundreds of entries listed in short, succinct statements of historical fact.[54] Cases of violence against the Jews from the eleventh century to the turn of the twentieth century cover 89 pages of condensed, straightforward, and shocking historical text that should be read by every Christian in the world. It is a chilling account of the senseless and ceaseless terror and cruelty that were continually imposed by nominal Christians upon Jewish men, women, and children for virtually an entire millennium.

Throughout the unrelenting barrage of violence against the Jewish people, however, the indomitable Jewish spirit has always come to the fore. Their simple and quiet confidence in the God of Scripture has buoyed their spirits to believe that their God, the sovereign of the universe, loved the descendants of Abraham, Isaac, and Jacob with an unending love and that he was irrevocably committed to their survival. A veritable parade of Gentile empires tried every way possible to obliterate Israel and the Jews. The Assyrians destroyed Israel's cities; the Babylonians took Judah into exile; the Greeks tried to destroy Judaism through syncretism; and the Romans obliterated Jerusalem and scattered the Jews throughout the world.[55] Erik Peterson said it well, however: "No power in the world will be able to extirpate Judaism. Indeed not even the Jews themselves will be able to extirpate themselves so long as God's long-suffering endures."[56] Against all the laws of history concerning the assimilation of conquered peoples, the Jews have maintained their separate identity as God instructed them to do.[57] Right in the face of death, they have confessed their faith in the one who is Lord of death and life. For countless Jewish martyrs, the last words that escaped their lips were, "*Shema, Yisrael, Adonai Elohenu, Adonai Echad*" ("Hear, O Israel, the LORD our God, the LORD is One"). Even in death, the Jewish people have remained triumphant, for they have known that their God is the one who is always faithful, even—and especially—to those who sleep in the dust of the earth.

---

54 Máttis Kantor, *Codex Judaica: Chronological Index of Jewish History* (New York: Zichron Press, 2005), pp. 185–274.

55 Richard Bell, *The Irrevocable Call of God: An Inquiry into Paul's Theology of Israel* (Tübingen, Germany: Mohr Sïebeck, 2005), p. 347.

56 Erik Peterson, *Die Kirche aus Juden und Heiden*, p. 18, quoted in Karl Barth, *Church Dogmatics, II/2: The Election of God; the Command of God* (New York: Bloomsbury Academic, 2004), p. 226.

57 Steven Beller, *Vienna and the Jews, 1867-1938: A Cultural History* (Cambridge, UK: Cambridge University Press, 1989), p. 74. As an example of how the Jewish people defied total assimilation, Beller noted that in nineteenth- and twentieth-century Vienna, Jews "had some idea of what being Jewish entailed. Full assimilation would have meant that this sense of a Jewish identity would have disappeared. . . . This is not what happened." The Jewish self-identity as Jews could never be obliterated.

CHAPTER 12

RESTORATIONISM AND ZIONISM
CHRISTIAN FAITH IN GOD'S PROMISES TO ISRAEL

Through the centuries of the great Diaspora following Hadrian's forced exile of the Jewish people from the land of Israel, the hope of return to the land never faded from the individual or corporate Jewish consciousness. Every time a Jew opened parchment scrolls or texts of the Hebrew Scriptures, the covenant of the Promised Land leapt from the Torah,[1] the *Nevi'im*,[2] and the *Ketuvim*,[3] causing faith to rise in their hearts that one day God would restore the people, the nation, and the land of Israel. Many, if not most, connected this expectation with the hope of the coming Messiah, and over the centuries, they prayed the following *Kaddish* hymn of praise: "Exalted and hallowed be God's great Name in this world of His creation. (Amen.) May His will be fulfilled by the revelation of His sovereignty and the flowering of His salvation. (Amen.) May He hasten the coming of his anointed Messiah in your lifetime and in the life of the whole House of Israel, speedily and soon, and let us say, Amen."[4]

Some of the prophetic texts, to be sure, could have been interpreted in preterist[5] fashion as having already been fulfilled historically in the restoration that followed the Babylonian captivity; however, many, if not most, of them undoubtedly spoke either obliquely or explicitly concerning what could only be understood as a still future event. Among the most absolute of these was Amos 9:11: "In that day I will raise up

---

[1] The Torah is composed of the five books of Moses, the Pentateuch.
[2] The *Nevi'im* is made up of the books of prophecy in the Hebrew Scriptures.
[3] The *Ketuvim* contains the historical and poetic books of the Hebrew Scriptures.
[4] Shmuel Kaplan, *Beneath the Sheltering Wings* (Bloomington, IN: ExLibris Press, 2011), p. 119.
[5] Preterism interprets most prophecies of the Bible, including the apocalyptic predictions of Daniel and the Apocalypse, in terms of events which have already occurred.

David's fallen *sukkah* and wall up its breaches . . . and rebuild it as in the days of old. . . . And I will restore the captivity of my people Israel, and they will rebuild the ruined cities and live in them. . . . I will also plant them on their land, and *they will not again be rooted out from their land which I have given them*, says the LORD your God."[6] This prophecy of the restored people and the restored land surely could not possibly have been fulfilled in the sense of having been "filled full"[7] in the post-exilic restoration,[8] for it is a simple fact of history that the Jewish people were uprooted and driven from their land both by Vespasian in AD 70 and by Hadrian in AD 135.

Though realistic prospects for the restoration of the Jewish people to the land may have seemed increasingly remote, if not impossible, still the God-intoxicated heart of the Torah-observant Jew[9] refused to relinquish the hope (*ha-tikvah*) that the Eternal would move to fulfill the Abrahamic promise. Many Jews, however, for their own safety and survival, chose to sublimate this hope and to make every reasonable effort possible to assimilate into the nations where their journeyings had brought them.

---

6 Emphasis added.

7 Craig L. Bloomberg, *Jesus and the Gospels: An Introduction and Survey* (Nashville, TN: B&H Publishing Group, 2009), p. 234. In discussing the fulfillment of Isaiah's prophecies regarding Immanuel (chapters 7–9), Bloomberg says, "[T]he semantic range of 'fulfill' that could include the concepts of 'completing' or 'filling full' allowed for multiple fulfillments of prophecy of varying kinds."

8 The various events that have been viewed as "fulfillments" of Amos' prophecy establish a principle of biblical hermeneutics wherein some prophecies can actually have multiple fulfillments. This principle is based on the concept of divine immutability, in which God's actions remain consistent and constant—unchanging—within given circumstances. The restoration of David's fallen *sukkah* was certainly "fulfilled" historically at the end of the Babylonian captivity, when the leaders of Judah returned to Jerusalem and restored the city and the temple. It was, however, "fulfilled" spiritually in the restoration of the house of David through the ministry of Jesus and his apostles, as was affirmed by James in Acts 15:11–16. It may well be in the process of acquiring yet another spiritual "fulfillment" in the return of Christian believers to the Jewish roots of their faith which began in the sixteenth century and has continued unabated until this day. It certainly is being "fulfilled" as the Jewish people are being restored to their land for what prayerfully will be the penultimate fulfillment in which they will "never be removed again." And, it will doubtless be finally "fulfilled"—and, indeed, "filled full"—when the Messiah comes to restore the House of David, including the throne of David, and establish the kingdom of God in the *Olam ha-Ba* (the Age to Come). See Sidney Greidanus, *Preaching Christ from the Old Testament: A Contemporary Hermeneutical Method* (Grand Rapids MI: Wm. B. Eerdmans Publishing Co., 1999), p. 143. In a discussion of the interpretive methodology of John Calvin, Greidanus concludes, "Fulfillment of a promise, therefore, is not a static entity but continues the process to ever greater fulfillments." Also, Bruce Corley, Steve Lemke, and Grant I. Lovejoy, eds., *Biblical Hermeneutics: A Comprehensive Introduction to Interpreting Scripture* (Nashville, TN: B&H Publishing Group, 2002), pp. 143–144; and Bloomberg, p. 234.

9 Samuel Umen, *Jewish Concepts and Reflections* (New York: Philosophical Library, 1962), p. 32. Umen has said, "Jewish history is the record of a god-intoxicated, god-thirsty people."

Christian Expectation for the Restoration of Israel

Long before the nation of Israel was resurrected from the ashes of the Holocaust, Christians had begun to join their Jewish brothers and sisters in praying for the peace of Jerusalem and for the restoration of the holy nation of Israel. As a matter of fact, early Christian hopes and expectations regarding the rebirth of Israel were called simply "Restorationism"[10] because they focused on a renewal of the ancient faith and practices of both the Jews and earliest Christianity. Restorationism developed three centuries before largely secular Jewish leaders coined the term *Zionism* to describe their vision for the reestablishment of Jewish sovereignty over the land of Israel. Christian Restorationism originated at the turn of the seventeenth century, long before the term *Christian Zionism* came to be employed by Christians in the mid-twentieth century to show their support for the Jewish people and for the restoration of Israel. Restorationists saw "the Jews as continuers of the biblical children of Israel, heirs to the covenant between God and Abraham, and the object of biblical prophecies about a restored Davidic kingdom in the land of Israel."[11] Goran Gunner points out that "in restorationism, the relation of Christianity to the Jews remains one of universalism to particularism. But instead of negating Jewish particularism and demanding that it obliterate itself into Christian universalism, it seeks to restore Jews to their status as a nation in their national land under Christian imperial patronage."[12] While this position was not without ulterior motive, at least it was a step in the right direction toward enlisting Christian support for restored Jewish sovereignty over their own nation and their own land.

It is not inconsequential that the greatest Christian advocacy for the restoration of the Jewish state arose during the birth and development of

---

[10] Stephen R. Haynes, *Reluctant Witnesses: Jews and the Christian Imagination* (Louisville, KY: Westminster/John Knox Press, 1995), p. 51. Hayes observes that "Restorationism denotes the Christian belief that Jews will be restored to their homeland in biblical Israel as a sign of God's impending millennial reign, usually just before, after or during a mass conversion of Jews to Christianity." He points out that Restorationist thought was a feature of all the various millenarian movements in the sixteenth through the eighteenth centuries and that Restorationism was also central to Puritan theology in Holland, Britain, and America during that time. Also, Yohanna Katanacho, *The Land of Christ: A Palestinian Cry* (Eugene, OR: Wipf and Stock Publishers, 2013), p. 9.

[11] Jonathan Rynhold, *The Arab-Israeli Conflict in American Political Culture* (Cambridge, UK: Cambridge University Press, 2015), p. 98.

[12] Goran Gunner and Robert O. Smith, *Comprehending Christian Zionism: Perspectives in Comparison* (Minneapolis, MN: Augsburg Fortress Press, 2014), p. 178.

the Protestant Reformation. Protestant emphases on the restoration of the people and nation of Israel were likely spawned by the early sixteenth-century *veritas Hebraica* teachings[13] promoted by self-styled Christian Hebraists.[14] With their emphasis on the importance of returning to Hebrew texts of Holy Scripture and recovering the Hebraic foundations of the Christian faith, these Christian Hebraists created the climate which produced the Reformation.[15] They certainly provided the intellectual foundation for the Reformers' emphasis on faith and Scripture.

Reformation Christians, especially those who espoused the restoration of Israel, were often expelled from their own homelands because of their views. As Heiko Oberman observed, "Once the homeless, fugitive Christians were compelled to share the destiny of the Jews, expulsion no longer bore the unambiguous marks of a God-sent punishment. The destiny of worldwide diaspora, formerly the proof of the obstinate Jew's guilt, was now the badge of faith of the avowed Christian."[16] It is obvious that as reformed and reforming Christians reconnected with the authority of Holy Scripture—evidenced by their motto *Sola Scriptura*[17]—they began

---

[13] The term *veritas Hebraica* was probably coined in the early fifth century by Jerome as description of his desire to go *ad fontes* ("[back] to the sources") for accurate translation of Holy Scripture. Jerome espoused studying both Hebrew and Greek in his efforts to translate the Scriptures more accurately into Latin. The result was his Latin Vulgate, which was *the* "Bible" of the Western Church for centuries. By the turn of the sixteenth century, however, the Christian Hebraists had concluded that they could no longer trust either Jerome's Vulgate or church tradition, so they advocated a return to studying the Hebrew texts of the "Old Testament," along with analyzing the Hebraic thought and the innumerable Hebraicisms that are found to be underlying the Greek text of the "New Testament."

[14] Through the centuries, the term *Christian Hebraist* has been given to scholars who have believed that the study of Hebrew is necessary for proper exegesis of Holy Scripture. Though it can be applied to scholars who lived from 450 AD to 1800 AD, it is generally used to describe such scholars who lived and worked from the sixteenth century forward. Stephen G. Burnett, *Christian Hebraism in the Reformation Era (1500–1660)* (Leiden, The Netherlands: Koninklijke Brill, 2012), p. 139. Burnett notes, "By the end of the sixteenth century Christian Hebraists of all confessions had developed both a rationale for studying the Hebrew language and Jewish texts and the necessary expertise to do so." See John D. Garr, *Christian Fruit–Jewish Root: Theology of Hebraic Restoration* (Atlanta, GA: Golden Key Press, 2014), pp. 379–380, and John D. Garr, *Life from the Dead: The Dynamic Saga of the Chosen People* (Atlanta, GA: Golden Key Press, 2014), pp. 293–294.

[15] Both Huldrych Zwingli, in the reformed tradition, and Philipp Melanchthon, the premier sixteenth-century Lutheran theologian, were Christian Hebraists. See Robert J. Wilkinson, *Tetragrammaton: Western Christians and the Hebrew Name of God* (Leiden, The Netherlands: Koninklijke Brill, 2015), p. 399, and Hans-Martin Kirn, "Traces of Targum Reception in the Work of Martin Luther," in *A Jewish Targum in a Christian World*, Alberdina Houtman, E. van Staalduine-Sulman, and Hans-Martin Kim, eds. (Leiden, The Netherlands: Koninklijke Brill, 2014), p. 270.

[16] Heiko Oberman, *The Origins of Anti-Semitism in the Age of Renaissance and Reformation*, tr. James I. Porter (Philadelphia, PA: Fortress Press, 1984), p. 140.

[17] *Sola Scriptura* means "Scripture Alone" or "Scripture Only." It was accompanied by other Reformation slogans, including *Sola Fide* ("Faith Alone") and *Sola Gratia* ("Grace Alone").

to understand the power and perdurability of God's promises to Abraham and his descendants. They could no longer subscribe to the tradition of the Western Church which, from the time of Augustine, had promoted an entrenched amillennialism, which was focused on maintaining the politico-ecclesiastical power and privilege of the church. Because they endured persecution and violence from the church, the Protestant Christians more readily empathized with the plight of the Jewish people and the suffering that they had endured at the hand of those "Christian" civil authorities whose actions were either overtly or tacitly condoned and were often endorsed by the same church that was harassing them.

Apostles and Church Fathers

These Christians, however, were not creating something new in Christian theology, for many leaders in the church after the destruction of Jerusalem in AD 70 and the exile of the Jews in AD 135 had shared the same expectation that the Jews themselves had long held for the restoration and renewal of their nation and land. For those early Gentile leaders of the Christian church, the prophetic theme of the eschatological resurrection of the dead at the end of days—in which they believed implicitly because of their faith in the resurrected Jesus—was specifically associated in the biblical languages with the restoration of the Jewish people to their ancestral home in the land of Israel. In fact, the two events—resurrection and restoration—were inextricably connected in the pages of Scripture itself.

Beginning with Paul's magisterial argument in Romans 11 for Gentile inclusion without Jewish exclusion,[18] recognition of God's parallel dealings with Israel and the church—though mystifying at best[19]—was part of the ongoing evaluation of what God was doing and how he might accomplish

---

[18] Jeffrey S. Siker, *Disinheriting the Jews: Abraham in Early Christian Controversy* (Louisville, KY: Westminster John Knox Press, 1991), p. 197. Siker notes that "Paul did not equate Jewish rejection of the gospel with God's rejection of the Jews. Nor would he allow such an equation to be inferred. Rather, Jewish rejection of the gospel served God's purpose of Gentile inclusion within the gospel. . . . Paul would not affirm the theological doctrine that became entrenched among later generations of Christians, namely, that Gentile inclusion necessitates Jewish exclusion."

[19] Paul specifically used the word *mystery* to describe Israel's "hardness in part" (Romans 11:25). His use of this term indicated that what was unfolding in holy history was not completely understood and ultimately had to be entrusted to the wisdom of God. His level of insight into God's actions regarding both Israel and the Christian community prompted him to exclaim through this doxology: "O, the depth of the riches both of the wisdom and knowledge of God! How unsearchable are his judgments and unfathomable his ways!" (Romans 11:33).

his "plan of salvation."[20] Karl Barth encapsulated the nature of God's act of including Gentiles without voiding his covenant with Israel and excluding Jews: "Without a doubt the Jews are to this very day the chosen people of God in the same sense as they have been so from the beginning. . . . They have the promise of God; and if we Christians from among the gentiles have it too, then it is only as those chosen with them; as guests in their house, as new wood grafted onto their old tree."[21]

The church in history, however, reversed the clear intentions of both Jesus and Paul by arguing that the Jews were required to come under the domain of the church in order to continue to be included in the covenant. In contrast, Paul understood that even the branches of God's family tree that were broken off because of unbelief could be regrafted into their own tree,[22] an expectation that was based on his assurance from Scripture that the calling of God is irrevocable.[23] Perhaps Paul himself wondered how and when this would take place, but, then, less than twenty years before that time, who would have even remotely suspected that Gentiles would come to faith in the God of Israel *en masse*?[24] Brad Young answers very simply the paradox of God's hardening Israel while maintaining their election when he asks the rhetorical question: "Does God break covenant with one to fulfill a promise with another?"[25] Pope John Paul II answered this question succinctly: "The permanence of Israel (while so many ancient peoples have disappeared without a trace) is a historic fact and a sign to be interpreted within God's design. We must in any case rid ourselves of the traditional idea of a people *punished*, preserved as a *living argument* for Christian apologetic. It remains a chosen people, 'the pure olive' on which were grafted the branches of the wild olive which are the gentiles."[26]

---

[20] Brian J. Abasciano, *Paul's Use of the Old Testament in Romans 9.1–18: An Intertextual and Theological Exegesis* (New York: T & T Clark International, 2011), p. 68. Abasciano says that "the parallel [in Paul's teaching] runs deeper. Not only is God presented as sovereign over both Israel and the Gentiles, but he also declares that his sovereign dealings with the Gentiles will glorify him and move Israel to acknowledge his greatness and covenant faithfulness."

[21] Karl Barth, *Against the Stream: Shorter Post-war Writings, 1946–1952*, Ronald Gregor Smith, ed. (London, UK: SCM Press, 1954), p. 200.

[22] Romans 11:23.

[23] Romans 11:29. For an excellent discussion of Jewish perspectives on Romans 9–11, see Mark D. Nanos, *The Mystery of Romans: The Jewish Context of Paul's Letters* (Minneapolis, MN: Augsburg Fortress Press, 1996).

[24] Matthew 10:5–6; Ephesians 3:5; Acts 15:15.

[25] Brad H. Young, *Paul the Jewish Theologian* (Peabody, MA: Hendrickson Publishing, 1997), p. 139.

[26] John Paul II, 6 March, 1982, in *1985 "Notes"* issued by the Holy See's Commission for Religious Relations with Judaism, quoted in *Selected Works of Joseph Cardinal Bernardin*, Alphonse P. Spilly, ed. (Collegeville, MN: The Liturgical Press, 2000), p. 291.

Paul's understanding of the "mystery" of Gentile inclusion[27] prompted him to issue this warning to those to whom he had been commissioned with the church's apostolate to the Gentiles:[28] "Do not be arrogant toward the [natural] branches."[29] It was not long after Paul's death, however, when church leaders began to surmise that Gentile inclusion must, in some way, have meant Jewish exclusion. By the middle of the second century AD, Justin Martyr had become the first Christian church father to identify the church as Israel and, by doing so, added credibility to teachings that would grow into Christian triumphalism and supersessionism vis-à-vis the Jews. Justin, however, was not a total supersessionist, for he still affirmed his belief in a future salvation of Israel and in an eschatological earthly kingdom that would be established in Israel with its capital in Jerusalem. This is what Justin said: "And what the people of the Jews shall say and do, when they see Him coming in glory, has been thus predicted by Zechariah the prophet."[30] Shortly thereafter, other church fathers further connected the restoration of Israel directly with the Christian expectation of the resurrection at the end of days. Kevin Madigan and Jon Levenson note that these "ancient Christian writers were well aware of both potential meanings" in the texts of the Hebrew Scriptures. Indeed, "they could be remarkably sensitive to the interwoven meanings — restoration and resurrection — in the original text."[31]

In the second century AD, Irenaeus, a church apologist from Gaul, "expected that Jerusalem would be rebuilt"[32] and restored to the Jews. He quoted "the prophecies of the restoration of the children of Israel" despite the fact that he applied the majority of his thought on that "restoration" to the church rather than to the Jewish people where it should have belonged.[33] Irenaeus' views were shared by the third-century Roman theologian Hippolytus, who argued for the return of the Jewish people from the lands into which they had

---

27 Ephesians 3:1–6.
28 Galatians 2:9; Romans 11:13; 2 Timothy 1:11.
29 Romans 11:18.
30 Justin, *First Apology* 52. See *The Ante-Nicene Fathers*, A. Cleveland Coxe, James Donaldson, and Alexander Roberts, eds. (Peabody, MA: Hendrickson Publishers, 1994), vol. 1, p. 180.
31 Kevin J. Madigan and Jon D. Levenson, *Resurrection: The Power of God for Christians and Jews* (New Haven, CT: Yale University Press, 2009), pp. 227–228.
32 Irenaeus, *Against Heresies* 5.25.4, 28.2, 30.2–4.
33 T. L. Frazier, *A Second Look at the Second Coming: Sorting Through the Speculations* (Ben Lomond, CA: Conciliar Press, 1999), p. 91. Also, Carole Monica Burnett, "Eastern Orthodox Perspectives on Zionism and Christian Zionism," in *Zionism and the Quest for Justice in the Holy Land*, Donald E. Wagner and Walter T. Davis, eds. (Cambridge, UK: The Lutterworth Press, 2014), p. 98.

been dispersed by the Assyrians, Babylonians, and Romans.[34] Irenaeus maintained that this restoration would take place despite the fact that the Jews did not believe in Jesus as Messiah and Lord. Because a number of other church fathers interpreted the prophecies of the Hebrew Scriptures literally, they believed "in a rather worldly millennium involving a far-reaching, miraculous transformation of the natural world,"[35] says Carey Newman. Prominent among these were the second-century Apostolic Father Papias, bishop of Hierapolis,[36] and the fourth-century bishop of Salamis, Epiphanius.[37] Similarly, the Montanist movement, which, from the second to the sixth centuries, was widespread with many adherents, also believed in the restoration of Israel.[38]

As late as the third century AD, the North African polemicist Tertullian argued for the restoration of the Jewish state by interpreting texts like Ezekiel 37 as speaking first about Israel's restoration and then about the eschatological resurrection. "For Tertullian, it is obvious," Madigan and Levenson say, "that the reincorporation and recompacting of bones symbolizes the 'restoration of the Jewish state,' 'tribe to tribe, people to people'—for the text itself supplies its own interpretation."[39] Tertullian also made this argument: "[God] will favour with his acceptance and blessing the circumcision, even the race of Abraham, which by and by is to acknowledge him."[40] On another occasion, he also observed, "It will be fitting for the Christian to rejoice, and not to grieve, at the restoration of Israel, if it is to be true (as it is) that the whole of our hope is intimately united with the remaining expectation of Israel."[41] Other third-century church fathers who believed in and taught the restoration of Israel included Lactantius[42] and Commodian,[43] who even predicted that the ten "lost"[44] tribes of Israel would return to the land of Israel.

---

34 Romanus Hippolytus, *Treatise on Christ and the Anti-Christ* Sn. 54, tr. Philip Schaff, in Coxe, Donaldson, and Roberts, eds., vol. 5, pp. 522, 527–528.

35 Carey C. Newman, *Jesus & the Restoration of Israel: A Critical Assessment of N. T. Wright's* Jesus and the Victory of God (Downers Grove, IL: InterVarsity Press, 1999), p. 130.

36 Papias, noted in Eusebius, *Ecclesiastical History* 3.39.12.

37 Epiphanius, *Against Heresies*, 49.1.2–3.

38 The Montanists were widely considered to be a heretical group because they were thought to take matters of Scripture too literally, emphasizing ecstatic and prophetic experiences and disregarding ecclesiastical authorities. Their understanding and teachings relating to the restoration of Israel were included among their literalist views of the beliefs and experiences of those in pre-Christian Israel and then within the earliest Christian church.

39 Madigan and Levenson, p. 228.

40 Tertullian, *Against Marcion*, 5.9, in Cox, Donaldson, and Roberts, eds., vol. 3, p. 448.

41 Tertullian, *On Modesty* 8, in Cox, Donaldson, and Roberts, eds., vol. 4, p. 82.

42 Lacantius, *Divine Institutes* 7.24–26.

43 Commodian, *Carmen Apologeticum*, 941–946.

44 Garr, *Christian Fruit*, p. 290, n. 59.

Polar Opposites: The Christian Supersessionists

During the same general timeframe, however, other Christian leaders had begun to descend in the downward spiral toward the arrogant, triumphalist heresy of supersessionism,[45] the "replacement theology" which argued that Christianity had forever replaced Judaism as God's religion, that Christians had forever replaced Jews as God's Chosen People, and that the divine particularity accorded to Israel in Scripture had been replaced by the universality of the inclusion of the entire world in the "City of God" or in the amillennial kingdom on earth.[46] Because a majority of the ante-Nicene, Nicene, and post-Nicene church fathers embraced the heresy of supersessionism, they generally rejected the validity of the Jewish claim to being the Chosen People and the rightful heirs of the Promised Land. Since Christian views of the hereafter had come to be focused on the neo-Platonic philosophy of escaping the evil material earthly and inheriting the heavenly realm, there was increasingly less room for a this-worldly understanding of God's dealings with humanity wherein the meek would inherit the earth forever.[47] By embracing the Greek view of the hereafter, the church transformed the land promises of the Abrahamic covenant into a heavenly inheritance.

With this approach to divine callings, the idea of a millennial kingdom on earth that might have included Jews and Christians essentially became anathema to most of the church fathers.[48] Indeed, the idea of the existence of such an

---

[45] The definition of heresy as "a deliberate denial of revealed truth coupled with the acceptance of error," is a perfect description of supersessionism or replacement theology. See Walter A. Elwell, ed., *Evangelical Dictionary of Theology* (Grand Rapids, MI: Baker Academic, 2011), p. 508. For a discussion of the heretical nature of supersessionism, see David Zaslow, *Jesus: First-Century Rabbi* (Brewster, MA: Paraclete Press, 2014), p. 218; James H. Charlesworth, *The Historical Jesus: An Essential Guide* (Nashville, TN: Abingdon Press, 2008), p. 57; and Peter Ochs, *Another Reformation: Postliberal Christianity and the Jews* (Grand Rapids, MI: Baker Academic, 2011), pp. 51–52.

[46] Roger E. Olson, *The Mosaic of Christian Belief: Twenty Centuries of Unity & Diversity* (Downers Grove, IL: InterVarsity Press, 2002), p. 353.

[47] Psalm 37:11; Matthew 5:5; 25:34; Daniel 7:18.

[48] Most church fathers denied the possibility of premillennialism, the coming of the Messiah to establish God's kingdom on earth, largely because the major sources for the idea were Jewish; therefore, the teaching of chiliasm (from the Greek word *chilias*, meaning 1,000), which spoke of the literal thousand-year reign of Christ as predicted by John in Revelation 20:6, was renounced as a "Jewish heresy" and was even anathematized at the Council of Ephesus in 431 AD. See Gershom G. Scholem and R. J. Zwi Werblowsky, *Sabbatai Sevi: The Mystical Messiah, 1626–1676* (Princeton, NJ: Princeton University Press, 1976), p. 98. Scholem and Werblowsky note that "the ancient struggle between the heritage of Greek thought—which never inclined to apocalypse—and that of Judaism reached a new climax inside the Christian church with the chiliast controversy. The theological spokesmen of the 'Greek' mentality denounced chiliasm as a 'Jewish heresy' and argued that a kingdom limited in time was devoid of religious value." In other words, they essentially denied the authority of the Apocalypse as Holy Scripture.

earthly kingdom was even negatively portrayed as being "sensual" in Origen's letters, as well as in the thought of other church fathers.[49] This emerging emphasis represented a renunciation of the Hebraic apocalypticism of Jesus and the apostles that featured their expectation of the kingdom *on earth*, a position that was consistent with what was envisioned throughout the Hebrew Scriptures.[50] "The Greek Church's philosophic preference for Heaven over a Messianic Kingdom on Earth may have been a concession to Gnosticism,"[51] says Hughes. It was certainly a concession to the neo-Platonism that also permeated Gnostic thought. The truth is that many church fathers were thoroughly infected with the dualism of both neo-Platonism and Gnosticism which posited the holiness of the heavenly and the realm of ideas while excoriating the evil of the earthly and everything related to it.[52] In such a context, the idea of an earthly kingdom rather than a heavenly domain was considered to be impossible.

Clement of Alexandria claimed that Israel had "denied the Lord" and thereby had "forfeited the place of the true Israel."[53] Other notable supersessionists

---

[49] Paul Hughes, *Finishing History Well* (Maitland, FL: Xulon Press, 2012), p. 47. Also Robert H. Mounce, *The Book of Revelation* (Grand Rapids, MI: Wm. B. Eerdmans Publishing Co., 1977), p. 368, and Matthew H. G. Francis, "Blessed is the One Who Reads Aloud. . .": The Book of Revelation in Orthodox Lectionary Traditions," in *Exegesis and Hermeneutics in the Churches of the East*, Vahan S. Hovhanessian, ed. (New York: Peter Lang Publishing, 2009), p. 71.

[50] One of the supreme ironies of ecclesiastical history is that for centuries the Greek and Latin church fathers utterly rejected the clear teaching of the Hebrew Scriptures that the Messiah would come and establish God's dominion on the earth. Daniel 7:18 stated this truth unequivocally: "But the holy people of the Most High will receive the kingdom and will possess it forever," and Zechariah 14:19: "Then the LORD will go forth and fight . . . his feet will stand on the Mount of Olives. . . . And the LORD *will be king over all the earth*" (emphasis added). The supersessionist, amillennialist church fathers also rejected the apocalyptic teaching of Jesus, who said, "The meek shall *inherit the earth*" (Matthew 5:5, emphasis added), and "Then the king will say to those on his right, 'Come, you who are blessed of my Father, *inherit the kingdom* prepared for you from the foundation of the world" (Matthew 25:34, emphasis added). They also rejected the chiliastic teachings of the apostles: "You have made them to be a kingdom of priests to our God; and *they will reign upon the earth*" (Revelation 5:10, emphasis added). According to both the Hebrew and Apostolic Scriptures, the Messianic Kingdom will be the fulfillment of the Abrahamic promise of dominion over the earth. It will involve the ultimate outworking of the land clause of the Abrahamic covenant that was expanded in the New Covenant: "The promise to Abraham or to his descendants that he would be *heir of the world* was . . . through the righteousness of faith" (Romans 4:13, emphasis added). This is the covenant that is made sure to the lineal descendants of Abraham as well as to those who have become heirs of the promises by faith (Galatians 3:29: "If you belong to the Messiah, then you are Abraham's descendants, *heirs according to the promise*" [emphasis added]).

[51] Hughes, p. 47.

[52] Vincent P. Branick, *Understanding the New Testament and Its Message: An Introduction* (Mahwah, NJ: Paulist Press, 1998), p. 166. Also Mary Ellen Waithe, ed., *Ancient Women Philosophers: 600 B.C.–500 A.D.* (Dordrecht, The Netherlands: Martinus Nijhoff Publishers, 1987), p. 142.

[53] Michael J. Vlach, *The People, the Land, and the Future of Israel: Israel and the Jewish People* (Grand Rapids, MI: Kregel Publications, 2014), p. 36.

like Augustine, John Chrysostom, and Gregory of Nyssa discouraged Christians from even making pilgrimages to Israel.[54] Because he was profoundly influenced by Greek philosophy, Origen was perhaps the strongest Ante-Nicene advocate of hyper-allegorized interpretations of Scripture that promoted supersessionism.[55] He posited "two callings of Israel" and suggested that "the church was called between the two callings of Israel; that is to say, first Israel was called, and afterwards when Israel had stumbled and fallen, the church of the Gentiles was called. 'But when the fullness of the Gentiles has come in, then will all Israel, having been called again, be saved.'"[56] Origen also argued that "the people of Israel are still missing from the complete picture. But when the fullness of the Gentiles has come in and Israel comes to salvation at the end of time, then it will be the people, which, although it existed long ago, will come at the last and complete the fullness of the Lord's portion and inheritance."[57] Origen, therefore, was ambivalent, wavering between absolute supersessionism and the possibility of a residual restoration of Israel after the church had fulfilled its destiny. Origin seemed to be an advocate of what would be called the "parenthesis theory of the church" in which the church has been viewed as

---

[54] Augustine: Epistle 78, *Migne Patrologie Latina* XXII, col. 489; Chrysostom: *Ad Populum Antiochenum* V, *Migne Patrologie Graeca* XLIX, col. 49; Gregory of Nyssa, *Migne Patrologie Graeca* XLIX, col. 49, noted in Walter Zander, *Israel and the Holy Places of Christendom* (London: Weidenfeld & Nicolson, 1991), pp. 6–8. The common discouragement of pilgrimage to Israel in Christian history was sometimes based on the words of Jesus to the Samaritan woman, "The hour is coming when neither on this mountain nor in Jerusalem will you worship the Father" (John 4:21). John Calvin even described pilgrimages to Jerusalem as "counterfeit worship." John Calvin, *The Acts of the Apostles*, tr. Oliver and Boyd, Ltd. (Grand Rapids, MI: Wm. B. Eerdmans Publishing Co., 1965), p. 225. Also, Robert L. Wilken, "Christian Pilgrimage to the Holy Land," in *City of the Great King: Jerusalem from David to the Present*, Nitza Rosovsky, ed. (Cambridge, MA: Harvard University Press, 1996), p. 121. Additionally, the reformers who drafted the Augsburg Confession denounced pilgrimages as "childless and useless works." Hunt Janin, *Four Paths to Jerusalem: Jewish, Christian, Muslim, and Secular Pilgrimages* (Jefferson, NC: McFarland & Company, Publishers, 2002), p. 149.

[55] Thomas Finan, *Scriptural Interpretations in the Fathers: Letter and Spirit* (Dublin, Ireland: Four Courts Press, 1995), p. 15. Also, Henri de Lubac, *Theological Fragments*, tr. Rebecca Howell Balinski (San Francisco, CA: Ignatius Press, 1989), pp. 129–164. Lubac says that "patristic allegorization of Scripture constituted a uniquely Christian transformation of the Philonic and Greek modes of interpretation." Also Eugen J. Pentiuc, *The Old Testament in Eastern Orthodox Tradition* (New York: Oxford University Press, 2014), p. 170. Pentiuc maintains that "the excess of a high allegorization of biblical texts, while underestimating or even eschewing historical and literary contexts, represents probably one of the obvious downsides of patristic interpretation as a whole."

[56] Origen, *The Song of Songs*, in *Ancient Christian Writers*, J. Quasten and J.C. Plumpe, eds. (Westminster, MD: Newman Press, 1957), p. 26.

[57] Origen, *Commentary on the Epistle to the Romans*, in *Ancient Christian Commentary on Scripture*, Gerald Bray, ed. (Downers Grove, IL: InterVarsity Press, 1998), vol. 6, p. 291.

having been inserted parenthetically, and unexpectedly, in salvation history because the Jewish people rejected Jesus as the Messiah.[58]

Even as Christian supersessionism was gaining traction throughout the church and as allegorical hermeneutics became the standard for biblical interpretation, honest brokers of Christian theology were still expecting the words of the prophets to be literally fulfilled in the restoration of the Jewish people to their land. Christians simply could not take all of the blessings from the Hebrew Scriptures, apply them to the church (as the allegorists did), and then leave all the curses for the Jews.[59] If they had been faithful to the Hebrew-based hermeneutical principles that were employed by Jesus and the apostles, they would have readily concluded that God's gifts and callings relating to the Jews were irrevocable[60] and that, in the end, God would move heaven and earth to fulfill the literal, material, and historical aspects of his covenant, his oath, and his promises to Abraham and his descendants.

The Restorationist Awakening

For centuries, Christians lost sight of the purposes of God toward Israel and haughtily displayed contempt for the Jews, a malady that continues even to this day in some circles.[61] Before and during the time of prophetic restoration, however, increasing numbers came forward to support the restoration of the nation of Israel.[62] In the thirteenth century,

---

58 Stanley Grentz, *The Millennial Maze* (Downers Grove, IL: InterVarsity Press, 1992), p. 97. Grentz describes the "parenthesis theory of the church" thus: "The Israel phase, which began with Abraham, was suspended when the Jews rejected Jesus as their Messiah. Consequently, the church phase, which is a parenthesis in God's Israel program, was inaugurated at Pentecost. The advent of the church, however, did not spell the end of God's program for Israel. God neither abrogated the divine promises to his Old Testament people nor enmeshed them into the church."

59 W. H. Griffith Thomas, "The Lord's Coming and the Supreme Theme of the Bible," in *The Christian Workers Magazine*, Charles Force Deems, John Bancroft Devins, and Amory Howe Bradford, eds., vol. XX, no. 1, September, 1919, p. 96.

60 Romans 11:29.

61 Recently, the Latin Patriarchate of Jerusalem even argued that Christian use of Hebrew liturgy was only a modern phenomenon and complained about Christian use of "Jewish customs" when, in fact, the most ancient Christian church maintained continuity with the synagogal model of fellowship, study, and worship by employing Hebrew liturgy and prayers. Acts 2:42 makes this clear, noting that the earliest Christians "continued faithful . . . in *the* prayers" (emphasis added), obviously connecting the "prayers" of the church with the prayers of the synagogue by employing the definite article in Greek, παῖς (*pais*), "*the*," with "prayers." This passage is frequently mistranslated as "in prayer"; however, the Greek text is explicit: They continued "in *the prayers*" (emphasis added).

62 Michael J. Vlach, *Has the Church Replaced Israel? A Theological Evaluation* (Nashville, TN: B & H Publishing Group, 2010).

Thomas Aquinas confessed that he expected a future salvation of the Jews: "It is possible to designate a terminus, because it seems that the blindness of the Jews will endure until all the pagans chosen for salvation have accepted the faith." During that same time in France, Gerardo di Borgo San Donnino displayed grace that had no ulterior motive or expectation by teaching that "some Jews would be blessed as Jews in the end time and would return to their ancient homeland."[63] In the fourteenth century, John of Ruperscissa believed that "the converted Jews would become God's new imperial nation and Jerusalem would be completely rebuilt to become the center of the purified faith."[64] Though some, if not most, Christian leaders did have ulterior motives for their support of Israel—e.g., eliciting conversion of the Jews to Christianity or believing Jewish conversion to be a precondition to the second coming of Jesus—at least they did voice their faith in the restoration of the people and the land.

While the French took the lead in promoting millennialism on the European continent, perhaps the strongest movement of Restorationism developed in England, where it emerged from the ranks of pietistic Protestants. Stephen Spector points out that there were "Christian proto-Zionists in England 300 years before modern Jewish Zionism emerged."[65] One of the first of these Restorationists was Frances Kett who, in 1585, called for the Jewish people to return to Palestine. Because of his position on Israel, Kett was declared a heretic and burned at the stake by the Church of England.[66] The death of a martyr, however, did not stop the march of prophecy toward the restoration of Israel. Amazingly—and only thirty years later—Thomas Brightman fathered what would be the British perspective on "the Restoration of the Jews."[67] His views were rapidly expanded by men like Sir Henry Finch, a member of the British Parliament, who made this distinct argument regarding what Scripture meant when it spoke of the restoration of Israel: "Where Israel, Judah,

---

63 Carl F. Ehle, Jr., "Prolegomena to Christian Zionism in America: The Views of Increase Mather and William E. Blackstone Concerning the Doctrine of the Restoration of Israel," Ph.D. Dissertation for New York University, 1977, pp. 41–42. Ehle notes that because Gerardo supported millenarian eschatology, he was sentenced to life in prison by Pope Alexander IV.

64 Robert E. Lerner, "Millennialism," in The Encyclopedia of Apocalypticism, John J. Collins, Bernard McGinn, and Stephen J. Stein, eds. (New York: Continuum Press, 2000), vol. 2, p. 353.

65 Stephen Spector, Evangelicals and Israel: The Story of American Christian Zionism (New York: Oxford University Press, 2009), p. 16.

66 Spector, p. 16.

67 Regina Sharif, Non-Jewish Zionism: Its Roots in Western History (London, UK: Zed Books, 1983), p. 25.

Zion, and Jerusalem are named, the Holy Ghost meant not the spiritual Israel, or the church of God collected of the Gentiles or of the Jews and Gentiles both . . . but Israel properly descended out of Jacob's loynes."[68]

By the mid-seventeenth century, Restorationism had become well entrenched in England, especially among the Puritans, who, though they viewed themselves as a reembodied Israel, also believed that the Abrahamic covenant still applied to the patriarch's physical descendants.[69] The strong interest that the Puritans maintained in the restoration of Israel in all likelihood resulted primarily from the fact that they placed much greater emphasis on the Hebrew Bible than other dissenters[70] of their time did.[71] It was the Puritans who were also largely responsible for bringing Restorationism to the New World when they emigrated from England in search of religious freedom.[72]

In the eighteenth century—especially in its second half—Christian support for the restoration of the nation of Israel in the land of Israel was widespread and growing, especially in England. "It was during these years that the *social* and *political* foundations of a Jewish homeland converged with the centuries-old *biblical* and *theological* foundations," says Timothy Demy.[73] What was developing in late eighteenth-century Christianity provided the foundation for nineteenth-century events that would allow Jewish restoration to their ancient land to be worked out practically through the resettlement of the land and the building of a social order that would eventuate in the reestablishment of the long-dormant nation

---

[68] Finch made these and other insightful arguments in his book, *The World's Great Restoration or the Calling of the Jews, and of all the Nations and Kingdoms of the Earth, to the Faith of Christ.* See Michael J. Vlach, "Israel in Church History," in *The People, the Land,, and the Future of Israel: Israel and the Jewish People*, Darrell L. Bock and Mitch Glaser, eds. (Grand Rapids, MI: Kregel Publications, 2014), p. 206. Also, Mayir Verete, "The Restoration of the Jews in English Protestant Thought, 1790-1840," in *Middle Eastern Studies*, vol. 8, no. 1 (1972), p. 14.

[69] Iain Murray, *The Puritan Hope* (Edinburgh, Scotland: Banner of Truth Publishers, 1971), p. 326.

[70] Christians who separated from the Church of England in the sixteenth, seventeenth, and eighteenth centuries were called dissenters. The dissenters opposed the interference of the state in religious and educational matters and simply wanted to have freedom to worship God according to the dictates of their own consciences.

[71] Rynhold, p. 98.

[72] Gerhard Falk, *The Restoration of Israel: Christian Zionism in Religion, Literature, and Politics* (New York: Peter Lang Publishing, 2006), pp. 81–82. Falk points out that the Puritans believed the Jews would be restored to their land, "but only after they became Christians."

[73] Timothy Demy, *Marching to Zion: Social and Political Foundations of Nineteenth-Century Christian Zionism*, posted at www.pre-trib.org/articles/view/marching-to-zion-social-and-political-foundations-of-nineteenth-century-christian-zionism.

of Israel. "The coalescing of history, politics, and theology in the events of the era reassured Christians of God's continued divine plan for the Jewish people,"[74] and increasing numbers of them made bold and public demonstrations of their support for both the Jewish people wherever they were and for what they perceived as a prophetic movement to bring about the restoration of the people, nation, and land of Israel. Of the many prominent eighteenth-century Restorationism activists was Thomas Newton, Bishop of Bristol in England, who supported the return of the Jews to their land while condemning anti-Jewish prejudice in his own country.[75] During this time, Joseph Priestly, a clergyman who, as a polymath, had attained fame as the co-discover of oxygen, believed and taught that the Jews would be restored to "Canaan."[76]

The passion that many Christians had for the restoration of Israel as a people, a nation, and a land was reflected in a hymn composed by Charles Wesley and published in 1762. Entitled "Almighty God of Love," this work enshrined the vision that God would regather the Jewish people to a restored Israel and then employ them to proclaim the gospel to all the nations. John Wesley considered this theme so important that he selected it for *A Collection of Hymns for the Use of the People Called Methodists*, a hymnal published in 1789. The third, fourth, and fifth stanzas of this hymn are particularly revealing of the insight and passion of eighteenth-century Protestant Christians, especially Methodists, for the restoration of Israel:

> O that the chosen band
> Might now their brethren bring
> And gathered out of every land
> Present to Sion's King.
> Of all the ancient race
> Not one be left behind
> But each impelled by secret grace
> His way to Canaan find!
>
> We know it must be done
> For God hath spoke the word
> All Israel shall their Saviour own
> To their first state restored.

---

[74] Demy, *Marching*.
[75] Verete, p. 3.
[76] Spector, p. 18.

Rebuilt by His command
Jerusalem shall rise
Her temple on Moriah stand
Again, and touch the skies.

Send then Thy servants forth
To call the Hebrews home
From west and east, and south, and north
Let all the wanderers come.
Where'er in lands unknown
Thy fugitives remain
Bid every creature help them on
Thy holy mount to gain.

The influence that the Restorationists had at that time and the impact that they made upon governments was considerable. When Napoleon Bonaparte invaded Palestine in 1799, the French Restorationist movement petitioned him to approve the restoration of the Jewish homeland in Palestine. In response to this request, Napoleon issued a "Proclamation to the Jewish Nation," in which he emphatically encouraged the Jewish people to begin work on restoring their ancient nation: "Hasten!" he exclaimed, "Now is the moment that may not return for thousands of years, to claim the restoration of your rights among the population of the universe that had been shamefully withheld from you for thousands of years, your political existence as a nation among the nations, and the unlimited natural right to worship Yehovah in accordance with your faith, publicly and in likelihood for ever."[77]

Whatever Napoleon's political or religious motives may have been for making this proclamation, when he urged the Jewish people to reclaim their long-denied right to nationhood, their right to self-determination, and their right to worship as they chose, he set forth a powerful and positive position that was free from traditional underlying Christian motives. This official recognition of the fundamental human rights of the Jewish people, including their legal right to possess their ancestral homeland, represented a profound shift from the positions that had been taken by the leaders of all European and Middle-Eastern governments before that time.

---

[77] Napoleon Bonaparte, quoted in Lawrence J. Epstein, *A Treasury of Jewish Inspirational Stories* (Northvale, NJ: Jason Aronson, 1993), p. 180.

Tragically, the window of opportunity that this Proclamation clearly opened would prove to be short lived. The dispersed and oppressed Jewish populace was simply not prepared at that time to take advantage of the emperor's largesse. What could well have been a *kairos*[78] moment of opportunity for the Jewish people vanished into thin air with the unfolding vicissitudes of European political and military engagements.

Ulterior Motives, Latent Antisemitism

"With the rise of philosemitism in the seventeenth century, Protestant interpreters . . . boldly announced the return of the Jewish people to the land of Israel as a prelude to the Millennium."[79] Generally speaking, the Restorationist belief that the Jewish people would be restored to their nation in the land of Israel was accompanied, if not driven, by their eschatological projections regarding the return of Jesus. Most Restorationists believed that immediately prior to that event, the Jewish people would accept Jesus as Messiah and Lord. It was at least partially for this reason that they adopted philosemitic feelings and visions toward the Jewish people. The danger of basing support for the return of the Jewish people to the land of Israel upon the view that such action was necessary to ensure the fulfillment of the Christian hope of the *parousia* of Jesus could not have been more tragically manifest than in the case of Martin Luther.

Early in his career, Luther expressed great love and admiration for the Jewish people; however, because he had also created his own personal eschatological scenario in which the Jews would be converted *en masse* to Protestantism and because he did not witness the fulfillment of that vision, Luther's initial philosemitism was transformed into virulent antisemitism which prompted him to produce some of the most vile pronouncements against the Jewish people in all of Christian literature. Mark Levene observes that

---

[78] The Greek word καιρός (*kairos*) refers to an opportune moment in time. Literally, it speaks of two metaphorical images: 1) the "moment in which an arrow may be fired with sufficient force to penetrate the target" and 2) "the moment in which the shuttle could be passed through the threads on the loom." For more details, see Hunter W. Stephenson, *Forecasting Opportunity: Kaziros, Production, and Writing* (Lanham, MD: University Press of America, 2005), p. 4. In the Apostolic Scriptures, the word *kairos* is used some 80 times, often signifying "God's appointed time" as in Mark 1:15: "The *kairos* is fulfilled, and the kingdom of God is at hand." Success in divine initiatives is achieved when preparation meets the *kairos* moment that allows for their fulfillment.

[79] David Brown, *The Restoration of the Jews* (Charleston, SC: BiblioLife, 2008), pp. 38–64. Also David S. Katz, *Philo-Semitism and the Readmission of the Jews to England 1603–1655* (Oxford, UK: Clarendon Press, 1982), pp. 94, 98, 123.

Luther's "briefly moderated tone" toward the Jews was based on "his own eschatological wish-fulfillment that imminent mass Jewish conversion would prove him right in the face of his papal detractors."[80] When he was "disabused of this notion by leading German rabbis," however, Luther embarked on "diatribes against the Jews" that "were couched in language as vitriolic and ugly as anything in the annals of anti-Semitism."[81] Thankfully, most Restorationists did not follow Luther's example and drift into antisemitism as a result of their unfulfilled eschatological expectations. Still, their primary interest in the restored people, nation, and land of Israel was not always purely for the sake the Jewish people themselves but was significantly motivated by their beliefs about Christianity itself. It was not surprising, therefore, that many Restorationists even had varying degrees of ambivalence toward the Jewish people. First, they supported the creation of the state of Israel and the return of the Jewish people to their own land; however, they often did not support equal rights for Jews in their own lands, nor did they welcome Jewish immigration into their own societies. Eventually, this ambivalence was to foster some of the greatest tragedies in human history.

One of many prime examples of this paradox was mid-nineteenth-century Englishman Anthony Ashley-Cooper, Earl of Shaftesbury, a prime mover in the London Society for Promoting Christianity Amongst the Jews, an organization which considered the promotion of the "restoration of the Jews to their national existence in Palestine" as being integral to its purpose.[82] While Ashley-Cooper was a vocal proponent of a restored nation of Israel,[83] at the same time, he also "opposed the Emancipation Bill that would have removed disabilities from Jews to full participation in English political and cultural life."[84] The irony was that

---

[80] Mark Levene, *Genocide in the Age of the Nation State, Volume 2: The Rise of the West and the Coming of Genocide* (New York: I.B. Tauris & Co., 2005), p. 135.

[81] Levene, p. 135.

[82] Rosemary Radford Ruether, "The Quest for Peace with Justice in the Middle East: Christian Zionist and Palestinian Theologies," in *Theologies of Liberation in Palestine-Israel: Indigenous, Contextual, and Postcolonial Perspectives*, Nur Masalha and Lisa Isherwood, eds. (Eugene, OR: Wipf and Stock Publishers, 2014), p. 129.

[83] Shaftesbury also promoted the establishment of the first Anglican bishopric in Jerusalem. Gunner and Smith report that Shaftesbury "envisioned a vast redemptive project in which unconverted Jews would return to Palestine" and become Christians. Like many Christians before, during, and after that time, Shaftesbury probably believed that the return of the Jewish people to Israel and their conversion to Christianity were two of the major events that would prepare the way for the second coming of Jesus. See Gunner and Smith, p. 181.

[84] Ruether, p. 129.

for the Earl of Shaftesbury, Jews could be fully Jewish with self-determination as long as they would do so in some location besides Britain. Yet another example of such ambivalence—and perhaps surprisingly so—was British Foreign Secretary Arthur James Balfour, who openly promoted the restoration of the Jewish homeland in either Uganda or Palestine and ultimately formalized such a proposal in his 1917 Balfour Declaration. When he became prime minister of Britain, however, Balfour was a prominent supporter of the Alien Immigration Act of 1905,[85] and he "worked tirelessly for the enactment of stringent anti-immigration legislation meant primarily to prevent Jewish immigrants who were fleeing the pogroms of Eastern Europe from entering Britain."[86] Balfour's positions were, to say the least, inconsistent.

It is entirely likely, however, that a great deal of such incipient, though shrouded, Judaeophobia and antisemitism may have made the eventual establishment of the nation of Israel possible. Shlomo Sand may well have had a point when he said that significant numbers of Jews might never have been able to emigrate to the Promised Land if Western countries had not refused to accept massive immigration of Jews into their societies. And it is doubtful whether what Sand erroneously considered the "fictitious *ethos*" of a Jewish people would have been created at all. "But the elimination of all other options," he mused, "forced a minority of the displaced to make their way to the Holy Land, which they initially regarded as an extremely unpromising destination."[87] Without a doubt, the exigencies and intricacies of international relations and the machinations of human prejudices worked together to produce the climate and circumstances that eventuated in the emigration of Jews from the countries of their dispersion to the land of their ancient ancestors and, finally, in the reestablishment of the nation of Israel. Wrong, impure, or compromised motivations could not obviate the divine initiative.

Some Christian leaders, however, actually had entirely pure motives for their support of the Jews and of the restoration of Israel wherein there was no inherent Christian self-interest. In 1800, James Cicheno,

---

[85] Andrew Prescott and Elizabeth M. Hallam, eds., *The British Inheritance: A Treasury of Historic Documents* (Berkeley, CA: The University of California Press, 1999), p. 125

[86] Brian Klug, *Being Jewish and Doing Justice* (London, UK: Vallentine Mitchell, 2011), pp. 199–299.

[87] Shlomo Sand, *The Invention of the Land of Israel: From Holy Land to Homeland*, tr. Jeremy Forman (London, UK: Verso Books, 2012), p. 257.

mirroring the thirteenth-century views of Gerardo di Borgo San Donnino, concluded that the restoration of the Jews to their ancient homeland "was not conditional on conversion to Christianity."[88] Cicheno was accurate in his assessment because the terms of the Abrahamic covenant: "I will give you this land," were not predicated on whether or not Jews would accept Jesus as Messiah four millennia later. The unilateral nature of God's particularist covenant with Abraham placed no performance demands upon the patriarch or upon his descendants. The fulfillment of the covenant's land grant was contingent upon one thing and one thing only: the immutable faithfulness of the Almighty to fulfill his covenant oath and promise to the patriarch of faith and to his lineal progeny. Those Christians who would be faithful to the "heavenly vision" would support the cause of restoration as God had designed it and had described it in Scripture rather than clouding the issue with their own expectations, no matter how noble they may have been.

Growing Numbers and Intensifying Support

As the nineteenth century continued to unfold, Christians in even greater numbers joined the ranks of the Restorationists. Derek Prince suggests that "the names of nineteenth-century Christians who embraced the concept of a restored Jewish state read like a section of Who's Who."[89] One of the greatest preachers of that time, Charles Haddon Spurgeon, was a leading supporter of Restorationism.[90] Another stream of evangelical belief, which would come to be called dispensationalism, developed in this timeframe and was also highly supportive of Restorationism. Leaders of this movement included John Nelson Darby in Britain and later Cyrus Scofield in the United States. As time progressed, dispensationalists would become some of the most ardent Restorationists and Christian Zionists.

Authors and poets joined in the rising chorus of support for the Jewish people and their right to return to the land of their ancestors.

---

88 Derek Prince, *The Key to the Middle East: Discovering the Future of Israel in Biblical Prophecy* (Bloomington, MN: Chosen Books, 1982), p. 35.

89 Prince, p. 35.

90 Clifford A. Kiracofe, *Dark Crusade: Christian Zionism and US Foreign Policy* (New York: I.B. Tauris & Co., 2009), p. 55. Spurgeon followed in the tradition of Jonathan Edwards, American Calvinism's most effective preacher, who in his eighteenth-century, posthumously published book, *The History of the Work of Redemption*, affirmed his support for "the restoration of the Jews as a nation." See Falk, p. 82.

Herman Melville penned this poignant statement in his *Clarel: A Poem and Pilgrimage in the Holy Land*:

> The Hebrew seers announce in time
> The return of Judah to her prime;
> Some Christians deemed it then at hand
> Here was an object. Up and On.
> With Seed and tillage help renew—
> Help reinstate the Holy Land.[91]

During this time, however, "Palestine was seen and presented as empty, wretched, and desolate," for "at the beginning of the twentieth century, Palestine was indeed sparsely populated outside the interior hill and mountain range."[92] Indeed, this was the famous evaluation of the land of Israel offered by Mark Twain in his book *The Innocents Abroad* in which he described his own visit to the Holy Land in 1867. After generally depicting Palestine as a "blistering, naked, treeless land,"[93] he continued to say, "There is not a solitary village [in Galilee]. . . . There are two or three small clusters of Bedouin tents, but not a single permanent habitation. One may ride ten miles, hereabouts, and not see ten human beings."[94] In describing ancient Samaria, he observed, "There was hardly a tree or a shrub anywhere." As he continued his trek, what he observed prompted him to conclude, "No landscape exists that is more tiresome to the eye than that which bounds the approaches to Jerusalem.[95]

Though Twain also described areas like Shechem (Nablus) as "under high cultivation" and "well watered,"[96] and though he found isolated spots between Jerusalem and the Elah Valley where there were "luxuriant orchards of figs, apricots, pomegranates," he also observed that these scenes contrasted with the vast majority of the land, which was "rugged, mountainous, verdureless, and forbidding."[97] He also remarked that "in

---

[91] Herman Melville, *Clarel, I.17: Nathan*, lines 259–264. See Herman Melville, *Clarel: A Poem and Pilgrimage in the Holy Land* (Evanston, IL: Northwestern University Press, 1991), p. 62.
[92] Gudrun Krämer and Graham Harman, *A History of Palestine: From the Ottoman Conquest to the Founding of the State of Israel* (Princeton, NJ: Princeton University Press, 2008), p. 128.
[93] Mark Twain, *The Innocents Abroad: The New Pilgrims' Progress* (Hartford, CT: The American Publishing Co., 1869), p. 482.
[94] Twain, p. 485.
[95] Twain, p. 555.
[96] Twain, p. 551.
[97] Twain, p. 604.

the flush of spring," there were "small shreds" of "very beautiful" spaces near Jaffa that were "all the more beautiful by contrast with the far-reaching desolation that surrounds them on every side."[98] Twain's descriptions of such isolated pockets of verdant, productive land were confirmed by Bayrard Taylor who pictured the Jezreel Valley in 1852 as "one of the richest districts in the world" where the soil "produces annually superb crops of wheat and barley,"[99] and by Laurence Oliphant who in 1886 identified the same area as "a huge green lake of waving wheat . . . one of the most striking pictures of luxuriant fertility which is possible to conceive."[100] Despite the mention of these few and far-between examples of verdurous landscapes, Twain's conclusion regarding the then-current state of the Promised Land was this: "It truly is monotonous and uninviting. . . . It is a hopeless, dreary, heart-broken land. . . . Palestine sits in sackcloth and ashes . . . and why should it be otherwise? Can the curse of the Deity beautify a land?"[101]

The sad state of affairs in what at one time had been described as a "land flowing with milk and honey" with abundant agricultural produce could be traced to the fact that the few who inhabited the land at that time had no real value for agriculture. The Bedouin Arabs were largely nomadic people, dependent upon flocks for their livelihood. Additionally, a cruel form of taxation had been imposed on the land by the Ottoman Empire wherein taxes were levied upon trees,[102] prompting the residents to engage in a virtual deforestation of the land, including the removal of untold numbers of fruit trees.[103] "When trees died they were never replanted because of the Turkish law taxing fruitbearing, or indeed any tree from time of planting."[104] J. V. Thirgood pointed out that in order to "escape the tree tax, the men from a village in Hebron district one winter cut down some five hundred trees."[105] In another incident, apricot trees on the

---

[98] Twain, p. 607.

[99] Bayard Taylor, *The Lands of the Saracen* (Alexandria, Egypt: The Library of Alexandria, 1854), p. 32.

[100] Laurence Oliphant, *Haifa: Life in Modern Palestine* (London, England: William Blackwood, 1887), p. 96. Oliphant was a Christian who was an advocate for the Jewish resettlement of Palestine.

[101] Twain, pp. 606–608.

[102] Alon Tal, *Pollution in a Promised Land: An Environmental History of Israel* (Berkeley, CA: The University of California Press, 2002), p. 39.

[103] Shaul Ephraim Cohen, *The Politics of Planting: Israeli-Palestinian Competition for Control of Land in the Jerusalem Periphery* (Chicago, IL: The University of Chicago Press, 1993), p. 45.

[104] J. V. Thirgood, *Man and the Mediterranean Forest* (London, England: 1880), p. 113, cited in Cohen, p. 45.

[105] Thirgood, p. 113.

Mount of Olives that were destroyed by locusts in 1864 "were never re-planted because of the severity of the Turkish law."[106] The Ottoman assault on the flora of Israel, though indirect, produced an environmental disaster that literally changed the climate of Palestine with rain patterns of the land altered to such a degree that desertification of the land became even more intense.[107] The tragically barren condition of the land of Palestine further prompted Christian Restorationists to support the return of the Jews to their ancient homeland not only to reestablish their own sovereignty but also to save and restore the land itself.

In the 1890's, Restorationists joined the early Zionists in repeating Israel Zangwill's sardonic aphorism: "Palestine is a land without a people for a people without a land."[108] To the Restorationists and Zionists who followed, there was no logical reason why the desolate land of the Bible should not be restored to the Jewish people. The land that had been largely neglected for centuries was surely the very place where the restored Jewish nation would bring about the miraculous renewal of that land in fulfillment of Isaiah's prediction that the desert would bloom like a crocus.[109] Though they had been landless for two millennia, the Jewish people would become landed again, they would do so in the same Promised Land that had been ceded by God to their father Abraham as the material evidence of his divine promise, covenant, and oath, and they would again make their land flow with milk and honey.

Christian Zionists

"Covenantal restorationism helped to prepare the public mood for the later, more sharply defined Christian Zionism that was to follow,"[110] says Clifford Kirakofe. By the late nineteenth century, the Restorationist

---

[106] Thirgood, p. 113.
[107] This situation was not reversed until the Israeli Jews engaged in a massive tree-planting exercise that eventually restored the climate of Israel to what it had been before the Ottoman occupation. One of the greatest of these efforts was Theodore Herzl's call for the planting of 10 million trees. See Cohen, pp. 46–51. Also, Alon Tal, "Combating Desertification: Evolving Perceptions and Strategies," in *Between Ruin and Restoration: An Environmental History of Israel*, Daniel E. Orenstein, Alon Tal, and Char Miller, eds. (Pittsburgh, PA: The University of Pittsburgh Press, 2013), pp. 106–127.
[108] Beverley Milton-Edwards, *The Israeli-Palestinian Conflict: A People's War* (New York: Routledge, 2009), p. 16. Zangwill coined the dictum that was to become a mantra for the early Jewish and Christian Zionist movements.
[109] Isaiah 35:1.
[110] Clifford A. Kiracofe, *Dark Crusade: Christian Zionism and US Foreign Policy* (New York: I.B. Tauris & Co., 2009), p. 55.

movement had taken on the title of Christian Zionists, and they had become involved in pro-Zionist lobbying efforts in the United States.[111] Perhaps the most prominent Restorationist who supported the early Zionist movement was American real estate tycoon William E. Blackstone. After renouncing his material pursuits, Blackstone took up the Restorationist cause by publishing a book entitled *Jesus Is Coming*, which was translated into 48 languages and sold millions of copies worldwide. Although Blackstone was an evangelical Methodist, he maintained that the Jews were not required to convert to Christianity either before or after the return of the Messiah. Avi Beker reports that "before promoting the political restoration of the Jews in their Promised Land, Blackstone had to recognize their Chosen role and reject the prejudices of traditional Christianity toward the Jews and absolve them from the need to convert."[112] With positions such as this, Blackstone's book was published in Yiddish, which allowed it to have considerable impact on the Jewish community of Europe. Paul Boyer points out that late in his career, Blackstone even warned European and American Jews, almost vatically, that "[Jewish] assimilationists [who] wish[ed] to remain in the various nations enjoying their social, political, and commercial advantages" would suffer difficult consequences for not having embraced Zionism.[113]

Then, in 1890, Blackstone organized the Conference on the Past, Present, and Future of Israel at the First Methodist Episcopal Church in Chicago. While this conference produced strong resolutions of sympathy for the oppressed Jews living in Russia, Blackstone remained unconvinced that simple resolutions were adequate, so he began to promote resettlement of Jewish people, especially those from Russia, in Palestine. In 1891, Blackstone promoted what came to be known as the Blackstone Memorial,[114] a petition that was to be presented to U.S. President Benjamin Harrison asking him to "consider the situation of the Israelites and their claims to Palestine as their ancient home."[115] When this petition was

---

[111] Rynhold, pp. 98–99.

[112] Avi Beker, *The Chosen: The History of an Idea, and the Anatomy of an Obsession* (New York: Palgrave Macmillan, 2008), p. 143.

[113] Paul Boyer, *When Time Shall Be No More: Prophecy Belief in Modern American Culture* (Cambridge, MA: Harvard University Press, 1992), p. 219.

[114] Rosemary Radford Ruether and Herman J. Ruether, *The Wrath of Jonah: The Crisis of Religious Nationalism in the Israeli-Palestinian Conflict* (Minneapolis, MN: Augsburg Fortress Press, 2002), p. 83. Ruether points out that Blackstone and others suggested "that President Harrison might be the modern-day Cyrus who would return the Jews from exile."

[115] Ruether and Reuther, p. 83.

signed by over 400 of the most prominent Americans of the day—including an impressive list of legislators, Supreme Court justices, industrialists, newspaper editors, and religious leaders—Blackstone was able to lobby President Harrison to begin to promote the migration of American Jews to Palestine, laying foundations for the restoration of Israel.[116]

Blackstone was one of the first to argue that the "law of dereliction" did not apply to the Jews and their relationship to the land of Israel. "They never abandoned the land," he said. "They made no treaty; they did not even surrender. They simply succumbed, after months of conflict, to the overwhelming power of the Romans."[117] Eventually, his viewpoints were resurrected by Supreme Court Justice Louis D. Brandeis, who asserted that Blackstone could be called the "Father of Zionism" because his work antedated that of Herzl. Brandeis, in turn, championed the Restorationist cause to U.S. President Woodrow Wilson, who, as a devout Presbyterian and the son of a minister, was probably "the last President of the United States who was disposed to be persuaded by the arguments of the Blackstone Memorial."[118] Before his death, Wilson marveled, "To think that I, a son of the manse, should be able to help restore the Holy Land to its people."[119] Though much of this action took place in private, it served to assure the British that there was American support for the Balfour Declaration.[120] It was also strongly instrumental in the unanimous drafting of the League of Nations Covenant for Palestine of 1922 and its British Mandate, which became

---

[116] Naim S. Ateek, "Foreword," in *Zionism through Christian Lenses: Ecumenical Perspectives on the Promised Land*, Carole Monica Burnett, ed. (Eugene, OR: Wipf and Stock Publishers, 2013), p. xiv.

[117] William E. Blackstone, "May the United States Intercede for the Jews?" in *Our Day* VIII, October, 1891, p. 46.

[118] Paul C. Merkley, *The Politics of Christian Zionism 1891–1948* (New York: Routledge, 1998), p. 93. Merkley says that "while it would be reckless to claim that we can trace a clear line of cause and effect from Blackstone's Memorial of 1891 to the Creation of the State of Israel in 1948, it is not at all far-fetched to say that the Memorial is the place to go to find the clearest expression of the motivation that won President Woodrow Wilson, and which would continue to be the surest, the most constant course of American Christian Zionism." He also succinctly noted the political and religious situation that succeeded Wilson: "The Presidents of the 1920s were not men of the same intellectual and mental and moral type. . . . The 1920s was the decade when the hegemony of American Protestantism was finally broken up—in the realms of thought and learning and in the realm of politics, and within the increasingly beleaguered house of Protestantism itself, Fundamentalism, though it won many battles, finally lost the war for control of thought and policy in all the major denominations."

[119] Woodrow Wilson, quoted from memory by Stephen S. Wise in Levi Soshuk and Azriel Louis Eisenberg, eds., *Momentous Century: Personal and Eyewitness Accounts of the Rise of the Jewish Homeland and State 1875–1878* (Cranbury, NJ: Cornwall Books, 1984), p. 118.

[120] Isaiah L. Kenen, *Near East Report—Volumes 18–20* (Washington, DC: Near East Report, 1974), p. 41.

the foundation for the 1947 United Nations Resolution 181 that recommended the partitioning of Palestine at the termination of the British Mandate in 1948.[121] The concern that high-ranking members of the United States government had for the plight of the Jewish people created a climate in which events could emerge that would eventuate in the restoration of their ancient homeland in the land of Israel. Though the actual outworking of the visions of those who lobbied for U. S. government support for the restoration of the Jewish people to their land would unfold over more than five decades, the seeds that had been planted centuries earlier were sprouting and beginning to bear fruit.

In the twentieth century, a significant portion of evangelical Christianity continued the tradition of the nineteenth-century Restorationists by maintaining some degree of support for the Jewish people and the eventual establishment of a Jewish state in the ancient Holy Land.[122] Though evangelicalism's influence in United States politics waned as the nation became increasingly influenced by the secular humanism of modernity, still a significant force of Christian support for the Jewish people and continuing prayer for the restoration of the nation of Israel placed public pressure on secular leaders to maintain at least some degree of sensitivity toward the plight of the Jews. This Christian influence helped prepare the way for the restored statehood of Israel.

---

[121] When the League of Nations was disbanded following World War II, the United Nations Organization, which was established in its place, "inherited all the agreements made by its predecessor, including the Mandate for Palestine." Cynthia D. Wallace, *Foundations of the International Legal Rights of the Jewish People and the State of Israel and Implications for the Proposed Palestinian State* (Lake Mary, FL: Creation House, 2012), p. 19. Wallace observes that even though Britain notified the United Nations of its intention to terminate its stewardship of the Mandate of the League of Nations Covenant for Palestine in 1947, "*the Mandate itself was not terminated*" (author's emphasis). Eli Hertz notes that "the 'Mandate for Palestine' was not a naive vision briefly embraced by the international community in blissful unawareness of Arab opposition to the very notion of Jewish historical rights in Palestine." The Mandate was created in 1920 and modified in 1922. Then on April 18, 1946, when the League of Nations "was dissolved and its assets and duties transferred to the United Nations, the international community, in essence, reaffirmed the validity of this international accord and reconfirmed that the terms for a Jewish National Home were the will of the international community, a 'sacred trust,'" says Hertz. The League of Nations Mandate for Palestine established "Jewish legal rights in Palestine. Then, the League of Nations commissioned the British with the mandate of "responsibility to administrate the area delineated by the League's 'Mandate for Palestine.'" The League of Nations Mandate for Palestine was a Trust, and the British Mandate was the Trustee. For a comprehensive discussion of the history and legal rights of the Jewish people to the land of Israel, see Eli E. Hertz, "'Mandate for Palestine': The Legal Aspects of Jewish Rights, posted at http://www.mythsandfacts.org/conflict/mandate_for_palestine/mandate_for_palestine.htm#top. For maps of the land designated for the Jewish state in the League of Nations Covenant for Palestine and its Mandate to Britain, see the appendices on pages 423–424 of this volume.

[122] Not all Evangelicals were strong supporters of the Jewish peoples right to restore their nation in the land of Israel. Before, during, and after the establishment of the nation of Israel, some segments of Evangelicalism had either antipathy for or ambivalence toward Restorationism and Zionism.

CHAPTER 13

THE HEBREW REVIVAL

RESURRECTING ISRAEL'S LANGUAGE

Because of the extent and duration of the dispersion of the Jews following the destruction of Jerusalem, first by the Babylonians in 587 BC, then by the Romans in AD 70 and in AD 132, the sacred tongue that the prophets, kings, and sages of Israel had used eventually became essentially a dead language.[1] Indeed, the language that God had used to communicate with this Chosen People[2]

---

[1] The term *dead language* means that a language is no longer used in everyday conversation. Clarisse Herrenschmidt argues that "a language is dead when it is no longer heard by any baby from when it is born." Clarisse Herrenschmidt, "Writing—and Some Thoughts on Hebrew and Greek," in *Ancestor of the West: Writing, Reasoning, and Religion in Mesopotamia, Elam, and Greece*, Jean Boltéro, Clarisse Herrenschmidt, and Jean-Pierre Dermant, eds. (Chicago, IL: The University of Chicago Press, 2000), p. 130.

[2] Though some scholars insist that Hebrew had been replaced by Aramaic at least by the time of the Roman occupation of Israel in 63 BC, it is clear that Hebrew was still being spoken during and after the time of Jesus. The *titulus crucis* at Jesus' crucifixion was inscribed in Hebrew, Latin, and Greek (Luke 23:38). Also, Paul declared in Acts 26:14–16 that when Jesus appeared to him on the Damascus Road, the Master addressed him in "the Hebrew tongue" ('Εβραΐδι διαλέκτω—*Hebraidi dialékto*). Then, decades later, Paul addressed some of his audiences in "the Hebrew tongue" so that they could better understand him (Acts 21:40; 22:2). Most Christian scholars have argued that the Greek term 'Εβραΐδι (*Hebraidi*) used in these texts denoted Aramaic, and some modern translations (*e.g.* NIV, ESV) render 'Εβραΐδι (*Hebraidi*) as "Aramaic." In his *Antiquities of the Jews*, however, Josephus made a clear distinction between the Greek terms that were used to describe Hebrew and Aramaic by appealing to 2 Kings 18:26 where Hebrew and Aramaic were clearly distinguished in this manner: "When Rabshakeh had made this speech in the Hebrew tongue ('Εβραϊστι—*Hebraisti*) . . . Eliakim . . . desired him to speak in the Syrian tongue (Συριστί—*Syristi* or Aramaic)." Flavius Josephus, *Antiquities of the Jews*, 10, 1, 2. The Hebrew text of 2 Kings 18:26 says that Eliakim asked Rabshakeh to speak in אֲרָמִית (*'Aramit*), Aramaic, rather than in יְהוּדִית (*Yehudit*), the Jews' language, Hebrew. The Septuagint translates אֲרָמִית (*'Aramit*) as Συριστί—*Syristi*) and יְהוּדִית (*Yehudit*) as Ιουδαϊστί, (*Ioudaisti*). Since Josephus wrote after the destruction of the temple, it is clear that Hebrew was still commonly spoken in Israel after AD 70. For centuries, however, Christian scholars have argued that Jesus did not speak Hebrew. This has given rise to such incidents as when Israeli Prime Minister Benjamin Netanyahu said to Pope Francis, "Jesus was here, in this land. He spoke Hebrew," only to be corrected (wrongly) by the pontiff: "Aramaic!" (Elizabeth Dias, "Pope Corrects Israeli Leader: Actually, Jesus Did Not Speak Hebrew," Time, May 27, 2014). For a detailed discussion of the continuing use of Hebrew in the first century, see Doug Hamp, *Discovering the Language of Jesus: Hebrew or Aramaic?* (Santa Ana, CA: Calvary Chapel Publishing, 2005), pp. 23–38.

gradually diminished in conversational use until it was essentially lost for that purpose.[3] By the time when Hadrian forcibly evicted all the Jewish people from Jerusalem in AD 132, Hebrew was no longer spoken as the vernacular of the Jewish people. Though the language was preserved through the centuries for rabbinic studies of Scripture and Jewish literature and for synagogue rituals and prayers, its loss as the everyday conversational tongue of the Jews had a significant impact upon what was to become a truly international Jewish community, as Jews came to be influenced progressively by the languages of the Diaspora.

Language is a powerful aspect of human thought patterns and, hence, also of human beliefs. The capacity for speech was a significant and essential element of human creation in the beginning. *Targum Onkelos*, an ancient Aramaic paraphrase of Scripture, underscored this fact when it rendered the final phrase of the human creation narrative, which says that "*ha-adam* [humanity] became a living being," as "humanity became a *speaking spirit*."[4] Humanity was made in the image of a "speaking being"—God. The capacity to speak intelligibly is certainly one aspect of the theomorphic nature of humankind in that it images God's ability to speak. It is the gift of language that empowers human beings to communicate with God and to worship him. In truth, it is language that "gives to all beings their own form, it makes them creatures in themselves with their own characteristics and peculiarities. As soon as a community on a particular piece of land speaks a particular language, it constitutes a people apart, and the land where that people has settled is the state of that people."[5] David Blumenthal says, "Each language has an elegance of its own and a power of expression which is peculiar to it, and these constitute the identity and character of the people who speak it."[6]

The Hebrew language, therefore, has always been central to Jewish self-identity. Hebrew even goes beyond Jewish self-identity, for it was the holy language before it became the vernacular of the Hebrew peoples. As Peter Wortsman has said, "It was with Hebrew words that the Judeo-Christian God

---

[3] Sara E. Karesh and Mitchell M. Hurvitz, eds., *Encyclopedia of Judaism* (New York: Infobase Publishing, 2006), p. 52. Karesh and Hurvitz argue that Hebrew did not finally become a dead language until after the destruction of the temple in AD 70.

[4] Moses Aberbach and Bernard Grossfeld, *Targum Onkelos to Genesis: A Critical Analysis Together with an English Translation of the Text* (Jersey City, NJ: KTAV Publishing House, 1982), p. 29.

[5] Eliezer ben-Yehuda, quoted in Alain Dieckhoff, *The Invention of a Nation: Zionist Thought and the Making of Modern Israel* (New York: Columbia University Press, 2003), p. 121.

[6] David R. Blumenthal, *God at the Center: Meditations on Jewish Spirituality* (Northvale, NJ: Jason Aronson, 1994), p. 134.

quite literally called the world into being. . . . The Hebrew language as such is a bridge, a lasting link between God and man."[7] Tragically, some degree of this sense of continuing intimate relationship between God and the Jewish people in daily life was lost to most of the world when the language of Scripture was replaced by the babel of the polyglot world. Translations, no matter how objective they may be, still fail to capture the full essence of the original words of Scripture. It is a simple fact that many important aspects of biblical faith are difficult to express or understand when they are wrenched from their Hebrew matrix. Indeed, many of the Hebrew words of Scripture are virtually untranslatable.

Preparation for Restoration

Unlike the Jews who had remained connected to the language of Scripture through the synagogue liturgy, the Christian church endured a long absence of Hebrew in scholarly reflection from the time of Jerome until the turn of the sixteenth century when, after at least eleven centuries of benign neglect—and even outright contempt—an interest in Hebrew erupted spontaneously across the European religious academic landscape. At that time, Johann Reuchlin and other Roman Catholic scholars began to insist that it was vital "to delve into a linguistic domain that [has] long been considered at best obsolete."[8] Reuchlin and his colleagues became enthusiastic students of Jewish sacred literature because they saw in it "the spiritual foundation of Christianity."[9] They came to understand that "just as the Jews themselves were reviled as . . . an alien body that had long since outlived its usefulness, so too was their language and literary heritage . . . held in ill repute."[10] They determined to do something about this historical aberration. The growing Christian interest in Hebrew, even if it represented a small minority of Christians, reintroduced the church to the importance of both the culture and the language of the Jewish people. The scholars who led this effort were styled *Christian Hebraists*, and they described their teaching as *"veritas Hebraica"* ("Hebrew truth"). This Christian movement was driven by a passion to restore the original language of Scripture to Christian exegesis and exposition, and, in the process of doing so, it set the stage for acceleration of the

---

[7] Peter Wortsman, "Foreword," in Johann Reuchlin, *Recommendation Whether to Confiscate, Destroy, and Burn All Jewish Books*, Peter Wortsman, ed. and tr. (Mahwah, NJ: Paulist Press, 2000), p. 3. Originally published as Johannsen Reuchlin, *Doctor Johannsen Reuchlins Augenspiegel* (Tübingen, Germany: Thomas Anshelm, 1511).

[8] Wortsman, p. 4, author's emphasis.

[9] Wortsman, p. 3.

[10] Wortsman, p. 3.

Restorationist Movement which created the climate for acceptance of the Jewish Zionist movement and its practical, political efforts to restore the nation of Israel.

Restoration and Hebrew

As time progressed, calls began to arise in the Jewish community for the restoration of ancient Hebrew to the larger Jewish community. During late eighteenth and early nineteenth centuries, *Maskilim*,[11] members of the Jewish enlightenment or *Haskalah*, had begun this process in earnest.[12] "Much like the humanists of the Renaissance era, who wanted to rescue Latin from the clutches of the Roman church and reclaim its original literary and scientific qualities, *Maskilim* wanted to return to the beauty and grace of ancient Hebrew and rediscover its more secular (literary, intellectual) qualities."[13] They also wanted "to turn written Hebrew into a secular language," even though the very idea "provoked traditionalists."[14] Among the leaders of the *Maskilim* who advocated restoring the Hebrew language for everyday Jewish discourse was Isaac Satanov, who expressed a view that would prove sagacious when he argued that "the political restoration of the people to Zion would enrich the language."[15] God was setting the stage for an important restoration that would accompany the resurrection of the Jewish nation. He was preparing the people for the restoration of the language with which the prophets, kings, and sages of Israel had communicated.

Through the efforts of Restorationists and the *Maskilim*, the attention of the Jews was increasingly turned toward a redefinition of Jewish identity. "Jewish communities experienced a new need for Jewish identification, something Jewish nationalism was able to provide."[16] As it turned out, this "new Jewish nationalism focused on two issues: the restoration of a Jewish language . . . and some sort of political autonomy."[17] When Jews from around the world began to immigrate into Israel, "the question of language was one of

---

[11] *Maskilim* is the plural of the Hebrew *maskil*, which means "scholar" or "enlightened man."

[12] Eli Lederhendler, *Jewish Responses to Modernity: New Voices in America and Eastern Europe* (New York: New York University Press, 1994), pp. 161–164.

[13] Eran Kaplan and Derek J. Penslar, eds., *The Origins of Israel, 1882–1948: A Documentary History* (Madison, WI: The University of Wisconsin Press, 2011), p. 168.

[14] Raymond Lillevik, *Apostates, Hybrids, or True Jews?: Jewish Christians and Jewish Identity* (Cambridge, UK: James Clarke & Co., 2014), p. 241.

[15] Isaac Satanov, noted in Nahum M. Waldman, *The Recent Study of Hebrew: A Survey of the Literature with Selected Bibliography* (Winona Lake, IN: Eisenbrauns, Inc., 1989), p. 218.

[16] Lillevik, p. 241.

[17] Lillevik, p. 241.

the most critical cultural issues that the early Zionists faced."[18] Would it be Yiddish, the blend of Hebrew and German that was popular in Western Europe? Would it be Ladino, a combination of Hebrew and Spanish with elements of other languages? Or would the restored Israel be a polyglot nation like Switzerland? At first, Theodor Herzl, the founder of Zionism, opted for the latter solution.[19] Such an approach to language in the restored state of Israel, however, would surely have resulted in the Balkanization of Israeli society.

Language Restoration

"A small number of intellectuals and activists believed that a revolutionary movement that aims to upend the course of Jewish history should not rely on the languages of the Diaspora but rather resurrect the ancient Jewish national tongue, Hebrew."[20] Even before the Zionist movement came to prominence, therefore, another advocate of what would come to be known as Zionism had an entirely different—and, as it turned out, correct—view that would have a powerful impact upon the emergence of the restored nation. This man was Eliezer Ben-Yehuda, a Lithuanian Jewish linguist, who "came to believe that the Jewish people could also revive the Jewish nation on its ancient national soil."[21] Even while he was still a student and Francophile at the Sorbonne in Paris, he came to understand the decisive role that French literature had had in the arousal of French nationalism.[22] In 1880, he reached a conclusion that stunned even him: "I have decided that a national revival of the Jewish people could only be successfully accomplished if it were accompanied by a revival of the Jews' ancient language, Hebrew."[23]

After he immigrated to Palestine in 1881 and saw the social and political realities there, Ben-Yehuda at first dismissed the claim that Jews did not count as a nation because they lacked a common spoken language, citing the example of multilingual Switzerland; however, he later changed his views. "Just as the Jews cannot really become a living nation other than through their returning to their ancestral land, so too, they are not able to become a living nation other than through their returning to their ancestral language."[24] Ben-Yehuda came to

---

[18] Kaplan and Penslar, eds., p. 168.
[19] Anton La Guardia, *War Without End: Israelis, Palestinians, and the Struggle for a Promised Land* (New York: Macmillan, 2003, p. 83.
[20] Kaplan and Penslar, eds., p. 168.
[21] Karesh and Hurvitz, p. 52.
[22] Alexander Murinson, *Turkey's Entente with Israel and Azerbaijan: State Identity and Security in the Middle East and Caucasus* (New York: Routledge, 2010), p. 33.
[23] Lawrence Jeffrey Epstein, *A Treasury of Jewish Anecdotes* (Northvale, NJ: Jason Aronson, Inc., 1989), p. 35.
[24] Eliezer Ben-Yehuda, quoted in La Guardia, p. 81.

understand that language was one of the most important core identities of any nation or people. The one thing that distinguished him from his fellow Zionists, therefore, was his understanding that the restored nation of Israel needed a restored language and that that language could only be the language of its Jewish ancestors. Ben-Yehuda came to believe that a conjunctive symbiosis existed between Zionism and the Hebrew language. His agenda was simple: "The Hebrew language can live only if we revive the nation and return it to the fatherland."[25] He also understood that the long-term success of the nation would depend to a large degree upon whether or not it would adopt a common language—in this case, Hebrew, the language common to the ancient ancestors of the Jewish people.

Ben-Yehuda decided to begin restoring Hebrew in the right place, in the Jewish home, and he chose his own home for his experiment. He and his wife decided that they would speak Hebrew exclusively in their home. As a result, their son, Ben-Zion, "became the first all-Hebrew speaking child in modern Jewish history."[26] By implementing his personal vision in his own family, Ben-Yehuda created the first Hebrew-speaking family in over 1600 years.[27] At the same time, he proved that a total revival or resurrection of the Hebrew language was both possible and practical. While he had made his own grand experiment in the context of his own family, Ben-Yehuda believed that the full restoration of Hebrew as the Israeli language would unfold in a process: "The Hebrew language will go from the synagogue to the house of study, and from the house of study to the school, and from the school it will come into the home, and . . . become a living language."[28]

"Zionists were faced with more practical considerations—to turn Hebrew into a living, everyday language."[29] Ben-Yehuda's task, therefore, was daunting. His undertaking was profoundly stressful not only because of the incredible amount of work that that had to be done in order to transform the 8,000-word vocabulary of biblical Hebrew into a modern language but also because he was confronted with significant opposition from traditionalists of the Jewish society of Palestine who objected to his

---

[25] Eliezer Ben-Yehuda, quoted in William M. Schniedewind, *A Social History of Hebrew: Its Origins Through the Rabbinic Period* (New Haven, CT: Yale University Press, 2013), p. 206.
[26] The Ben-Yehudas abandoned the European Ashkenazi pronunciation of Hebrew in favor of one influenced by Sephardic pronunciation and spoken Arabic. Karesh and Hervitz, p. 52.
[27] Jack Fellman, *The Revival of Classical Tongue: Eliezer Ben Yehuda and the Modern Hebrew Language* (The Netherlands: Mouton & Co., 1973), p. 37.
[28] Eliezer Ben-Yehuda, *Ha-Zevi* 31 (1886/87), p. 146.
[29] Kaplan and Penslar, eds., p. 168.

"profaning" the sacred language of Scripture by promoting it for everyday use. In fact, Ben-Yehuda "was excommunicated by the ultra-Orthodox because they rejected the use of the holy tongue for day-to-day discourse,"[30] and he and his family were targeted for verbal—and sometimes physical—abuse. Ultimately, however, the intellectuals of the Zionist movement were "joined by the broader Jewish population in Palestine that by the second decade of the twentieth century in their schools, public institution, and their homes embraced Hebrew as their national language."[31]

With Ben-Yehuda's work, Hebrew became the unifying language of the Jewish people and the nation of Israel. Regardless as to what nation and language the Jewish people left when they made *aliyah* to the Promised Land, when they arrived in Israel, they found a polyglot people speaking one universal language, Hebrew. They did so largely because Ben-Yehuda labored tirelessly, despite his ongoing battle with tuberculosis, to complete the work that he knew he had been called to do on behalf of his people. His works culminated in his seventeen-volume *Complete Dictionary of Ancient and Modern Hebrew*. A month before Ben-Yehuda died in December, 1922, the British Mandate for Palestine declared Hebrew to be the official language of the Jewish community in Palestine.[32] What the pioneer of Hebrew restoration had envisioned had come to fruition in the unification of the diverse Jewish communities of Israel around one language, the language of their ancestors of antiquity.

In reality, Eliezer Ben-Yehuda was a prophet,[33] though a prophet of a different sort.[34] He was not an ecstatic voice bubbling up with spiritual insight; however, he was a prophet of restoration. He even spoke of his mission in life in highly mystical terms: "During this time, suddenly—it was as if the heavens opened and a light shone forth—a pure and gleaming ray flashed before my eyes, and a mighty inner voice called in my ears. Israel's Rebirth on the Soil of

---

[30] David Horovitz, ed., *Shalom, Friend: The Life and Legacy of Yitzhak Rabin* (New York: William Morrow, 1996), p. 281.

[31] Kaplan and Penslar, eds., 168.

[32] The declaration of the British Mandate said, "English, Arabic, and Hebrew shall be the official languages of Palestine." See Anat Stavans, "Challenges Faced by a Medium-Sized Language Community in the 21st Century: The Case of Hebrew," in *Survival and Development of Language Communities: Prospects and Challenges*, F. Xavier Vila, ed. (Bristol, UK: Multilingual Matters, 2013), p. 82.

[33] For an excellent personal account of the life of Eliezer Ben-Yehuda written his grandson, Rabbi Eliezer Ben-Yehuda, see Eliezer Ben-Yehuda, *Fulfillment of Prophecy: The Life Story of Eliezer Ben-Yehuda* (Charleston, SC: BookSurge Publishing, 2009).

[34] Kenneth Katzner, *The Languages of the World* (New York: Taylor & Francis Group, 2002); Robert St. John, *Tongue of the Prophets: The Fascinating Biography of Eliezer Ben-Yehuda, the Father of Modern Hebrew* (Beverly Hills, CA: Wilshire Book Co., 1972).

the Fathers!"[35] Cecil Roth encapsulated Ben-Yehuda's mission well when he said, "Before Ben-Yehuda, Jews could speak Hebrew, after him, they did."[36]

A Living Language for a Living People

Another great miracle connected with the restoration of Israel as a people, a nation, and a land was the resurrection of the dead language of an "as-good-as-dead" people. Hebrew became a living language for a rejuvenated, revived, reinvigorated people. What happened with the Jews also happened with their language, and it too was something that had never taken place in history. "No nation has ever lost its language (which is a country's national identity), only to have it restored and revived after 2000 years. It has happened to NO other nation,"[37] says Alan Turner. In 1930, Shalom Spiegel spoke of the importance that Hebrew would have for the Jewish nation: "The revival of Hebrew and its transformation into a colloquial tongue with all the defects and virtues of a living language . . . and such progress in vocabulary as would have filled any civilized people with pride—these things have proven beyond a doubt the physiological genuineness of our rejuvenation as a people."[38]

Shortly after Israel was restored in 1948, Menahem Ribalow said, "Only through communication, through some communion with the Hebrew language, will [our children] behold the full revelation of Judaism and become initiated into the mystery that preserved the Jewish people since the beginning of its history to this day of the renewal of Jewish sovereignty."[39] Today, Hebrew is the living language of Israel, spoken by 6 million Israelis and studied by much of world Jewry. Anton La Guardia says, "Hebrew is the mortar holding together Israel's disparate ethnic traditions."[40] David Blumenthal observes that "the natural place for Hebrew is the land of Israel. The proper locus of the holy tongue is the holy land. There, the language and environment resonate together. There, the echoes of the one rebound naturally from the landscape of the other."[41] Hebrew is the language "which unites all the children of Israel from the four corners of the globe . . . it is the language of our forefathers, the language of our prophets, the language of our

---

[35] Eliezer Ben-Yehuda, quoted in La Guardia, p. 80.
[36] Cecil Roth, "Was Hebrew Ever a Dead Language?" in *Personalities and Events in Jewish History* (Philadelphia, PA: Jewish Publication Society of America, 1953), pp. 136–142.
[37] Alan Turner, *Is God Finished with Israel?* (Maitland, FL: Xulon Press, 2008), p. 66, author's emphasis.
[38] Shalom Spiegel, *Hebrew Reborn* (New York: Meridian Books, 1930), pp. 19–20.
[39] Menahem Ribalow, *Jewish Education* 22 (Summer, 1951), p. 69.
[40] La Guardia, p. 84.
[41] Blumenthal, p. 134.

sages."[42] Though there are many cultural and socio-economic distinctions in Israel, there is one thing that is common to all Israelis: the Hebrew language.

Cosmic, Spiritual Dimensions?

Could it be that the restoration of the Hebrew language to the Hebrew people, the Jews, in their own nation and land is even the fulfillment of the words of prophecy? The God of Israel declared through the prophet Zephaniah, "For then I will restore to the peoples a pure language that they all may call on the name of the LORD, to serve him with one accord."[43] The timing of this prophetic word certainly points to the eschatological denouement of all things when, at the end of the age, God prepares the world for the Messianic dominion. "In that day," God says to Israel, "it will be said to Jerusalem: Do not be afraid, O Zion. . . . The LORD your God is in your midst, a victorious warrior. . . . At that time I will bring you in, even at the time when I gather you together, indeed, I will give you renown and praise among all the peoples of the earth, when I restore your fortunes before your eyes, says the LORD."[44]

Over a century ago, Charles Forster interpolated Zephaniah's prophecy in this manner: "As, at the beginning of your existence as a nation, I gave you 'a pure language' from Mount Sinai; so, at the end, I will restore you 'a pure language,' a vehicle of thought and expression meet to celebrate my praise, and in which to call upon my name."[45] For this reason, Forster said, "the Hebrew of the Pentateuch, thenceforward to become the language of the whole Hebrew people, may be regarded as a pure language or idiom revealed from heaven, less simple, because more regularly constructed than any of the primeval tongues; in order that no tongue polluted by heathen profligacy or idolatry might profane, by becoming their receptacle, the lively oracles of God."[46] This is why Hebrew is "commonly known as 'the holy tongue' (lashon ha-kodesh)."[47]

In Zephaniah's prophecy, God declared that when he finally restores his people in their land, he will also restore "a pure language," שָׂפָה בְרוּרָה (sapah

[42] Eliezer Ben-Yehuda and Eisig Silberschlag, *Eliezer Ben-Yehudah: A Symposium in Oxford* (Oxford, UK: Oxford Centre for Postgraduate Hebrew Studies, 1981), p. 41.

[43] Zephaniah 3:9.

[44] Zephaniah 3:16–17, 20.

[45] Charles Forster, *The One Primeval Language Traced Experimentally through Ancient Inscriptions* (London, England: Richard Bentley, 1852), p. 78.

[46] Forster, p. 78.

[47] Ronald L. Eisenberg, *Dictionary of Jewish Terms: A Guide to the Language of Judaism* (Lanham, MD: Taylor Trade Publishing, 2011), p. 182.

b'rurah). This "pure language" will doubtless be the opposite of that of Babel, where "confusion of tongues" perpetuated established idolatry among the nations. The Hebrew tongue is the language of divine discourse, the one that was fully revealed to humankind when God himself audibly thundered the Ten Words from Mount Sinai.[48] "Because they heard God speak in an audible voice," says Jack Deere, "the Israelites realized . . . that their God was unique among all the pagan deities."[49] William Schniedewind even suggests that Hebrew "was the language of heaven" and, as the sages have also argued, that it was "the vernacular of God's creative acts."[50] What Israel heard, then, was the spoken word that had summoned all creation in existence![51] M. Rubin suggests that this *lashon ha-kodesh* "will prevail once more in the end of the days, when all nations will once again speak this primordial language in which the world was created."[52]

It may be that an as-yet-unrevealed manner of communicating with the Divine will ultimately be manifest; however, the foundation for whatever "pure language" finally emerges was established in biblical Hebrew. The implications of the Hebrew language for prefacing God's ultimate work of redemption, renewal, and restoration cannot be minimized. The restoration of Hebrew to the Jewish people, therefore, is just as important as the restoration of the land of Israel to the Jews, for as Blumenthal notes, "the language of the people in its land is the language of revelation. It is the language of the foreparents and the prophets—Hebrew."[53] Judah Magnes said it well, "In every Jewish cultural revival the Hebrew language has played an important part, and today when the Jewish nation is again witness to the marvel of its own renaissance, when, like an old tree in springtime, it is shooting forth new cultural blossom, the Hebrew language is again fulfilling its mission as the natural vehicle through which young Judah expresses his fears and hopes."[54]

---

48 Deuteronomy 4:15.
49 Jack Deere, *Surprised by the Voice of God: How God Speaks Today Through Prophecies, Dreams, and Visions* (Grand Rapids, MI: Zondervan Publishing Co., 1996), p. 131.
50 Schniedewind, p. 171. Schniedewind underscores his argument by noting that the apocryphal book of Jubilees defines Hebrew as "the tongue of creation" (Jubilees 12:16).
51 John 1:1–4; Romans 4:17.
52 M. Rubin, "The Language of Creation or the Primordial Language: A Case of Cultural Polemics in Antiquity," in *Journal of Jewish Studies* XLIX (1998), p. 317, quoted in Masanobu Endo, *Creation and Christology: A Study on the Johannine Prologue in the Light of Early Jewish Creation Accounts* (Tübingen, Germany: Mohr Siebeck, 2002), p. 139.
53 Blumenthal, p. 136.
54 Judah L. Magnes, quoted in W. Gunther Plaut, *The Growth of Reform Judaism* (New York: World Union for Progressive Judaism, 1965), p. 320.

CHAPTER 14

ZIONISM AND DIVINE DESTINY

FAITH IN GOD'S CALL FOR *ALIYAH*

All of the dreams and prayers of Christian Restorationists, whether driven by pure love and altruism toward the Jewish people or by eschatological scenarios or conversionist triumphalism, would have been for naught if it had not been for the fact that God, the God of Israel, placed a deep and abiding love for the land of Israel in the hearts of his Chosen People. From the time of Abraham, it was clear that connectedness to the Holy Land would be intrinsic to the self-definition of the Hebrews/Israelites/Jews. It was as though the Jewish heart could never be severed from the Jewish land. It was, therefore, inevitable that the passion that had driven individual Jewish families to return to the land of Israel, regardless as to what name had been imposed upon it by Gentile powers, would drive increasing numbers of Jews to reconnect themselves with the land of their patriarchs and matriarchs.

During the second half of the nineteenth century, a growing realization of the dangers that threatened the persecuted Jewish population of most of Europe began to foster insight in the hearts of avant-garde Jews into the need for the creation of an independent, modern Jewish nation.[1] Some believed that this emerging viewpoint was a contrived, illegitimate idea based on a myth of the "ancient site from which the 'ethnic' tribe [of Israel] had ostensibly sprouted."[2] The passion for creating a modern state of Israel in the land of Israel as a vision for the survival of the Jewish people was, in fact, more than simply a good idea: it was a prophetic vision, the accuracy of which would be shockingly confirmed a century later in Nazi Germany. This national territorialization birthed from

---

[1] *Jewish Quarterly*, (Braintree, UK: Jewish Literary Trust, 1977), vol. 25–27, p. 7.
[2] Shlomo Sand, *The Invention of the Land of Israel: From Holy Land to Homeland*, tr. Jeremy Forman (London, UK: Verso Books, 2012), p. 256.

religious philosophies may well have been "one of Zionism's most important, even if not completely original, achievements,"[3] but in reality, it was the outworking of the Jewish soul's longing for restoration to the matrix from which it had been birthed some four millennia earlier.

This phenomenon of return to the land came to be called *aliyah*. The Hebrew word עֲלִיָּה (*'aliyah*), meaning "ascent," comes from the verb עָלָה (*'alah*), which means "to go up." The word *'aliyah* refers to the Psalm of Ascents (Psalm 122) in which the ancients said, "Let us *go up* to the house of the LORD. . . . Jerusalem is a city that is bound firmly together, to which the tribes *go up* . . . to give thanks to the name of the LORD."[4] The "origin of the term *'aliyah* is," therefore, "purely sacred, or religious" in that "it initially referred to the pilgrimage made three times a year during the Second Jewish Commonwealth period, when, on the three major holidays, Jews were obliged to ascend to the Jerusalem Temple and to bring tributes and sacrifices to God and his holy servants, the priests of the Temple."[5] After the destruction of the temple and the dispersion of the Jewish people, the word *'aliyah* came to describe "making *aliyah* to the Torah," the act of being called to the *bema* of the synagogue to read the Torah.[6] *Aliyah* was also used to describe immigration to Israel, primarily for burial purposes. It was from this background of figurative applications that the literal application of "making *aliyah*" as the act of moving to the land of Israel in order to take up residence there was born. This was the meaning of the word *'aliyah* that the early Zionists adopted to describe their intentions for the Jews regarding the land of Israel, and it became a focal point for encouraging Jews to immigrate into Israel following the establishment of the State of Israel.

It is not insignificant that the word *'aliyah* is the very last word in the *Tanakh*, appearing in the record of the decree of Cyrus, King of Medo-Persia, when he recounted the fact that God had instructed him to sponsor the reconstruction of the Temple in Jerusalem. This is what Cyrus decreed: "The LORD . . . has charged me to build him a house at Jerusalem, which is in Judah. Whoever is among you of all his people, may the LORD his God be

---

[3] Sand, *The Invention of the Land*, p. 256.

[4] Isaiah 2:3.

[5] Baruch Kimmerling, "Academic History Caught in the Cross-Fire," in *Postzionism: A Reader*, Laurence Jay Silberstein, ed. (New Brunswick, NJ: Rutgers, the State University Press, 2008), p. 108.

[6] Rich Cohen, *Israel Is Real: An Obsessive Quest to Understand the Jewish Nation and Its History* (New York: Macmillan, 2009), p. 58. Cohen points out that in each synagogue, the *Aron Kodesh* that contains the Torah is elevated on a *bema* (platform), which represents Mt. Sinai. Those who are called upon to read the Torah make *aliyah* by ascending to the *bema*.

with him. Let him go up (*'alah*)."[7] Since the commandment for the restoration of the temple and the rebuilding of Jerusalem concluded with the word *'alah*, it is altogether appropriate that the same term, in the form *'aliyah*, should be used to describe the work of the Jewish people to "go up" to the land of Israel and there to do the work of restoring Israel, the Chosen People; Israel, the Jewish nation; and Israel, the Holy Land. Just as it was a sacred quest for the Israelites to "go up" to Jerusalem to worship their God three times each year during the pilgrimage festivals, and just as it has been a sacred responsibility for Jews to "go up" to read the Torah in their synagogues around the world, it has also been a sacred opportunity for Jews from the nations of the world—east, west, north, and south—to hear the voice of God beckoning them to "go up" from the nations of their dispersion to the land of their ancestors. Answering the call for *aliyah* is the fundamental key to restoring the people of Israel to the land, restoring the land of Israel to the people of Israel, and restoring the people of Israel to their God. Perhaps the imperative of Cyrus to the post-exilic Judean community will be seen to have been God's prophetic word to his Chosen People in this day: "Go up!"

Remaining Faithful to God and to the Holy Land

Despite centuries of efforts by an unending array of Gentile powers to evict them from the Promised Land, Jews tenaciously maintained their connection to the real estate that God had conveyed to them through their father Abraham. The Babylonian *Galut* had scattered the vast majority of their ancestors in 597 BC; the Roman destruction of the Temple in 70 AD had begun the Diaspora;[8] and when Hadrian razed Jerusalem and constructed *Aelia Capitolina* on its ruins, the

---

[7] 2 Chronicles 36:23, ESV. This verse is the last statement in the Hebrew Scriptures because the *Tanakh* is organized in a different order from that of the Christian canon of the Hebrew Scriptures ("Old Testament"). The word *Tanakh* (sometimes written *TaNaKh*) is an acronym for Torah, *Nevi'im*, and *Ketuvim* (Law, Prophets, and Writings, respectively). The *Ketuvim* begins with the Book of Psalms, and it includes all the poetic and historical books of the Hebrew Scriptures. These books conclude with 2 Chronicles, the last word of which is *'alah*, the root of *'aliyah*. Interestingly, then, the Hebrew Scriptures begin with the word *b'reshit* ("In the beginning"), and they end with the command *'alah* ("Go up"). The Hebrew word עֲלִיָּה (*'aliyah*) appears in the Hebrew Scriptures only in 2 Chronicles 9:4: "[Solomon's] ascent (*'aliyah*—*'aliyato*) by which he went up into the house of the LORD." The antonym of *'aliyah* is *yerida* ("descent"). The final imperative of King Cyrus is one word in Hebrew: וְיָעַל (*v'ya'al*), "And go up!"

[8] Heidi Thomann Tewareson, "Jews among Christians in Germany," in *Encyclopedia of Diasporas: Immigrant and Refugee Cultures Around the World*, Melvin Ember, Carol R. Ember, and Ian Skoggard, eds. (New York: Springer Science+Business Media, Inc., 2005), p. 466. Also, Amos Perlmutter, *The Social and Philosophical Profile of the Zionist-Socialist Labor Movement in Palestine, 1897–1947* (Berkeley, CA: The University of California Press, 1054), p. 51.

expulsion of the Jews from Jerusalem and all of Israel seemed a *fait accompli*. Still the passion of the Jewish people for the land could not be quenched, and at incredible risk to their lives, Jews insisted on remaining in the land of their ancestors because they understood that this was the Holy Land that was consecrated by God himself and given to them, as he himself said, "forever." Abba Eban argued that the prayers in Jewish memory had the effect of infusing "Jewish life with a peculiar nostalgia, strong enough to prevent any sentiment of finality or permanence in any other land." Consequently, he said, "The physical link was never broken. A thin but crucial line of continuity had been maintained by small Jewish communities and academies in Jerusalem, Safed, Jaffa, and Hebron."[9]

Abraham Heschel has pointed out just one of the many continuously surviving Jewish communities in Israel: "In the mountain village of Peki'in in Galilee a flawless line of descent can be traced from the Hebrews of yore to the present-day inhabitants."[10] And this is but one example of the incredible tenacity of the Jewish people to maintain their claim on the land of the Bible. In addition to the small percentage of world Jewry who insisted on remaining connected with the land of their ancestors, virtually all of the Jews who have lived outside the land of Israel (because of the exiles and evictions) have continually "referred to themselves as living in the 'Diaspora,'" and have "never abandoned their claim to return to the land from which so many of their ancestors had been forcibly driven."[11] Throughout the Diaspora, therefore, the Jewish hope of reclamation of the land of Israel continued to be encapsulated in the concept of "making *aliyah*," of "going up" to the land of their forefathers. Though "the center of gravity of the Jews and Judaism had moved from the Middle East to Europe,"[12] still a Jewish presence remained in the land of Israel.

It is quite significant that the first recorded effort of the Jewish people to make an organized return to their ancestral land was initiated during the same timeframe when the Christian Restorationist movement began to call for the revival of the nation of Israel. Heschel describes this unique and profound effort thus: "In the sixteenth century, Joseph, the Duke of

---

[9] Abba Solomon Eban, *Heritage: Civilization and the Jews* (New York: Simon & Schuster, 1984), p. 244.

[10] Abraham Joshua Heschel, *Israel: An Echo of Eternity* (New York: Macmillan, 1967), p. 71.

[11] Alan M. Dershowitz, "Countering Challenges to Israel's Legitimacy," in *Israel's Rights as a Nation-State in International Diplomacy*, Alan Baker, ed. (Jerusalem, Israel: Jerusalem Center for Public Affairs, 2011), p. 160.

[12] Gavin I. Langmuir, "Continuities, Discontinuities and Contingencies of the Holocaust," in *Studies in Contemporary Jewry: Volume XIII: The Fate of the European Jews*, Jonathan Frankel, ed. (New York: Oxford University Press, 1997), p. 10.

Naxos . . . seemed to have realized the necessity of finding not a temporary haven of refuge for the Jews, but a permanent one. There was only one safe place for persecuted Jewry: Palestine. He intended to make Tiberias in Galilee a Jewish center. With astonishing tenacity, the original Jewish settlement managed to survive through a long succession of invasions and catastrophes until late in the Middle Ages."[13] Whereas organized efforts at Jewish immigration into Palestine sometimes failed, the determination of individuals and families to return to and occupy the land ensured a continuing Jewish presence even in the most difficult of times.

Assimilation: A Strategy for Failure

After more than fifteen centuries of being scattered to the four winds and then being persecuted, assaulted, and murdered, the Jewish people would have had every reason to despair of their hope that one day they would be restored as a people to one nation and one land—Israel. For many, that dream had faded into the very pragmatic necessity for making efforts to assimilate into the nations where they lived. Such efforts, however, often had the same "boomerang effect of Jewish efforts to assimilate into Greek civilization—resentment instead of integration, hatred instead of acceptance."[14] In fact, the "modern attempts to force Jews to assimilate—ideally, to convert to Christianity—as a quid pro quo for emancipation" were met with the same "inbuilt ambivalence to Judaism and the Jews" that "helped justify European anti-Semitism."[15] As the future would prove incontrovertibly, however, efforts toward assimilation were doomed to failure, for when one had been born a Jew, nothing could change that fundamental identity in the non-Jewish nations, especially those of Europe, where national identity was often founded on theories like Germany's *Blut und Boden.*[16]

---

[13] Heschel, *Israel,* p. 71.

[14] Moshe Aberbach, *Jewish Education and History: Continuity, Crisis and Change* (New York: Routledge, 2009), pp. 74–75.

[15] Aberbach, p. 75.

[16] The German phrase *Blut und Boden* means "Blood and Soil." This perspective on national self-identity made it possible for Nazi theories to emerge that promoted Aryan superiority based on concepts of eugenics and social Darwinism that were in vogue at that time. Such ideas that asserted the natural superiority of the Aryan peoples made it possible for some Germans to view Jews and others as subhuman species, even as vermin that surely needed to be exterminated for the wellbeing of the society as a whole. See Daniel Bar-Tal, *Shared Beliefs in a Society: Social Psychological Analysis* (Thousand Oaks, CA: Sage Publications, 2000), p. 133. Bar-Tal reports that for Germans, "Jews were devils, destroyers of civilization, parasites, demons, bacteria, vermin, and pests . . . maggots and bedbugs." Also, Caroline Alice Wiedmer, *The Claims of Memory: Representations of the Holocaust in Contemporary Germany and France* (Ithaca, NY: Cornell University Press, 1999), p. 3.

The Jewish people could not be faulted, however, for their efforts toward assimilation. Many considered themselves to be Germans or French or British citizens first and then Jews secondarily. By the time of the nineteenth and early twentieth century, many of them had become only semi-religious, adopting the philosophy of Reformed Judaism. Many had also become agnostic. As a matter of fact, "as their assimilation and patriotism increased, some Jews came to view traditional Judaism as weak, out of touch with the modern world."[17] In Germany, some had gone as far as to distance themselves from their ghetto-dwelling, poorer, and less educated—but more religious—distant relatives in Eastern Europe whom they stereotyped as the *Ostjuden*.[18] This should not have been surprising, moreover, for in societies at large, "even assimilated Jews remained embarrassments and outcasts . . . insecure in their environs, lacking peace of mind, overanxious to fit in yet feeling shame for doing so, and generally clinging to a frail existence. The Jews remained an anomalous mixture of race, religion, and nation."[19] None of the efforts toward assimilation, however, would be enough, as unfolding history would prove. As it turned out, even conversion to Christianity would not ensure Jewish survival in the cataclysm that was to come.

For nearly a millennium, Jews had been hated, persecuted, abused, and murdered in virtually every part of Europe. Even the Age of Reason and the Enlightenment could not cure the pathology of European antisemitism, for the emancipation of suppressed people groups and other egalitarian efforts that moved Europe from the evils of the Dark Ages to the utopian dreams of modernity just could not be fully extended to the Jewish people. If anything, Judaeophobia and antisemitism became ever more virulent. It was in this milieu that the modern Jewish Zionist movement was birthed. Francis Nicosia describes the emergence of Zionism: "In the second half of the nineteenth century, Jewish emancipation and assimilation as well as the increasing virulence of secular racial anti-Semitism generated conflicts within Jewish communities in Europe that contributed to the beginnings of modern Zionism. While nationalism, along with Enlightenment principles of freedom and equality, compelled most Jews to opt for some degree of assimilation into gentile society, those principles along with an increasingly virulent anti-Semitism throughout

---

[17] Aberbach, p. 86.
[18] The German term *Ostjuden* means Eastern Jews, or Jews from the East. For an excellent discussion of this nineteenth-century fissure between German and Eastern Jews, see Laurel Plapp, *Zionism and Revolution in European-Jewish Literature* (New York: Routledge, 2008), p. 25ff.
[19] Michael Makovsky, *Churchill's Promised Land: Zionism and Statecraft* (New Haven, CT: Yale University Press, 2007), p. 40.

Europe induced a relatively small minority of Jews, particularly among the young, to seek the alternative path of Zionism."[20]

At the same time, the rise of antisemitism in Russia and Eastern Europe led to a resurgence of pogroms that shattered whatever hopes the Jews had for tolerance and equality that may have existed in these societies. Because a door was opening to immigration into Palestine, Russian and Eastern European Jews began to make *aliyah* to the land of their ancestors. Simultaneously, significant numbers of Jews from Turkey, Iraq, Morocco, and Yemen, who were completely unaware of the Zionist movement, were motivated both by fear of increasing intolerance in the Muslim world and by the longstanding Jewish dream of returning to Zion, and they, too, began the challenge of immigrating to Palestine. David Novak sums up the overriding reason for the Jewish immigration: "The quasi-totality of Jewish immigrants in Israel came to escape anti-Semitic persecution."[21]

A New Movement for the Restoration

When the Jews began a revival of their rightful claim to their nation and their land, the verve and vigor of the young Jews who coalesced into the Zionist movement were certainly the motive force behind their efforts; however, it is a simple fact of history that "the rise of Christian Zionism prepared the ground for the emergence of European Jewish Zionism in the late nineteenth century," and "Political (Jewish) Zionism . . . was inspired and directly influenced by its contemporary, Christian Zionism."[22] Perhaps in the sovereignty of God, the seeds of the divine plan for restoring the Jewish nation had ironically been planted in the world's corporate consciousness by Christians who had forsaken the sins of their fathers that brought so much pain to the larger Jewish community and had embraced varying degrees of philosemitism and love for Israel. For the first time in nearly two thousand years, these Christians had heard the plain and simple words that God spoke to the patriarchs and prophets of Israel: "I will give you this land." For four centuries before the rise of Jewish political Zionism, Christian Restorationists had been proclaiming what could only be seen as the clear word of the Lord: "Let my people go. . . . I will plant them in their land never to be uprooted again."[23] And,

---

[20] Francis R. Nicosia, *Zionism and Anti-Semitism in Nazi Germany* (Cambridge, UK: Cambridge University Press, 2008), p. 31.

[21] Roger Garaudy, "Religious and Historical Pretexts of Zionism," in *The Link*, vol. 10, no. 3, p. 13.

[22] Merkley, 1998, pp. 15–21.

[23] Exodus 5:1; Amos 9:5.

more importantly, they had been working in the halls of governments to sound the alarm against antisemitism in their nations and to promote means by which the security of self-sovereignty could be restored to the Jewish people.

David Novak notes the supreme irony of the history of Zionism: "In fact, it is sometimes embarrassing for Jewish Zionists to learn that there are Christian Zionists who have better biblically based arguments for their Zionism than many Jews have for their own Zionism."[24] Anita Shapira, a contemporary Israeli historian, suggests that evangelical Christian Zionists of the 1840s "passed this notion on to Jewish circles."[25] This fact rests on the 500-year-long continuing quest by Restorationists and Christian Zionists to pray for, support, and work to effect the restoration of the land of Israel to the sovereignty of the Jewish people. What may be even more ironic, however, is the fact that a few early Jewish Zionists took their argument for the importance of the restored Jewish state in Israel even further by maintaining that "a Jewish state would be 'a light unto the nations.'"[26] While Christian Restorationists had had significant influence on the birth of Zionism, Zionism would have a much more powerful impact on the church because the restoration of Israel would force the church to come face to face with the fallacy of its supersessionist triumphalism vis-à-vis the Jews. There can be no doubt that restored Eretz Yisrael has radically influenced the theology of virtually all Christian denominations![27] Perhaps the greatest light that Restored Israel has brought and will bring to Christianity is the restoration of the inherent Jewish roots of the Christian faith that will enable Christianity to recognize its supreme debt to Judaism and to the Jewish people.

Restorationism had to be transformed, however, from a Christian eschatological hope into a physical reality, and only the Jewish people themselves could effect this seemingly impossible accomplishment. Fortunately, the

---

[24] David Novak, *Zionism and Judaism* (Cambridge, UK: Cambridge University Press, 2015), p. 21.

[25] Anita Shapira, *Israel: A History*, tr. Anthony Berris (London, UK: Weidenfeld and Nicolson, 2014), p. 15.

[26] Freedman, p. 2.

[27] Eva Fleischner, *Judaism in German Christian Theology Since 1945* (Lanham, MD: Scarecrow Press, 1975), p. 27. Fleischner says that "the concrete fact of Israel's existence is effecting a major change in Christianity's view of Judaism." Also, Herman N. Ridderbos, "The Future of Israel," in *Prophecy in the Making: Messages Prepared for Jerusalem Conference on Biblical Prophecy*, Carl F. H. Henry, ed. (Carol Stream, IL: Creation House, 1971), p. 316. Ridderbos notes the dilemma that Israel's restoration has presented to Christian theology: "The existence of Israel once again becomes a bone of contention, this time in a theoretical and theological sense. Do the misery and suffering of Israel in the past and in the present prove that God's doom has rested and will rest upon her, as has been alleged time and again in so-called Christian theology? Or is Israel's lasting existence and, in a way, her invincibility, God's finger in history, that Israel is the object of His special providence (*providential specialissima*) and the proof of her glorious future, the future that has been beheld and foretold by Israel's own seers and prophets?"

God of history had the power to transform into material substance a dream to which Christians, after centuries of blindness, had come to share with their Jewish brothers: the vision of a restored Zion. What some Christians had come to believe and to act upon in the spheres of their influence, Jews would labor intensely and incessantly to bring into reality with all the vigor and determination steeled into the very fiber of their being by centuries of fire and pressure. The Zionist Movement was ready to emerge on the human scene and effect one of history's most amazing miracles, the full restoration of the long-dormant nation and land of Israel. It would not be an easy task, however, for "most of the Jewish world at the beginning of the twentieth century was non-Zionist or anti-Zionist."[28]

By far the most important leader of the Zionist movement that emerged in the late nineteenth century was Theodore Herzl, a Jewish journalist with a doctorate in law who was both a thinker and an organizer. As writer for the liberal Viennese newspaper, Herzl had encouraged Jews to assimilate in the various nations where they lived.[29] "In 1896, after witnessing the anti-Jewish rioting in France connected to the Dreyfus affair, in which a French Jewish army officer was falsely accused of giving military secrets to the Germans," however, "Herzl concluded that there was no safe place for the Jews of Europe and that assimilation was not possible."[30] It was at this time that Herzl wrote his defining work *Der Judenstaat* (*The Jewish State*), in which made two seminal arguments: 1) the Jews throughout the world were "one people" and 2) the only solution to the Jewish plight was "the establishment of their own nation.[31] At first, Herzl suggested "that any tract of land big enough to accommodate the Jews would suffice,"[32] and he even suggested that a part of Uganda could serve that purpose. When this matter was considered during the Sixth Zionist Congress (also known as the Uganda Congress), however, Franz Oppenheimer argued poignantly and correctly: "Allocating [the Jewish people] the most magnificent expanses of farm

---

28 Chaya Herman, *Prophets and Profits: Managerialism and the Restructuring of Jewish Schools* (Cape Town, South Africa, HSRC Press, 2006), p. 84.
29 Richard D. Bank, *The Everything Jewish History and Heritage Book: From Abraham to Zionism* (Avon, MA: F+W Publications, 2003), p. 256.
30 Robert I. Freedman, "Introduction," in *Contemporary Israel: Domestic Politics, Foreign Policy, and Security Challenges*, Robert O. Freedman, ed. (Boulder, CO: Westview Press, 2009), p. 2.
31 Bank, p. 256.
32 Bank, p. 256. Bank points out that some of the first ideas for a location for the Jewish state included land in Argentina where Baron de Hirsch had funded the settlement of 6,000 Jews in an agricultural colony. Also included was Rothschild's work of funding Jewish settlements in Palestine. Ultimately, with the Balfour Declaration, even Uganda was considered as a possibility for a new Jewish homeland.

land in Canada or Argentina will not enhance the strength of the wandering Jew as much as settling on the lowly Plain through which the Jordan flows and upon which the Lebanon looks out."[33] Ultimately, however, Herzl eventually came to believe that a Jewish state in Palestine was necessary for the security and survival of the Jewish people. Herzl envisioned a new Jewish nation as a "socialist utopia" which he described in his novel, *Altneuland* ("The Old New Land"),[34] as "a secular, socialist, and peace-loving society, a vision not entirely detached from Torah and the message of Israel's prophets."[35]

In 1897, Herzl organized the First Zionist Congress in Basel, Switzerland,[36] a meeting with 200 participants from seventeen nations. On the second day of the meeting, the congress established the goal of the emerging Zionist movement in what became known as The Basel Program: "Zionism aims at establishing for the Jewish people a publicly and legally assured home in Palestine. For the attainment of this purpose, the Congress considers the following means serviceable: 1) the promotion of the settlement of Jewish agriculturists, artisans, and tradesmen in Palestine; 2) the federation of all Jews into local or general groups, according to the last of the various countries; 3) the strengthening of the Jewish feeling and consciousness; 4) preparatory steps for the attainment of those governmental grants which are necessary to the achievement of the Zionist purpose."[37] The Zionists called for the restoration of "the Jewish national home in Palestine, where Jews could find sanctuary and self-determination, and work for the renascence of their civilization and culture."[38]

Shortly after the congress, Herzl summed up the significance of the three-day meeting as he wrote in his diary, "At Basel I founded the Jewish

---

[33] Franz Oppenheimer, quoted in Shmuel Almog, *Zionism and History: The Rise of a New Jewish Consciousness* (New York: St. Martin's Press, 1987), p. 259. Also, Chaim Gans, *A Just Zionism: On the Morality of the Jewish State* (New York: Oxford University Press, 2008), p. 33.

[34] Bank, p. 256.

[35] Isaac C. Rottenberg, "Israelic Christians," in *Restore!*, Issue 52, p. 32. Rottenberg also observed this truism: "Rare, indeed, is the Jewish soul so secular that all remnants of Israel's spiritual heritage have been erased." Rottenberg was able to maintain and promote balance in the Christian support of Israel's right to exist with complete self-determination while at the same time avoiding the extremes of political party endorsements that have impacted many Christians. See Isaac C. Rottenberg, *Christian-Jewish Dialogue: Exploring Our Commonalities and Our Differences* (Atlanta, GA: Hebraic Heritage Press, 2005), and Isaac C. Rottenberg, *Judaism, Christianity, Paganism: A Judeo-Christian Worldview and Its Cultural Implications* (Atlanta, GA: Hebraic Heritage Press, 2007), p. 108.

[36] Freedman, p. 2.

[37] Isidore Singer, Cyrus Adler, *et. al.*, eds. "The Basel Program," in *The Jewish Encyclopedia* (New York: Funk and Wagnalls Company, 1906), vol. II, pp. 570–571.

[38] Leonard J. Davis, *Myths and Facts: A Concise Record of the Arab-Israeli Conflict*, Eric Rozenman and Jeff Rubin, eds. (Washington, DC: Near East Report, 1989), p. 3.

state. If I said this out loud today I would be greeted by universal laughter. In five years perhaps, and certainly in fifty years, everyone will perceive it."[39] What may have seemed presumptuous at that time was to become a reality as history progressed toward the establishment of the nation of Israel and proving that Herzl had perhaps even been prescient in his claim. "What began as an evanescent movement whose most ardent supporters never believed that the objective of Jewish sovereignty in Palestine would be achieved in their lifetime became a real national movement that shaped a society and nation and built a state."[40]

Only seven years after that historical event, Herzl, exhausted from his supreme devotion to the Zionist cause, died an untimely death at the age of 44. Significantly, however, the death of Zionism's founder "marked the beginning of the Second Aliyah (1904–1914)," which brought to Palestine forty thousand Jews. Primarily from Russia, these socialist Jews founded the enduring Israeli institution of *kibbutzim* (national farms)[41] that did wonders in reclaiming the barren land for agriculture. At the same time, with their philosophy of egalitarianism, they helped foster the first democratic nation in the Middle East. The principles outlined by the early Zionists established a solid basis not only for the dream of a Jewish nation but also for the practical principles through which that dream could be achieved. John Judis points out that "the outward logic of Zionism was impeccable," for "the nations of Europe, where Jews had dwelt for hundreds of years, were treating them as a nation in their midst," and "nationalist politicians and intellectuals in central and Eastern Europe called for purging their countries of this alien nation."[42] Who could argue, then, with the Zionist leaders' call for the establishment of a genuine Jewish nation where "they could be secure from persecution and oppression"?[43]

From its inception, the Zionist movement began to encourage Jewish migration into Ottoman-controlled Palestine,[44] confirming the long-standing view of the Jewish community, as well as that of significant parts of the Christian community, that the restoration of the Jewish people to their ancestral homeland was

---

[39] Theodor Herzl, quoted in Naomi E. Pasachoff, *Great Jewish Thinkers: Their Lives and Work* (Springfield, NJ: Behrman House, 1992), p. 98.
[40] Shipira, p. 3.
[41] Bank, p. 257.
[42] John B. Judis, *Genesis: Truman, American Jews, and the Origins of the Arab/Israeli Conflict* (New York: Macmillan, 2014), p. 15.
[43] Judis, p. 15.
[44] Robin Cohen, *The Cambridge Survey of World Migration* (Cambridge, UK: Cambridge University Press, 1995), p. 504. Also, James Gelvin, *The Israel-Palestine Conflict: One Hundred Years of War* (Cambridge, UK: Cambridge University Press, 2007), p. 51.

absolutely essential for Jewish survival in an increasingly hostile world filled with Judaeophobia and antisemitism. The bravery that individual Jews and Jewish families manifest by enduring the inhospitable conditions of a long-neglected land and overcoming the constant dangers of violence against their persons that were lurking in the shadows was key to the restoration of the land and nation of Israel. These brave and determined Jews were merely following in the footsteps of others before them who, despite the exile of the vast majority of the Jewish people from Israel, had continued to cling tenaciously to the land of their ancestors. As a matter of fact, large communities were present in Jerusalem and Tiberias in the ninth century,[45] and in the eleventh century, Jews grew and prospered in Rafah, Gaza, Ashkelon, Jaffa, and Caesarea.[46] This inherent Jewish bravery was indubitably confirmed when, after the disastrous slaughter of all the Jews in Jerusalem during the Crusades, "Jews reestablished centers of Jewish learning and commerce in the Land of Israel. From this time on, Palestine was never without a significant and well-documented Jewish presence."[47] After the Crusades, significant immigrant rabbis and Jewish pilgrims also established major religious communities in Tzfat and Jerusalem.[48]

The Jewish families that made possible the eventual establishment of the Jewish state in Israel were the ones who made the trek to the Holy Land and then purchased and developed property. Sandra Teplinksy points out that during the time of Ottoman rule, "About 50,000 Jews lived on legally purchased or inherited real estate that would eventually become Israel."[49] By the early nineteenth century, more than 10,000 Jews lived throughout what is today Israel.[50] These long-standing historical facts are important to current circumstances in Israel because they further confirm the unbroken history of Jewish settlement in Palestine and establish the fact that those Jews were not the object of the intense genocidal antipathy that had come to characterize world Islam since the restoration of Israel in the twentieth century. Such simple continuing Jewish ownership of land in Israel maintained the right of the Jewish people to continue to live in the homeland of their ancient ancestors.

---

[45] Danny Danon, *Israel: The Will to Prevail* (New York: Macmillan, 2013), p. 141.

[46] Davis, p. 10.

[47] Dershowitz, p. 160.

[48] Simon Federbusch, *World Jewry Today* (New York: Thomas Yoseloff, 1959), p. 75.

[49] Sandra Teplinsky, *Why Care about Israel? How the Jewish Nation Is Key to Unleashing God's Blessings in the 21st Century* (Grand Rapids, MI: Baker Publishing Group, 2004), p. 190.

[50] Dan Bahat, ed., *Twenty Centuries of Jewish Life in the Holy Land* (Jerusalem: The Israel Economist, 1976), pp. 61–63.

The unbroken line of Jewish patriots who loved the land given by God to their patriarchal ancestors so much that they were willing to suffer constant hardship and risk their lives to maintain residence in that land ensured the right of the Jewish people for reclaiming their land and their nation.[51] The Zionist movement merely strengthened and expanded what had been maintained in some form throughout all the centuries of the history of Israel. The Zionists purposed to add to those numbers the millions of Jews who still suffered oppression across Europe and in other parts of the world. All the advocates of Zionism, Jewish and Christian, have had one common agenda: the repatriation of the Jewish people to the homeland from which their ancestors were dispersed millennia earlier.[52] Michael Brown states the truth well: "At no time was Palestine considered an independent Arab nation, and throughout the millennia, only one group claimed this land as its ancestral homeland: the Jews!"[53] For more than a century, Zionism's one common denominator has been what is succinctly noted by Gideon Shimoni: "At the heart of the Zionist ideology was the claim to Eretz Israel, or Zion, as the national homeland of the Jews, hence, as the legitimate locus for the national self-determination of the Jews."[54]

The Jewish *Aliyah*

In the early nineteenth century, only a few Jews lived in Palestine, concentrated primarily in the Jewish Quarter of the city of Jerusalem in "a dismal ghetto where scholars and other observant Jews subsisted on charitable contributions sent by their European brethren."[55] In the 1870s, however, a new approach to settlement in Israel was initiated by Yehudi Shlomo Hai Alkali, who became one of the first Jewish leaders to promote "taking

---

51 The continuing presence of Jews in Palestine is confirmed by the fact that significant numbers of Jews were slaughtered by the Crusaders in the invasion of Jerusalem in 1099. If Palestine were an exclusively Arab (*qua* "Palestinian") land at that time—as some stridently claim—how is it that there was a Great Synagogue in which the Jewish population of Jerusalem was immolated by the Christian crusaders?

52 Ran Aronson, "Settlement in Eretz Israel—A Colonialist Enterprise? 'Critical' Scholarship and Historical Geography," in *Israel Studies*, Indiana University Press, vol. 2, no. 2, (1997) pp. 214–229. Also, Michael J. Cohen, "Zionism and British Imperialism II: Imperial Financing in Palestine" in *Journal of Israeli History: Politics, Society, Culture*, vol. 30, no. 2 (2011), pp. 115–139.

53 Michael L. Brown, *What Do Jewish People Think about Jesus? And Other Questions Christians Ask about Jewish Beliefs, Practices, and History* (Grand Rapids, MI: Baker Publishing Group, 2007), p. 32.

54 Gideon Shimoni, *The Zionist Ideology* (Boston, MA: Brandeis University Press, 1995), p. 333.

55 Bank, p. 254.

active measures towards Jewish resettlement in Eretz-Israel."[56] The idea was to encourage Jewish people around the world to return to Israel to reclaim the land by purchasing individual plots of ground and settling there. When the call went out for resettlement, many Jews from various parts of the world began to trickle into Palestine to join the few Jews[57] whose ancestors had somehow managed to remain in the land through the centuries[58] and to begin what was a formidable task of reclaiming the desolate, barren landscape.

Shortly after Alkali's effort to promote such resettlement efforts, Baron Edmund James de Rothschild began to take an active interest in Jewish resettlement of Palestine by supporting significant land purchases and assisting Jewish reclamation of *Eretz Yisrael* by means of agricultural settlements. With Rothschild's help, Jews who immigrated to Palestine were able to secure rights to property through long-term leases which made it practical for them to invest enormous energies in reclaiming the land and making it agriculturally productive. Rothschild's interest and extensive financial support began to change the odds for Jewish reclamation of the ancient land of their ancestors from the status of "slim to none" as had been the case for centuries and moving them into the realm of possibility. This small group of immigrants was soon joined by those of the "first wave of Jewish immigration" of 1882–1903 which was prompted by "the Russian pogroms of

---

[56] Efraim Karsh, ed., *Israel: The First Hundred Years, Volume I: Israel's Transition from Community to State* (London, UK: Frank Cass Publishers, 2000), p. 99.

[57] In the late nineteenth century, Laurence Oliphant wrote of his encounter with an enclave of Jews in Bukeia (Peki'in) who were believed to be lineal descendants of ancestors who had lived uninterruptedly in the Holy Land from Second Temple times: "There were the Jews—the only group of Jews existing in the world whose ancestors have clung to the soil" ever since the time of Jesus, representing "the faith which was the repository of the highest moral teaching prior to Christianity, prior to Mohammedanism." Laurence Oliphant, *Haifa: Life in Modern Palestine* (London, England: William Blackwood, 1887), p. 111. Dennis Prager and Joseph Telushkin maintain that "Jews have lived continuously as a community in Palestine since approximately 1200 B.C.E. Dennis Prager and Joseph Telushkin, *Why the Jews?: The Reason for Antisemitism* (New York: Simon and Schuster, 1983), p. 105. Also, Michael Bard, *The Complete Idiot's Guide to the Middle East Conflict* (New York: Penguin Books, 2008), p. 288, and Shalom Goldman, *Zeal for Zion: Christians, Jews, & The Idea of the Promised Land* (Chapel Hill, NC: The University of North Carolina Press, 2009), p. 69.

[58] From a sweep of history, it is clear that Jews have lived continuously as Jews in the land of Israel since they inherited the land in the time of Joshua. One needs only to look at the history of Jews who were persecuted and murdered in Jerusalem through the centuries to confirm this fact, a prime example of which was the hundreds who were burned alive in the Great Synagogue by the Crusaders in 1099. Every effort to obliterate the Jews so as to make Jerusalem either a Christian or a Muslim city failed to eradicate the Jewish people, who, despite indescribable suffering continued to cling to their native land.

1881–1882."[59] Because of harsh conditions in the land and onerous Turkish taxation, coupled with growing hostility from the Arabs, fully half of the 35,000 settlers who made up the First Aliyah[60] returned to Europe.[61] Those who remained, however, were steeled in their determination to reclaim their right to the land of Israel. Additionally, a steady stream of new immigrants added to the total Jewish population in Palestine. These early resettlement efforts resulted in a Jewish majority in the city of Jerusalem by the end of the nineteenth century.[62] In the 1918 census, Jews "formed the largest community in Jerusalem."[63] The increasing numbers of Jews who had immigrated to the Holy Land set the stage for the restoration of the nation of Israel in the land of Israel.

Moving from Vision toward Reality

The intense work of both Christian Restorationists and the original Zionists had not only visionary aspects but practical applications, particularly those that were lobbied in the halls of government in both the Britain and the United States. One such meeting that was to have profound impact on establishing the cause of Jewish national restoration as something that could reasonably be accomplished occurred when Chaim Weizmann met with Arthur James Balfour, the foreign secretary of the United Kingdom. When Balfour suggested that the Jews settle for a state in Uganda, Weizmann responded, "Mr. Balfour, supposing I was to offer you Paris instead of London, would you take it?" Balfour said, "But Dr. Weizmann, we have London," to which Weizmann responded, "That is true, but we had Jerusalem when London was a marsh." This exchange prompted Balfour to ask, "Are there many Jews who think like you?" Weizmann assured the Foreign Secretary, "I believe I speak the mind of millions of Jews," prompting Balfour to exclaim, "If that is so, you will one day be a force."[64]

---

[59] Bank, p. 99.
[60] Bank, p. 99. Bank notes that there were five *Aliyah's* in total that occurred as the Jewish settlement of Palestine unfolded.
[61] Bank, p. 99.
[62] Arthur Lourie, "Palestine Under the British Mandate (1918–1948)" in *A History of Israel and the Holy Land*, Michael Avi-Yonan, ed. (New York: The Continuum International Publishing Group, 2003), p. 322. Lourie points out that from census statistics of that time, there were more Jews living in Jerusalem than there were Christians or Muslims.
[63] Roberto Mazza, *Jerusalem: From the Ottomans to the British* (New York: I.B. Tauris & Co., 2009), p. 40.
[64] Chaim Weizmann, *Trial and Error: The Autobiography of Chaim Weizmann* (Westport, CT: Greenwood Publishing Group, 1972), p. 111.

Weizmann's relationship with Balfour had begun much earlier in 1905, and their interactions continued for years. It was propitious for Weizmann that, as a chemist, he had invented a new process for producing acetone, one of the key ingredients in cordite, an important military propellant that facilitated the British army's execution of World War I.[65] This fact alone had opened to Weizmann doors to then British minister of munitions, David Lloyd-George, who later became Britain's prime minister. Lloyd-George recalled a meeting he had had with Weizmann in 1916 wherein the Jewish inventor and Zionist "explained his aspirations as to the repatriation of the Jews to the sacred land they had made famous." Their conversation was to be "the fount and origin of the famous declaration about the National Home for the Jews in Palestine," said Lloyd-George, for "as soon as I became Prime Minister, I talked the whole matter over with Mr. Balfour."[66]

These and other behind-the-scenes activities eventually elicited the issuance of what came to be called the Balfour Declaration, which was actually a November 2, 1917, letter written by James Balfour to Walter Rothschild for transmission to the Zionist Federation of Great Britain and Ireland. This document made the following momentous statement: "His Majesty's government view with favour the establishment in Palestine of a national home for the Jewish people, and will use their best endeavours to facilitate the achievement of his object, it being clearly understood that nothing shall be done which may prejudice the civil and religious rights of existing non-Jewish communities in Palestine, or the rights and political status enjoyed by Jews in any other country."[67] The Balfour Declaration of 1917 became the foundation for the 1922 League of Nations Covenant for Palestine and its Mandate to Britain, which, in turn, was the basis for the November 29, 1947, United Nations Resolution 181 that called for the establishment of the Jewish state in Palestine and set the stage for the Declaration of the Statehood of Israel on May 14, 1948.[68]

---

[65] James Wei, *Great Inventions that Changed the World* (Hoboken, NJ: John Wiley & Sons, 2012), p. 177. Weitzmann developed a process for "producing acetone through bacterial fermentation of starch."

[66] David Lloyd George, *Memoirs of the Peace Conference* (New Haven, CT: Yale University Press, 1939), vol. II, pp. 724–734.

[67] Alex Bein, *The Jewish Question: Biography of a World Problem* (Madison, NJ: Fairleigh Dickinson University Press, 1990), p. 692.

[68] Howard Grief, *The Legal Foundation and Borders of Israel Under International Law: A Treatise on Jewish Sovereignty over the Land of Israel* (Jerusalem, Israel: Mazo Publishers, 2008), pp. 136–147. May 14, 1948, was chosen as the date for the Israeli Declaration of Independence because the League of Nations Covenant for Palestine and its Mandate to the British expired at midnight on that date.

It reality, however, neither the United Nations Resolution, the League of Nations Covenant for Palestine, the British Mandate, the Balfour Declaration, nor any other document or action by individuals, nations, or groups of nations created the State of Israel. This action was accomplished by the hand of God over three millennia before when the Almighty summoned the Israelites from the land of Egypt and joined with them in a covenant that formed the people of Israel into the nation of Israel. Then, it was the God of Israel who brought the people and nation of Israel to the land that he had promised to Abraham, Isaac, and Jacob where he established his "holy nation" on irrevocable promises. The growing Jewish *aliyah* and the emergence of a new nation of Jews were not to be the result of international altruism. It was not the product of political or military machinations. What had happened and what would happen was to be solely the work of the Almighty to fulfill the divine destiny of his Chosen People! God himself, the God of Israel, had been and would be the architect of the amazing, the author of the impossible. He alone had orchestrated and would continue to orchestrate the interactions of millions of characters and the intersection of thousands of incidents that would produce the unattainable but the inevitable. The Restorationist and Zionist dream was gradually moving toward ultimate reality as God used human instruments to effect divine purposes, but it was the hand of God that was doing what was impossible for humans to achieve.

Ultimate Tragedy on the Horizon

Amazing and even miraculous events had been occurring in the lives of the international Jewish community for most of the nineteenth and early twentieth centuries. Four centuries of enlightened Christian support for the resurrection of the Jewish nation in the Jewish land had begun to bear practical fruit. The spirit of *aliyah* had seized upon growing numbers of the Jewish people in what was more than a desperate attempt to escape the persecution inflicted upon them in their Diaspora. This was more than an escape mechanism. This was a rebirth, a resurrection, a renewal of ancient promises. In fact, what is called the First Aliyah was defined by the goal of "the political, national, and spiritual resurrection of the Jewish people in Palestine."[69] What Christians could only envision, Jews accomplished by

---

[69] Mitchell Geoffrey Bard and Moshe Schwartz, *One Thousand and One Facts Everyone Should Know about Israel* (Lanham, MD: Rowman & Littlefield Publishers, 2005), p. 14.

returning to the land of their ancestors and beginning the arduous tasks of reclaiming and renewing that land in preparation for the ultimate miracle that was to come. In this milieu, "the image of the romantic pioneer, the hard-working agricultural colonist, the brawny Jewish farmer" answered the long-standing Gentile caricature of the Jews as "mere parasites, racially incapable of 'productive' labor."[70] Operating within the parameters of a renewed concern for the welfare of the Jewish people in ecclesiastical and political circles, there was hope for good things to come. Surely visions of Jewish restoration to their native land were about to be fulfilled.

By the time of the rise of the Nazi Party in Germany, however, Judaeophobia and antisemitism had come to cloud the vision and sensitivities of far too many in world governments as well as in far too many parts of the Christian church. None of this boded well for the Jewish people anywhere in the world and in particular for those who were trapped in Germany and Europe when the doors for immigration into Western Europe and America were gradually closed and finally slammed shut. What had been on track for nearly four centuries was suddenly derailed. The work of restoration was sidetracked. Conspiracy after conspiracy was launched in the halls of Western governments to close every avenue of escape for the Jewish people from the confines of Europe where the cruelest, most diabolical tragedy in human history awaited them.

Lawrence Epstein described the situation both accurately and succinctly: "The Zionists were completely and presciently correct about the principal moral reason why a state for the Jews was needed. There was a deadly 'racial' hatred of the Jews charging through history and aiming right at them. The Zionists were frighteningly correct in their assessment of the dangers the Jews faced. Not only was hatred of the Jews loose in the world, but soon there would be no escape from it. After the 1924 immigration act in the United States, there would be no remaining haven for Jews in trouble."[71] All the voices of conscience that had sounded the alarm of impending doom for the Jewish people were soon drowned out in vociferous promotions of nationalism and isolationism, based on economic despair, fear, and impending manifest evil. The ultimate catastrophe was on the horizon.

---

[70] Allon Gal, *Envisioning Israel: The Changing Ideals and Images of North American Jews* (Jerusalem: The Magnes Press, 1996), p. 41.
[71] Lawrence J. Epstein, "The Moral Case," p. 1.

CHAPTER 15

HOLOCAUST

ANTISEMITISM'S FINAL SOLUTION

Judaeophobia, anti-Judaism, and antisemitism first appeared in recorded history in the diabolical schemes of Haman in ancient Persia. Then all of these pathologies were manifest in the remnants of the Grecian Empire by Antiochus IV Epiphanes, who sought to stamp out Judaism by imposing Hellenism upon the Jews.[1] Later, they influenced the Roman Empire to react violently against the inextinguishable yearning of the Jewish heart for liberty and self-determination. Finally, they came to characterize the Christian church,[2] which emerged from the matrix of biblical and Second Temple Judaism but then all too rapidly lost its bearings and turned against the Jewish people in a psychosis of fratricidal carnage wherein the church of Jesus despised and abused the family of Jesus.

Sadly, this Haman spirit sprayed its venom far and wide, especially throughout Christian Europe so that, for a thousand years, Europeans engaged in religiously excused, even religiously endorsed, persecution and violence against the Jews. In decade after decade and in nation after nation

---

[1] The antisemitic actions of Antiochus were perhaps more insidious than other overt and frontal attacks on Judaism and the Jewish people, for initially his efforts were designed to bring about a syncretism between Hellenism and Judaism. When this failed, however, he sought viciously to impose Hellenism upon the Jewish people, polluting the temple by offering swine on its altar in homage to Zeus and killing significant numbers of the Jews. See Mark Adam Elliott, *The Survivors of Israel: A Reconsideration of the Theology of Pre-Christian Judaism* (Grand Rapids, MI: Wm. B. Eerdmans Publishing Co., 2000), p. 192.

[2] These three dynamics of disdain for the Jews and their faith gradually gained control of much, if not most, of Christianity. The first to be manifest was Judaeophobia, wherein early leaders of the church feared debate with the more learned Jewish rabbis and sought to ingrain an almost morbid fear of legalism in the hearts of their constituents in order to combat the perceived threat that the rabbis would somehow convert them to Judaism. Second, an ever-increasing anti-Judaism began to invade Christianity, with church leaders attacking the Jewish faith as antiquated and superseded by Christian faith. Ultimately, full-blown antisemitism took over when Christians began to hate Jews themselves and to seek to do them emotional and physical harm.

across the European continent, the Jewish people were subjected to decidedly unchristian attitudes and actions that kept them under constant fear of the next spark that would ignite another pogrom.[3] Violence, mayhem, and murder against Jews were systematic and unrelenting as "Christian" nations, often encouraged by "Christian" clerics, incited the masses to rain down terror upon the Jewish communities among them. It is not insignificant that Christian holy days were the most terrifying times for the Jewish people!

This Christian-endorsed persecution of the Jews would not reach its nadir, however, until the twentieth century. Ironically, this was the century when the long-anticipated utopia of modernity had been expected to manifest itself and bring a seismic change in the human situation.[4] This was to be the age when the evolution of the human species would finally produce the peace and prosperity that philosophers thought the essential nature of humanity demanded. Secular humanists were convinced that the evolving physical, intellectual, emotional, and social makeup of humankind could not help but actualize the utopian dream.[5] It was inevitable, and it was close at hand!

Whereas antisemitism in the Middle Ages had been based largely on religion, it took on a new and even more treacherous form in the post-Enlightenment era, basing itself in "science" or, more accurately, in two pseudosciences. First was the "scientific study of race," which drew support from anthropology and a philosophy of racial difference. Jonathan Sacks explains: "Different races had different civilisational attributes and these could be traced by physical markers, such as the color of a person's skin or shape of the nose."[6] At the same time, "the other pseudo-science was the curious hybrid of biology and sociology known as social Darwinism" which argued that "the evolution of society followed the same laws as the evolution of species."[7] In this schema, "Nature is a battleground in which the ruthless survive and the weak perish. So is human

---

[3] The word *pogrom*, which is taken directly from the Russian word *pogróm* (meaning "destruction" or "devastation") describes an organized massacre of a particular ethnic group, particularly the Jewish people.

[4] James K. Dew, *Science and Theology: An Assessment of Alister McGrath's Critical Realist Perspective* (Eugene, OR: Wipf and Stock Publishers, 2011), p. ix.

[5] Modernity was based on the idea that the human race was constantly evolving, ever improving in and of itself, and moving inexorably toward a utopia of universal peace. The foundations of modernity came crashing down in the twentieth century with two world wars, the development of nuclear weapons of mass destruction, and the unthinkable Holocaust. Over 68 million soldiers and civilians were killed in the two world wars, and over 6 million Jews, including over 1 million women and children, were murdered in the Holocaust.

[6] Jonathan Sacks, *Future Tense: Jews, Judaism, and Israel in the Twenty-first Century* (New York: Schocken Books, 2009), p. 100.

[7] Sacks, p. 100.

history. The strong prevail; the weak die and disappear. There is nothing moral or immoral about this process. It is simply how things are."[8] This climate of irrational Enlightenment "rationalism" and "scientific" pseudoscience stripped anti-semitism of its inherent religious element (at least in the minds of secularists, agnostics, and atheists) and transmogrified it into an even more insidious form.

At the turn of the twentieth century, Europe was embroiled in the constant warfare that had characterized its entire recorded history. The Europeans were a bellicose people, and across the landscape of time, the bloodletting between competing nations and factions was incessant. Nothing could seem to prevent the nations of Europe from attacking one another. Since the first century AD, at least 417 wars had been fought on European soil. Then, by 1914, ten more wars had already been fought there in the twentieth century. Finally, the war came that everyone believed would be the "war to end all wars," the Great War,[9] which drew into its conflict not only most European nations but also other countries from around the world. Because of new military inventions such as machine guns, tanks, chemical weapons, grenades, and aircraft, this conflict resulted in the loss of more than 20 million lives and produced untold suffering for the wounded and maimed, both in the military and in civilian ranks. Death from warfare swept across Europe on a scale that had never been seen before as the Western Entente Powers of France, Britain, and Russia met the Triple Alliance made up of Germany, Austria-Hungary, and Italy in a fight to the finish. In the end, the defeated and dispirited German people bore the brunt of the blame for the conflict, and after their defeat on the battlefield, they were punished severely by enforced disarmament and demands for reparations and other economic strictures. After years of ever deepening economic hardships, in 1933, the German people were fully ripe for the ascent of Adolf Hitler and his Nazi Party and the great tragedy that was to follow.

Blame the Jews

In order to advance his autocratic agenda, Hitler needed a scapegoat on which to blame the woes of post-war Germany. And an easy target was readily available, one that had been attacked and blamed for virtually every malady in European history for at least ten centuries. Hitler used the one scapegoat that he had already attacked in his reflection on political theory and his personal

---

8 Sacks, p. 100.
9 With the advent of World War II, the Great War came to be called World War I.

memoir, *Mein Kampf.* He targeted the Jews.[10] This tactic had been used repeatedly throughout the Middle Ages and beyond, so it was very simple to use it again.[11] Hitler, however, took antisemitism to extremes never imagined by anyone in the history of the world.[12] He planned, plotted, and began the implementation of his *Endlösung der Judenfrage* (Final Solution to the Jewish Question)[13] which, if it had been completely successful, would have resulted in the total annihilation of the entire Jewish population of Europe and perhaps of the world. Steven Sage demonstrates that from his youth till his death, Hitler was obsessed with the genocide of the Jews.[14] Everything that happened in interwar Germany had been the fault of the Jews. Hitler deemed "Jewish journalists to be a seminal factor in Germany's interwar malaise."[15] The Nazis carefully orchestrated the libel against the Jews, whom they "blamed for every ill: the loss of the war, the *Diktat* of Versailles, and the inflation, from which Jews were said to have profiteered."[16] Indeed, the Weimar Republic, which had been instituted in Germany at the end of the war, came to be known as the "Jew Republic."[17] At the same time, "the influx of eastern Jews, who were looked on as aliens and suspected of swindling" was "fantastically exaggerated in the anti-Jewish

---

[10] Sarah Ann Gordon, *Hitler, Germans, and the "Jewish Question"* (Princeton, NJ: Princeton University Press, 1984), p. 134.

[11] Martin Collier, Bill Marriott, and Rosemary Rees, *Colonisation and Conflict 1750–1990* (Oxford, UK: Heinemann Educational Publishers, 2002), p. 176.

[12] While some elements of the German church openly supported the Nazis or acquiesced to them, and while the church in general (including Roman Catholicism) raised little protest against the Third Reich, the antisemitism that resulted in the Holocaust was not a Christian invention. Instead, it was "carried out for the purpose of a neopagan, modernist, progressive, racial Darwinist agenda." Though Christians participated to varying degrees in the Holocaust, "this agenda was not itself defined primarily in theological terms." Robert W. Bleakney, personal communication. Also Richard Weikart, *Hitler's Ethic: The Nazi Pursuit of Evolutionary Progress* (New York: Palgrave Macmillan, 2009); Richard Weikart, *From Darwin to Hitler: Evolutionary Ethics, Eugenics, and Racism in Germany* (New York: Palgrave Macmillan, 2004); and Lukman Harees, *The Mirage of Dignity on the Highways of Human 'Progress': The Bystanders' Perspective* (Bloomington, IN: AuthorHouse, 2012), p. 296.

[13] The term *Endlösung der Judenfrage* was actually a German euphemism designed to disguise the true nature of the Third Reich's intention, which was simply the systematic extermination of the entire Jewish population of Europe through genocide. Donald Bloxham, *The Final Solution: A Genocide* (New York: Oxford University Press, 2009).

[14] Steven F. Sage, *Ibsen and Hitler: The Plagiarist, the Poet, and the Plot for the Third Reich* (New York: Carroll & Graf Publishers, 2006). Sage does a brilliant job of demonstrating that Hitler drew upon Henrik Ibsen's plays, *Emperor and Galilean, The Masterbuilder, and An Enemy of the People*, for his lifelong obsession with the quest for the genocide of the Jews.

[15] Paul Reitter, *The Anti-Journalist: Karl Kraus and Jewish Self-Fashioning in Fin-de-Siècle Europe* (Chicago, IL: The University of Chicago Press, 2008), p. 32.

[16] Edward Flannery, *The Anguish of the Jews: Twenty-Three Centuries of Antisemitism* (Mahwah, NJ: Paulist Press, 2004), p. 206.

[17] Flannery, p. 207.

propaganda."[18] Additionally, all of the Jewish people "were suspected of ties with Communism, which was commonly referred to as 'Jewish Bolshevism.'"[19] No matter what the problem may have been, the Jews were responsible for it!

Anything that was perceived to be evil was blamed on the Jewish people. "If capitalism was bad, Jewish capitalism . . . was worse. . . . If socialism was bad, Jewish-led socialism was infinitely more damnable."[20] Whatever could be warped or twisted to the advantage of the Nazis was used to make Hitler's program for the eradication of the Jewish people more palatable to the German people. As had been the case throughout history, the Jewish people were once again set up as the "default scapegoats" for every ill in society, and they continued to be the victims of "Christian paranoia by proxy."[21] This disorder was being fanned to a frenzy as the Nazis used Christians to advance an occult, neopagan agenda that was rife with racial Darwinism and radically perverse eugenics philosophy.

Without the Jews as scapegoats, Hitler and the Nazi party likely would not have succeeded in gaining control of German society as they did. "How did [Hitler], mediocre in so many ways, so quickly attract to his standard" such a cross section of German society? Edward Flannery concluded that "the one catalyst that above all else enabled him to reconcile oppositions and finally transform Germany from a liberal republic into a totalitarian state in a single decade was his anti-semitism."[22] Indeed, in Nazi Germany, the "ultimate limit of antisemitism—as an *ersatz* religion—was reached."[23] Daniel Goldhagen confirmed this fact: "The German people were more dangerously oriented towards Jews than they had been during any other time since the dawn of modernity," and this orientation was easily transformed by the Nazis into "eliminationist antisemitism."[24] In Germany, antisemitism was much more intense than it was anywhere else in Europe; therefore, when the Nazis came to power, Germans, "equipped with little more than the cultural notions current in their country, would easily become genocidal executioners."[25]

---

[18] Flannery, p. 206.
[19] Flannery, p. 207.
[20] Bruce F. Pauley, *From Prejudice to Persecution: A History of Austrian Anti-Semitism* (Chapel Hill, NC: The University of North Carolina Press, 1992), p. 319.
[21] Daniel Rancour-Laferriere, *The Sign of the Cross: From Golgotha to Genocide* (Piscataway, NJ: Transaction Publishers, 2011), p. 217.
[22] Flannery, p. 209.
[23] Flannery, p. 211.
[24] Daniel Jonah Goldhagen, *Hitler's Willing Executioners: Ordinary Germans and the Holocaust* (New York: Random House, 1996), pp. 463–466.
[25] Goldhagen, p. 185.

At All Cost, Kill the Jews!

Transforming Jews into caricatures was the order of the day as the Nazi party rose to power in Germany. Their Final Solution to the Jewish Question, however, was not just caricature or social isolation: it was extermination, the complete genocide of the people group that had been derogated, derided, hated, and persecuted in Europe for nearly a thousand years. In the end, the Nazis considered Jews to be vermin, subhuman creatures that deserved to be exterminated for the public good.[26] So Hitler and his cohorts launched a well-planned, well-organized, and systematically implemented program designed to ensure the complete liquidation of all the Jewish people—men, women, and children—in Europe. The ultimate goal was a *Judenrein*[27] Europe, with the Jewish population entirely eradicated.

On November 9, 1938, the Nazi plan for the extermination of the Jews was launched in a four-day pogrom that came to be called *Kristallnacht* ("Crystal Night" or the "Night of Broken Glass").[28] In this and the ensuing days, a hundred Jews were killed, and 30,000 were arrested and placed in concentration camps, while over 1,000 synagogues were burned and over 7,000 Jewish businesses were damaged or destroyed.[29] On the last day of the *Kristallnacht* riots, Joseph Goebbels, the Nazi Reich Minister of Propaganda, attributed the events to the German people's "healthy instincts," noting that "the German people are anti-Semitic. It has no desire to have its rights restricted or to be provoked in the future by parasites of the Jewish race."[30] Dehumanizing language such as this was designed to make the Nazis' program for the extermination of the Jews more acceptable to the German people. And it worked.

---

[26] Christopher R. Browning, "The German Bureaucracy and the Holocaust," in *Genocide, Critical Issues of the Holocaust: A Companion Volume to the Film "Genocide,"* Alex Grobman and Daniel Landes, eds. (West Orange, NJ: Behrman House, 1983), p. 148. Also Caroline Alice Wiedmer, *The Claims of Memory: Representations of the Holocaust in Contemporary Germany and France* (Ithaca, NY: Cornell University Press, 1999), p. 3. Wiedmer notes that "vermin such as spiders and rats were the common figures for Jews in Nazi propaganda, and the German populace was supposed to define the Jews as inhuman and parasitic, as vermin to be feared and ultimately destroyed—robbed of all personal belongings and put into gas chambers to be exterminated with pesticide."

[27] *Judenrein* in German means "clean of Jews." Another German word which was used to describe the actions of the Nazis against the Jews was *Judenfrei*, meaning "free of Jews."

[28] *Kristallnacht* was also called *Pogromnacht* ("Pogrom Night"). The term *Kristallnacht* was applied to this event because of the millions of shards of broken glass that littered the streets in German and Austrian cities after the windows of Jewish stores, buildings, and synagogues were smashed by Nazi-led paramilitary forces and civilians.

[29] Michael Berenbaum and Arnold Kramer, *The World Must Know* (Washington, DC: United States Holocaust Memorial Museum, 1993), p. 49.

[30] Joseph Goebbels, quoted in *The Daily Telegraph,* November 12, 1938, cited in Martin Gilbert, *Kristallnacht: Prelude to Destruction* (New York: Harper Collins, 2006), p. 142.

In an organized and well-coordinated effort, the German *Schutzstaffel* (SS) and the *Gestapo* raided Jewish homes in Germany and Austria and imprisoned the Jews in German concentration camps in Dachau, Buchenwald, and Sachsenhausen. Then, in Lithuania, Russia, Ukraine, and Poland, they herded Jewish families into killing zones where they were shot and dumped into long trench-like mass graves.[31] This liquidation process was begun several years before the infamous crematoria were ever built.[32] During this operation, mobile firing squads called *Einsatzgruppen* killed an estimated 1.3 million Jews.[33] When Heinrich Himmler, *Reichsführer* of the SS,[34] heard of complaints from firing-squad executioners who were being repulsed by the fact that they were required to murder unarmed men, women, and children, he decided that other, more efficient means had to be developed for killing Jews.[35] In 1941, the Nazis experimented with loading Jews into rear compartments of mobile vans, driving them to places prepared for their execution, there introducing carbon monoxide gas from engine exhaust into those compartments in order to asphyxiate the Jews, and then throwing the Jewish bodies into mass graves and burying them with bulldozers.

It became increasingly clear to the SS, however, that an even more efficient killing system had to be created if the goal of exterminating all of Europe's Jews was to be realized. In order to implement their Final Solution, the Nazis built concentration camps in Poland and equipped them with gas chambers and crematoria designed for mass murder. The first opened at Chelmno in December, 1941, followed by others in Belzec, Sobidor, Treblinka, Auschwitz, and Birkenau, all of which became infamous for their killing efficiency. In Birkenau alone, up to 6,000 Jews were murdered daily. The Nazis also made use of Europe's rail systems, herding into cattle cars the Jews whom they had arrested in France, Belgium, Italy, the Netherlands, and other nations and transporting them to the killing centers.[36]

---

31 James R. Norton, *The Holocaust: Jews, Germany, and the National Socialists* (New York: The Rosen Publishing Group, 2008), p. 33. Also, Patrick Desbois, *The Holocaust by Bullets: A Priest's Journey to Uncover the Truth Behind the Murder of 1.5 Million Jews* (New York: Palgrave Macmillan, 2008). Desbois documents the murder by firing squads of Jews in virtually every village across Eastern Europe.

32 Avraham Burg, *The Holocaust Is Over; We Must Rise from Its Ashes* (New York: Palgrave Macmillan, 2008), p. 15.

33 Norton, p. 33.

34 The term *Schutzstaffel* meant "Protective Squadron." At first,the SS served as Hitler's personal bodyguards. In time, however, it grew to one of the most powerful and feared organizations in Nazi Germany.

35 Yitzhak Arad, *Belzec, Sobidor, Treblinka: The Operation Reinhard Death Camps* (Bloomington, IN: Indiana University Press, 1987), p. 379.

36 Paul Azous, *In the Plains of the Wilderness* (Jerusalem, Israel: Mazo Publishers, 2006), p. 146.

Hitler and the leading Nazis were utterly consumed by a maniacal obsession for ridding Europe of all Jews. Hannah Arendt has observed that "Hitler could rejoice even in the midst of military setbacks over the extermination of the Jews and the establishment of death factories."[37] Even when it was clear that the Nazis had lost the war, they continued to service the killing centers in their determined march toward the genocide of all European Jews. Troop trains destined for the front lines were shunted onto sidings to avoid delaying trains that were transporting Jews to the death camps. Then, when transportation systems became scarce, Jewish victims were force-marched to the killing centers.[38] The Nazis considered the Final Solution to be more important than winning the war. This strategy reflected not only the ultimate insanity of the leaders of the Third Reich but also that of thousands of ordinary Germans.[39] These psychotic sociopaths orchestrated the death of six million Jews, including more than one million children. This was the Holocaust[40] of staggering and unprecedented proportions, the *Shoah*[41] that came very close to the total annihilation of European Jewry.

The Blood-Stained Hands of the Western Allies

While Nazi Germany bears full responsibility for the Holocaust and its atrocities, antisemitism in Great Britain and the United States played significant

---

[37] Hannah Arendt, *The Origins of Totalitarianism* (Orlando, FL: Harcourt-Brace, Inc., 1968), p. 442.

[38] Suzette Cotte, *Criminological Theories: Bridging the Past to the Future* (Thousand Oaks, CA: Sage Publications, 2002), p. 37. Cotte notes that "the forced marches of camp inhabitants over hundreds of miles in the last days of the war were meant to kill Jews, even though the guards knew that the German war effort was lost." Also, see the website: http://www.scetv.org/education/holocaust_forum/contents/lesson_6.cfm.

[39] Even when leaders of the Third Reich ordered local commanders to desist from the brutality against the Jews in an effort to achieve better surrender terms from the allied armies, those commanders continued with the atrocities. See Cotte, p. 47. With this in mind, Cotte observed that "the destruction of the Jews did not derive from structures of higher authority but from the close and cruel handiwork of thousands of ordinary Germans operating within an exterminationist anti-Semitic culture."

[40] The word *Holocaust* is from the Greek word ὁλόκαυστος (*holókaustos*), meaning "burnt whole." The Greek term originally was a translation of the Hebrew word עוֹלָה (*'olah*), the "whole burnt offering" (*korban 'olah* in the Hebrew Scriptures), which was an animal sacrifice that was completely burned.

[41] The Hebrew word שׁוֹאָה (*sho'ah*) means "the catastrophe" or "devastation." In Scripture (Job 30:3), it is translated "waste." Many Jewish scholars have maintained the term *Shoah* is to be preferred over the word *Holocaust* as a description of the Nazi's genocide of the Jews because the word *holocaust* implies a "burnt offering to God" and in no way can the six million who died be considered to be a "burnt offering to God." Walter Laqueur rightly argued, "It was not the intention of the Nazis to make a sacrifice of this kind and the position of the Jews was not that of a ritual victim." Walter Laqueur, quoted in Richard Evans, *In Hitler's Shadow: West German Historians and the Attempt to Escape from the Nazi Past* (New York: Pantheon Books, 1989), p. 142. Also Richard L. Rubenstein and John K. Roth, *Approaches to Auschwitz: The Holocaust and Its Legacy* (Louisville, KY: Westminster John Knox Press, 2003), p. 5.

roles first in not preventing the Holocaust altogether and then in not saving millions of Jewish lives by facilitating their emigration from Germany and Eastern Europe to the West. In a very real way, rampant antisemitism in both the British Foreign Secretary's Office and the U.S. State Department conspired against those Jews who found themselves in the path of the Nazi *blitzkrieg* by making it virtually impossible for them to escape the Holocaust.

Long before the rise of the Nazis, the League of Nations had promised the Jewish people a state in Palestine. In an action unanimously viewed as a sacred duty by the 51 nations that comprised the League of Nations, a Covenant for Palestine was created, and Britain was given this Mandate: "The Mandatory shall be responsible for placing the country [Palestine] under such political, administrative, and economic conditions as will secure the establishment of the Jewish National Home."[42] In its first draft in 1920, this Covenant was to have given Palestine[43] and the Trans-Jordan, to the Jews.[44] In its final form in 1922, the Covenant prescribed that all of the land west of the Jordan River and the Golan Heights were to comprise "Jewish Palestine,"[45] while the eastern portion of the land, the Trans-Jordan, would be designated as "Arab Palestine."[46] This League of Nations Covenant for Palestine eventually became the basis in international law for Resolution 181 of the United Nations which, in 1947, formalized the right of the Jews to their ancient homeland.[47]

---

[42] Article 2 of the League of Nations Covenant for Palestine.

[43] Before 1948, the term *Palestinian* was almost exclusively used to refer to Jews. Virtually all of the Muslims living in Palestine preferred to be called "Arabs" and considered being called Palestinian an insult.

[44] Charles River Editors, *Decoding the Conflict Between Israel and the Palestinians: The History and Terms of the Middle East Peace Process* (Cambridge, MA: Create Space, 2013), p. 1970. This ebook notes that "The British Mandate for Palestine gave the British control over the lands that have since become Jordan, Israel, the West Bank, and the Gaza Strip. The terms of the British Mandate incorporated the language of the Balfour Declaration, recognizing the 'historical connection of the Jewish people with Palestine.' The British were also tasked by the League of Nations with creating a Jewish state, an action which the United States Congress also endorsed in 1922." It is ironic—yet absurd—that the British were somehow able to create the nations of Jordan and Iraq as homelands for Palestinian Arabs and yet, at the same time, were totally unable to create the Jewish homeland that the Covenant and Mandate required. It is also ironic that after 26 years of British dithering and Machiavellian manipulation failed to fulfill the mandate of the Covenant, the nation of Israel was born on the very next day after the British Mandate expired!

[45] Ze'ev Shemer, *Israel and the Palestinian Nightmare* (Bloomington, IN: iUniverse, 2010), p. 25. In 1923, the Golan Heights was ceded to Syria by the British even though it was part of the League of Nations Mandate.

[46] For maps of the League of Nations Covenant for Palestine, see Appendices on pp. 423–424.

[47] The power of the League of Nations Covenant for Palestine was transferred intact to the United Nations when the League of Nations was dissolved and transferred its assets to the United Nations. This, "in essence reaffirmed the validity of this international accord and reconfirmed that the terms for a Jewish National Home were the will of the international community, a 'sacred trust.'" See Eli E. Hertz, "'Mandate for Palestine': The Legal Aspects of Jewish Rights," posted at http://www.mythsandfacts.org/conflict/mandate_for_palestine/mandate_for_palestine.htm.

If the British had fulfilled the League of Nations Mandate between 1922 and 1933, virtually all of the Jews who died in the Holocaust could have immigrated into Palestine and there have escaped the killing machines.[48] Sabina Citron notes that "twenty years were wasted while the British played up to the Arabs. Even after the 1939 outbreak of World War II, there were still many possibilities to save the Jews of Europe. But even those ships with refugees from Europe were mercilessly turned away practically from the very shores of the Land! British perfidy knew no bounds!"[49] Additionally, for the first half of the twentieth century, antisemitism in both the British Foreign Secretariat and the United States State Department[50] was demonstrated in their refusal to allow immigration of Jews from Germany and Eastern Europe. When World War II began, "Britain banned all emigration [including Jews] from Nazi-controlled territories" and then banned Jewish immigration into Palestine in 1939,[51] a policy they enforced rigorously.[52]

---

[48] Alexander Zephyr, *State of Israel: Its Friends and Enemies: Prophetic Future* (Bloomington, IN: iUniverse, 2013), p. 58. Zephyr points out that "the State of Israel was not created because of the Holocaust." This conclusion is true because most of the 1948 Jewish population of Palestine had arrived there before the Holocaust and World War II began.

[49] Sabina Citron, *The Indictment* (Jerusalem: Gefen Publishing House, 2006), p. 149.

[50] Alan M. Dershowitz, *The Vanishing American Jew: In Search of Jewish Identity for the Next Century* (New York: Touchstone, 1997), p. 83. Dershowitz says, "Even in the United States—historically among the least anti-Semitic nations in the world—the State Department was rife with anti-Semitism in the 1930s and the 1940s." Regarding Britain, Dershowitz says, "Great Britain was even worse, as evidenced by its active suppression during the war of documented information about the Holocaust and its adamant refusal to open Palestine to Jewish immigration." See also Thomas Adam, ed., *Germany and the Americas: Culture, Politics, and History* (Santa Barbara, CA: ABC-CLIO, Inc., 2005), p. 88. Adam notes that "the late 1930s marked a high point in American antisemitism, and many U.S. State Department officials, themselves antisemitic, refused to make full use of the quota allotments available to Germans. Notable among these antisemitic officials was Assistant Secretary of State Breckenridge Long, who ordered U.S. consulates to hinder Jewish immigration as far as possible and who personally acted illegally to do so." See also Alan M. Kraut and Richard D. Breitman, "Anti-Semitism in the State Department, 1933–44: Four Case Studies," in *Anti-Semitism in American History*, David A. Gerber, ed. (Urbana, IL: The University of Illinois Press, 1986), pp. 150–174, and David S. Wyman, *The Abandonment of the Jews: America and the Holocaust, 1941–1945* (New York: The New Press, 1998).

[51] Robert Rozett and Shmuel Spector, eds., *Encyclopedia of the Holocaust* (Jerusalem, Israel: The Jerusalem Publishing House, 2000), p. 249. Also Patrick J. Hearden, *Architects of Globalism: Building a New World Order During World War Two* (Fayetteville, AR: The University of Arkansas Press, 2002), p. 136; Rebecca Boehling and Uta Larkey, *Life and Loss in the Shadow of the Holocaust: A Jewish Family's Untold Story* (Cambridge, UK: Cambridge University Press, 2011), p. 166; and Mati Alon, *Holocaust and Redemption* (Victoria, Canada: Trafford Publishing, 2003), p. 198.

[52] The most infamous case of British denial of immigration to Palestine was that of the *Struma*, a ship carrying Jewish refugees from Rumania. After the ship was denied entry into Palestine, it sank in the Black Sea, drowning all but two of its passengers. Edgar S. Marshall, *Israel: Current Issues and Historical Background* (Hauppauge, NY: Nova Science Publishers, 2002), p. 113. In another case, after denying passengers of the *Exodus* entry into Palestine, the British embarrassingly changed their minds when "the world saw that the Jews of the *Exodus* would rather die than be denied entry to their homeland." Eugene Korn, *The Jewish Connection to Israel, the Promised Land: A Brief Introduction for Christians* (Woodstock, VT: Jewish Lights Publishing, 2008), p. 88.

This action was taken in order to placate British allies among the Middle East Arabs.[53] Then, in 1941, a "sudden reversal of U.S. refugee policy during World War II had catastrophic consequences for Europe's Jews," for, until that time, "the Nazis had emphasized a policy of forcing Jews to emigrate, initially through social and economic pressures and later through widespread use of violence and terror."[54] If antisemitism had not been so pervasive in the West, significant numbers of the six million could have escaped the clutches of the Third Reich.

Tragically, even with the League of Nations Covenant and Mandate[55] and the decisions of the United Nations to endorse the creation of the Jewish State of Israel, backhanded dealings prevented the implementation of those plans and created the regional and territorial circumstances that continue to plague the land of Israel to this day. First, the territory east of the Jordan River was taken over by Abdullah Ibin al-Hussein and became Jordan. Then, after Abdullah's forces killed unknown numbers of "Palestinian"[56] residents of the

---

[53] David M. Keithly, *The USA and the World* (Lanham, MD: Rowman & Littlefield Publishers, 2007), p. 101. Also, Irwin M. Berent, *Norfolk, Virginia: A Jewish History of the 20th Century* (Norfolk, VA: United Jewish Federation of Tidewater, 2001), p. 168.

[54] James Ciment and John Radzilowski, eds., *American Immigration: An Encyclopedia of Political, Social, and Cultural Change* (New York: Routledge, 2014), p. 217. Ciment and Radzilowski point to scholars who have argued that "Hitler turned to the 'Final Solution' of genocide after the continued failure of the forced emigration policy, due in large part to the international community's refusal to provide sanctuary to Jewish refugees."

[55] The League of Nations Covenant and Mandate of July 24, 1922, made this declaration: "Whereas recognition has thereby been given to the historical connection of the Jewish people with Palestine and to the grounds for reconstituting their national home in that country. . . . The Mandatory [Britain] shall be responsible for placing the country under such political, administrative, and economic conditions as will secure the establishment of the Jewish national home . . . and also for safeguarding the civil and religious rights of all the inhabitants of Palestine, irrespective of race and religion." See Alan Baker, ed., *Israel's Rights as a Nation-State in International Diplomacy* (Jerusalem, Israel: Jerusalem Center for Public Affairs, 2011), p. 76. Also, see maps and commentary in the Appendices, pp. 423–42 of this volume. The original League of Nations Covenant for Palestine on April 24, 1920, had set aside all the land west of the Jordan River from Lebanon to Eilat and all the land of the Trans-Jordan east of the Jordan River (along with the Golan Heights) for a Jewish National Homeland. On December 23, 1923, the Paulet-Newcombe Agreement carved out the Golan Heights from the original Covenant and ceded it to Syria under the French Mandate. Finally, on September 16, 1922, with the collusion of the British, the Mandatory was further modified by the Trans-Jordan Memorandum, which annulled the articles of the original Covenant regarding the Jewish National Homeland in the territory east of the Jordan River, ceding control of the Trans-Jordan to Abdullah bin al-Hussein and the land further east to his brother, Faisal bin al-Hussein, as part of the newly created Iraq. In effect, the British carved away 77% of the land originally mandated for the Jewish National Homeland and created two emirates, one for Abdullah and the other for Faisal, to reward them for their support for the British against the remnants of the Ottoman Empire in World War I. See Ira M. Lapidus, *A History of Islamic Societies* (Cambridge, UK: Cambridge University Press, 1988), pp. 587–597.

[56] Masses of Arabs, natives of the Trans-Jordan, who would later be called "Palestinians," were expelled to consolidate the "Hashemite Kingdom" that was created through Abdullah's complicity with Great Britain.

Trans-Jordan and expelled many of the remaining ones in the East Bank to the West Bank. The British Empire was bent on protecting its own interests in the Middle East and, as a result, it miserably failed in fulfilling the Mandate for Palestine that had been entrusted to it by the League of Nations Covenant for Palestine. Except for the political machinations designed to further British colonialism, the entire land of Israel, including the West Bank that was later illegitimately annexed by Abdullah in 1949,[57] could well have been a place of refuge for millions of Jews who wished to escape the Nazi reign of terror. If even a small concession to the fulfillment of the Mandate had been made, most, if not all, of the Holocaust could have been avoided, and untold numbers of Jewish lives could have been spared. Israeli Prime Minister Benjamin Netanyahu stated a powerful truth when he retorted to the erroneous idea that the Holocaust somehow "produced" the nation of Israel by saying, "There are those who say that if the Holocaust had not occurred, the State of Israel would never have been established. But I say that if the State of Israel would have been established earlier, the Holocaust would not have occurred."[58]

The Western nations that were complicit in exercises to postpone the restoration of the nation of Israel and to restrict the emigration of Jews from Europe bear a significant responsibility for the extent of the Holocaust. When the British Foreign Secretary's office demonstrated its inherent antisemitism by closing Britain's doors to Jewish immigration and then manipulated the political scene in the Middle East to preclude Jewish emigration to that area, they effectively slammed the door shut on Germany and Eastern Europe and, whether knowingly or unknowingly, ensured that the killing machines would operate without any restraint. The United States Department of State also bears considerable responsibility because it denied Jewish immigration into the "Land of the Free." The Canadian government likewise considered calls from church leaders to facilitate Jewish immigration into that nation "an exercise in impractical idealism"[59] and refused to permit it. Endemic antisemitism in Western governments, therefore, kept the "Free World" from being free when it came to Jews.

---

[57] Interestingly, when Abdullah annexed the West Bank, the only nations in the world that approved his actions were Great Britain and Pakistan.
[58] Benjamin Netanyahu, Foreign Policy Speech in June, 2009, quoted in Pieter Vermeulen, "The Novel Form and the Timing of the Nation," in *See Under: Shoah: Imagining the Holocaust with David Grossman*, Marc De Kesel, Bettine Giertsmea, and Katarzyna Szurmiak, eds. (Leiden, The Netherlands: Koninklijke Brill NV, 2014), p. 155.
[59] Alan Davies and Marilyn F. Nefsky, *How Silent Were the Churches?: Canadian Protestantism and the Jewish Plight during the Nazi Era* (Waterloo, Canada: Wilfrid Laurier University Press, 1997), p. 129.

The Holocaust: Beyond Any Comparison

Claude Lanzmann argues that it is impossible to "engender the Holocaust" because "there is an unbreachable discrepancy" between "the gassing of three thousand persons, men, women, children, in a gas chamber" and any conditions that might be construed to have been causes of those atrocities.[60] "There is no solution of continuity between the two; there is rather a gap, an abyss, and this *abyss* will never be bridged."[61] Elie Wiesel was correct, therefore, when he said that the Holocaust "transcends history."[62] Because of its nature and substance, David Ben-Gurion said that "the Holocaust . . . is not like other atrocities . . . [of] the Nazis . . . but a unique episode that has no equal, an attempt to totally destroy the Jewish people."[63] Indeed, Dan Gillerman was totally right when he said, "The Holocaust constituted a systematic and barbarous attempt to annihilate an entire people in a manner and magnitude that have no parallel in human history."[64] While millions have been murdered by empire builders, no other atrocity in history has targeted an entire multinational people group for utter extermination solely because of the uniqueness of its ethnic self-identity and its religion.[65] The Holocaust stands alone as a singular event in human history for which there is can be no explanation.[66] Louise Vasvári sums up this truth well: "The Holocaust is essentially different from any other historical events; it is unexplainable because the extension and dreadfulness of the Holocaust are beyond human reason."[67] While many have tried to explain it—or explain it away—the Holocaust is simply the Holocaust.

---

[60] Claude Lanzmann, "The Obscenity of Understanding: An Evening with Claude Lanzmann," in *American Imago*, vol. 48, no. 4 (Winter 1991), pp. 473–495.

[61] Lanzmann, p. 481.

[62] Elie Wiesel, p. 158.

[63] David Ben-Gurion, quoted in Tom Segev, *The Seventh Million: The Israelis and the Holocaust* (New York: Hill and Wang, 1993), p. 329.

[64] Dan Gillerman, Statement to the United Nations General Assembly 31 October 2005. See http://mfa.gov.il/MFA/InternatlOrgs/Speeches/Pages/Israel%20submits%20draft%20UN%20resolution%20on%20Holocaust%20remembrance%2031-Oct-2005.aspx.

[65] Robert Bleakney makes a succinct summation: "The Holocaust was the only case of an international, indeed intercontinental, campaign of mass murder of an entire people group as defined by the religious affiliation of grandparents (thus victims were targeted both religiously and genetically), with a goal of complete destruction of that group wherever in the world its members might be found" (Robert W. Bleakney, personal communication).

[66] For a comprehensive discussion of the uniqueness of the Holocaust, see Eliezer Schweid, "Is the *Shoah* a Unique Event?" in *Wrestling with God: Jewish Theological Responses during and after the Holocaust*, Steven T. Katz, Shlomo Biderman, and Gershon Greenberg, eds. (New York: Oxford University Press, 2007), pp. 219–229.

[67] Tamás Kistanal, "The Holocaust as a Paradigm for Ethical Thinking and Representation," in *Comparative Central European Holocaust Studies*, Louise O. Vasvári and Steven Tötösy de Zepetnek, eds. (West Lafayette, IN: Purdue University Press, 2009), p. 19.

Many Jews have wondered, "Where was God during the Holocaust?" Elie Wiesel gave an account of a group of religious Jewish inmates at Auschwitz who had experienced the horrors committed in the concentration camp. They decided to put God on trial, with a judge, a jury, and counsel for both prosecution and defense. When the time came to pronounce judgment, there was unanimity: God was guilty as charged. Then, with the announcement that it was time for evening prayers, the "court" adjourned, and the court officers went off to worship the God whom they had just found guilty,[68] pausing to recite the *Shema* and the *Amidah*, thereby expressing their continuing faith in God.[69] Although they could never understand the apparent silence of God in the face of evil unparalleled in human history, perhaps they had the assurance that God could deliver them from their circumstances and that even if they were not physically delivered, God would keep faith with them while they slept in the dust of the earth.

These Jewish men arrived at the conclusion that Issachar Jacobsohn made when he said, "We must give up the idea of arriving at a rational explanation of the Holocaust in order to remain believers."[70] Death for the Jews in the gas chambers and crematoria was not the end: it was only the beginning, the door to a resurrection of the people, the nation, and the land of Israel. Two dynamic post-Holocaust truths, therefore, remain. The first truth is that the Jewish people survived the insidious force of manifest evil. "Without entering into a discussion of the metaphysics of history, let this point just stand for further reflection, i.e., that the Jews survived Hitler and Jewish history did not end at Auschwitz," says Steven Katz. The second and perhaps more significant truth is that the Jews not only survived the Holocaust but also thrived by recreating the long-destroyed Jewish commonwealth in the land of Israel. "This event, too, is remarkable in the course of Jewish existence," says Katz. "Logic and conceptual adequacy require that if in our discussion of the relation of God and history we want to give theological weight to the Holocaust, then we *must* also be willing to attribute *theological* significance to the state of Israel."[71]

---

[68] Anne Geldart, *Judaism, Second Edition* (Portsmouth, NH: Heinemann Library, 2001), p. 58.

[69] Elie Wiesel paraphrased from Stefan Einhorn, *A Concealed God: Religion, Science and the Search for Truth* (Radnor, PA: Templeton Foundation Press, 1998), p. 3.

[70] Adele Berlin, ed., *The Oxford Dictionary of the Jewish Religion* (New York: Oxford University Press, 2011), p. 356. For excellent examples of positive and uplifting testimonies of Holocaust survivors, see also Itta Halberstan and Judith Leventhal, *Small Miracles of the Holocaust: Extraordinary Coincidences of Faith, Hope, and Survival* (Guilford, CT: The Globe Pequot Press).

[71] Steven T. Katz, "The Issue of Confirmation and Disconfirmation in Jewish Thought after the Shoah," in *The Impact of the Holocaust on Jewish Theology*, Steven T. Katz, ed. (New York: New York University Press, 2005), pp. 15–16.

CHAPTER 16

A NATION REBORN

RESURRECTED FROM THE DUST AND THE ASHES

"Can a nation be born in a single day?"[1] Better yet, "Can these [dry] bones live?"[2] God, the God of Israel, asked two different Hebrew prophets these seemingly unanswerable questions. The obvious and logical answer to both questions would have been, *No!* But, the obvious answer was not the correct one. God was not looking for a logical answer —or even for an illogical answer, for that matter. In his infinite wisdom and foreknowledge, the Almighty knew that there was a supralogical answer, one that would transcend human reasoning and tap into his own infinite logic and power. The restorative action that God had planned for the Jewish nation was "not simply *super*natural; it [was] *contra*natural,"[3] in that it defied all the known laws of nature and of history. God was planning to do something that no one could have reasonably expected. He was going to do the impossible.

Can a nation, indeed, be born in a day? While it might have seemed impossible, there was every reason for the Jewish people in the twentieth century to believe that such a miracle could—and would—occur, for the nation of Israel had already been born in a day over three millennia before that time. God had summoned the descendants of Abraham, Isaac, and Jacob out of Egyptian slavery and had brought them to Mt. Sinai for the express purpose of celebrating one of his festivals.[4] Then, in one day, *Shavuot* (the Day of Pentecost), when the Israelites assembled before the

---

[1] Isaiah 66:8.
[2] Ezekiel 37:3.
[3] Jon D. Levenson, *The Death and Resurrection of the Beloved Son: The Transformation of Child Sacrifice in Judaism and Christianity* (New Haven, CT: Yale University Press, 1993), p. 155.
[4] Exodus 9:1.

smoking, quaking mountain, God constituted them as a "holy nation," a "kingdom of priests,"[5] and gave t hem their national constitution—the Torah. In reality, such a thing must have seemed as utterly impossible then as it did when Zionism was birthed at the end of the nineteenth century. Indeed, how could an enslaved, abused, rag-tag, motley group of people ever in their wildest dreams have expected to be molded into a nation in years, much less in a day? The answer was, Yes! because God was birthing this nation, the only nation in history that was born in one day!

Nearly 3,500 years later, after an experience among the nations of the world that was far more devastating than the Egyptian bondage that their ancestors had encountered, the distant descendants of the ancient Israelites finally reached the appointed time for them to experience an event similar to what had occurred at Sinai. This time, the nation would be reborn. Israel, which had seemed long dead, would be resurrected from the dust and ashes of the Holocaust through the miraculous power of the Creator.[6] Mark Lindsay described the miracle poignantly in this way: "In religious rather than mythological terms, Israel's re-birth was a 'resurrection', after the 'crucifixion' of the Jews in Auschwitz."[7] What seemed like an utterly destroyed nation would rise again after being buried for nearly two thousand years in the dust of history. The dry bones of the long decimated Israelite army would, indeed, live again. God's nation would once more stand as a sovereign dominion among the diverse nations of the world. This was to be far more than what Paul Johnson described as Israel's slipping "into existence through a fortuitous window of history."[8] It was more, far more: this was a divinely orchestrated miracle.

When God asked the prophet, "Can a nation be born in a day?" he continued with the exclamatory rhetorical question: "Who has ever heard of such a thing?" The answer to the questions, however, was obvious, for the Lord God immediately said, "As soon as Zion travailed, she also brought

---

5 Exodus 19:6.
6 Eliezer Berkovits, *Faith After the Holocaust* (New York: KTAV Publishing House, 1973), p. 156. Berkovits connected the Holocaust spiritually with the resurrection of Israel: "If at Auschwitz . . . we have witnessed 'The Hiding Face of God,' in the rebirth of the State of Israel and its success 'we have seen a smile on the face of God.'" Eliezer Berkovits cited in Mark R. Lindsay, *Barth, Israel, and Jesus: Karl Barth's Theology of Israel* (Burlington, VT: Ashgate Publishing Co., 2007), p. 60
7 Mark R. Lindsay, *Barth, Israel, and Jesus: Karl Barth's Theology of Israel* (Burlington, VT: Ashgate Publishing Co., 2007), p. 60. Lindsay reports Richard Rubenstein's observation that if the Holocaust and the establishment of Israel are not kept independent of each other, "one runs the risk of retrospectively infusing the Holocaust with positive significance."
8 Paul Johnson, *A History of the Jews* (London, UK: Orion Press, 1993), p. 526.

forth her sons."[9] Israel's rebirth was not, however, to be predicated solely on the ingenuity or strength of the Jewish people. This work of the *Ruach HaKodesh* was an outworking of the utter faithfulness of Israel's God: "'Shall I bring to the point of birth and not cause to bring forth?' says the LORD. . . . 'Rejoice with Jerusalem, and be glad for her.' . . . For thus says the LORD, 'Behold, I will extend peace to her like a river, and the glory of the nations like an overflowing stream.'"[10] God himself was the one who signed Israel's birth certificate, guaranteeing the right of the Jewish people to corporate and national sovereignty, and God has never signed—nor will he ever sign—Israel's death certificate! He who was the midwife who birthed Israel has been her constant protector and sustainer, and he will ever continue to be so forever.

After appearing to be in the grave of history for almost two millennia, Israel would be reborn in a resurrection, just as Ezekiel had witnessed in his prophetic vision concerning the revivified dry bones. Most of the Jewish people had surely concluded what the prophet had predicted, "Our bones are dried up and our hope is gone; we are cut off."[11] What looked like a hopeless boneyard, the remnants of a long-since defeated army, was to become the site of a miracle of resurrection and restoration. God promised, "Behold, I will open your graves and cause you to come up out of your graves, my people; and I will bring you into the land of Israel."[12] God would summon his people from the four corners of the earth and bring them again out of exile to their own land: "I will say to the north, 'Give them up!' And to the south, 'Do not hold them back.' Bring my sons from afar and my daughters from the ends of the earth."[13] Yes, the dead bones would live again, and they would "stand up a mighty army." As Jon Levenson has pointed out, "The revitalization of the downtrodden and despondent people is clearly patterned on the old legends of their having come into being against all odds, historical and natural."[14]

Declarations and Independence

John Stuart Mill summed up basic principles of sociology and politics: "A portion of mankind may be said to constitute a Nationality, if

---

9 Isaiah 66:8, NIV, ESV, NASB paraphrased.
10 Isaiah 66:9, 10, 12, ESV.
11 Ezekiel 37:11, NIV.
12 Ezekiel 37:12.
13 Isaiah 43:6.
14 Levenson, p. 145.

they are united among themselves by common sympathies, which do not exist between them and any others which make them co-operate with each other more willingly than with other people, desire to be under the same government, and desire that it should be government by themselves or a portion of themselves, exclusively."[15] These principles that were descriptive of the ancient Israelites and their descendants through the centuries also defined the Jewish people in the twentieth century. The long-delayed League of Nations Covenant for Palestine, which had been enacted on July 24, 1922, and entrusted as a Mandate to the British government for its fulfillment was coming to a point of fulfillment. "The Jewish People were ripe for independence because, unlike the situation that existed at the start of the Mandate, it was now able to stand alone and exercise the powers of self-government . . . which was the only requirement for terminating the Mandate under Article 22 of the Covenant of the League of Nations that was an integral part of the Mandate for Palestine."[16] The excuse that Britain had used to continue its domination of all of Palestine and to deny the Jewish people the right of self-determination had become a moot issue,[17] for at that time, "the consent of the League of Nations or the British Mandatory was not formally needed because declaring independence was not a 'modification' of the terms of the Mandate but the realization or fulfillment of its purpose for which it existed."[18]

It should have come as no surprise that something powerfully spiritual and prophetic was taking place in the Holy Land. The British Mandate over Palestine had expired after Britain had notified the United Nations in 1947 of its intention to terminate its stewardship of its Mandate from the League of Nations Covenant for Palestine. On November 29, 1947, the United Nations passed Resolution 181 which included its plan to partition the territory of the Mandate for Palestine into two independent countries, one Arab, the other Jewish.[19] On the very next day after the United Nations had passed its resolution for the creation of an

---

[15] John Stuart Mill, *Considerations on Representative Government* (Chicago, IL: Gateway Publishing, 1962), p. 303.

[16] Howard Grief, *The Legal Foundation and Borders of Israel Under International Law: A Treatise on Jewish Sovereignty over the Land of Israel* (Jerusalem, Israel: Mazo Publishers, 2008), p. 167.

[17] Charles River Editors, *Decoding the Conflict Between Israel and the Palestinians: The History and Terms of the Middle East Peace Process* (Cambridge, MA: Create Space, 2013), p. 1970.

[18] Grief, p. 167.

[19] In 1922, the second iteration of the original League of Nations Mandate for Palestine had assigned all the land west of the Jordan River to the Jewish state and the land east of the Jordan to the Arab state.

Arab state in the Trans-Jordan and a Jewish state in Judea, Samaria, and Galilee, the Arabs launched an uprising in an effort to negate the United Nations action. When the Jews defeated the Arabs, the Jordanian army counterattacked and occupied land west of the Jordan River, including areas in and around Jerusalem. Then, Jordanian King Abdullah brought 2,000 loyal Arabs to the West Bank,[20] initiating what was to be the birth of the "West-Bank" Palestinian myth. Abdullah was intent upon maintaining control of his own kingdom by precluding the formation of a Palestinian state on the east side of the Jordan River,[21] where its existence had been mandated by the international community of nations (the League of Nations) for some 26 years.

Despite the bellicosity of its neighbors, the state of Israel was emerging. Finally, on May 14, 1948, the very day that the British Mandate had expired at midnight, David Ben-Gurion became the first person to sign the Israeli Declaration of Independence, and then he formally proclaimed The Declaration of the Establishment of the State of Israel, which said, in part:

> ERETZ-ISRAEL was the birthplace of the Jewish people. Here their spiritual, religious and political identity was shaped. Here they first attained statehood, created cultural values of national and universal significance and gave to the world the Book of Books.
>
> After being forcibly exiled from their land, the people kept faith with it throughout their Dispersion and never ceased to pray and hope for their return to it and for the restoration in it of their political freedom.

---

[20] With the help of the British, Abdullah circumvented the allotment to the Arab (Palestinian) state and formed the "Hashemite" kingdom of Jordan, for which there was no legitimacy. Abdullah, who was an Arabian born in Mecca, not a "Jordanian," exploited his relationship of support for the British during World War I in order to create his own "kingdom" out of thin air. This, in turn, produced the "West Bank" controversy that continues to this day. See Mary Christian Wilson, *King Abdullah, Britain and the Making of Jordan* (Cambridge, UK: Cambridge University Press, 1987), pp. 179–181, 195.

[21] William W. Haddad and Mary M. Hardy, "Jordan's Alliance with Israel and its Effects on Jordanian-Arab Relations" in *Israel, the Hashemites, and the Palestinians: The Fateful Triangle,* Efraim Karsh and P. R. Kumaraswam, eds. (London, UK: Frank Cass Publishers, 2003), pp. 31–48. Haddad and Hardy point out that when Israel retook the West Bank in 1957 nearly twenty years after Abdullah's invasion, "they did not conquer the Palestinians; they made war with Jordan. Jordan had occupied the territory in 1948, and it was not their territory to begin with." In reality, Israel was the liberator, not the occupier of the West Bank. This territory had been "occupied" by Jordan for nineteen years before it was liberated by the Israeli army in the Six-Day War. The West Bank, therefore, has not been "occupied territory" since the time when it was controlled by Jordan from 1948 until 1967. It has been, and continues to be, part of Israel.

Impelled by this historical and traditional attachment, Jews strove in every successive generation to re-establish themselves in their ancient homeland. In recent decades they returned in their masses. Pioneers, *ma'pilim*, [immigrants coming to Eretz-Israel in defiance of restrictive legislation] and defenders, they made deserts bloom, revived the Hebrew language, built villages and towns, and created a thriving community controlling its own economy and culture, loving peace but knowing how to defend itself, bringing the blessings of progress to all the country's inhabitants, and aspiring towards independent nationhood. . . .

We, members of the People's Council, representatives of the Jewish community of Eretz-Israel and of the Zionist movement, are here assembled on the day of the termination of the British Mandate over Eretz-Israel and, by virtue of our natural and historic right and on the strength of the resolution of the United Nations General Assembly, hereby declare the establishment of a Jewish state in Eretz-Israel, to be known as the State of Israel. . . . Placing our trust in the "Rock of Israel", we affix our signatures to this proclamation at the session of the Provisional Council of State, on the soil of the homeland, in the city of Tel-Aviv, on this Sabbath eve, the 5th day of Iyar, 5708 (14th May, 1948).[22]

Within minutes of Ben-Gurion's historic proclamation of the statehood of Israel, United States President Harry Truman "rejected the advice of his State Department and made the United States the first nation to recognize the new country."[23] This was another example of divine orchestration of world events, for Truman was a Baptist who "believed that the Jewish people and the Holy Land had distinct roles in God's plan. And because of the great suffering that they had endured over two millennia as a dispersed people, he strongly identified with Jews' quest for a homeland, especially in the aftermath of the Holocaust."[24] The fact that

---

22 The *Official Gazette*, No. 1 of the 5th, Iyar, 5708 (14th May, 1948).
23 Michael Nelson, *Guide to the Presidency* (New York: Routledge, 2015), p. 611.
24 Mark R. Amstutz, *Evangelicals and American Foreign Policy* (New York: Oxford University Press, 2014), p. 130.

Truman was able to withstand the objections of the clearly antisemitic U.S. State Department is testimony to the strength of his personal convictions, but it is also a greater testimony to divine providence that positioned the right person at the right time to do the right thing in recognizing Israel, for with the endorsement of Israel by the United States, worldwide acceptance of Israel's existence was a *fait accompli*.

What had been in the making for more than fifty years since the earliest Zionists[25] had been moved by their passion for the holy land to begin working toward recreating a Jewish nation came to fruition on that day. The centuries-long struggle of individual Jews, a struggle to make *aliyah* by "going up" to the land of Israel—living there, purchasing land there, and praying there that God would one day completely fulfill his promise to their ancestors—was finally realized. Against all odds, Jews had begun to return to the land of the Bible. At first it had been a mere trickle, then a stream, then a torrent. After nineteen centuries in exile, the Jews were finding their way back home again. The legendary stereotypical "wandering Jew" would wander no more: Jews were going home. They were not to be in a remote and alien plot of ground assigned to them by other nations and people; they were home in the land contracted to them by their God, the God of the universe, in the eternal, irrevocable covenant that he had made with Abraham four millennia earlier!

Immediately after its rebirth, however, Israel was attacked by Muslim and Arab nations that had done everything possible to abort the Jewish nation before it could be born and were then intent on inflicting infanticide on the newly born nation. They were utterly determined to destroy forever what had suddenly and spontaneously come to life in their midst. Consequently, on the very next day after the Israeli Declaration of Independence had been signed and the proclamation of the formation of the State of Israel had been made, seven Arab nations—Egypt, Transjordan (now Jordan), Syria, Iraq, Yemen, Saudi Arabia, and Lebanon—along with the Arab Liberation Army, invaded Israel with what appeared to be an overwhelming force that would simply crush the newly born Jewish nation and eradicate the Jews once and for all from the land of Israel.[26]

---

[25] In 1897, Theodor Herzl, the father of the movement that would eventually produce the Jewish State, convened the First Zionist Congress where the right of the Jewish people to a national rebirth in their own country was proclaimed.

[26] Alex Wolf, *The Arab-Israeli War Since 1948* (Chicago, IL: Capstone Global Library, 2012), p. 14.

The Arab forces sprang into action to fulfill the pre-World War II prom-ise of the Arab Higher Committee: "Whenever the English remove their hands from this land, we will throw and chase all the Jews in a stampede into the sea!"[27] As the Arab nations discovered, however, Israel was not nearly as easy a foe to defeat as they had thought. Finally, after ten months of intense warfare, the Israelis prevailed against their invaders, the Islamists nations were repelled, and an armistice agreement was signed, ending the hostilities—at least for the moment.

A Jewish State Resurrected from the Ashes of the Holocaust

There is no direct connection either materially or spiritually between the Holocaust and the rebirth of the nation of Israel. The Holocaust was not some cosmic price that the Jews had to pay for the birth of Israel. "The State of Is-rael is not an atonement. It would be blasphemy to regard it as a compensa-tion," says Abraham Heschel.[28] The Holocaust was not a penalty exacted upon the Jewish people for some perceived evil or sin on their part. The evil—monstrous and unprecedented—emerged entirely from the hearts of the Nazis and their antisemitic collaborators in Europe. The Holocaust was a wholly undeserved monstrosity imposed upon the Jews by evil personified in Hitler and his henchmen. In reality, the Holocaust did not precipitate the creation of the Nation of Israel, for the stage had already been set politically and practical-ly for the formation of Israel by the continuing *aliyah* of the Jewish people that began in earnest in the nineteenth century and by the Balfour Declaration and the League of Nations Covenant for Palestine of the early twentieth century.

The miracle of post-Holocaust Jewish existence stands as a memorial to the indomitable will of the Jewish people not only to survive but also to thrive. This is why Elie Wiesel has argued that any attempt to link the Holocaust and reborn Israel diminishes both because they are two differ-ent mysteries.[29] At the same time, however, for Jews in the land of Israel, "the 'Holocaust-Israel' motif of 'death/rebirth' became a central dogma of Jewish civil religion,"[30] says Byron Sherwin. He also argued that, quite amazingly, "this blatantly Christian motif of death and resurrection,

---

27 Klaus-Michael Mallmann and Martin Cüppers, *Nazi Palestine: The Plans for the Extermination of the Jews in Palestine*, tr. Krista Smith (New York: Enigma Books, 2010), p. 18.
28 Abraham Joshua Heschel, *Israel: An Echo of Eternity* (New York: Farrar, Straus and Giroux, 1969), p. 113.
29 Elie Wiesel noted in Berlin, p. 356.
30 Byron L. Sherwin, *Faith Finding Meaning: A Theology of Judaism* (New York: Oxford University Press, 2009), p. 26.

death and salvation, proclaimed an indisputable nexus between the Holocaust and the State of Israel."[31] Irving Greenberg has rightly argued that "the lesson of the Holocaust is that powerlessness is immoral, because it is not compatible with survival."[32] He also has pointed out that "the existence of the State of Israel validates continuing faith in God and constitutes a redeeming act, which matches the great catastrophe."[33]

After the incredible numbers of deaths that were experienced by the Jewish people during the Holocaust, the rebirth of the nation of Israel has to be seen as a profound act of divine resurrection, the restoration of the nation and its people to the ancient land. Emmanuel Lévinas was entirely correct to assert that "the Shoah re-establishes the link—which up until then had been incomprehensibly hidden—between present-day Israel and the Israel of the Bible."[34] Abraham Heschel even saw the act of restoring the Nation of Israel as making the Holy Land even more holy: "No act is as holy as the act of saving human life. The Holy Land, having offered haven to more than two million Jews . . . has attained a new sanctity."[35]

The corporate consciences of the nations of Western Europe and the United States were awakened by the Holocaust from an abyss of dark contempt for the Jewish people and of utter disdain for their right to their own Jewish state in the land of their ancestors. The Christian church likewise felt the imprint of nails driven by the Holy Spirit into its corporate consciousness that made eternal truth undeniable.[36] For centuries, the church had been overwhelmed by the darkness of abject evil in its evaluation of and attitude toward the Jewish people and their inalienable right to their homeland. All Christians in history should have been deeply distressed by the condition in which Jewish believers in the same God that the church worshipped were subjected to unrelenting and systematic

---

31 Sherwin, p. 26. Sherwin apparently did not understand that the death and resurrection motif has never been blatantly or exclusively "Christian." As a matter of fact, Christians inherited the entire resurrection idea and theme from the Jews and Judaism, particularly from the Pharisees, the progenitors of Rabbinic Judaism. Paul made this clear: "I am a Pharisee, a son of Pharisees; I am on trial for the hope and resurrection of the dead" (Acts 23:6).
32 Irving Greenberg, paraphrased in Berlin, p. 356.
33 Greenberg, in Berlin, p. 356. Greenberg also observed that the "embrace of modernity was a profound blunder, and Jews must learn to resist the absoluteness of the secular." Indeed, it was the absolute secularity of modernity that denied the spiritual altogether and created the climate for the Holocaust.
34 Emmanuel Lévinas, *Difficult Freedom: Essays on Judaism,* tr. Sean Hand (Baltimore, MD: Johns Hopkins University Press, 1990), p. 12.
35 Heschel, *Israel,* p. 113.
36 Ecclesiastes 12:11.

persecution, torture, and death. Instead, the vast majority of Christians had fully experienced the condition that Paul had observed in the lives of many people who had far less evil intentions than many in later generations had against the Jewish people: "Such teachings come through hypocritical liars whose consciences have been seared as with a hot [branding] iron."[37]

The branding iron of abject evil and perversion had for centuries left a deep and wide scar on Christianity's conscience, so much so that, for all intents and purposes, it had very little conscience at all when it came to the Jewish people and their plight. Occasionally, isolated Christian voices did arise in history to condemn efforts to harm the Jews, to encourage Christian commiseration with the plight of the Jews, and to support the rights of Jews to life and liberty.[38] Generally speaking, however, both official Christianity and individual Christians were so blinded by centuries of the heresies of supersessionism and contempt for the Jews that they either engaged in actions that were utterly non-Christian or they remained silent in the face of such evil,[39] neither of which was acceptable conduct for those who took the teachings of Jesus seriously.

The corporate consciences of the nations of Europe and, for that matter, of the United States, were in worse shape than the conscience of the church. Perhaps it took something of the magnitude of the Holocaust to convict those nations of their arrogance and contempt toward the Jews and of their need to make restitution to the Chosen People by recognizing their rights to nationhood and homeland. God did not inflict the Holocaust upon the Jewish people for what some Christians viewed as

---

[37] 1 Timothy 4:2, NIV.

[38] Some voices were raised during the time of the Holocaust; however, those raised by Christians and others were drowned out by the cacophony of self-serving arguments that were at bottom merely reiterations of ancient antisemitism. See Hubert G. Locke, *Learning from History: A Black Christian's Perspective on the Holocaust* (Westport, CT: Greenwood Press, 2000), p. 115. Locke is correct when he notes that "those who spoke out in the United States" against the Nazis and antisemitism "did so in a national climate of isolationism, racism, and antisemitism that made their views not only unpopular but, in many circles, unpatriotic." Even the outcry of some British churches against the unfolding atrocities of the time "ended in futility," Locke says. The US State Department and the British Foreign Secretariat were simply not nearly as concerned about the genocide of Europe's Jews as they were with winning the war.

[39] One of the things that troubled post-Holocaust Jewish and Christian children in the United States and in Germany was the Christian silence in the face of the atrocities of the Holocaust. See Björn Krondorfer, *Remembrance and Reconciliation: Encounters Between Young Jews and Germans* (New Haven, CT: Yale University Press, 1995), p. 105. In an analysis of the lack of response German response to the Holocaust, Krondorfer notes that "the American Jewish and Christian students were astounded by the ubiquity of the conspiracy of silence their German peers had experienced in their families; and the East and West German students came to realize how deeply they themselves were invested in that conspiracy."

obduracy and unbelief, nor did he make the Holocaust a *quid pro quo* for the establishment of the nation of Israel. "There is no salvation to be extracted from the Holocaust," says Michael Wyschogrod. "If there is hope after the Holocaust, it is because to those who believe, the voices of the Prophets speak more loudly than did Hitler, and because the divine promise sweeps over the crematoria and silences the voice of Auschwitz."[40] The Holocaust was entirely the product of pure evil incarnated in the hearts of utterly conscienceless human beings. Here is what God did: he orchestrated the events before and after the Holocaust that brought about the rebirth of the nation of Israel in the Promised Land, thereby foiling the Nazi's planned genocide of the Jewish people and forging their determination to fulfill Emil Fackenheim's 614th commandment, which he said forbids the Jews from giving Hitler posthumous victories.[41] Ever since that time, the cry, "Never again!" has continued to resound across the landscape of Israel and to echo in the hearts of Jews around the world.

Renewal of the "Forever" Land Contract

If the Christian church at large had really believed the Scriptures on which it claimed that its faith was established, it would have known that it should have given unequivocal support for the establishment of the nation of Israel, for imbedded in the very fiber of its Bible is God's irrevocable commitment that this specific land would be deeded to the descendants of Abraham, Isaac, and Jacob *forever*.[42] This land was conveyed by God to Abraham with no deed restrictions. There would never be a time when the ownership of the land would be revoked or permitted to go into foreclosure, and the law of adverse possession has never applied.[43] God's covenant with Abraham and its land provisions were unilateral. God simply said, "I

---

[40] Michael Wyschogrod, *Abraham's Promise: Judaism and Jewish-Christian Relations* (Grand Rapids, MI: Wm. B. Eerdmans Publishing Co., 2004) p. 120.

[41] Emil L. Fackenheim, *To Mend the World: Foundations of Post-Holocaust Jewish Thought* (Bloomington, IN: Indiana University Press, 1982), pp. xix–xx.

[42] The land provision of the covenant was first made to Abraham (Genesis 13:15). It was confirmed to Isaac (Genesis 17:21) and then to Jacob (Genesis 28:13; 35:9–15). In none of these cases did God attach deed restrictions to the promise or attach expiration clauses to the deed.

[43] The law of adverse possession, so-called "squatters rights," could never be applied to the land of Israel because the Jewish people never abandoned the land, nor did they leave it in a state of disrepair. They also never relinquished title to the land voluntarily. The eviction of the Jews from Israel was carried out time and time again by violent dispossession, and their God-given land was literally plundered from them by oppressors.

will give you this land," no ifs, ands, or buts about it! Though God said that the land might, on occasion, actually "vomit out" the Israelites because of their disobedience and idolatry,[44] he constantly assured his people that their title to the land could never be nullified[45] or revoked because it was based on his own faithfulness, not on their performance.[46]

From the time of Abraham, the Hebrews, the Israelites, and the Jewish people had been inextricably connected with the land of Israel. Whenever the people had been exiled from the land, they had cried out to God from the depths of their souls for restoration to their sacred space. And because they had the assurance that the land clause of their irrevocable covenant would never be abrogated, they never doubted that they or their descendants would be fully restored to the Promised Land and that the land would be restored to them. It was simply inevitable!

No wonder Emil Fackenheim attributed the restoration of the people of Israel in the land of Israel and in the state of Israel to the power and authority of the Hebrew Scriptures: "We must ask whether this ever happened that, after two millennia, a people was returned to its language, its state, its land. *Without a Book—this Book—this return could not possibly have taken place.* This is the shared astonishment behind all religio-secular diversities. This is the shared experience that makes possible a bond between all Israel and Torah."[47] Fackenheim concluded his thoughts with this startling and challenging declaration: "Where once the existence of God guaranteed the existence of Israel, today the continued existence of the people Israel guarantees the existence of God."[48]

Miracle after Miracle: The Israeli Reality

In what has to be one of the most amazing miracles in history, a Jewish state exists and grows stronger every day despite the unrelenting efforts of a host of enemies that have been committed to the cause of destroying

---

[44] Leviticus 18:26–30. Jacob Blumenthal and Janet Liss, *Etz Hayim Study Companion* (Philadelphia, PA: The Jewish Publication Society, 2005), p. 203, and Elliot N. Dorff, *For the Love of God and People: A Philosophy of Jewish Law* (Philadelphia, PA: Jewish Publication Society, 2007), p. 105.

[45] Michael Rydelnik, *Understanding the Arab-Israeli Conflict: What the Headlines Haven't Told You* (Chicago, IL: Moody Publishers, 2003), p. 158.

[46] Rydelnik, p. 158.

[47] Fackenheim, *To Mend*, p. 328.

[48] Emil L. Fackenheim, paraphrased in Steven L. Jacobs, ed., *The Holocaust Now: Contemporary Christian and Jewish Thought* (East Rockaway, NY: Cummings & Hathaway, 1996), p. 333.

what God and the Jewish people have done. Right out of the ashes of the Holocaust, the miracle of life was manifest in the resurrection of the corporate body of world Jewry and their proclamation of the Jewish state in precisely the same geographical setting of God's promise to Abraham 4,000 years ago. Miracle of life upon miracle of life has been demonstrated in the more than sixty years of modern Israel's existence. As David Ben-Gurion once said, "Anyone in Israel who does not believe in miracles is not a realist."[49]

In reality, as George Steiner observed, Israel itself "is an *indispensable miracle*. . . . Its coming into being, its persistence against military, geopolitical odds, its civic achievement, defy reasoned expectation."[50] The very survival of the Jewish people themselves is a miracle. The existence of the Jewish state is an even greater miracle. Karl Barth exclaimed that seeing the Jews being restored to their ancient homeland was "like seeing an ancient map come alive, like the bursting forth of a living nation and people, at once ancient and new."[51] No greater living witness to the existence of God can be advanced than his utter faithfulness to his covenant with the Jewish people.[52] If anyone wonders whether or not there is a God, he needs only to turn his eyes toward the Jewish nation and the Jewish people for incontrovertible evidence and proof.[53] Both the Jewish people and the Jewish state are living testimonies to the utter faithfulness and dependability of the God who, as "the Father of lights" simply "does not change like shifting shadows."[54] In defiance of all the norms of history for the assimilation of conquered peoples, still the Jewish people and their nation are clearly identifiable in person and on the world map. Barth well observed, "By all analogies of world history, the Jews as a race

---

49 David Ben-Gurion, quoted in Charles A. Garfield, *Psychosocial Care of the Dying Patient* (New York: McGraw-Hill, 1978), p. 8.

50 George Steiner, *Errata: An Examined Life* (London, UK: Weidenfeld and Nicolson, 1997), p. 54, author's emphasis.

51 Karl Barth, quoted in Katherine Sonderegger, "The Cup of Wrath," a sermon delivered at Virginia Theological Seminary, April 8, 2003. Noted in Mark R. Lindsay, *Barth, Israel, and Jesus: Karl Barth's Theology of Israel* (Burlington, VT: Ashgate Publishing, 2007), p. 59.

52 Richard H. Bell, *The Irrevocable Call of God: An Inquiry into Paul's Theology of Israel* (Tübingen, Germany: Mohr Siebeck, 2005), p. 347.

53 In the eighteenth century, when the avowed skeptic Frederick the Great, king of Prussia, demanded, "Give me in one word a proof of the divine origin of the Bible," his chaplain replied, "The Jews, your Majesty, the Jews." W. A. Cook, "The Jews in History," in *The Park Review*, vol. 5, no. 1 (October, 1903), p. 97.

54 James 1:17, NIV.

should no longer have existed after the Fall of Jerusalem in A.D. 70."[55] Instead, *Am Yisrael chai*!

The resurrection of the Jewish people from the death that the Holocaust imposed on six million of their global family has been the ultimate expression of the Israelite vision of redemption and restoration. Joseph Soloveitchik had a convincing answer to the post-Holocaust argument that the death camps disproved God's existence: "The reborn State of Israel supplies powerful evidence of God's existence and His continued love affair with the Jewish people."[56] Jon Levenson notes the results of God's love for Israel: "There is perhaps nothing more characteristic of the ancient Israelite vision of redemption than renewed fertility and new life—fertility where there had been sterility, life where there had been death."[57] The resurrection of the state of Israel after nearly nineteen centuries of sleeping in the dust of the earth is further testimony to the absolute faithfulness and utter dependability of the God of the Jews. The God of Scripture who created the entire universe *ex nihilo* demonstrated his same omnipotence when he created the nation of Israel *ex nihilo*, virtually out of nothing, but that is a testimony to the one who holds death and life in his hands,[58] who sets up and takes down rulers,[59] and who has promised to establish his Chosen People forever,[60] not only by sustaining the living but also by keeping faith with those who sleep in the dust of the earth and by being faithful to give life to the dead.[61]

---

[55] Karl Barth, "The Jewish Problem and the Christian Answer," in *Against the Stream: Shorter Post-War Writings 1946–52* (London, UK: SCM Publishing, 1954), pp. 196, 200.

[56] Joseph Soloveitchik, noted in *Wrestling with God: Jewish Theological Responses during and after the Holocaust* (New York: Oxford University Press, 2007), p. 381.

[57] Levenson, p. 152.

[58] 1 Samuel 2:6.

[59] Psalm 75:7; Daniel 2:21.

[60] 2 Samuel 7:25–26.

[61] These are the words of the *Gevurot Berakah*, the second benediction of the *Amidah, the* prayer *par excellence* in the synagogue which praises the God of Israel for his "powers": "You are mighty forever, O Lord. You give life to the dead. You are great to save. You sustain life with lovingkindness. You give life to the dead with great mercy. You support the falling, and heal the sick, freeing the prisoners and keeping faith with those who sleep in the dust. Who is like you, master of powers, and who resembles you, king of death and of life, and the one who causes salvation to spring up! You are reliable and faithful to give life to the dead. Blessed are you, O Lord, giving life to the dead."

CHAPTER 17

SURVIVING AND THRIVING
RESTORED ISRAEL: STRESSED, BUT BLESSED

After some nineteen centuries of dispersion, disparagement, and despair, the Jews who made *aliyah* to the newly reconstituted nation of Israel were simply overjoyed when they finally witnessed the reestablishment of their nation in the land of their ancestors. These relatively new citizens of Israel were determined to continue the tradition that had been established for over a century by settlers who had braved the deserts, the swamps, and the hostile environs of Palestine; therefore, they continued to accept the challenge of making the desert bloom by establishing agricultural marvels, of building modern, bustling cities like Tel Aviv to replace the swamps that those before them had drained, and of living day-to-day life with the stress of dwelling in close proximity to neighbors who were far too often inhospitable and violent.

"With great love," the Sabras—those Jews who had been born in the land —"received the uprooted Jews from many lands, taught them Hebrew, helped them adjust, and transformed them into proud and productive citizens."[1] Like the established Israelis, the new citizens of the renewed state of Israel often found themselves stressed, but they were at the same time blessed. Their lives were filled with hard work and struggle, but they knew that they had been blessed to experience realities about which their ancestors could only have dreamed. In spite of all the challenges, they both survived and thrived, transforming a backwater and largely barren land into an agricultural, industrial, and technological wonder. "Today, Israel is a modern agricultural and industrial state, her desert serrated by fertile fields, her swamps drained . . . her cities growing, bustling with health."[2]

---

[1] Leo Trepp, *Judaism: Development and Life* (Belmont, CA: Dickenson Publishing Co., 1966), p. 62.
[2] Max I. Dimont, *The American Zionist* (1971), vol. 62, p. 18.

Stuart Eisenstat said it well when he discussed the incredible perseverance of the Jewish people. Through the Babylonian captivity, the Roman
destruction and dispersion, the pogroms, the expulsions, the *Shoah*, and
the continuing state of war by the Arab world against the restored nation—"through all of this, the Jewish people have survived and thrived,
while the empires that conquered, dispersed, or threatened us are in the
dustbin of history."[3] Lawrence Epstein accurately described the circumstances, contrasting the manner in which Muslims had come to dominate
not only Palestine but also the entire Middle East and the high moral approach that the Jews had taken when they reclaimed the land of Israel:
"The modern Palestinian Arabs couldn't then morally complain if the
Jews wished to reclaim the land, even by force. However, the Jews were
not doing it by force the way the Muslims did. The Jews did it by building homes, reclaiming swamps, and by employing Arab labor. They
didn't conquer the land. They moved back to their old neighborhood and
were willing to live beside their new neighbors."[4]

Employing the words of the Talmud in which the Jews swore that they
would neither resist their persecutors nor prematurely "climb the wall" to
return to Jerusalem,[5] Emil Fackenheim graphically and poignantly discussed the real walls over which they had to climb in their struggle to
reclaim the land of their ancestors, the title of which land they neither
corporately nor individually had ever surrendered. David Patterson elab-
orated on Fackenheim's theme in this manner: "Which wall have the Jews
climbed?" he asked. "It is not the wall surrounding Jerusalem but the
electrified fence surrounding Auschwitz, the walls whose gates are em-
bossed with the words *Arbeit Macht Frei*, the walls that would wall the
Jews out from the world and into a graveyard without a single grave.
Therefore the Jewish return to Jerusalem is nothing less than a resurrection."[6] It was not, however, merely the historical and physical walls of the
death camps that the Jews figuratively "climbed over" in order to escape

3 Stuart E. Eisenstat, *The Future of the Jews: How Global Forces Are Impacting the Jewish People, Israel,
and Its Relationship with the United States* (Lanham, MD: Rowman & Littlefield Publishers, 2012), p. 317.
4 Lawrence J. Epstein, "The Moral Case of Zionism: If Both Jews and Palestinian Arabs Start Their
Historical Narrative with Beginning of Zionism, Jews Have Deeper Moral Claim to the Land of Israel," in *Israel
Opinion*, April 17, 2014, p. 1, posted at http://www.ynetnews.com/articles/0,7340,L-4509231,00.html.
5 Babylonian Talmud, *Ketuvot* 111a.
6 David Patterson, *Emil L. Fackenheim: A Jewish Philosopher's Response to the Holocaust* (Syracuse, NY:
Syracuse University Press, 2008), p. 143.

death itself. "The walls that the Jews have climbed in their return to Jerusalem are the walls that the Holocaust deniers would deconstruct and that the anti-Zionists would reconstruct."[7] It is these walls that "all who oppose the existence of the Jewish state—from the 'benign' left-wing liberal to the murderous fanatic Jihadist—erect which even now threaten the annihilation of the resurrection of the Jews and Israel.[8]

Despite the fact that their neighbors were largely inhospitable and even bellicose, the Jews who reclaimed their ancestral land were not deterred or limited by fear and the threat of violence. Instead, they persevered with such determination—and, indeed, faith—that the Jewish state of Israel "has become a major player on the world scene, raising its head unashamedly high among the nations."[9] Consequently, "the modern State of Israel has enabled the Jewish people to emerge from the shadows of history, to cast aside centuries of living at the caprice of rules and hostile populations; to serve as an example of democratic nation building; to become a center of the technologies that will be the keys to the twenty-first century's prosperity and security."[10] Considering the amazing successes of the Jewish people in the land of Israel in the midst of such ongoing conflict, one can only wonder what they might have accomplished had the history of Israel always been one of peace, tranquility, and mutual respect among all of the inhabitants of the Middle East. Doubtless, it would have been an economic powerhouse for the three continents that are contiguous with it.

Conflict and Violence

For nearly seven decades since the establishment of the nation of Israel, the Jewish people have continually sought peace with their Arab neighbors. For the same seven decades, however, the Arab nations and the Arabs living in the Israeli portion of the Covenant for Palestine that was allotted to the Jewish state, have seized every opportunity to inflict violence on the Jewish people by maiming and murdering innocent civilians—men, women, and children. The pages of restored Israel's short history have been littered with armed insurgencies, suicide bombings of Israeli restaurants and

---

[7] David Patterson, *Anti-Semitism and Its Metaphysical Origins* (Cambridge, UK: Cambridge University Press, 2015), p. 206.
[8] David Patterson, *Anti-Semitism*, p. 206.
[9] Eisenstat, p. 317.
[10] Eisenstat, p. 317.

buses, Scud missile attacks, and almost innumerable mortar and rocket barrages—all of which have been aimed specifically (to the greatest degree possible, given the limitations of Arab weaponry) at Israeli civilian population centers. Except for the 1948 Arab war against Israel and the Six-Day War, which were waged against both Jewish civilian centers and Israeli military facilities, virtually all of the Arab violence directed against Israel has taken the form of guerrilla actions specifically designed to inflict horrific suffering and death upon Jewish civilians in efforts to terrorize and weaken the resolve of the rest of the populace.

In the years immediately after the restoration of the nation of Israel, those Jewish people who had boldly accepted the challenge to return to the land of their ancestors found themselves constantly "vulnerable to terrorist attacks."[11] The borders of Israel were porous, and the nation was not well equipped to defend incursions from those who are intent on murder and mayhem. The violence that the Arabs had regularly fomented in Palestine since the days of British rule was merely escalated and redirected.[12] Then, in the 1950s, outright terrorism against Israel began in earnest "with cross-border attacks launched from neighboring states, particularly Egypt and Jordan, both of which were known as 'sanctuary states.'"[13] Palestinian *fedayeen*[14] "crossed the Israeli border and attacked Israeli civilians and targets of strategic importance such as irrigation systems, electric supplies, agricultural equipment, and buses,"[15] while avoiding military installations and posted Israel Defense Forces personnel at all cost. The cowardice of the Arab Muslim population knew no bounds.

The strategy of the Arabs was essentially the same as that of the ancient Amalekites, who were the first people to oppose God's plan to bring his Chosen People into the Promised Land. The Amalekites "always operated as terrorists, particularly in their attacks against Israel,"[16] says Paul Williams. Here is how God himself described the Amalekite strategy: "Remember what the Amalekites did to you along the way when you came out of Egypt. When you were weary and worn out, they met you on your journey and cut off all who were lagging behind;

---

[11] Benjamin Pogrund, *Drawing Fire: Investigating the Accusations of Apartheid in Israel* (Lanham, MD: Rowman & Littlefield, 2014), p. 49.
[12] Gary A. Tobin and Dennis R. Ybarra, *The Trouble with Textbooks: Distorting History and Religion* (Lanham, MD: Rowman & Littlefield Publishers, 2008), p. 135.
[13] James Ciment, *World Terrorism: An Encyclopedia of Political Violence from Ancient Times to the Post-9/11 Era* (Armonk, NY: M. E. Sharpe Publishing, 2011), p. 295.
[14] The Arabic word *fedayeen* means "fighters."
[15] Ciment, p. 295.
[16] Paul R. Williams, "The Spirit of Amalek," in *Restore!*, Issue 25, pp. 16–18.

they had not fear of God."[17] Williams maintains that "the Amalekite strategy was one of terrorism, avoiding the heart of the Israelite military and attacking the weak and weary, the innocent and undefended."[18] The Amalekite plan was simple: launch surprise attacks on the perimeters and prey on the weak and defenseless. The warfare method that Agag, the king of the Amalekites, employed was certainly manifest in one of his direct descendants, Haman, the Persian prime minister, who planned and orchestrated the devious stratagem for the first attempted genocide of the Jewish people.[19] Some scholars have suggested that Islam's prophet, Muhammad, may also have been a descendant of Amalek.[20] Others have argued that Adolph Hitler was either an Amalekite or, at the very least, operated in the spirit of Amalek.[21] Perhaps this history of terrorism proves the truth of the declaration that God made to Moses immediately after the first Israelite engagement with the Amalekites: "Write this on a scroll as something to be remembered. . . . The LORD will be at war against the Amalekites from generation to generation."[22] The Palestinian Arabs may not have any direct ancestry that is traceable to the Amalekites; however, their strategy of terrorism certainly has mirrored that of King Agag. Whenever Israel has been vulnerable, horrendous terrorist events have continued on a regular basis as there has always been plenty of volunteers willing to launch suicide attacks in hopes of gaining a heavenly reward for their *jihad*.

A Dramatic Change

The overall scene of violence in Israel changed dramatically, however, with the Six-Day War in 1967 when Israel responded to increasing threats

---

17 Deuteronomy 25:17–18, NIV.
18 Williams, pp. 16–18. Williams argues that "the spirit of Amalek is still manifest today in world terrorism, particularly that of the Muslim Arabs whose hatred for Israel and the Jewish people knows no bounds. . . . The spirit of terrorism is . . . clearly manifest in those who will 'die to the last man' in order to drive Israel into the Mediterranean."
19 Esther 3:8.
20 Irving M. Zeitlin, *The Historical Muhammad* (Cambridge, UK: Polity Press, 2007), p. 27. Zeitlin quotes William Muir's observation: "We learn from the Muslim tradition that the earliest inhabitants of Mecca, Medina, and the deserts of Syria, were Amalekites." Also, William Muir, *The Life of Mahomet and History of Islam* (London, England: Smith, Elder, and Co., 1858), vol. II, p. 207.
21 Konrad Kwiet and Jürgen Matthaus, *Contemporary Responses to the Holocaust* (Westport, CT: Greenwood Publishing Group, 2004), p. 9. Also Steven T. Katz, *The Impact of the Holocaust on Jewish Theology* (New York: New York University Press, 2005), pp. 143–147; Aaron Rakeffet-Rothkoff and Joseph Epstein, *The Rav: The Word of Rabbi Joseph B. Soloveitchik* (Hoboken, NJ: KTAV Publishing House, 1999), vol. 2, p. 152; and Reuven Firestone, *Holy War in Judaism: The Fall and Rise of a Controversial Idea* (New York: Oxford University Press, 2012), pp. 99–107. Firestone is of the opinion that "the Amalekite line was finally destroyed in Persia" when Haman was executed (Firestone, p. 102).
22 Exodus 17:14–16, NIV.

by its Arab neighbors by launching an invasion of Egypt and following it up with attacks on Jordan and Syria. In the bellicosity that had led up to and precipitated this war, Egyptian President Gamal Abdel Nasser had blocked the Straits of Tiran, thereby closing Israel's access to the Red Sea through the port of Eilat. Then, on May 27, Nasser boasted, "We intend to open a general assault against Israel. This will be total war. Our basic aim will be to destroy Israel."[23] Syrian defense minister Hafez al-Assad had also declared, "I, as a military man, believe that the time has come to enter into a battle of annihilation."[24] Then, on May 31, Iraqi president Abdul Rahman Aref arrogantly proclaimed, "This is our opportunity to wipe out the ignominy which has been with us since 1948. Our goal is clear—to wipe Israel off the map."[25] King Faisal of Saudi Arabia also warned, "Every Arab who does not participate in this conflict will seal his fate. He will not be worthy of being called an Arab."[26] Earlier, in 1954, the Saudi king had summed up the seriousness with which he viewed the necessity of annihilating Israel: "The Arab nations should sacrifice up to 10 million of their 50 million people, if necessary to wipe out Israel. . . . Israel to the Arab world is like a cancer to the human body, and the only way to remedy is to uproot it, just like a cancer."[27]

Believing that the leaders of the Arab nations meant precisely what they had said, Israel wisely initiated a preemptive attack on Egypt on June 5 in which the Israeli Air Force destroyed more than three hundred Egyptian airplanes on the ground, and the Israeli Defense Force subsequently routed the Egyptian army of 100,000 in the Sinai Peninsula.[28] At the same time, Jordan's King Hussein chose to ignore the message sent to him by the Israeli forces in which they gave the Jordanians assurances that they had no intentions of attacking them and ordered his troops to begin hurling shells into Jewish Jerusalem's city center and suburbs.[29] This prompted the Israeli Defense Force to undertake a counterattack

[23] Gamal Abdel Nasser, quoted in Pogrund, p. 49.
[24] Hafez al-Assad, quoted Eli E. Hertz, "UN Security Council Resolution 242," in *Myths and Facts* 2009, pp. 1–2, posted at http://www.mythsandfacts.org/conflict/10/resolution-242.pdf.
[25] Abdur Rahman Aref, quoted in Mark A. Tessler, *A History of the Israeli-Palestinian Conflict* (Bloomington, IN: Indiana University Press, 1994), p. 393.
[26] King Faisal, quoted in Steven Pressfield, *The Lion's Gate: On the Front Lines of the Six Day War* (New York: Penguin Group, 2014), p. 128.
[27] King Faisal, quoted in Alan M. Dershowitz, *Chutzpah* (New York: Simon & Schuster, 1991), p. 214.
[28] Pogrund, p. 50.
[29] An estimated 6,000 Jordanian shells were fired on the Jewish section of then-partitioned Jerusalem.

that routed Jordan's vaunted Arab Legion, chasing them out of Jerusalem, out of the West Bank, and across the Jordan River.[30] In the process of this action, Israel reclaimed the Temple Mount, Judaism's holiest shrine, from which all Jews had been denied access since King Abdullah's invasion of Israel and his occupation of East Jerusalem and the West Bank in 1948.[31] Finally, as the Six-Day War was winding down, when the well-provoked Israelis were attacked by Syria, they defeated those forces and secured the Golan Heights. This action removed Arab armies from the plateau of high ground situated above the east side of Sea of Galilee and its surrounding area and brought an end to the periodic and indiscriminate Arab shelling of the greater Galilee.

"The outcome of the 1967 Six-Day War radically altered the geographical status quo in the Arab-Israeli conflict. Not only had Israel completely pulverized the Egyptian, Jordanian, and Syrian armies, but it had also captured large tracts of Egyptian, Jordanian, and Syrian territory."[32] It was these acquisitions that "provided [Israel] with a measure of strategic depth for the first time in its history, particularly vis-à-vis Egypt in the south and Jordan in the east. Israel's major population centers, industrial assets, and military bases no longer remained within easy reach of Arab armies and terrorist organizations."[33] Amazingly, however, despite one of the most resounding, rapid, and total defeats in the history of warfare, the Arab nations and

---

[30] Pogrund, p. 50.

[31] During their two decades of control of East Jerusalem and other parts of Israel, the Jordanians denied the Jews access to their shrines and holy places in the Jordanian-occupied territory. This Muslim strategy should be strongly contrasted to the Israeli posture of not only permitting Muslims access to their shrines but also allowing the Mosque of Omar (the Dome of the Rock) and the Al-Aqsa Mosque, which are situated on the site of the ancient Jewish Temple, to be controlled by the Arabs and giving Muslims free access to these shrines. Israel paid a high price for allowing Arab control of the Temple Mount, however, when the Palestinian Authority destroyed priceless treasures that they had excavated from under the Temple Mount in their perverse attempt to negate Israeli claims to Jerusalem as the site of the Temple. See Terry Brennan, *The Sacred Cipher* (Grand Rapids, MI: Kregel Publications, 2009) p. 139. Brennan reports the following fiery declaration by Dr. Richard Johnson, former chair of the Antiquities College at Columbia University and fellow of the British Museum: "The most infuriating thing is that the Waqf [the Islamic organization responsible for managing Islamic edifices on the temple mount] is simply raping the Mount with impunity and destroying irreplaceable artifacts. Again, I believe it is a blatant effort to destroy any evidence of a Jewish temple, and therefore any Jewish claim on the Temple Mount. Do you know that in the last few years, the Waqf has had the audacity to bring bulldozers—*bulldozers*—into the area under the Mount that some have called Solomon's Stables? And the bulldozers have dug out thousands of yards of dirt, poured it into dump trucks, and hauled the dirt to a dump, all without any oversight or supervision from international archaeological agencies."

[32] David Rodman, *Sword and Shield of Zion: The Israel Air Force in the Arab-Israeli Conflict* (Eastbourne, UK: Sussex Academic Press, 2014), p. 3.

[33] Rodman, p. 3.

the Palestinian Arabs continued to persist with their demands for the destruction of Israel. As Abba Eban, the Israeli Foreign Minister of that time, wryly observed, "This is the first war in history that on the morrow the victors sued for peace and the vanquished called for unconditional surrender."[34]

Continuing and Unrelenting Hostility

In every conflict between the Arabs and the Jews, Israel had won handily. As former Israeli Prime Minister Golda Meir said, "We don't thrive on military acts. We do them because we have to, and thank God we are efficient."[35] Still, the Arab nations have simply refused to recognize the right of the Jews to live in their ancestral land with complete self-determination. From 1969–1970, Israel fought a war of attrition with Egypt, in which the Arab nation was backed by the Soviet Union. This conflict ended in a stalemate. Then, in 1973, the Yom Kippur War took place when Egypt, Syria, Jordan, Iraq, Algeria, Morocco, and Tunisia, supported by Cuba and North Korea, invaded Israel on the highest and holiest day of the Jewish year, *Yom Kippur* (the Day of Atonement). When Israel succeeded in repelling the invasion, Egypt negotiated a peace treaty with Israel, and Syria agreed to a disengagement.

Then in 1978, Israel forced the withdrawal of the Palestine Liberation Organization, the epitome of terrorist organizations, from Southern Lebanon. In 1982, a mere four years after that event, Israel's action in the First Lebanon War forced the complete expulsion of the PLO from Lebanon. Only five years later in 1987, the Palestinian Arabs initiated the First Intifada,[36] a terrorist action which continued for six years, ending only with the Oslo I Accords. This peace, like every other "peace" initiative with the Arabs,[37] did not last, for in 2000, the Palestinian Arabs launched the Second Intifada, a conflict that continued for five years and ended with Israel's victory and the construction of the Israeli West Bank barrier. One year later, in response to

---

[34] Abba Eban, quoted in Jack Bloom, *Out of Step: Life-story of a Politician: Politics and Religion in a World at War* (Bloomington, IN: The Indiana University Press, 2005), p. 302.

[35] Golda Meir, quoted in *Vogue* (July 1969).

[36] The Arabic word *intifada* means "uprising," "insurrection," "revolt," or "rebellion." It is an organized opposition to authority in which one faction attempts to wrest control from another. It describes the campaign of protest and violent resistance that the Palestinian Arabs directed at Israel as protest against Israeli occupation of so-called "Palestinian" territories.

[37] The Arabic word for "truce" or "ceasefire," is *hudna*, which does not mean "peace treaty," but actually means a "negotiated halt to fighting intended to be used for rearming" or "a pause until a better fighting opportunity arises." See Joshua Spurlock, "Analysis: Hate and Hudna—The True Face of Hamas' Approach to 'Ceasefires,'" posted at www.themideastupdate.com, July 27, 2014.

missile and mortar attacks from Hezbollah in southern Lebanon, Israel launched the Second Lebanon War, which ended in a stalemate. Two years after that, in 2008, Israel was forced to initiate Operation Cast Lead in order to stop rocket fire that had been directed at Israeli territory from Gaza.

In 2005, a grand "land-for-peace" experiment was undertaken by Israeli Prime Minister Ariel Sharon with Israel's unilateral disengagement from Gaza. This action, however, resulted in the establishment of an "independent Palestinian State" in Gaza. Almost immediately, the Israeli territory in Gaza that was ceded to the Palestinian Authority was coopted by the inveterate terrorist organization Hamas and turned into little more than a launching pad for the missiles and rockets that the terrorists would thereafter hurl indiscriminately toward Israeli population centers. Only four years after that time, Operation Pillar of Defense became a necessary measure by the Israeli military in order to ensure the (temporary) cessation of Hamas rocket fire from Gaza into Israel. Then again, in 2014, in response to Hamas missile and rocket fire, Israel was forced to launch Operation Protective Edge in order again to destroy the Hamas rocket launchers. In the process, the Israeli forces discovered and destroyed the elaborate system of tunnels that the terrorist organization had surreptitiously designed, dug, and fortified under Israel's border with Gaza in order to make the Israeli civilian population even more vulnerable to attacks by its *jihadists*.

The unending litany of violence initiated by the Palestinian Arabs and equipped and funded by terror-sponsoring states that at one time or another has included virtually all of the Arab nations, as well as other non-Arab but Muslim-dominated nations such as Iran and Pakistan, has continually exposed the Jewish population to mayhem and murder. An overwhelming and irrational hatred has been directed at the Jewish state for the near seven decades of its existence by the international Muslim population. The Jews have had to live their lives in constant fear of terrorist attacks, the ubiquitous sound of sirens directing them to bomb shelters, and the all-too-frequent reports of murdered and maimed Israeli citizens, almost always civilian women and children. The construction of the West Bank barrier has limited suicide bomber access to Israel;[38] however,

---

[38] The installation of the West Bank barrier has cut Palestinian Arab terrorist attacks on Israel by an estimated 90%. Elgin F. Hunt and David C. Colander, *Social Science: An Introduction to the Study of Society* (Boston, MA: Pearson, 2006), p. 388. Also, Mitchell Bard, "West Bank Security Fence: Background & Overview, Jewish Virtual Library, posted at www.jewishvirtuallibrary.org.

depraved Muslim individuals have continued to launch individual attacks against Jews, shooting them from motorcycles, driving vehicles into crowds of innocent Jews waiting at city bus stops, and generally continuing the Muslim reign of terror by targeting innocent civilians. "Some historical and political context reveals that it is actually the Palestinian leaders who routinely incite and train their people towards the desired goal of the annihilation of the Jews."[39] And it is an undeniable fact that virtually all the terrorism employed by the Palestinian Arabs against Israel is funded by those Muslim nations that are intent on Israel's destruction.

Such acts of Muslim violence against the Jews, however, certainly come as no surprise because some thirteen centuries have been littered with the impact of Muslim-on-Muslim violence, principally in the ongoing conflicts between Shia and Sunni Muslims. The news is punctuated almost daily with reports of violent attacks launched by either of these prominent denominations of Islam against the other or of brutal barrages of Muslim splinter groups targeting various other Muslim communities. Then, there are continuing guerrilla actions undertaken by Muslims against various governments and religious groups—Christian, Buddhist, Hindu, Sikh, and others. It has been estimated that fully 90% of all terrorist incidents in the world have been sponsored, led, and perpetrated by Muslims.[40]

James F. Gauss is right when he maintains that the ancient "pattern of Islamic barbarity continues into the modern era and the 21st century."[41] Steve Koehane observes that from 1970–2000, "there were 43,721 terrorist attacks worldwide; 113,425 people were killed; over 82,126 were injured. Over 90% of these barbaric acts were committed by Muslims."[42] Listing some 14 nations "where the plague of Islamic aggression is bearing its vicious fangs and encroaching upon others with its marauding tentacles," Ahamkaari says that today, "over three fourths of the world's armed conflicts involve Muslim 'issues' and individuals."[43] Then, he draws the following conclusion: "For a community that accounts for one fifths of the human

---

[39] Tricia Aven and Tricia Miller, *Jews and Anti-Judaism in Esther and the Church* (Cambridge, UK: James Clark & Co, 2015), p. 176.

[40] Ryszard Stemplowski, *Transnational Terrorism in the World System Perspective* (Warsaw, Poland: Polish Institute of International Affairs, 2002), p. 176.

[41] James F. Gauss, *Islam & Christianity: A Revealing Contrast* (Alachua, FL: Bridge-Logos Publishing, 2009), p. 275.

[42] Steve Keohane, "Muhammad: Terrorist or Prophet?", posted at http://bibleprobe.com/muhammad.htm.

[43] Ahamkaari, *Will I Be Killed? (for writing the following contents. . .)* (Lincoln, NE: iUniverse, 2003), p. 151.

head count, their hogging such a disproportionate share of troubles cannot be deemed purely coincidental."[44] In virtually every conflict in which Muslim extremists are involved anywhere in the world, they employ the standard *jihadist* terrorist tactics by targeting civilian populations rather than engaging military targets. The obsession of Muslim extremists with the spread of Islam on the edge of the sword is legendary, and it continues unabated to this day.

The facts speak for themselves: a significant portion of the Muslim population of the world engages in extremist interpretations of the *Qur'an* and act on their interpretations by seeking to spread Islam through violence and warfare.[45] Muhammad himself set the precedent and established this course of action for unfolding world events involving his disciples when he boasted, "I, last of the Prophets, am sent with a sword. The sword is the key to heaven and hell. All who draw it in the name of the faith will be rewarded."[46] The ensuing history also clearly speaks for itself: "Within less than 100 years after Islam's appearance, Arab Muslim warriors had swept out of Arabia into the Middle East and North Africa, bringing about the downfall of Byzantium and Persia and inaugurating a succession of Islamic states that would rule a large part of the known world until the collapse of the Ottoman dynasty after World War I,"[47] writes Juan Campo. "On the basis of the success of the Muslim conquests, it has become a

---

[44] Ahamkaari, p. 151.

[45] A cursory review of the unspeakable atrocities of ISIS, the newly declared Muslim "caliphate" and the latest incarnation of Muslim evil, serves to underscore the extent to which extremist and fanatical interpretations of the *Qur'an* can stoop in their depraved determination to spread their own version of Islam on the edge of the sword. These include staging mass executions of Christians, Yazidis, Druze, and Muslims of different sects, crucifying Christians, organizing public mass beheadings (with the decapitations posted on social media), burning prisoners of war alive, carrying out mass drownings, burying people alive *en masse*, staging firing-squad executions of large numbers of children whose only "sin" was not "properly" celebrating Ramadan, engaging in vicious child rape, forcing women to submit to "circumcision" (a euphemism for excision of the clitoris), offering women as sex-slave prizes in contests for the best observance of Islam, engaging in the systematic mass rape of women of other religions including those of other Muslim sects, engaging in slave trade with women and children, and a long, virtually interminable, list of other atrocities. ISIS glories in its barbarism, releasing slick pamphlets justifying child rape and sex slavery as well as promoting and glamorizing its atrocities and crimes against humanity in well-crafted propaganda videos for distribution on social media. Considering the brutal, barbaric tactics that ISIS employs against civilian populations in its ever-widening sphere of influence, it should be easy for anyone to understand the continuing danger that Israel faces from Hamas, which is simply another incarnation of the same Muslim evil that ISIS represents. The philosophy that ISIS espouses undergirds Hamas, which also brutalizes the citizens of Gaza, routinely and summarily executing suspected Israeli collaborators without trial or due process, using women and children as human shields to protect its military assets and to stand between its militants and the Israeli Defense Forces, and launching missiles against Israeli population centers from its own civilian centers, including hospitals and even United Nations complexes.

[46] Morris Katz, *The Journey: A Trip to Eternity* (Victoria, Canada: Trafford Publishing, 2004), p. 139.

[47] Juan Eduardo Campo, *Encyclopedia of Islam* (New York: Infobase Publishing, 2009), p. xxix.

commonplace to assert that Islam is a violent religion that was spread by the sword," Campo admits. At the same time, however, he argues that "scholars specializing in the early history of Islam and its transregional expansion have found that the historical factors involved were much more varied and complex than the 'conquest by the sword' thesis would suggest."[48]

The Ancient and Enduring Struggle over the Promised Land

The controversy over the Promised Land can actually be traced to the time of Abraham, for the patriarch "had two sons."[49] Ishmael, Abraham's firstborn, was born to the Egyptian bondservant Hagar when his wife Sarah despaired of ever having a son herself and invoked the ancient custom of surrogate motherhood. Ishmael was not, however, the answer to God's promise to Abraham. As a matter of fact, when the Almighty gave the command for the *Akedah* ("binding") of Isaac, Abraham and Sarah's son, he instructed the patriarch, "Take now your son, *your only son*, whom you love, Isaac, and go to the land of Moriah, and offer him there as a burnt offering on one of the mountains of which I will tell you."[50] It was specifically through the lineage of Isaac, not Ishmael, that God's covenant would be perpetuated: ". . . through Isaac your descendants shall be named."[51]

Rivalry for the inherited blessing of Abraham may well have been the underlying cause of the contention between Sarah and Hagar[52] and later between the young Isaac and Ishmael.[53] It is certain that Ishmael was not inclined to follow the divine instructions that God had given to Abraham. In fact, as God so accurately predicted to Abraham, "He will be a wild ass of a man, his hand will be against everyone,"[54] an apropos descriptive of many of Ishmael's descendants to this day. Despite the fact that Abraham prayed for Ishmael, imploring God with these words: "O that Ishmael might live before you [the LORD],"[55] and

---

[48] Campo, p. xxix.
[49] Galatians 4:22.
[50] Genesis 22:2, emphasis added.
[51] Genesis 21:12.
[52] Genesis 16:4–5. Having borne a son to Abraham by means of surrogate motherhood, Hagar may well have thought she had the upper hand over the childless Sarah and that her son would eventually inherit Abraham's estate as his "firstborn."
[53] Genesis 21:9. Ishmael may very well have "mocked" Isaac because he thought that he, Abraham's firstborn, should and would receive the inheritance, including the Abrahamic covenant and blessing. Some Jewish scholars have suggested that there were even deeper and far more nefarious elements at play in Ishmael's mocking.
[54] Genesis 16:12.
[55] Genesis 17:18.

despite the fact that God responded by promising Abraham, "I will bless [Ishmael],"[56] it was clear that the descendants of the son of the Egyptian bondwoman would not be allegiant to the faith of Abraham and that they would not inherit the blessing of the Abrahamic covenant, including its real estate clause.

The conflict over the land of Israel that developed between Ishmael's descendants and those of Isaac continued and became one of the most enduring and intractable struggles in history. In Genesis *Rabbah*, an account is given of an instance of just such controversy that took place during the time of Alexander the Great when Ishmaelites, joined by Canaanites and Egyptians, initiated a challenge to Israel's right to the Promised Land and appeared before Alexander to pursue their claim.[57] "Who is laying claim against whom?" Alexander asked. The Ishmaelites responded, "We are the claimants, and we base our claim on [the Jews'] Torah, for it is written, 'But he shall acknowledge the first born, the son of the hated, and Ishmael was the firstborn.'"[58] Israel's respondent, Gebia of Qosem, countered their argument by asking Alexander, "My lord, the king, cannot a man do as he likes with his sons?" When Alexander responded in the affirmative, Gebia continued his argument in this manner: "Thus it is written, 'Abraham gave all that he had to Isaac.'"[59] Then the sage asked rhetorically, "Where is the deed of gift to the other sons?" When he answered his own question, saying, "But unto the sons of the concubines that Abraham had, Abraham gave gifts," Gebia rested his case, prompting the Ishmaelite, Canaanite, and Egyptian claimants to withdraw in embarrassment.[60] This rabbinic *midrash* simply recounts yet another of the continuing efforts that have been put forth by the Arabian descendants of Ishmael to claim title to the land of Israel.

Around a millennium after this incident, an illiterate Arabian merchant named Muhammad[61] purloined and redesigned biblical history[62] to make

---

[56] Genesis 17:20.

[57] For an in-depth study of the history of the Ishmaelite background of the Arabs, see Carol Bakhos, *Ishmael on the Border: Rabbinic Portrayals of the First Arab* (Albany, NY: The State University of New York Press, 2006), pp. 77–78.

[58] Deuteronomy 21:17.

[59] Genesis 25:2.

[60] This account is found in Genesis *Rabbah* 61:7.

[61] Some scholars suggest that Muhammad was actually invented by seventh-century Arabians to justify their military conquests and to legitimize their preexisting religious and philosophical traditions. See Robert Spencer, *Did Muhammed Exist? An Inquiry into Islam's Obscure Origins* (Wilmington, DE: ISI Books, 2012).

[62] Tom Holland, "When I Questioned the History of Muhammad," *The Wall Street Journal*, January 9, 2015, posted at http://www.wsj.com/articles/when-i-questioned-the-history-of-muhammad-1420821462. Holland writes, "Did the Quran, the supposed corpus of Muhammad's revelations, in fact derive from a whole multiplicity of preexisting sources? . . . The answer to all these questions, I gradually came to conclude, was yes."

Ishmael and the Arabs the leading characters in the Abrahamic drama, to appropriate the Abrahamic blessing for his own people, and to assert that his own newly minted religion superseded both Judaism and Christianity.[63] He even coopted Israel's God, YHWH, renaming him *Allah*, the name that before Muhammad's time had been applied to one member of the pantheon of "deities in Arabian polytheistic tradition."[64] He also expropriated Israel's foremost commandment, the *Shema*: "*Shema, Yisrael, YHWH eloheinu, YHWH echad*" ("Hear, O Israel, YHWH, our God, is YHWH alone"),[65] and replaced it with the Muslim *Shahada*:[66] "*La 'ilaha 'illa-llah, muhammadur rasulu-llah*" ("There is no God but

---

[63] Muhammad initially "tried to use Judaism as the basis" for his religion; however, when he was rejected by the Jews, he turned against them, either "wiping out or sending into exile the Jewish tribes of Mecca and Medina." Naomi E. Pasachoff and Robert Littman, *A Concise History of the Jewish People* (Lanham, MD: Rowman & Littlefield Publishers, 1995), p. 111.

[64] John M. Duffey, *Science and Religion: A Contemporary Perspective* (Eugene, OR: Wipf and Stock Publishers, 2013), p. 182. Also, David W. Shenk, *Journeys of the Muslim Nation and the Christian Church: Exploring the Mission of Two Communities* (Nairobi, Kenya: Uzima Publishing House, 2006), p. 22; and Karen Armstrong, *Islam: A Short History* (New York: Random House, 2000), p. 11. Armstrong says that the *Ka'aba*, Islam's holiest site, was originally a shrine to a Nabatean god known as Hubal and that it originally contained 360 images representing deities for each day of the year that were enshrined as tutelary guardians of the Arab year. See Patrick Fairbairn, *The Imperial Bible-Dictionary: Historical, Biographical, Geographical, and Doctrinal* (London, England: Blackie and Son, 1866), p. 113. The enshrined gods included images of each of the gods of the various Arabian tribes. Herodotus (*Thalia*, 8) noted that among these gods, two, Urotalt and Ailat, were the prominent gods that the ancient Arabians worshipped. See John Ramsay McCulloch, *A Dictionary, Geographical, Statistical, and Historical* (London, England: Longman, Orme, Brown, Green, and Longmans, 1841), vol. 1, p. 139. One of these lesser deities was named Allah. Apparently by Muhammad's time, says Armstrong, Allah had become "the High God," supplanting Hubal, Urotalt, and Ailat. Because the *Ka'aba* contained idols dedicated to all of the gods in the Arabian polytheistic pantheon, the structure was dedicated to peace; therefore, when warring Arabian clans sought to make peace, they brought their gods with them to the *Ka'aba* where they found those same gods living in peace inside the shrine. The *Ka'aba*, therefore, became "the centre of a peace zone (*haram*), where tribal hostilities were put aside." See F. Donald Logan, *A History of the Church in the Middle Ages* (New York: Routledge, 2013), p. 36. This fact was thought to have contributed to the making of peace among warring tribes, especially during the month of *Dhu al-Hijja*, which required a cessation of the hostilities that were all too common among the competing, bellicose tribes of Arabia. See James Wynbrandt, *A Brief History of Saudi Arabia* (New York: Infobase Publishing, 2004), p. 26. When the sacred site of the *Ka'aba* was taken over by Muhammad and became the central shrine of Islam, the theme of making peace carried over. This is probably the historical background of the claim that Islam is a "religion of peace," even though the term is essentially more a modern political fabrication used to describe Islam than it is a practical reality. Etymologically, the Arabic word *Islam* is, in fact, cognate with the word *salam* ("peace"), even though technically the word Islam means "submission" or "surrender to Allah's will." See Norio Suzuki, "The Problem of Peace and World Order in an Islamic Context: The Cast of Modern Japan," in *Peace Movements and Pacifism After September 11*, Shin Chiba and Thomas J. Schoenbaum, eds. (Cheltenham, UK: Edward Elgar Publishing, 2008), p. 114.

[65] Deuteronomy 6:4–9. In context with the faith of his Jewish community, Jesus affirmed that the *Shema* was the first and greatest commandment in the Torah (Matthew 22:36–40).

[66] The Arabic word *shahada* means "testimony."

Allah. Muhammad is the messenger of Allah").[67] Indeed, the *Qur'an* even went so far as to place Abraham with Ishmael at the *Ka'aba* in Mecca "praying that Allah will send Muhammad as a messenger."[68] It is a simple fact, however, that Muhammad could not have "written"—nor could he have created—the traditions and principles of the *Qur'an*[69]—especially with many of its concepts and narratives being so closely parallel with those of Judaism and Christianity—if he had not plagiarized[70] the sacred writings and traditions of both faiths.[71] By far Muhammad's worst perversion of the Hebrew Scriptures, however, occurred when he commandeered the *Akedah*, the binding of Isaac, and misrepresented what was by then a 2700-year-old biblical truth by saying that instead of presenting Isaac as a sacrifice on Mt. Moriah, Abraham offered Ishmael near Mecca. "Since Ishmael went on to become the founding father of the Arabic peoples in the Hebrew Bible as well as the Koran, Muhammad thus expropriated Judaism's

---

[67] The *Shahada* was first used in the late seventh century, AD. See James E. Lindsay, *Daily Life in the Medieval Islamic World* (Indianapolis, IN: Hackett Publishing Co., 2005), p. 140.

[68] *Qur'an* 2:129. John Kaltner, *Ishmael Instructs Isaac: An Introduction to the Qur'an for Bible Readers* (Collegeville, MN: The Liturgical Press, 1999), p.117. For an excellent discussion of the expropriations and aberrations of the *Qur'an* as they relate to biblical history see all of Kaltner's *Ishmael Instructs Isaac.*

[69] In point of fact, Muhammad did not write the *Qur'an*; therefore, its opening verse, "This book has been sent down to you," is inaccurate. The *Qur'an* was not compiled into a book until a century after Muhammad's death. See Ira M. Lapidus, *A History of Islamic Societies* (Cambridge, UK: Cambridge University Press, 1988), p. 22. Lapidus points out what many scholars believe: "The traditional story of the origins and early history of Islam was a later invention intended to demonstrate, via historical narrative, the mythical, doctrinal, and other beliefs of Muslims and their superiority to religious rivals, including pagan Arabians, Jews, and Christians."

[70] David James Burrell, *The Religions of the World: An Outline of the Great Religious Systems* (Philadelphia, PA: Presbyterian Board of Publication and Sabbath-School Work, 1888), pp. 274–275. Burrell observed that the *Qur'an* is "made up of visions, legends, plagiarized and distorted Bible-stories, apocryphal traditions, dogmas, moral maxims, and civil laws."

[71] An example of Muhammad's plagiarism from Christian Scripture is this: "The Prophet said, "Allah said, 'I have prepared for my righteous slaves [such things] as no eye has ever seen, nor an ear has ever heard, nor a human heart can ever think of" (*Sahih Al-Bukhari*, vol. 9, book 93, no. 589). This is virtually a verbatim expropriation of 1 Corinthians 2:9. Unlike Muhammad, however, Paul rightfully attributed his declaration to Isaiah 64:4 in the Hebrew Scriptures. Since Paul wrote seven centuries before Muhammad lived and Isaiah wrote eight centuries before Paul, Muhammad's use of this statement can only be seen as plagiarism. Muhammad expropriated other stories of Scripture while mixing them with legends and ideas of his own. In some cases, Muhammad actually did give attribution, albeit rather oblique, to Judaism as when he wrote, "For this we prescribed to the children of Israel that whoever kills a person, unless it be for punishing murder or for violence in the land, it would be as if he had killed all mankind; and if anyone saves a life, it would be as if he saved all mankind" (Sura 5:31–33). This is a quote, not from Scripture, but from the Jerusalem Talmud, *Sanhedrin* 37a, which says, "Whoever destroys a soul, it is considered as if he destroyed an entire world. And whoever saves a life, it is considered as if he saved the entire world." Since the Jerusalem Talmud was compiled from centuries-old oral traditions in the fourth and fifth centuries AD, it predated the time of Muhammad by at least two centuries. The oral tradition which was finally codified in the Talmud, however, predated the first century AD and, according to rabbinic tradition, dated from the time of Moses.

foundational sacrifice for his desert tribes and their own ancestral place of pilgrimage near Mecca."[72] Then, in order to lend authenticity to his religion, Muhammad even claimed that Abraham (*Ibrahim* in Arabic) was somehow given the cuboid-shaped black stone[73] which was to become the center of Islamic worship and that the patriarch and Ishmael traveled from Jerusalem to Mecca in order to build the *Ka'aba* and the first mosque to house the black stone.[74] In an effort to establish the ancient nature of monotheism among the Arabs, Muhammad maintained that Abraham and Ishmael also smashed the idols of the pre-Islamic polytheistic tribes that were housed in the *Ka'aba*,[75] in an alleged incident that was designed to parallel the rabbinic *midrash* that described young Abraham as destroying stone idols in his father Terah's workshop in Ur of the Chaldeans.[76]

According to the *Qur'an*, Muhammad, early in his career, is said to have encouraged relative tolerance for the Jewish people, whom, along with the Christians, he characterized as "People of the Book."[77] As time went on and both the Jews and Christians rejected him and his message, however, he turned increasingly violent against both people groups. Richard Booker confirms this fact: "Initially, Muhammad spoke kindly toward Jews and Christians. He even called the Jews God's chosen people and acknowledged that God gave them the Promised Land. He said that the Jews and Christians should not be forced to accept Islam. But when they did not accept him as a true prophet of Abraham, he turned against them."[78] Jacob Pressman further explained Muhammad's reaction to Jewish and Christian rejection: "The Jews in Arabia, from whom Muhammad learned the biblical tradition, refused to recognize him as God's chosen prophet. . . . Enraged and frustrated, Muhammad turned against the Jews and there ensued a series of massacres . . . [for] there was no one left against whom the spirit of intolerance could be exercised—no one but the Jews."[79]

The *Qur'an* specifically said, "We [Allah] said to the Israelites: 'Dwell in this land [Israel]. When the promise of the hereafter comes to be fulfilled, We

---

[72] Patrick Tierney, *The Highest Altar: The Story of Human Sacrifice* (New York: Viking Press, 1989), p. 371.
[73] The black stone is probably a meteorite.
[74] *Qur'an* 2:127; 14:39.
[75] *Qur'an* 21:51–73. See David R. Topper, *Idolatry and Infinity: Of Art, Math, and God* (Boca Raton, FL: Universal Publishers, 2014), p. 4.
[76] Genesis *Rabbah* 38:13.
[77] *Qur'an* 29:46.
[78] Richard Booker, *Radical Islam's War Against Israel, Christianity, and the West* (Shippensburg, PA: Destiny Image Publishing, 2008), p. 70.
[79] Jacob Pressman, *Dear Friends: A Prophetic Journey Through Great Events of the 20th Century* (Jersey City, NJ: KTAV Publishing House, 2002), p. 71.

[Allah] shall assemble you [the Israelites] all together [in the land of Israel]."[80] Islam originally did not consider Jews and Christians to be "infidels"[81] as it did polytheists, pagans, and idolaters, who had the option of accepting Islam or being killed. Muhammad even offered Jews and Christians a *dhimma* ("contract" or "covenant"), stating that "if they submitted peaceably to Islamic authority, they would be permitted the freedom . . . to practice their own faiths."[82] Likewise, they could live in relative peace if they would pay the *jizyah* (poll tax) to their Islamic rulers. If, however, Jews and Christians refused to convert to Islam or pay the poll tax, they were to be killed.[83] Finally, at the end of his career, Muhammad issued a general decree approving the killing of Jews: "Kill any Jew that falls into your power."[84] Immediately after this decree was issued, when one of Muhammad's zealots killed a Jewish merchant and was rebuked by his younger brother for the cruelty of his act, he replied, "Had the one [Muhammad] who ordered me to kill him ordered me to kill you, I would have cut your head off."[85]

Though some apologists make excuses for Islamic terrorism and insist that "Islam is a religion of compassion and love, as much as any religion like Buddhism or Christianity is,"[86] the fact remains that a significant percentage of Muslims, by their continuing acts of warfare and terrorism, cause their religion to be viewed as the most violent in the world by every reasonable person, except those who are driven by postmodernist multiculturalism and political correctness.[87] When the *Qur'an* specifically says, "I will cast terror into the hearts of those who disbelieved. Therefore strike off their heads and

---

[80] *Qur'an* 17:100–104.

[81] Muhammad Shafiq and Mohammed Abu-Nimer, *Interfaith Dialogue: A Guide for Muslims* (Herndon, VA: The International Institute of Islamic Thought, 2011), p. 51.

[82] Letty M. Russell, *Hagar, Sarah, and Their Children* (Louisville, KY: Westminster John Knox Press, 2006), p. 12.

[83] *Qur'an* 9:30.

[84] Ibn Ishaq, *Sirat Rasul Allah* [*The Life of Muhammad*], tr. Alfred Guillaume (New York: Oxford University Press, 1955), p. 369.

[85] Ishaq, p. 369.

[86] Asghar Ali Engineer, *Islam in Contemporary World* (Elgin, IL: New Dawn Press Group, 2007), p. xi.

[87] Peter Berger, "Religion and Global Civil Society," in *Religion in Global Civil Society*, Mark Juergensmeyer, ed. (New York: Oxford University Press, 2005), p. 18. Berger says, "We have been urged not to identify Islam as such with its most violent element . . . but it seems to me that Islam, even in its moderate forms, has certain characteristics that are unfavorable to the development of civil society. I would particularly emphasize two aspects—the understanding of religious law and the role of women." He continues to note that despite all of the useful cautions to the effect that the term *jihad* and its applications can also be understood in nonviolent ways, the term has mainly been used throughout Muslim history to describe the extension of Islamic sovereignty through warfare. "It hardly needs emphasizing that this is an understanding inimical to civility," Berger notes.

strike off every fingertip of them,"[88] viewing Islam as a religion of violence cannot be judged as radically unfair. In fact, as Katerina Dalacoura notes, "Many observers of Islamist terrorism see its causes as primarily ideational. Islamist terrorism is driven by the ideas of Islam as a religion—and occasionally as culture—or Islamism as a political ideology. . . . Their argument is that the precepts of Islam, including the Koran, contain an intolerant view which enables or encourages terrorism's emergence; that the core principles of Islam as a religion or Islamism as a political ideology are *inherently* prone to terrorism; and that the causes of Islamism and Islamist terrorism overlap."[89] Walter Laqueur further develops this premise: "Radical Muslims exhibit hostility toward all those who are different, a free-floating rage, and a tradition of violence that favors the appearance of terrorism. Popular Western perception equates radical Islam with terrorism. While many Muslim purists do not support terrorism, the perception is still more accurate than the apologist's claim that Western fears are 'mythical' in character, based on unfounded apprehensions, prejudices, and insufficient knowledge about Islam."[90]

The simple truth is that Muslims consider the establishment of the state of Israel to be an unlawful intrusion into the *Dar al-Islam*,[91] for "all of historical Palestine [was] conquered by jihad in the fourth decade of the seventh century"[92] and must remain "a permanent part of the *Dar al-Islam*, where Islamic law must forever prevail." In Muslim tradition, the land "occupied" by the state of Israel must be returned to Muslim suzerainty[93] and rightfully ruled only by Muslims. The foundational covenant[94] of the terrorist organization Hamas, which rules Gaza with an iron fist, asserts its right to the land of Israel because it says,

---

[88] *Qur'an* 8:12.

[89] Katerina Dalacoura, *Islamist Terrorism and Democracy in the Middle East* (Cambridge, UK: Cambridge University Press, 2011), p. 32.

[90] Walter Laqueur, *The New Terrorism: Fanaticism and the Arms of Mass Destruction* (New York: Oxford University Press, 1999), p. 129.

[91] *Dar al-Islam* is a classical Muslim legal term used to designate the places in which Islam and *Sharia* law dominates. The *Dar al-Islam* includes any territory that has ever been conquered by the armies of Islam. Once a portion of land or a people has come under Islamist control, it is thereafter sacred to Islam and must forever be controlled by Muslims and ruled by *Sharia* law.

[92] Andrew G. Bostom, *The Legacy of Islamic Antisemitism: From Sacred Texts to Solemn History* (New York: Prometheus Books, 2008), p. 52.

[93] Jacob Neusner, *Comparing Religions Through Law: Judaism and Islam* (Routledge, 1999), p. 201. Also Paul Charles Merkley, *Christian Attitudes Towards the State of Israel* (Kingston, Canada: McGill-Queen's University Press, 2001), p. 122.

[94] The Hamas covenant is officially called "The Covenant of the Islamic Resistance Movement." Its motto says, "Allah is its goal, the Prophet its model to be followed, the Koran its constitution, Jihad its way, and death for the sake of Allah its loftiest desire."

"The land of Palestine is an Islamic *Waqf* consecrated for future Muslim generations until Judgment Day. Neither it nor any part of it may be squandered or given up. The law governing the land of Palestine is to be in accordance with the Islamic Sharia (law) . . . because during the times of (Islamic) conquests the Muslims consecrated these lands to Muslim generations until the day of Judgment."[95]

Continuing, Unabated Conflict

The ancient conflict over the sacred space that God promised to Abraham and his descendants through Isaac and Jacob has continued to be the object of contention from the descendants of Ishmael and other distant relatives of the ancient Israelites. From the time of Abraham until the present day, the controversy has continued. As has been the case for Muslims since the time of Muhammad, most of the Arab and Muslim nations and a significant portion of the Muslim people remain intractable, refusing to recognize the right of the Jewish people to exist in their own nation and in their own land with the right of self-determination, free from all coercion, whether political, economic, or religious. Shlomo Sharan and Dawid Bûqay this pertinent question: "From whence comes the seeming importance of the Land of Israel for Arabs/or Muslims?"[96] for simple antisemitism "does not purport to explain the Arab's 'attachment' to Judea and Samaria and parts of [the] present day State of Israel."[97] They conclude that "given the overwhelming significance of Arabia in the history of Islam, plus early Islam's explicit recognition of Jewry's divine right to the Land of Israel," the only explanation for Arab intransigence toward the Jewish state and the land of Israel must be viewed in this light: "The Palestinian objective is to transfer the historic rights of Jewish people to the Land of Israel accrued over four thousand years of existence to the Palestinians who have no history and who emerged only recently. The Palestinian Arabs are trying to implement a policy that aims to appropriate the identity and legitimacy of the Jews for themselves. They demand that the world recognize them as the sole legitimate owner of Palestine."[98]

---

95 Jamal Khader, "Opportunities and Threats for Religions in Conflict and Violence: How (Not) to Use the Name of God," in *Postcolonial Europe in the Crucible of Cultures: Reckoning with God in a World of Conflicts,* Jacques Haers, Norbert Hintersteiner, and Georges de Schrijver, eds. (Amsterdam, The Netherlands: Editions Rodopi B.V., 2007), p. 145.

96 Shlomo Sharan and Dāwid Bûqay, *Crossovers: Anti-Zionism and Anti-Semitism* (Piscataway, NJ: Transaction Publishers, 2010), p. 7.

97 Sharan and Bûqay, p. 7.

98 Sharan and Bûqay, p. 7.

Amazingly, at the same time when many Muslim nations loudly boast of their intentions to destroy the "cancer of Zionism" and Palestinian Arabs engage in wave after wave of violence against Israel with the avowed motive of driving the Jews into the Mediterranean, Israel is urged by the international community to show restraint even while missiles and mortar shells rain down on Israeli population centers. The question that demands to be asked is this: What other nation in the world would tolerate its neighbor's firing even one missile into its sovereign territory without responding in kind? The answer is, not one![99] Yet, the Israelis are constantly urged to show restraint[100] when missiles and mortar shells land indiscriminately in Israel as do those coming almost continually from Hamas-dominated Gaza and from Hezbollah-controlled southern Lebanon. There seems to be no end to the demands that the Islamists and their allies around the world can make for Israel to absorb attacks on its citizenry without retaliating in kind so as to discourage further jihadist violence. Militant Muslims have free course to inflict acts of terror, mayhem, and murder upon Israeli citizens while being justified in their actions by the Western press on the grounds of "Israeli oppression." At the same time, Israel is warned that if it responds by fighting fire with fire, it is engaging "crimes against humanity" and "genocide."

When Israel does respond to such terrorist attacks, it announces its intentions to the civilian populations in advance of their response and then attempts to remove missile and rocket launchers with almost surgical precision. Inevitably, however, it is accused of "disproportionate response" and "war crimes" because the terrorist entities hide their missiles in hospitals, schools, libraries, and even United Nations facilities[101] and also use women and children of their own populations as human shields[102] to discourage Israeli response. They even go so far as to launch missiles and shells that fall on their own population centers

---

99 What would Russia do if Poland suddenly started firing missiles at Moscow? What would the US do if Cuba launched a barrage of missiles at Miami? What would England do if France began shelling London? The answers to all of these questions is purely academic: they would all counterattack with overwhelming force!

100 Katarina Engberg, *The EU and Military Operations: A Comparative Analysis* (New York: Routledge, 2014), p. 63. Engberg reported the observations of the G8 Summit in St. Petersburg, "The G8 group stated that Israel had the right to exist, but called for restraint. . . . The French President . . . called for 'a show of moderation' in the Middle East."

101 Terrence McCoy, "Why Hamas Stores Its Weapons Inside Hospitals, Mosques and Schools," *The Washington Post*, July 31, 2014, posted at http://www.washingtonpost.com/news/morning-mix/wp/2014/07/31/why-hamas-stores-its-weapons-inside-hospitals-mosques-and-schools/.

102 Yaakov Katz, "Hamas Used Kids as Human Shields," in *The Jerusalem Post*, 03/15/2010, posted at http://www.jpost.com/Israel/Hamas-used-kids-as-human-shields. Also, Ellen Lust, *The Middle East, 13th Edition* (Thousand Oaks, CA: SAGE Publications, 2014), p. 361.

and then blame Israel for the atrocities.[103] These facts prompted Israeli Prime Minister Benjamin Netanyahu to observe, "The difference between us is that we're using missile defense to protect our civilians and they're using their civilians to protect their missiles."[104] Ironically, the one time that Israel was persuaded to show restraint was during the United States war to expel Saddam Hussein's Iraqi forces from Kuwait. When some forty scud missiles from Iraq were raining upon Tel Aviv and other population centers, the Israelis acquiesced when the U.S. implored them not to respond in kind. Immediately after the war was concluded, however, Israel was betrayed by the U.S. government when it refused to grant loan guarantees to help Israel absorb recent immigrants from the Soviet Union.[105] So much for international cooperation!

Hamas also argues that its military actions and Israel's responses are not proportional because Israel has bomb shelters whereas Gaza has none. "Has anyone thought to ask the talking heads on TV . . . why there are no bomb shelters in Gaza?" Jonathan Tobin wonders.[106] The answer is simple: the labyrinth of underground tunnels that honeycomb virtually all of the Gaza Strip are reserved exclusively for military personnel and are closed to civilians! Tobin then poses an amazingly simple question that the worldwide media also ignores: "What if, instead of devoting all of their resources and cash in an effort to turn Gaza into an armed fortress, bristling with thousands of rockets and honeycombed with tunnels and shelters where only Hamas members and their dangerous toys are allowed, the people of Gaza had leaders who had devoted their efforts to improving the lot of the Palestinian people since they took over the strip after Israel's complete withdrawal in 2005?"[107] The answer should be obvious to any thoughtful,

---

103 Yair Lapid, "Gaza Conflict: Hamas chooses to Let Children Die for Its Own Crazy Ends," *The Telegraph,* July 23, 2014, posted at http://www.telegraph.co.uk/news/worldnews/middleeast/israel/10987095/Gaza-conflict-Hamas-chooses-to-let-children-die-for-its-own-crazy-ends.html. Lapid made this observation: "Islamic terror is absolutely cynical, it always was and always will be, and its greatest specialty is taking advantage of every democracy's main weakness—the fact that we sanctify life. . . . Hamas intentionally builds its missile factories and bunkers underneath civilian homes, stores its ammunition in schools and kindergartens (including United Nations schools), launches its rockets surrounded by civilian families, despite knowing beyond any doubt that it will lead to innocent casualties. . . . The absurd result is that Israel does much more to protect Palestinian children than Hamas [does] and yet many Europeans and many Britons accuse us of being responsible for their deaths."
104 Benjamin Netanyahu in an interview on CBS television's *Face the Nation,* July 12, 2014.
105 Meron Medzini, *Israel's Foreign Relations: Selected Documents* (Jerusalem, Israel: Israel Ministry for Foreign Affairs, 1988), p. 720.
106 Jonathan S. Tobin, "Why Gaza Doesn't Have Bomb Shelters," in *Commentary,* 07.12.2014, posted at https://www.commentarymagazine.com/2014/07/12/why-gaza-doesnt-have-bomb-shelters-hamas-israel-terrorism/.
107 Tobin, "Why Gaza."

fair-minded person. Since Hamas controls a "Palestinian State" called Gaza, the only reason for their continued acts of violence against Israel is their commitment to the philosophy of *jihad* and their intractable and deep-seated antisemitism. Instead of working to improve Gaza's economy, Hamas leaders spend millions of dollars, most of which have been donated to them by the West as "humanitarian" relief, to smuggle arms into its territory and conceal them in population centers.

"Despite the frightening religious bigotry, homophobia, misogyny, violent persecution of Christians in the Middle East, and the chilling Judeophobia," says Robert Wistrich, "Islamists have garnered considerable sympathy in the West as authentic representatives of the Palestinian cause."[108] At the same time, however, "Israel—despite being the region's only free, tolerant, and open society—has been continually vilified by much of the mainstream Western media and by large sectors of public opinion. While Israel is denounced for a purely fictional 'genocide,' the lethal character of Hamas' Jew-hatred has been largely ignored."[109] In its rush toward political correctness, tolerance, and inclusivity, the West utterly ignores the root cause of radical Islamist violence that is solidly anchored in Islam's apocalypticism and its vision for genocide of the Jewish people. "For Islamists today, it is the Prophet himself who points them forward to an apocalyptic genocidal resolution of the conflict with the Jews."[110]

The conflict in the Middle East, therefore, "is not a war between Palestinians and Zionists or between the Arab States and Israel, but strictly between Muslims and Jews in which no compromise is possible."[111] This religious dimension to the conflict makes it virtually unsolvable by any normal means of peaceful negotiation, for religious zealotry is based on a reported *hadith* from Muhammad himself: "The Day of Judgment will not come until Muslims fight the Jews, when the Jew will hide between stones and trees. The stones and trees will say, O Muslims, O Abdullah, there is a Jew behind me, come and kill him."[112] Physical attacks upon Israel and the Jewish community, therefore, are not merely a political matter for the most violent of radical Islamists. Instead, they are founded in a deeply held religious conviction which produces actions that transcend reason (despite the fact

---

[108] Robert S. Wistrich, "Gaza, Hamas, and the Return of Antisemitism," in *Israel Journal of Foreign Affairs*, VIII: 3 (2014).
[109] Wistrich, "Gaza."
[110] Wistrich, "Gaza."
[111] Wistrich, "Gaza."
[112] Daniel Jonah Goldhagen, *The Devil That Never Dies: The Rise and Threat of Global Antisemitism* (New York: Little, Brown, and Co., 2013), p. 221.

that apologists make every effort to justify such actions in the name of "freedom fighting," struggles against oppression, and the like). "In spite of Israel's readiness to offer concessions, the rhetoric for destroying Israel 'remains much more ubiquitous than the gospel of co-existence' in the Arab world."[113]

Jewish Resiliency and Divine Faithfulness

Despite every effort by the Palestinian Arabs and their cohorts in Arab and other Muslim nations to terrorize the Israelis, the Jews have refused to be intimidated.[114] Today, as in every day in the nearly seven decades of life in their ancestral land, they boldly go about their everyday lives, refusing to cower in fear in the face of a cloak-and-dagger enemy that hides its face behind masks, launches "lone-wolf" attacks on urban streets, digs cross-border tunnels in order to reach civilian population centers with terrorist attacks, and fires rockets and missiles indiscriminately into schools and other civilian sites.[115] These Jews "are teaching the world how to 'love life more than they fear death.'"[116] They have refused to give Hitler even the smallest posthumous victory either by denying their Jewishness or their faith in the God of Scripture[117] or by

---

[113] Raphael Israeli, *Islamikaze: Manifestations of Islamic Martyrology* (London: UK: Frank Cass Publishers, 2003), p. 363.

[114] Eugene B. Borowitz, *Reform Judaism Today* (Springfield, NJ: Behrman House, Inc., 1983), p. 65.

[115] Contrast the Israeli posture toward terrorism with that of the Western world which Rabbi Eric Carlson says "remains silent, cowering in fear of upsetting Muslims while they torture and abuse women, forbid freedom of speech, behead Jews and Christians, and murder innocent people in the name of Islam. . . . The majority of American News and Press agencies refuse to report the danger and truth of Radical Islam!" Eric Carlson, *Is God Done with America?* (New York: Morgan James Publishing, 2011), p. 16. In fact, the West cannot bring itself to acknowledge that terrorism actually exists! Randall Marshall says that as a consequence, "we cannot develop ways to reduce the impact of fear of terrorism, in its entire spectrum, if we don't acknowledge that it exists." Randall Marshall, "Learning from 9/11: Implications for Disaster Research and Public Health," in *9/11: Mental Heath in the Wake of Terrorist Attacks*, Yuval Neria, Raz Gross, and Randall Marshall, eds. (Cambridge, UK: Cambridge University Press, 2012), p. 625.

[116] Phyllis Chesler, *Living History: On the Front Lines for Israel and the Jews 2003–2015* (Jerusalem, Israel: Gefen Publishing House, 2015), p. 180.

[117] Steven T. Katz, "The Issue of Confirmation and Disconfirmation in Jewish Thought after the Shoah," in *The Impact of the Holocaust on Jewish Theology*, Steven T. Katz, ed. (New York: New York University Press), pp. 22–24. Katz discusses the implications of Emil Fackenheim's famous 614th commandment: "Jews are forbidden to hand Hitler posthumous victories!" by explaining Fackenheim's philosophy: "After Auschwitz, Jews are under a sacred obligation to survive; Jewish existence is itself a holy act; Jews are under a duty to remember the martyrs; Jews are, as Jews, forbidden to despair of redemption, or to become cynical about the world and humanity, for to submit to cynicism is to abdicate responsibility for the here and now and to deliver the future into the hands of the forces of evil. Above all, Jews are 'forbidden to despair of the God of Israel, lest Judaism perish.' Hitler's demonic passion was to eradicate Israel from history. For the Jew to despair of the God of Israel as a result of Hitler's monstrous actions would be, ironically, to do Hitler's work and to aid in the accomplishments of Hitler's goal. . . . To say no to Hitler is to say yes to the God of Sinai; to say no to the God of Sinai is to say yes to Hitler."

shrinking into the shadows and living in fear, and they have also refused to have their visions for their personal and corporate lives diminished by the terrorist attacks of a shameless and cowardly enemy. They refuse to be terrorized by the terrorists! They boldly go on with their lives and achieve the highest levels of success—all while living in one of the most dangerous parts of the world. As former Israeli Prime Minister Golda Meir said, "Above all this country is our own. Nobody has to get up in the morning and worry what his neighbors think of him. Being a Jew is no problem here."[118]

The Jews in Israel continually seek peace, simply wanting to be allowed by their Arab neighbors and by constantly meddling world powers to live their lives in peace and tranquility. They would like to have the whole world keep its hands off their children. They have no innate hostility toward their neighbors, no designs on aggression, and no intentions of expanding of their domain.[119] Golda Meir spoke for virtually all Jews when she said, "We hate war. We do not rejoice in victories. We rejoice when a new kind of cotton is grown, and when strawberries bloom in Israel."[120] Still, Israel has no choice but to be vigilant in the face of the forces of mass destruction that surround them. With the constant acts of violence that are directed against them, the Israelis would be foolish not to expend every effort to protect and defend themselves. Meir summed up the reason for the Israeli vigilance this way: "We have always said that in our war with the Arabs we had a secret weapon—no alternative. The Egyptians could run to Egypt, the Syrians into Syria. The only place we could run was into the sea, and before we did that we might as well fight."[121]

Though the Israelis have never sought war, they have also never shied away from confrontation because they have a horrible reminder of what can happen when a people or a nation does not stand up against intimidation, terrorism, and aggression by others. That utterly unforgettable reminder is the Holocaust which systematically, relentlessly, and unmercifully destroyed

---

[118] Golda Meir, quoted in Ashton Applewhite, William R. Evans III, and Andrew Frothingham, eds., *And I Quote: The Definitive Collection of Quotes, Sayings, and Jokes for the Contemporary Speech-Maker* (New York: Macmillan, 1992), p. 437.

[119] There have been times when Israel has expanded the territory that it possessed; however, even with its acquisition of the Golan Heights and what has been called the "West Bank," it has done so with the primary motive of providing security for its citizens in the face of Arab rockets and mortars and various terrorist attacks. Then, in fact, the acquisition of both the Golan and the West Bank has only fulfilled the land reserved for Israel in the original League of Nations Covenant for Palestine and, more importantly, in the Holy Scriptures.

[120] Gold Meir, quoted in Israel Shenker and Mary Shenker, eds., *As Good as Golda: The Warmth and Wisdom of Israel's Prime Minister* (New York: McCall Publishing Co., 1970), p. 28.

[121] Golda Meir, quoted in *Life* magazine, October 3, 1969, p. 32.

over six million Jews in a short twelve-year time period[122] while the rest of the world either did not know what was occurring or turned a blind eye and a deaf ear to the unimaginable genocide of European Jewry. Israel, therefore, does not seek a fight; however, it does not back down from one, and it usually finishes it. The Israelis, however, do not live in fear. Instead, they live their lives to the fullest, trusting and believing that no matter what comes their way, their incredible resolve and trust in their God will ensure their survival.

Israel continues to exist in the midst of profound saber rattling and chest thumping that would cause a less resolute people to cower in fear. The Middle East playbook that the Arab nations have used for a hundred years or more has never changed. The bellicose rhetoric echoes across years and years of ongoing threats. "Right from the start," says Zeev Maoz, "the Arab leaders knew that destroying Israel was an unrealistic dream. At the same time, they could not afford to change the anti-Israel rhetoric from an extremely hostile one to a peaceful one; many of those who tried paid with their lives."[123] So, the news never changes. Iran's self-styled "supreme leader," Ayatollah Seyyed Ali Khamenei, continually refers to Israel as "a cancerous tumor that should be cut and will be cut."[124] Hassan Nasrallah, leader of Hezbollah in southern Lebanon says, "The only solution is to destroy [Israel] without giving it the opportunity to surrender."[125] Khaled Mashaal, political leader of Hamas, which controls Gaza, boasted, "We are not giving up any inch of Palestine. . . . Jihad and armed resistance is the only way."[126] So, the verbal threats remain the same; however, the physical means of achieving them improve as technology advances.

Israel, therefore, lives daily with the threat of religion-inspired acts of barbarity. When small instances of what occurs with regularity in Israel take place in the

---

[122] Timothy W. Ryback, "The First Killings of the Holocaust," in *The New York Times*, Jan. 3, 2012, posted at http://www.nytimes.com/2012/01/04/opinion/the-first-killings-of-the-holocaust.html?_r=0. Ryback says that the Holocaust officially began Wednesday, April 12, 1933, when four Jews "were executed in the obscure Bavarian hamlet of Prittlbach." The Holocaust was concluded on May 8, 1945, when World War II officially ended in Europe.

[123] Zeev Maoz, *Defending the Holy Land* (Ann Arbor, MI: The University of Michigan Press, 2009), p. 576. A prime example of those who have paid with their lives is Egyptian President Anwar Sadat, who was assassinated by Muslim Brotherhood terrorists after he concluded a peace agreement with Israel.

[124] Seyyed Ali Khamenei, quoted in "Khamenei: Israel Is a Cancerous Tumor," *Jerusalem World News*, February 3, 2011, posted at http://jerusalemworldnews.com/2012/02/03/khamenei-israel-is-a-cancerous-tumor/.

[125] Hassan Nasrallah, quoted in "Nasrallah, in Vicious Public Address, Calls for the Destruction of Israel," *The Times of Israel*, August 2, 2015, posted at http://www.timesofisrael.com/hezbollah-leader-rallies-shiites-with-highly-sectarian-speech/.

[126] Khaled Mashaal, quoted in Aaron Kalman, "Abbas Condemns Hamas Head's Statements," *The Times of Israel*, December, 2012, posted at http://www.timesofisrael.com/abbas-condemns-hamas-leaders-call-for-the-destruction-of-israel/.

West, shock, amazement, and consternation arise only to be tamped down by postmodernist politicians and media. If what has been everyday life for Israeli citizens for decades were constantly manifest on a regular basis in virtually any other nation of the world, postmodern tolerance would give way to unconditional war. This, then, is the level of hypocrisy in the West. Israel is expected to bear with patience and non-retaliation levels of violence against its citizenry that no other government would tolerate. Since Jews have long been expendable in the minds of non-Jewish nations and peoples, they are still expected to sacrifice themselves—even their lives—on the altar of expediency to accommodate for the psychotic impulses of others. Jewish citizens of Israel do not deserve protection, for "no matter whose side history is on, Jews have always been expendable. As long as we are expendable, to talk of 'Jewish power' is obscene,"[127] says Ellen Willis.

Perhaps in order to conceal his regime's real goal of annihilating Israel with nuclear weapons, Ayatollah Khamenei has unveiled another strategy which advocates "a long period of low-intensity warfare designed to make life unpleasant if not impossible for a majority of Israeli Jews so that they leave the country."[128] He assumes that dual-citizenship Jews "would prefer to live in the U.S. or Europe as opposed to facing death threats on a regular basis" and that "Israel fatigue" will cost the nation support from its allies.[129] The Jewish people in Israel, however, have an iron will to survive and thrive because they are assured by four thousand years of history that they have been chosen to endure even the greatest hardship and to emerge victorious. For most Jews, this is much more than mere self-confidence. It is a simple, deep-seated assurance that God, the God of Israel, is with them and that he ensures not only their survival but also their blessing. Michael Wyschogrod encapsulates this history of the Jewish people and their expectation not only to survive but also to thrive: "[Israel] survives the mightiest nation-states, many of which have long disappeared from history, while Israel, against all human calculation, endures. Israel is thus a living witness that the God who chose it is the Lord of history and that his purpose will be achieved."[130]

[127] Ellen Willis, *Beginning to See the Light: Sex, Hope, and Rock-and-Roll* (Minneapolis, MN: The University of Minnesota Press, 2013), p. 244.

[128] Seyyed Ali Khamenei, *Palestine*, reported in "Iran's Khamenei Reportedly Publishes Book on How to Destroy Israel," *Haaretz*, Aug. 02, 2015, posted at http://www.haaretz.com/news/middle-east/1.669241.

[129] Seyyed Ali Khamenei, reported in Vincent Funaro, "Iran's Supreme Leader Ayatollah Ali Khamenei Pens Book With Plan to Destroy Israel," in *Christian Post*, August 5, 2015, posted at http://www.christianpost.com/news/irans-supreme-leader-ayatollah-ali-khamenei-pens-book-with-plan-to-destroy-israel-142301/.

[130] Michael Wyschogrod, *Abraham's Promise: Judaism and Jewish-Christian Relations* (Grand Rapids, MI: Wm. B. Eerdmans Publishing Co., 2004), p. 182.

CHAPTER 18

ANTI-ZIONISM
THE FÜHRER'S NEW CLOTHES

A new and improved version of the ancient and continuing antisemitism that has plagued the Jewish community for centuries has been introduced in the post-modern world of consequentialism and multiculturalism. The old antisemitism is now being marketed in an acceptable, even glitzy, package called anti-Zionism.[1] After lying low for a time, the ugly and abominable spirit that produced the Holocaust has emerged from the shadows in Europe, the Middle East, and in a shocking number of nations around the world. Far and wide, it has become fashionable for ultraliberal politicians and the extreme leftist secular press to sport the garments of anti-Zionism, the new antisemitism. Now being clothed in the newest fabrics and styles of anti-Israel *haute couture* has become a badge of hauteur in far too many societies around the world. This is especially true in the elite, rarified air of avant-garde leftist media, academia, and politics. In much of Western Europe, the delegitimization of Israel has become a cottage industry,[2] and anti-Zionism has become "a 'respectable' anti-Semitism."[3] At the same time, ancient Eastern European hotbeds of antisemitism that had flourished for centuries only to be driven underground by post-World-War-II civility have now

---

[1] Jonathan Freedland, "Is Anti-Zionism Antisemitism?" in *A New Antisemitism? Debating Judeophobia in 21st-Century Britain*, Paul Iganski and Barry Kosmin, eds. (London, UK: Profile Books, 2003).

[2] Jerold S. Auerbach, *Jewish State, Pariah Nation: Israel and the Dilemmas of Legitimacy* (New Orleans, LA: Quid Pro Books, 2014). Auerbach points to British-produced books such as Uri Davis, *Israel: An Apartheid State* (London, UK: Zed Books, 1987) and many of the tomes published by the anti-Zionist Pluto Press, including John Rose, *The Myths of Zionism* (London, UK: Pluto Press, 2004); Jonathan Cook, *Blood and Religion: The Unmasking of the Jewish and Democratic State* (London, UK: Pluto Press, 2006); Joel Kovel, *Overcoming Zionism* (London, UK: Pluto Press, 2007) and Ben White, *Israeli Apartheid: A Beginners Guide* (London, UK: Pluto Press, 2009).

[3] Alvin H. Rosenfeld, *Anti-Zionism in Great Britain and Beyond: A 'Respectable' Anti-Semitism?* (New York: American Jewish Committee, 2004).

begun to erupt with the intensity and regularity of Old Faithful.[4] Now, the old, pustule-infested emperor thinks he has a gleaming new wardrobe of politically correct garments! The naked truth, however, is that, when clothed with the garments of anti-Zionism, the old antisemitism, though subtle and politically correct, is even more heinous and insidious than its source, the evil Haman, and its most recent incarnation, the Führer himself.

Interestingly, it was Hitler who set the stage for clothing antisemitism in the garments of anti-Zionism: "While the Zionists try to make the rest of the world believe that the national consciousness of the Jew finds its satisfaction in the creation of a Palestinian state, the Jews again slyly dupe the dumb *Goyim*. It doesn't even enter their heads to build up a Jewish state in Palestine for the purpose of living there; all they want is a central organization for their international world swindle."[5] Hitler's ideas are alive and well, as is evidenced by 1998 Nobel Prize winner José Saramago's[6] depiction of Israel a "racist state by virtue of Judaism's monstrous doctrines — racist not just against the Palestinians, but against the entire world, which it seeks to manipulate and abuse."[7]

Very subtly, anti-Zionists have discarded the foundation of eugenics, race, and social Darwinism that the Third Reich employed for its antisemitism and have adopted a new, politically correct foundation for their perverse hatred of Jews, which they trumpet as "human rights." Recognizing this transition from racial to socio-political antisemitism, Anthony Chase said, "The twentieth century brought with it anti-Zionist and anti-colonialist movements in the Arab world, some currents of which looked to human rights as a basis of support."[8] The Arabs were joined immediately by Europeans, Latin Americans, and others who had discovered the new and universally approved means of vaunting their inherent and long-held antisemitism. The major promulgator of this new antisemitism, however,

---

[4] Stephan M. Horak and Richard Blanke, *Eastern European National Minorities, 1919–1980: A Handbook* (Santa Barbara, CA: Libraries Unlimited, 1985), p. 56. In Eastern Europe, it was during "the aftermath of the Arab-Israeli war of 1967" that "official anti-Semitism came to the fore again in the form of anti-Zionism."

[5] Adolf Hitler, *Mein Kampf*, tr. Ralph Manheim (Boston: Houghton Mifflin, 1971), p. 56. Interestingly, when Hitler referenced the "creation of a Palestinian state," he was talking about the *Jewish* state of *Palestine*, Israel. At that time, therefore, all the "Palestinians" were Jews!

[6] Portugal's Saramago was awarded the Nobel Prize in Literature.

[7] José Saramago, quoted in Robert S. Wistrich, *A Lethal Obsession: Anti-Semitism from Antiquity to the Global Jihad* (New York: Random House, 2010), p. 7.

[8] Anthony Tirado Chase, "Nongovernmental Organizations: Arab NGOs," in *Encyclopedia of Human Rights*, David P. Forsythe, ed. (New York: Oxford University Press, 2009), vol. 1, p. 98.

has been the United Nations, which has not hesitated to accuse Israel of "racism, apartheid, ethnic cleansing, crimes against humanity, and attempted genocide."[9] When the United Nations General Assembly passed Resolution 3329 in 1975, declaring, "Zionism is a form of racism and racial discrimination," many Western nations tacitly endorsed this indictment by their silence and their acquiescence to it.[10]

Robert Wistrich described the emergence of the new, socially acceptable antisemitism that is marketed as anti-Zionism: "Anti-Semitism did not dissolve or significantly diminish, let alone disappear, after the establishment of Israel in 1948. Instead, Israel itself would gradually be identified as the new 'Jewish question.'"[11] This new antisemitism would even be so inane as to maintain that "Jews benefited from exploiting their suffering during the Holocaust."[12] Anti-Zionism, therefore, has become a socially acceptable way to advocate for the elimination of the state of Israel.[13] Jonathan Sacks says it well: "The new antisemitism is clearly continuous with the old. It has recycled all the old myths, from the Blood Libel to The Protocols of the Elders of Zion.[14] Yet it is different. It is not Christian anti-Judaism, nor is it the racial antisemitism of Nazi Germany. It is . . . focused not on Jews as individuals but on Jews as a nation in their land."[15] As David Blumenthal says, "Jew-haters in the West who feel uneasy labeling themselves 'antisemites' find in 'anti-Zionism' an easy way to sustain their Jew-hatred under a socially acceptable label."[16]

Today, old underlying currents of antisemitism can hide behind what is euphemistically called a "critique" of Israel. "This new expression of anti-Semitism

---

[9] Jonathan Sacks, *Future Tense: Jews, Judaism, and Israel in the Twenty-first Century* (New York: Schocken Books, 2009), p. 101.

[10] In 1991, Israel forced the passage of Resolution 46/86, which revoked Resolution 3379's charge that Zionism is a form of racism, by making Resolution 46/86 a precondition for its participation in the Madrid Peace Conference. Otherwise, Resolution 3379 would still be in force, and Israel would still be condemned by its vile indictments.

[11] Wistrich, *A Lethal Obsession*, p. 22.

[12] Andreas Zick, "Anti-Semitism," in *Encyclopedia of Group Processes and Intergroup Relations*, John M. Levine and Michael A. Hogg, eds. (Thousand Oaks, CA: SAGE Publications, Inc., 2010), p. 24.

[13] Bernard Harrison, "Anti-Zionism, Antisemitism, and the Rhetorical Manipulation of Reality," in *Resurgent Antisemitism: Global Perspectives*, Alvin H. Rosenfeld, ed. (Bloomington, IN: Indiana University Press, 2013), p. 11.

[14] Hadassa Ben-Itto, *The Lie That Wouldn't Die: The Protocols of the Elders of Zion* (Estree, UK: Vallentine Mitchell Publishers, 2005).

[15] Sacks, p. 99

[16] David Blumenthal, "Antisemitism," in *A Dictionary of the Jewish-Christian Dialogue*, Leon Klenicki and Geoffrey Wigoder, eds. (Mahwah, NJ: Paulist Press, 1984), p. 11.

is found in right wing populism, Islamist propaganda, and sometimes left wing ideologies," says Andreas Zick. Additionally, "Israeli policies against Palestinians are sometimes defined as 'Jewish'[17] and thus attributed to religious rather than nationalistic causes. This anti-Semitic critique is linked to two other themes: first, a comparison of Israeli policies to the crimes of the Nazis in the Third Reich; and second, a separatist ideology categorizing Jews as a strange community that is not part of society."[18] No matter how it is disguised, however, "anti-Zionism contains anti-Semitism like a cloud contains a storm,"[19] says Auschwitz survivor Jean Amery. And no matter how it is presented, "the antisemitism that is anti-Zionism has permeated respectable public discourse, incorporating the hoary antisemitic stereotypes of Jews as vindictive and bloodthirsty."[20] Even though anti-Zionists have tried desperately to mask their anti-semitism with a thick layer of politically correct cosmetics, the hideous, pock-marked ugliness remains. The underlying reality is what Emmanuel Lévinas described when he spoke of the Jewish perspectives on anti-Zionist antisemitism: "Do we not smell here . . . beyond all violence which still submits to will and reason, the odor of the camps? Violence is no longer a political phenomenon of war and peace, beyond all morality. It is the abyss of Auschwitz or the world at war."[21]

Jonathan Sacks speaks of three degrees of anti-Zionism: 1) "Jews are not entitled to a nation-state of their own," which is, in effect, a denial "of the right of Israel to exist"; 2) "the existence of Israel is merely an aberration" which "is responsible for all the evils of the world"; and 3) "all Jews are Zionists; therefore all Jews are responsible for the sufferings caused by Israel; therefore all Jews are legitimate targets of attack." This

---

[17] It is ironic that anti-Zionists describe Israeli policies as "Jewish" but they could never define the nation of Israel as a "Jewish state."

[18] Zick, p. 24.

[19] Jean Amery, quoted in Benjamin Weinthal, "Why Europe Blames Israel for the Holocaust: Post-1945 Anti-Semitism," in *The Jerusalem Post*, 01/28/2014, posted at http://www.jpost.com/Jewish-World/Jewish-Features/Why-Europe-blames-Israel-for-the-Holocaust-Post-1945-anti-Semitism-339571. Accusations that Jews are "separatists" and a "strange community that is not part of society" clearly echo from the fifth-century-BC antisemitic diatribe Haman delivered in the court of Xerxes: "There is a certain people dispersed among the peoples in the provinces of your kingdom who keep themselves separate" (Esther 3:9).

[20] David Matas, *Aftershock: Anti-Zionism & Anti-Semitism* (Toronto, Canada: Dundurn Press, 2005), p. 218.

[21] Emmanuel Lévinas, *Nine Talmudic Readings*, tr. Annette Aronowicz (Bloomington, IN: Indiana University Press, 1990), p. 190, quoted in David Patterson, *Open Wounds: The Crisis of Jewish Thought in the Aftermath of Auschwitz* (Seattle, WA: The University of Washington Press, 2006), p. 102.

third degree, says Sacks, is the "bridge from anti-Zionism to anti-Semitism."[22] This is why, as Walter Laqueur has argued, "There is no clear borderline" between antisemitism and anti-Zionism.[23] Whatever the case, Rosemary Ruether hit the nail on the head when she said, "There is no doubt that anti-Zionism has become a way of reviving the myth of the 'perennial evil nature of the Jews.'"[24] Clearly, in today's world, the "enemies of the Jews nearly always use the word 'Zionist' when they mean Jews."[25] In fact, antisemitism's new garments are becoming less and less subtle and more and more crude and vulgar.

"Like all anti-Semites, the anti-Zionists oppose the Jewish state *not for any action* [that it has committed] but for its *presence*," says David Patterson.[26] "Whatever the current evil might be—racism, colonialism, imperialism, apartheid, ethnic cleansing, crimes against humanity, or genocide—one can be sure that the anti-Zionists will hang the label on the Jewish state. Like the religious and secular anti-Semites of the nineteenth century, the religious and secular anti-Zionists, from rabid Jihadists to radical liberals, share a self-righteous indignation over the very existence of the Jewish state precisely because they themselves would be the moral measure of humanity."[27] What is amazing about such anti-Zionist moralizing is that many—if not most—of those who make such judgments against Israel are generally amoral agnostics who have arrogated to themselves the right to adjudicate morality and "fairness" while living lives of complete hypocrisy often void of constraint and lacking any true ethical boundaries! In reality, many are postmodern nihilists who ultimately believe in nothing—even denying the possibility of objective truth—and accept no moral restrictions except what they in their narcissistic subjectivity wish to impose on others.[28]

---

[22] Sacks, *Future Tense*, pp. 97–98.

[23] Walter Laqueur, *The Changing Face of Antisemitism: From Ancient Times to the Present Day* (Oxford, UK: Oxford University Press, 2006), p. 7.

[24] Rosemary Radford Ruether, *Faith and Fratricide: The Theological Roots of Anti-Semitism* (New York: Seabury Press, 1974), p. 227.

[25] Dennis Prager and Joseph Teluskin, *Why the Jews? The Reason for Antisemitism* (New York: Simon & Schuster, 2003), p. 157.

[26] David Patterson, *Anti-Semitism*, p. 199, author's emphasis.

[27] David Patterson, *Anti-Semitism*, p. 199.

[28] Ken Wilber, *The Eye of Spirit: An Integral Vision for a World Gone Slightly Mad* (Boston, MA: Shambhala Publications, Inc., 2001), p. 132. An American philosopher who is strongly influenced by Buddhism, Wilber says that increasingly in today's world, "truth is whatever you want, which leaves us nothing at all, except that shell of nihilism filled with the thickest of narcissism, a postmodern pastry from hell."

Anti-Zionism, the New Christian Antisemitism

Any reasonable person would think that the Holocaust would have forever destroyed the historical Christian antisemitism that before that time had raged throughout Europe and elsewhere for nearly a millennium, beginning at the turn of the eleventh century. Sadly, this has not been the case, for the brutality of the Holocaust did not bring many Christians to true biblical repentance[29] for the church's complicity in the breeding ground for the Holocaust and in the mechanics of its manifestation. Sadly, it served only to drive much of Christian antisemitism underground where it continued to seethe, awaiting an opportunity and an excuse to erupt. That excuse came when Palestinian Arab and Muslim propaganda, which had been directed relentlessly against the state and people of Israel, began to impact mainstream Christian denominations and, more recently, even some Evangelicals. Anti-Zionism is the new antisemitism that is now in vogue in far too many Christian circles, where attacks on Zionist "colonialism" give vent to latent, but insidious, antisemitism.

Patterson, however, makes the historical connection that anti-Zionist Christians would like to ignore: "The diatribes of the anti-Zionist anti-Semites reek of the odor of the camps, and they reek most disgustingly in the sanctimonious denunciations of the Israelis that erupt from the mouths of well-meaning liberal Christians and not-so-well-meaning liberal intellectuals. In both we discover that time-worn manifestations of Jew hatred turn out to be timeless. Liberal Christian anti-Zionism has implications that play into the hands of supersessionist theology. Left-wing intellectual anti-Zionism is the fashionable expression of Jew hatred traceable to what we have seen in the Enlightenment and the socialist liberalism that followed in its wake."[30] Franklin Littell identified the source of the new, improved version of the old Christian antisemitism: "The rage for universal truths, accompanied by abandonment of holy events and the Scriptures that record them, came to dominate university thinking following

---

[29] The problem with Christian "repentance" is that its dynamics flow from the Greek word μετάνοια (metánoia), which means "to change one's *mind*," instead of from the dynamics of repentance described by the Hebrew word תְּשׁוּבָה (teshuvah), which means to "turn [the whole person] around and go in the opposite direction." The prophets, sages, and apostles understood that the whole person, not just the mind, was necessary for repentance. The church's repentance for antisemitism represented a change of mind, but in some cases, it did not represent making a 180-degree turn and going in the opposite direction. *Teshuvah* requires recognition of sin, confession of sin, resolution never to repeat the sin again, and overcoming the sin when the temptation reappears.

[30] David Patterson, *Anti-Semitism*, p. 207.

the Enlightenment. It is this style of thinking that is the most fertile single source of liberal Antisemitism—whether religious or secular."[31]

While the Roman Catholic Church has led the way in identifying and removing historical and theological foundations for outright Christian antisemitism,[32] it has still maintained a posture toward the state of Israel that is not-so-subtle anti-Zionism. This posture can be traced to the beginning of the Zionist movement. "When in 1903 Herzl visited Pope Pius X, the latter declared that whereas the Church could not prevent a Jewish return to Jerusalem, it could never sanction it."[33] This policy was maintained until 1993,[34] when the Vatican finally granted the state of Israel official recognition. Even then, the Vatican policy was not one of full acceptance of the Jewish right to the whole land of Israel, including its undivided capital city, Jerusalem. In fact, when all of the old city of Jerusalem, including the Temple Mount, was returned to Jewish control during the Six Day War, "the Vatican began to issue a series of calls" for the internationalization of Jerusalem, something that it had never requested "during the nineteen years that the city [had been] under Jordanian control."[35] Even during the historical deliberations of Vatican II and the development of its *Nostra Aetate* declaration—which rejected the historical Christian charge of deicide that had been lodged against the Jews for centuries—Muslim pressure, together with that of "Arabophile Catholic factions," succeeded in having its original draft replaced "with a watered-down version."[36] As a matter of fact, "the *dhimmi* Arab clergy considered the passage which annulled the collective accusation of deicide against the Jews as untimely and demanded its removal."[37] The Arab Catholic clergy even argued that Muslim protests

---

31 Franklin Littell, *The Crucifixion of the Jews: The Failure of Christians to Understand the Jewish Experience* (Macon, GA: Mercer University Press, 1986), pp. 38–39.

32 With the almost prophetic fervor of Pope John XXII for Vatican II and its enactment of *Nostra Aetate* and its radical and sweeping changes of Christian thought concerning the Jews, the Roman Catholic Church clearly outpaced and outdistanced most Protestant denominations in acknowledging the church's historical sins against the Jews, recognizing the continuing dimensions of God's relationship with Israel, and promoting repentance and restitution for evils perpetrated by Christians against the Jews.

33 Emil L. Fackenheim, *What Is Judaism?* (New York: Macmillian, 1987), pp. 231–232.

34 Interestingly enough, though it took 45 years for the Vatican to recognize the state of Israel, the Holy See, in a deal that was brokered by the then-future Pope, Pius XII, was the first entity to give Nazi Germany diplomatic recognition with the signing of the *Reichskonkordat* on July 20, 1933.

35 Fackenheim, *What*, pp. 231–232.

36 Bat Ye'or, *Islam and Dhimmitude: Where Civilizations Collide* (Cranbury, NJ: Associated University Presses, 2002), p. 272.

37 Ye'or, p. 272.

"against the disculpation of the Jewish people" were made in "a perfectly authentic pursuit" of the Koran, a demand "for the honor of God and of both Christ and the Virgin."[38]

Among mainstream Protestant denominations, the World Council of Churches has long championed the cause of Christian anti-Zionism—and, indeed, of Christian antisemitism both before and after the declaration of the statehood of Israel. Before that time, mainstream Protestant denominations lobbied against the formation of the Israeli state, arguing that the land of Israel (Palestine) should be a cultural center for Jews and nothing more. In 1948, "pressure from Arab Protestants and local missionaries, supersessionist theology, oil ties, dislike of Jews and the emphasis on peace and justice issues led the new World Council of Churches to be ambivalent or even hostile to the new state [Israel]."[39] From its earliest days, the WCC Middle East media were "composed of people from Arab countries"[40] and did not have even one Israeli or Jewish voice. In 1948, the *Christian Century* "supported the internationalization of Jerusalem" and "blamed the creation of Israel on New York Jewish voters."[41]

As a result of the liberal Protestant press promotions, the WCC was —and has continued to be—the leading Christian voice denouncing Israel. Melanie Phillips notes that in WCC-backed publications "the critique of some Israeli sin would be severe, while Arab countries were spared any kind of condemnation in order not to jeopardize Christian missionary interests there."[42] This position became particularly true after the Six-Day War "when the influential Protestant journal *Christianity and Crisis* switched from a pro-Israel position to the Palestinian camp on the grounds that nothing could 'sanctify the right of conquest in the twentieth century.'"[43] Phillips states the obvious when she says, "If one wonders how it could possibly be that both the liberal churches in particular and the West in general consistently blame Israel not just for

---

[38] Ye'or, p. 272.

[39] Jonathan Adelman, *The Rise of Israel: A History of a Revolutionary State* (New York: Routledge, 2008), p. 96.

[40] Melanie Phillips, *The World Turned Upside Down: The Global Battle over God, Truth, and Power* (New York: Encounter Books, 2010), p. 377.

[41] Adelman, p. 96. For a comprehensive study of the anti-Zionist posture of the World Council of Churches, see Adelman, pp. 95–99.

[42] Phillips, p. 377. The primary concern of Christian denominations has never been for justice for Israel and the Jewish people. Their agendas have always been driven by self-interest in protecting their own properties and parishioners in Arab and Muslim nations.

[43] Phillips, p. 377.

crimes it has not committed but *of which it is often the victim*, one need look no further than the WCC."[44] This posture of the World Council of Churches was particularly on display in the major role that it played in the 2001 United Nations Conference on Racism, Racial Discrimination, Xenophobia, and Related Intolerance, which branded Israel as a racist state.[45] Continuing WCC anti-Zionism and antisemitism have been so pervasive as to produce innumerable examples of the duplicity of double standards wherein Israel is condemned for offenses that are minor in contrast to those of its persecutors from the Muslim world for which there is little, if any, condemnation.

Jewish Anti-Zionism

Amazingly, not insignificant numbers of the Jewish people have expressed either apathy or antipathy toward Zionism—and for a variety of reasons. On the one extreme, are the *Haredim*, the ultra-conservative Jews whose anti-Zionist stance has been maintained for purely religious and halakhic reasons. The *Haredim* establish their position on rabbinic rulings that anything that is new "is prohibited from the Torah in all places" as well as on rabbinic prohibitions against "hastening the day of redemption" since Zionism has formed a secular state that is not the Messianic state.[46] On the opposite end of the spectrum, large numbers of socialist and liberal European and American Jews were against the formation and continuation of the State of Israel from the earliest days of the Zionist movement primarily because they believed that assimilation into the nations and cultures where Jews lived was the best-case scenario for Jewish survival and prosperity. Thomas Kolsky confirmed that "the longest, fiercest, and most persistent resistance

---

[44] Phillips, p. 378. Phillips gives a withering account of the impact that World Council of Churches' positions of anti-Zionism had upon European nations, particularly Great Britain where incipient and longstanding antisemitism within the Anglican Church has found an avenue of release in anti-Zionism (pp. 380–381). She points to Canon Andrew White, the archbishop of Canterbury's former envoy to the Middle East and now vicar of Baghdad, who charged that "replacement theology has now gone viral within the Church of England" and that "the establishment of the State of Israel would probably have had more opposition from the church had it not been for the Holocaust." Now, however, Phillips observes with White that "with modern Israel being represented as behaving in an analogous fashion to the Nazis, that brake on prejudice has been removed." Phillips says that Anglican tradition concludes that "the Promised Land is where the church will be established, that Jerusalem is the heavenly city, and that it will eventually be the home of all Christians." This liberation-theology-founded position "was drawn in large measure from the radical ideas of the World Council of Churches."

[45] Phillips, p. 378.

[46] For a full discussion of the *Haredim* and their views regarding the Zionist state, see Sami Shalom Chetrit, *Intra-Jewish Conflict in Israel: White Jews, Black Jews* (New York: Routledge, 2010), pp. 165–166.

to [Zionism] in America came from Reform Jews."[47] While in the earliest days of the Zionist movement, "Jews opposing Zionism were surely more common than Jews supporting it,"[48] this situation gradually changed with discourse and was reversed with the Holocaust, though some ambivalence still existed in many Jewish circles. Regardless as to the circumstances, a small minority of Jewish intellectuals has continued to be anti-Zionist. Paul Eidelberg describes some of these intellectuals in this manner: "Jewish socialists sought to dissolve not only class distinctions but also their own Jewishness in the amorphous sea of egalitarianism," which has rendered them "all the more prone to demophrenia" in which "they identify with their enemies" and "jeopardize their own interests."[49]

Then, there are some Jews who have a strong distaste for the state of Israel based on the Zionist agenda that helped form it. Shlomo Sand, among others, attacks the historicity of Jewish legitimacy as a people, as a nation, and as rightful possessors of the land: "The myth of the historical claim to Eretz Israel, which fortified the self-sacrificing endeavors of the first Zionist settlers and legitimized the acquisition of the territorial base for the future state, led it after nineteen years of independence to become immured in an oppressive colonialist situation."[50] Some rabbis have also joined the chorus of anti-Zionist rhetoric, even adopting some of the language, if not the philosophy, of the anti-Zionists. As an example, Mark Ellis points to a Jewish Voice for Peace Passover Seder observance in which, rather than following the tradition of reciting the Ten Plagues that God visited on Egypt in order to secure the release of Pharaoh's Israelite slaves, the group's rabbis listed the ten Israeli plagues of "occupation, poverty, restrictions on movement, water shortage, destruction of olive trees, home demolitions, settlements, political prisons, profiteering, denial of the right

---

[47] Thomas Kolsky, *Jews Against Zionism: The American Council for Judaism, 1942–1948* (Philadelphia, PA: Temple University Press, 1990), p. 28. Kolsky points out that the "only American Jewish organization ever formed to fight against Zionism was founded by Reform rabbis" (p. 29). This fact now seems staggering; however, it reflects the controversy in the early twentieth century as to what was the best approach for ensuring Jewish safety and success.

[48] Jeffrey Herf, *Anti-Semitism and Anti-Zionism in Historical Perspective: Convergence and Divergence* (New York: Routledge, 2007), p. 41.

[49] Paul Eidelberg, *An American Political Scientist in Israel: From Athens to Jerusalem* (Lanham, MD: Roman & Littlefield, 2010), p. 102. Eidelberg defines demophrenia as "a deeply rooted malady" that involves a compulsive application of democratic principles to moral problems and ideological conflicts which are impervious to, and intensified by, those principles—especially the principle of equality."

[50] Shlomo Sand, *The Invention of the Land of Israel: From Holy Land to Homeland*, tr. Jeremy Forman (London, UK: Verso Books, 2012), p. 307.

of return, and erasures of histories."[51] In the end, Patterson probably has a good point when he says that "the Jew's Anti-Zionism is rooted in a certain rebellion against the Zion from which the Torah goes forth, against the Torah that comes from the Holy One, and against the holiness that lies at the core of the Jew's humanity."[52] Perhaps virulent anti-Zionism, even among Jews, is akin to antisemitism in that it is rebellion against—even a hatred of —the God of the Jews and his moral demands upon Israel and the world.

As a result of historical and even present-day postures in which either antipathy or ambivalence toward Israel exists among Jews, nearly all anti-Zionists have formed the habit of pointing to supposedly anti-Zionist Jews as examples of those who are truthful in sharing the objections of Palestinian Arabs and others to the existence of the state of Israel.[53] Dennis Prager and Joseph Telushkin counter this argument, however, by saying, "Anti-Zionists would be hard put to find any affirmatively identifying Jew who would not view them as mortal enemies. Studies and opinion polls have shown that 99 percent of American Jewry identifies with the right of Jews to the Jewish state."[54] Perhaps this is why after Alvin Rosenfeld had recounted "the infinitely varied attempts, mostly by Jewish progressives, to depict Israel as the devil's own experiment station, the epitome of apartheid, and the one genuine inheritor of Nazism," he concluded that "when a man can no longer be a Jew, he becomes an anti-Zionist."[55] For Jews no longer bound by religion or tradition or peoplehood, there seemed to nothing left of Jewish "identity" except to attack the Jewish state.[56]

The New Blood Libel: False Indictments

Every accusation imaginable—and some, unimaginable—has been hurled at the Jewish people through the centuries. Perhaps the most damnable has

---

[51] Marc H. Ellis, *Future of the Prophetic: Israel's Ancient Wisdom Re-Presented* (Minneapolis, MN: Augsburg Fortress Press, 2014), p. 46.

[52] David Patterson, *Anti-Semitism*, p. 248.

[53] Edward H. Flannery, *The Anguish of the Jews: Twenty-three Centuries of Antisemitism* (Mahwah, NJ: Paulist Press, 1985), p. 344.

[54] Dennis Prager and Joseph Telushkin, *Nine Questions People Ask About Judaism* (New York: Simon & Schuster, 1975), p. 125.

[55] This statement was a play on words from Haim Hazas' novel, *Hadrashah* (The Sermon), in which the author has a kibbutznik say, "When a man can no longer be a Jew, he becomes a Zionist." Haim Hazas, *Hadrashah* (Tel Aviv, Israel: Haim Publishing, 1942), p. 283.

[56] Alvin H. Rosenfeld, *"Progressive" Jewish Thought and the New Anti-Semitism* (New York: American Jewish Committee, 2006), recounted in Edward Alexander, "Paying a Debt: Bernard Harrison versus the Old-New Antisemitism," in *Reality and Culture: Essays on the Philosophy of Bernard Harrison*, Patricia Hanna, ed. (Amsterdam, The Netherlands: Rodopi B.V., 2014), p. 119–120.

been the unrelenting Christian charge that all Jews were guilty of deicide because they were said to have been solely responsible for the death of Jesus.[57]
Of almost equal magnitude to the diabolical charge of deicide has been the
Blood Libel, which was the Medieval Christian myth that accused the Jews of
kidnapping and murdering Christian children in order to use their blood in
religious rituals during Jewish holy days.[58] A third vile accusation against the
Jews was another Medieval Christian fabrication, the so-called "desecration of
the host," in which "Jews have been accused of stealing the bread of the Eucharist and then breaking it, torturing it, transfixing it, even causing it to bleed
so that they can reenact the crucifixion of Jesus through the host.[59]

What has been all too common among the superstitious and ignorant masses
of history, however, has continued to be maintained during humanity's most
knowledgeable era, the time of modernity and postmodernity. Fabrications as
specious as the Blood Libel[60] and the charge of deicide continue to be leveled
against the international Jewish community and more specifically against the
nation and people of Israel. Whatever charge is in vogue in the politically correct
world of post-modern "tolerance" finds an easy target in the Jews and
Israel.[61] The Western media are especially devious and corrupt in adopting

---

[57] Hyam Maccoby, *Antisemitism and Modernity: Innovation and Continuity* (New York: Routledge, 2006),
p. 18. Also, Todd D. Baker, *Matthew 27:25: "His Blood Be on Us.": Are the Jewish People Racially
Condemned for the Death of Christ?* (Bloomington, IN: iUniverse, 2008), p. 38; and Eliezer Berkovits,
"European and American Responses during and following the War," in *Wrestling with God: Jewish
Theological Responses during and after the Holocaust*, Steven T. Katz, Shlomo Biderman, and Gershon
Greenberg, eds. (New York: Oxford University Press, 2007), p. 480.

[58] For a comprehensive analysis of the Blood Libel charge, see Alan Dundes, *The Blood Libel Legend: A
Casebook in Anti-Semitic Folklore* (Madison, WI: The University of Wisconsin Press, 1991).

[59] Dean Phillip Bell, "Host Desecration," in *Antisemitism: A Historical Encyclopedia of Prejudice and
Persecution*, Richard S. Levy, ed. (Santa Barbara, CA: ABC-CLIO, Inc., 2005), vol. 1, p. 325. This idea is
based on the Roman Catholic doctrine of transubstantiation, which maintains that the bread of the
Eucharist is transubstantiated into the actual body of Christ during Holy Communion. If such were the
case, then abusing that bread would be, in effect, abusing the literal transubstantiated body of Christ.

[60] Amazingly, the Medieval Blood Libel myth has transmogrified into twentieth-century Muslim charges
that Israel engages in "organ trafficking (of dead Palestinian children)"! Rusi Jaspal, *Antisemitism and
Anti-Zionism: Representation, Cognition and Everyday Talk* (Farnham, UK: Ashgate Publishing Limited,
2014), p. 52. Also Robert S. Wistrich, "Gaza, Hamas, and the Return of Antisemitism," in *The Israel
Journal of Foreign Affairs*, July, 2014, p. 38. Wistrich points to a racist Muslim movie called *Valley of the
Wolves*, which contains "scenes that show an American Jewish doctor removing organs from injured
civilian prisoners to be sold to his wealthy clients in New York, London, and Tel Aviv."

[61] Alan Dershowitz, *The Case Against Israel's Enemies: Exposing Jimmy Carter and Others Who Stand in the
Way of Peace* (Hoboken, NJ: John Wiley & Sons, Inc., 2008). Dershowitz methodically counters charges of
apartheid policies made against Israel by former U.S. President Jimmy Carter. He also makes a defense
against arguments that many have made for boycotting Israeli academic institutions and for divesting from
Israeli businesses. Additionally, he builds a strong case against the violent and militant Islamist nation of Iran.

and promulgating such accusations as "undeniable facts." In actually believing such utterly preposterous Palestinian Arab myths, some Western journalists demonstrate an incredible level of naïveté, especially they when ignore the simple fact "that the Arab world does not maintain journalistic standards according to western values."[62] When they are "exposed to the popular 'Palestinian story' . . . their sympathy for that narrative grows and, eventually, they become dependent on those Palestinian sources" for their information.[63] Then, such deceitful Muslim "media"[64] create totally unbelievable and outrageous claims like this: "[Palestinian villagers] spoke spontaneously how Nablus, Ramallah, and al-Khalil [Hebron] turned into modern-day Aushwitzes [sic], Treblinkas, and Bergen-Belsens," and they make comparisons of the "Nazi holocaust [sic] against the Jews" with the "Jewish-perpetuated holocaust [sic] against [the Palestinian Arabs]."[65] Such media-generated — or at least media-perpetuated — propaganda is void of reason and is totally lacking in traditional standards for ethical and responsible journalism.

Ultra-hyperbolical propaganda of this sort does not always reach media audiences in the West; however, it does influence naïve and sympathetic Western reporters and writers to such a degree that the vitriol filters down in other accusations against Israel that are equally preposterous though less sensationalized. As Akbar Ahmed observes, "Hyperbole may be thought appropriate for the mob gathered in the Muslim city—wiping the enemy from the face of the earth, the mother of battles which would claim thousands of lives, and so on—but it translates badly in the international press."[66] On the other hand, some Western media journalists and analysts—particularly television personalities—gleefully report some of the most highly toxic Muslim propaganda as though it were true, and they report some extreme incidents of supposed Israeli brutality as true when, in fact, those

---

[62] Ron Schleifer and Jessica Snapper, *Advocating Propaganda—Viewpoints from Israel: Social Media, Public Diplomacy, Foreign Affairs, Military Psychology, and Religious Persuasion Perspectives* (Eastbourne, UK: Sussex Academic Press, 2015), p. 58.

[63] Schliefer and Snapper, p. 58.

[64] The reports that follow were taken from comments on the 2001 Holocaust Memorial Day in Israel that were published in the English-language *Iran Daily*. Meir Litvak, "The Islamic Republic of Iran and the Holocaust: Anti-Semitism and Anti-Zionism," in *Anti-Semitism and Anti-Zionism in Historical Perspective: Convergence and Divergence,* Jeffrey Herf, ed. (New York: Routledge, 2007), p. 260.

[65] Litvak, p. 260. It is highly unlikely that most, if any, "Palestinian villagers" actually know anything about Treblinka and Bergen-Belsen, including the names of the places themselves!

[66] Akbar S. Ahmed, *Islam Today: A Short Introduction to the Muslim World* (London, UK: I.B. Tauris & Co, 1999), p. 219.

incidents have been deliberately staged by the Palestinian Arabs, sometimes in collusion with those Western reporters themselves.[67] Some Western television crews have even "manipulated images of Palestinian youth throwing stones to portray them as very skilled fighters,"[68] and others have paid Palestinian Arab youth to add drama to their on-camera reports by engaging in rock-throwing incidents. With such duplicity common in the Muslim media and even not infrequent in the Western media, is it any wonder that the real issues of the Israeli–Palestinian conflict are barely covered and what is covered is more sensationalism designed to boost television ratings than serious journalism that seeks to discover and report the real issues and events?

The false accusations hurled against Israel—and Jews, in general—take many forms, generally stretching to the patently absurd and often to the insane, a fact which only marginalizes any legitimate claims that the Palestinian Arabs may have against Israeli government policies or practices. The outrageous indictments that have been leveled against Israel include the following:

Maintaining an Apartheid State

Former US President Jimmy Carter famously made the accusation that Israel is an apartheid state, though when his hand was called on the matter, he walked back his blanket statements by saying they applied to the "West Bank" and not to all of Israel.[69] Alan Dershowitz said, "One thing is certain:

---

[67] Some incidents of supposed Israeli attacks on Palestinian Arabs have actually been produced and directed by Western television "news" crews. One example is the incident that sparked the Second Intifada in 2001 when, with cameras rolling, France 2's Jerusalem correspondent, Charles Enderlin, reported that twelve-year-old Mohammed al-Dura had been "gunned down in cold blood, even as he cowered for his life." Later, when Ederlin's camera footage was reviewed in a French court, a completely different story emerged. Melanie Phillips reports that "for whatever people think they saw in those 55 seconds, it was not the death of that boy. He was not killed by Israeli bullets; he was not killed at all. At the end of France 2's famous footage, he was still alive and unharmed. The whole thing was staged, a fantastic piece of play-acting, an elaborate fabrication designed to blacken Israel's name and incite the Arab and Muslim mobs to mass murder." Phillips explained that "after Enderlin pronounces the boy dead, the corpse mysteriously assumes four different positions." Then, amazingly, "you see the cameraman's fingers making the "take-two" sign to signal the repeat of a scene," whereupon, "you see the lifeless martyr raise his arm and peep through his fingers—presumably to check whether his thespian services are still required or whether he can now get up and go home." Besides the other widespread bloodshed and destruction of property that this "incident" launched, a "mob of Palestinians shouting, 'Revenge for the blood of Mohammed al-Dura,' lynched two Israeli army reservists and dragged their mutilated bodies through the streets of Ramallah." Melanie Phillips, "Remember This? Palestinian Arab Propaganda Stages Fake Israeli 'Attacks' for Media," in *The Muslim Issue*, September 28, 2012, posted at www.themuslimissue.wordpress.com.
[68] Nariman Awwad, *Beleaguered Word: Documentation of Israeli Aggression Against the Palestinian Media* (Palestine: Itithad al-Suhufiyin al-'Arab Press, 2000), p. 21.
[69] Jimmy Carter, *Palestine: Peace Not Apartheid* (New York: Simon & Schuster, 2006).

[Carter's] book has fed the anti-Israel hatred that helps keep the conflict going. He has granted undue legitimacy to the claims of a once-marginal group of extremists that has sought for years to equate Israel with apartheid South Africa."[70] Leftist luminaries like Anglican Archbishop Desmond Tutu have supported such insidious and ridiculous claims, even accusing Israelis of "fighting against God"[71] and comparing the Jews with Hitler and other mass murderers. "The Jewish lobby is powerful—very powerful," said Tutu. "The apartheid government was very powerful, but today it no longer exists. Hitler, Mussolini, Stalin, Pinochet, Milosevec, and Idi Amin were all powerful, but in the end they bit the dust,"[72] he continued, perhaps even trying, by implication, to prophesy of Israel's future demise.

Indictments of Israel for "apartheid" policies gained ascendancy in 2001 when the United Nations World Conference Against Racism, Racial Discrimination, Xenophobia, and Related Intolerance focused primarily on Israeli treatment of Palestinians and only secondarily on human-rights violations and attempts at genocide in the rest of the world. Using the backdrop of Durban, South Africa, where this conference was convened, the U.N. leaders attempted to reify the charge of apartheid against Israel. The draft of its resolutions included "statements equating Zionism with racism, and alleging that it is an 'apartheid' state guilty of 'genocide' and 'ethnic cleansing' designed to ensure a Jewish state."[73] Journalist Benjamin Pogrund, himself of South African heritage, was shocked—"gobsmacked," as he called it—to see these draft resolutions. "I knew apartheid and had already learned enough about Israel to know that the draft was a concoction of lies and distortions. . . . The actual text accused Israel of 'a new kind of apartheid, a crime against humanity'; it singled out Israel for alleged 'ethnic cleansing of the Arab population of historic Palestine'; it said Zionism was 'based on racial superiority'."[74]

The charges that purported Israel to be an apartheid state have always been designed to undercut the right of both the people and the nation of Israel to exist. In fact, it was the Palestinian Liberation Organization, one of history's most

---

[70] Dershowitz, *The Case*, p. 44.

[71] Desmond Tutu, quoted in Dershowitz, *The Case*, p. 45.

[72] Desmond Tutu, quoted in Jay Nordlinger, *Peace, They Say: A History of the Nobel Peace Prize, the Most Famous and Controversial Prize in the World* (New York: Encounter Books, 2012), p. 255.

[73] Anne Bayefsky, "Human Rights Watch Coverup," in *The Jerusalem Post*, April 13, 2004, posted at http://ngo-monitor.org/archives/op-eds/041304-1.htm.

[74] Benjamin Pogrund, *Drawing Fire: Investigating the Accusations of Apartheid in Israel* (Lanham, MD: Rowman & Littlefield, 2014), p. xviii.

mendacious and vicious terrorist movements, which "invented the apartheid canard in the mid-1960s, years before Israel's occupation of the West Bank and Gaza."[75] As Yehuda Bauer says, "Israel is being accused of being an apartheid state, with the obvious conclusion that as an apartheid state, it has no legitimacy of any kind and has to be destroyed, and the same genocidal and antisemitic attitude is propagated as with the antisemitic liberals."[76] Victor Sharpe makes a strong but true rebuttal of such claims: "The Left refuses to admit that it is the Arab-Muslim culture that actively engages in the very evil practices that they falsely hurl at Israel. And where do you find apartheid, racism, repression and torture? Why, in the very Arab-Muslim world the Left supports and embraces." Instead of exposing Arab-Muslim hypocrisy, however, the leftist apologists always retreat "to the tawdry defense of hurling charges of Islamophobia and racism at all who attempt to correct it."[77]

The charge of *apartheid* Israel is demonstrably false. "There is no Israeli ideology, policy or plan to segregate, persecute or mistreat the Arab population. . . . Arab citizens of Israel enjoy the full range of civil and political rights, including the right to organize politically, the right to vote and the right to speak and publish freely. Israeli Arabs and other non-Jewish Israelis serve as members of Israel's security forces, are elected to parliament and appointed to the country's highest courts. . . . These facts serve as a counter to the apartheid argument and demonstrate that Israel is committed to democratic principles and equal rights for all its citizens."[78] In truth, "Israel actually is the only apartheid-free state in the Middle East,"[79] says Efraim Karsh. If this were not true, Evelyn Gordon could not have written that "back in 2011, when the Arab Spring revolutions were at their height, *Haaretz* correspondent Anshel

---

[75] Efraim Karsh, "The Middle East's Real Apartheid," in *The Jerusalem Post*, 03/05/2012, posted at http://www.jpost.com/Opinion/Op-Ed-Contributors/The-Middle-Easts-real-apartheid. Some scholars maintain that the both the PLO and its "apartheid" and "racism" canards were inventions of the Soviet Union propagandists. See Emmett Laor, *The Invention of the "Palestinians": 27 Theses They Won't Let You Hear* (Bloomington, IN: Xlibris Corp., 2012), pp. 115, 135. This should come as no surprise since Russia has long been one of the most antisemitic nations on the face of the earth. Theodore S. Hamerow, *Why We Watched: Europe, America, and the Holocaust* (New York: W. W. Norton & Co., 2008), p. 371. The Russian Orthodox Church is also one of the world's most antisemitic Christian denominations. Richard S. Levy, *Antisemitism: A Historical Encyclopedia of Prejudice and Persecution* (Santa Barbara, CA: ABC-CLIO, Inc., 2005), vol. 1, p. 637.

[76] Yehuda Bauer, *The Jews: A Contrary People* (Zürich, Switzerland: Lit Verlag GmbH & Co., 2014), p. 114.

[77] Victor Sharpe, *Politicide: The Relentless Attempts by the Arab and Muslim World to Destroy the State of Israel* (Raleigh, NC: Lulu Press, Inc., 2011), p. 45.

[78] Response to the charge that Israel is an apartheid state by the Anti-Defamation League posted at http://www.adl.org/israel-international/israel-middle-east/content/AG/inaccuracy-israel-apartheid-state.html.

[79] Karsh, http://www.jpost.com/Opinion/Op-Ed-Contributors/The-Middle-Easts-real-apartheid.

Pfeffer reported being stunned to hear from demonstrators in both Tunis and Cairo—neither of whom knew he represented an Israeli newspaper—that they wanted 'a democracy like in Israel,'" nor could she have reported that "the Middle East Media Research Institute published excerpts from articles in the Arab press over the last year that held up Israel as a model Arab states should learn from—in some cases, because of its economic, scientific, and democratic achievements, but in others, because of its democracy and even its morality."[80]

The truth is that Israel is just the opposite of an apartheid state, for it promotes and lives by values that are diametrically opposed to those of the prototypical apartheid regime in South African. "Israel has not since its inception taken away vested Israeli citizenship of even one Palestinian for the sole reason that the person is ethnic Palestinian. Israel has not created designated territories within its border to which it has forcibly removed its own citizens who are ethnic Palestinian. Indeed, when one starts to look at what apartheid really was, any comparison between Israel today and South Africa at the time of apartheid becomes ludicrous."[81] It is for this reason that Jean-Christophe Rufin recommended that the charge of apartheid against Israel should be criminalized because is so ridiculously opprobrious. "What should be penalised," he said, "is the perverse and defamatory use of the charge of racism against those very people who were victims of racism to an unparalleled degree. The accusations of racism, of apartheid, of Nazism carry extremely grave moral implications. These accusations have, in the situation in which we find ourselves today, major consequences which can, by contagion, put in danger the lives of our Jewish citizens."[82] Sadly, as Alan Dershowitz points out, "The slander that portrays Israel as a 'racist colonialist apartheid state' is already so widespread as to be part of the international community's ordinary parlance."[83] The rush to make moral equivalencies based on imagined parallels between one set of circumstances and another has not helped anyone except the smugly self-righteous who perpetrate such nonsense.

If any of the nations in the Middle East could be accused of being apartheid states, it would certainly have to be the Arab states. Efraim Karsh confirms the longstanding nature of this truth: "Apartheid has been an

---

[80] Evelyn Gordon, "Israeli Apartheid? To Arabs, It's a Model Democracy," in *Commentary*, 05.09.2014, posted at https://www.commentarymagazine.com/2014/05/09/israeli-apartheid-to-arabs-its-a-model-democracy/.

[81] David Matas, *Aftershock: Anti-Zionism and Anti-Semitism* (Toronto, Canada: Dundurn Press, 2005), p. 54.

[82] Jean-Christophe Rufin, "Chantier sur la lutte contre le racisme et l'antisémitisme," In *La Monde*, October 19, 2004, cited in Matas, pp. 54, 243.

[83] Dershowitz, *The Case*, p. 136.

integral part of the Middle East for over a millennium, and its Arab and Muslim nations continue to legally, politically, and socially enforce this discriminatory practice against their hapless minorities."[84] A prime example is the "religious apartheid" of which Pakistan is guilty, wherein Muslims are "a separate—and privileged—class from others." In reality, the very origin of Pakistan is "traceable to religious apartheid," says India's *Foreign Affairs Record*.[85] What can be said of the social and religious practices of Pakistan can also be said of many other Muslim nations whose radical interpretations of the *Qur'an* and Islam in general establish and reinforce institutions of discrimination that are the essence of apartheid against minority religious populations. This is clearly the case in Saudi Arabia which even denies non-Muslims entrance to Mecca.

Comparing Zionism with Nazism

Increasingly, in both Arab nations and in other parts of the world, Zionism is being compared with Nazism in what may be one of the most psychotic accusations in history. This despicable tactic of anti-Zionists simply carries forward and expands the false indictment that the Communists made in the 1930s when they said that "Zionism and Nazism were collaborating to produce mass hysteria, a situation most favorable to Zionist plans of mass immigration into Palestine."[86] One of the prominent Middle Eastern agents of the Communist Comintern[87] even suggested that "Hitler should be elected honorary president of the Zionist movement."[88] These arguments are today mirrored in the thinking and rhetoric of Palestinian Arabs: "In general, academic Palestinian historical discourse does not deny the Holocaust, but there is an attempt to describe its 'instrumental' aspects, especially when certain aspects of cooperation between Zionism and Nazism are emphasized."[89] In fact, in the larger Muslim world, "Zionism is actually considered to be a far more heinous

[84] Karsh, http://www.jpost.com/Opinion/Op-Ed-Contributors/The-Middle-Easts-real-apartheid.

[85] *Foreign Affairs Record* (New Delhi, India: Ministry of External Affairs, 1964), vols. 10–11, p. 141. Interestingly, despite overwhelming evidence to the contrary in Pakistani society, Pakistan's Foreign Minister Zulfikar Bhutto maintained that "Pakistan is truly founded on Islam which admits of no apartheid, racial or religious." Zulfikar Ali Bhutto, *A South Asian View: A Collection of Speeches and Excerpts* (Information Division, Embassy of Pakistan, 1964), p. 79.

[86] Jacob Hen-Tov, *Communism and Zionism in Palestine: The Comintern and the Political Unrest* (Cambridge, MA: Schenkman Publishing Co., 1974), p. 83.

[87] Founded in 1915, the Comintern (an abbreviation for Communist International) was the official advocate and propaganda mouthpiece for world communism.

[88] Hen-Tov, p. 83. This quote is attributed to Avigdor, who was probably Egyptian communist Constantine Weiss.

[89] Meir Litvak, *Palestinian Collective Memory and National Identity* (New York: Palgrave Macmillan, 2009), p. 159.

crime than Nazism."[90] In the words of the so-called "moderate" Muslim prime minister of Turkey, Recep Erdogan, "[The Israelis] curse Hitler morning and night; however, now their barbarism has surpassed even Hitler's."[91] To say that Erdogan's accusation is absurd is a gross understatement!

The very idea of comparing the movement to establish the Jewish people in the safety and security of their own ancestral land with Adolph Hitler and the German Third Reich, whose goal it was to preside over the genocide of the Jewish people, is so repugnant that it is unclear how anyone with a scintilla of conscience and even a cursory knowledge of the Holocaust could even conceive the idea of making such a comparison. In case politicians, autocrats, and media people of the Muslim world have not noticed, Israel has not murdered even one Palestinian Arab with cyanide gas or firing squads, and until recently there has never been a single crematorium in Israel.[92] Yet, it seems that there is no depth to which Muslim anti-Zionists will not stoop in order to stigmatize the Jewish state of Israel, and, sadly, Western media generally march in lockstep with Muslim polemicists and libelists.

Bernard Harrison says, "Coupling the Star of David with the swastika, and Israel with the Nazis . . . is not to engage in 'criticism of Israel'; it is rather to engage in political anti-Semitism in its most traditional form."[93] Alan Dershowitz agrees, "Comparing Israel to Nazi Germany is anti-Semitism, pure and simple. There is no other explanation for it, especially in light of the reality that there is no actual similarity between Hitler's systematic genocide against the Jews and Israel's efforts to defend itself from genocidal threats against its

---

[90] Robert Satloff, *Among the Righteous: Lost Stories from the Holocaust's Long Reach Into Arab Lands* (Philadelphia, PA: Perseus Books Group, 2006), p. 167. Satloff reports that when al-Jazeera television polled the Muslim world and posed this question: "What Is Worse: Zionism or Nazism?" 84.6 percent of the respondents said that Zionism is worse than Nazism, 11.1 percent said that Zionism is equal to Nazism, and just 2.7 percent said that Nazism is worse than Zionism. These findings represent either mass illiteracy and prejudice in the Muslim world or the lack of a moral compass in the hearts and minds of 97.3 percent of Muslims.

[91] Recep Tayyip Erdogan, quoted in Richard Cohen, "With Israel, the World Is Blaming the Victims," in *The Washington Post*, July 28, 2014, posted at http://www.washingtonpost.com/opinions/richard-cohen-with-israel-the-world-is-blaming-the-victims/2014/07/28/104bcc4c-1680-11e4-9349-84d4a85be981_story.html.

[92] Eva Etzioni-Halevy, *The Divided People: Can Israel's Breakup Be Stopped?* (Lanham, MD: Lexington Books, 2002), p. 95. When a crematorium was opened in Israel in 2007 for the use of private Israeli citizens, its existence was roundly condemned. The obvious reason for this reaction was the association of such an operation with the crematoria of the Nazi death camps of Europe. Even now, any Israelis who choose cremation are not entitled to state funding for the procedure. For details, see Matthew Wagner, "Israel's Only Crematorium To Re-open," *The Jerusalem Post*, 10/28/2007, posted at http://www.jpost.com/Israel/Israels-only-crematorium-to-re-open.

[93] Bernard Harrison, *The Resurgence of Anti-Semitism: Jews, Israel, and Liberal Opinion* (Lanham, MD: Rowman & Littlefield Publishers, 2006), p. x.

Jewish population."[94] When people in Germany, of all places, have the audacity to equate Zionism with Nazism, they manifest the pathology that Israeli psychiatrist Zvi Rex described in these terms: "The Germans will never forgive the Jews for Auschwitz."[95] French philosopher Vladimir Jankelevitch is said to have remarked that the Germans would not be alone in this regard, for the Holocaust was an immense crime for which the Germans were chiefly responsible but for which the list of coconspirators is long.[96]

Charges that Zionism Is Racism

The opponents of the Jewish state of Israel "claim that in pursuing their aims Zionists have actually created a *new* oppressed and homeless people. Moreover, they charge, the sources of Zionism are the same ones that bred western colonialism and racism, meaning that its ideas must be rejected by all right-thinking human beings."[97] This was the theme of the infamous 2001 United Nations Conference Against Racism, Racial Discrimination, Xenophobia, and Related Intolerance, which specifically labeled Zionism as racism. A study of what prefaced this absurd accusation is revealing. While speaking before the 1985 session of the United Nations Special Political Committee, the Representative of Syria summed up the recurring and unending anti-Zionist Muslim charges of Nazism and racism against Israel: "Palestinians are the victims of Zionism, the real heir of Nazism, which not only professes its racism but to this day also exploits the painful memory of the victims of Nazism to justify its crimes and atrocities against the Arab citizens suffering under the yoke of Zionist occupation."[98] Unfortunately for Israel, says Thomas Idinopulos, "the charge that Zionism is racist revives old obfuscations that have bedeviled Zionists for the past 50 years."[99] It extrapolates principles from real cases of racism around the world and applies them unfairly to the Jewish people.

The lies that have been fabricated against the Jews for more than a millennium simply will not die: they are merely reincarnated in new circumstances and venues by those antisemites around the world who camouflage their real

---

94 Dershowitz, *The Case*, p. 136.
95 Zvi Rex, quoted in Richard Cohen, *Israel: Is It Good for the Jews?* (New York: Simon & Schuster, 2014), p. 100.
96 Cohen, pp. 100–101.
97 David Engel, *Zionism* (New York: Routledge, 2013), p. xii.
98 Toufic Abouchaer, quoted in Yoram Dinstein and Mala Tabory, eds., *Israel Yearbook on Human Rights 1987* (Dordrecht, The Netherlands: Kluwer Academic Publishers Group, 1988), p. 69.
99 Thomas A. Idinopulos, "Zionism and Racism," in *Christian Attitudes on Jews and Judaism*, Issues 40–54 (New York: Institute of Jewish Affairs, 1975), pp. 7–8.

pathological hatred for the Jews under the banner of anti-Zionism. The 2001 formulation of Zionism as racism merely continued the parade of such charges. Is it any wonder that US Ambassador Daniel Moynihan called the Zionism-racism resolution "obscene" and thundered to the UN's Thirtieth General Assembly, "Today we have drained the word 'racism' of its meaning"[100] or that Yale University political scientist Charles H. Fairbanks wrote, "To call Zionism a form of racism makes a mockery of the struggle against racism as the emperor Caligula made a mockery of the Roman Senate when he appoint to it his horse"? Fairbanks was even more incisive and insightful when he said that the UN General Assembly's majority had inflicted "the most crippling blow yet dealt in the irreversible decline of concern with human rights as we know it."[101]

The racism charges that have been made against Israel are "not a constructive call for change in Israeli policies," says Yosef Mazur. Instead, they are "meant to strike at the very foundations of Israel's legitimacy as a nation" by associating "the Jewish state with a system declared a 'crime against humanity.'"[102] Mazur also points out the utter fallacy of the "racism" charge: "The Jews of Israel themselves comprise multiple racial and ethnic groups. Jewish Israelis comprise Europeans, Africans, Ethiopians, Georgians, Persians and other groups. Race, therefore, cannot form the basis for alleged institutionalized discrimination in Israel because the alleged discriminators (Jewish Israelis) are multiracial themselves."[103] Moreover, many Druze, Baha'is, Circassians, Bedouins, and Christians are also citizens of Israel even though they certainly come from different ethnic backgrounds.[104]

Even in the United States, where an overwhelming percentage of the population is supportive of Israel, some politicians have "used the chimerical Zionism-racism charge to cast the Palestinians as blacks and the Israelis as rednecks," a feeble attempt to parallel the Israeli-Palestinian conflict with the history of slavery, segregation, and racism in the United States. Although U.S. President Barack Obama protested, "We

---

[100] Daniel Moynihan, quoted in Thomas M. Franck, *Nation Against Nation: What Happened to the U.N. Dream and What the U.S. Can Do About It* (New York: Oxford University Press, 1985), p. 209.
[101] Charles H. Fairbanks, quoted in Franck, p. 209.
[102] Yosef Mazur, *Zionism, Post-Zionism & the Arab Problem: A Compendium of Opinions About the Jewish State*, Mike Cohen, ed. (Bloomington, IN: WestBow Press, 2012), p. 217.
[103] Mazur, p. 217.
[104] The Druze highly support the Israeli government and serve in the Israel Defense Forces. While Israel has often encouraged the Bedouins to give up their nomadic lifestyles and integrate more fully into Israeli society, it still respects their lifestyle preferences and does not attempt to force them to make changes with which they are not comfortable.

will always reject the notion that Zionism is racism," Gil Troy says that this analogy has "reduced the story [of the Israeli-Palestinian conflict] to one of racial oppression, rather than what it is—national conflict."[105]

Apparently, those who attack Israel as being a racist nation do not know the difference between nationalism and racism.[106] If nationalism is racism, then virtually every nation in the world is racist. In reality, however, even though some nations do consider their citizens to be racially superior to other nationalities and ethnicities,[107] most nations simply take pride in their own cultures and governments in what can be described as patriotism. Christopher Wellman notes that "we are right to distinguish between racism and patriotism. . . . We not only confirm that patriotism is benign and racism malignant" and "we [also] see better why (and in what forms) patriotism is healthy and why racism is so deplorable."[108]

From its inception, Zionism has simply sought to restore the Jewish nation of Israel that was destroyed nearly two millennia ago, when its people were forced into worldwide dispersion. Regardless as to the extent of their dispersion and persecution, the Jewish people were able to cling to their sense of corporate—even national—identity; consequently, the restoration of the people, the nation, and the land was transformed from a hope to an expectation and finally to a reality. There is every reason, therefore, for the Israeli people to be patriotic about their nation and their land, considering the fact that for so many centuries their ancestors were involuntarily nationless and landless and were condemned to the status of being the Wandering Jew, stripped of human rights and dignity and without any means of protecting themselves and their families from the unending violence of thieves, rapists, and murderers that nearly effected their genocide. The truth is that Jewish nationalism and ethnic pride is far more removed from racism than the patriotism of most European nations and certainly of virtually all Muslim nations.

---

[105] Gil Troy, *Moynihan's Moment: America's Fight Against Zionism as Racism* (New York: Oxford University Press, 2013), p. 12.

[106] George L. Mosse, "Racism and Nationalism," in *Nationalism: Critical Concepts in Political Science*, John Hutchinson and Anthony D. Smith, eds. (New York: Routledge, 2000), pp. 1382–1393. Also, Guntram H. Herb and David H. Kaplan, *Nations and Nationalism: A Global Historical Overview* (Santa Barbara, CA: ABC-CLIO, Inc., 2008), p. 1425.

[107] For example, most Japanese people have long considered themselves to be superior to other cultures. See Chin-ning Chu, *Asian Mind Game* (New York: Rawson Associates Scribner, 1991), p. 102. Chu points out that "the Japanese consider the 'pure blood' of the Japanese people to be the wellspring of their superiority."

[108] Christopher Heath Wellman, *Liberal Rights and Responsibilities: Essays on Citizenship and Sovereignty* (New York: Oxford University Press, 2014), p. 48.

Accusations of War Crimes and Genocide

Palestinian Arab propaganda mills constantly churn out indictments against Israel, accusing the Jews of war crimes and attempted genocide. William Cook argues that "the Palestinian people are defending themselves and their land and their homes against Israeli war crimes and Israeli war criminals, both military and civilian."[109] Once again, the United Nations endlessly supports these specious indictments through a complicit and willing Western press. With furrowed brow, the UN Commission on Human Rights expressed its grave concern about atrocities inflicted upon the Palestinian people, calling them "war crimes, flagrant violations of international humanitarian law and crimes against humanity."[110] Such oft-repeated diatribes have even affected some Israeli Arabs as is evidenced by the pronouncement of a Committee for Arab Citizens of Israel that the nation was "committing genocidal actions, war crimes, and crimes against humanity" in its military responses to Hamas missile attacks from Gaza.[111] Needless to say, plenty of hyperventilated charges, filled with extremist rhetoric, have been and continue to be hurled against Israel for initiating exercises to protect its people and their land from indiscriminate violence and terrorism. For simply providing for the common defense of its citizens—one of the most basic responsibilities of any nation—Israel is continually charged with racism, war crimes, crimes against humanity, and attempted genocide.

Canadian philosophy professor Michael Neumann may have summed up all the new incarnations of the old Blood Libel against the Jews when he charged Israel with engaging in a "race war" against Palestinians and "specifically accused Jews of pure racism" simply for suggesting that "any shedding of Jewish blood is a world-shattering calamity."[112] As if to lay a capstone on his litany of libels, he also inculpated Israel for "genocide" against Palestinians and of "crimes worse than that of the German people in World War II." Because Newmann is an academic and apparently

---

109 William A. Cook, *The Plight of the Palestinians: A Long History of Destruction* (New York: Palgrave Macmillan, 2010), p. 260.

110 UNHCR, quoted by Cook, p. 260. Ironically, the term *crime against humanity* comes directly from the Nuremberg trials where it was applied to the atrocities perpetrated against the Jews by the Nazi regime. See Alexander Mikaberidze, *Atrocities, Massacres, and War Crimes: An Encyclopedia* (Santa Barbara, CA: ABC-CLIO, 2013), p. 322.

111 Ilan Peleg and Dov Waxman, *Israel's Palestinians: The Conflict Within* (Cambridge, UK: Cambridge University Press, 2011), p. 88, n. 36.

112 Robert S. Wistrich, *From Ambivalence to Betrayal: The Left, the Jews, and Israel* (Lincoln, NE: The University of Nebraska Press, 2012), p. 64.

because his preposterous charges were so patently irrational and absurd, he appended his diatribe by making the equally absurd argument that "it can be reasonable to be anti-Semitic"![113]

Demands for Divestiture

One of the growing tactics of the radical left against those with whom they disagree has been the call for divestiture of investments in the businesses that support the economies of those nations or people groups that they oppose or that provide resources and equipment for those nations.[114] For some time now, Palestinian Arabs and their supporters have promoted the use of the same tactic against Israel. Amazingly, but not unexpectedly,[115] the many organizations that have taken up this challenge include virtually all of the mainstream denominations of Protestant Christianity.[116] Most prominent among these is the Presbyterian Church USA, which voted to divest $21 million from Caterpillar (maker of the D9 bulldozer that it says has been used to "destroy Palestinian homes"), Motorola (makers of surveillance equipment used in the West Bank), and Hewlett-Packard (creators of technology that is employed in Israel's blockade of Gaza).[117] To one degree or another, the United Church of Christ, the Episcopal Church USA, and the United Methodist Church have followed the lead of the PCUSA.[118] Additionally, the Evangelical Lutheran Church, while not calling for total divestiture of investments, has instituted a "diversion of all denominational resources and aid to 'those who need it most,' code language for the Palestinians."[119]

It is for this reason that Diana Appelbaum has written op-ed articles in the conservative *American Thinker* accusing Presbyterians of anti-Semitism

---

[113] Michael Newmann, quoted in Wistrich, *From Ambivalence*, p. 64. The problem with rationalism is that it can be used to rationalize virtually anything, including the utterly irrational! See Alasdair C. MacIntyre, *Whose Justice? Which Rationality?* (South Bend, IN: The University of Notre Dame Press, 1989).

[114] This tactic was used effectively in the drive to bring down the apartheid government in South Africa.

[115] Indeed, it could only be expected that the Christian denominations that have not supported the restoration of the nation of Israel, including some that have openly fought against it since before 1948, would jump on the divestiture bandwagon with both feet! Old prejudices never really die; they simply lie dormant until a fresh opportunity arises for them to flourish again.

[116] These are denominations in which historical Christian antisemitism has found a new incarnation in anti-Zionism.

[117] Sandy Tolan, *Children of the Stone: The Power of Music in a Hard Land* (New York: Bloomsbury Publishing, 2015), p. 423.

[118] C. J. Conner, *Jesus and the Culture Wars: Reclaiming the Lord's Prayer* (Mustang, OK: Tate Publishing & Enterprises, 2007), p. 157.

[119] Conner, p. 157.

and false allegations against Israel.[120] Another opinion piece in the *Jewish World Review* took the charge even further by accusing the Presbyterians Church of committing a sin against God.[121] One would think that if Christians of conscience sincerely desired to divest their resources from nations or organizations that engage in racism, terrorism, crimes against humanity, and even genocide and from the international business organizations that facilitate such actions, their prime target would be those Muslim nations and businesses as well that sponsor terrorism not only against Israel and the Jewish people but also against Christians and people of other religions. Neither Christians nor Jews are terrorists while Muslim *jihadists* clearly are. If Christians desire to stand against oppression and human suffering, the choice of whom to challenge is very clear, and it is not Jews or Christians!

While such atrocities can be incontrovertibly ascribed to organizations like the Islamic State of Iraq and al-Sham (ISIS), Al Qaeda, and Boko Haram, they can also be leveled at Palestinian Arab organizations like Hamas and the Palestinian Authority as well as neighboring Hezbollah in Lebanon. One thing is for certain: the nation of Israel has never ordered the murder of even one Christian or the destruction of even one Christian shrine. At the same time, the murder of Coptic Christians and the destruction of their properties, including sanctuaries, have become routine practices of the Muslim Brotherhood in Egypt. Similarly, ISIS butchers have committed virtual genocide against the historical Chaldean Church of Babylon that has continually functioned since 1552 but increasingly faces extinction because of the systematic slaughter of its people and the confiscation or destruction of its properties. Doubtless Christian intolerance for Israel's self-defense coupled with its tolerance for Palestinian Arab aggressive terrorism is patently absurd!

Though he advocates criticism of Israel's policies toward the Palestinian Arabs, Marc Ellis observes what is becoming more and more a tragedy of the ongoing, and increasingly one-sided, Christian debate about Israel: "Holocaust remembrance events suffer from a loss of energy and attendance" as "more and more Christians see that the Holocaust now functions to limit dissent about Israeli policies toward Palestinians." Ellis says that "the Holocaust as a lifeline to

---

[120] Diana Appelbaum, "Presbyterians Bearing False Witness," in *The American Thinker*, June 3, 2006. Also, Nathan Guttman, "Presbyterians Divest Themselves from Israel," in *Haaretz*, July 22, 2004, posted at www.haaretz.com/print-edition/features/presbyterians-divest-themselves-from-Israel-1.129171; and Maia Carter Hallward, *Transnational Activism and the Israeli-Palestinian Conflict* (New York: Palgrave Macmillan, 2013), p. 149.

[121] Prager and Telushkin, *Why the Jews?*, p. 204.

Israel is coming to an end. So, too, the endless discussion of antisemitism is seen as a relic rather than a contemporary challenge."[122] What Ellis describes in mainstream denominations is also beginning to take root in Evangelicalism, which was once the bastion of Christian support for the restoration of Israel. Apparently a new generation of Evangelicals is emerging that is like the Pharaoh "to whom Joseph meant nothing."[123] These Evangelicals are being infected with a subtle form of anti-Zionism that diminishes support for Israeli Jews in favor of standing with Palestinian Christians against supposed Israeli injustices.

Sadly, during the Third Lausanne Congress of World Evangelization in 2010, a Pew survey of evangelical leaders revealed that only a minority sympathized primarily with Israel.[124] Additionally, some Evangelicals, second and third generations removed from those unequivocal supporters of Israel who founded their organizations, have been influenced by the antisemitic drumbeat of the secular media and now empathize totally with the plight of Palestinian Christians at the expense of support for Israel, and they often express blatant antisemitism in their anti-Zionist diatribes.[125] While no one should have been surprised at mainstream Protestant Christianity's abandonment of support for Israel and the Jews since most of those denominations were largely antisemitic in their supersessionist teachings even before Zionism arose, declining Evangelical support for Israel is another matter that few would have predicted fifty, even twenty, years ago.[126]

Surely it is time at the very least for Christians, if not for the secular, postmodern, neopagans of Western societies, to take off the blinders and see the picture that is much bigger than the propaganda of the anti-Zionist antisemites that is vaunted

---

[122] Ellis, p. 46.

[123] The waning support for Israel and the Jewish community in some Christian circles parallels the loss of celebrity that the Israelites experienced after Joseph had saved the Egyptian civilization from a protracted seven-year famine when he was Egypt's prime minister. When a later Pharaoh came to power in Egypt "to whom Joseph meant nothing," the once celebrated Israelites rapidly found themselves enslaved (Exodus 1:8, NIV). Could history repeat itself with even Evangelical Christians turning against Israel and embracing Palestinian Arab and Palestinian Christian propaganda?

[124] Alison Weir, "Christian Evangelicals Increasingly Support Palestinian Human Rights," in *CounterPunch*, September 29, 2014, posted at http://www.counterpunch.org/2014/09/29/christian-evangelicals-increasingly-support-palestinian-human-rights/.

[125] For a comprehensive study of this phenomenon, see Tricia Miller, *Jews and Anti-Judaism in Esther and the Church* (Cambridge, UK: James Clarke & Co., 2015), pp. 178–190. Also David Brog, "The End of Evangelical Support for Israel?: The Jewish State's International Standing," in *Middle East Quarterly*, Spring 2014, posted at http://www.meforum.org/3769/israel-evangelical-support. Both Miller and Brog name specific evangelical ministries that are becoming increasingly anti-Zionist and antisemitic.

[126] While some Evangelical groups have never supported Israel, a significant portion of Evangelicalism has stood in solidarity with the international Jewish community and the nation of Israel.

in the liberal media. Christians who sit in churches and listen to diatribes against Israel or read reports of such charges in denominational literature should engage in divestiture themselves by divesting themselves of their membership in and support for such churches and denominations. Organizations that call for the boycott of Israeli-made goods and services should themselves be boycotted by tithe-paying parishioners. If one claims to be a Christian, it is time to take a stand for what the Bible, the founding document of the Christian faith, says! And, much to the chagrin of many nominal Christians, the Bible just happens to be a Jewish book![127] It is time to open this Jewish book, read it, and live by it—all of it, not just a few selected passages that serve as pious platitudes for many Christian leaders who are more dedicated to political correctness than they are to divine truth. Jesus and Paul did not encourage believers to learn the views of the godless societies in which they lived and syncretize their Hebraic faith with those views. In the richest of Jewish tradition, they instructed believers to read and practice Holy Scripture.[128] It is far better to be biblically correct than to be politically correct! At best, political correctness will gain only ephemeral recognition and evanescent validation in the constantly changing relativism of atheistic, secularist, and neopagan societies. Biblical correctness will ensure blessings that will endure in eternity.

Myths and Fantasies about Palestine

Many Palestinian Arabs, including Yasir Arafat and Faisal Husseini, have claimed that the Palestinians are descendants of autochthonous Canaanite tribes, particularly of the Jebusites.[129] Some have even gone as far as to argue that since Abraham was an "Arab,"[130] the Jews were "descendants of the Arabs [and that] the Arabs, who were Abraham's original offspring . . . possessed prior rights to the land of Palestine."[131] Ted Swedenburg maintains that "by such means the [Palestinian Arabs] meant to affirm that their originary title to the land of Palestine predated and took precedence over rival Israeli Jewish claims."[132] The obvious hope of these Muslim historical

---

[127] John D. Garr, *Christian Fruit—Jewish Root: Theology of Hebraic Restoration* (Atlanta, GA: Golden Key Press, 2015), pp. 35–48.

[128] John 5:39; 2 Timothy 3:15–16.

[129] Eric H. Cline, *Jerusalem Besieged: From Ancient Canaan to Modern Israel* (Ann Arbor, MI: The University of Michigan Press, 2004), pp. 12, 33.

[130] This allegation is patently untrue, for Abraham was first a Babylonian by birth (Genesis 11:31), then an Assyrian by nationality (Genesis 12:4–5), and finally a Hebrew by divine covenant (Genesis 14:13).

[131] Ted Swedenburg, *Memories of Revolt: The 1936–1939 Rebellion and the Palestinian National Past* (Fayetteville, AR: The University of Arkansas Press, 2003), p. 80.

[132] Swedenburg, p. 80.

revisionists is to place the Palestinian Arabs in Canaan before the arrival of the Jews and to hope thereby to invalidate Israel's claim to the land.

Muslims have even had the nerve to co-opt the Jewish Scriptures in an effort to support their argument since the *Tanakh* says that Jerusalem was a possession of the Jebusites before Israel entered the Promised Land[133] and long before David conquered Jerusalem from them in the tenth century BC.[134] David Wenkel, who has done an extensive study of the Palestinian Arab claim of historical and genealogical connection with the Jebusites, concludes that "the claim to Jebusite heritage within the Palestinian community is a recent construct."[135] Palestinian activist Rashid Khalidi even confessed that Palestinian nationalists "anachronistically read back into the history of Palestine over the past few centuries, and even millennia, a nationalist consciousness and identity that are in fact relatively modern," creating a "predilection for seeing in peoples such as the Canaanites, Jebusites, Amorites, and Philistines the lineal ancestors of the modern Palestinians."[136] Randall Price maintains that while some scholars have traced Canaanite artistic traditions to as late as 149 BC, there is simply no evidence in any historical document that indicates any of the Canaanite peoples continued to exist in the land of Israel.[137] On the other hand, says Price, "Arab heritage is traceable in secular history no earlier than references in the Neo-Assyrian annals of the ninth to seventh centuries B.C.," and "even this preserved influence of Canaanite art still leaves another 1,000 years until the coming of the Arabian nomads of Islam to the Land."[138]

This evidence could well explain the reason why neither the *Qur'an* nor any other Muslim document before, during, or immediately after the Muslim conquest of Israel mentions any "ancestral connection going back to the Canaanites (or to the Philistines or Jebusites)."[139] Even Grand

---

[133] Numbers 13:29; Joshua 11:3.

[134] 2 Samuel 5:6.

[135] David Wenkel, "Palestinians, Jebusites, and Evangelicals," in *Middle East Quarterly*, Summer 2007, pp. 49–56. Wenkel's analysis of this subject is comprehensive, informative, and well documented.

[136] Rashid Khalidi, *Palestinian Identity: The Construction of Modern National Consciousness* (New York: Columbia University Press, 1997), pp. 149, 253, n. 13, quoted in Wenkel, pp. 49–56. Wenkel points out that Khalidi has been accused of failing to give attribution to the original sources on which he based his observations.

[137] Randall Price, *Fast Facts on the Middle East Conflict* (Eugene, OR: Harvest House Publishers, 2003), p. 61.

[138] Price, p. 61.

[139] Price, p. 61.

Sharif Hussein bin Ali, Emir of Mecca, King of the Arabs, and guardian of the Islamic Holy Places in Arabia and Jerusalem, said in the early twentieth century that the Palestinians' ancestors had only been in the area of the Holy Land for 1,000 years,[140] which, if accurate, would have made their first appearance there around the time of Muhammad. A statement by the British Government also confirms that Palestinians themselves have long acknowledged the fact that their connection with the land reached back in history no further than Muhammad's conquest of Palestine in the seventh century, which was more than a millennium after the Israelites/Jews settled the land.[141] Even then, says Eliezer Schweid, "no other separate national entity based on this land alone had come into being in the land of Israel. That is to say, foreign conquest had not turned into the establishment of a new nation. The Arabs who lived in the land belonged, in terms of their national affiliation, to the greater Arab people, for whom the land of Israel was but one of many conquests."[142]

Yehuda Bauer has reached the conclusion that "there was no Palestinian people before the early 20th century, because local Arabs thought of themselves as inhabitants of Southern Syria (*Sooriyah djanoobiyah*)."[143] In fact, for centuries before the founding of the state of Israel until long after that event, the term *Palestinian* was applied to Jews living in Palestine.[144] Since the word *Palestinian* for centuries had referred to the Jews, the Arabs did not want to be associated with the term. As a matter of fact, some of the Arabs "denounced the term *Palestine* as 'a Zionist invention.'" Daniel Gordis agrees with this assessment: "When Israel was created, there *was* no Palestinian national movement. Palestinian Arabs had long thought of themselves as Southern Syrians, and the term *Palestinian* was actually used to refer to the

---

140 *Al-Qibla*, (March 23, 1918), quoted in Samuel Katz, *Battleground—Fact and Fantasy in Palestine* (New York: Bantam Books, 1977), p. 126.

141 British Government, *Report of the Anglo-American Committee of Enquiry, 1946, Part VI*, (April 20, 1946).

142 Eliezer Schweid, *The Land of Israel: National Home or Land of Destiny* (Cranbury, NJ: Associated University Presses, 1985), p. 193.

143 Yehuda Bauer, *The Jews: A Contrary People* (Zürich, Switzerland: Lit Verlag GmbH & Co., 2014), p. 277.

144 Jews living in Israel and in southern Syria were referred to as "Palestinian Jews" during the Ottoman Empire (AD 1299–1922). Those who lived in two of the provinces of the Byzantine Empire that were called *Palaestina Prima* (the land east of the Mediterranean from Gaza to Acco stretching to the Dead Sea) and *Palaestina Secunda* (the land east of a line from Acco to Jericho and stretching to Phoenicia on the north and Arabia on the east) were also called "Palestinian Jews" from AD 390–636.

Jews of Palestine."[145] Interestingly, using the word *Palestinian* to describe both the land of Israel and those Jews who returned to their ancient homeland was so common that when the news of Israel's declaration of independence was announced, it was published in the *Palestine Post*![146]

It is ironic, therefore, that the first time that the term *Palestinian People* was used to describe Arabs in Palestine was when it appeared in the preamble of the 1964 Palestine Liberation Organization (PLO) Charter that was drafted in Moscow. It is no wonder, then, that Yasser Arafat proudly boasted in his authorized biography, "If there is any such thing as a Palestinian people, it is I, Yasser Arafat, who created them."[147] In fact, one of Arafat's military lieutenants, Zuheir Muhsin, made it clear that "the existence of a separate Palestinian identity serves only tactical purposes. The founding of a Palestinian state is a new tool in the continuing battle against Israel."[148] Doubtless, then, Palestinian Arab claims to be related to the Canaanites are a recent phenomenon, and they are contrary to historical evidence. How could the PLO resort to such utterly fallacious arguments to support its agenda? The answer is simple, says Roger Carasso: "The Arabs learned their disinformation tactic from the Nazis: If you repeat the lie long enough, and loud enough, people will actually believe you. As a result, most people now believe there is something called the 'Palestinian' people, a total fabrication, complete with a phony history and a phony culture." Carasso concludes that "there is only one truth here, that there are 1.75 million people, a hodgepodge of Arabs and Turks, intentionally or maybe unwittingly, masquerading as a 'people,' and made into a 'people' by the PLO and many in the world community who relished attacking the Jews in yet another novel way."[149]

---

[145] Daniel Gordis, *The Promise of Israel: Why Its Seemingly Greatest Weakness Is Actually Its Greatest Strength* (Hoboken, NJ: John Wiley & Sons, 2012), p. 38, author's emphasis. Also, Stuart Arden, *Sense and Nonsense: Everything You Need to Know About the Arab-Israeli Conflict* (Jerusalem, Israel: Gefen Publishing House, 2013), p. 10.

[146] *The Palestine Post*, founded in 1932, was not renamed *The Jerusalem Post* until 1950.

[147] Yasser Arafat, quoted in Lawrence Solomon, "Playing Make-Believe over Gaza," in *The Financial Post*, August 7, 2014, posted at http://business.financialpost.com/fp-comment/lawrence-solomon-playing-make-believe-over-gaza.

[148] Zuheir Muhsin, quoted in the Dutch *Daily Trouw*, March, 1977.

[149] Roger David Carasso, "What's in a Name: The Western Palestinian Arabs," posted at http://www.carasso.com/israel/palestineterms.html. The real truth is that Yasir Arafat, whose real name was Rahman Abdel-Raouf Arafat al-Qudwa al-Husseini, was born to an Egyptian textile merchant and later became a member of the Egyptian Muslim Brotherhood. His claim to being a "refugee" and a "Palestinian" was a total fraud.

Based on these historical facts and arguments, former Israeli Prime Minister Golda Meir said, "There were no such thing as Palestinians. When was there an independent Palestinian people with a Palestinian state? It was either southern Syria before the First World War, and then it was a Palestine including Jordan. It was not as though there was a Palestinian people in Palestine considering itself as a Palestinian people and we came and threw them out and took their country away from them. They did not exist."[150] By the terms of the Balfour Declaration and the subsequent League of Nations Covenant for Palestine and its British Mandate, the "occupied territory," then, is not—and has never been—the Israeli-occupied West Bank. Instead, it is the Arab-occupied West Bank and the Hashemite-occupied Transjordan.

The Real Truth about Muslim National Traditions

Ironically, virtually all of the charges made by the Palestinian Arabs and their allies in the West are far more applicable to the Palestinian Arabs and the Muslim nations that support them than they are to Israel. Efrain Karsh lists the many strategies which Arab and Muslim nations regularly employ to enforce their ideologies and to exercise virtually total dominance over their citizens:

1) *"Religious intolerance:* Muslims historically viewed themselves as distinct from, and superior to, all others living under Muslim rule, known as 'dhimmis.' . . . Christians, Jews, and Baha'is remain second-class citizens throughout the Arab/Muslim world."

2) *"Ethnic inequality:* Arabs, Turks and Iranians continue to treat long-converted [to Islam] populations that retained their language, culture and social customs, as inferior."

3) *"Racism:* The Middle East has become the foremost purveyor of anti-Semitic incitement in the world. . . . Likewise, Africans of sub-Saharan descent are held in deep contempt, a vestige of the region's historic role as epicenter of the international slave trade."

4) *"Gender discrimination:* Legal and social discrimination against women is pervasive throughout the Arab-Islamic world."

5) *"Slavery:* The Arabic-speaking countries remain the world's foremost refuge of slavery, from child and sex trafficking in Saudi Arabia and the Gulf states to actual chattel slavery in Sudan and Mauritania."[151]

---

[150] Golda Meir, quoted in the *Washington Post* (June 16, 1969).
[151] The Arabic word *abeed* means "slave," but it is usually used as an insult to Africans of sub-Saharan, non-Muslim descent.

6) *"Political Oppression:* Many Middle Eastern regimes are little more than elaborate repressive systems aimed at perpetuating apartheid-style domination by a small minority: Alawites in Syria . . . the Saudi royal family; the Hashemite dynasty in Jordan."[152]

Political Corruption

The Palestinian Arabs continue to be almost hopelessly bellicose primarily because they are dominated—as they have always been—by shamelessly corrupt political leaders who transfer multiplied millions, if not billions, of dollars of Western "humanitarian aid" into private European bank accounts while keeping their people in abject poverty.[153] If these "foreign aid" and "relief" efforts of Western nations alone had been directed to the Palestinian Arab populace rather than to its political leaders, the people could be secure and comfortable. If the oil-rich Arab nations who purport to support the "Palestinians" had simply given to the Palestinian Arab people the billions of dollars that they continually distribute to terrorist organizations, the status and situation of those people would be elevated exponentially, easing a great deal of their frustration and anger and eliminating one of their supposed motivations for terrorism. To be sure, Muslim autocrats and Palestinian Arab leaders do not have a monopoly on world political corruption; however, there has been and continues to be a tradition within their ranks that makes too few profoundly wealthy and powerful and too many poor and exploited.[154] The very existence of such conditions foment anger and frustration which is vented, not against the corrupt Palestinian Arab leaders, but against the easiest target available—in this case, the perennial scapegoat of history, the Jewish people.

---

[152] Karsh, http://www.jpost.com/Opinion/Op-Ed-Contributors/The-Middle-Easts-real-apartheid.

[153] Stuart Arden describes Yasser Arafat's widow Suha's lifestyle: "[S]he wandered about at Gucci, Chanel, Yves St. Laurent, Christian Dior, and other 'thrift(less) shops' she frequents in Paris on the millions of dollars she received from Yasser Arafat's secret Swiss bank accounts. Meanwhile, the PA [Palestinian Authority] bilks European and American donor countries, allowing their leaders to live in luxury while many average citizens live in near squalor." Arden, p. 132. Aaron Manes observes that "reports of corruption have plagued the [Palestinian Authority] since its inception. The Palestinian Legislative Council launched several investigations, finding massive misappropriation of funds. The investigations found that PA money had been embezzled by PA leaders. . . . An independent audit of the 1997 budget could not account for $323 million." Aaron Mannes, *Profiles in Terror: The Guide to Middle East Terrorist Organizations* (Lanham, MD: Rowman & Littlefield Publishers, 2004), p. 294.

[154] The Palestinian Arab leaders have kept the Palestinian Arab people in poverty and squalor in order to foment their hatred for the Jews and to incite them to violence against Israel.

Comparing Sacred Scripture: Teachings of Peace, Teachings of War

A comparison of the teachings of the sacred writings of both Judaism and Islam produces some revealing truth. For the Jews, the *Torah* stipulates that no human being is ever to commit homicide (murder).[155] This commandment is so important that it is included in the Ten Words that were thundered by God himself when Israel gathered at Sinai. In Jewish thought, the commandment proscribing murder is considered to be inviolable and cannot be suspended even to save one's own life.[156] For Muslims, while the *Qur'an* also condemns murder, it also says that when Muslims are engaged in *jihad* (holy war), they are to "kill [the infidels] whenever you overtake them and expel them from wherever they have expelled you . . . if they fight you, then kill them."[157] Ultimately, radical Islam and many in mainstream Islam mandate three choices for non-Muslims, especially Jews and Christians: conversion to Islam, subjugation to Muslim rule and taxes, or death, because the *jihad* ("holy war") will continue until all who resist are killed.[158] The killing in *jihad* is not limited to self-defense: the holy war is a war of aggression against infidels in which even the innocent can be slaughtered with impunity.

For Jews, the *Torah* commands: "You shall not bear false witness."[159] This commandment is "a bulwark not only against trivial lying but especially against perjury in the court."[160] For Muslims, the *Qur'an* specifies not only their right but also their obligation to engage in prevarication and deception if by doing so they can advance the cause of Islam: "And they [the disbelievers] schemed, and Allah schemed [against them]: and Allah is the best of schemers."[161] The Arabic word for "scheme" (or plot) in this passage is *makara*, which literally means "deceit." There can be no doubt that "if Allah is supremely deceitful toward

---

155 Exodus 20:13.

156 Judaism teaches that all of the commandments in the Hebrew Scriptures can be suspended in order to save human life, including one's own life, except three of the Ten Commandments: the prohibitions against idolatry, murder, and adultery. If one is ordered upon penalty of death to break one of these commandments, he must accept martyrdom rather than violate the commandment. See Barry S. Kogan, *A Time to Be Born and a Time to Die: The Ethics of Choice* (Hawthorne, NY: Aldine De Gruyter, Inc., 1991), p. 123. The principle in Jewish law of *Pikuach Nefesh* (literally "saving of human life") even says that almost any negative commandment of the Torah may become inapplicable when a human life is at stake. See Joseph Telushkin, *The Book of Jewish Values* (New York: Bell Tower Publishing, 2000), pp. 100–105.

157 *Qur'an* 61:11.

158 *Qur'an* 9:29.

159 Exodus 20:16.

160 W. Sibley Towner, "Exodus 20:1–17, Exegetical Perspective," in *Feasting on the Word: Lent through Eastertide*, David Lyon Bartlett and Barbara Brown Taylor, eds. (Louisville, KY: Westminster John Knox Press, 2008), p. 79.

161 *Qur'an* 3:54.

unbelievers, then there is little basis for denying that Muslims are allowed to do the same."[162] Islam teaches that there are three types of deception when dealing with non-believers, *taqiyya* (sacred deception and dissimulation),[163] *kitman* (lying by omission), and *khodeh* (trickery and deceit). In addition, "*adarorah*, meaning 'the ends justify the means,' has become the Sunni version for permitting or commanding deceit in order to protect the faith [of Islam]."[164] If the cause of Islam can be advanced in any way, a Muslim is permitted to lie and is encouraged to do so, especially if he can "gain the trust of non-believers in order to draw out their vulnerability and defeat them."[165] This is why Islam says, "The prophet said, 'War is deceit.'"[166] The context from which this saying was drawn was likely the story of the incident when Muhammad's associates murdered Usayr ibn Zarim and thirty unarmed men with him after Muhammad had "guaranteed" them safe passage.[167] Abi Hamid Al Gahazali, founder of Sufism, the inner mystical dimension of Islam, goes even further with these arguments by saying, "You can lie if that will keep you from evil or if it will result in prosperity."[168]

For Jews, the *Torah* makes no exceptions when it says, "You shall not steal."[169] This means that the right of each individual to life, liberty, and property are protected by this commandment.[170] For Muslims, while the *Qur'an* prescribes stiff penalties for those who are caught in petty theft, it also permits theft from unbelievers who are perceived as warring against Islam, even giving

---

[162] "Lying (Taqiyya and Kitman)," posted at http://www.thereligionofpeace.com/quran/011-taqiyya.htm.

[163] The idea that deception and dissimulation could be "sacred" is inimical to both Judaism and Christianity; however, it is built into the Muslim faith and even the Arabic language. See Nonie Darwish, *The Devil We Don't Know: The Dark Side of Revolutions in the Middle East* (Hoboken, NJ: John Wiley & Sons, 2012), p. 60. Darwish says, "For the sake of protecting Mohammed and Islam, practically anything is allowed, and the individual Muslim is taught that protection of Islam is a sacred communal obligation that is more important than family, life, or happiness." This principle has also been used to undergird so-called "honor" killings (for which the Arabic term is *ghayra*) in which Muslims sometimes abuse and even kill their own relatives—including wives and children—with impunity in order to protect the "honor" of their families against perceived transgressions of Muslim traditions. For a comprehensive study of the Islamic foundations for such internecine violence see Daniel Akbari and Paul Tetreault, *Honor Killing: A Professional's Guide to Sexual Relations and Ghayra Violence from the Islamic Sources* (Bloomington, IN: AuthorHouse, 2014).

[164] Bill Siegel, *The Control Faction: Our Struggle to See the True Threat* (Lanham, MD: Hamilton Books, 2012), p. 27.

[165] Robert Spencer, *The Politically Incorrect Guide to Islam (and the Crusades)* (Washington, DC: Regnery Publishing, Inc., 2005), pp. 79–81.

[166] *Haddith, Bukhari* 42:269.

[167] Ibn Ishaq/Hisham, 981.

[168] Abi Hamid Al Gahazali, quoted in Mark A. Gabriel, *Islam and Terrorism* (Lake Mary, FL: Charisma Media, 2002), p. 95. Muslims are encouraged to lie in negotiations with a non-Muslim if it will bring them a profit.

[169] Exodus 20:15.

[170] Andrew Knowles, *The Bible Guide: An All-in-one Introduction to the Book of Books* (Oxford, UK: Lion Publishing, 2001), p. 54.

rules mandating the manner in which the spoils of war are to be divided.[171] This ruling easily extends to the positions of Muslim police who do not enforce laws against "thieves who steal from infidels," and it is extrapolated as a means of identifying "infidel business for theft and ransom."[172]

Considering the contrast of moral and ethical positions in the *Torah* and the *Qur'an*, one must wonder how anyone—journalist, politician, diplomat, or military commander—could ever trust radical and reactionary Muslims in any matter when their religion not only does not prohibit but also excuses and even commands murder, deception, and theft.

Turning the Tide of Antisemitic Anti-Zionism

The state of Israel has made many mistakes in its near seventy-year history, and it has suffered considerably for them. Since all human beings err, Jews should be held to no higher standard than anyone else, even though the prophets tended to hold "their own people up to higher moral standards than they [did] other people . . . because the Hebrews were introduced to a moral and religious code that made certain demands on them."[173] On the stage of world politics, however, Jews cannot be expected to lay down their lives so their enemies can bolster their self-worth and expand their power and resources. The murderous spirit that is determined to annihilate the Jews must not be allowed to triumph.

Now is the time for Christians to take the lead in helping to turn the tide of lies and deceptions that have become the staple of radical Muslim propagandists and Western media. Surely it is time to stop supporting individuals and movements which, with their distortions and outright prevarications, make it possible for people like the young Palestinians in Germany to express the views of most fundamentalist Muslims regarding Israel and Jews in general by saying outrageous things like, "The damned Jews should be burnt," and, "They should be slaughtered like pigs," and, "I would eradicate all Jews, shooting them into the sea and goodbye."[174] What insanity it is that anyone could mouth such abominable statements—and all in the name of God and religion!

---

171 *Qur'an* 8:41. Muhammad even promised his followers spoils, which were assets stolen from unbelievers (*Qur'an* 48:18–20).

172 Marvin W. Heyboer, *Journeys into the Heart and Heartland of Islam* (Pittsburgh, PA: Dorrance Publishing Co., 2009), p. 218.

173 Mordecai Schreiber, *The Man Who Knew God: Decoding Jeremiah* (Lanham, MD: Rowman & Littlefield Publishers, 2010), p. 141.

174 Günther Jikeli, *European Muslim Antisemitism: Why Young Urban Males Say They Don't Like Jews* (Bloomington, IN: Indiana University Press, 2015), p. 125.

A groundswell of support for the people and the nation of Israel must arise, especially among those who seek peace on earth.[175] It is time to recognize the bountiful oasis of peace-loving Jews in Israel that is surrounded by a desiccated desert of anger, hate, violence, terror, and war. Christians everywhere must come to the understanding that "what the anti-Zionists would obliterate is precisely the voice of the Torah—and with the Torah, God and Israel as well."[176] Ultimately, any plan to annihilate the Jews is at bottom a plan to neutralize, if not destroy, the God of the Jews. The promises of God to the descendants of Abraham are, however, secure, and nothing can prevent their fulfillment. The time has come for the world to admit that the Jewish people have suffered enough.[177] Those who recognize the righteous precepts of the God of Scripture must grant the Jews the blessings of freedom and security. It is time to stop both Holocaust deniers who "deny the Jews their deaths and their past" and anti-Zionists who "deny the Jews their lives and their future."[178]

The spirit of anti-Zionism, the new unholy garments of the ancient and enduring antisemitism, must be discarded. Of a truth, anti-Zionism's days are numbered, for when the Messiah comes, he will not establish his throne in New York, London, Rome, Athens, Geneva, Moscow, Tokyo, Bejing, Damascus, Istanbul, or Mecca. His universal dominion will be headquartered on Mount Zion in the city of Jerusalem, and from that foundation, he will extend peace like a river to all the inhabitants of Israel and from them to all the inhabitants of the earth.[179] It is time for songs of peace to echo around the world, for "peace sown by peacemakers brings a harvest of justice."[180] This is what YHWH, the God of Israel says of his holy nation and his holy land: "I will return to Zion and will dwell in the midst of Jerusalem. . . . Old men and old women will again sit in the streets of Jerusalem . . . and the streets of the city shall be filled with boys and girls playing in its streets."[181]

---

[175] Luke 2:14.
[176] David Patterson, *Anti-Semitism*, pp. 100–101.
[177] This is true for some Christians whose eschatological scenarios anticipate yet another "time of Jacob's trouble" (Jeremiah 30:7) that will result in the destruction of two-thirds of the Jewish population of the earth (Zechariah 13:8). Surely such prophecies have already been fulfilled enough to have been "filled full." At some point, an end must come to "restoration followed by destruction" in the prophetic pronouncements. Whatever the case, all Christians, like Father Abraham, should be interceding for mercy and against judgment!
[178] David Patterson, *Anti-Semitism*, p. 197.
[179] Isaiah 66:12.
[180] James 3:18.
[181] Zechariah 8:3–5.

CHAPTER 19

FOUNDATION OF PEACE
THE HOLY CITY AND THE HOLY LAND

From its beginning, Israel was designed by God to be a land of peace. This fact is clearly reflected in the name of Israel's capital city, Jerusalem, which is one of the oldest cities on the face of the earth.[1] Because of its name, ancient Jerusalem must have been focused on peace. Amazingly, the same ethos that characterized the Holy City then still thrives in the modern nation of Israel. The Hebrew word that is translated *Jerusalem* in Holy Scripture, יְרוּשָׁלַיִם (*Yerushalayim*), almost certainly means "people, house, or habitation of peace," with the first half of the word, יְרוּ (*Yeru*), meaning "men or people and hence house or habitation" and its second half, שָׁלַיִם (*shalayim*), meaning "peace." The focal point of the term *Jerusalem*, however, is the word *salem* (*shalem or shalayim*), which is the root of the Hebrew word שָׁלוֹם (*shalom*), meaning peace, not just as an absence of war, but in the sense of wholeness, completeness, health, and prosperity.

Yerushalayim was first used in Scripture in Joshua 10, where, according to a rabbinic *midrash*, the word is a combination of the name which Abraham gave to the site of the *Akedah* of Isaac, *YHWH-yireh* (God's personal name *YHWH* joined with the Hebrew word *yireh*, which means meaning "to see" or "to provide"), coupled with the name of the town "*Shalem*,"[2] where Melchizedek

---

[1] Eric H. Cline, *Jerusalem Besieged: From Ancient Canaan to Modern Israel* (Ann Arbor, MI: The University of Michigan Press, 2004), p. 161. Some scholars have suggested that Jerusalem may have been established as early as the fourth millennium BC. See David Wood, "My Place in the Sun," in *Interpreting Nature: The Emerging Field of Environmental Hermeneutics*, Forrest Clingerman, Brian Treanor, Martin Drenthen, and David Utsler, eds. (Bronx, NY: Fordham University Press, 2014), p. 293.

[2] Most English translations use the form *Salem* for the name of Melchizedek's town; however, the Hebrew text is *Shalem* (שָׁלֵם).

served as king and priest.[3] Wilhelm Gesenius maintained that the Hebrew word *Yerushalayim* can also take the meaning of "foundation of peace,"[4] an opinion that George Adam Smith[5] shares and that Harold Mare confirms: "The element *yeru* ('foundation') is seen in the form *Yeruel*,[6] meaning 'founded by God,' and *shalem*,[7] meaning 'peace.'"[8] Selah Merrill has also suggested that yet another alternative translation for the word *Yerushalayim* may be "the foundation of security."[9] Could it be that the real foundation of world peace and security is revealed in the very city where God chose to place his own name?[10] Doubtless, there will no peace on earth until peace comes to Jerusalem and the land of Israel.[11] Peace in the Holy Land is, therefore, the foundation of peace for the world. From the fact that the word *Jerusalem* has also been identified in rabbinic thought as one of the names of God,[12] it is certain, however, that Jerusalem is not like any other city on the earth.

Ironically, however, from the pages of the most ancient of recorded history to the headlines of today's newspapers, Jerusalem, the city of peace, has been the scene of ongoing violence, as a veritable cavalcade of princes, kings, megalomaniacs, despots, religious leaders, messianic pretenders, and zealots of different religious persuasions have vied for domination over this city. "The fact that Jerusalem may be the most contested piece of real estate in history," however,

---

[3] Dore Gold, *The Fight for Jerusalem: Radical Islam, the West, and the Future of the Holy City* (Washington, DC: Regnery Publishing, Inc., 2007), p. 45.

[4] Heinrich Friedrich Wilhelm Gesenius, *Gesenius' Hebrew and Chaldee Lexicon to the Old Testament Scriptures*, tr. Samuel Prideaux Tregelles (London, England: Samuel Bagster and Sons, 1847), p. 367. Gesenius says that the first part of the name *Jerusalem,* יְרוּ (*yeru*) comes from the root word יָרָה (*yarah*), which means "foundation."

[5] George Adam Smith, *Jerusalem: The Topography, Economics and History from the Earliest Times to A.D. 70* (Cambridge, UK: Cambridge University Press, 2013), vol. 1, p. 258.

[6] The form *yeruel* can be seen in 2 Chronicles 20:16.

[7] The Hebrew word *Shalem* first appears in Genesis 14:18.

[8] W. Harold Mare, *The Archaeology of the Jerusalem Area* (Eugene, OR: Wipf and Stock Publishers,1987), p. 20. Mare points to 1 Chronicles 20:16 and Job 38:6 for biblical instances where the form *yeruel* is used.

[9] Selah Merrill, "An Archaeological Visit to Jerusalem," in *The Biblical World*, vol. 14, no. 4, Oct., 1899, p. 270. Merrill observed that interpreting the word *Jerusalem* to mean "foundation of security" would be "singularly appropriate to the situation and history of the place" because "Jerusalem was always 'strong' [and] 'secure.'"

[10] 1 Kings 9:3; 11:36; 2 Chronicles 6:6; 7:16.

[11] Warren Wiersbe, *The Wiersbe Bible Commentary: Old Testament* (Colorado Springs, CO: David C. Cook Publishing, 2007), p. 818. Wiersbe says, "There can be no peace in this world until there is peace in Jerusalem, and there can be no peace in Jerusalem unless God's people obey this command and pray, 'Thy kingdom come.'"

[12] Joseph Albo, *Sefer Ha'Ikkarim: Book of Principles* (Philadelphia, PA: Jewish Publication Society of America, 1929), vol. 2, p. 28. Cf. Matthew 5:35: "The City of the Great King."

"makes the idealized notion of a 'city of peace' all the more compelling,"[13] says Sid Schwartz. It is not surprising, therefore, that Jerusalem—and, by extension, all of Israel—is the most prayed-for piece of real estate in the history of the world, with millions of Jews and Christians interceding for the its peace in obedience to God's explicit instructions: "Pray for the peace of Jerusalem. May all who love this city prosper. O Jerusalem, may there be peace within your walls and prosperity in your palaces."[14] Doubtless, Clinton McCann is right when he says that "the psalmist's invitation is at least implicit recognition of Jerusalem's turmoil, the world's turmoil."[15] Otherwise, there would be no need for anyone to pray for its peace. The words of the Psalm could well have been prophetic of the coming conflict over God's Holy City[16] and the need for intercession in behalf it is peace and security, for, in its history, Jerusalem "has been destroyed at least twice, besieged 23 times, attacked 52 times, and captured and recaptured 44 times."[17] It would be just like ha-Satan[18] to attempt to heap violence and war on God's foundation of peace in an effort to foil the Almighty's plan.

The Ideal and the Real

The sad and ironic history of the city of Jerusalem, wherein God's "foundation of peace" has been afflicted with continuing violence and war, has simply demonstrated the hard reality that the inhabitants of the restored nation of Israel and their capital city, Jerusalem, have continued to experience for nearly seven decades. While the vast majority of Israelis—and Jews around the world, for that matter—seek peace and tranquility in their lives, the dilemma for those living in the land of Israel is that of trying to balance their idealistic passion for peace with their practical need for safety, security, and self-defense. Peace is a central part of Jewish self-identity. In fact, "seeking peace is a basic Jewish and Israeli

---

[13] Sid Schwartz, *Judaism and Justice: The Jewish Passion to Repair the World* (Woodstock, VT: Jewish Lights Publishing, 2006), p. 68.

[14] Psalm 122:6–7.

[15] J. Clinton McCann, Jr., *A Theological Introduction to the Book of Psalms: The Psalms as Torah* (Nashville, TN: Abingdon Press, 1993), p. 154.

[16] Nehemiah 11:1, 18; Isaiah 52:1; Daniel 9:24; Matthew 27:53. The sobriquet *Holy City* was probably applied to Jerusalem shortly after the Babylonian captivity. See David Patterson, *Anti-Semitism and Its Metaphysical Origins* (Cambridge, UK: Cambridge University Press, 2015), p. 204.

[17] Eric Cline, "Jerusalem Besieged: 4,000 Years of Conflict in the City of Peace," *Archaeological Institute of America,* posted at https://www.archaeological.org/lectures/abstracts/9873.

[18] *HaSatan*, meaning "The Adversary," is the Hebrew term describing the "devil." This can be seen in Peter's statement, "Your *adversary*, the *devil*, prowls around like a roaring lion, seeking someone to devour" (1 Peter 5:8, emphasis added). Delitzsch translates the Greek for "adversary," ἀντίδικος (*antídikos*), as הַשָּׂטָן (*ha-Satan*).

ethos."[19] The Israelis, however, continually live with the harsh reality of being bordered by hostile neighbors whose ethos focuses on *jihad*, which, though it may, for the average Muslim, describe a personal spiritual struggle to overcome sin through obedience to the tenets of Islam,[20] nevertheless, means "holy war" for an increasingly significant percentage of Muslims, especially in the Middle East.[21]

The nation of Israel was restored in 1948 in order to provide a safe haven where Jews could live in peace and security and not be subject to the whims of the dominant forces that for centuries had heaped so much suffering on them and their ancestors. As Israel's rebirth unfolded, however, the Muslim Arabs immediately sought to obliterate the fledgling nation from the face of the earth. Unfortunately, that same objective has continued to dominate Muslim and Palestinian Arab communities since that time. Seemingly, Israel's quest for peace has not changed much since the time when King David exclaimed, "Too long my soul had its dwelling with those who hate peace. I am for peace, but when I speak, they are for war."[22]

It is a simple fact that one cannot seek peace and pursue it when one's intention is to effect the genocide of one's adversary. On the other hand, one can still be engaged in the pursuit of peace even when it is necessary to engage in counter-offensive military actions in order to ensure survival in the face of violence and terrorism. Of a truth, peace that is punctuated with violence is not really peace at all. Such is the dilemma that Israel has continued to face for the nearly seven decades of its existence. Lasting peace is attainable only when all parties to a conflict lay down their arms and pursue peace. With regard to the ongoing Israeli-Palestinian conflict and calls by world leaders for peace, Israeli

---

[19] Dalia Gavriely-Nuri, *Israeli Peace Discourse: A Cultural Approach to CDA* (Amsterdam, The Netherlands: John Benjamins Publishing Co., 2015), p. 4.

[20] Ian Richard Netton, *A Popular Dictionary of Islam* (New York: Routledge, 1992), p. 136. Netton says that "all Muslims are obliged to wage a spiritual jihad in the sense of striving against sin and sinful inclinations within themselves." See N. C. Asthana and Anjali Nirmal, *Urban Terrorism: Myths and Realities* (Jaipur, India: Aavishkar Publishers, 2009), p. 44. Asthana and Nirmal maintain that "the word 'jihad' means 'struggle' or 'striving' or to work for a noble cause with determination." Also, Reuven Firestone, *Jihad: The Origin of Holy War in Islam* (New York: Oxford University Press, 1999), pp. 16–18. Firestone gives an excellent discourse on *jihad* as personal struggle for good both internal and external to the individual.

[21] Various dictionaries define *jihad* as "holy war." *Random House Dictionary of the English Language* gives it as "a holy war undertaken as a sacred duty to Muslims." *Collins Cobuild English Language Dictionary* makes it "a holy war which Islam allows merely to fight against those who reject its teachings." *The American Heritage Dictionary of the English Language* calls it "A Moslem holy war against infidels." See David Perusek, *Between Jihad and McWorld: Voices of Social Justice* (Cambridge, UK: Cambridge University Press, 2010), p. 146.

[22] Psalm 120:6–7.

Prime Minister Benjamin Netanyahu spoke an incontrovertible truth when he said, "If Palestine were to lay down their guns tomorrow, there would be no war. If Israel were to lay down theirs, there would be no Israel."[23]

While the Israelis pursued peace, "buses were still exploding and shopping centers and café shops were no longer safe,"[24] prompting Israel to respond militarily to punish the actions and practically by building a wall to deny suicide bombers access to Israel. While the Israelis pursued peace, Scud missiles rained down upon their population centers from Iraq, and Israel's gestures of restraint accomplished nothing towards bringing peace to the land. While the Israelis pursued peace, Hezbollah launched mortars into northern Israel, prompting Israel to respond in kind and even to invade southern Lebanon in an effort to root out the terrorists' launching devices. While the Israelis pursued peace, thousands of missiles launched from Gaza by Hamas terrorists landed in southern Israel, prompting Israel to launch military counterattacks in order to protect its citizens.

The "Land for Peace" Myth

For decades, Israel has been bombarded with "land-for-peace" demands not only from the Palestinian Arabs and their allies but also from nations around the world, including Israel's own Western allies. This has been especially true since Israel regained control of the "West Bank" from the Jordanians during the Six-Day War.[25] It is quite ironic, therefore, that the international "land-for-peace" clamor which has incessantly demanded that Israel surrender the "occupied territory" was not even a faint whisper when Jordan's King Abdullah attacked the newly constituted nation of Israel in 1948 and annexed the West Bank.[26] It was under the Jordanian regime, therefore, that the West Bank became "occupied territory." The subsequent Israeli action during the Six-Day War actually liberated the "occupied territory" and restored it to Israel to

---

[23] Benjamin Netanyahu in a speech at the Knesset, 2006, quoted in "Olmert: We Will Continue to Pursue Hisbullah Leaders" in *The Globes*, August 14, 2006, posted at http://www.globes.co.il/en/article-1000122795.

[24] Robert L. Rothstein, *The Israeli-Palestinian Peace Process* (Brighton, UK: Sussex Academic Press, 2002), p. 119.

[25] Jordan had "occupied" the West Bank for nineteen years after its invasion of the territory in 1948.

[26] In fact, the only nations that objected to Abdullah's annexation of the territory of the West Bank to Jordan and his proclamation of himself as "king of united Palestine" were other Arab states. The West was curiously silent in the face of this aggression. See "Jerusalem; Keystone of an Arab-Israeli Settlement," in *Legislative and Special Analyses* (1969), Issue 13, p. 28. Also, Ronen Yitzhak, *Abdullah Al-Tall, Arab Legion Officer: Arab Nationalism and Opposition to the Hashemite Regime* (Eastbourne, UK: Susses Academic Press, 2012), p. 95.

which it had belonged since the League of Nations Covenant in 1922 and certainly since United Nations Resolution 181 in 1947. Since there was no international outrage when Abdullah invaded Israel and annexed the West Bank and yet there has been unrelenting pressure on Israel to surrender the West Bank to the Palestinian Arabs, one can only conclude that land-for-peace demands are reserved only for Israel and do not apply to Arab Muslim nations.

The truth is that Israel has already experienced up close and personal the results of a "land-for-peace" gesture. This occurred when Israel unilaterally withdrew from Gaza in 2005, displacing 8,000 of its own citizens, some of whom were literally dragged from their homes and synagogues by Israeli Defense Forces personnel in order to accommodate the "land-for-peace" effort.[27] The newly constituted "nation" almost instantly became a haven for the Palestinian Arab terrorist organization Hamas when it brutally seized control of Gaza, slaughtering innocent Arab civilians in the process. The result? It certainly was not peace, for Hamas was simply positioned directly on Israel's border from which it could more effectively stage its *jihad* against the Jewish nation by moving missile launchers much nearer to Israel's population centers and by implementing a diabolical plan for gaining direct, surreptitious access to Israel through a labyrinth of tunnels that it excavated under the new Israel-Gaza border! So, even in a "land-for-peace" initiative that displaced Israelis and enfranchised terrorists, there was no peace to be gained when dealing with the Muslim terrorist organization, the Palestine Liberation Organization, which in 1994 morphed into the more politically correct Palestinian Authority!

The Palestinian Christian Dilemma

Perhaps the most often overlooked tragedy in the unfolding Muslim Palestinian conflict with Israel is the dilemma of Palestinian Christians. While Palestinian Christians who live in Israel have had freedom of religion, those who live in the West Bank and Gaza have found that virtually all of their freedoms have been restricted, if not totally denied—and especially so in Gaza—after Israel ceded control of those areas to the Palestinian Authority.[28] Additionally,

---

[27] Gregory Morgan, "Gaza Strip Disengagement," in *The Encyclopedia of the Arab-Israeli Conflict: A Political, Social, and Military History*, Spencer C. Tucker, ed. (Santa Barbara, CA: ABC-CLIO, Inc., 2008), p. 385.

[28] Michael Prior, "Holy Places, Unholy Domination: The Scramble for Jerusalem," in *My Jerusalem: Essays, Reminiscences, and Poems*, Salma Khadra Jayyusi and Safar Ishaq Ansari, eds. (Northampton, MA: Olive Branch Press, 2005), p. 84. Prior reports that in 2005, some 114,000 Palestinian Christians lived in Israel, while 50,352 lived in the "Occupied Territories" of the West Bank and Gaza.

Palestinian Christians have suffered from the inconveniences[29] that are inevitable consequences of Israel's exercise of control over Judea and Samaria which has been driven by its responsibility to provide for the security of its citizens.[30]

Nowhere is the Palestinian Christian dilemma more clearly manifest than in Bethlehem, the birthplace of Jesus. In the shadow of the city of Jerusalem, the town of Bethlehem has long been "a major center for Palestinian Christianity" because "it contains one of Palestine's most significant Christian churches and because it has long constituted a major site of Christian pilgrimage."[31] Because Palestinian Christians are, indeed, Christians, they can connect their faith and experience with the earliest forays of Jewish Christian missionaries into the non-Jewish world population, beginning, as Jesus instructed them, at Jerusalem and continuing through Judea and Samaria into the "remotest part of the earth."[32] Munib Younan speaks for this embattled people when he says, "We believe that we represent the continuity of the Old Testament and New Testament peoples' existence on the land. This is not merely an emotional attachment, but one that has geographical, historical, traditional, cultural, and social, as well as spiritual roots. We are tied to the land as the land belongs to us." Younan probably expresses the sentiments of a significant portion of the Palestinian Christian community when he says, "We will exist and coexist [with the Jews] as long as the land is also our land of milk and honey."[33] For Palestinian Christians, therefore, "the security of Israel is interdependent with the issues of justice in the land and freedom for Palestinians."[34]

Palestinian Christians do, indeed, have a much stronger reason for claiming a right to live in the land of Israel than Muslims do, for their

---

[29] Prominent among these often embarrassing and demeaning inconveniences is the Israeli West Bank Barrier which, in effect, has walled off those who live in the area. While this barrier has effectively reduced the wave of suicide bombings and other terrorist attacks in Israel by 90%, the inconvenience it has imposed upon the residents of the West Bank has been considerable and has elicited much negative response, including from Palestinian Christians.

[30] Reza Aslan, *Muslims and Jews in America: Commonalities, Contentions, and Complexities* (New York: Palgrave Macmillan, 2011), p. 1. With regard to the security fence, Aslan says, "For Jewish Israelis, the separation is necessary to keep Israel's citizens safe from Palestinian terrorists. For Muslim and Christian Palestinians, the divide is merely the most physical manifestation of what they view as Israel's policy of ethnic and religious segregation."

[31] Philip Mattar, *Encyclopedia of the Palestinians* (New York: Facts on File, Inc., 2000), p. 101.

[32] Acts 1:8.

[33] Munib Younan, *Witnessing for Peace: In Jerusalem and the World* (Minneapolis, MN: Augsburg Fortress Press, 2003), p. 64.

[34] Younan, p. 64.

lineal heritage in the land could exceed all Muslim claims by as much as eight centuries.[35] Unfortunately, in efforts to establish historical connections to the land in which they live, some within the larger ranks of Palestinian Christians have resorted to a revisionist approach to both Christian theology and church history that invokes elements of the heresy of supersessionism and is, therefore, inherently antisemitic.[36] A new Palestinian form of South American liberation theology, which some have called "Marxized Christianity,"[37] has revived the Christian supersessionism and triumphalism that the Holocaust and Vatican II drove underground. "Now it's back," says Melanie Phillips, "kick-started by Palestinian Christian liberation theology, which states falsely that the Palestinian Arabs were the original possessors of the land of Israel."[38]

One such effort that supports Palestinian Christian liberation theology has been advanced by Bethlehem Bible College, which hosts a biennial "Christ at the Checkpoint Conference" that is designed to seek "justice" for Palestinian Christians by advancing such revisionist ideas. The name of the college's conference, "as well as [its] logo—which depicts a church behind the security barrier built by Israel to prevent suicide bombers from targeting Israeli civilians—demonstrates the focus of these meetings," says Tricia Miller.[39] Though the college asserts its commitment "to the great truths and abiding fundamentals of the Christian faith,"[40] it simply ignores or distorts inconvenient theological truths that are set forth incontrovertibly in Holy Scripture. Amazingly, some leaders of the movement that supports this agenda boldly proclaim that

---

[35] Michael Kohn, *Israel & the Palestinian Territories* (Footscray, Australia: Lonely Planet Publications, 2007), p. 43. Kohn points out that while some Muslim Palestinians "argue that they arrived in Jerusalem with Caliph Omar, which would mean they have been on the land for 1400 years," at the same time, "Palestinian Christians claim to be the descendants of the first Christians—those that guided Queen Helena on her tour of the Holy Land in the 5th century," which, if true, would have placed them in the land hundreds of years before any Muslims arrived.

[36] Salim J. Munayer, "Reconciliation as a Christian Response," in *Christians and the Middle East Conflict*, Paul S. Rowe, John H. A. Dyck, and Jens Zimmermann, eds., (New York: Routledge, 2014), p. 17. Munayer points out that within the Palestinian Christian community "attitudes towards replacement theology vary greatly"; however, for Palestinian Christians, supersessionism "tends to be a largely theological and non-political issue."

[37] David Horowitz, *The Professors: The 101 Most Dangerous Academics in America* (Washington, DC: Regnery Publishing, 2006), p. 143.

[38] Melanie Phillips, *The World Turned Upside Down: The Global Battle Over God, Truth, and Power* (New York: Encounter Books, 2010), p. 379. Phillips quotes Riah Abu El-Assal, former Anglican bishop of Jerusalem, as claiming that Palestinian Christians "are the true Israel," and then adding, "no-one can deny me the right to inherit the promises, and, after all, the promises were first given to Abraham and Abraham is never spoken of in the Bible as a Jew. . . . He is the father of the faithful."

[39] Tricia Miller, *Jews and Anti-Judaism in Esther and the Church* (Cambridge, UK: James Clarke & Co., 2015), p. 198.

[40] Miller, p. 198.

"if Jesus lived in Bethlehem today, he would have to go through the checkpoints just like the Palestinians do."[41] Others even promote a Palestinian version of supersessionism in which it is said that "Palestinians replace Jews as the indigenous people of the Holy Land" and that "Jesus and the early Christians were all Palestinians."[42] Aside from being utterly fallacious and lacking both historical and scriptural support, such arguments are rife with anti-Judaism and antisemitism, both of which are inimical to the faith of Jesus and the apostles, all of whom were Jews and citizens of Israel.

Whether subtle or blatant, supersessionism flies in the face of the Apostolic Scriptures which affirm that Jesus[43] and all of the apostles were Jews,[44] not Arabs or Canaanites. It is a simple fact of history that earliest Christianity was exclusively Jewish—indeed, one of the many Judaisms or sects of Judaism that existed in the first century of the Common Era. There were no non-Jews in earliest Jewish community that recognized Jesus as Messiah. This is clear from the specific instructions that Jesus gave to his disciples: "Do not go in the way of the Gentiles, and do not enter any city of the Samaritans; but rather go to the lost sheep of the house of Israel."[45] It is further confirmed by the fact that Jesus initially refused to respond to a "Canaanite" woman who had petitioned him to exorcise a demon from her daughter, replying to his disciples when they questioned his actions, "I was sent only to the lost sheep of the house of Israel,"[46] and answering the woman, "It is not right to take the children's bread and toss it to the dogs."[47]

---

41 Miller, p. 198. The fact is that since Jesus was—and still is—a Jew, he would simply go through the checkpoints like the Israelis do!

42 Miller, p. 198.

43 Hebrews 7:14.

44 Mike Liles, Jr., *Christian Faith in Contemporary Society: The Framework for Belief* (Lincoln, NE: iUniverse, 2005), p. 366. Liles notes the fact that "Jesus' apostles and the leaders of the early Christian Church were all ethnically Jewish," though he also observes correctly that "within a few centuries, indeed even decades, Jewish Christian leadership of the Christian Church all but vanished." See also Cecil E. Sherman, *Formations Commentary: Luke–Acts* (Macon, GA: Smyth & Helwys Publishing, 2006), p. 174. Sherman notes that "all the disciples were Jews. Because they were Jews, they were expected to have the loyalties, traditions, patriotism that goes with being a good Jew. That meant that when the Council (the Sanhedrin) commanded them to do something, they obeyed." This statement is categorically true in light of Jesus' instruction to his disciples: "The teachers of the law and the Pharisees sit in Moses' seat. So you must be careful to do everything they tell you" (Matthew 23:2–3, NIV).

45 Matthew 10:6, NIV.

46 Matthew 15:24, NIV.

47 Matthew 15:26, NIV. Jesus used the term *dogs* that was then commonly used by Jews to describe Gentiles. See Cynthia A. Jarvis and E. Elizabeth Johnson, *Feasting on the Gospels—Mark* (Louisville, KY: Westminster John Knox Press, 2014), p. 209. This incident proves that Jesus and his disciples were not "Canaanites."

Coupled with Jesus' foray into Galilee of the Gentiles[48] where he delivered a demon-possessed Gadarene,[49] the Master's ultimate response to the Canaanite woman's faith wherein he delivered her daughter, was, no doubt, predictive of the fact that the mission of his community would eventually include the non-Jews of the world. Indeed, it had to do so in order to fulfill God's promise to Abraham: "In your offspring all the nations of the earth will be blessed."[50] It was not until after his resurrection, however, that Jesus commanded his disciples to herald the gospel of the kingdom into all the world.[51] The Christian Scriptures also affirm that there were no non-Jews in the church until some ten years after Jesus' resurrection when Peter was commissioned by the Holy Spirit to visit the household of Cornelius in Caesarea Maritima.[52] Even then, the apostle could be compelled to undertake that mission only after having received divine instructions in a vision that was set in the context of Jewish kosher laws.[53] Saying that Jesus and his apostles were Arabs or Canaanites is not only absurd; it is also highly antisemitic.

The final truth is that if Palestinian Christians and their supporters in mainstream Protestant Christianity, as well as some in Evangelical circles, actually believe that the resurrected Jesus will ultimately return to earth, then they must get used to the idea that when he returns, he will not be a cosmic Christ or a universal man. Instead, he will still be the same Jew that he was when he ascended into heaven.[54] This truth was confirmed unequivocally and unambiguously in Peter's Pentecost sermon, in which he said that because King David knew that "God had sworn to him with an oath to seat one of his descendants on his throne, he looked ahead and spoke of the resurrection of the Messiah, that he was neither abandoned in Hades, nor did his flesh suffer decay."[55] Christian Scripture proves that Jesus was born to a Jewish mother,[56] lived his life as a Jew,[57]

---

48 Isaiah 9:1 speaks of an area "beyond Jordan, in Galilee of the Gentiles." This same term is used in Matthew 4:15, where it describes the territory east of the Jordan River, which included eight of the ten cities of the Decapolis (Greek for "Ten Cities") in what is now Jordan and Syria. (The other two cities of the Decapolis, Scythopolis [Beit-Shean] and Hippos, were in Israel.) Gadara, the town and territory where the demoniac whom Jesus delivered lived, was also included in the area of "Galilee of the Gentiles."
49 Mark 5:1-10.
50 Genesis 22:18.
51 Acts 1:8.
52 Luke 10:1–31.
53 Acts 10:14.
54 Acts 1:11. The two angels who witnessed Jesus' ascension assured the disciples, "This same Jesus . . . will come back in the same way you have seen him go into heaven." Jesus was a Jew, and he never changed his ethnicity. Since Jesus ascended in a glorified Judean body, he will return in the same body.
55 Acts 2:30–31.
56 Matthew 2:2.
57 John 4:9.

died as a Jew,[58] was resurrected as a Jew,[59] ascended into heaven as a Jew,[60] is seated at God's right hand as a Jew,[61] and will also return as a Jew.[62] Any attempt to make Jesus the cosmic Christ[63] or universal man[64] instead of the Jewish Jesus, or to ascribe to him any ethnicity except his inherent Jewishness, perpetuates historical Christian anti-Judaism and mirrors Nazi antisemitism.[65]

Attempts to disconnect Jesus and his apostles from their Jewish families and the Jewish milieu in which they lived or to wrench their message from the matrix of biblical and Second Temple Judaism from which it emerged diminish the credibility of any who engage in such efforts, including Palestinian Christians. The connection of many Palestinian Christians with their Arab heritage has, therefore, created a dilemma for them. Kathleen Christison says that "in a milieu so strongly perceived by the non-Arab world to be Islamic and therefore alien, Arab Christians have always been the poor relatives of Western Christianity. . . . Western Christians, if they know of their Arab co-religionists at all, are unsympathetic to this unique theological and national dilemma."[66]

It is a sad twist of history that Arab intransigence obviated the opportunity for the League of Nations Covenant and Mandate for Palestine to produce a homeland not only for the Jews but also for both Christian and Muslim Palestinians, especially the Christians. "That a 'national home' materialized for the Jewish inhabitants of Palestine is an unfortunate consequence of a mandate that had as its original aim to enable the inhabitants of the lands once ruled by the

---

[58] Luke 23:38.

[59] Romans 1:2–3.

[60] Acts 2:34.

[61] Hebrews 7:14–17.

[62] Acts 1:11.

[63] John R. Levison and Priscilla Pope-Levison, "The New Contextual Christologies: Liberation and Inculturation," in *Global Dictionary of Theology: A Resource for the Worldwide Church*, William A. Dyrness and Veli-Matti Kärkkäinen, eds. (Downers Grove, IL: InterVarsity Press, 2008), p. 185. The Levisons maintain that Jesus is manifest as the cosmic Christ across ethnic lines and in all of the world's major religions.

[64] Patrick Carnegie Simpson, *The Fact of Christ: A Series of Lectures* (Grand Rapids, MI: Fleming H. Revell Co, 1901), p. 51. In an effort to establish the universal appeal of Jesus, Simpson has magnanimously, but wrongly, said that Jesus "transcends all ethnic limitations and divisions."

[65] Nigel Leaves, "Who Do You Say that I Am? Preaching Jesus Today," in *Wisdom and Imagination: Religious Progressives and the Search for Meaning*, Rex A. E. Hunt and Gregory C. Jenks, eds. (Eugene, OR: Wipf and Stock Publishers, 2014), p. 126. Leaves discusses the dangers of denying the Jewishness of Jesus by pointing out that in pre-World War II Germany "pastors, bishops, professors of theology, religion teachers, and laity" advanced a "perverted scholarship, that denied the Jewishness of Jesus and falsely promoted his Aryan roots, [which] laid the foundations for anti-Semitism that was a short-step away from countenancing the horrors of the concentration camp."

[66] Kathleen Christison, "Dilemmas of Arab Christianity," *Journal of Palestinian Studies* vol. 22, no. 1 (Autumn 1992), pp. 117–119.

Ottoman Empire one day to 'stand by themselves.'"[67] Will Stalder observes that when the British "endeavored to establish a home for both peoples . . . the nature of that home was unsatisfactory in the eyes of the 'non-Jewish communities of Palestine' and was the cause of much opposition from the land's Arab inhabitants."[68] Benny Morris points out that a settlement of the League of Nations Covenant for Palestine and its British Mandate that would have been satisfactory to the Palestinian Arabs at the time was virtually precluded by the fact that most of the Arabs had supported the Ottoman Empire in World War I. Because these Arabs had aligned themselves against the Christian Allied powers that were led by Britain, the British were not inclined to help them. "At the same time," he observes, neither a "Palestinian Arab national movement nor any separate Palestinian Arab national consciousness"[69] existed. The self-identity preferred by Arab Palestinians of the time was that of Arabs, not Palestinians.

In reality, Palestinian Christians have been caught in a no-man's-land, "squeezed by Israel's crippling military blockage of the West Bank and the rise of Muslim fundamentalism."[70] Now, "in Bethlehem, the once-prosperous hub of Palestinian Christian life, [Christians] no longer represent a majority [of the population]."[71] Tom Doyle notes that "Palestinian Christians are already suffering under Hamas rule. And if a Palestinian State becomes a reality, it will only get worse. Religious freedom will be nonexistent."[72] Then, he observes that "this is vastly different [from] what the Palestinians have experienced with Israel's government. The Israelis have destroyed no mosques since 1948," and they have destroyed no Christian churches. In reality, Israel is the only nation in the Middle East that truly protects Christians and allows them to coexist in peace and security alongside the majority population.[73] Leaders in most

---

[67] This provision was a key declaration of the original League of Nations Covenant with Palestine, Article 22. See Will Stalder, *Palestinian Christians and the Old Testament History, Hermeneutics, and Ideology* (Minneapolis, MN: Augsburg Fortress Press, 2015), pp. 145–146.

[68] Stalder, p. 146.

[69] Benny Morris, *1948: A History of the First Arab-Israeli War* (New Haven, CT: Yale University Press, 2008), p. 10.

[70] Mat Spetalnick, "War-Weary Christians Seek Escape from Holy Land," *Reuters News Service*, 12/17/2003, posted at http://www.unitedjerusalem.org/index2.asp?id=384317&Date=12/25/2003.

[71] Spetalnick, "War-Weary."

[72] Tom Doyle, *Two Nations Under God: Why You Should Care about Israel* (Nashville, TN: B&H Publishing Group, 2004), pp. 145–146.

[73] To affirm this statement, one only has to recall the unrelenting Muslim Brotherhood violence against Coptic Christians in Egypt, the rape, torture, enslavement, and slaughter of Iraqi Christians by ISIS, the fate of Syrian Christians caught between ISIS and Bashar al-Assad's vicious regime, and the total abuse, debasement, and violence that is constantly experienced by Christians in Pakistan.

Muslim nations give lip service to Christian religious freedom; however, Christians who live in these societies are always second-class citizens, for they remain vulnerable to the whims of autocratic leaders, and they periodically experience violence, rape, murder, and the destruction of their properties, including their churches and schools.[74]

A few Palestinian Christians have come to understand the right relationship that they should have with the Jewish people as co-heirs of God's promises to Abraham. These brave and visionary believers have begun to work toward rapprochement with the Jewish community by engaging in dialogue and striving for mutually supportive relationships with Jews who love peace and want to share it and who understand human suffering and wish to help alleviate it within the Palestinian Christian community. Those Palestinian Christians who have made such efforts have been roundly criticized by other Christians and have been threatened with significant violence by Muslim Arab Palestinians. Efforts toward cooperation between these Palestinian Christians and Jews represent small beginnings, but they could well have significant short-term and long-term consequences. It would only be fitting if two parallel streams of faith in the God of Scripture, Christians and Jews, could demonstrate to the rest of the Arab and Muslim world—as well as to the antisemitic anti-Zionists—that the family of Abraham can have peace among themselves when they fully demonstrate once and for all Abraham's unequivocal faith in God and his magnanimous deference toward all. Only time will tell.

Peace and Justice

When King David recorded the divine injunction to "pray for the peace of Jerusalem," he also said, "May there be peace within your walls and security within your citadels."[75] The commitment to pray for peace, however, "is not

---

[74] Doyle, p. 146. In fact, even after the Six-Day War wrested control of East Jerusalem from the Jordanians, Israel continued to allow Jordanian Muslims to oversee the Al-Aqsa Mosque and the Dome of the Rock that were built on the ruins of the ancient Jewish Temple complex by Caliph Abd al-Malik in the late seventh century AD. This was quite an amazing Jewish gesture for peace considering the fact that when Jordan seized control of the West Bank and much of Jerusalem in 1948, its armies looted and destroyed 58 synagogues, ransacked Jewish cemetery on the Mount of Olives where Jews had buried their dead for more than two millennia, and then, for nineteen years, denied all Jews access to their holiest shrine, the Western Wall of the Temple Mount. The grace and mercy that the Israeli government has shown in its efforts to promote peace and religious freedom even in the face of the cynical banality of religious bigotry that has been—and is still being—directed against its citizens by the Muslim authorities has been, and continues to be, simply incredible!

[75] Psalm 122:7, NIV.

facile optimism nor mere wishful thinking."[76] In reality, it is "eschatological," for when the Psalmist speaks of entering Jerusalem, he "*really does* mean to enter a new world."[77] His speaking of living for God's sake[78] and for the sake of others[79] is a call "to experience, embody, and extend the justice God intends for the world."[80] The prophets of Israel, says Paul Steinberg, "place the welfare of Israel at the epicenter of the struggle for peace. That peace is not simply geographical, but rather peace for all peoples. . . . In praying for the security of Israel, we pray, too, for morality and peace everywhere."[81] Jerusalem is the foundation of peace!

The Psalmist also made a profound declaration when he said, "Shun evil and do good: seek peace and pursue it."[82] One rabbinic *midrash* interprets this command to mean that the believer is to seek peace in his own place and then pursue it everywhere else.[83] It is not enough to seek peace only in one's family or community or in one's small personal sphere of influence. *Shalom bayit* (peace in the home)[84] and peace in one's community are only the beginning of the peace continuum. One must also pursue peace among all people. "Wishing for peace will not get the job done. Nor will thinking good thoughts. Judaism's call is to dedicated action, the tireless pursuit of peace."[85] Interestingly, the only other passage in the Hebrew Scriptures that issues the imperative *pursue* is Deuteronomy 16:20, which says, "Justice, justice, you shall pursue, so that you may thrive and occupy the land that the LORD your God is giving you."[86] Sid Schwartz expands on the connection between the two *Tanakh* passages that employ the imperative *pursue*: "It is interesting that the challenge, 'pursue it [peace],' added as a device to underscore the imperative ['seek peace'], is also used to emphasize the importance of pursuing justice as in 'Justice, justice shall you pursue.'"[87] From the parallel of these two passages that command Israel—and, indeed, the world—to pursue peace and justice, it is clear that there

---

[76] McCann, Jr., p. 154.
[77] McCann, Jr., p. 154.
[78] Psalm 120:9.
[79] Psalm 120:8.
[80] McCann, Jr., p. 154.
[81] Paul Steinberg, *Celebrating the Jewish Year: The Spring and Summer Holidays: Passover, The Omer, Shavuot, Tisha b'Av*, Janet Greenstein Potter, ed. (Philadelphia, PA: The Jewish Publication Society, 2009), p. 117.
[82] Psalm 34:15.
[83] *Midrash* Leviticus *Rabbah* 9:9.
[84] For an extensive discussion of *shalom bayit*, see John D. Garr, *Feminine by Design: The God-Fashioned Woman* (Atlanta, GA: Golden Key Press, 2014), pp. 306–308.
[85] Schwartz, p. 68.
[86] Deuteronomy 16:20, TNK.
[87] Schwartz, p. 68.

can be no peace in the absence of justice. Because of the words of the Torah, the Jewish people remember that their rightful claim to "live in and occupy" the land God has given them is predicated on their pursuit of justice. "When you pursue justice," God says, "you will occupy the land I am giving you."

The pursuit of both justice and peace characterized Abraham's life. The primary reason that God gave for choosing Abraham was this: "I know him, that he will command his children . . . *to do justice* and judgment, so that the LORD may bring upon Abraham what he has spoken about him."[88] Abraham's understanding of the dynamics of justice prompted God to say of him, "Abraham obeyed me and kept my charge, my commandments, my statutes, and my instructions."[89] Since Abraham knew that God's judgment is always tempered with mercy,[90] he also balanced his own righteous conformity to God's commandments with a strong sense of mercy and grace. Doing justice while loving mercy is what the prophet Micah described as "walking humbly with God."[91] Jewish tradition speaks of the balance of justice and mercy as a quality of the Divine, pointing out that the most sacred name of God, the Tetragrammaton, specifically "symbolizes the attribute of Mercy, and its obverse, the attribute of Judgment."[92]

Abraham epitomized both of these virtues as he obeyed God's command, "Walk before me and be perfect."[93] He proved his sense of justice by his instant response to divine commands,[94] but he also demonstrated true justice tempered with mercy through the amazing deference that he

---

[88] Genesis 18:19, emphasis added.

[89] Genesis 26:5.

[90] Ronald L. Eisenberg, *What the Rabbis Said: 250 Topics from the Talmud* (Santa Barbara, CA: ABC-CLIO, 2010), p. 11. Eisenberg says, "God's strict judgment is always tempered by Divine mercy. Indeed, the Talmud relates that God prays that 'My mercy may suppress My anger,' so that when forced to punish His children (the Israelites), His mercy will make Him 'stop short of the limit of strict justice'" (*Berachot* 7a).

[91] Micah 6:8.

[92] Jacob Culi, Isaac ben Moses Magriso, Zvi Faier, Areh Kaplan, Shmuel Yerushalmi, and Eliyahu Touger, *The Torah Anthology* (Brooklyn, NY: Moznaim Publishing Co., 1987), vol. 14, p. 122. Jewish thought suggests that God's name *Elohim* identifies the divine attribute of justice because "every reference to Elohim means His attribute of justice." See Israel Konowitz, *The God Idea in Jewish Tradition* (Jerusalem, Israel: Jerusalem Publishing House, 1989), p. 8. At the same time, Jewish thought maintains that God's personal name YHWH identifies his attribute of mercy. In fact, when God revealed his name YHWH to Moses, he said of himself, "YHWH, YHWH *El*, merciful (*rachum*) and gracious (*channum*), longsuffering ('arek), and abounding in stedfast love (*chesed*) and truth ('*emet*)" (Exodus 34:6, author's translation). See Isidore Singer, Cyrus Adler, et. al, eds., *The Jewish Encyclopedia* (New York: Funk and Wagnalls Co., 1902), vol. 5, p. 299.

[93] Genesis 17:1. The Hebrew word that is translated "perfect" in this passage is תָּמִים (*tameem*), which means "complete," "whole," or "healthful," not the attainment of an apex of righteousness or holiness.

[94] The Scriptures repeatedly say that when God gave a command to Abraham, he "rose up early in the morning" and proceeded to fulfill that command (Genesis 19:27; 21:14; 22:3).

demonstrated in his life. When conflict arose between his herdsmen and those of his nephew Lot, Abraham made peace by being content to take what was left of the Promised Land after he allowed Lot to choose the part that he wanted.[95] Likewise, at the very moment when God covenanted with Abraham that he and his wife would witness the birth of their promised son Isaac, he exclaimed incongruously, "O that Ishmael may live before you."[96] Instead of relishing the moment of the fulfillment of the hopes and prayers that had dominated his heart for decades, Abraham believed God's promise but also prayed immediately that its fulfillment "should not lead to the rejection and exclusion of Ishmael."[97] Finally, when God announced to his friend Abraham that he intended to destroy two of the most evil cities on earth, Abraham was compelled by his own mercy to intercede for those cities to see if peradventure God might spare them the full execution of his wrath.[98] In fact, Abraham actually had the *chutzpah* to negotiate with God over the fate of Sodom and Gomorrah.[99]

Both Jews and Christians understand the prime importance of the divine commandment: "Love your neighbor as yourself."[100] There is, however, another commandment in the Torah that says, "The foreigner residing among you must be treated as your native-born. Love them as yourself, for you were foreigners in Egypt. I am the LORD your God."[101] This commandment is all the more powerful because it concludes, just as the commandment to love one's neighbor does, with the declaration: "I am the LORD your God."[102] Perhaps this was the foundation for the parable of the Good Samaritan in which Jesus gave a

---

[95] Genesis 13:8.

[96] Genesis 17:18.

[97] Melancthon Williams Jacobus, *Notes, Critical and Explanatory, on the Book of Genesis* (New York: Robert Carter & Brothers, 1865), p. 290.

[98] In interceding for both Ishmael and Sodom and Gomorrah, Abraham proved his divine call as a prophetic intercessor for blessing that was based on God's covenant promise to him that "in you all the nations of the earth will be blessed" (Genesis 18:18).

[99] Maleah Bell, B. C. Blackwell, Misty Bourne, *et. al.*, eds., *The Voice Bible: Step Into the Story of Scripture* (Nashville, TN: Thomas Nelson, Inc., 2012), p. 21: "Scripture records here an amazing exchange between the Lord and Abraham. In all of the Bible there is nothing quite like it. In these verses Abraham is negotiating with God over the fate of Sodom and its inhabitants. But this is no game. . . . Abraham has followed God long enough and knows Him well enough to stand confident as he presses and probes the extent of God's mercy."

[100] Leviticus 19:18; Matthew 22:39. Jesus said that the commandment to "love you neighbor as yourself" is second only in importance to the commandment to "love the LORD God with all your heart, mind, and strength." The apostle John went even further by saying, "If someone says, 'I love God,' and hates his brother, he is a liar, for the one who does not love his brother whom he has seen, cannot love God whom he has not seen" (1 John 4:20).

[101] Leviticus 19:34.

[102] Exodus 20:2.

graphic answer to the classical question, "Who is my neighbor?"[103] While the word *neighbor* can be variously interpreted,[104] the term *foreigner* (גֵר—*ger* in Hebrew) is unmistakable. Abraham was a גֵר (*ger*) in Canaan, and the Israelites were גֵרִים (*gerim*) in Egypt; therefore, the גֵרִים (*gerim*) among the Israelites were no different in God's eyes from Abraham and the Israelites. They were to be loved as the Israelites loved themselves, and they were to be treated as native-born. Doubtless, "a concern for resident aliens was etched into the [Israelite] legal system."[105]

Pursuing justice is seeking diligently to do what is right in God's sight and to engage in proper conduct towards all people. When one loves God, one's neighbor, and the foreigner who has no connection with him or his people, that person is not only praying for peace: he is also pursuing it. Such pursuit of peace is not just wishful thinking. It is an activity of "walking faith," the kind of faith that through action works itself out in faithfulness.[106] It is the faith that is conjoined with good works—in this case the action of praying and pursuing peace—thereby bringing faith to life through positive fulfillment.[107] This attitude can even empower one with the capacity to love one's enemy,[108] hoping to rescue him from his deception, as Abraham attempted to do for Sodom.

Jerusalem is also the foundation of justice.[109] Herein, therefore, lies the key for achieving peace in Jerusalem and working outward from God's "foundation of peace" into all the world. Righteous claims to the Promised Land must also be tempered by Abrahamic deference. Jesus set a high standard when he said that Abraham's children must evidence their patrimony by doing the works of Abraham,[110] and this includes both Jews, who are lineal descendants of Abraham, and Christians, who are spiritual descendants of the patriarch of faith.[111] Righteous claims to the Holy Land should be made in the context of the love

---

[103] Matthew 22:39.
[104] The great Rabbi Akiva said "neighbor" included all humanity; however, his colleagues limited its meaning to "Isdraelites." Others said it applied only to one's nearest kin. Louis Finkelstein, "The Jewish Vision of Human Brotherhood," in *Religious Pluralism and World Community*, Edward Jabra Juri, ed. (Leiden, The Netherlands: E. J. Brill, 1969), pp. 87–88. Finkelstein referenced *Abot of R. Nathan* I, chap. 16, 32b and *Mekilta Mishpatim*, chap. 12, p. 290; chap. 15, p. 302.
[105] Stephen G. Dempster, "Foreigner," in *Evangelical Dictionary of Biblical Theology*, Walter A. Elwell, ed. (Grand Rapids, MI: Baker Books, 1996), p. 265.
[106] This kind of faith transcends the Greek idea of πίστις (*pistis*), faith as "agreement with a premise," and moves into the arena of the Hebrew concept of אֱמוּנָה (*emunah*), faith as "faithfulness."
[107] James 2:17.
[108] Matthew 5:44.
[109] Isaiah 2:3; Micah 4:2: "The Torah will go forth from Zion, and the word of the LORD from Jerusalem."
[110] John 8:39.
[111] Galatians 3:29.

that the Torah required for those who are not Israelites but are, nevertheless, objects of God's blessing and inclusion among his native-born Chosen People despite the fact that they are foreigners. God blessed Abraham and Isaac, but he also blessed Ishmael. In the great tradition of Abraham, therefore, the Israelis are to be careful not to allow righteous nationalism to devolve into unjust exclusivity and racism. In truth, however, modern Israel already manifests an exceptional degree of respect for diversity. Israeli Jews come from a wide range of racial, ethnic, and even religious backgrounds, and Bedouins, Druze, and Arabs are Israeli citizens. Despite living in an atmosphere that is often bellicose and violent, Israel has already established a climate for peace among its own diverse citizenry. This needs only to be expanded to be even more inclusive of the *gerim* among them and those who are in their extended neighborhood. And, indeed, the Jews do understand very well "that if they were to build their house securely," they cannot "live in a narrow nationalism or isolationism and must be good neighbors to their Arab brothers, or cousins."[112]

At the same time, the Palestinian Arabs must also learn to embrace their distant cousins. Sadly, "Arab rejection of direct negotiations [for peace] is not based on a preference for some other procedure of settlement; they have rejected any procedure for terminating the conflict. They have rejected every gradual or staged settlement unless an opening is left for them to revert to their fundamental position advocating the liquidation of Israel."[113] The Muslims must find a way to respect the Jews whom Muhammad originally called the "People of the Book."[114]

---

[112] *Palestine, Volumes 1–5* (New York: American Zionist Emergency Council, 1943), p. 4.

[113] Yehoshafat Harkabi, *Palestinians and Israel* (Jerusalem, Israel: Israel Universities Press, 1974), p. 176. In fact, in 2002, when Israeli Prime Minister Ehud Barak offered to accept all of the PLO's demands for "peace," offering Yasir Arafat 97% of the original land of Israel, the Egyptian terrorist extraordinaire flatly rejected the offer, proving that his strategy for "peace" was to demand and negotiate while engaging in relentless acts of terrorism with no intention of ceasing and desisting from his violent agenda until Israel no longer existed. "Peace" for the PLO and for other terrorist organizations like Hamas and Hezbollah has long meant—and still means—the obliteration of the nation of Israel and the genocide of the Jewish people. Only then would they be able to achieve their "land-for-peace" objectives.

[114] Muhammad Abdel Haleem, *Understanding the Qur'an: Themes and Style* (New York: I.B. Tauris & Co., 1999), p. 75. Haleem says that "Christians and the Jews who lived among an overwhelming Muslim majority are referred to in the Qur'an by the honorific term *ahl al-kitab* (the 'People of the Book') not as 'minorities.' . . . The Qur'an does not brand the 'People of the Book' as a whole as unacceptable. It says: 'There are some among the People of the Book who are upright, who recite God's revelations during the night, who bow down in worship, who believe in God and the Last Day, who order what is right and forbid what is wrong, who are quick to do good deeds. These people are among the righteous, and they will not be denied [the reward] for whatever good deeds they do: God knows exactly who is conscious of Him" (*Qur'an* 3:113-115). While this statement was not a blanket acceptance of those who were not Muslims, it did at least offer some measure of respect that could make peaceful coexistence possible.

Perhaps Golda Meir understood the key to peace: "Peace will come when the Arabs will love their children more than they hate us."[115] She certainly evoked the profound nature of the Jewish view concerning the sanctity of all human life—which undoubtedly is central to any quest for peace—when she poignantly declared, "When peace comes, we will perhaps in time be able to forgive the Arabs for killing our sons, but it will be harder for us to forgive them for having forced us to kill their sons."[116]

Continual Prayer for Peace

Around the world, people of virtually all faiths are praying for world peace. Ultimately, however, universal peace upon this planet is impossible without peace first in Jerusalem and in the land of Israel. Of all those who pray for peace, however, none prays more consistently than the Jewish people. Three times daily in synagogues around the world, observant Jews pray the *Amidah*. Each time this prayer is prayed, it concludes with these words: "He who makes peace in the Heavens, May he make peace upon us and upon all Israel." This is not, however, a vainly repeated, mindless mantra. It is an outpouring of the heart of every Jew who prays it. But, more than that, it is a collective prayer of the whole house of Israel, including the people in the Promised Land. Dalia Gavriely-Nuri says it well: "This ethos has been an integral part of Israel's declared political culture since the beginning of the Zionist movement in the late 19th century."[117]

So Jews pray for and pursue peace. Muslims, however, often pray for and pursue *jihad*. With this intractability of the Muslim nations and the Arab peoples in relationship to Israel, one could easily despair of prospects for peace in the Middle East or resign oneself to believing that peace in Israel can be achieved only in the eschatological future. While the Hebrew Scriptures do point to a final denouement of the ages when the Messiah comes as the *Sar Shalom* (Prince of Peace), the Jewish and Christian ethos requires that one pray for and to pursue peace in every day that will precede that event. Believers in God can dream of a day when peace will cover the earth; however, they are also expected to work assiduously for peace. In fact, Jesus made this duty clear when he said, "Blessed are the peacemakers; for they shall be called the children of God."[118] What Jesus said

---

[115] Golda Meir during a 1957 speech, quoted in Paul Carlson, *Media Bias and the Middle East* (2003), p. 10.
[116] Golda Meir, *A Land of Our Own: An Oral Autobiography,* Marie Syrkin, ed. (New York: G. P. Putnam's Sons, 1973), p. 242.
[117] Gavriely-Nuri, p. 4.
[118] Matthew 5:9.

was in context with rabbinic tradition which teaches that "the messianic hope for a peaceful world" is "an ideological premise about the real world and not merely a sweet dream or vision of the future."[119] It was also in context with the Jewish concept of *Tikkun Olam* ("Restoration of the World"), in which God and his children are to work together in partnership to improve the world in every generation.[120] The Psalmist echoed the vision of Messianic peace: "The LORD bless you from Zion, and may you see the prosperity of Jerusalem all the days of your life. May you live to see your children's children. Peace be upon Israel."[121]

Peace and Messianic Expectation

Rabbi Judah ben Yosi once said, "Great is peace, for God's name is peace. . . . Great is peace, for it encompasses all blessings. . . . Great is peace for when the Messiah comes, he will commence with peace, as it is said: "How beautiful upon the mountains are the feet [footsteps] of the messenger of good tidings, who announces peace."[122] The Jewish Scriptures speak poignantly of such a time: "They shall hammer their swords into plowshares and their spears into pruning hooks. Nation will not lift up sword against nation, and never again will they learn war."[123] This event will occur when many people say, "Come, let us go up to the mountain of the LORD, to the house of the God of Jacob; that he may teach us concerning his ways and that we may walk in his paths. For the Torah will go forth from Zion and the word of the LORD from Jerusalem."[124] Chaim Weizmann made this very astute observation: "The prophetic vision that out of Zion comes forth the word of the Lord is not a legacy of the past but is the

---

119 Joseph Isaac Lifshitz, "War and Aesthetics in Jewish Law," in *War and Peace in Jewish Tradition: From the Biblical Word to the Present*, Yigal Levin and Amnon Shapira, eds. (New York: Routledge, 2012), p. 107.

120 Blair P. Grubb, "Tikkun Olam," in *Jewish Stories from Heaven and Earth: Inspiring Tales to Nourish the Heart* (Woodstock, VT: Jewish Lights Publishing, 2008), p. 113. Grubb says that the process of *tikkun olam*, "repairing the world is accomplished by individual conscious acts of compassion, mercy, justice, and kindness." Also, Philip D. Ben-Shmuel, "*Hagshamah*: A Theology for an Alternate Messianic Jewish Zionism," in *The Land Cries Out: Theology of the Land in the Israeli-Palestinian Context*, Salim J. Munayer and Lisa Loden, eds. (Eugene, OR: Wipf and Stock Publishers, 2012), p. 154. Ben-Shmuel says, "In Jewish terms, this active pursuit of the kingdom of heaven on earth is called *tikkun 'olam*—the restoration of the *cosmos*." For this reason, he says, a truly biblical Zionism "cannot be concerned only with the redemption of Israel in their land, but rather with the redemption of all the families of the earth." He concludes by saying that "this can be referred to as 'general Zionism,' because it looks towards the establishment of New Jerusalem." Pursuit of peace is not just an eschatological expectation, it is a daily endeavor.

121 Psalm 128:5–6.

122 Leviticus *Rabbah* 9:9.

123 Isaiah 2:4; Micah 4:3.

124 Isaiah 2:3.

commandment of the present and the hope of the future."[125] The foundation and fountainhead of global peace will be Jerusalem, and its agent will be the God's Torah. "Rejoice greatly, O daughter Zion! Shout aloud, O daughter Jerusalem! Behold, your king comes to you; just and endowed with salvation . . . [T]he battle bow will be broken. He will proclaim peace to the nations. His dominion will be from sea to sea and from the River to the ends of the earth."[126] The prophet Isaiah further spoke of the profound impact of God's peace: "I will extend peace to her like a river. . . . As one whom his mother comforts, so I will comfort you; and you will be comforted in Jerusalem."[127]

Through the agency of the Holy Spirit, God is seeking righteous Gentiles who will renew biblical Ruth's affirmation, "Your people shall be my people," confirming their identity with and among the ancient people of God. Such intercessors from among all the nations of the earth must stand shoulder-to-shoulder with the Jewish people, imploring the God of peace to bring peace first to Jerusalem and then to the whole world. They must join the ranks of those about whom the God of Israel spoke when he said, "I have posted watchmen on your walls, O Jerusalem; they will never be silent day or night. You who remind the LORD, give yourselves no rest, and give him no rest until he establishes and makes Jerusalem a praise in the earth."[128]

The passion that the Jewish people have for the peace of Jerusalem, of Israel, and of the whole world is an outworking of their calling as the Chosen People. It is not so much that they have chosen God and the land where the Almighty has placed his name as it is that God has chosen them, placed his name on them, and brought them to his land to be his people and his nation. David Patterson confirms this truth when he says that "the Jews do not lay claim to Jerusalem— Jerusalem lays claim to the Jews."[129] The magnet of the holy Presence that resides in the Holy City draws this people inexorably toward God and his land. Like King David, they know that the Lord is great and "greatly to be praised in the city of our God, his holy mountain."[130] Patterson concludes that "when Jews pray to the Holy One, they never refer to Jerusalem as 'our city,' but rather

[125] Chaim Weizmann, quoted in Ferdynand Zweig, *Israel: The Sword and the Harp: The Mystique of Violence and the Mystique of Redemption; Controversial Themes in Israeli Society* (Cranbury, NJ: Associated University Presses, 1969), p. 216.
[126] Zechariah 9:9–10, NIV, NRS, NASB, edited.
[127] Isaiah 66:13.
[128] Isaiah 62:6–7, NIV, NRS, NASB, edited.
[129] David Patterson, *Anti-Semitism and Its Metaphysical Origins* (Cambridge, UK: Cambridge University Press, 2015), p. 204.
[130] Psalm 48:1.

as *irkha*, 'Your city,' that is, God's city, invoking God as the *Boneh Yerushalyim*, the 'Builder of Jerusalem.'"[131] The God of Israel has promised to make peace and he will not be thwarted in fulfilling his purposes. "The LORD will give strength to his people; the LORD will bless his people with peace."[132] In that day, "the LORD of hosts shall reign in Mount Zion, and in Jerusalem, and before his ancients gloriously."[133] This is God's final promise: "I will fill this house with glory . . . the latter glory of this house will be greater than the glory of the former, and in this place I will give peace, declares the LORD of hosts."[134]

Hope in a Morass of Hopelessness

Without God, human beings are hopeless creatures for whom the banality of barbarity knows no bounds. Although the Age of Reason and the Enlightenment of the seventeenth and eighteenth centuries postulated that human beings were inherently good and were moving toward a perfect social form[135] and although Social Darwinism of the nineteenth century fully expected the human animal to continue evolving until it reached Utopia,[136] the events of the twentieth century destroyed that hope[137] and opened the door for secular nihilist postmodernity wherein neither truth nor secular ethics are possible and humanity is doomed to continue in a downward spiral that will inevitably lead it to self-obliteration.[138] Two violent world wars confirmed the fact that, apart

---

[131] Patterson, p. 204.

[132] Psalm 29:11.

[133] Isaiah 24:23.

[134] Haggai 2:7–9, NASB, NIV edited.

[135] Markus Mühling, *T & T Clark Handbook of Christian Eschatology* (London, UK: Bloomsbury T & T Clark, 2015), p. 231. Mühling lists five significant characteristics of Enlightenment thinking as 1) "Humans are not bad according to their nature," 2) "Humans are first located on morally lower stages," 3) "Knowledge of what is morally good is universally accessible," 3) "Humans are therefore morally perfectible," and 5) "In the future, the perfect human social form will be realized within history."

[136] Dave Breese, *Seven Men Who Rule the World from the Grave* (Chicago, IL: Moody Publishers, 1990), p. 32. Breese notes that Social Darwinism assumed that "the social structure is engineered and controlled by impersonal forces rather than by God," that Western society has moved and will move "through progressive states of secularization from Christianity to atheism," and that "society is moving upward from a mean past to an improving future" and will continue to do so "until perfect culture comes into being," which is Utopia.

[137] Christopher Falzon, *Philosophy Goes to the Movies: An Introduction to Philosophy* (New York: Routledge, 2007), p. 188. Falzon observes that instead of moving toward a social Darwinian utopia, the twentieth century instilled "more pessimistic, dystopian visions of the future."

[138] Nietzsche's "Pessimistic Nihilism" leads "to the obliteration and self-destruction of life." His Optimistic Nihilism leads only to the obliteration of "the currently reigning table of values." See Nikos Kazantzakis, *Friedrich Nietzsche on the Philosophy of Right and the State* (Albany, New York: The State University of New York Press, 2006), p. 17.

from God, human beings are hopelessly violent and self-destructive. The Holocaust was the final nail in the coffin of modernity and its lofty expectations for human self-achievement and self-generated peace.[139] And the continuing and unrelenting violence that has taken countless innocent human lives during and after the second half of the twentieth century has done nothing but add to the ominous sense of the inevitable death-spiral of the human race. All that seems to be left in today's secularist arena is hedonism and barbarism—the ultimate demonstration of humankind's destiny after its complete rejection of God and the restraints imposed by his commands and its embrace of consequentialism and its intolerance of tolerance of every perversion that the human mind can conceive.

What is true in the macrocosm of the world is true also in the microcosm of the Middle East where competing worldviews and mindsets have created and maintained a dilemma of human suffering that seems to have no pragmatic resolution, much less utopian conclusion. The difference between the adherents to Judaism and Christianity and those of other religions in the postmodern world—and particularly those who eschew any religious persuasion whatsoever—is at least a minimal belief in God's biblical design for humanity. This is the fundamental knowledge that the God of Scripture created theomorphic human beings and infused within them a spark of the Divine. Because humans breathe the *neshamah* of the Eternal, they have the potential to manifest the divine likeness, and, therefore, they have the capacity to join in partnership with the Eternal to bring to pass his primordial design for Planet Earth. This can be accomplished, however, only when humans recognize the existence of manifest evil in the world and its utter rejection of the God of Scripture and his specific and uncompromisable instructions for human existence. If evil is not recognized and acknowledged for what it is, "good" becomes entirely a perspective of subjective relativism so that, in effect, there is no objective good. In this case, anything can be rationalized as good such that the ends always justify the means, no matter how heinous they may be.

In spite of all the reasons for despair, "Hope springs eternal in the human breast,"[140] as Alexander Pope said over five centuries ago. This is particularly true for believers in the God of Scripture, who know above all things that Israel's God is faithful, and he does "great and unfathomable things."[141] What has appeared to be a hopeless morass of intractable conflict that has bedeviled the Jewish people

---

[139] J. Richard Middleton and Brian J. Walsh, *Truth Is Stranger Than It Used to Be: Biblical Faith in a Postmodern Age* (Downers Grove, IL: InterVarsity Press, 1995), p. 23.
[140] Alexander Pope, *An Essay on Man* (London, England: Thomas Tegg, 1811), p. 48.
[141] Job 9:10.

for centuries can be resolved by God in one moment of time. The same God who has restored his people, his nation, and his land in this day[142] can build a "highway from Assyria to Egypt,"[143] and he can also reconcile Isaac and Ishmael, the long-estranged sons of Abraham, and call Egypt, Assyria, and Israel "my people."[144]

Is it possible for the seemingly incurable proclivity toward violence that has characterized so much of the Muslim Arab world to be abated? Is it possible for Islam to undergo a reformation that would move it away from its militant and violent past and toward a more peaceful future? Appeals for such a reformation have become increasingly numerous in recent times and in various places. In a speech before Al-Azhar and the Awqaf Ministry, a gathering of Islamic clerics, scholars, and leaders, Egyptian President Abdel Fattah al-Sisi boldly called for a "religious revolution" in the world of Islam, saying, "It's inconceivable that the thinking that we hold most sacred should cause the entire Islamic world to be a source of anxiety, danger, killing, and destruction for the rest of the world. Impossible!"[145] Ayaan Hirsi Ali, however, underscores the difficulty of such a revolutionary quest, noting that "neither Muslim reformers nor Western liberals have so far been able to articulate a coherent program for a Muslim Reformation." At the same time, however, she still has hope, believing that "the Muslim Reformation has begun."[146]

Abdeslam Maghraoui goes further, suggesting that under the name of *tajdid*,[147] a "systematic reconsideration and rationalization of Islamic doctrines, institutions, beliefs, and practices" is taking place in Islam.[148] Many other scholars

---

[142] Isaiah 11:11.

[143] Isaiah 19:23.

[144] Isaiah 19:24–25.

[145] Abdel Fattah al-Sisi, quoted in John Hayward, "Egyptian President Al-Sisi Calls for an Islamic Reformation," *Breitbart News*, 9 Jan 2015, posted at http://www.breitbart.com/national-security/2015/01/09/egyptian-president-al-sisi-calls-for-an-islamic-reformation/.

[146] Ayaan Hirsi Ali, quoted in Clifford D. May, "The Case for Islamic Heresy: Ayaan Hirsi Ali Risks All with Her Call for a Muslim Reformation," *The Washington Times*, April 14, 2015, posted at http://www.washingtontimes.com/news/2015/apr/14/clifford-may-ayaan-hirsi-ali-risks-life-with-call-/. Also, Ayaan Hirsi Ali, *Heretic: Why Islam Needs a Reformation Now* (New York: HarperCollins, 2015).

[147] *Tajdid* is the Arabic word for "renewal." When used in its Islamic context, it refers to a revival of Islam to bring society to greater justice.

[148] Abdeslam Maghraoui, "American Foreign Policy and Islamic Renewal," in *Conflict, Identity, and Reform in the Muslim World: Challenges for U.S. Engagement*, Daniel Brumberg and Dina Shehata, eds. (Washington, DC: United States Institute of Peace, 2009), p. 51. Maghraoui says that the systematic approach to Islamic Reformation includes efforts 1) "to reclaim the Islamic heritage from traditional clerics (associated with autocratic states), extremist Islamist groups (bent on waging holy war against the West and their own 'adulterated' societies), and fundamentalist movements (whose goal is to apply strict Sharia law once they gain power through democratic elections or through informal *da'wa*—a religious call to fellow Muslims to abide by Islamic principles), and 2) "to adapt Islamic principles, values, and institutions to the modern world while recognizing the importance of Islam as a cultural frame of reference."

like Zuhdi Jasser,[149] Asra Nomani,[150] Tawfiq Hamid,[151] Irshad Manji,[152] and Tarip Ramadan[153] have made arguments for Islamic reformation that are increasingly being heard. Is it possible that a religion which has been more exploited for violence than any other can become a religion of peace? Perhaps dormant seeds in Islamic sacred literature which envision a Muslim messianic event[154] have at least a chance of flowering into a new Islamic focus on peace, rather than conflict.

Could it also be that some Islamic reformers might actually come to recognize and acknowledge the Jewish foundations on which many aspects of the Muslim faith were built? The bedrock absolute monotheism of Islam certainly rests on the monotheism of Judaism which preceded monotheistic belief in Arabian tradition by over two millennia.[155] Other concepts were also borrowed, if not expropriated, from the Jews and Judaism by Muhammad and his associates.[156] Could it be that, in a fashion similar to the twentieth-century Christianity experience vis-à-vis the Jews and Judaism, Islam, the world's most triumphalistic and supersessionist religion,[157] might also come to acknowledge that some, if not most, of its theological foundations were established in the faith of Abraham as defined and codified by Jewish patriarchs and prophets and by

---

[149] Zuhdi Jasser is featured regularly on major television news programs, and he contributes many articles to various newspapers and journals.

[150] Asra Quratulain Nomani, *Standing Alone in Mecca: An American Woman's Struggle for the Soul of Islam* (New York: HarperCollins Publishers, 2006).

[151] Tawfiq Hamid, *Inside Jihad: How Radical Islam Works, Why It Should Terrify Us, How to Defeat It* (Pembroke, VA: Mountain Lake Press, 2015).

[152] Irshad Manji, *The Trouble with Islam Today* (New York: St. Martin's Press, 2003).

[153] Tariq Ramadan, *Radical Reform: Islamic Ethics and Liberation* (New York: Oxford University Press, 2009).

[154] Though the Muslim messianic idea of the *Mahdi* was clearly expropriated from Christianity, at least it anticipates a final eschatological denouement when justice and peace will reign supreme on Planet Earth.

[155] There was no concept of monotheism in the most ancient Arabian traditions where tribal gods dominated and polytheism was common.

[156] Acknowledgement by Muslims of Islam's Jewish roots would not be new as Ross Brann points out when he cites eleventh-century Muslim Qadi Sa'id al-Andalusi's statement in his *Al-tarif bi-tabaqat al-umam* (*Exposition of the Generations of Nations*) that "their scholars [i.e., the Banu Isra'il = the Jews] were best informed in the story of creation and in knowledge of the prophets. Muslim scholars such as 'Abd Allah ibn 'Abbas, *ka'b al-Ahbar*, and *Wahb ibn Munabbih* acquired this knowledge from them" (author's emphasis). Ross Brann, *Power in the Portrayal: Representations of Jews and Muslims in Eleventh and Twelfth Century Islamic Spain* (Princeton, NJ: Princeton University Press, 2002), p. 31.

[157] While it has recognized Moses as the prophet of Judaism and Jesus as the prophet of Christianity (and thus two of its own prophets), Islam has always claimed that Muhammad was the ultimate and greatest prophet and that the religion of Muhammad superseded both Judaism and Christianity. This, of course, is supersessionism *par excellence*. At the same time, through the centuries, Islam has proven its triumphalistic mindset by expanding its dominion on the edge of the sword at the expense of unknown and unimaginable human suffering and death. Islam, therefore, has achieved and maintained a level of triumphalism to which neither Judaism nor Christianity ever aspired and which neither has attained.

the sages of Judaism?[158] Some Jewish scholars have already demonstrated distinct parallels between Judaism and Islam.[159] Could such insights prompt a reformation of restoration in Islam to abandon non-Abrahamic concepts[160] and return to the purity of Abrahamic faith?

Less than a century ago, who could have imagined that nearly a millennium of Christian violence against the Jewish people would finally come to an abrupt end? Yet, the Holocaust-shocked conscience of the Christian church finally exclaimed, "Never again!" prompting increasing numbers of Christians to confess that their own faith is deeply rooted in the soil of Judaism and to acknowledge the Jewish people as continuing co-participants with them in the faith of Abraham. Surely, the God who produced this miracle can also work wonders in the world of Islam by making the quest for world peace far more important than any other theological, sociological, or political agenda! This holy vision can be worked out practically. As Jonathan Sacks says, "We must raise a generation of young Jews, Christians, Muslims and others to know that it is not piety but sacrilege to kill in the name of the God of life, hate in the name of the God of love, wage war in the name of the God of peace, and practice cruelty in the name of the God of compassion."[161]

With God, all things are possible! With God, many things are plausible and likely. With God, what he has proclaimed and prophesied in his Holy Word is not only possible but also inevitable! Nothing can be taken from it or added to it, and nothing on the earth can ever prevent its ultimate accomplishment. *YHWH-Shalom*,[162] the God of peace, will surely and finally bring peace on earth to people of good will, and he will create the divine *shalom* that infinitely exceeds all human comprehension or imagination.[163]

---

158 Studies in the Jewish roots of Islam have been ongoing since the nineteenth century when Jewish scholars such as Abraham Geiger and Ignaz Goldziher "stressed the Judaizing nature of early Islam." Sander Gilman, *Multiculturalism and the Jews* (New York: Routledge, 2006), p. 5. Some have even argued that the similarities that Christianity and Islam share with Judaism have produced within all three religions what Sigmund Freud called the "narcissism of minor differences." Stephen Brooks, *The Challenge of Cultural Pluralism* (Westport, CT: Greenwood Publishing Group, 2002), p. 39.

159 J. R. Wegner, "Islamic and Talmudic Jurisprudence: The Four Roots of Islamic Law and their Talmudic Counterparts," *American Journal of Legal History* 26 (1982), pp. 26–29. Also, Patricia Crone and Michael Cook, *Hagarism: The Making of the Islamic World* (Cambridge, UK: Cambridge University Press, 1980).

160 Steven Bayme, *Understanding Jewish History: Text and Commentaries* (Jersey City, NJ: KTAV Publishing House, 1997), p. 128. Bayme maintains that perhaps Islam's most important departure from Jewish thought has been its "conflict over territory and territorial imperatives" which "divided the world into *dar al-Islam*, or 'territory of Islam' and *dar al-harb* or 'territory of the nations.'"

161 Jonathan Sacks, "How to Defeat Religious Violence," *The Wall Street Journal*, Oct. 2, 2105, posted at http://www.wsj.com/articles/how-to-defeat-religious-violence-1443798275.

162 Judges 6:24.

163 Philippians 4:7.

CHAPTER 20

UNEQUIVOCALLY PRO-ISRAEL

CHRISTIANS AND ISRAEL

Because of its theological and historical connection with Judaism, the Jewish people, and the land of Israel, Christian support for Israel should be as natural as breathing! As a matter of fact, philosemitism should be a part of the Christian autonomic nervous system, for the foundations of the Jewish faith are responsible for the very core of the Christian faith. Indeed, there would be no Christians if there had been no Hebrews, no Israelites, and no Jews.[1] And there would be no Christianity if there had been no biblical Judaism or Second Temple Judaism.[2] Also, since God had joined himself in an irrevocable covenant with the Israelites, it was impossible for Jesus to have come from any people group other than the Jewish people.

Jesus was a Jew, and his religion was Judaism, and he never changed either his ethnicity or his religion. To those among his fellow Israelite compatriots who entertained the thought that he might have come to start a new religion, he emphatically affirmed this truth: "Do not even begin to think that I have come to abolish the Torah or the prophets. I have not come to abolish them but to fulfill them."[3] Then, he became

---

[1] Robert A. Ashworth, quoted in Don A. Pitman, "Reflections on Religious Pluralism," in *The Theologically Formed Heart: Essays in Honor of David J. Gouwens*, Warner M. Bailey, Lee C. Barrett, and James O. Duke, eds., (Eugene, OR: Wipf and Stock Publishers, 2014), p. 22.
[2] Richard W. Rosseau, ed., *Christianity and Judaism: The Deepening Dialogue* (Montrose, PA: Ridge Row Press, 1983), vol. 3, p. 186. Also Lemuel Baker, *The Many Faces of Judaism: Jewish Studies for the Busy Person* (Bloomington, IN: Xlibris Corp., 2012), p. 92. Baker observes that if Israel had been annihilated by Antiochus Epiphanes in the time of the Maccabees, "Jesus Christ would not have come and thus Christianity as a religion or belief system would not exist." He concludes, therefore, that "without Judaism and Israel there would be no Christianity."
[3] Matthew 5:17, author's translation.

even more eloquent and specific: "Of a truth, I tell you, until heaven and earth disappear, not one *yud* or the smallest crown [stroke of the pen] will by any means disappear from the Torah until everything is accomplished."[4] Finally, Jesus affirmed that "whoever then annuls one of the least of these commandments, and teaches others to do the same, shall be called least in the kingdom of heaven; but whoever keeps and teaches them, he shall be called great in the kingdom of heaven."[5] If anything, therefore, Jesus strengthened the Torah by promoting a reformation of restoration[6] in order to return the faith of his people to the original spirit of the Torah.[7]

Even the apostle Paul, who has been both applauded[8] and excoriated[9] for being the supposed creator of Christianity, followed the example of Jesus and never intended to foster a new religion. To his dying day, he professed to be a Pharisee,[10] and he affirmed in legal proceedings that as a member of a Jewish sect called "The Way," he believed—and practiced— everything that was in accordance with the Torah and that was written the prophets.[11] Evan Freed rightly confirms that Paul "did not even change from Judaism to Christianity because he never gave up his Jewish beliefs."[12] Paul also said of his co-religionists, the Jews, "They *are* beloved for the sake

---

4 Matthew 5:18, NIV.
5 Matthew 5:19.
6 Hebrews 9:10. The nature of Jesus' reformation as that of restoration is seen in the antitheses of the Sermon on the Mount (Matthew 5:21–48) in which he strengthened the Torah by emphasizing its original intent and giving greater emphasis to its heart issues rather than its external punctilious performance.
7 Per Bilde, *The Originality of Jesus: A Critical Discussion and a Comparative Attempt* (Göttingen, Germany: Vandenhoeck & Ruprecht GmbH & Co., 2013), p. 145. Bilde says that "the most important feature of Jesus' relationship to the Mosaic Law is that Jesus tightened, strengthened and intensified the Law of Moses partly by referring to the more original, authentic and stricter 'law of creation.'"
8 Geza Vermes, *The Changing Faces of Jesus* (New York, Penguin Books, 2000), p. 64. Vermes says that Paul "is hailed by independent scholars as the true founder of the Christian religion and its institutions," and he cites the *Oxford Dictionary of the Christian Church* as describing "Paul as 'the creator of the whole doctrinal and ecclesiastical system presupposed in his Epistles.'" William Wrede also called Paul "the second founder of Christianity." See William Wrede, *Paul*, tr. E. Lummis (London, England: Green & Hull, 1907), p. 179. Paul was also illogically and falsely called "the great pathologist of Judaism" by Julius Wellhausen, who further noted that "in the Mosaic theocracy the cultus became a pedagogic instrument of discipline. It is estranged from the heart; its revival was due to old custom, it would never have blossomed again of itself." See Julius Ferminger Wellhausen, *Prolegomena to the History of Israel*, tr. J. Sutherland Black and Allan Menzies (Edinburgh, Scotland: Adam and Charles Black, 1885), p. 366.
9 Susannah Heschel, *Abraham Geiger and the Jewish Jesus* (Chicago, IL: The University of Chicago Press, 1998), p. 151.
10 Acts 23:6.
11 Acts 24:14.
12 Edwin D. Freed, *The Apostle Paul, Christian Jew: Faithfulness and Law* (Lanham, MD: University Press of America, 1994), p. 8.

of the fathers; for the gifts and the calling of God are irrevocable,"[13] and he fully expected them to be included in the eschatological denouement at the end of the age: "And so, all Israel will be saved."[14]

While it is manifestly true that Christianity can and must be contextualized by being indigenized for every culture on earth, it is also incontrovertibly true that every authentic expression of the Christian faith has a Jewish root.[15] In fact, Christianity owes a profound debt of gratitude to the Jewish people of history—and by association, to the Jewish people of the present day—for being the source of the foundational elements of its faith. The God that Christians worship is the God of the Jews,[16] the Bible that Christians read is a Jewish book,[17] the Messiah whom Christians revere and follow was and is a Jew,[18] and the salvation that Christians experience is "from the Jews."[19] In truth, Christianity is, in effect, "the other Jewish religion."

Tragically though, millions of Christians have been denied access to the Hebrew foundations—the Jewish roots—of their faith by one of history's greatest aberrations—the Hellenization, Latinization, and paganization of Christian faith. Christians have been robbed of the richness of their faith in Jesus that is readily understood when the Master and his teachings are

---

[13] Romans 11:28–29, emphasis added.

[14] Romans 11:26.

[15] For a comprehensive study of the inherent Jewishness of the Christian faith, see John D. Garr, *Christian Fruit—Jewish Root: Theology of Hebraic Restoration* (Atlanta, GA: Golden Key Press, 2015).

[16] Christians received the understanding of monotheism from the Jews. The God whom Jesus called "Father" is YHWH, the God of the Jews. See Darrell J. Fasching, *The Jewish People in Christian Preaching* (Lewiston, NY: The Edwin Mellen Press, 1984), p. 24.

[17] It has been said that the Bible is a Jewish book from Genesis to maps! The Bible is a book written by Jews for Jews in the language of the Jews about the God of the Jews. Indeed, both the Hebrew Scriptures and the Apostolic Scriptures were written, compiled, and edited by Jews, including the books of Luke (Luke and Acts) that were written by a proselyte to Judaism who became an associate of the apostle Paul. In *Questiones Hebraicae in Genesim*, Jerome argued that Luke was a proselyte from paganism to Judaism before he became a believer in Jesus. See Richard Watson, *An Exposition of the Gospels of St. Matthew and St. Mark and Some Other Detached Parts of Holy Scripture* (London, UK: John Mason, 1833), p. 532.

[18] That Jesus was a Jew is so obvious that the author of Hebrews said that "it is evident that our Lord came from the tribe of Judah," from the name of which the term *Jew* was derived as a contracted form. Both of the genealogies of Jesus recorded in Christian Scripture prove incontrovertibly that Jesus was a Jew (Matthew 1:1–17; Luke 3:23–38). As a matter of fact, Apostolic Scripture (the "New Testament") begins with these words: "A record of the origin of Jesus Christ, the son of David, the son of Abraham." See Katherine Sonderegger, *That Jesus Christ Was Born a Jew: Karl Barth's Doctrine of Israel* (State College, PA: Pennsylvania State University Press, 1992).

[19] John 4:22. Jesus himself said that "salvation is from the Jews." Rosemary Ruether, *Faith and Fratricide: The Theological Roots of Anti-Semitism* (Eugene, OR: Wipf and Stock Publishers, 1995), p. 256. Ruether says that "the Christian messianic experience in Jesus was a Jewish experience, created out of Jewish hope."

returned to the Jewish matrix from which they emerged. Especially important in Christianity's lost legacy is the Christian connection to the people, the nation, and the land of Israel.[20] Because of the Judaeophobia, anti-Judaism, and antisemitism that emerged in the church in the centuries following the days of the apostles, Christians in general do not understand the importance of their connection with the Jewish people and with the Jewish nation of Israel. In fact, historical Christianity's missing link has been its Jewish connection, and for postmodern Christianity, that link has become even more obscure.

For far too long, Christianity has defined itself as being "not Jewish," while Judaism, often in response, has defined itself as being "not Christian." Now, both Christianity and Judaism must fully understand that they are kindred faiths, springing from the common root of biblical and Second Temple Judaism. As a matter of fact, of the many Judaisms that existed in the first century, they are the only two that survived. The Pharisees developed into Rabbinic Judaism. The *Notzrim*,[21] the followers of Jesus, evolved into Christianity. Michael Kogan captured the essence of this historical fact very well: "In the first century of the present era a number of Jewish sects flourished, each with its own faith-based reading of the texts available to them and many with their own messianic expectations. . . . But of all these schools of thought, only two survived the Jewish revolt and Romans conquest of 64–70 C.E. The Nazarene movement and the Pharisee movement emerged and grew into Christianity and rabbinic Judaism." Then, Kogan suggested the kind of mutual respect that makes Christian support for Jews and Judaism possible: "Both began as sects of Judaism, and each cherished its own messianic vision. Why should they be expected to agree? One is no more legitimate than the other, but they are different. Only the ultimate messianic advent will settle the matter."[22]

Prophetic Promise

Various Jewish prophets and sages predicted the amazing restoration of the people, the nation, and the land of Israel. God, himself, promised that following what would be more than two millennia of Jewish dispersion

---

[20] John D. Garr, *Our Lost Legacy: Christianity's Hebrew Heritage* (Atlanta, GA: Golden Key Press, 2000).

[21] The disciples of Jesus called themselves the *Notzrim* because they were the followers of the one whom they recognized as the *Netzer*, the "branch" or "shoot" from the stem of Jesse, about whom Isaiah 11:1 prophesied.

[22] Michael S. Kogan, *Opening the Covenant: A Jewish Theology of Christianity* (New York: Oxford University Press, 2008), p. 126.

among the nations of the world that began with the Babylonian captivity, he would once again set his hand to regather the outcasts of the Diaspora into their own land never to be removed again: "I will restore the captivity of my people Israel. . . . I will also plant them on their land, and they will not again be rooted out from their land which I have given them, says the LORD."[23] God also declared that the regathering would be from the entire earth: "In that day the LORD will reach out his hand a second time to reclaim the surviving remnant of his people. . . . He will gather the dispersed of Judah from the four corners of the earth."[24] He even predicted that this exodus to *aliyah* from the north, east, south, and west would eclipse the archetypal Exodus from Egyptian slavery in both scope and importance: "The days are coming, declares the LORD, when they will no longer say, 'As the LORD lives, who brought up the children of Israel from the land of Egypt.' but, 'As the LORD lives, who brought up and led back the descendants of the household of Israel from the north land and from all the countries where I had driven them.' Then they will live on their own soil."[25] Israel was to be a renewed nation: "Who has heard such a thing? Can a nation be brought forth all at once? As soon as Zion travailed, she also brought forth her children."[26]

Israelite prophets also declared that the restoration of Israel would be accompanied by an impartation of loving concern and support from Gentile peoples for the restored nation and the renewed people. God said to Israel through Isaiah: "Arise, shine; for your light is come, and the glory of the LORD has risen upon you . . . and Gentiles will come to your light . . . and foreigners will build up your walls, and their kings will minister to you."[27] These inspired prophetic words predicted Gentile support for rebuilding the city of Jerusalem and the nation of Israel following the exile in Babylon. And, true to his word, God called Cyrus, the king of Medo-Persia, his "anointed" and instructed him to commission Jewish leaders to return to the land of their ancestors and to rebuild their ancient capital city and its temple.[28] This historical event, however, was merely a foretaste of an even greater restoration that was to occur centuries later: the modern-day rebirth of the nation of Israel. God predicted that the restoration of Israel that had occurred historically

---

23 Amos 9:14–15.
24 Isaiah 11:11–12.
25 Jeremiah 23:7–8.
26 Isaiah 66:8.
27 Isaiah 60:1, 3, 10.
28 Isaiah 44:28; 45:1.

in post-exilic times would be completed in a yet-future time when the Jewish people would be returned to their land "never to be plucked out again."[29]

Christian Ambivalence

While it is the hand of God that has regathered the Jewish people to their land, the restoration of the people to the land and of the land to the people has received significant support from among the Gentile nations of the world, particularly from the international Christian community. The kind of massive, unequivocal support that the prophets envisioned, however, has not yet been fully realized. Many Christian denominations have at best vacillated in their stand for Jewish people's right of self-determination in the land that God himself deeded to their ancestors and their descendants in perpetuity. Even moderate support for Jewish causes in recent times has been a radical departure from the norm in Christian circles. Christian leaders, including some Evangelicals, have learned from secularists how to mask antisemitism as "anti-Zionism." This, however, has simply been a further manifestation of heretical theologies and practices that have characterized historical Christianity for centuries.

Since the beginning of the second century, most of Christianity has been characterized by Judaeophobia, anti-Judaism, and antisemitism.[30] Despite the fact that the Christian patriarch Paul enjoined upon the Gentiles a profound sense of humility and appreciation for being included in God's family tree of covenant salvation,[31] Christian triumphalism has continued to be manifest in the heresy of supersessionism[32] that has relegated Judaism to the role of a failed, fossil religion, the Jewish people to a subhuman species of Christ-killers, and Israel to an irredeemable relic of the past.[33] Far from anticipating—much less supporting—Israel's restoration, much of the church in history and even in the present has reveled in Jewish dispersion as "evidence" of their divine rejection.[34] Some, like

---

[29] Amos 9:11–15.

[30] Donald J. Dietrich, *God and Humanity in Auschwitz: Jewish-Christian Relations and Sanctioned Murder* (Piscataway, NJ: Transaction Publishers, 1995), p. 15. Dietrich says, "For centuries before 1945, Christian antisemitism (anti-Judaism) thrived and was reinforced as a religious as well as a cultural norm, which ultimately became a self-fulfilling social and political prophecy."

[31] Romans 11:11, 18.

[32] Kogan, p. 163. Kogan says that before Vatican II, "Christians had seen the Jewish people and faith largely through the twin lenses of triumphalism and supersessionism."

[33] Isaac S. Moses, "The Growth of Ethical Monotheism," in *The Christian Register*, June 17, 1886, vol. 67, no. 24, p. 376. Moses exclaimed that "Israel still lives, not merely as a relic of the past, but as a living wonder and testimony of the indestructibility of Israel's faith and race."

[34] Jeremy Cohen, *Essential Papers on Judaism and Christianity in Conflict* (New York: New York University Press, 1990), p. 27.

Steven Bryan, have even dared to attribute such ideas to Jesus. "In Jesus' view the announcement of Israel's judgement meant the end of Israel's election,"[35] he said.

To Support or Not to Support

Anyone who has studied pro-Israel Christianity in the twentieth century has noted that most of this support has come from Evangelical Christians. While mainstream Protestant denominations[36] have been characteristically supportive of Judaism, they have generally refrained from support of Israel, even championing Palestinian and other Muslim causes instead and criticizing virtually everything about Israel. Leon Klenicki has observed that "the constant criticism of the State of Israel" from mainstream Protestants "is the new way of theological anti-Judaism, of the teaching of contempt. Before they denied us a role in God's plan and now they want to deny us a place in history."[37] Evangelical churches, on the other hand, have offered general endorsement for Israeli statehood and independence, while lagging behind mainstream churches in support for Judaism and Jewish communities outside the land of Israel.[38] Evangelical support has sometimes vacillated, however, depending upon individual eschatological scenarios and sympathies or lack thereof for the "Palestinian" people.

Ulterior motives have also impacted Christian support for Israel from the time when Martin Luther transitioned from being strongly philosemitic to being virulently antisemitic because the Jewish people did not convert *en masse* to Lutheran Protestantism in accordance with his own personal eschatology in which he anticipated the return of Jesus in his time.[39] Much of dispensationalism is also supportive of Israel because it sees rapprochement with the Jewish community as necessary for the realization of an eschatology that

---

[35] Steven M. Bryan, *Jesus and Israel's Traditions of Judgement and Restoration* (Cambridge, UK: Cambridge University Press, 2002), p. 87.

[36] Mainstream Protestant denominations include the following: the Presbyterian Church (U.S.A.), the Episcopal Church, the United Methodist Church, the American Baptist Churches, the Evangelical Lutheran Church in America, the United Church of Christ, the Reformed Church in America, and the Disciples of Christ.

[37] Leon Klenicki, quoted in David Singer, ed., *American Jewish Year Book, 1998* (Atlanta, GA: The American Jewish Committee, 1998), p. 97.

[38] Henry L. Lantner, *What? Again Those Jews!* (Jerusalem, Israel: Gefen Publishing House, 1997), p. 28. Lantner observes that "many Protestant Churches . . . still tend to be highly critical of Israel's policies, while the doctrine of denying the Jews any role in the Christian Divine scheme also affects their attitude. Evangelical Churches, on the other hand, have been highly supportive of Israel. Their support is connected with the return of Jews to the Promised Land, which is in accordance with their religious belief."

[39] Allison P. Coudert, "Seventeenth-Century Christian Hebraists," in *Judaeo-Christian Intellectual Culture in the Seventeenth Century*, A. P. Coudert, S. Hutton, and R. H. Popkin, eds. (Dordrecht, The Netherlands: Kluwer Academic Publishers, 1999), p. 47.

ultimately requires the "conversion" of the Jews as a precondition to the return of Jesus.[40] Additionally, it is sometimes easy for Western evangelical Christians to love Israel while being indifferent to and even hating Jews who live near them because Israel is on the other side of the world and is mentioned in their Bibles, while they are generally ignorant of Jewish culture and religion.

Then, there are some Christians who have had a "love" for Israel and the Jews that has been founded on their hope of converting individual Jews to Christianity. A virtual big-game-hunter mentality dominates their proselytizing agenda and forces them to "love" the Jewish people, all in hopes of being able to boast of having "converted" a Jew to Christianity. Fortunately, growing numbers of Christians have learned to be faithful to Jesus' *Mega Mitzvah* (the Great Commission),[41] which requires them to bear universal witness to their faith, while at the same time supporting the international Jewish community and the nation of Israel without preconditions.

What the Christian church needs for its own health, as well as for the benefit of the Jewish community, is a balanced, no-strings-attached position that affirms support for Israel and the international Jewish community that is not dominated by ulterior motives and, at the same time, prayerfully seeks social justice for all people everywhere.[42] Unequivocal Christian support for Israel must also be accompanied by corresponding support for all the peoples of the world so that, as believers in the God of Scripture, Christians become intercessors for peace, first in Jerusalem, then throughout the Middle East, and finally in the uttermost parts of the earth.

Solving Christian Vacillation

How does the church get beyond the confusing mixed signals of its historical love/hate relationship with the Jews? How can Christians come to manifest unequivocal support for the Jewish community and for the nation of Israel that is based on pure, biblical motives? How can Christians arise

---

[40] Stephen Spector, *Evangelicals and Israel: The Story of American Christian Zionism* (New York: Oxford University Press, 2009), p. 23. Spector says that "it has been widely reported that evangelicals have a dangerous ulterior motive for backing Israel: the belief that the Jews' return to their biblical home will lead to their mass conversion or death and will hasten the Rapture and the Second Coming. The reality is far more complicated than that, however."

[41] Mark 16:15. The Mega Mitzvah for Christians is this command from Jesus: "Go into all the world and preach the gospel to every creature."

[42] Sadly, some Christians fall into the trap of believing that in order to be pro-Israel, one must be anti-Palestinian Arab. This decidedly unchristlike attitude differs little from those who fall into the same trap of believing that in order to be pro-Palestinian, one must also be anti-Israel.

in this time of restoration of the nation of Israel to become unequivocally pro-Israel,[43] thereby fulfilling in a spiritual dimension the words of the prophets that Gentiles would come to Israel's light and build up her walls? A simple marketing axiom teaches that if one is to become highly supportive of a product or an idea, he must be enfranchised with a sense of ownership in that object or concept. Human beings are loyal to and supportive of what they own or that to which they have a sense of belonging. This profoundly simple concept must be applied to Christians in order to enlist their unequivocal support for Israel. Christians must be enfranchised with a sense of ownership of the vision of the restoration of Israel. They must come to see themselves as partners in the development of Israel and in the security of both Israel and the international Jewish community.

How can this be? First, the church around the world must be educated concerning the truth that Christianity is inherently a Jewish religion, birthed from the matrix of Second Temple Judaism. Gentile Christians who have come to faith in the God of the Hebrew Scriptures have been grafted into God's family tree of salvation and covenant relationship[44] and together with the Jewish people have become fellow citizens in the commonwealth of God's eternal Israel.[45] Gentiles are naturalized citizens of this commonwealth, but citizens nonetheless, and, as such, they have entitlements of citizenship. They are Abraham's children and "heirs according to the promises" that God made to Abraham.[46] This fact of Christian Scripture permits Christians to join the Jewish people and the nation of Israel as part of the greater family of God, sharing both the blessings and the responsibilities of biblical faith.

Taking the Initiative

Christians have the greater responsibility for establishing the means of coming alongside the Jewish community in true fraternal relationship because the church has been the greater source of division through its overt persecution of the Jewish people for the past eighteen centuries. Christianity has been the agent of the triumphalism and the supersessionist claims that have sought to disenfranchise the Jewish people from God's

---

[43] Being unequivocally pro-Israel does not mean that one must endorse and support every political, social, and military action undertaken by the government of Israel, nor does it mean that one must be anti-Arab.

[44] Romans 11:11.

[45] Ephesians 2:11–19.

[46] Galatians 3:29.

promises by saying that Christianity replaced Judaism, Christians re-placed the Jews, and the church replaced Israel in the purposes of God. Isaac Rottenberg said it well: "Divorced from Israel, torn from the nurtur-ing Hebraic roots of biblical faith (Romans 11:17ff.), the church becomes *ipso facto* a wayward church adhering to a (supersessionist) theology that is sadly off course."[47] Now, it is time to right historical wrongs, for Christians to bridge the gap that their forebears created.

When all of Christianity has been made aware of the richness of its heritage with and among the Jewish people, one of the largest people groups on the planet — the 2.3 billion Christians in the world — can be en-listed in unequivocal support of the international Jewish community and the nation of Israel. This support will not be a blanket endorsement of any particular political party, agency, or action in Israel.[48] It will not be "an unnuanced loyalty to Israel that looks very much like 'blank-check solidarity.'"[49] It will, however, be an affirmation of the fundamental right of the Jewish people to exist in the land of Israel as Jews with complete self-determination, void of any political, economic, or religious coercion, with full entitlement to establish and maintain their nation as they collec-tively see fit and proper. When Christians fully realize that the Jews are to be restored to their land, not because of some Christian eschatological scenario,[50] but because of Jewish entitlement to the land by virtue of God's unilateral covenant with their father Abraham and by virtue of God's irrevocable commitment to Abraham's posterity in perpetuity, Christians by the millions will come to support the Jewish people and their nation without all the self-interest-driven ecclesiastical vacillation that has produced so much suffering for the Jews in the past.

Sigmund Freud was completely correct when he argued that Christ-ian "hatred for Judaism is at bottom hatred for Christianity."[51] He also zeroed in on one of the real causes of such antipathy: "The peoples who

---

47 Isaac C. Rottenberg, "Israelic Christians," in *Restore!*, Issue 52, p. 33.
48 Unequivocal support for the people and nation of Israel is not putting the biblical message "into the service of ideological interests" or allowing "propaganda to be presented as gospel truth—all in the name of relevancy and prophecy." See Rottenberg, p. 34.
49 Rottenberg, p. 32.
50 Rottenberg, p. 32. Rottenberg notes that eschatological scenarios tend to be apocalyptic in nature, making "Israel's role in end-time speculations key" and "Armageddon and the Rapture . . . central theological foci." These often place Jews in the position of "being treated as marionettes in an almost mechanical Christian end-time scenario."
51 Sigmund Freud, *Moses and Monotheism* (New York: Random House, 1939), pp. 116–117.

now excel in the practice of anti-Semitism became Christians only in relatively recent times, sometimes forced to it by blood compulsion. One might say that they are 'badly christened' under the thin veneer of Christianity [and] they have remained . . . barbarically polytheistic."[52] Freud's maxim is true: Christian hatred for Jews is, in essence, a form of self-hatred. Christians who are ignorant of the foundations of their faith do not realize that when they hate Jews and Israel or even are apathetic toward that people and that nation, those same emotions redound toward their own Christian faith. Rather than define themselves *in contrast to* Judaism, the Jewish community, and the nation of Israel as Christianity has historically done, it is time for Christians to define themselves fully *in context with* Judaism, the Jewish community, and the nation of Israel just as Jesus and the apostles of original Christianity did two millennia ago.

When Christians fully realize that their faith was and remains a branch of biblical and Second-Temple Judaism, they will gain a profound sense of ownership in the vision of Jewish well-being and Israeli security. They will then be far more inclined to utter these immortal words and to mean them: "Wherever you go, I will go, and wherever you live, I will live; your people will be my people, and your God will be my God. Where you die, I will die, and there I will be buried. May YHWH punish me, and do so severely, if anything but death separates you and me."[53] These words that a Moabite Gentile woman named Ruth expressed over three millennia ago to her mother-in-law and, in effect, to the Jewish people of her day must echo from the heart of every Christian on the planet in this time. Old prejudices must melt away in the loving warmth of face-to-face relationship when Christians embrace their ancient, long-abandoned family. When Christians are led out of the ignorance of their heritage by the

---

[52] Freud's description of Christian antisemites as those with only a thin veneer of Christianity covering the barbaric polytheism of their past certainly described those German citizens who supported the Nazi regime and joined in its horrific acts of depravity against the Jews. Those "Christians" had been inoculated with just enough Christianity to make them immune to the Judaic-based conscience of true Christianity and, therefore, readily vulnerable to recidivism into their former polytheistic religion and its ethos. Many of them were outright advocates of neopaganism, and many of their Nazi leaders who professed to be Christians were actually atheistic occultists. For a discussion of neopaganism in Germany, see Abir Taha, *Nietzsche, Prophet of Nazism: The Cult of the Superman* (Bloomington, IN: AuthorHouse, 2005), p. 11ff. For an analysis of the impact of the occult on the Nazi party, see Nicholas Goodrick-Clark, *The Occult Roots of Nazism: Secret Aryan Cults and Their Influence on Nazi Ideology* (New York: New York University Press, 2004).

[53] Ruth 1:16–17, HCSB.

educational process that has so long been the hallmark of the Jewish community, they will abandon old prejudicial caricatures of Jews and Judaism. They will unequivocally and fully embrace the faith of Abraham, who Paul declared is the father of us all.[54]

It is profoundly difficult to hate one's own family, even when some members of that family are dysfunctional. When Christians embrace Jews as members of the divine family that was birthed in Abraham, nurtured in the prophets and sages of Israel, and expanded by the rabbi from Nazareth who, like his people before him, welcomed Gentiles into the faith of God, familial love overlooks faults and failures of the past and anticipates joy and success in future relationships of true mutuality. As Alain Weaver has said, "collaboration and mutual support between Jews and Christians can become possible around the task of recovering exilic traditions within Christianity and Judaism, even as Jews and Christians recognize and affirm the differences that separate them and the possibility of mutual learning from and challenge to those differences."[55]

Education

Racists, bigots, and antisemites will always slither from under their rocks, rear their ugly heads, shout their obscenities, and spew their hateful venom, and they must always be challenged when they do so. Rather than expending excessive energies, emotions, and resources counterattacking such evil, however, Christians should exercise themselves to the task of educating the church, bringing it out of the dark ages of prejudice into the light of its rightful biblical relationship with the international Jewish community. Then Christians will be able to extend to Israel and to the Jewish people the loving support that Jesus and the earliest Christian leaders demanded that they demonstrate to all people.

Though Christians by their own Scriptures have no literal entitlement to the land of Israel at least until the Messianic Age that is yet to come, they must still realize that, in spirit, Israel is their land and that the Jews are their people. Education is the key. By self-definition, education leads those who acquire it out of ignorance, superstition, and prejudice.[56] And prejudice is

---

[54] Romans 4:16.

[55] Alain Epp Weaver. *Mapping Exile and Return: Palestinian Dispossession and Political Theology* (Minneapolis, MN: Augsburg Fortress Press, 2014), p. 72.

[56] The word *education* is from the Latin *ex* ("from" or "out of") and *ducere* ("to lead").

nothing more than being down on something one is not up on! Could Christian Judaeophobia and antisemitism be any better defined? At the same time, knowledge is power. In this case, knowledge of Christianity's Judaic heritage is the dynamic antidote to Judaeophobia, anti-Judaism, antisemitism, anti-Zionism, and anti-Israelism.

The words of Edward Flannery bear repeating: "The over-Hellenized, over-Latinized Christian church needs a re-Judaization process in order to return it to its original ideal."[57] This process is not the conversion of Christians to Judaism or the replacing of faith with what has been characterized as legalism. It is merely embracing the faith of Jesus and the apostles, all of whom were observant Jews who were faithful to the teachings of the Hebrew Scriptures. In fact, it is discovery that Christianity is established on faith in the God of the Jews as understood through the Scriptures of the Jews, and realized by faith in the Jew whom the apostles recognized as Messiah and Lord. It is making the sincere effort to go where the church has not gone in nineteen centuries—back to the "faith once delivered to the saints,"[58] the faith of Abraham, Moses, David, Isaiah, Jesus, and Paul, and to true salvation which is from the Jews.[59]

In order to restore what has been lost, Christians must become proactive. A significant place to begin is in learning something about the language of Jesus and the apostles, biblical Hebrew. Despite the fact that most traditional historical Christian scholars do not believe Jesus was conversant with Hebrew, the truth is that he was well versed in the language of the Hebrew Scriptures. He certainly had no problem reading the *parashah* (Torah portion) and the *haftarah* in the synagogue of Galilee.[60] Paul was probably a polyglot, but his theology was taken from the Hebrew Scriptures,[61] and he

---

[57] Edward Flannery, quoted in George Cornell, "The Church after Jesus Loses Is Jewish Context," Fredericksburg, VA *Free Lance-Star*, Friday, March 28, 1975, p. 16.

[58] Jude 1:3.

[59] John 4:22.

[60] Luke 4:16–19; Isaiah 61:1.

[61] That Paul used the Hebrew text of Scripture for his theological arguments is proven in 1 Corinthians 15:54, where he renders Isaiah 25:8, "Death is swallowed up *in victory*." Most translations render Isaiah 25:8 as "Death is swallowed up *forever*." The Hebrew word translated "forever," however, is נֶצַח (*netzach*), which usually means "perpetuity" or "forever" but also can take the rare and obscure meaning of "victory." Paul used this meaning and translated the Hebrew *netzach* with the Greek νῖκος (*nikos*), "victory." It is certain that the apostle used the Hebrew *Tanakh* as his source rather than the Septuagint, for the Septuagint renders Isaiah 25:8, Κατέπιεν ὁ θάνατοσ ἰσχύσας (*katéphien ho thánatos*), "Death has prevailed and swallowed *men* up." In the Hebrew text, eternity or eternal life swallows up death. In Paul's Isaiah 25:8 translation, therefore, eternal life is victorious over death; in the Septuagint, death is victorious over men. It was easy for Paul to extrapolate his meaning from the *Tanakh*; however, it was impossible to get the same meaning from the Septuagint.

did not hesitate to address Jewish audiences in the Hebrew tongue that they understood.[62] Reconnecting with the language of Jesus and the primary language of Paul, therefore, will help Christians gain a better understanding of the worldview, mindset, and practices of the earliest Christian community which cannot help but make their own Christianity more vibrant.

When Christian understanding of the church's Jewish connection becomes universal, Christianity, the one people group that should always have stood alongside the Jewish people and the nation of Israel in unswerving, loving support, will once again become unequivocally pro-Israel, just as its Jewish Lord and his Jewish disciples were two millennia ago. This means that the largest religion in the world, representing one-third of the world population, would stand proudly alongside the Jewish people and the land of Israel. It means that there would be 2.3 billion unequivocal Israel supporters!

Taking a Stand

The restoration of the nation of Israel has been an unfolding act of God's hand to fulfill his covenant with Abraham including his promise that the patriarch's descendants would inherit the land of Canaan forever.[63] As such, it portends of even greater things that the God of Israel will do as he fulfills all his promises to the Jewish community and to the world. As Abraham Joshua Heschel wisely said, "The state of Israel is not the fulfillment of the messianic promise, but it makes the messianic promise possible."[64] The miracle of Israel's rebirth confirms to a skeptical world that "the gifts and callings of God are irrevocable,"[65] and it gives hope to both Jews and Christians that the Messianic Age will yet come, bringing God's gift of universal peace and blessing. As Rottenberg so eloquently said, "The nation of Israel, blessed with the gift of Torah, can and should manifest signs of the coming reign of God. So should countries and continents where the Gospel of the Kingdom has been proclaimed. The world desperately needs such pointers to the promises of Zion. This is the best model for those who seek to pursue what might be called the 'Shalomization' of the world along the way revealed in the Jewish Torah and the Christian Kerygma."[66]

---

[62] Acts 21:40; 22:2.
[63] Genesis 13:15.
[64] Abraham Joshua Heschel, *Israel: An Echo of Eternity* (New York: Macmillan, 1967.), p. 223.
[65] Romans 11:29.
[66] Rottenberg, p. 34.

CHAPTER 21

GOD'S "FINAL SOLUTION"

ISRAEL PLANTED, NEVER TO BE UPROOTED

A veritable parade of tyrants has marched across the annals of history, each one seeking to solve the "Jewish problem" and impose his own "final solution" on God's Chosen People. From Pharaoh, to Nebuchadnezzar, to Haman, to Antiochus, to Titus, to Hadrian, and, finally, to Hitler, "history's worst tyrants have always reserved a special hatred for the Jewish people."[1] At the same time, however, Israel—and especially the city of Jerusalem—has long been an "unmovable rock"[2] to such megalomaniacal despots and an almost unending succession of others who have sought to dominate the Jewish people, their body politic, and their land. Without exception, however, all the nations in history that have meddled in the affairs of Israel have herniated themselves, broken their backs, or become paralyzed and incapacitated as a result of their attitudes and actions toward Israel.[3] And as the Prophet Zechariah declared of what could well be a yet future attempt to destroy this people, this nation, and this land, "All who try to move [this stone] will injure themselves."[4]

Any present or future efforts by nations or peoples to align themselves against Israel will be met with the same catastrophic events that have afflicted the magnificent and mighty in history who have attempted to brutalize and enslave the Jewish people. They will find themselves "staggering" from

---

[1] George W. Bush in an April, 2001, speech, quoted in David B. MacDonald, *Thinking History, Fighting Evil: Neoconservatives and the Perils of Analogy* (Lanham, MD: Rowman & Littlefield Publishers, 2009), p. 98.
[2] Zechariah 12:3a, NIV.
[3] Even when those nations, including Babylon and Rome, that God commissioned to bring judgment upon Israel met the same fate when they exceeded their commission and began to brutalize the Chosen People.
[4] Zechariah 12:3b, NIV.

the profound inebriation imposed upon them by God himself.[5] Indeed, God declared that when the all the nations of the world launch the final eschatological assault against Israel and its capital, Jerusalem, they will run headlong into the only omnipotent entity in the universe, God himself, who declared that he would personally "set about to destroy all the nations that come against Jerusalem."[6] Any person, social entity, or political system that threatens any part of the Abrahamic covenant and its land contract will be cursed by God, for the Almighty has declared incontrovertibly, "The one who curses you I will curse."[7] Likewise any person or social entity that blesses what God has blessed by supporting, defending, and facilitating the fulfillment of the Abrahamic promise and its land contract will also be blessed by God, who also has pledged, "I will bless those who bless you."[8] And, indubitably, the Lord of heaven has categorically and irrevocably assured the world that he is ever on guard and alert to recognize and deal with affronts of any kind against his Chosen People and their land: "Behold, he who keeps Israel will neither slumber nor sleep."[9]

Inflicting pain on Israel causes God to suffer. Isaiah said it well when he quoted God as saying, "I was appalled that no one gave support, so my own arm achieved salvation for me. . . . So he became their Savior. In all their distress he too was distressed, and the angel of his presence saved them."[10] A rabbinic *midrash* on the prophetic declaration *in all their distress he too was distressed* suggests that anyone "who hates Israel is as if he hated God. . . . And he who helps Israel is as if he helped God. Whenever Israel is enslaved, the Shechinah is enslaved with them, as it says, 'In all their afflictions He was afflicted (Isa. LXIII, 9).'"[11]

Sadly, "instead of accepting Israel's election with humility," the Gentile nations "rail against it, mocking the God of the Jews," says Michael Wyschogrod. "Israel's presence is a constant reminder to them that they were not chosen but that this people was, and that this people remains in their midst as a thorn in the flesh. Minute by minute, the existence of Israel mocks the pagan gods, the divine

---

[5] Zechariah 12:2.
[6] Zechariah 12:9.
[7] Genesis 12:3.
[8] Genesis 12:3.
[9] Psalm 121:4.
[10] Isaiah 63:5, 8–9.
[11] *Sifre* to Numbers 64.4.5, in *A Theological Commentary to the Midrash: Sifre to Numbers and Sifre to Deuteronomy,* Jacob Neusner, ed. (Lanham, MD: University Press of America, 2001), pp. 21–22. Also Paul M. van Buren, *A Theology of the Jewish-Christian Reality: A Christian Theology of the People of Israel* (Lanham, MD: University Press of America, 1995), p. 166.

beings who rise out of the consciousness of all peoples but which are gentile gods because they are deifications of humanity and the forces of nature rather than the true, living God of Abraham."[12] In the name of their gods, the Gentile nations have repeatedly shaken their fists in the face of the God of Israel. Naftali Rothenberg rightly observes, however that "the paradox is that those people who left only monuments behind as a record of their existence have vanished with time, whereas the Jews, who left ideas, have survived."[13] Egyptians, Assyrians, Babylonians, Hittites, and Philistines "disappeared from the stage of history, leaving behind archaeological remains, but no living way of life."[14]

The Final Vindication of God's Honor

God is "a deity whose fierce passion and covenant commitment to His people knows no limitation and whose ardor for His chosen people guarantees their eventual restoration."[15] The Almighty went so far as to declare that his own personal honor would be at stake in the restoration of the land of Israel to the people of Israel. Listen to his declaration to the prophet Ezekiel: "It is not for your sake, O house of Israel, that I am about to act, but for my holy name. . . . I will vindicate the holiness of my great name. . . . Then the nations will know that I am the LORD, declares the LORD God, when I prove myself holy among you in their sight. For I will take you from the nations, gather you from all the lands and bring you into your own land."[16]

To a degree, the return of the Jewish people to their own land has already vindicated God's eternal promise to them. It has validated the passion for peoplehood, nationhood, and land that God himself has placed in their hearts. Israel's final restoration will, in fact, be the ultimate vindication of both the God of the Jews and his Chosen People. First, YHWH himself will be vindicated, as he said through the prophet Ezekiel, "'The nations will know that I am the LORD,' declares the LORD God, 'when through you I vindicate my holiness before their eyes.'"[17] Then, the Hebrews/Israelites/Jews who have been mocked, despised, ex-

---

[12] Michael Wyschogrod, *Abraham's Promise: Judaism and Jewish-Christian Relations*, P. Kendall Soulen, ed. (Grand Rapids, MI: Wm. B. Eerdmans Publishing Co., 2004), p. 182.

[13] Max I. Dimont, *Jews, God, and History* (New York: Penguin Books, 2004), cover.

[14] Naftali Rothenberg and Eliezer Schweid, eds., *Jewish Identity in Modern Israel: Proceedings on Secular Judaism and Democracy* (Jerusalem, Israel: Urim Publications, 2002), p. 69.

[15] Tim F. LaHaye and Edward E. Hindson, eds., *The Popular Bible Prophecy Commentary: Understanding the Meaning of Every Prophetic Passage* (Eugene, OR: Harvest House Publishers, 2006), p. 21.

[16] Ezekiel 36:22–24.

[17] Ezekiel 36:23, ESV.

iled, persecuted, and murdered for centuries will have their faith in God fully vindicated. After millennia of sorrow, pain, and agony, they will experience the blessing of God's promise to Zephaniah: "'Sing, Daughter Zion; shout aloud, Israel! Be glad and rejoice with all your heart, Daughter Jerusalem! The LORD has taken away your punishment. . . . The LORD, the King of Israel, is with you; never again will you fear any harm. . . . At that time I will gather you, at that time I will bring you home. I will give you honor and praise among all the peoples of the earth when I restore your fortunes before your very eyes,' says the LORD."[18]

Who Is on the Lord's Side?

God can no more forsake his land promise to Abraham's progeny than he can decide not to send the Messiah to earth. If God can forsake Israel, he can forsake the whole world, withdraw himself into the heavenlies, and nullify the promise of the resurrection. But, if he did any of these things, he would not be God, for God "cannot lie."[19] For this reason, God has given his personal assurance: "The LORD will not abandon his people on account of his great name, because the LORD has been pleased to make you a people for himself."[20] David Klinghoffer asks, "We are confronted here with the choice between the instrumentalist theory of faith, and the truth theory. Is religion about man, or is it about God?"[21] Marvin Wilson says that Klinghoffer's question is a reminder that "the religion and calling of Israel have their origin either in the eternal counsel of God or in the changeable theories of man. If the permanence of Israel's election is in doubt, the trustworthiness of God's Word is likewise in doubt."[22]

Most of historical Christianity, however, has placed the Jewish people outside salvation history with a status very little different from those who espouse polytheistic religions. Instead of recognizing the continuing impact of the Abrahamic covenant upon the Jewish people and affirming their inclusion in that covenant, the church has insisted that they be excluded, thereby violating Paul's unequivocal imperative: "Do not boast against the natural branches [the Jews]."[23] Judith

---

[18] Zephaniah 3:14–15, 20, NIV.
[19] Numbers 23:19; Titus 1:2.
[20] 1 Samuel 12:22, NIV.
[21] David Klinghoffer, "God Is Not a Pluralist," in *The Role of Religion in Politics and Society*, Arthur A. Cohen and Paul Mendes-Flohr, eds. (New York: Free Press, 1987), p. 152.
[22] Marvin R. Wilson, *Exploring Our Hebraic Heritage: A Christian Theology of Roots and Renewal* (Grand Rapids, MI: Wm. B. Eerdmans Publishing Co., 2014), p. 250. In support of his statement, Wilson references Genesis 17:7; Deuteronomy 7:7-9; 2 Samuel 7:24; and Jeremiah 31:35-36.
[23] Romans 11:18.

Gundry Volf maintains that "Paul argues against the mistaken conclusion that the hardened majority within Israel is permanently excluded from salvation,"[24] suggesting that the apostle includes them in his recapitulation: "All Israel shall be saved."[25] David Holwerda similarly declares that "the category of election still applies to the Jewish people, even those who do not now believe in Jesus."[26] The future of the Jewish people is guaranteed because it is based on God's faithfulness to bring to fruition the vision and work for which he elected them from among the nations in the first place.

Since God has never excluded the Jews from salvation history, why would anyone think he has the right to do so?[27] The question of who is saved and who is not saved is best left in the hands of the one and only Savior, who alone knows the thoughts and intents of every heart.[28] Everyone can rest assured that "the Lord knows those who are his."[29] The historical Christian church would have done well to have made Paul's exclamation its own theme song: "The gifts and calling of God are irrevocable."[30] Then, it could have passed what George Gilder describes as the "Israel test," the question of how people respond to the success of the nation of Israel.[31] What is true in the natural is also true in the spiritual: Those who hate Israel fail the "Israel test." Those who love Israel pass the "Israel test."

---

[24] Judith M. Gundry Volf, *Paul & Perseverance: Staying in and Falling Away* (Louisville, KY: Westminster John Knox Press, 1990), p. 171.

[25] Romans 11:26.

[26] David E. Holwerda, *Jesus and Israel: One Covenant or Two?* (Grand Rapids, MI: Wm. B. Eerdmans Publishing Co.,1995), p. 25.

[27] This position lets God be God in the determination of the outworking of the Abrahamic covenant. It does not presuppose a dual covenant theology—one covenant for the Jews, another for the Christians (Gentiles)—that some Christian denominations and theologians have developed. Paul says unequivocally, "There is one Lord, one faith, one baptism" (Ephesians 4:5). There is one covenant, the Abrahamic covenant, that has been renewed and expanded through the New Covenant and extended to all the people whom God promised to bless through Abraham and his descendants. The proper work of the church is to embrace the dynamic tension that includes Israel and the church in the covenant without requiring the exclusion of one in order to permit the inclusion of the other. In the final analysis, this approach recognizes that the right to define the covenant belongs to the one created it.

[28] Hebrews 4:12. For a variety of opinions on this issue, see Clark H. Pinnock, *The Wideness of God's Mercy: The Finality of Jesus Christ in a World of Religions* (Grand Rapids, MI: Zondervan Publishing House, 1992); John Sanders, *No Other Name: An Investigation into the Destiny of the Unevangelized* (Eugene, OR: Wipf & Stock Publishing, 2001); Al Truesdale with Keri Mitchell, *With Cords of Love: A Wesleyan Response to Religious Pluralism* (Kansas City, MO: Beacon Hill Press, 2013); and Terrance L. Tiessen, *Who Can Be Saved? Reassessing Salvation in Christ and World Religions* (Downers Grove, IL: InterVarsity Press, 2004).

[29] 2 Timothy 2:19.

[30] Romans 11:29.

[31] George Gilder, *The Israel Test: Why the World's Most Besieged State is a Beacon of Freedom and Hope for the World Economy* (Minneapolis, MN: Richard Vigilante Books, 2009). Also, Bill Federer, "What Happens When You Mess with Israel?" *WorldNetDaily,* 7 Sept. 2015, posed at http://www.wnd.com/2015/09/what-happens-when-you-mess-with-israel/.

Ultimately, God will bring an end to the litany of Gentile "final solutions" to the "Jewish problem" when he initiates his own "final solution" to the "Gentile problem" by reversing the Gentile trend of engaging in downward spirals of condemnation, caricature, and violence against his Chosen People. This he will do when he reestablishes the faith of the Jewish people on the new covenant of the Torah written on their hearts.[32] In fact, then the nations will understand that resurrected Israel *is*, as Jacob Neusner describes it, "God's final solution to the human problem."[33] May the entire earth join in joyous expectation of the fulfillment of what Paul envisioned as God's final solution for the Jewish people: "All Israel shall be saved."[34] Those who do will also be able to share in the apostle's doxology by exclaiming with him, "Oh, the depth of the riches both of the wisdom and knowledge of God! How unsearchable are his judgments and unfathomable his ways! . . . For from him and through him and to him are all things. To him be the glory forever. Amen."[35]

The Ultimate Restoration

While numerous prophecies are set forth in the Hebrew Scriptures predicting the restoration of the Jewish people to their land, there is one that has a ring of finality. This is the prophecy of Amos in which he recorded this promise from God to Israel, "In that day I will restore David's fallen *sukkah*—I will repair its broken walls and restore its ruins—and will rebuild it as it used to be."[36] The restoration that YHWH promised was to be accompanied with agricultural wonders: "Behold, days are coming, declares the LORD, when the plowman will overtake the reaper and the treader of grapes him who sows seed; when the mountains will drip sweet wine."[37] In that day, the restored Israeli people is to enjoy the richness of the land: "They will plant vineyards and drink their wine; they will make gardens and eat their fruit."[38] Finally, however, God established perhaps the most important prophetic promise about this restoration that had ever been made when he said, "I will plant Israel in their own land, *never again to be uprooted from the land I have given them*, says the LORD your God."[39]

---

[32] Jeremiah 31:31.
[33] Jacob Neusner, *The Native Category-Formations of the Aggadah: The Earlier Midrash-Compilations* (Lanham, MD: University Press of America, 2000), p. 150.
[34] Romans 11:26.
[35] Romans 11:33, 36.
[36] Amos 9:11, NIV.
[37] Amos 9:13.
[38] Amos 9:14.
[39] Amos 9:15, emphasis added.

While other prophecies promised restoration to the land, an abundance of miracles in the land, and abiding peace in the land, Amos heard God say that his final solution for Israel would feature this promise: *Israel will never again be uprooted from its land!* Once and for all time, the people who have been dislodged from their land again and again by violence will be restored to the land with the promise that they will never be uprooted from it.

Yet another miracle that God promised to Israel through Amos is the final reconciliation of the non-Jewish nations to the Chosen People. Here is what God predicted: "[Israel will] possess the remnant of Edom and all the nations that bear my name, declares the LORD, who will do these things."[40] The culmination of the "never-to-be-uprooted" promise includes the full application of Israel's Abrahamic blessing to the nations, the expansion of God's particularity into his universality by extending to the nations the unilateral covenant of inclusion. This was the mystery[41] to which Paul alluded when he discussed Gentile inclusion in God's family tree[42] and their adoption as naturalized citizens of the commonwealth of Israel.[43] Amos' Gentile inclusion in Israel's blessing was echoed by Isaiah's divine message to Israel: "Arise, shine; for your light has come. . . . Nations will come to your light. . . . [T]he flocks of Kedar [and] the rams of Nebaioth will minister to you. They will go up with acceptance on my altar. . . . Foreigners will build up your walls, and their kings will minister to you."[44] God had already promised Isaiah that foreigners (Gentiles) would be added to his Chosen People: "Many peoples will come and say, 'Come, let us go up the mountain of the LORD, to the temple of the God of Jacob. He will teach us his ways, so that we may walk in his paths.'" The prophet said that this prediction would be possible because "the Torah will go forth from Zion and the word of the LORD from Jerusalem."[45] Then God even predicted that the Gentiles who would lay hold on his Torah would be given a name "better than that of sons and daughters . . . which will not be cut off."[46]

Jacob Neusner discusses Jewish thought on the manner in which this Gentile inclusion in Israel can take place: "Israel is Israel by reason of accepting the Torah . . . that conviction . . . represents the final solution to the gentile-problem:

---

[40] Amos 9:121, NIV.
[41] Ephesians 3:4–9.
[42] Romans 11:11.
[43] Ephesians 2:12–19.
[44] Isaiah 60:1, 3, 7. Here, Kedar and Nabaioth, the first two of Ishmael's twelve sons, represent the Gentiles.
[45] Isaiah 2:3, NIV.
[46] Isaiah 56:5.

how the gentile overcomes his alienation from God and becomes Israel. His condition is not beyond remediation but readily corrected. And when the gentile becomes Israel, then he or she joins Israel without differentiation as to origin or status."[47] Within the general mystery of God's sovereign dealings with all the people of the earth, another Jewish rabbi, the apostle Paul proclaimed this solution: "If you belong to the Messiah, then you are Abraham's offspring, heirs according to the promise,"[48] and he also predicted that a "full number of the Gentiles" would be included in the Abrahamic covenant in the same timeframe in which "all Israel will be saved."[49] This all-inclusive work of divine sovereignty is intrinsically connected with the full restoration of David's *sukkah*, the tabernacle of Israel, to its glory. God's word to the prophet Haggai best describes this miraculous event: "The latter glory of this house will be greater than the former . . . and in this place I will give peace, declares the LORD of hosts."[50]

The return of the Jewish people who have made *aliyah* from the four corners of the earth has certainly set the stage for the final fulfillment of God's prophetic promise to Amos. The prayers and hopes of both Jews and Christians have to be that the restoration of Israel—the people, the nation, and the land— that has taken place in the modern era will transcend the post-exilic restoration in the days of Ezra, Nehemiah, Zerubbabel, and Joshua and will have the permanency that God predicted to Amos. Prayerfully, it will be the final restoration, the one that will firmly and securely place the Jewish people in their land so that they will never be removed again. With the extraordinary miracle that occurred in 1948 and with the continuing miracles of preservation that have taken place since that time, all people of biblical faith must affirm God's words of final truth and say, Amen! May today's restoration, indeed, be the final restoration.[51]

Final Borders for the Land

How much real estate is included in God's land promises to Abraham, Isaac, Jacob, the Israelites, and the Jews? It is quite ironic that many of the people who think that they have the definitive answer to this question seem more preoccupied with defining the borders of Israel than the Jews, including those who live in Israel, are. Some Christians think they have a divine right,

---

[47] Jacob Neusner, *A Theological Commentary to the Midrash: Ruth Rabbah and Esther Rabbah I* (Lanham, MD: University Press of America, 2001), p. 46.
[48] Galatians 3:29.
[49] Romans 11:25–26.
[50] Haggai 2:9.
[51] Daniel 2:44; 4:3; 7:14, 18, 27.

based on their interpretation of the biblical land promises or on their eschatological expectations, to condemn Israeli leaders for negotiating land settlements with Palestinian Arabs or with their neighbors, Egypt, Lebanon, Syria, and Jordan. Others would even encourage Israel to launch invasions across its present borders to secure land that has been included in biblical iterations of the land promises.

Perhaps the answer to this question is as simple as the fact that when God first made a land promise to Abraham, he merely said, "To your descendants I will give this land."[52] The real estate contract of the first promise was not, therefore, based on a GPS perimeter survey with a margin for error of less than 100 millimeters. "What the Bible emphasizes," says Marvin Wilson, "is not precisely defined borders but simply the land of Canaan."[53] As God's relationship with Abraham unfolded the simple "this-land" promise was further delineated and expanded. First, in response to Abraham's "land-for-peace" gesture toward Lot, God said, "Now lift up your eyes and look from the place where you are, northward and southward and eastward and westward; for all the land which you see, I will give it to you and to your descendants forever."[54] Later, when God finalized his covenant with Abraham, he said, "To your descendants I give this land, from the River of Egypt to the great river, the Euphrates."[55]

In time, God further clarified to Moses the extent of the land promise: "I will fix your boundary from the Red Sea to the sea of the Philistines, and from the desert to the River Euphrates."[56] Then, centuries later, the Almighty gave the prophet Ezekiel even more extensive and definitive details regarding Israel's boundaries: "This shall be the boundary of the land: on the north side, from the Great Sea by the way of Hethlon, to the entrance of Zedad. The boundary shall extend from the sea to Hazar-enan at the border of Damascus. . . . This is the north side. The east side, from between Hauran, Damascus, Gilead and the land of Israel, shall be the Jordan . . . from the north border to the Dead Sea. This is the east side. The west side shall be the Great Sea, from the south border to a point opposite Lebo-hamath. This is the west side. The south side toward the south shall extend from Tamar as far as the waters of Meribath-kadesh, the brook of Egypt and to the Great Sea. This is the south side toward the south."[57]

---

[52] Genesis 12:7.
[53] Marvin R. Wilson, *Our Father Abraham: Jewish Roots of the Christian Faith* (Grand Rapids, MI: Wm. B. Eerdmans Publishing Co., 1989), p. 274.
[54] Genesis 13:15.
[55] Genesis 15:18, NIV.
[56] Exodus 23:31.
[57] Ezekiel 47:15–20.

Perhaps this systematic unfolding, delineation, and expansion of the land contract of the Abrahamic covenant was emblematic of the fact that the Land of Israel would be defined in different times by different borders. Regardless as to the extent of the borders on a map, however, the "land" was the land of Israel. The land reached its greatest expanse during the reign of Solomon, stretching virtually to the limits of the Abrahamic promise, but it was still the land when Gentile neighbors encroached on its definitive ultimate boundaries. Throughout history, boundary definitions for the landmass of Israel have been in a constant state of flux, and this condition continues to the present day.

For this and other reasons, absolutist "real estate theology," especially absolutist real estate eschatology, is fraught with potential for misunderstanding and abuse.[58] This is why Wilson urges caution in considering "the return of the Jews to the land as a realization of eschatological promises in Scripture."[59] Perhaps the most important hermeneutical principle for interpreting biblical prophecy is this: no prophecy of the Scriptures can be fully understood until *after* it has been fulfilled. In the meantime, even the wisest of teachers and seers must acknowledge with Paul that they "see only a reflection as in a mirror."[60] While the restoration of the land of Israel to the Jewish people may well have eschatological implications, it is — and will be — primarily the fulfillment of the terms of the Abrahamic covenant, not an absolutist precondition of a particular eschatological scenario. It is an established fact of Christian insight that those who take an absolutist perspective on eschatological events more often than not "miss the time of their visitation."[61]

This is why even Jewish claims to the land of Israel must be tempered by the universal Jewish sensitivity to social justice. The Jewish people's reclamation of the Holy Land is a testimony to a divine miracle. They did not have to muster a great army to invade and conquer the land. Instead, little by little, they made *aliyah* to their native land and gradually reclaimed it from centuries of neglect and disrepair. The independence of the Jewish state and its global recognition were the result of peaceful action, not violent conquest, even though it was immediately followed by Arab invasions designed to abort the birth — or rebirth — of God's nation. Thankfully, the resurrected state of Israel

---

[58] Christians who make judgments and land boundary demands on Israel based on proof-texting of Scripture would do well to understand that, in the final analysis, God is in charge of his Holy Land and he will effect his divine will in the time that he chooses.

[59] Wilson, p. 268.

[60] 1 Corinthians 13:12.

[61] Luke 19:44.

has been guided by the ongoing Jewish quest for justice and peace and its expectation of working in partnership with God in the process of *Tikkun Olam*. Israel has sought to conquer no territory, and it has expanded its borders only in the face of invasions by its neighbors—and even then only as a means of providing for its own security and not just to acquire more territory.

Regarding land boundaries for Israel, one guiding principle should be clear: the body politic of Israel—and no other person or entity—has the right to determine the parameters of the Israelis' land inheritance.[62] At the same time, the final borders of the land will ultimately be set by God himself, who may extend them in whatever manner he wills, for "the earth is the LORD's and the fullness thereof."[63] Uriel Tal offers a wise word of caution to those who wonder about present-day boundaries: "Is our time—our era—one of eschatological fulfillment or even of apocalyptical salvation? Or are we in the realm of historical time? Is the sacrosanctity of space, the domain in which the State of Israel expands, dependent on politically fixed boundaries, or are territorial boundaries conceived in terms of historical, hence, changing space?"[64] Since the eschatological events that will inaugurate God's kingdom on earth have not yet arrived, humanity must still be operating in the realm of historical time.[65] As the earth moves from the historical to the ahistorical *Olam Ha-Ba*, however, sacrosanct space will be delineated by God himself, who will make the land of Israel his dwelling place forever. In the final analysis, the "land" included in the Abrahamic covenant will ultimately encompass "all the earth," for the Messiah will establish the dominion that will consume all others and will stand forever.[66]

What God Says about Israel's Future

The foundation of what God has planned for Israel's future rests in the fiery passion that he has for both his people and his land. Here is what God himself said: "This is what the LORD Almighty says: I am very jealous for

---

[62] The boundaries of Israel were often imposed upon the Jewish people by foreign powers rather than by their own initiative. Whatever the case may be, God will ultimately orchestrate the circumstances which will eventuate in the full conveyance of all the land that he promised Abraham's descendants forever.

[63] Psalm 24:1.

[64] Uriel Tal, "Totalitarian Democratic Hermeneutics and Policies in Modern Jewish Religious Nationalism," in *Totalitarian Democracy and After*, Yehoshua Arieli and Nathan Rotenstreich, eds., (London, UK: Frank Cass Publishers, 2002), p. 141.

[65] Just as Miriam's Song by the Sea spoke not only of the liberation of Israel from Egypt but also of the breaking forth of God's kingdom, as evidenced by its concluding refrain, "The LORD reigns for ever and ever" (Exodus 15:18), so the gathering of Israel must also speak of both historical and ahistorical time in the *Olam Ha-Ba*.

[66] Daniel 2:44.

Zion; I am burning with jealousy for her. . . . I will return to Zion and dwell in Jerusalem. Jerusalem will be called The Faithful City, and the mountain of the LORD Almighty will be called the Holy Mountain."[67]

God will renew his eternal covenant with his people Israel: "Behold, days are coming, declares the LORD, when I will make a new covenant with the house of Israel and with the house of Judah, not like the covenant which I made with their fathers in the day I took them by the hand to bring them out of the land of Egypt. . . . [T]his is the covenant which I will make with the house of Israel after those days, declares the LORD, I will put my Torah within them and on their heart I will write it; and I will be their God, and they shall be my people.'"[68] It is clear that in this prophecy, "Jeremiah specifically pictures the eschatological fulfillment of God's purposes for Israel as the making of a new covenant, that is, the eschatological renewal of God's covenant with Israel."[69]

Because God is passionate about his people Israel, he will gather them and return them to their land: "I will gather the remnant of my flock out of all the countries where I have driven them and bring them back to their pasture, and they will be fruitful and multiply."[70] There is no place on earth to which the Jews have been dispersed that will not witness their regathering to their own land: "Though those of you who have been scattered were in the most remote part of the heavens, I will gather them from there and will bring them to the place where I have chosen to cause my name to dwell."[71] God will assemble his people from every part of the earth to which they have been dispersed: "Do not fear, for I am with you; I will bring your offspring from the east, and gather you from the west. I will say to the north, Give them up! And to the south, Do not hold them back. Bring my sons from afar and my daughters from the ends of the earth."[72]

God will fully restore to his Chosen People all the land that he promised to Abraham: "Thus says the LORD God, This shall be the boundary by which you shall divide the land for an inheritance among the twelve tribes of Israel . . . each one equally with the other; for I swore to give it to your forefathers, and this land shall fall to you as an inheritance."[73] In fact,

---

[67] Zechariah 8:2–3, NIV.
[68] Jeremiah 31:32–33.
[69] M. Eugene Boring, *An Introduction to the New Testament: History, Literature, and Theology* (Louisville, KY: Westminster John Knox Press, 2012), pp. 3–4.
[70] Jeremiah 23:3.
[71] Nehemiah 1:9.
[72] Isaiah 43:5–6.
[73] Ezekiel 47:13–14.

the Almighty was even more specific regarding the inheritance of the twelve tribes: "This is the land which you shall divide by lot to the tribes of Israel for an inheritance, [and] the gates of the city will be named after the tribes of Israel."[74] Israel's ultimate borders were also described in great detail by the prophet Ezekiel,[75] reflecting the fullness of the land that God conveyed to Abraham's descendants "forever," the land from the river of Egypt to the Euphrates.[76] Even then, God declared that he would expand Israel's borders: "You have increased the nation, O LORD . . . you have enlarged all the borders of the land."[77] Before the Israelites had entered the Promised Land over three millennia ago, God had promised them: "I will drive out nations before you and enlarge your borders, and no man shall covet your land when you go up three times a year to appear before the LORD."[78] God's promise to Jacob, however, was even greater than this: "You will spread out to the west and to the east and to the north and to the south; and in you and your descendants shall all the families of the earth be blessed."[79] Ultimately, Abraham's descendants are destined to inherit the entire earth: "The promise to Abraham and his descendants that he would be heir of the *kosmos* was . . . through the righteousness of faith."[80]

The land of Israel will be profoundly blessed with fertility and productivity: "I will restore the captivity of my people Israel, and they will rebuild the ruined cities and live in them; they will also plant vineyards and drink their wine, and make gardens and eat their fruit."[81] God will fulfill this promise by bringing forth "offspring from Jacob, and an heir of my mountains from Judah; even my chosen ones shall inherit it, and my servants will dwell there. Sharon will be a pasture land for flocks, and the valley of Achor

---

74 Isaiah 48:29–31.
75 Ezekiel 47:14–21.
76 Genesis 15:18.
77 Isaiah 26:15.
78 Exodus 34:24. The promise that "no one" would covet the land of Israel was certainly never fulfilled in Israelite history, and it has not been fulfilled even to this day, for there has never been a time when someone has not coveted the land of Israel. In fact, throughout history to the present day, the land of Israel has been among the most coveted pieces of real estate in the world! This divine promise, therefore, must have been eschatological in nature, speaking of the *Olam Ha-Ba*.
79 Genesis 28:14.
80 Romans 4:13. The Greek word translated "world" is κόσμος (*kósmos*), which indicates that the scope of Abraham's inheritance was expanded from "this land" (Genesis 12:7), to "all that you can see" (Genesis 28:14), to "from the river of Egypt to the Euphrates" (Genesis 15:18), and ultimately to the entire earth. Paul clearly understood that through the Messiah, Abraham's inheritance would ultimately include the entire cosmos!
81 Amos 9:14.

a resting place for herds."[82] In that day, "the wilderness and the desert will be glad, and the Arabah will rejoice and blossom; like the crocus it will blossom profusely."[83] Amazingly, "instead of the thorn bush the cypress will come up, and instead of the nettle the myrtle will come up, and it will be a memorial to the LORD, for an everlasting sign which will not be cut off."[84] All the land of Israel will be fruitful in this time when God blesses Israel in greater proportions than when Israel was a "land flowing with milk and honey."[85] Here is God's promise for the future: "But you, O mountains of Israel, you will put forth your branches and bear your fruit for my people Israel; for they will soon come. For, behold, I am for you, and I will turn to you, and you will be cultivated and sown. I will multiply men on you, all the house of Israel, all of it; and the cities will be inhabited and the waste places will be rebuilt. . . . I will treat you better than at the first. Thus you will know that I am the LORD."[86]

God will make Israel a place of permanent security and safety for his Chosen People: "Behold, I will gather them out of all the lands to which I have driven them in my anger. . . . I will bring them back to this place and make them dwell in safety."[87] The Lord of Israel will accomplish his promise as he also said: "I will provide a place for my people Israel and will plant them so that they can have a home of their own and no longer be disturbed. Wicked people will not oppress them anymore."[88] This includes the city of Jerusalem: "All the fields as far as the brook Kidron, to the corner of the Horse Gate toward the east, shall be holy to the LORD; it will not be plucked up or overthrown anymore forever."[89] God could not be clearer about his intentions: "I will plant them, and not pluck them up. . . . I will rejoice in doing good to them, and I will plant them in this land in faithfulness, with all my heart and all my soul. . . . I will plant you, and not pluck you up."[90] Furthermore, he promised, "I will also plant them on their land, and they will not again be rooted out from their land which I have given them, says the LORD your God."[91]

---

[82] Isaiah 65:9–10.
[83] Isaiah 35:1–2.
[84] Isaiah 55:13.
[85] Exodus 3:8.
[86] Ezekiel 36:9–10.
[87] Jeremiah 32:37–38.
[88] 2 Samuel 7:10, NIV.
[89] Jeremiah 31:40.
[90] Jeremiah 24:6; 32:41; 42:10.
[91] Amos 9:15

God himself will personally fight to secure peace for his Chosen People:
When God will "gather all nations against Jerusalem to battle," then, "the
LORD will go forth" and stand "on the Mount of Olives" so he can "fight
against those nations." At that time, "living waters will flow out of Jerusalem
. . . and the LORD will be king over all the earth." Finally, "on that day there
will be one LORD, and his name the only name."[92] God himself will set foot
on earth in order to fight for his people and their land, and he will rescue
them: "As a lion or lion cub growls at its prey and is not frightened away . . .
so likewise the LORD of hosts will descend to fight on Mount Zion. Like
hovering birds, so will *YHWH Tzva'ot* protect Jerusalem, shielding and saving, protecting and rescuing."[93]

***God will send the Messiah to Israel with the mission of restoring all things
and even superseding what he created in Eden:*** The prophet Daniel made this
prediction: "Behold, with the clouds of heaven one like a son of man was coming, and he came to the Ancient of days . . . and to him was given dominion,
glory, and a kingdom, that all the peoples, nations and men of every language
might serve him. His dominion is an everlasting dominion which will not pass
away."[94] King David also envisioned this event: "Give the king your judgments, O God, and your righteousness to the king's son. May he judge your
people with righteousness and your afflicted with justice. In his days may the
righteous flourish, and abundance of peace till the moon is no more. May he
also rule from sea to sea and from the River to the ends of the earth. . . . And
let all kings bow down before him, all nations serve him."[95]

God will bring deliverance and salvation to his people in their land: "The
LORD has sent out word to the end of the earth, Say to the daughter of Zion, See
your salvation comes; behold, his reward is with him, and his recompense before
him."[96] This is the time about which God predicted, "And it shall come to pass
that whoever calls on the name of the LORD shall be delivered. For in Mount
Zion and in Jerusalem there shall be deliverance."[97] In that day, "on Mount Zion
there will be deliverance. . . . Jacob will possess his inheritance."[98] When God

---

92 Zechariah 14:1-8.
93 Isaiah 31:4–5, CJB, TNK.
94 Daniel 7:13–14.
95 Psalm 72:1–2, 7–8, 11. David's prayer clearly transcended his own dominion and that of his son
Solomon. It speaks in terms of events that will occur during the messianic kingdom at the end of the age.
96 Isaiah 62:11.
97 Joel 3:1.
98 Obadiah 1:17.

fully restores his people in their land, "then they will know that I, the LORD their God, am with them, and that they, the house of Israel, are my people, declares the LORD God."[99] When this occurs, "they will come and shout for joy on the height of Zion, and they will be radiant over the bounty of the LORD. . . . Then the virgin will rejoice in the dance, and the young men and the old, together, for I will turn their mourning into joy and will comfort them and give them joy for their sorrow."[100] When everything is accomplished, "God will save Zion and build the cities of Judah, that they may dwell there and possess it. The descendants of his servants will inherit it, and they that love his name shall dwell in it."[101]

The land of Israel will be the focal point from which the divine word will flow to all nations: "And many peoples will come and say, Come, let us go up to the mountain of the LORD, to the house of the God of Jacob; that he may teach us concerning his ways and that we may walk in this paths. For the Torah will go forth from Zion and the word of the LORD from Jerusalem."[102] Psalms of praise will echo from Zion: "Great is the LORD, and greatly to be praised in the city of our God, in His holy mountain. Beautiful in elevation, the joy of the whole earth, is Mount Zion on the sides of the north, the city of the great King."[103] Divine worship will even be extended from Mt. Zion to all the Gentile lands: "In that day there will be an altar to the LORD in the heart of Egypt, and there will be a monument to the LORD at its border."[104]

God will see to it that righteous non-Jews are included in Israel's land inheritance: God reiterated to Ezekiel what he had commanded the Israelites in the Torah: "You shall divide [the land] by lot for an inheritance among yourselves and among the foreigners who stay in your midst . . . and they shall be to you as the native-born among the sons of Israel; they shall be allotted an inheritance with you among the tribes of Israel. In whatever tribe a foreigner resides, there you are to give them their inheritance, declares the Sovereign LORD."[105] Isaiah described Gentile inclusion in Abraham's blessing, "In you all the nations of the earth will be blessed," when he predicted: "In that day Israel will be the third party with Egypt and Assyria, a blessing in the midst of the earth, whom the LORD of hosts

99 Ezekiel 34:30.
100 Jeremiah 31:12–13.
101 Psalm 69:35–36.
102 Isaiah 2:3.
103 Psalm 48:1–2.
104 Isaiah 19:19.
105 Ezekiel 47:22.

has blessed, saying, Blessed is Egypt my people, and Assyria the work of my hands, and Israel my inheritance."[106] Of a truth, "the conversion of the nations . . . is a broad thematic expression of the promise made to Abraham that 'in you all the families of the earth shall be blessed . . . as well as the promise of the land, both integral parts of the Abrahamic promise."[107]

All nations will know that the God of Israel is the true God, and they will worship him together with the Jews: "The nations will fear the name of the LORD, and all the kings of the earth will revere your glory. For the LORD will build up Zion and appear in His glory."[108] This is the vision that King David so succinctly encapsulated in these words: "All nations whom you have made shall come and worship before you, O LORD, and they shall glorify your name. . . . All the ends of the earth will remember and turn to the LORD, and all the families of the nations will worship before you. For the kingdom is the LORD's and he rules over the nations."[109] Zechariah confirmed the finality of this action in the *Olam Ha-Ba*: "Then it will come about that any who are left of all the nations that went against Jerusalem will go up from year to year to worship the King, the LORD of hosts, and to celebrate the Festival of Tabernacles."[110]

God's Final Word for Israel

In the final analysis, God will have the last word regarding Israel. Based on the principle of divine immutability which establishes the truth that God is utterly faithful to fulfill his covenants and promises, it can be asserted that God's ultimate word for his Chosen People will be the same as the final word in his own ancient blessing for Israel. When God composed this everlasting benediction for Israel and dictated it to Moses, he instructed the prophet to make sure that the following words would be continually spoken over the children of Israel in all their generations:

יְבָרֶכְךָ יהוה וְיִשְׁמְרֶךָ׃

יָאֵר יהוה פָּנָיו אֵלֶיךָ וִיחֻנֶּךָּ׃

יִשָּׂא יהוה פָּנָיו אֵלֶיךָ וְיָשֵׂם לְךָ שָׁלוֹם׃

---

106 Isaiah 19:24–25.
107 David Mathewson, "Abraham, the Father of Many Nations in the Book of Revelation," in *Perspectives on Our Father Abraham: Essays in Honor of Marvin R. Wilson*, Steven A. Hunt, ed. (Grand Rapids, MI: Wm. B. Eerdmans Publishing Co., 2014), p. 170.
108 Psalm 102:15–16.
109 Psalm 86:6; Psalm 22:27.
110 Zechariah 14:16.

> May the LORD bless you, and keep you;
> May the LORD cause his face to shine upon you
> and be gracious unto you;
> May the LORD turn his face toward you and give you *shalom*.

The final Hebrew word of this divine benediction is שָׁלוֹם (*shalom*), which, in itself, is a self-contained blessing that means far more than peace in the sense of an absence of conflict. Trevor Bechtel describes the word *shalom* in this manner: "The most common meaning of shalom is material well-being and prosperity. This means our physical health, our access to food and care and shelter . . . an integrated state of well-being or health."[111] This is what is meant in Isrel when someone inquires of another, "*Ma sh'lom-cha?*" (literally, "What is your peace [well-being]?" but colloquially, "How are you?"). Interestingly, in Israel the word *shalom* is also a common form of greeting which means both "hello" and "goodbye." In contemporary use in Israel, *shalom* is also viewed as a sense of justice, "the restoration or creation of right relationships between individuals or groups."[112] Yet another use of *shalom* connects with "personal integrity and honesty." Since true *shalom* does involve "physical well-being, justice, and integrity," it essentially means that "everything is exactly as it should be."[113]

God's final word for Israel, then, is, "The LORD turn his face toward you and give you *shalom* [health, justice, and integrity]," thereby making "everything precisely as it should be" in the individual and corporate lives of his Chosen People. No matter what anyone else may have to say to the Jewish people, the nation of Israel, and the Promised Land, God's final word to Israel is *Shalom*, and God will always have the last word! It is no wonder, then, that God said to Jerusalem, "I will extend peace to her like a river," and promised his people, "No weapon that is formed against you will prosper. . . . [T]his is the heritage of the servants of the LORD, and their vindication is from me."[114] Ultimately, God will have the last word—the final solution—in the conflict with humanity, and he has already spoken, he still speaks, and, through the terms of his eternal covenant, he will continue to speak his everlasting *shalom* to the Chosen People, the Holy Nation, and the Promised Land.

---

[111] Trevor George Bechtel, *The Gift of Ethics: A Story for Discovering Lasting Significance in Your Daily Work* (Eugene, OR: Wipf and Stock Publishers, 2014), p. 38.
[112] Bechtel, p. 38.
[113] Bechtel, p. 38.
[114] Isaiah 66:12; 54:17.

Appendix A
League of Nations Mandate for Palestine
April 24, 1920

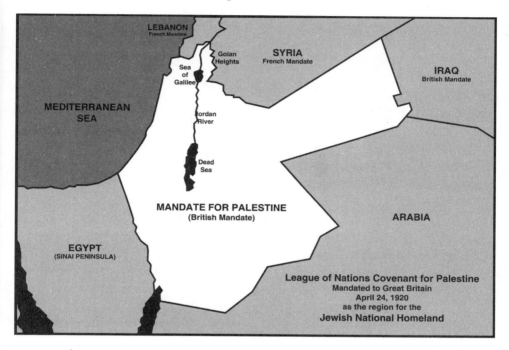

The map above depicts the original League of Nations Covenant for Palestine that was established on April 24, 1920. In the terms of the original League of Nations Covenant, the entire land west and east of the Jordan River (the area in white) was mandated to Great Britain for the purpose of establishing a national homeland for the Jewish people just as soon as the people were strong enough and organized enough to be able to constitute an independent nation.[1]

---

[1] Eli E. Hertz, "'Mandate for Palestine': The Legal Aspects of Jewish Rights,"posted at http:// www.mythsandfacts.org/conflict/mandate_for_palestine/mandate_for_palestine.htm. Hertz documents in great detail the nature and scope of the League of Nations Covenant and Mandate for Palestine which "laid down the Jewish legal right to settle anywhere in western Palestine" in the area "between the Jordan River and the Mediterranean Sea. He also notes that "the Mandate weathered the test of time: On April 18, 1946, when the League of Nations was dissolved and its assets and duties transferred to the United Nations, the international community, in essence, reaffirmed the validity of this international accord and reconfirmed that the terms for a Jewish National Home were the will of the international community, a 'sacred trust." See pp. 218, 255, 257 in this text.

Appendix B
League of Nations Mandate for Palestine
July 24, 1922

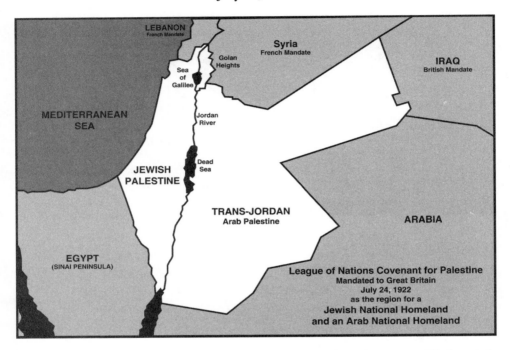

The map above depicts the League of Nations Covenant for Palestine modified on July 24, 1922. The Covenant mandated to Great Britain for the Jewish State included all of the land west of the Jordan River (the West Bank) and the Golan Heights and was the basis for the 1947 United Nations Resolution 181, which prepared the way for the establishment of the nation of Israel on May 14, 1948, the day after the British Mandate ended. The Golan Heights was ceded to Syria by the British on February 3, 1922. Jordan invaded and occupied the West Bank in 1948. The 45-year Golan occupation and the 19-year West Bank occupation were ended with the Israeli victory in the Six-Day War.[2]

---

[2] Eli E. Hertz, "'Mandate for Palestine': The Legal Aspects of Jewish Rights," posted at http://www.mythsandfacts.org/conflict/mandate_for_palestine/mandate_for_palestine.htm. Hertz documents the fact that the British removed sections of the League of Nations Mandate for Palestine and gave the territory to Faisal bin Hussein (forming Iraq) and Abdullah (forming Trans-Jordan [now Jordan]) to reward their loyalty to the British in their fight against the Ottoman Turks during World War I. This was in violation of the Mandate which said, "The mandatory shall be responsible for placing the country [Palestine] under such political, administrative and economic conditions as will secure the establishment of the Jewish National Home. . ." See pp. 218, 255, 257 in this book.

BIBLIOGRAPHY

Abasciano, Brian J. *Paul's Use of the Old Testament in Romans 9.1–18: An Intertextual and Theological Exegesis*. New York: T & T Clark International, 2011.

Aberbach, Moses, and Bernard Grossfeld. *Targum Onkelos to Genesis: A Critical Analysis Together with an English Translation of the Text*. Jersey City, NJ: KTAV Publishing House, 1982.

Aberbach, Moshe. *Jewish Education and History: Continuity, Crisis and Change*. Abingdon, UK: Routledge, 2009.

Adelman, Jonathan. *The Rise of Israel: A History of a Revolutionary State*. New York: Routledge, 2008.

Ahamkaari. *Will I Be Killed: For Writing the Following Contents*. Lincoln, NE: iUniverse, 2003.

Ahlström, Gösta W. *History of Ancient Palestine*. Sheffield, UK: Sheffield Academic Press, 1993.

Ahmed, Akbar S. *Islam Today: A Short Introduction to the Muslim World*. London, UK: I.B. Tauris & Co, 1999.

Albo, Joseph. *Sefer Ha'Ikkarim: Book of Principles*. Philadelphia, PA: Jewish Publication Society of America, 1929.

Alexander, Edward. "Paying a Debt: Bernard Harrison versus the Old-New Antisemitism," in *Reality and Culture: Essays on the Philosophy of Bernard Harrison*, Patricia Hanna, ed. Amsterdam, The Netherlands: Rodopi B.V., 2014.

Ali, Ayaan Hirsi. *Heretic: Why Islam Needs a Reformation Now*. New York: HarperCollins, 2015.

Aling, Charles F. *Egypt and Bible History*. Grand Rapids, MI: Baker Books, 1981.

Almog, Shmuel. *Zionism and History: The Rise of a New Jewish Consciousness*. New York: St. Martin's Press, 1987.

Alon, Mati. *Holocaust and Redemption*. Victoria, Canada: Trafford Publishing, 2003.

Amstutz, Mark R. *Evangelicals and American Foreign Policy*. New York: Oxford University Press, 2014.

Appelbaum, Diana . "Presbyterians Bearing False Witness," in *The American* Thinker, June 3, 2006.

Applewhite, Ashton, William R. Evans III, and Andrew Frothingham, eds. *And I Quote: The Definitive Collection of Quotes, Sayings, and Jokes for the Contemporary Speech-Maker*. New York: Macmillan, 1992.

Arad, Yitzhak. *Belzec, Sobidor, Treblinka: The Operation Reinhard Death Camps*. Bloomington, IN: Indiana University Press, 1987.

Arden, Stuart. *Sense and Nonsense: Everything You Need to Know About the Arab-Israeli Conflict*. Jerusalem, Israel: Gefen Publishing House, 2013.

Arendt, Hannah. *The Origins of Totalitarianism*. Orlando, FL: Harcourt-Brace, Inc., 1968.

Armstrong, Karen. *Holy War: The Crusades and Their Impact on Today's World*. New York: Anchor Books, 1988.

_____ *Islam: A Short History*. New York: Random House, 2000.

Aronson, Ran. "Settlement in Eretz Israel—A Colonialist Enterprise? 'Critical' Scholarship and Historical Geography," in *Israel Studies*, vol. 2, no. 2. Bloomington, IN: Indiana University Press, 1997.

Aslan, Reza. *Muslims and Jews in America: Commonalities, Contentions, and Complexities*. New York: Palgrave Macmillan, 2011.

Asthana, N. C., and Anjali Nirmal. *Urban Terrorism: Myths and Realities*. Jaipur, India: Aavishkar Publishers, 2009.

Astley, Jeff. Leslie J. Francis, and Mandy Robbins, *Peace or Violence: The Ends of Religion and Education?* South Glamorgan, UK: The University of Wales Press, 2007.

Ateek, Naim S. "Foreword," in *Zionism through Christian Lenses: Ecumenical Perspectives on the Promised Land*, Carole Monica Burnett, ed. Eugene, OR: Wipf and Stock Publishers, 2013.

Auerbach, Jerold S. *Jewish State, Pariah Nation: Israel and the Dilemmas of Legitimacy*. New Orleans, LA: Quid Pro Books, 2014.

_____ *Rabbis and Lawyers: Journey from Torah to Constitution*. New Orleans, LA: Quid Pro Books, 1990.

Austin, Samuel. *A View of the Economy of the Church of God*. Newburyport, England: Thomas & Whipple, 1807.

Aven, Tricia, and Tricia Miller. *Jews and Anti-Judaism in Esther and the Church*. Cambridge, UK: James Clark & Co, 2015.

Awwad, Nariman. *Beleaguered Word: Documentation of Israeli Aggression Against the Palestinian Media*. Itithad al-Suhufiyin al-'Arab, 2000.

Azous, Paul. *In The Plains of the Wilderness*. Jerusalem, Israel: Mazo Publishers, 2006.

Bahat, Dan, ed. *Twenty Centuries of Jewish Life in the Holy Land*. Jerusalem: The Israel Economist, 1976.

Bailey, Kenneth E. *Jesus Through Middle Eastern Eyes: Cultural Studies in the Gospels*. Downers Grove, IL: InterVarsity Press, 2008.

Baker, Lemuel. *The Many Faces of Judaism: Jewish Studies for the Busy Person.* Bloomington, IN: Xlibris Corp., 2012.

Baker, Todd D. *Matthew 27:25: "His Blood Be on Us": Are the Jewish People Racially Condemned for the Death of Christ?* Bloomington, IN: iUniverse, 2008.

Bakhos, Carol. *Ishmael on the Border: Rabbinic Portrayals of the First Arab.* Albany, NY: The State University of New York Press, 2006.

Baldwin, Joyce G. *The Message of Genesis 15–20.* Downers Grove, IL: IVP Academic, 1986.

Bank, Richard D. *The Everything Jewish History and Heritage Book: From Abraham to Zionism.* Avon, MA: F+W Publications, 2003.

Banks, Diane. *Writing the History of Israel.* London, UK: T & T Clark International, 2006.

Barclay, William. *The Gospel of John,* vol. 2. Edinburgh, UK: Saint Andrew Press, 1975.

Bard, Michael. *The Complete Idiot's Guide to the Middle East Conflict.* New York: Penguin Books, 2008.

Bard, Mitchell Geoffrey, and Moshe Schwartz. *One Thousand and One Facts Everyone Should Know about Israel.* Lanham, MD: Rowman & Littlefield Publishers, 2005.

Baron, Salo Wittmayer. *Social and Religious History of the Jews.* New York: Columbia University Press, 1974.

Bar-Tal, Daniel. *Shared Beliefs in a Society: Social Psychological Analysis.* Thousand Oaks, CA: Sage Publications, 2000.

Barth, Karl. *Against the Stream: Shorter Post-war Writings, 1946–1952,* Ronald Gregor Smith, ed. London, UK: SCM Press, 1954.

_____ *Church Dogmatics: II/2: The Election of God; the Command of God.* New York: Bloomsbury Academic, 2004.

_____ *Church Dogmatics III/2: The Doctrine of Creation.* London, UK: T & T Clark International, 2004.

_____ *Church Dogmatics III/3, The Creator and His Creature,* G. W. Bromley, ed. London, UK: T&T Clark International, 2000.

_____ "The Jewish Problem and the Christian Answer," in *Against the Stream: Shorter Post-War Writings 1946–52.* London, UK: SCM Publishing, 1954.

Barthélemy, Dominique. *God and His Image: An Outline of Biblical Theology.* San Francisco, CA: Ignatius Press, 2007.

Baskin, Judith R. *The Cambridge Dictionary of Judaism and Jewish Culture.* Cambridge, UK: Cambridge University Press, 2001.

bat Meir, Rivkah. *Rivkah Meneket: A Manual of Wisdom and Piety for Jewish Women.* Philadelphia, PA: The Jewish Publication Society, 2008.

Bauckham, Richard. "Biblical Theology and the Problems of Monotheism," in *Out of Egypt: Biblical Theology and Biblical Interpretation,* Craig Bartholomew, ed. Carlisle, UK: Paternoster, 2004.

_____ *Jesus and the God of Israel: God Crucified and Other Essays on the New Testament's Christology of Divine Identity.* Crownhill, UK: Authentic Media, 2008.

Bauer, Yehuda. *The Jews: A Contrary People.* Zürich, Switzerland: Lit Verlag GmbH & Co., 2014.

Bayefsky, Anne. "Human Rights Watch Coverup," in *The Jerusalem Post,* April 13, 2004.

Bayme, Steven. *Understanding Jewish History: Text and Commentaries.* Jersey City, NJ: KTAV Publishing House, 1997.

Bechtel, Trevor George. *The Gift of Ethics: A Story for Discovering Lasting Significance in Your Daily Work.* Eugene, OR: Wipf and Stock Publishers, 2014.

Bein, Alex. *The Jewish Question: Biography of a World Problem.* Madison, NJ: Fairleigh Dickinson University Press, 1990.

Beker, Avi. *The Chosen: The History of an Idea, and the Anatomy of an Obsession.* New York: Palgrave Macmillan, 2008.

Bell, Dean Phillip. "Host Desecration," in *Antisemitism: A Historical Encyclopedia of Prejudice and Persecution,* Richard S. Levy, ed. Santa Barbara, CA: ABC-CLIO, Inc., 2005.

_____ *Jews in the Early Modern World.* Lanham, MD: Rowman & Littlefield Publishers, 2008.

Bell, Maleah, B. C. Blackwell, Misty Bourne, et. al, eds. *The Voice Bible: Step into the Story of Scripture.* Nashville, TN: Thomas Nelson, Inc., 2012.

Bell, Richard C. *The Irrevocable Call of God: An Inquiry into Paul's Theology of Israel.* Tübingen, Germany: Mohr Siebeck, 2005.

Beller, Steven. *Vienna and the Jews, 1867–1938: A Cultural History.* Cambridge, UK: Cambridge University Press, 1989.

Bentley, Douglas T. *Abraham's Seed and Covenant.* Springville, UT: Cedar Fort Publishing, 2003.

Ben-Itto, Hadassa. *The Lie That Wouldn't Die: The Protocols of the Elders of Zion.* Estree, UK: Valentine Mitchell, 2005.

Ben-Sasson, Haim Hillel. *A History of the Jewish People.* Cambridge, MA: Harvard University Press, 1976.

Ben-Shmuel, Philip D. "*Hagshamah*: A Theology for an Alternate Messianic Jewish Zionism," in *The Land Cries Out: Theology of the Land in the Israeli-Palestinian Context*, Salim J. Munayer and Lisa Loden, eds. Eugene, OR: Wipf and Stock Publishers, 2012.

Ben-Yehuda, Eliezer, and Eisig Silberschlag. *Eliezer Ben-Yehudah: A Symposium in Oxford.* Oxford, UK: Oxford Centre for Postgraduate Hebrew Studies, 1981.

_____*Ha-Zevi* 31, 1886/87.

Ben-Yehuda, Eliezer. *Fulfillment of Prophecy: The Life Story of Eliezer Ben-Yehuda.* Charleston, SC: BookSurge Publishing, 2009.

Ben-Yehudi, Nachman. *Masada Myth: Collective Memory and Mythmaking in Israel.* Madison, WI: The University of Wisconsin Press, 1995.

Berenbaum, Michael, and Arnold Kramer. *The World Must Know.* Washington, DC: United States Holocaust Memorial Museum, 1993.

Berent, Irwin M. *Norfolk, Virginia: A Jewish History of the 20th Century.* Norfolk, VA: United Jewish Federation of Tidewater, 2001.

Berger, Peter. "Religion and Global Civil Society," in *Religion in Global Civil Society*, Mark Juergensmeyer, ed. New York: Oxford University Press, 2005.

Berkhouwer, G. C. *General Revelation: Studies in Dogmatics.* Grand Rapids, MI: Wm. B. Eerdmans Publishing Co., 1955.

Berkovits, Eliezer. "European and American Responses during and following the War," in *Wrestling with God: Jewish Theological Responses during and after the Holocaust*, Steven T. Katz, Shlomo Biderman, and Gershon Greenberg, eds. New York: Oxford University Press, 2007.

_____ *Faith After the Holocaust.* New York: KTAV Publishing House, 1973.

Berlin, Adele, ed. *The Oxford Dictionary of the Jewish Religion.* New York: Oxford University Press, 2011.

Berman, Louis Arthur. *The Akedah: The Binding of Isaac.* Northvale, NJ: Jason Aronson, Inc., 1997.

Berrett, LaMar C. *Discovering the World of the Bible.* Provo, UT: Grandin Book Co., 1996.

Bertinoro, Ovadiah, ed. *The Mishnah.* Brooklyn, NY: Mesorah Publications, 1979.

Bhutto, Zulfikar Ali. *A South Asian View: A Collection of Speeches and Excerpts.* Information Division, Embassy of Pakistan, 1964.

Biale, David. *Power & Powerlessness in Jewish History.* New York: Schocken Books, 1986.

Bilde, Per. *The Originality of Jesus: A Critical Discussion and a Comparative Attempt.* Göttingen, Germany: Vandenhoeck & Ruprecht GmbH & Co., 2013.

Bird, Michael F. *Jesus and the Origins of the Gentile Mission.* New York, T & T Clark International, 1988.

Blackstone, William E. "May the United States Intercede for the Jews?" in *Our Day* VIII, October, 1891.

Blaising, Craig A. "The Structure of Biblical Covenants: The Covenants Prior to Christ," in *Progressive Dispensationalism*, Craig A. Blaising and Darrell L. Bock, eds. Grand Rapids, MI: Baker Academic, 1993.

Blaschke, Andreas. *Beschneidung: Zeugnisse der Bibel und verwandter Texte*, TANZ 28. Tübingen, Germany: A. Francke Verlag, 1998.

Blech, Arthur. *The Causes of Anti-Semitism: A Critique of the Bible.* Amherst, NY: Prometheus Books, 2006.

Bloch, Abraham P. *The Biblical and Historical Background of Jewish Customs and Ceremonies.* Jersey City, NJ: KTAV Publishing House, 1980.

Block, Daniel I. *The Book of Ezekiel, Chapters 1–24.* Grand Rapids, MI: Wm. B. Eerdmans Publishing Co., 1997.

Bloom, Jack. *Out of Step: Life-story of a Politician: Politics and Religion in a World at War.* Bloomington, IN: The Indiana University Press, 2005.

Bloomberg, Craig L. *Jesus and the Gospels: An Introduction and Survey.* Nashville, TN: B&H Publishing Group, 2009.

Bloxham, Donald. *The Final Solution: A Genocide.* New York: Oxford University Press, 2009.

Blumenthal, David R. "Antisemitism," in *A Dictionary of the Jewish-Christian Dialogue*, Leon Klenicki and Geoffrey Wigoder, eds. Mahwah, NJ: Paulist Press, 1984.

_____*God at the Center: Meditations on Jewish Spirituality.* Northvale, NJ: Jason Aronson, 1994.

Blumenthal, Jacob, and Janet Liss. *Etz Hayim Study Companion.* Philadelphia, PA: The Jewish Publication Society, 2005.

Bock, Darrell L. "Covenants in Progressive Dispensationalism," in *Three Central Issues in Contemporary Dispensationalism: A Comparison of Traditional and Progressive Views*, Herbert W. Bateman, ed. Grand Rapids, MI: Kregel Publications, 1999.

Boehling, Rebecca, and Uta Larkey, *Life and Loss in the Shadow of the Holocaust: A Jewish Family's Untold Story.* Cambridge, UK: Cambridge University Press, 2011.

Boehm, Omri. *Binding of Isaac: A Religious Model of Disobedience.* New York: T & T Clark International, 2007.

Bolaffi, Guido. *Dictionary of Race, Ethnicity, and Culture.* Thousand Oaks, CA: SAGE Publications, 2003.

Boman, Thorlief. *Hebrew Thought Compared with Greek,* tr. Jules L. Moreau. New York: W. W. Norton & Co., 1960.

Booker, Richard. *Radical Islam's War Against Israel, Christianity, and the West.* Shippensburg, PA: Destiny Image Publishing, 2008.

Boring, M. Eugene. *An Introduction to the New Testament: History, Literature, and Theology.* Louisville, KY: Westminster John Knox Press, 2012.

Borowitz, Eugene B. *Reform Judaism Today.* Springfield, NJ: Behrman House, Inc., 1983.

Bostom, Andrew G. *The Legacy of Islamic Antisemitism: From Sacred Texts to Solemn History.* New York: Prometheus Books, 2008.

Bowen, Nancy R. *Abingdon Old Testament Commentaries: Ezekiel.* Nashville, TN: Abingdon Press, 2010.

Boyarin, Daniel. *Border Lines: The Partition of Judaeo-Christianity.* Philadelphia, PA: The University of Pennsylvania Press, 2004.

Boyer, Paul. *When Time Shall Be No More: Prophecy Belief in Modern American Culture.* Cambridge, MA: Harvard University Press, 1992.

Boys, Mary C. *Redeeming Our Sacred Story: The Death of Jesus and Relations between Jews and Christians.* Mahwah, NJ: Paulist Press, 2013.

Branick, Vincent P. *Understanding the New Testament and Its Message: An Introduction.* Mahwah, NJ: Paulist Press, 1998.

Brann, Ross. *Power in the Portrayal: Representations of Jews and Muslims in Eleventh- and Twelfth-Century Islamic Spain.* Princeton, NJ: Princeton University Press, 2002.

Braun, Emily. "The Faces of Modigliani: Identity Politics under Fascism," in Voljtech Jirat-Wasiutynski, *Modern Art and the Idea of the Mediterranean.* Toronto, Canada: The University of Toronto Press, 2007.

Breese, Dave. *Seven Men Who Rule the World from the Grave.* Chicago, IL: Moody Publishers, 1990.

Breslauer, S. Daniel. *The Seductiveness of Jewish Myth: Challenge or Response?* Albany, NY: The State University of New York Press, 1997.

Brog, David. "The End of Evangelical Support for Israel?" in *The Middle East Quarterly,* vol. 21, no. 2. Spring 2014.

Brooks, Stephen. *The Challenge of Cultural Pluralism.* Westport, CT: Greenwood Publishing Group, 2002.

Brown, David. *The Restoration of the Jews.* Charleston, SC: BiblioLife, 2008.

Brown, Michael L. *What Do Jewish People Think about Jesus?: And Other Questions Christians Ask about Jewish Beliefs, Practices, and History.* Grand Rapids, MI: Baker Publishing Group, 2007.

Browning, Christopher R. "The German Bureaucracy and the Holocaust," in *Genocide: Critical Issues of the Holocaust: A Companion Volume to the Film* Genocide, Alex Grobman and Daniel Landes, eds. West Orange, NJ: Behrman House, 1983.

Brueggemann, Walter. *An Introduction to the Old Testament: The Canon and Christian Imagination.* Louisville, KY: Westminster John Knox Press, 2003.

_____ *The Land: Place as Gift, Promise, and Challenge in Biblical Faith.* Minneapolis, MN: Augsburg Fortress Press, 2002.

Brunner, Emil. *Dogmatics III: Christian Doctrine of the Church, Faith & the Consummation.* London, UK: James Clark & Co., 2002.

Bryan, Steven M. *Jesus and Israel's Traditions of Judgement and Restoration.* Cambridge, UK: Cambridge University Press, 2002.

Bullinger, Ethelbert W. *Number in Scripture: Its Supernatural Design and Spiritual Significance.* Grand Rapids, MI: Kregel Publications, 1967.

Burg, Avraham. *The Holocaust Is Over; We Must Rise from Its Ashes.* New York: Palgrave Macmillan, 2008.

Burnett, Carole Monica. "Eastern Orthodox Perspectives on Zionism and Christian Zionism," in *Zionism and the Quest for Justice in the Holy Land,* Donald E. Wagner and Walter T. Davis, eds. Cambridge, UK: The Lutterworth Press, 2014.

Burnett, Stephen G. *Christian Hebraism in the Reformation Era (1500–1660).* Leiden, The Netherlands: Koninklijke Brill, 2012.

Burrell, David James. *The Religions of the World: An Outline of the Great Religious Systems.* Philadelphia, PA: Presbyterian Board of Publication and Sabbath-School Work, 1888.

Byfield, Ted. *The Christians: Their First Two Thousand Years; A Glorious Disaster: A.D. 1100 to 1300: The Crusades: Blood, Valor, Iniquity, Reason, Faith.* Edmonton, Canada: Society to Explore and Record Christian History, 2003.

Byron, John. *Cain and Abel in Text and Tradition: Jewish and Christian Interpretations of the First Sibling Rivalry.* Leiden, The Netherlands: Koninklijke Brill NV, 2011.

Callen, Barry L. *Discerning the Divine: God in Christian Theology.* Louisville, KY: Westminster John Knox Press, 2004.

Calvin, John. *Commentaries on the First Book of Moses Called Genesis,* vol. 1, tr. John King. Edinburgh, UK: The Edinburgh Printing Co., 1847.

_____*The Acts of the Apostles,* tr. Oliver and Boyd, Ltd. Grand Rapids, MI: Wm. B. Eerdmans Publishing Co., 1965.

Campo, Juan Eduardo. *Encyclopedia of Islam.* New York: Infobase Publishing, 2009.

Carabind, Deirdre. *The Unknown God.* Eugene, OR: Wipf and Stock Publishers, 1995.

Cargas, Harry J. *Holocaust Scholars Write to the Vatican.* Westport, CT: Greenwood Publishing Group, 1998.

Carlson, Eric. *Is God Done with America?* New York: Morgan James Publishing, 2011.

Carter, Jimmy. *Palestine: Peace Not Apartheid.* New York: Simon & Schuster, 2006.

Cassius Dio, *Historia* 69, 13.

Chafer, Lewis Sperry. *Systematic Theology.* Grand Rapids, MI: Kregel Publications, 1948.

Charles River Editors. *Decoding the Conflict Between Israel and the Palestinians: The History and Terms of the Middle East Peace Process.* Cambridge, MA: Create Space, 2013.

Charlesworth, James H. *The Historical Jesus: An Essential Guide.* Nashville, TN: Abingdon Press, 2008.

Chase, Anthony Tirado. "Nongovernmental Organizations: Arab NGOs," in *Encyclopedia of Human Rights,* David P. Forsythe, ed. New York: Oxford University Press, 2009.

Chazan, Robert, ed. *Church, State, and Jew in the Middle Ages.* New York: Behrman House, 1980.

Chemotsky, Harry I., and Heidi H. Hobbs. *Crossing Borders: International Studies for the 21st Century.* Thousand Oaks, CA: SAGE Publications, Inc., 2016.

Chesler, Phyllis. *Living History: On the Front Lines for Israel and the Jews 2003–2015.* Jerusalem, Israel: Gefen Publishing House, 2015.

Chetrit, Sami Shalom. *Intra-Jewish Conflict in Israel: White Jews, Black Jews.* New York: Routledge, 2010.

Chisholm, Robert B. "Evidence from Genesis," in *A Case for Premillennialism: A New Consensus,* Donald K. Campbell and Jeffrey L. Townsend, eds. Chicago, IL: Moody Publications, 1992.

Christison, Kathleen. "Dilemmas of Arab Christianity," *Journal of Palestinian Studies* vol. 22, no. 1 (Autumn 1992).

Ciment, James, and John Radzilowski, eds. *American Immigration: An Encyclopedia of Political, Social, and Cultural Change.* New York: Routledge, 2014.

_____*World Terrorism: An Encyclopedia of Political Violence from Ancient Times to the Post-9/11 Era.* Armonk, NY: M. E. Sharpe Publishing, 2011.

Citron, Sabina. *The Indictment.* Jerusalem: Gefen Publishing House, 2006.

Cline, Eric H. *Jerusalem Besieged: From Ancient Canaan to Modern Israel.* Ann Arbor, MI: The University of Michigan Press, 2004.

Cohen, Hermann. *Religion of Reason: Out of the Sources of Judaism,* tr. Simon Kaplan. New York: Frederick Ungar Publishing Co., 1972.

Cohen, Jeffrey M. *Prayer and Penitence: A Commentary on the High Holy Day Machzor.* Northvale, NJ: Jason Aronson, 1994.

Cohen, Jeremy. *Essential Papers on Judaism and Christianity in Conflict.* New York, NY: New York University Press, 1990.

Cohen, Michael J. "Zionism and British Imperialism II: Imperial Financing in Palestine" in *Journal of Israeli History: Politics, Society, Culture,* vol. 30, no. 2, 2011.

Cohen, Rich. *Israel Is Real: An Obsessive Quest to Understand the Jewish Nation and Its History.* New York: Macmillan, 2009.

Cohen, Richard. *Israel: Is It Good for the Jews.* New York: Simon & Schuster, 2014.

_____"With Israel, the World Is Blaming the Victims," in *The Washington Post,* July 28, 2014.

Cohen, Robin. *The Cambridge Survey of World Migration.* Cambridge, UK: Cambridge University Press, 1995.

Cohen, Shaul Ephraim. *The Politics of Planting: Israeli-Palestinian Competition for Control of Land in the Jerusalem Periphery.* Chicago, IL: The University of Chicago Press, 1993.

Cohen, Shaye J. D. *The Beginnings of Jewishness: Boundaries, Varieties, Uncertainties.* Berkeley, CA: The University of California Press, 1999.

Coke, Karl D. "Jerusalem and the Letter *Shin,*" in *Restore!,* vol. 10, no. 4.

Collier, Martin, Bill Marriott, and Rosemary Rees. *Colonisation and Conflict 1750–1990.* Oxford, UK: Heinemann Educational Publishers, 2002.

Commodian, *Carmen Apologeticum,* 941–946.

Conner, C. J. *Jesus and the Culture Wars: Reclaiming the Lord's Prayer.* Mustang, OK: Tate Publishing & Enterprises, 2007.

Conway, Kevin P. *The Promises of God: The Background of Paul's Exclusive Use of 'Epangelia' for the Divine Pledge.* Berlin, Germany: Walter de Gruyter GmbH, 2014.

Coogan, Michael David, Marc Zvi Brettler, Carol Ann Newsom, and Pheme Perkins, eds. *The New Oxford Annotated Bible.* New York: Oxford University Press, 2007.

Cook, Jonathan. *Blood and Religion: The Unmasking of the Jewish and Democratic State.* London, UK: Pluto Press, 2006.

Cook, William A. "The Jews in History," in *The Park Review*, vol. 5, no. 1 (October, 1903).

_____*The Plight of the Palestinians: A Long History of Destruction.* New York: Palgrave Macmillan, 2010.

Copan, Paul, and Matt Flannagan. *Did God Really Command Genocide? Coming to Terms with the Justice of God.* Grand Rapids, MI: Baker Books, 2014.

_____*How Do You Know You're Not Wrong? Responding to Objections that Leave Christians Speechless.* Grand Rapids, MI: Baker Books, 2005.

Corley, Bruce, Steve Lemke, and Grant I. Lovejoy, eds. *Biblical Hermeneutics: A Comprehensive Introduction to Interpreting Scripture.* Nashville, TN: B&H Publishing Group, 2002.

Cornell, George. "The Church after Jesus Loses Is Jewish Context," in Fredericksburg, VA, *Free Lance-Star*, Friday, March 28, 1975.

Cotte, Suzette. *Criminological Theories: Bridging the Past to the Future.* Thousand Oaks, CA: Sage Publications, 2002.

Couch, Mal, ed. *Dictionary of Premillennial Theology: A Practical Guide to the People, Viewpoints, and History of Prophetic Studies.* Grand Rapids, MI: Kregel Publications, 1996.

Coudert, Allison P. "Seventeenth-Century Christian Hebraists," in *Judaeo-Christian Intellectual Culture in the Seventeenth Century*, A. P. Coudert, S. Hutton, and R. H. Popkin, eds. Dordrecht, The Netherlands: Kluwer Academic Publishers, 1999.

Coxe, A. Cleveland, James Donaldson, and Alexander Roberts, eds. *The Ante-Nicene Fathers.* Peabody, MA: Hendrickson Publishers, 1994.

Creyer, F. H. "On the Recently-Discovered 'House of David' Inscription," *Scandinavian Journal of the Old Testament* 8 (1994).

Crone Patricia, and Michael Cook. *Hagarism: The Making of the Islamic World.* Cambridge, UK: Cambridge University Press, 1980.

Cross, Frank Moore. *Canaanite Myth and Hebrew Epic: Essays in the History of the Religion of Israel.* Cambridge, MA: Harvard University Press, 1973.

Culi, Jacob, Isaac ben Moses Magriso, Zvi Faier, Areh Kaplan, Shmuel Yerushalmi, and Eliyahu Touger. *The Torah Anthology*, vol. 14. Brooklyn, NY: Moznaim Publishing Co., 1987.

Dalacoura, Katerina. *Islamist Terrorism and Democracy in the Middle East.* Cambridge, UK: Cambridge University Press, 2011.

Daly, Robert J. "The Soteriological Significance of the Sacrifice of Isaac," in *Catholic Biblical Quarterly* 39 (1977).

Danon, Danny. *Israel: The Will to Prevail.* New York: Macmillan, 2013.

Darwish, Nonie. *The Devil We Don't Know: The Dark Side of Revolutions in the Middle East.* Hoboken, NJ: John Wiley & Sons, 2012.

Davies, Alan, and Marilyn F. Nefsky. *How Silent Were the Churches?: Canadian Protestantism and the Jewish Plight during the Nazi Era.* Waterloo, Canada: Wilfrid Laurier University Press, 1997.

Davies, Jon. *Death, Burial and Rebirth in the Religions of Antiquity.* New York: Routledge, 1999.

Davies, Philip R. "'House of David' Built on Sand," *Biblical Archaeology Review*, July/August, 1994.

_____*In Search of Ancient Israel.* Sheffield, UK: Sheffield Academic Press, 1992.

Davies, William D. *The Territorial Dimension of Judaism.* Berkeley, CA: The University of California Press, 1982.

Davis, Leonard J. *Myths and Facts: A Concise Record of the Arab-Israeli Conflict.* Washington, DC: Near East Report, 1989.

Davis, Uri. *Apartheid Israel: Possibilities for the Struggle Within.* London, UK: Zed Books, 2003.

_____*Israel: An Apartheid State.* London, UK: Zed Books, 1987.

Dawkins, Richard. *The God Delusion.* Boston: Houghton Mifflin, 2006.

de Lubac, Henri. *Theological Fragments*, tr. Rebecca Howell Balinski. San Francisco, CA: Ignatius Press, 1989.

Dempster, Stephen G. "Foreigner," in *Evangelical Dictionary of Biblical Theology*, Walter A. Elwell, ed. Grand Rapids, MI: Baker Books, 1996.

Dershowitz, Alan M. *Chutzpah.* New York: Simon & Schuster, 1991.

_____"Countering Challenges to Israel's Legitimacy," in *Israel's Rights as a Nation-State in International Diplomacy*, Alan Baker, ed. Jerusalem, Israel: World Jewish Congress, 2011.

_____*The Case Against Israel's Enemies: Exposing Jimmy Carter and Others Who Stand in the Way of Peace.* Hoboken, NJ: John Wiley & Sons, Inc., 2008.

_____*The Case for Peace: How the Arab-Israeli Conflict Can be Resolved.* Hoboken, NJ: John Wiley & Sons, 2005.

_____*The Vanishing American Jew: In Search of Jewish Identity for the Next Century.* New York: Touchstone, 1997.

Desbois, Patrick. *The Holocaust by Bullets: A Priest's Journey to Uncover the Truth Behind the Murder of 1.5 Million Jews.* New York: Palgrave Macmillan, 2008.

Dew, James K. *Science and Theology: An Assessment of Alastair McGrath's Critical Realist Perspective.* Eugene, OR: Wipf and Stock Publishers, 2011.

Dieckhoff, Alain. *The Invention of a Nation: Zionist Thought and the Making of Modern Israel.* New York: Columbia University Press, 2003.

Dietrich, Donald J. *God and Humanity in Auschwitz: Jewish-Christian Relations and Sanctioned Murder.* Piscataway, NJ: Transaction Publishers, 1995.

Dimont, Max I. *Jews, God, and History.* New York: Penguin Books, 2004.

_____*The American Zionist*, vol. 62, 1971.

Dinstein, Yoram, and Mala Tabory, eds. *Israel Yearbook on Human Rights 1987.* Dordrecht, The Netherlands: Kluwer Academic Publishers Group, 1988.

Dockery, David S., ed. *Holman Concise Bible Commentary.* Nashville, TN: B&H Publishing Group, 2010.

Donelson, Lewis R. *From Hebrews to Revelation: A Theological Introduction.* Louisville, KY: Westminster John Knox Press, 2001.

Dorff, Elliot N. *For the Love of God and People: A Philosophy of Jewish Law.* Philadelphia, PA: Jewish Publication Society, 2007.

_____*To Do the Right and the Good: A Jewish Approach to Modern Social Ethics.* Philadelphia, PA: The Jewish Publication Society, 2002.

Doyle, Tom. *Two Nations Under God: Why You Should Care about Israel.* Nashville, TN: B&H Publishing Group, 2004.

Drazin, Israel. *Maimonides and the Biblical Prophets.* Jerusalem, Israel: Gefen Publishing House, 2009.

Duffey, John M. *Science and Religion: A Contemporary Perspective.* Eugene, OR: Wipf and Stock Publishers, 2013.

Dundes, Alan. *The Blood Libel Legend: A Casebook in Anti-Semitic Folklore.* Madison, WI: The University of Wisconsin Press, 1991.

Eban, Abba Solomon. *Heritage: Civilization and the Jews.* New York: Simon & Schuster, 1984.

Eckardt, Alice L., and A. Roy Eckardt. *Long Night's Journey into Day: A Revised Retrospective on the Holocaust.* Detroit, MI: Wayne State University Press, 1982.

Edelman, Diana. "The Nile in Biblical Memory," in *Thinking of Water in the Early Second Temple Period.* Berlin, Germany: Walter de Gruyter GmbH, 2014.

Edwards, Jonathan. *A History of the Word of Redemption.* Worcester, MA: Thomas & Whipple, 1808.

Ehle, Jr., Carl F. "Prolegomena to Christian Zionism in America: The Views of Increase Mather and William E. Blackstone Concerning the Doctrine of the Restoration of Israel," Ph.D. Dissertation for New York University, 1977.

Einhorn, Stefan. *A Concealed God: Religion, Science and the Search for Truth.* Radnor, PA: Templeton Foundation Press, 1998.

Eisenberg, Ronald L. *What the Rabbis Said: 250 Topics from the Talmud.* Santa Barbara, CA: ABC-CLIO, 2010.

_____*Dictionary of Jewish Terms: A Guide to the Language of Judaism.* Lanham, MD: Taylor Trade Publishing, 2011.

_____*Jewish Traditions: A JPS Guide.* Philadelphia, PA: Jewish Publication Society, 2004.

Eisenstat, Stuart E. *The Future of the Jews: How Global Forces Are Impacting the Jewish People, Israel, and Its Relationship with the United States.* Lanham, MD: Rowman & Littlefield Publishers, 2012.

Eising, H. "Ne'um," in *Theologisches Wörterbuch zum Alten Testament*, G. J. Botterweck, H. J. Fabry, and H. Ringgren, eds. Stuttgart, Germany: W. Kohlhammer, 1986.

Elazar, Daniel J. *Covenant & Polity in Biblical Israel: Biblical Foundations & Jewish Expressions.* Piscataway, NJ: Transaction Publishers, 1995.

_____"Jewish Religious, Ethnic, and National Identities," in *National Variations in Jewish Identity: Implications for Jewish Education*, Steven M. Cohen and Gabriel Horenczyk, eds. Albany, NY: The State University of New York Press, 1999.

Eldemann, Richard. "Ahasuerus, the Wandering Jew: Origin and Background," in *The Wandering Jew: Essays in the Interpretation of a Christian Legend*, G. Hasan-Roken and A. Dundes, eds. Bloomington, IN: Indiana University Press, 1986.

Elliott, Mark Adam. *The Survivors of Israel: A Reconsideration of the Theology of Pre-Christian Judaism.* Grand Rapids, MI: Wm. B. Eerdmans Publishing Co., 2000.

Ellis, Marc H. *Future of the Prophetic: Israel's Ancient Wisdom Re-presented.* Minneapolis, MN: Augsburg Fortress Publishers, 2014.

Elwell, Walter A., ed. *Evangelical Dictionary of Theology.* Grand Rapids, MI: Baker Academic, 2011.

_____and Philip W. Comfort. *Tyndale Bible Dictionary.* Wheaton, IL: Tyndale House Publishers, 2001.

Endo, Masanobu. *Creation and Christology: A Study on the Johannine Prologue in the Light of Early Jewish Creation Accounts.* Tübingen, Germany: Mohr Siebeck, 2002.

Engar, Ann W. "Old Testament Women as Tricksters," in *Mappings of the Biblical Terrain: The Bible as Text,* Vincent L. Tollers and John R. Maier, eds. Cranbury, NJ: Associated University Presses, 1990.

Engberg, Katarina. *The EU and Military Operations: A Comparative Analysis.* New York: Routledge, 2014.

Engel, David. *Zionism.* New York: Routledge, 2013.

Engineer, Asghar Ali. *Islam in Contemporary World.* Elgin, IL: New Dawn Press Group, 2007.

Enns, Paul P. *The Moody Handbook of Theology.* Chicago, IL: Moody Publications, 2014.

Enns, Peter. *Exodus.* Grand Rapids, MI: Zondervan Publishing Co., 2000.

Epiphanius, *Heresies* 49.1.2–3.

Epstein, Lawrence J. *A Treasury of Jewish Inspirational Stories.* Northvale, NJ: Jason Aronson, 1993.

_____ *A Treasury of Jewish Anecdotes.* Northvale, NJ: Jason Aronson, Inc., 1989.

_____ "The Moral Case of Zionism: If Both Jews and Palestinian Arabs Start Their Historical Narrative with Beginning of Zionism, Jews Have Deeper Moral Claim to the Land of Israel," in *Israel Opinion,* April 17, 2014, p. 1.

Erlewine, Robert. *Monotheism and Tolerance: Recovering a Religion of Reason.* Bloomington, IN: Indiana University Press, 2010.

Etzioni-Halevy, Eva. *The Divided People: Can Israel's Breakup Be Stopped?* Lanham, MD: Lexington Books, 2002.

Evans, Craig A. *Jesus and His Contemporaries: Comparative Studies.* Leiden, The Netherlands: E. J. Brill, 1995.

Evdokimov, Paul. *Woman and the Salvation of the World,* tr. Anthony P. Gythiel. Crestwood, NY: St. Vladimir's Seminary Press, 1994.

Exodus *Rabbah* 24:1.

Fackenheim, Emil L. "Post-Holocaust Anti-Jewishness, Jewish Identity and the Centrality of Israel," in *World Jewry and the State of Israel,* Moshe Davis, ed. New York: Arno Press, 1977.

_____ *The Jewish Bible after the Holocaust: A Re-Reading.* Bloomington, IN: Indiana University Press, 1991.

_____ *To Mend the World: Foundations of Post-Holocaust Jewish Thought.* Bloomington, IN: Indiana University Press, 1982.

_____ *What Is Judaism?* New York: Macmillian, 1987.

Fackre, Gabriel. *The Christian Story, Vol. 2: Authority: Scripture in the Church for the World.* Grand Rapids, MI: Wm. B. Eerdmans Publishing Co., 1987.

Fairbairn, Patrick. *The Imperial Bible-Dictionary: Historical, Biographical, Geographical, and Doctrinal.* London, England: Blackie and Son, 1866.

Falk, Gerhard. *The Restoration of Israel: Christian Zionism in Religion, Literature, and Politics.* New York: Peter Lang Publishing, 2006.

Falk, W. Avner. *Anti-Semitism: A History and Psychoanalysis of Contemporary Hatred.* Westport, CT: Greenwood Publishing Group, 2008.

_____*A Psychoanalytic History of the Jews.* Madison, NJ: Fairleigh Dickinson University Press, 1996.

Falzon, Christopher. *Philosophy Goes to the Movies: An Introduction to Philosophy.* New York: Routledge, 2007.

Fasching, Darrell J. *The Jewish People in Christian Preaching.* Lewiston, NY: The Edwin Mellen Press, 1984.

Federbusch, Simon. *World Jewry Today.* New York: Thomas Yoseloff, 1959.

Federer, Bill. "What Happens When You Mess with Israel?" *WND,* 7 Sept. 2015.

Feinberg, John S. *"No One Like Him,"* in *The Doctrine of God.* Wheaton, IL: Crossway Books, 2001.

Feinstein, Edward. *Tough Questions Jews Ask: A Young Adult's Guide to Building a Jewish Life.* Woodstock, VT: Jewish Lights Publishing, 2012.

Fellman, Jack. *The Revival of Classical Tongue: Eliezer Ben Yehuda and the Modern Hebrew Language.* The Netherlands: Mouton & Co., 1973.

Finan, Thomas. *Scriptural Interpretations in the Fathers: Letter and Spirit.* Dublin, Ireland: Four Courts Press, 1995.

Finkelstein, Israel, and Neil Asher Silberman, *David and Solomon: In Search of the Bible's Sacred Kings and the Roots of the Western Tradition.* New York: Simon & Schuster, 2006.

_____and Amihai Mazar, *The Quest for the Historical Israel: Debating Archaeology and the History of Early Israel.* Atlanta, GA: The Society of Biblical Literature Press, 2007.

Finkelstein, Louis. "The Jewish Vision of Human Brotherhood," in *Religious Pluralism and World Community,* Edward Jabra Juri, ed. Leiden, The Netherlands: E. J. Brill, 1969.

Firestone, Reuven. *Holy War in Judaism: The Fall and Rise of a Controversial Idea.* New York: Oxford University Press, 2012.

_____*Jihad: The Origin of Holy War in Islam.* New York: Oxford University Press, 1999.

Fisher, Eugene J. and Dennis D. McManus, "Good Friday Prayer for the Perfidious Jews," in *A Dictionary of Jewish-Christian Relations,* Kessler, Edward. and Neil Wenborn, eds. Cambridge, UK: Cambridge University Press, 2005.

Fishman, Sylvia Barack. *Jewish Life and American Culture.* Albany, NY: The State University of New York Press, 2000.

Flannery, Edward. *The Anguish of the Jews: Twenty-Three Centuries of Antisemitism.* Mahwah, NJ: Paulist Press, 2004.

Forbes, Christopher. *Prophecy and Inspired Speech in Early Christianity and its Hellenistic Environment.* Tübingen, Germany: J.C.B. Mohr, Siebeck, 1995.

Forster, Charles. *The One Primeval Language Traced Experimentally through Ancient Inscriptions.* London, England: Richard Bentley, 1852.

Francis, Matthew H. G. "Blessed is the One Who Reads Aloud. . .": The Book of Revelation in Orthodox Lectionary Traditions," in *Exegesis and Hermeneutics in the Churches of the East,* Vahan S. Hovhanessian, ed. New York: Peter Lang Publishing, 2009.

Franck, Thomas M. *Nation Against Nation: What Happened to the U.N. Dream and What the U.S. Can Do About It.* New York: Oxford University Press, 1985.

Franke, John R. *The Character of Theology: An Introduction to Its Nature, Task, and Purpose.* Grand Rapids, MI: Baker Academic, 2005.

Frazier, T. L. *A Second Look at the Second Coming: Sorting Through the Speculations.* Ben Lomond, CA: Conciliar Press, 1999.

Freed, Edwin D. *The Apostle Paul, Christian Jew: Faithfulness and Law.* Lanham, MD: University Press of America, 1994.

Freedland, Jonathan. "Is Anti-Zionism Antisemitism?" in *A New Antisemitism? Debating Judeophobia in 21st-Century Britain,* Paul Iganski and Barry Kosmin, eds. London, UK: Profile Books, 2003.

Freedman, David. "Woman, a Power Equal to Man," *Biblical Archaeological Review,* Jan/Feb 1983.

Freedman, Robert I. "Introduction," in *Contemporary Israel: Domestic Politics, Foreign Policy, and Security Challenges,* Robert O. Freedman, ed. Boulder, CO: Westview Press, 2009.

Freud, Sigmund. *Moses and Monotheism.* New York: Random House, 1939.

Fretheim, Terence E. *Abraham: Trials of Family and Faith.* Columbia, SC: The University of South Carolina Press, 2007.

Fritz, Glen A. *The Lost Sea of the Exodus: A Modern Geographical Analysis.* Ph.D. Dissertation, Texas State University, 2006.

Frymer-Kensky, Tikva. *Studies in Bible and Feminist Criticism.* Philadelphia, PA: Jewish Publication Society, 2006.

Fuller, Daniel. *Gospel and Law.* Grand Rapids, MI: Wm. B. Eerdmans Publishing Co., 1980.

Gal, Allon. *Envisioning Israel: The Changing Ideals and Images of North American Jews.* Jerusalem: The Magnes Press, 1996.

Gans, Chaim. *A Just Zionism: On the Morality of the Jewish State.* New York: Oxford University Press, 2008.

Garaudy, Roger. "Religious and Historical Pretexts of Zionism," in *The Link,* vol 10, no. 3.

Garfield, Charles A. *Psychosocial Care of the Dying Patient.* New York: McGraw-Hill, 1978.

Garr, John D. *Christian Fruit—Jewish Root: Theology of Hebraic Restoration.* Atlanta, GA: Golden Key Press, 2015.

_____*Coequal and Counterbalanced: God's Blueprint for Women and Men.* Atlanta, GA: Golden Key Press, 2012.

_____*Feminine by Design: The God-Fashioned Woman.* Atlanta, GA: Golden Key Press, 2012.

_____*God and Women: Woman in God's Image and Likeness.* Atlanta, GA: Golden Key Press, 2011.

_____*Life from the Dead: The Dynamic Saga of the Chosen People.* Atlanta, GA: Golden Key Press, 2014.

_____*Our Lost Legacy: Christianity's Hebrew Heritage.* Atlanta, GA: Golden Key Press, 2000.

_____*Passover: The Festival of Redemption.* Atlanta, GA: Golden Key Press, 2013.

Garr, W. Randall. *In His Own Image and Likeness: Humanity, Divinity, and Monotheism.* Leiden, The Netherlands: Koninkijke Brill, 2003.

Gauss, James F. *Islam & Christianity: A Revealing Contrast*. Alachua, FL: Bridge-Logos Publishing, 2009.

Gavriely-Nuri, Dalia. *Israeli Peace Discourse: A Cultural Approach to CDA*. Amsterdam, The Netherlands: John Benjamins Publishing Co., 2015.

Gavron, Daniel. *Holy Land Mosaic: Stories of Cooperation and Coexistence between Israelis and Palestinians*. Lanham, MD: Rowman & Littlefield Publishers, 2008.

Geldart, Anne. *Judaism, Second Edition*. Portsmouth, NH: Heinemann Library, 2001.

Gelvin, James. *The Israel-Palestine Conflict: One Hundred Years of War*. Cambridge, UK: Cambridge University Press, 2007.

Gesenius, Heinrich Friedrich Wilhelm. *Gesenius' Hebrew and Chaldee Lexicon to the Old Testament Scriptures*, tr. Samuel Prideaux Tregelles. London, England: Samuel Bagster and Sons, 1847.

Gilbert, Martin. *Kristallnacht: Prelude to Destruction*. New York: Harper Collins, 2006.

Gilder, George. *The Israel Test*. Minneapolis, MN: Richard Vigilante Books, 2009.

Gilman, Sander. *Multiculturalism and the Jews*. New York: Routledge, 2006.

Ginsburgh, Yitzchak. *The Alef-Beit: Jewish Thought Revealed through the Hebrew Letters*. Rechovot, Israel: Gal Einai Institute, 1990.

Ginzburg, Louis. *The Legends of the Jews*, tr. Henrietta Szold. Charleston, SD: BiblioBazaar, 2007.

_____*Rectifying the State of Israel: A Political Platform Based on Kabbalah*. Cedarhurst, NY: Gal Einai Institute, 2003.

Gish, Arthur G. *The New Left and Christian Radicalism* (Grand Rapids, MI: Wm. B. Eerdmans Publishing Co., 1970.

Glasser, Arthur F., Charles E. Van Engen, Dean S. Gilland, and Shawn B. Redford. *Announcing the Kingdom: The Story of God's Mission in the Bible*. Grand Rapids, MI: Baker Academic, 2003.

Gold, Dore. *The Fight for Jerusalem: Radical Islam, the West, and the Future of the Holy City*. Washington, DC: Regnery Publishing, Inc., 2007.

Goldhagen, Daniel Jonah. *Hitler's Willing Executioners: Ordinary Germans and the Holocaust*. New York: Random House, 1996.

_____*The Devil that Never Dies: The Rise and Threat of Global Antisemitism*. New York: Little, Brown and Co., 2013.

Goldin, Shmuel. *Unlocking the Torah Text: Shmot*. Jerusalem, Israel: Gefen Publishing House, 2008.

Goldman, Shalom. *Zeal for Zion: Christians, Jews, & the Idea of the Promised Land*. Chapel Hill, NC: The University of North Carolina Press, 2009.

Goldstein, David. *Jewish Panorama*. Boston, MA: Catholic Campaigners for Christ, 1940.

Goodman, Roberta Louis, and Sherry H. Blumberg, eds. *Teaching About God and Spirituality: A Resource for Jewish Settings*. Denver, CO: A.R.E. Publishing, 2002.

Goodrick-Clark, Nicholas. *The Occult Roots of Nazism: Secret Aryan Cults and Their Influence on Nazi Ideology*. New York: New York University Press, 2004.

Gordis, Daniel. *The Promise of Israel: Why Its Seemingly Greatest Weakness Is Actually Its Greatest Strength*. Hoboken, NJ: John Wiley & Sons, 2012.

Gordon, Evelyn. "Israeli Apartheid? To Arabs, It's a Model Democracy," in *Commentary*, 05.09.2014.

Gordon, Sarah Ann. *Hitler, Germans, and the "Jewish Question."* Princeton, NJ: Princeton University Press, 1984.

Gowan, Donald. *Eschatology in the Old Testament*. New York: T & T Clark International, 1986.

Green, Joel B., Jacqueline Lapsley, Rebekah Miles, and Allen Verhey, eds. *Dictionary of Scripture and Ethics*. Grand Rapids, MI: Baker Academic, 2011.

Gregg, Steve. *All You Want to Know About Hell: Three Christian Views of God's Final Solution to the Problem of Sin*. Nashville, TN: Thomas Nelson, 2013.

Greidanus, Sidney. *Preaching Christ from the Old Testament: A Contemporary Hermeneutical Method*. Grand Rapids MI: Wm. B. Eerdmans Publishing Co., 1999.

Grief, Howard. *The Legal Foundation and Borders of Israel Under International Law: A Treatise on Jewish Sovereignty over the Land of Israel*. Jerusalem, Israel: Mazo Publishers, 2008.

Grubb, Blair P. "Tikkun Olam," in *Jewish Stories from Heaven and Earth: Inspiring Tales to Nourish the Heart*. Woodstock, VT: Jewish Lights Publishing, 2008.

Gunner, Goran, and Robert O. Smith. *Comprehending Christian Zionism: Perspectives in Comparison*. Minneapolis, MN: Augsburg Fortress Press, 2014.

Gurkan, S. Leyla. *The Jews as a Chosen People: Tradition and Transformation*. Abingdon, UK: Routledge, 2009.

Guttman, Nathan, "Presbyterians Divest Themselves from Israel," in *Haaretz*, July 22, 2004.

Haddad, William W., and Mary M. Hardy. "Jordan's Alliance with Israel and its Effects on Jordanian–Arab Relations" in *Israel, the Hashemites, and the Palestinians: The Fateful Triangle*, Efraim Karsh and P. R. Kumaraswam eds. London, UK: Frank Cass Publishers, 2003.

Hahn, Scott. *Kinship by Covenant: A Canonical Approach to the Fulfillment of God's Saving Promises.* New Haven, CT: Yale University Press, 2009.

Hachlili, Rachel. *Ancient Jewish Art and Archaeology in the Land of Israel.* Leiden, The Netherlands: E. J. Brill, 1988.

Halberstan, Itta, and Judith Leventhal. *Small Miracles of the Holocaust: Extraordinary Coincidences of Faith, Hope, and Survival.* Guilford, CT: The Globe Pequot Press.

Haleem, Muhammad Abdel. *Understanding the Qur'an: Themes and Style.* New York: I.B. Tauris & Co., 1999.

Hallward, Maia Carter. *Transnational Activism and the Israeli-Palestinian Conflict.* New York: Palgrave Macmillan, 2013.

Halkin, Hillel. *Yehuda Halevi.* New York: Random House, 2010.

Halpern, Baruch. "Erasing History: The Minimalist Assault on Ancient Israel," in V. Phillips Long, ed., *Israel's Past in Present Research: Essays on Ancient Israelite Historiography.* Winona Lake, IN: Eisenbrauns, Inc., 1999.

Hamerow, Theodore S. *Why We Watched: Europe, America, and the Holocaust.* New York: W. W. Norton & Co., 2008.

Hamid, Tawfiq. *Inside Jihad: How Radical Islam Works, Why It Should Terrify Us, How to Defeat It.* Pembroke, VA: Mountain Lake Press, 2015.

Hammer, Jill. *Sisters at Sinai: New Tales of Biblical Women.* Philadelphia, PA: Jewish Publication Society, 2001.

Hamp, Doug. *Discovering the Language of Jesus: Hebrew or Aramaic?* Santa Ana, CA: Calvary Chapel Publishing, 2005.

Hanna, Kenneth G. *From Moses to Malachi: Surveying the Old Testament.* Bloomington, IN: Lifeway Publishers, 2014.

Harees, Lukman. *The Mirage of Dignity on the Highways of Human 'Progress': The Bystanders' Perspective.* Bloomington, IN: AuthorHouse, 2012.

Harkabi, Yehoshafat. *Arab Attitudes to Israel.* Jerusalem, Israel: Keter Publishing House, 1972.

_____*Palestinians and Israel.* Jerusalem, Israel: Israel Universities Press, 1974.

Harless, Hal. *How Firm a Foundation: The Dispensations in the Light of the Divine Covenants.* New York: Petr Lang Publishing, 2004.

Harris, Sam. *The End of Faith: Religion, Terror, and the Future of Reason.* New York: W. W. Norton & Co., 2004.

Harris, Stephen L., and Robert L. Platzner. *The Old Testament: An Introduction to the Hebrew Bible.* New York: McGraw-Hill, 2003.

Harrison, Bernard. "Anti-Zionism, Antisemitism, and the Rhetorical Manipulation of Reality," in *Resurgent Antisemitism: Global Perspectives*, Alvin H. Rosenfeld, ed. Bloomington, IN: Indiana University Press, 2013.

_____*The Resurgence of Anti-Semitism: Jews, Israel, and Liberal Opinion.* Lanham, MD: Rowman & Littlefield Publishers, 2006.

Hart, Michael B. "Jews and Race: An Introductory Essay," in *Jews and Race: Writings on Identity and Difference, 1880–1940*, Mitchell Bryan Hart, ed. Boston, MA: Brandeis University Press, 2011.

Hartin, Patrick J. *A Spirituality of Perfection: Faith in Action in the Letter of James.* Collegeville, MN: The Liturgical Press, 1999.

Hayes, John Haralson. *Interpreting Ancient Israelite History, Prophecy, and Law*, Brad E. Kelle, ed. Eugene, OR: Wipf and Stock Publishers, 2013.

Haynes, Stephen R. *Reluctant Witnesses: Jews and the Christian Imagination.* Louisville, KY: Westminster John Knox Press, 1995.

Hayward, John. "Egyptian President Al-Sisi Calls for an Islamic Reformation," *Breitbart News*, 9 Jan 2015.

Hazas, Haim. *Hadrashah.* Tel Aviv, Israel: Haim Publishing, 1942.

Hearden, Patrick J. *Architects of Globalism: Building a New World Order During World War Two.* Fayetteville, AR: The University of Arkansas Press, 2002.

Hen-Tov, Jacob. *Communism and Zionism in Palestine: The Comintern and the Political Unrest.* Cambridge, MA: Schenkman Publishing Co., 1974.

Herb, Guntram H., and David H. Kaplan. *Nations and Nationalism: A Global Historical Overview.* Santa Barbara, CA: ABC-CLIO, Inc., 2008.

Herf, Jeffrey. *Anti-Semitism and Anti-Zionism in Historical Perspective: Convergence and Divergence.* New York: Routledge, 2007.

Herman, Chaya. *Prophets and Profits: Managerialism and the Restructuring of Jewish Schools.* Cape Town, South Africa, HSRC Press, 2006.

Herodotus, *Thalia*, 8.

Herrenschmidt, Clarissse. "Writing—and Some Thoughts on Hebrew and Greek," in *Ancestor of the West: Writing, Reasoning, and Religion in Mesopotamia, Elam, and Greece*, Jean Boltéro, Clarisse Harrenschmidt, and Jean-Pierre Dermant, eds., tr. Teresa Lavender Fagan. Chicago, IL: The University of Chicago Press, 2000.

Hertz, J. H. ed. *The Pentateuch and Haftorahs*. London: Soncino Press, 1975.

Heschel, Abraham Joshua. *Between God and Man: An Interpretation of Judaism*, Fritz A. Rothschild, ed. New York: Simon & Schuster, 1959.

_____*God in Search of Man: A Philosophy of Judaism*. New York: Farrar, Straus and Giroux, 1955.

_____*Israel: An Echo of Eternity*. New York: Macmillan, 1967.

_____*Man is Not Alone: A Philosophy of Religion*. New York: Farrar, Straus and Giroux, 1951.

_____*The Sabbath*. New York: Farrar, Straus and Giroux, 1951.

Heschel, Susannah. *Abraham Geiger and the Jewish Jesus*. Chicago, IL: The University of Chicago Press, 1998.

Heyboer, Marvin W. *Journeys into the Heart and Heartland of Islam*. Pittsburgh, PA: Dorrance Publishing Co., 2009.

Hill, Andrew E., and John H. Walton. *A Survey of the Old Testament Introduction*. Grand Rapids, MI: Zondervan Publishing, 1991.

Hippolytus, Romanus. *Treatise on Christ and the AntiChrist* Sn. 54.

Hitler, Adolf. *Mein Kampf*, tr. Ralph Manheim. Boston: Houghton Mifflin, 1971.

Hitti, Phillip K. *History of Syria, Including Lebanon and Palestine*. Piscataway, NJ: Gorgias Press, 2002.

Hoffmeier, James K. *Israel in Sinai: The Evidence for the Authenticity of the Wilderness Tradition*. New York: Oxford University Press, 2005.

Holland, Tom. "When I Questioned the History of Muhammad," *The Wall Street Journal*, January 9, 2015.

Holwerda, David E. *Jesus and Israel: One Covenant or Two?* Grand Rapids, MI: Wm. B. Eerdmans Publishing Co., 1995.

Horak, Stephan M., and Richard Blanke. *Eastern European National Minorities, 1919–1980: A Handbook*. Santa Barbara, CA: Libraries Unlimited, 1985.

Hordern, William. *The Case for a New Reformation Theology*. London, UK: Westminster Press, 1959.

Horovitz, David, ed. *Shalom, Friend: The Life and Legacy of Yitzhak Rabin*. New York: William Morrow, 1996.

Horowitz, David. *The Professors: The 101 Most Dangerous Academics in America*. Washington, DC: Regnery Publishing, 2006.

House, H. Wayne. *Israel: The Land and the People—An Evangelical Affirmation of God's Promises*. Grand Rapids, MI: Kregel Academic, 1998.

Hughes, Aaron W. *Rethinking Jewish Philosophy: Beyond Particularism and Universalism*. New York: Oxford University Press, 2014.

Hughes, Paul. *Finishing History Well*. Maitland, FL: Xulon Press, 2012.

Hughes, Robert B., and J. Carl Laney, *Tyndale Concise Bible Commentary*. Wheaton, IL: Tyndale House Publishers, 1990.

Hunsinger, George. *For the Sake of the World: Karl Barth and the Future of Ecclesial Theology*. Grand Rapids, MI: Wm. B. Eerdmans Publishing Co., 2004.

Hunt, Elgin F., and David C. Colander. *Social Science: An Introduction to the Study of Society*. Boston, MA: Pearson, 2006.

Hutton, Christopher. *Race and the Third Reich: Linguistics, Racial Anthropology, and Genetics in the Dialectic of Volk*. Cambridge, UK: Polity Press, 2005.

Ibn Habib, Jacob ben Solomon. *Ein Yaakov, The Ethical and Inspirational Teachings of the Talmud*, Yaakov ibn Chaviv, ed., Abraham Yaakov Finkel, tr. New York: Jason Aronson, 1999.

Idinopulos, Thomas A. "Zionism and Racism," in *Christian Attitudes on Jews and Judaism*, Issues 40–54. New York: Institute of Jewish Affairs, 1975.

Irenaeus, *Against Heresies* 5.25.4, 28.2, 30.2–4.

Ishaq, Ibn. *Sirat Rasul Allah [The Life of Muhammad]*, tr. Alfred Guillaume. New York: Oxford University Press, 1955.

Ivanski, Dariusz. *The Dynamics of Job's Intercession*. Rome, Italy: Editrice Pontificio Instituto Biblico, 2006.

Jackelén, Antje. *Time & Eternity: The Question of Time in Church, Science and Theology*, tr. Barbara Harshaw. West Conshohocken, PA: Templeton Foundation Press, 2005.

Jacobs, Steven L., ed. *The Holocaust Now: Contemporary Christian and Jewish Thought*. East Rockaway, NY: Cummings & Hathaway Publishers, 1996.

Jacobus, Melancthon Williams. *Notes, Critical and Explanatory, on the Book of Genesis*. New York: Robert Carter & Brothers, 1865.

Janin, Hunt. *Four Paths to Jerusalem: Jewish, Christian, Muslim, and Secular Pilgrimages.* Jefferson, NC: McFarland & Company, Publishers, 2002.

Jarvis Cynthia A., and E. Elizabeth Johnson. *Feasting on the Gospels—Mark.* Louisville, KY: Westminster John Knox Press, 2014.

Jaspal, Rusi. *Antisemitism and Anti-Zionism: Representation, Cognition and Everyday Talk.* Farnham, UK: Ashgate Publishing Limited, 2014.

Jeschke, Marlin. *Rethinking Holy Land: A Study in Salvation Geography.* Harrisonburg, VA: Herald Press, 2005.

Jestice, Phyllis G. *Holy People of the World: A Cross-Cultural Encyclopedia,* Vol. 1. Santa Barbara, CA: ABC-CLIO, Inc., 2004.

Jikeli, Günther. *European Muslim Antisemitism: Why Young Urban Males Say They Don't Like Jews.* Bloomington, IN: The Indiana University Press, 2015.

Johnson, Paul. *A History of the Jews.* London, UK: Orion Press, 1993.

Josephus, Flavius, *Antiquities of the Jews,* 10, 1, 2.

Judis, John B. *Genesis: Truman, American Jews, and the Origins of the Arab/Israeli Conflict.* New York: Macmillan, 2014.

Justin, *First Apology* 52.

Kaiser, Jr., Walter C. *The Old Testament Documents: Are They Reliable & Relevant?* Downers Grove, IL: InterVarsity Press, 2001.

_____*The Christian and the Old Testament.* Pasadena, CA: William Carey Library, 1998.

_____*Toward Rediscovering the Old Testament.* Grand Rapids, MI: Zondervan Publishing, 1987.

Kalman, Aaron. "Abbas Condemns Hamas Head's Statements," *The Times of Israel,* December, 2012.

Kaltner, John. *Ishmael Instructs Isaac: An Introduction to the Qur'an for Bible Readers.* Collegeville, MN: The Liturgical Press, 1999.

Kant, Immanuel. *Grounding for the Metaphysics of Morals,* tr. James W. Ellington. Indianapolis, IN: Hackett, 1981.

Kantor, Máttis. *Codex Judaica: Chronological Index of Jewish History.* New York: Zichron Press, 2005.

Kaplan, Eran, and Derek J. Penslar, eds. *The Origins of Israel, 1882–1948: A Documentary History.* Madison, WI: The University of Wisconsin Press, 2011.

Kaplan, Shmuel. *Beneath the Sheltering Wings.* Bloomington, IN: ExLibris Press, 2011.

Karesh, Sara E., and Mitchell M. Hurvitz, eds. *Encyclopedia of Judaism.* New York: Infobase Publishing, 2006.

Karsh, Efraim, ed. *Israel, The First Hundred Years, Volume I: Israel's Transition from Community to State.* London, UK: Frank Cass Publishers, 2000.

_____"The Middle East's Real Apartheid," in *The Jerusalem Post,* 03/05/2012.

Kasper, Walter. *Transcending All Understanding: The Meaning of Christian Faith Today.* San Francisco, CA: Ignatius Press, 1989.

Katanacho, Yohanna. *The Land of Christ: A Palestinian Cry.* Eugene, OR: Wipf and Stock Publishers, 2013.

Katz, David S. *Philo-Semitism and the Readmission of the Jews to England 1603–1655.* Oxford, UK: Clarendon Press, 1982.

Katz, Morris. *The Journey: A Trip to Eternity.* Victoria, Canada: Trafford Publishing, 2004.

Katz, Samuel. *Battleground—Fact and Fantasy in Palestine.* New York: Bantam Books, 1977.

Katz, Steven T. *The Impact of the Holocaust on Jewish Theology.* New York: New York University Press, 2005.

_____, Shlomo Biderman, and Gershon Greenberg, eds. *Wrestling with God: Jewish Theological Responses during and after the Holocaust.* New York: Oxford University Press, 2007.

Katz, Yaakov. "Hamas Used Kids as Human Shields," in *The Jerusalem Post,* 03/15/2010.

Katzner, Kenneth. *The Languages of the World.* New York: Taylor & Francis Group, 2002.

Kaufman, Michael. *Love, Marriage, and Family in Jewish Law and Tradition.* Northvale, NJ: Jason Aronson, Inc., 1992.

Kazantzakis, Nikos. *Friedrich Nietzsche on the Philosophy of Right and the State.* Albany, New York: The State University of New York Press, 2006.

Keil, Carl Friedrich, and Franz Delitzsch. *The Pentateuch,* vol. 1., tr. James Martin. Edinburgh, Scotland: T & T Clark, 1864.

Keith, Alexander. *The Land of Israel, According to the Covenant with Abraham, with Isaac, and with Jacob.* Edinburgh, Scotland: William Whyte and Co., 1843.

Keithly, David M. *The USA and the World.* Lanham, MD: Rowman & Littlefield Publishers, 2007.

Kenny, Anthony J. *Catholics, Jews, and the State of Israel.* Mahwah, NJ: Paulist Press, 1993.

Kessler, Edward, and Neil Wenborn, eds. *A Dictionary of Jewish-Christian Relations.* Cambridge, UK: Cambridge University Press, 2005.

Khader, Jamal. "Opportunities and Threats for Religions in Conflict and Violence: How (Not) to Use the Name of God," in *Postcolonial Europe in the Crucible of Cultures: Reckoning with God in a World of Conflicts,* Jacques Haers, Norbert Hintersteiner, and Georges de Schrijver, eds. Amsterdam, The Netherlands: Editions Rodopi B.V., 2007.

Khalidi, Rashid. *Palestinian Identity: The Construction of Modern National Consciousness.* New York: Columbia University Press, 1997.

Khamenei, Seyyed Ali. Quoted in "Khamenei: Israel Is a Cancerous Tumor," *Jerusalem World News,* February 3, 2011.

Kidd, Thomas S. *American Christians and Islam: Evangelical Culture and Muslims from the Colonial Period to the Age of Terrorism.* Princeton, NJ: Princeton University Press, 2009.

Kim, Heerak Christian. *Intricately Connected: Biblical Studies, Intertextuality, and Literary Genre.* Lanham, MD: University Press of America, 2008.

Kimmerling, Baruch. "Academic History Caught in the Cross-Fire," in *Postzionism: A Reader,* Laurence Jay Silberstein, ed. New Brunswick, NJ: Rutgers, the State University Press, 2008.

_____ *The Invention and Decline of Israeliness: State, Society, and the Military.* Berkeley, CA: The University of California Press, 2001.

Kippenberg, H. G. "Reading Religious Violence in Terms of Theories of Social Action," in *Control of Violence: Historical and International Perspectives on Violence in Modern Societies,* Wilhelm Heitmeyer, Heinz-Gerhard Haupt, Stefan Malthaner, eds. New York: Springer Science +Business Media, 2011.

Kiracofe, Clifford A. *Dark Crusade: Christian Zionism and US Foreign Policy.* New York: I.B. Tauris & Co., 2009.

Kirk, J. R. Daniel. *Unlocking Romans: Resurrection and the Justification of God.* Grand Rapids, MI: Wm. B. Eerdmans Publishing Co., 2008.

Kirn, Hans-Martin. "Traces of Targum Reception in the Work of Martin Luther," in *A Jewish Targum in a Christian World,* Alberdina Houtman, E. van Staalduine-Sulman, and Hans-Martin Kim, eds. Leiden, The Netherlands: Koninklijke Brill, 2014.

Kistanal, Tamás. "The Holocaust as a Paradigm for Ethical Thinking and Representation," in *Comparative Central European Holocaust Studies,* Louise O. Vasvári and Steven Tötösy de Zepetnek, eds. West Lafayette, IN: Purdue University Press, 2009.

Kitto, John. *The Pictorial Bible: Judges–Job.* London, England: W. and R. Chambers, 1855.

Klappert, Bertold. "An Alternative for Christian Substitution Theology and Christology," in *Humanity at the Limit: The Impact of the Holocaust Experience on Jews and Christians* Michael Alan Signer, ed. Bloomington, IN: Indiana University Press, 2000.

Klein, William. *The New Chosen People: A Corporate View of Election.* Eugene, OR: Wipf and Stock Publishers, 1990.

Klinghoffer, David. "God Is Not a Pluralist," in *The Role of Religion in Politics and Society,* Arthur A. Cohen and Paul Mendes-Flohr, eds. New York: Free Press, 1987.

Klug, Brian. *Being Jewish and Doing Justice.* London, UK: Vallentine Mitchell, 2011.

Knight, George A. F. *Theology as Narration.* Grand Rapids, MI: Wm. B. Eerdmans Publishing Co., 1976.

Knowles, Andrew. *The Bible Guide: An All-in-One Introduction to the Book of Books.* Oxford, UK: Lion Publishing, 2001.

Koestler, Arthur. "A Valedictory Message to the Jewish People (1949)," in Paul R. Mendes-Flohr, and Jehuda Reinharz, eds. *The Jew in the Modern World: A Documentary History.* New York: Oxford University Press, 1980.

Kogan, Barry S. *A Time to Be Born and a Time to Die: The Ethics of Choice.* Hawthorne, NY: Aldine De Gruyter, Inc., 1991.

Kogan, Michael S. *Opening the Covenant: A Jewish Theology of Christianity.* New York: Oxford University Press, 2008.

Kohn, Michael. *Israel & the Palestinian Territories.* Footscray, Australia: Lonely Planet Publications, 2007.

Kolsky, Thomas. *Jews Against Zionism: The American Council for Judaism, 1942–1948.* Philadelphia, PA: Temple University Press, 1990.

Koltun-Fromm, Ken. *Moses Hess and Modern Jewish Identity.* Bloomington, IN: Indiana University Press, 2001.

Konowitz, Israel. *The God Idea in Jewish Tradition.* Jerusalem, Israel: Jerusalem Publishing House, 1989.

Korn, Eugene. *The Jewish Connection to Israel, the Promised Land: A Brief Introduction for Christians.* Woodstock, VT: Jewish Lights Publishing, 2008.

Korn, Yitshak. *Jews at the Crossroads.* New Brunswick, NJ: Rosemont Publishing and Printing Corp., 1983.

Köstenberger, Andreas J. *John.* Grand Rapids, MI: Baker Academic, 2004.

Kovel, Joel. *Overcoming Zionism.* London, UK: Pluto Press, 2007.

Krämer, Gudrun, and Graham Harman. *A History of Palestine: From the Ottoman Conquest to the Founding of the State of Israel*. Princeton, NJ: Princeton University Press, 2008.

Kraut, Alan M., and Richard D. Breitman. "Anti-Semitism in the State Department, 1933–44: Four Case Studies," in *Anti-Semitism in American History*, David A. Gerber, ed. Urbana, IL: The University of Illinois Press, 1986.

Krondorfer, Björn. *Remembrance and Reconciliation: Encounters Between Young Jews and Germans*. New Haven, CT: Yale University Press, 1995.

Kuruvilla, Abraham. *Genesis: A Theological Commentary for Preachers*. Eugene, OR: Wipf and Stock Publishers, 2014.

Kwiet, Konrad, and Jürgen Matthaus. *Contemporary Responses to the Holocaust*. Westport, CT: Greenwood Publishing Group, 2004.

Kwon, Yon-Gyong. *Eschatology in Galatians*. Tübingen, Germany: Mohr Siebeck, 2004.

Lacantius, *Divine Institutes* 7.24–26.

La Guardia, Anton. *War Without End: Israelis, Palestinians, and the Struggle for a Promised Land*. New York: Macmillan, 2003.

LaHaye, Tim F., and Edward E. Hindson, eds. *The Popular Bible Prophecy Commentary: Understanding the Meaning of Every Prophetic Passage*. Eugene, OR: Harvest House Publishers, 2006.

Langmuir, Gavin I. "Continuities, Discontinuities and Contingencies of the Holocaust," in *Studies in Contemporary Jewry: Volume XIII: The Fate of the European Jews*, Jonathan Frankel, ed. New York: Oxford University Press, 1997.

Langworth, Richard. *Churchill by Himself: The Definitive Collection of Quotations*. London, UK: Ebury Press, 2008.

Lantner, Henry L. *What? Again Those Jews!* Jerusalem, Israel: Gefen Publishing House, 1997.

Lanzmann, Claude. "The Obscenity of Understanding: An Evening with Claude Lanzmann," in *American Imago*, vol. 48, no. 4. Winter 1991.

Laor, Emmett. *The Invention of the "Palestinians": 27 Theses They Won't Let You Hear*. Bloomington, IN: Xlibris Corp., 2012.

Lapid, Yair. "Gaza Conflict: Hamas chooses to Let Children Die for Its Own Crazy Ends," *The Telegraph*, July 23, 2014.

Lapidus, Ira M. *A History of Islamic Societies*. Cambridge, UK: Cambridge University Press, 1988.

Laqueur, Walter. *The Changing Face of Antisemitism: From Ancient Times to the Present Day*. Oxford, UK: Oxford University Press, 2006.

_____*The New Terrorism: Fanaticism and the Arms of Mass Destruction*. New York: Oxford University Press, 1999.

Leaves, Nigel. "Who Do You Say that I Am? Preaching Jesus Today," in *Wisdom and Imagination: Religious Progressives and the Search for Meaning*, Rex A. E. Hunt and Gregory C. Jenks, eds. Eugene, OR: Wipf and Stock Publishers, 2014.

Lederhendler, Eli. *Jewish Responses to Modernity: New Voices in America and Eastern Europe*. New York: New York University Press, 1994.

Lee, Chee-Chiew. *The Blessing of Abraham, the Spirit, and Justification in Galatians: Their Relationship and Significance for Understanding Paul's Theology*. Eugene, OR: Wipf and Stock Publishers, 2013.

Lemche, Niels Peter. *Prelude to Irsrael's Past: Background and Beginnings of Israelite History and Identity*. Peabody, MA: Hendrickson Publishers, Inc., 1998.

_____*The Israelites in History and Tradition*. Louisville, KY: Westminster John Knox Press, 1998.

Lerner, Robert E. "Millennialism," in *The Encyclopedia of Apocalypticism*, John J. Collins, Bernard McGinn, and Stephen J. Stein, eds. New York: Continuum Press, 2000.

Leslie, Charles. *A Short and Easy Method with the Jews, Wherein the Certainty of the Christian Religion Is Demonstrated*. Spitalfields, England: 1812.

Levene, Mark. *Genocide in the Age of the Nation State, Volume 2: The Rise of the West and the Coming of Genocide*. (New York: I.B. Tauris & Co., 2005.

Levenson, Jon D. *Resurrection and the Restoration of Israel: The Ultimate Victory of the God of Life*. New Haven, CT: Yale University Press, 2006.

_____"The Universal Horizon of Biblical Particularism," in *Ethnicity and the Bible*, Mark G. Brett, ed. Leiden, The Netherlands: E. J. Brill, 1996.

_____*The Death and Resurrection of the Beloved Son: The Transformation of Child Sacrifice in Judaism and Christianity*. New Haven, CT: Yale University Press, 1993.

Lévinas, Emmanuel. *Difficult Freedom: Essays on Judaism*, tr. Sean Hand. Baltimore, MD: Johns Hopkins University Press, 1990.

_____*In the Time of the Nations*, tr. Michael B. Smith. Bloomington, IN: The Indiana University Press, 1994.

_____Nine Talmudic Readings_, tr. Annette Aronowicz. Bloomington, IN: Indiana University Press, 1990.

_____"Zionisms," in Sean Hand, ed. _The Levinas Reader._ Oxford, UK: Basil Blackwell, 1989.

Levison, John R., and Priscilla Pope-Levison. "The New Contextual Christologies: Liberation and Inculturation," in _Global Dictionary of Theology: A Resource for the Worldwide Church_, William A. Dyrness and Veli-Matti Kärkkäinen, eds. Downers Grove, IL: InterVarsity Press, 2008.

Levy, Richard S. _Antisemitism: A Historical Encyclopedia of Prejudice and Persecution._ Santa Barbara, CA: ABC-CLIO, Inc., 2005.

Licona, Michael. _The Resurrection of Jesus: A New Historiographical Approach._ Downers Grove, IL: InterVarsity Press, 2010.

Lifshitz, Joseph Isaac. "War and Aesthetics in Jewish Law," in _War and Peace in Jewish Tradition: From the Biblical Word to the Present_, Yigal Levin and Amnon Shapira, eds. New York: Routledge, 2012.

Liles, Jr., Mike. _Christian Faith in Contemporary Society: The Framework for Belief._ Lincoln, NE: iUniverse, 2005.

Lillevik, Raymond. _Apostates, Hybrids, or True Jews?: Jewish Christians and Jewish Identity._ Cambridge, UK: James Clarke & Co., 2014.

Lindsay, James E. _Daily Life in the Medieval Islamic World._ Indianapolis, IN: Hackett Publishing Co., 2005.

Lindsay, Mark R. _Barth, Israel, and Jesus: Karl Barth's Theology of Israel._ Burlington, VT: Ashgate Publishing Co., 2007.

Lister, J. Ryan. _The Presence of God: Its Place in the Storyline of Scripture and the Story of Our Lives._ Wheaton, IL: Crossway 2015.

Littell, Franklin. _The Crucifixion of the Jews._ Macon, GA: Mercer University Press, 1986.

Litvak, Meir. _Palestinian Collective Memory and National Identity._ New York: Palgrave Macmillan, 2009.

_____"The Islamic Republic of Iran and the Holocaust: Anti-Semitism and Anti-Zionism," in _Anti-Semitism and Anti-Zionism in Historical Perspective: Convergence and Divergence_, Jeffrey Herf, ed. New York: Routledge, 2007.

Lloyd George, David. _Memoirs of the Peace Conference._ New Haven, CT: Yale University Press, 1939.

Locke, Hubert G. _Learning from History: A Black Christian's Perspective on the Holocaust._ Westport, CT: Greenwood Press, 2000.

Lockyer, Herbert. _All the Divine Names and Titles in the Bible._ Grand Rapids, MI: Zondervan Publishing House, 1988.

_____All the Women of the Bible._ Grand Rapids, MI: Zondervan Publishing Co. 1967.

Lodahl, Michael. _Claiming Abraham: Reading the Bible and the Qur'an Side by Side._ Grand Rapids, MI: Baker Books, 2010.

Logan, F. Donald. _A History of the Church in the Middle Ages._ New York: Routledge, 2013.

Lohfink, Norbert. _The God of Israel and the Nations: Studies in Isaiah and the Psalms._ Collegeville, MN: Liturgical Press, 2000.

Long, V. Phillips, ed. _Israel's Past in Present Research: Essays on Ancient Israelite Historiography._ Winona Lake, IN: Eisenbrauns, Inc., 1999.

Longman III, Tremper. _Old Testament Essentials: Creation, Conquest, Exile, and Return._ Downers Grove, IL: InterVarsity Press, 2014.

_____The Baker Illustrated Bible Dictionary._ Grand Rapids, MI: Baker Academic, 2013.

Lourie, Arthur. "Palestine Under the British Mandate (1918–1948)" in _A History of Israel and the Holy Land_, Michael Avi-Yonan, ed. New York: The Continuum International Publishing Group, 2003.

Lyle, Anthony. _Ancient History: A Revised Chronology._ Bloomington, IN: AuthorHouse, 2012.

Maccoby, Hyam. _Antisemitism and Modernity: Innovation and Continuity._ New York: Routledge, 2006.

Maimonides, Moses. _Guide for the Perplexed_, tr. M. Friedländer. London, England: George Routledge & Sons, 1919.

Mallmann, Klaus-Michael, and Martin Cüppers. _Nazi Palestine: The Plans for the Extermination of the Jews in Palestine_, tr. Krista Smith. New York: Enigma Books, 2010.

MacArthur, John. _MacArthur New Testament Commentary: 2 Corinthians._ Chicago, IL: Moody Publishers, 2003.

MacDonald, David B. _Thinking History, Fighting Evil: Neoconservatives and the Perils of Analogy._ Lanham, MD: Rowman & Littlefield Publishers, 2009.

MacDonald, Nathan, Mark W. Elliott, and Grant Macaskill, _Genesis and Christian Theology._ Grand Rapids, MI: Wm. B. Eerdmans Publishing Co., 2012.

MacIntyre, Alasdair C. _Whose Justice? Which Rationality?_ South Bend, IN: The University of Notre Dame Press, 1989.

Madigan, Kevin J., and Jon D. Levenson. *Resurrection: The Power of God for Christians and Jews*. New Haven, CT: Yale University Press, 2009.

Maghraoui, Abdeslam. "American Foreign Policy and Islamic Renewal," in *Conflict, Identity, and Reform in the Muslim World: Challenges for U.S. Engagement*, Daniel Brumberg and Dina Shehata, eds. Washington, DC: United States Institute of Peace, 2009.

Makovsky, Michael. *Churchill's Promised Land: Zionism and Statecraft*. New Haven, CT: Yale University Press, 2007.

Mangano, Mark. *The College Press NIV Commentary: Esther & Daniel*. Goshen, IN: College Press Publishing Co., 2001.

Manji, Irshad. *The Trouble with Islam: A Muslim's Call for Reform in Her Faith*. New York: St. Martin's Press, 2003.

Mannes, Aaron. *Profiles in Terror: The Guide to Middle East Terrorist Organizations*. Lanham, MD: Rowman & Littlefield Publishers, 2004.

Maoz, Zeev. *Defending the Holy Land*. Ann Arbor, MI: The University of Michigan Press, 2009.

Marcus, Ivan G. *The Jewish Life Cycle: Rites of Passage from Biblical to Modern Times*. Seattle, WA: The University of Washington Press, 2004.

Mare, W. Harold. *The Archaeology of the Jerusalem Area*. Eugene, OR: Wipf and Stock Publishers, 1987.

Marshall, Edgar S. *Israel: Current Issues and Historical Background*. Hauppauge, NY: Nova Science Publishers, 2002.

Marshall, Randall. "Learning from 9/11: Implications for Disaster Research and Public Health," in *9/11: Mental Heath in the Wake of Terrorist Attacks*, Yuval Neria, Raz Gross, and Randall Marshall, eds. Cambridge, UK: Cambridge University Press, 2012.

Martin, Troy W. "Circumcision in Galatia and the Holiness of God's Ecclesiae," in *Holiness and Ecclesiology in the New Testament*, Kent Brower and Andy Johnson, eds. Grand Rapids, MI: Wm. B. Eerdmans Publishing Co., 2007.

Martin, Vincent. *A House Divided: The Parting of the Ways between Synagogue and Church*. Mahwah, NJ: Paulist Press, 1995.

Masalha, Nur. *The Bible and Zionism: Invented Traditions, Archaeology, and Post-Colonialism*. London, UK: Zed Books, 2007.

Matas, David. *Aftershock: Anti-Zionism & Anti-Semitism*. Toronto, Canada: Dundurn Press, 2005.

Mathews, Kenneth A. *The New American Commentary: An Exegetical and Theological Exposition of Holy Scripture: Genesis 11:27–50:26*. Goshen, IN: Broadman & Holman Publishers, 2005.

Mathewson, David. "Abraham, the Father of Many Nations in the Book of Revelation," in *Perspectives on Our Father Abraham: Essays in Honor of Marvin R. Wilson*, Steven A. Hunt, ed. Grand Rapids, MI: Wm. B. Eerdmans Publishing Co., 2014.

Mattar, Philip. *Encyclopedia of the Palestinians*. New York: Facts On File, Inc., 2000.

May, Clifford D. "The Case for Islamic Heresy: Ayaan Hirsi Ali Risks All with Her Call for a Muslim Reformation," *The Washington Times*, April 14, 2015.

Mazur, Yosef. *Zionism, Post-Zionism & the Arab Problem: A Compendium of Opinions About the Jewish State*, Mike Cohen, ed. Bloomington, IN: WestBow Press, 2012.

Mazza, Roberto. *Jerusalem: From the Ottomans to the British*. New York: I.B. Tauris & Co., 2009.

McCann, Jr., J. Clinton. *A Theological Introduction to the Book of Psalms: The Psalms as Torah*. Nashville, TN: Abingdon Press, 1993.

McCulloch, John Ramsay. *A Dictionary, Geographical, Statistical, and Historical*. London, England: Longman, Orme, Brown, Green, and Longmans, 1841.

McKenzie, Steven L. *Covenant*. St. Louis, MO: Chalice Press, 2000.

McLaren, Brian D. *A New Kind of Christian: A Tale of Two Friends on a Spiritual Journey*. San Francisco, CA: John Wiley & Sons, 2001.

Meadors, Edward P. *Creation, Sin, Covenant, and Salvation: A Primer for Biblical Theology*. Eugene, OR: Wipf and Stock Publishers, 2011.

Medzini, Meron. *Israel's Foreign Relations: Selected Documents*. Jerusalem, Israel: Israel Ministry for Foreign Affairs, 1988.

Meir, Golda. *A Land of Our Own: An Oral Autobiography*, Marie Syrkin, ed. New York: G. P. Putnam's Sons, 1973.

Mekhilta R. Ishmael 48:I.20–21; 42: II.1; 43:I.2.

Melcher, Sarah J. "Lacan, the Phallus, and the Construal of Intergenerational Kinship in Genesis–Numbers," in *Relating to the Text: Interdisciplinary and Form-Critical Insights on the Bible*, Timothy Sandoval, Carleen Mandolfo, eds. New York: T & T Clark International, 2003.

Mendels, Doron. *The Rise and Fall of Jewish Nationalism*. Grand Rapids, MI: Wm. B. Eerdmans Publishing Co., 1992.

Merlkey, Paul C. *The Politics of Christian Zionism 1891–1948*. New York: Routledge, 1998.

_____*Christian Attitudes Towards the State of Israel.* Kingston, Canada: McGill-Queen's University Press, 2001.

Merrill, Eugene H. *Everlasting Dominion: A Theology of the Old Testament.* Nashville, TN: Broadman & Holman Publishers, 2006.

_____*The World and the Word: An Introduction to the Old Testament.* Mark F. Rooker, and Michael A. Grisanti, eds. Nashville, TN: B & H Publishing Group, 2001.

Merrill, Selah. "An Archaeological Visit to Jerusalem," in *The Biblical* World, vol. 14, no. 4. Oct., 1899.

Merriman, Scott A. *Religion and the Law in America: An Encyclopedia of Personal Belief and Public Policy.* Santa Barbara, CA: ABC–CLIO, Inc., 2007.

Middleton, J. Richard, and Brian J. Walsh. *Truth Is Stranger Than It Used to Be: Biblical Faith in a Postmodern Age.* Downers Grove, IL: InterVarsity Press, 1995.

Mikaberidze, Alexander. *Atrocities, Massacres, and War Crimes: An Encyclopedia.* Santa Barbara, CA: ABC-CLIO, 2013.

Miles, Jack. *God: A Biography.* New York: Knopf Doubleday Publishing Group, 1995.

Mill, John Stuart. *Considerations on Representative Government.* Chicago, IL: Gateway Publishing, 1962.

Miller, Chaim, ed. *Chumash, with Rashi's Commentary: Exodus.* New York: Kol Menachem, 2005.

Miller, Tricia. *Jews and Anti-Judaism in Esther and the Church.* Cambridge, UK: James Clarke & Co., 2015.

Milner, Larry Stephen. *Hardness of Heart/Hardness of Life: The Stain of Human Infanticide.* Lanham, MD: University Press of America, 2000.

Milton-Edwards, Beverley. *The Israeli-Palestinian Conflict: A People's War.* New York: Routledge, 2009.

Moltmann, Jürgen. *The Crucified God,* tr. R. A. Wilson and John Bowden. New York: Harper & Row, 1974.

Montefiore, C. G., and H. M. J. Loewe, eds. *A Rabbinic Anthology.* Cambridge, UK: Cambridge University Press, 1938.

Moore, Megan Bishop, and Brad E. Kelle, *Biblical History and Israel's Past: The Changing Study of the Bible and History.* Grand Rapids, MI: Wm. B. Eerdmans Publishing Co., 2011.

Morgan, Gregory. "Gaza Strip Disengagement," in *The Encyclopedia of the Arab-Israeli Conflict: A Political, Social, and Military History,* Spencer C. Tucker, ed. Santa Barbara, CA: ABC-CLIO, Inc., 2008.

Morris, Benny. *1948: A History of the First Arab-Israeli War.* New Haven, CT: Yale University Press, 2008.

_____*The Road to Jerusalem: Glubb Pasha, Palestine and the Jews.* London, UK: I.B. Tauris & Co, 2002.

Moses, Isaac S. "The Growth of Ethical Monotheism," in *The Christian Register,* vol. 67, no. 24, June 17, 1886.

Mosse, George L. *Nazi Culture: A Documentary History.* New York: Random House, 1966.

_____"Racism and Nationalism," in *Nationalism: Critical Concepts in Political Science,* John Hutchinson and Anthony D. Smith, eds. New York: Routledge, 2000.

Mounce, Robert H. *The Book of Revelation.* Grand Rapids, MI: Wm. B. Eerdmans Publishing Co., 1977.

Mühling, Markus. *T & T Clark Handbook of Christian Eschatology.* London, UK: Bloomsbury T & T Clark, 2015.

Muir, William. *The Life of Mahomet and History of Islam,* Vol. II. London, England: Smith, Elder, and Co., 1858.

Munayer, Salim J. "Reconciliation as a Christian Response," in *Christians and the Middle East Conflict,* Paul S. Rowe, John H. A. Dyck, and Jens Zimmermann, eds. New York: Routledge, 2014.

Murinson, Alexander. *Turkey's Entente with Israel and Azerbaijan: State Identity and Security in the Middle East and Caucasus.* New York: Routledge, 2010.

Murray, Iain. *The Puritan Hope.* Edinburgh, Scotland: Banner of Truth Publishers, 1971.

Nanos, Mark. *The Mystery of Romans: The Jewish Context of Paul's Letters.* Minneapolis, MN: Augsburg Fortress, 1996.

Nasrallah, Hassan, quoted in "Nasrallah, in Vicious Public Address, Calls for the Destruction of Israel," *The Times of Israel,* August 2, 2015.

Naveh, Joseph. "Hebrew Graffiti from the First Temple Period," in *Israel Exploration Journal,* vol. 51, no. 2.

Nelson, Michael. *Guide to the Presidency.* New York: Routledge, 2015.

Netton, Ian Richard. *A Popular Dictionary of Islam.* New York: Routledge, 1992.

Neufeld, Dietmar. *The Social Sciences and Biblical Translation.* Atlanta, GA: Society of Biblical Literature, 2008.

Neusner, Jacob. *A Theological Commentary to the Midrash, Vol. 9: Mikhilta Attributed to Rabbi Ishmael.* Lanham, MD: University Press of America, 2001.

_____*A Theological Commentary to the Midrash.* Lanham, MD: University Press of America, 2001.

_____*Comparing Religions Through Law: Judaism and Islam.* Routledge, 1999.
_____*Rabbinic Judaism: The Theological System.* Boston, MA: Brill Academic Publishers, 2002.
_____*Scripture and the Generative Premises of the Halakhah: A Systematic Inquiry.* Binghamton, NY: Global Publications, 1999.
_____*The Classics of Judaism: A Textbook and Reader.* Louisville, KY: Westminster John Knox Press, 1995.
_____*The Native Category-Formations of the Aggadah: The Earlier Midrash-Compilations.* Lanham, MD: University Press of America, 2000.
_____*The Theology of the Halakhah.* Leiden, The Netherlands: Koninklijke Brill NV, 2001.
Newman, Carey C. *Jesus & the Restoration of Israel: A Critical Assessment of N. T. Wright's* Jesus and the Victory of God. Downers Grove, IL: InterVarsity Press, 1999.
Nicosia, Francis R. *Zionism and Anti-Semitism in Nazi Germany.* Cambridge, UK: Cambridge University Press, 2008.
Nolan, Albert. *Jesus Before Christianity.* Maryknoll, NY: Orbis Books, 1978.
Noll, K. L. *Canaan and Israel in Antiquity: An Introduction.* New York: Sheffield Academic Press, 2001.
Nomani, Asra Quratulain. *Standing Alone in Mecca: An American Woman's Struggle for the Soul of Islam.* New York: HarperCollins Publishers, 2006.
Nordlinger, Jay. *Peace, They Say: A History of the Nobel Peace Prize, the Most Famous and Controversial Prize in the World.* New York: Encounter Books, 2012.
Norton, James R. *The Holocaust: Jews, Germany, and the National Socialists.* New York: The Rosen Publishing Group, 2008.
Novak, David. *Talking with Christians: Musings of a Jewish Theologian.* Grand Rapids, MI: Wm. B. Eerdmans Publishing Co., 2005.
_____*Zionism and Judaism.* Cambridge, UK: Cambridge University Press, 2015.
Nwachukwu, Mary Sylvia Chinyere. *Creation-Covenant Scheme and Justification by Faith: A Canonical Study of the God-Human Drama in the Pentateuch and the Letter to the Romans.* Rome, Italy: Gregorian University Press, 2002.
Oberman, Heiko. *The Origins of Anti-Semitism in the Age of Renaissance and Reformation,* tr. James I. Porter. Philadelphia, PA: Fortress Press, 1984.
Ochs, Peter. *Another Reformation: Postliberal Christianity and the Jews.* Grand Rapids, MI: Baker Academic, 2011.
O'Daly, Gerard. *Augustine's City of God: A Reader's Guide.* New York: Oxford University Press, 1999.
Oeste, Gordon K. *Legitimacy, Illegitimacy, and the Right to Rule: Windows on Abimelech's Rise and Demise in Judges 9.* London, UK: T & T Clark International, 2011.
Ohana, David. *The Origins of Israeli Mythology: Neither Canaanites Nor Crusaders.* Cambridge, UK: The Cambridge University Press, 2012.
O'Hare, Padraic. *The Enduring Covenant: The Education of Christians and the End of Antisemitism.* Valley Forge, PA: Trinity Press International, 1997.
Oliphant, Laurence. *Haifa: Life in Modern Palestine.* London, England: William Blackwood, 1887.
Olson, Roger E. *The Mosaic of Christian Belief: Twenty Centuries of Unity & Diversity.* Downers Grove, IL: InterVarsity Press, 2002.
Økland, Jorunn. *Women in Their Place: Paul and the Corinthians Discourse of Gender and Sanctuary Space.* London, UK: T & T Clark International.
Orenstein, Walter. *Teach Me about God: The Meaning and Significance of the Name of God.* Lanham, MD: Jason Aronson Publishing 2005.
Origen. *Commentary on the Epistle to the Romans* in *Ancient Christian Commentary on Scripture,* vol. 6., Gerald Bray, ed. Downers Grove, IL: InterVarsity Press, 1998.
_____*The Song of Songs* in *Ancient Christian Writers,* J. Quasten and J.C. Plumpe, eds. Westminster, MD: Newman Press, 1957.
Orlinsky, H. M. "The Biblical Concept of the Land of Israel," in *The Land of Israel: Jewish Perspectives,* L. A. Hoffman, ed. Notre Dame, IN: Notre Dame University Press, 1986.
Packer, J. I. *Keep in Step with the Spirit: Finding Fullness in Our Walk with God.* Grand Rapids, MI: Baker Books, 1984.
Paldiel, Mordecai. *Churches and the Holocaust, Unholy Teaching, Good Samaritans, and Reconciliation.* Jersey City, NJ: KTAV Publishing House, 2006.
Pannenberg, Wolfhart. *Systematic Theology,* vol. 3. Grand Rapids, MI: Wm. B. Eerdmans Publishing Co., 1998.
Pasachoff, Naomi E., and Robert Pittman. *A Concise History of the Jewish People.* Lanham, MD: Rowman & Littlefield Publishers, 1995.
_____*Great Jewish Thinkers: Their Lives and Work.* Springfield, NJ: Behrman House, 1992.
Patai, Raphael, and Jennifer Patai. *The Myth of the Jewish Race.* Detroit, MI: The Wayne State University Press, 1975.

Patterson, Ben. *Waiting: Finding Hope When God Seems Silent.* Downers Grove, IL: InterVarsity Press, 1989.

Patterson, David. *Anti-Semitism and Its Metaphysical Origins.* Cambridge, UK: Cambridge University Press, 2015.

_____*Emil L. Fackenheim: A Jewish Philosopher's Response to the Holocaust.* Syracuse, NY: Syracuse University Press, 2008.

_____*Open Wounds: The Crisis of Jewish Thought in the Aftermath of Auschwitz.* Seattle, WA: The University of Washington Press, 2006.

Pauley, Bruce F. *From Prejudice to Persecution: A History of Austrian Anti-Semitism.* Chapel Hill, NC: The University of North Carolina Press, 1992.

Peleg, Ilan, and Dov Waxman. *Israel's Palestinians: The Conflict Within.* Cambridge, UK: Cambridge University Press, 2011.

Pentecost, J. Dwight. *Things to Come: A Study in Biblical Eschatology.* Grand Rapids, MI: Zondervan Publishing, 1984.

_____, and Kenneth M. Durham, *Faith That Endures: A Practical Commentary on the Book of Hebrews.* Grand Rapids, MI: Kregel Publications, 1992.

Pentiuc, Eugen J. *The Old Testament in Eastern Orthodox Tradition.* New York: Oxford University Press, 2014.

Perusek, David. *Between Jihad and McWorld: Voices of Social Justice.* Cambridge, UK: Cambridge University Press, 2010.

Peters, Joan. *From Time Immemorial: The Origins of the Arab-Jewish Conflict Over Palestine.* Michael Joseph Publishers, 1985.

Phillips, Melanie. "Remember This? Palestinian Arab Propaganda Stages Fake Israeli 'Attacks' for Media," in *The Muslim Issue*, September 28, 2012.

_____*The World Turned Upside Down: The Global Battle over God, Truth, and Power.* New York: Encounter Books, 2010.

Philo, *De Decalogo* 33, *De Praemiis* 2.

Pinnock, Clark H. *The Wideness of God's Mercy: The Finality of Jesus Christ in a World of Religions.* Grand Rapids, MI: Zondervan Publishing House, 1992.

Pipes, Richard. *Russia Under the Bolshevik Regime.* New York: Alfred A. Knopf, 1994.

Pitman, Don A. "Reflections on Religious Pluralism," in *The Theologically Formed Heart: Essays in Honor of David J. Gouwens,* Warner M. Bailey, Lee C. Barrett, and James O Duke, eds., Eugene, OR: Wipf and Stock Publishers, 2014.

Plapp, Laurel. *Zionism and Revolution in European-Jewish Literature.* New York: Routledge, 2008.

Plaut, W. Gunther. *The Growth of Reform Judaism.* New York: World Union for Progressive Judaism, 1965.

_____, and David E. S. Stein, eds. *The Torah: A Modern Commentary.* New York: UJR Press, 2005.

Pogrund, Benjamin. *Drawing Fire: Investigating the Accusations of Apartheid in Israel.* Lanham, MD: Rowman & Littlefield, 2014.

Poliakov, Leon. *The History of Anti-Semitism, Volume One: From the Time of Christ to the Court Jews,* tr. Richard Howard. Philadelphia, PA: The University of Pennsylvania Press, 2003.

Pope, Alexander. *An Essay on Man.* London, England: Thomas Tegg, 1811.

Poythress, Vern S. *The Shadow of Christ in the Law of Moses.* Phillipsburg, NJ: P & R Publishing, 1995.

Prager, Dennis, and Joseph Telushkin. *Nine Questions People Ask About Judaism.* New York: Simon & Schuster, 1975.

_____, and Joseph Telushkin. *Why the Jews? The Reason for Antisemitism.* New York: Simon and Schuster, 1983.

Prescott, Andrew, and Elizabeth M. Hallam, eds. *The British Inheritance: A Treasury of Historic Documents.* Berkeley, CA: The University of California Press, 1999.

Prescott, Deborah Lee. *Imagery from Genesis in Holocaust Memoirs: A Critical Study.* Jefferson, NC : McFarland & Company, Publishers, 2010.

Pressfield, Steven. *The Lion's Gate: On the Front Lines of the Six Day War.* New York: Penguin Group, 2014.

Pressman, Jacob. *Dear Friends: A Prophetic Journey Through Great Events of the 20th Century.* Jersey City, NJ: KTAV Publishing House, 2002.

Price, Randall. *Fast Facts on the Middle East Conflict.* Eugene, OR: Harvest House Publishers, 2003.

Prince, Derek. *The Key to the Middle East: Discovering the Future of Israel in Biblical Prophecy.* Bloomington, MN: Chosen Books, 1982.

Prior, Michael. "Holy Places, Unholy Domination: The Scramble for Jerusalem," in *My Jerusalem: Essays, Reminiscences, and Poems,* Salma Khadra Jayyusi and Safar Ishaq Ansari, eds. Northampton, MA: Olive Branch Press, 2005.

Rakeffet-Rothkoff, Aaron, and Joseph Epstein. *The Rav: The Word of Rabbi Joseph B. Soloveitchik.* Hoboken, NJ: KTAV Publishing House, 1999.

Ramachandra, Vinoth. *Faiths in Conflict? Christian Integrity in a Multicultural World.* Downers Grove, IL: InterVarsity Press, 2000.

_____*The Recovery of Mission: Beyond the Pluralist Paradigm.* Grand Rapids, MI: Wm. B. Eerdmans Publishing Co., 1997.

Ramadan, Tariq. *Radical Reform: Islamic Ethics and Liberation.* New York: Oxford University Press, 2009.

Ramakrishnan, Ram. *Many Paths, One Destination: Love, Peace, Compassion, Tolerance, and Understanding Through World Religions.* Tucson, AZ: Wheatmark Publishing Services, 2009.

Rancour-Laferriere, Daniel. *The Sign of the Cross: From Golgotha to Genocide.* Piscataway, NJ: Transaction Publishers, 2011.

Rashi, *Perush al Hatorah.*

Rausch, David. *Legacy of Hatred: Why Christians Must Not Forget the Holocaust.* Grand Rapids, MI: Baker Publishing Group, 1990.

Rayner, John D. *An Understanding of Judaism.* Oxford, UK: Berghahn Books, 1997.

Reitter, Paul. *The Anti-Journalist: Karl Kraus and Jewish Self-Fashioning in* Fin-de-Siècle *Europe.* Chicago, IL: The University of Chicago Press, 2008.

Rejwan, Nissim. *Israel's Place in the Middle East: A Pluralist Perspective.* Gainesville, FL: The University of Florida Press, 1998.

Reuchlin, Johannsen. *Doctor Johannsen Reuchlins Augenspiegel.* Tübingen, Germany: Thomas Anshelm, 1511.

Rhetorica ad Herennium 4.9.13.

Ribalow, Menahem. *Jewish Education* 22, Summer, 1951.

Ridderbos, Herman N. "The Future of Israel," in *Prophecy in the Making: Messages Prepared for Jerusalem Conference on Biblical Prophecy,* Carl F. H. Henry, ed. Carol Stream, IL: Creation House, 1971.

Rodman, David. *Sword and Shield of Zion: The Israel Air Force in the Arab-Israeli Conflict.* Eastbourne, UK: Sussex Academic Press, 2014.

Rohl, David M. *Pharaohs and Kings: A Biblical Quest.* New York: Crown Publishers, 1995.

Rose, John. *The Myths of Zionism.* London, UK: Pluto Press, 2004.

Rose, Paul Lawrence. *Revolutionary Antisemitism in Germany from Kant to Wagner.* Princeton, NJ: Princeton University Press, 1990.

Rosenfeld, Alvin H. *Anti-Zionism in Great Britain and Beyond: A 'Respectable' Anti-Semitism?* New York: American Jewish Committee, 2004.

_____*"Progressive" Jewish Thought and the new Anti-Semitism.* New York: American Jewish Committee, 2006.

Rosseau, Richard W., ed. *Christianity and Judaism: The Deepening Dialogue,* vol. 3. Montrose, PA: Ridge Row Press, 1983.

Roth, Cecil. "Was Hebrew Ever a Dead Language?" in *Personalities and Events in Jewish History.* Philadelphia, PA: Jewish Publication Society of America, 1953.

Rothenberg, Naftali, and Eliezer Schweid, eds. *Jewish Identity in Modern Israel: Proceedings on Secular Judaism and Democracy.* Jerusalem, Israel: Urim Publications, 2002.

Rothstein, Robert L. *The Israeli-Palestinian Peace Process.* Brighton, UK: Sussex Academic Press, 2002.

Rottenberg, Isaac C. *Christian-Jewish Dialogue: Exploring Our Commonalities and Our Differences.* Atlanta, GA: Hebraic Heritage Press, 2005.

_____"Israelic Christians," in *Restore!,* Issue 52.

_____*Judaism, Christianity, Paganism.* Atlanta, GA: Hebraic Heritage Press, 2007.

Rozett, Robert, and Shmuel Spector, eds. *Encyclopedia of the Holocaust.* Jerusalem, Israel: The Jerusalem Publishing House, 2000.

Rosovsky, Nitza, ed. *City of the Great King: Jerusalem from David to the Present,* Cambridge, MA: Harvard University Press, 1996.

Rubenstein, Richard L. *After Auschwitz: History, Theology, and Contemporary Judaism.* Baltimore, MD: Johns Hopkins University Press, 1992.

_____, and John K. Roth. *Approaches to Auschwitz: The Holocaust and Its Legacy.* Louisville, KY: Westminster John Knox Press, 2003.

_____"The Dean and the Chosen People," in *Wrestling with God: Jewish Theological Responses during and after the Holocaust,* Steven T. Katz, Shlomo Biderman, and Gershon Greenberg, eds. New York: Oxford University Press, 2007.

Rubin, M. "The Language of Creation or the Primordial Language: A Case of Cultural Polemics in Antiquity," in *Journal of Jewish Studies* XLIX, 1998.

Rudin, Arnold James. *Christians & Jews Faith to Faith: Tragic History, Promising Present, Fragile Future.* Woodstock, VT: Jewish Lights Publishing, 2011.

Ruether, Rosemary Radford. *Faith and Fratricide: The Theological Roots of Anti-Semitism.* New York: Seabury Press, 1974.

_____ "The Quest for Peace with Justice in the Middle East: Christian Zionist and Palestinian Theologies," in *Theologies of Liberation in Palestine-Israel: Indigenous, Contextual, and Post-colonial Perspectives,* Nur Masalha and Lisa Isherwood, eds. Eugene, OR: Wipf and Stock Publishers, 2014.

_____, and Herman J. Ruether. *The Wrath of Jonah: The Crisis of Religious Nationalism in the Israeli-Palestinian Conflict.* Minneapolis, MN: Augsburg Fortress, 2002.

Rufin, Jean-Christophe. "Chantier sur la lutte contre le racisme et l'antisémitisme," in *La* Monde, October 19, 2004.

Runes, Dagobert David. *The War against the Jew.* New York: Philosophical Library, 1968.

Rydelnik, Michael. *Understanding the Arab-Israeli Conflict: What the Headlines Haven't Told You.* Chicago, IL: Moody Publishers, 2003.

Rynhold, Jonathan. *The Arab-Israeli Conflict in American Political Culture.* Cambridge, UK: Cambridge University Press, 2015.

Ryrie, Charles C. *A Survey of Bible Doctrine.* Chicago, IL: Moody Publishers, 1972.

Russell, Letty M. *Hagar, Sarah, and Their Children.* Louisville, KY: Westminster John Knox Press, 2006.

Sacks, Jonathan. "How to Defeat Religious Violence," *The Wall Street Journal,* Oct. 2, 2105.

_____ *Future Tense: Jews, Judaism, and Israel in the Twenty-first Century.* New York: Schocken Books, 2009.

Sage, Steven F. *Ibsen and Hitler: The Plagiarist, the Poet, and the Plot for the Third Reich.* New York: Carroll & Graf Publishers, 2006.

Sagi, Avi, and Daniel Statman. *Religion and Morality.* Amsterdam, The Netherlands: Rodopi B.V., 1994.

Sahih Al-Bukhari, vol. 9, book 93, no. 589

Sailhamer, John H. *Biblical Archaeology.* Grand Rapids, MI: Zondervan Publishing, 1998.

Saltman, Roy G. *Sacred Humanism Without Miracles: Responding to the New Atheists.* New York: Palgrave Macmillan, 2012.

Sand, Shlomo. *The Invention of the Land of Israel: From Holy Land to Homeland,* tr. Jeremy Forman. London, UK: Verso Books, 2012.

_____ *The Invention of the Jewish People,* tr. Yale Lotan. London, UK: Verso Books, 2009.

Sanders, John. *No Other Name: An Investigation into the Destiny of the Unevangelized.* Eugene, OR: Wipf & Stock Publishing, 2001.

Sandford, R. Loren. *The Prophetic Church: Wielding the Power to Change the World.* Grand Rapids, MI: Baker Publishing Group, 2009.

Santayana, George. *Reason in Common Sense, Vol. 1: The Life of Reason.* Mineola, NY: Dover Publications, 1980.

Sarna, Nahum M. "Isaac," in Cecil Roth, *et. al.,* eds., *The Encyclopedia Judaica.* Jerusalem, Israel: Keter Publishing House, 1994.

_____ *Understanding Genesis.* New York: Schocken Books, 1970.

Satloff, Robert. *Among the Righteous: Lost Stories from the Holocaust's Long Reach Into Arab Lands.* Philadelphia, PA: Perseus Books Group, 2006.

Schäfer, Peter. *The Origins of Jewish Mysticism.* Tübingen, Germany: Mohr Siebeck, 2009.

Scharfstein, Sol. *The Five Books of Moses.* Jersey City, NJ: KTAV Publishing House, 2005.

Schleifer, Ron, and Jessica Snapper. *Advocating Propaganda—Viewpoints from Israel: Social Media, Public Diplomacy, Foreign Affairs, Military Psychology, and Religious Persuasion Perspectives.* Eastbourne, UK: Sussex Academic Press, 2015.

Schloss, Chaim. *2000 Years of Jewish History: From the Destruction of the Second Bais HaMikdash until the Twentieth Century.* Jerusalem, Israel: Feldheim Publishers, 2002.

Schniedewind, William M. *A Social History of Hebrew: Its Origins Through the Rabbinic Period.* New Haven, CT: Yale University Press, 2013.

Schoeps, Hans-Joachim. *Paul: The Theology of the Apostle in the Light of Religious History,* tr. H. Knight. Philadelphia, PA: Westminster Press, 1961.

Scholem, Gershom G., and R. J. Zwi Werblowsky. *Sabbatai Sevi: The Mystical Messiah, 1626–1676.* Princeton, NJ: Princeton University Press, 1976.

Schönborn, Christoph. *Loving the Church: Spiritual Exercises Preached in the Presence of Pope John Paul II.* San Francisco, CA: Ignatius Press, 1998.

Schreiber, Mordecai. *The Man Who Knew God: Decoding Jeremiah.* Lanham, MD: Rowman & Littlefield Publishers, 2010.

Schwartz, Howard. *Tree of Souls: The Mythology of Judaism.* New York: Oxford University Press, 2004.

Schwartz, Sid. *Judaism and Justice: The Jewish Passion to Repair the World.* Woodstock, VT: Jewish Lights Publishing, 2006.

Schweid, Eliezer. "Is the *Shoah* a Unique Event?" in *Wrestling with God: Jewish Theological Responses during and after the Holocaust*, Steven T. Katz, Shlomo Biderman, and Gershon Greenberg, eds. New York: Oxford University Press, 2007.

_____*The Land of Israel: National Home Or Land of Destiny.* Madison, NJ: Fairleigh Dickinson University Press, 1985.

Seebass, Horst. "בחר *bachar*," in C. J. Botterweck and H. Ringgren, eds., *Theological Dictionary of the Old Testament.* Grand Rapids, MI: Wm. B. Eerdmans Publishing Co., 1975.

Segev, Tom. *The Seventh Million: The Israelis and the Holocaust.* New York: Hill and Wang, 1993.

Shafiq, Muhammad, and Mohammed Abu-Nimer. *Interfaith Dialogue: A Guide for Muslims.* Herndon, VA: The International Institute of Islamic Thought, 2011.

Shapira, Anita. *Israel: A History*, tr. Anthony Berris. London, UK: Weidenfeld and Nicolson, 2014.

Sharan, Shlomo, and Dawid Bûqay. *Crossovers: Anti-Zionism and Anti-Semitism.* Piscataway, NJ: Transaction Publishers, 2010.

Sharif, Regina. *Non-Jewish Zionism, Its Roots in Western History.* London, UK: Zed Books, 1983.

Sharpe, Victor. *Politicide: The Relentless Attempts by the Arab and Muslim World to Destroy the State of Israel.* Raleigh, NC: Lulu Press, Inc., 2011.

Shemer, Ze'ev. *Israel and the Palestinian Nightmare.* Bloomington, IN: iUniverse, 2010.

Shenk, David W. *Journeys of the Muslim Nation and the Christian Church: Exploring the Mission of Two Communities.* Nairobi, Kenya: Uzima Publishing House, 2006.

Shenker, Israel, and Mary Shenker, eds. *As Good as Golda: The Warmth and Wisdom of Israel's Prime Minister.* New York: McCall Publishing Co., 1970.

Sherman, Cecil E. *Formations Commentary: Luke–Acts.* Macon, GA: Smyth & Helwys Publishing, 2006.

Sherwin, Byron L. *Faith Finding Meaning: A Theology of Judaism.* New York: Oxford University Press, 2009.

Shimeall, Richard Cunningham. *The Second Coming of Christ.* New York: Henry S. Goodspeed & Co., 1873.

Shimoni, Gideon. *The Zionist Ideology.* Boston, MA: Brandeis University Press, 1995.

Siegel, Bill. *The Control Faction: Our Struggle to See the True Threat.* Lanham, MD: Hamilton Books, 2012.

Siker, Jeffrey S. *Disinheriting the Jews: Abraham in Early Christian Controversy.* Louisville, KY: Westminster John Knox Press, 1991.

Silberman, Neil Asher, and Israel Finkelstein, *The Bible Unearthed: Archaeology's New Vision of Ancient Israel and the Origin of Its Sacred Texts.* New York: Touchstone, 2001.

Simpson, Patrick Carnegie. *The Fact of Christ: A Series of Lectures.* Grand Rapids, MI: Fleming H. Revell Co, 1901.

Singer, David, ed. *American Jewish Year Book, 1998.* Atlanta, GA: The American Jewish Committee, 1998.

Singer, Isadore. Cyrus Adler, *et. al.*, eds. *The Jewish Encyclopedia: A Descriptive Record of the History, Religion, Literature, and Customs of the Jewish People from the Earliest Times to the Present Day.* New York: Funk and Wagnalls Co., 1907.

Sizer, Stephen. *Christian Zionism: Road Map to Armageddon.* Downers Grove, IL: InterVarsity Press, 2004.

Smith, George Adam. *Jerusalem: The Topography, Economics and History from the Earliest Times to A.D. 70.* Cambridge, UK: Cambridge University Press, 2013.

Smith, Steven B. *Spinoza, Liberalism, and the Question of Jewish Identity.* New Haven, CT: Yale University Press, 1997.

Solomon, Lawrence. "Playing Make-Believe over Gaza," in *The Financial Post*, August 7, 2014.

Soloviev, V. S. *Freedom, Faith, and Dogma: Essays by V. S. Soloviev on Christianity and Judaism.* Albany, NY: The State University of New York Press, 2008.

Sonderegger, Katherine. *That Jesus Christ Was Born a Jew: Karl Barth's Doctrine of Israel.* State College, PA: Pennsylvania State University Press, 1992.

Soshuk, Levi, and Azriel Louis Eisenberg, eds. *Momentous Century: Personal and Eyewitness Accounts of the Rise of the Jewish Homeland and State 1875–1878.* Cranbury, NJ: Cornwall Books, 1984.

Soulen, R. Kendall. *The God of Israel and Christian Theology.* Minneapolis, MN: Augsburg Fortress, 1996.

Spector, Stephen. *Evangelicals and Israel: The Story of American Christian Zionism.* New York: Oxford University Press, 2009.

Spencer, Robert. *Did Muhammed Exist? An Inquiry into Islam's Obscure Origins.* Wilmington, DE: ISI Books, 2012.

_____*The Politically Incorrect Guide to Islam (And the Crusades)*. Washington, DC: Regnery Publishing, Inc., 2005.

Spiegel, Shalom. *Hebrew Reborn*. New York: Meridian Books, 1930.

Sprinkle, Preston M. *Paul and Judaism Revisited: A Study of Divine and Human Agency in Salvation*. Downers Grove, IL: InterVarsity Press, 2013.

St. John, Robert. *Tongue of the Prophets: The Fascinating Biography of Eliezer Ben-Yehuda, the Father of Modern Hebrew*. Beverly Hills, CA: Wilshire Book Co., 1972.

Stalder, Will. *Palestinian Christians and the Old Testament History, Hermeneutics, and Ideology*. Minneapolis, MN: Augsburg Fortress Publishers, 2015.

Stanley, Christopher D. *The Hebrew Bible: A Comparative Approach*. Minneapolis, MN: Fortress Press, 2010.

Stark, Rodney. *One True God: Historical Consequences of Monotheism*. Princeton, NJ: Princeton University Press, 2001.

Stavans, Anat. "Challenges Faced by a Medium-Sized Language Community in the 21st Century: The Case of Hebrew," in *Survival and Development of Language Communities: Prospects and Challenges*, F. Xavier Vila, ed. Bristol, UK: Multilingual Matters, 2013.

Steinberg, Paul. *Celebrating the Jewish Year: The Spring and Summer Holidays: Passover, The Omer, Shavuot, Tisha b'Av*, Janet Greenstein Potter, ed. Philadelphia, PA: The Jewish Publication Society, 2009.

Steinbock, Steven E. *Torah: The Growing Gift*. New York: Union for Reform Judaism Books, 1993.

Steiner, George. *Errata: An Examined Life*. London, UK: Weidenfeld and Nicolson, 1997.

Stemplowski, Ryszard. *Transnational Terrorism in the World System Perspective*. Warsaw, Poland: Polish Institute of International Affairs, 2002.

Stephenson, Hunter W. *Forecasting Opportunity: Kaziros, Production, and Writing*. Lanham, MD: University Press of America, 2005.

Stroud, Dean Garrett, ed. *Preaching in Hitler's Shadow: Sermons of Resistance in the Third Reich*. Grand Rapids, MI: Wm. B. Eerdmans Publishing Co., 2013.

Strong, James. *Strong's Exhaustive Concordance to the Bible*. Peabody, MA: Hendrickson Publishers, 2007.

Strunk, Gary. *As He Is*. Ringgold, GA: Teach Services Publishing, 2012.

Sutton, Matthew Avery. *American Apocalypse: A History of Modern Evangelicalism*. Cambridge, MA: Harvard University Press, 2014.

Suzuki, Norio. "The Problem of Peace and World Order in an Islamic Context: The Cast of Modern Japan," in *Peace Movements and Pacifism After September 11*, Shin Chiba and Thomas J. Schoenbaum, eds. Cheltenham, UK: Edward Elgar Publishing, 2008.

Swedenburg, Ted. *Memories of Revolt: The 1936–1939 Rebellion and the Palestinian National Past*. Fayetteville, AR: The University of Arkansas Press, 2003.

Taha, Abir. *Nietzsche, Prophet of Nazism: The Cult of the Superman*. Bloomington, IN: AuthorHouse, 2005.

Tal, Alon. "Combating Desertification: Evolving Perceptions and Strategies," in *Between Ruin and Restoration: An Environmental History of Israel*, Daniel E. Orenstein, Alon Tal, and Char Miller, eds. Pittsburgh, PA: The University of Pittsburgh Press, 2013.

_____*Pollution in a Promised Land: An Environmental History of Israel*. Berkeley, CA: The University of California Press, 2002.

Tal, Uriel. "Totalitarian Democratic Hermeneutics and Policies in Modern Jewish Religious Nationalism,"in *Totalitarian Democracy and After*, Yehoshua Arieli and Nathan Rotenstreich, eds. London, UK: Frank Cass Publishers, 2002.

Talmon, Shemaryahu. "'The Dead Sea Scrolls' or 'The Community of the Renewed Covenant,'" in *The Echoes of Many Texts: Reflections on Jewish and Christian Traditions*, W. G. Dever and J. E. Wright, eds. Atlanta, GA: Scholars Press, 1997.

Taylor, Bayard. *The Lands of the Saracen*. Alexandria, Egypt: The Library of Alexandria, 1854.

Taylor, Joan E. *The Essenes, the Scrolls, and the Dead Sea*. New York: Oxford University Press, 2012.

Telushkin, Joseph. *The Book of Jewish Values*. New York: Bell Tower Publishing, 2000.

ten Boom, Corrie. *The Hiding Place*, Elizabeth Sherrill and John Sherrill, eds. Grand Rapids, MI: Baker Publishing Group, 1971.

Teplinsky, Sandra. *Why Care about Israel? How the Jewish Nation Is the Key to Unleashing God's Blessings in the 21st Century*. Grand Rapids, MI: Baker Publishing Group, 2004.

Tertullian, *Adversus Judaeos*, 10.

_____*Against Marcion*, 5.9.

_____*On Modesty* 8.

Tessler, Mark A. *A History of the Israeli-Palestinian Conflict*. Bloomington, IN: Indiana University Press, 1994.

Tewareson, Heidi Thomann. "Jews among Christians in Germany," in Encyclopedia of Diasporas: Immigrant and Refuge Cultures Around the World, Melvin Ember, Carol R. Ember, and Ian Skoggard, eds. New York: Springer Science+Business Media, Inc., 2005.

The Official Gazette, No. 1 of the 5th, Iyar, 5708 (14th May, 1948).

Thirgood, J. V. Man and the Mediterranean Forest. London, England: 1880.

Thomas, Reuen. Divine Sovereignty. Boston, MA: D. Lothrop & Company, 1885.

Thomas, W. H. Griffith. "The Lord's Coming and the Supreme Theme of the Bible," in The Christian Workers Magazine, Charles Force Deems, John Bancroft Devins, and Amory Howe Bradford, eds., vol. XX, no. 1, September, 1919.

Thompson, Thomas L. Early History of the Israelite People. Leiden, The Netherlands: Koninklijke Brill, 1992.

_____The Historicity of the Patriarchal Narratives. London: T & T Clark, 2002.

_____The Mythic Past: Biblical Archaeology and the Myth of Israel. New York: Basic Books, 1999.

Tiegreen, Chris. 90 Days Thru the Bible: A Devotional Journey from Walk Thru the Bible. Wheaton, IL: Tyndale House Publishers, 2012.

Tierney, Patrick. The Highest Altar: The Story of Human Sacrifice. New York: Viking Press, 1989.

Tiessen, Terrance L. Who Can Be Saved? Reassessing Salvation in Christ and World Religions. Downers Grove, IL: InterVarsity Press, 2004.

Tilley, Virginia. The One-State Solution: A Breakthrough for Peace in the Israeli-Palestinian Deadlock. Ann Arbor, MI: The University of Michigan Press, 2005.

Tobin, Gary A., and Dennis R. Ybarr. The Trouble with Textbooks: Distorting History and Religion. Lanham, MD: Rowman & Littlefield Publishers, 2008.

Tolan, Sandy. Children of the Stone: The Power of Music in a Hard Land. New York: Bloomsbury Publishing, 2015.

Topper, David R. Idolatry and Infinity: Of Art, Math, and God. Boca Raton, FL: Universal Publishers, 2014.

Torrance, Alan J. "On Deriving 'Ought' from 'Is'," in The Doctrine of God and Theological Ethics, Michael C. Banner and Alan J. Torrance, eds. New York: T & T Clark, 2006.

Torrance, David W. The Witness of the Jews to God, vol. 1. Edinburgh, UK: Handsel Press, 1982.

Torrance, Thomas F. "Salvation Is of the Jews," Evangelical Quarterly 22, 1950.

_____The Mediation of Christ. Grand Rapids, MI: Wm. B. Eerdmans Publishing Co., 1984.

Totten, Samuel. Teaching about Genocide: Issues, Approaches and Resources. Charlotte, NC: Information Age Publishing, Inc., 2004.

Towner, W. Sibley "Exodus 20:1–17, Exegetical Perspective," in Feasting on the Word: Lent through Eastertide, David Lyon Bartlett and Barbara Brown Taylor, eds. Louisville, KY: Westminster John Knox Press, 2008.

Trepp, Leo. Judaism: Development and Life. Belmont, CA: Dickenson Publishing Co., 1966.

Troy, Gil. Monihan's Moment: America's Fight Against Zionism as Racism. New York: Oxford University Press, 2013.

Truesdale, Al, with Keri Mitchell. With Cords of Love: A Wesleyan Response to Religious Pluralism. Kansas City, MO: Beacon Hill Press, 2013.

Tuchman, Shera Aranoff, and Sandra E. Rapoport. The Passions of the Matriarchs. Jersey City, NJ: KTAV Publishing House, 2004.

Turner, Alan. Is God Finished with Israel? Maitland, FL: Xulon Press, 2008.

Twain, Mark. The Innocents Abroad: The New Pilgrims' Progress. Hartford, CT: The American Publishing Co., 1869.

Ucko, Hans. The People and the People of God: Minjung and Dalit Theology in Interaction. Hamburg, Germany: Lit Verlag Münster, 2002.

Umen, Samuel. Jewish Concepts and Reflections. New York: Philosophical Library, 1962.

van Beeck, Frans Josef. God Encountered: A Contemporary Catholic Systematic Theology Vol. Two/2: The Revelation of the Glory: Part II: One God, Creator of All That Is. Collegeville, MN: The Liturgical Press, 1996.

van Buren, Paul M. A Theology of the Jewish-Christian Reality: A Christian Theology of the People of Israel. Lanham, MD: University Press of America, 1995.

Van Seters, John. Abraham in History and Tradition. Brattleboro, VT: Echo Point Books & Media, 2014.

_____Prologue to History. New Haven, CT: The Yale University Press, 1992.

Vander Laan, Ray. With All Your Heart. Grand Rapids, MI: Zondervan Publishing, 2010.

VanDrunen, David. Divine Covenants and Moral Order: A Biblical Theology of Natural Law. Grand Rapids, MI: Wm. B. Eerdmans Publishing Co., 2014.

Verete, Mayir. "The Restoration of the Jews in English Protestant Thought, 1790-1840," in Middle Eastern Studies, vol. 8, no. 1, 1972.

Verlin Jerome R., and Lee S. Bender. *Pressing Israel: Media Bias Exposed from A–Z*. Philadelphia, PA: Pavilion Press, 2012.

Vermes, Geza. *Jesus and the Word of Judaism*. London, UK: SCM Press, 1983.

_____"Redemption and Genesis xxii—The Binding of Isaac and the Sacrifice of Jesus," in *Scripture and Tradition in Judaism: Haggadic Studies*. Leiden, The Netherlands: Brill, 1983.

_____*The Changing Faces of Jesus*. New York, Penguin Books, 2000.

Vermeulen, Pieter. "The Novel Form and the Timing of the Nation," in *See Under: Shoah: Imagining the Holocaust with David Grossman*, Marc De Kesel, Bettine Giertsmea, and Katarzyna Szurmiak, eds. Leiden, The Netherlands: Koninklijke Brill NV, 2014.

Vlach, Michael J. *Has the Church Replaced Israel? A Theological Evaluation*. Nashville, TN: B & H Publishing Group, 2010.

_____*The People, the Land, and the Future of Israel: Israel and the Jewish People*. Grand Rapids, MI: Kregel Publications, 2014.

Volf, Judith M. Gundry. *Paul & Perseverance: Staying in and Falling Away*. Louisville, KY: Westminster John Knox Press, 1990.

Volfson, Mosheh. *Wellsprings of Faith: Perspectives on the Sources of Emunah*. Jerusalem, Israel: Feldheim Publishers, 2002.

von Orelli, Conrad. *Die hebräischen Synonyma der Zeit und Ewigkeit genetisch und sprachvergleichend dargestellt*. Leipzig, Germany: 1871; republished Ithaca, NY: Cornell University Library, 2009.

Waagenaar, Sam. *The Pope's Jews*. Chicago, IL: Open Court Pub. Co., 1974.

Wagner, Matthew. "Israel's Only Crematorium To Re-open," *The Jerusalem Post*, 10/28/2007.

Waithe, Mary Ellen, ed. *Ancient Women Philosophers: 600 B.C.–500 A.D.* Dordrecht, The Netherlands: Martinus Nijhoff Publishers, 1987.

Waldman, Nahum M. *The Recent Study of Hebrew: A Survey of the Literature with Selected Bibliography*. Winona Lake, IN: Eisenbrauns, Inc., 1989.

Wall, Gregory. "Man Is the Land," in *John Paul II and the Jewish People: A Jewish-Christian Dialogue*, David G. Dalin and Matthew Severing, eds. Lanham, MD: Rowman & Littlefield Publishers, 2008.

Wallace, Cynthia D. *Foundations of the International Legal Rights of the Jewish People and the State of Israel and Implications for the Proposed Palestinian State*. Lake Mary, FL: Creation House, 2012.

Walker, Peter. "Summarizing the Points of Dispute," in *The Land Cries Out: Theology of the Land in the Israeli-Palestinian Context*, Salim J. Munayer and Lisa Loden, eds. Eugene, OR: Wipf and Stock Publishers, 2011.

Waltke, Bruce K. *The Dance Between God and Humanity: Reading the Bible Today As the People of God*. Grand Rapids, MI: Wm. B. Eerdmans Publishing Co., 2013.

Walvoord, John. *The Millennial Kingdom: A Basic Text in Premillennial Theology*. Grand Rapids, MI: Zondervan Publishing, 1983.

Watson, Richard. *An Exposition of the Gospels of St. Matthew and St. Mark and Some Other Detached Parts of Holy Scripture*. London, UK: John Mason, 1833.

Weaver, Alain Epp. *Mapping Exile and Return: Palestinian Dispossession and Political Theology*. Minneapolis, MN: Augsburg Fortress Publishers, 2014.

Wegner, J. R. "Islamic and Talmudic Jurisprudence: The Four Roots of Islamic Law and their Talmudic Counterparts," *American Journal of Legal History* 26 (1982).

Wei, James. *Great Inventions that Changed the World*. Hoboken, NJ: John Wiley & Sons, 2012.

Weidner, Revere Franklin. *Biblical Theology of the Old Testament*. Philadelphia, PA: H. B. Garner, 1886.

Weikart, Richard. *From Darwin to Hitler: Evolutionary Ethics, Eugenics, and Racism in Germany*. New York: Palgrave Macmillan, 2004.

_____*Hitler's Ethic: The Nazi Pursuit of Evolutionary Progress*. New York: Palgrave Macmillan, 2009.

Wein, Berel. *Patterns in Jewish History: Insights into the Past, Present, and Future of the Eternal People*. Jerusalem, Israel: Koren Publishers, 2011.

Weinthal, Benjamin. "Why Europe Blames Israel for the Holocaust: Post-1945 Anti-Semitism," in *The Jerusalem Post*, 01/28/2014.

Weir, Alison. "Christian Evangelicals Increasingly Support Palestinian Human Rights," in *CounterPunch*, September 29, 2014.

Weissman, Moshe, ed., *The Midrash Says*. Brooklyn, NY: Bnay Yakov Publications, 1980.

Weizmann, Chaim. *Trial and Error: The Autobiography of Chaim Weizmann*. Westport, CT: Greenwood Publishing Group, 1972.

Wellhausen, Julius Ferminger. *Prolegomena to the History of Israel*, tr. J. Sutherland Black and Allan Menzies. Edinburgh, Scotland: Adam and Charles Black, 1885.

Wellman, Christopher Heath. *Liberal Rights and Responsibilities: Essays on Citizenship and Sovereignty.* New York: Oxford University Press, 2014.

Wenham, Gordon J. "The Akedah: A Paradigm of Sacrifice," in *Pomegranates and Golden Bells: Studies in Biblical, Jewish, and Near Eastern Ritual, Law, and Literature in Honor of Jacob Milgrom,* David P. Wright, David Noel Freedman, and Avi Hurvitz, eds. Winona Lake, IN: Eisenbrauns Publishers, 1995.

_____*Story as Torah: Reading Old Testament Narrative Ethically.* Grand Rapids, MI: Baker Academic, 2000.

_____*World Biblical Commentary: Genesis 16–50,* vol. 2. Nashville, TN: Word Publishing, 1994.

Wenkel, David. "Palestinians, Jebusites, and Evangelicals," in *Middle East Quarterly,* Summer 2007.

White, Ben. *Israeli Apartheid: A Beginners Guide.* London, UK: Pluto Press, 2009.

Whitelam, Keith. *The Invention of Ancient Israel.* Abingdon, UK: Routledge, 1996.

Wiedmer, Caroline Alice. *The Claims of Memory: Representations of the Holocaust in Contemporary Germany and France.* Ithaca, NY: Cornell University Press, 1999.

Wiersbe, Warren. *The Wiersbe Bible Commentary: Old Testament.* Colorado Springs, CO: David C. Cook Publishing, 2007.

Wilber, Ken. *The Eye of Spirit: An Integral Vision for a World Gone Slightly Mad.* Boston, MA: Shambhala Publications, Inc., 2001.

Wilcox, Howard D. *Divine Providence.* Bloomington, IN: Life Way Publishers, 2011.

Williams, Paul R. "The Spirit of Amalek," in *Restore!,* Issue 25.

Williams, Peter. *Israel and the Covenants in New Testament Times.* Dundee, UK: Paragon Publishing, 2012.

Williamson, Clark M. *A Guest in the House of Israel: Post-Holocaust Church Theology.* Louisville, KY: Westminster John Knox Press, 1993.

Williamson, Paul R. *Abraham, Israel and the Nations: The Patriarchal Promise and Its Covenantal Development in Genesis.* Sheffield, UK: Sheffield Academic Press, 2000.

Willis, Ellen. *Beginning to See the Light: Sex, Hope, and Rock-and-Roll.* Minneapolis, MN: The University of Minnesota Press, 2013.

Wilken, Robert L. "Christian Pilgrimage to the Holy Land," in *City of the Great King: Jerusalem from David to the Present,* Nitza Rosovsky, ed. Cambridge, MA: Harvard University Press, 1996.

Wilkinson, Robert J. *Tetragrammaton: Western Christians and the Hebrew Name of God.* Leiden, The Netherlands: Koninklijke Brill, 2015.

Wilson, Marvin R. *Exploring Our Hebraic Heritage: A Christian Theology of Roots and Renewal.* Grand Rapids, MI: Wm. B. Eerdmans Publishing Co., 2014.

_____*Our Father Abraham: Jewish Roots of the Christian Faith.* Grand Rapids, MI: Wm. B. Eerdmans Publishing Co., 1989.

Wilson, Mary Christian. *King Abdullah, Britain and the Making of Jordan.* Cambridge, UK: Cambridge University Press, 1987.

Wine, Sherwin T. *A Provocative People: A Secular History of the Jews.* Farmington Hills, MI: International Institute for Secular Humanistic Judaism, 2012.

Wistrich, Robert S. *From Ambivalence to Betrayal: The Left, the Jews, and Israel.* Lincoln, NE: The University of Nebraska Press, 2012.

_____"Gaza, Hamas, and the Return of Antisemitism," in *The Israel Journal of Foreign Affairs,* July, 2014.

_____*Lethal Obsession: Anti-Semitism from Antiquity to the Global Jihad.* New York: Random House, 2010.

Witham, Larry. *The God Biographers: Our Changing Image of God from Job to the Present.* Lanham, MD: Rowman & Littlefield Publishers, 2010.

Wolf, Alex. *The Arab-Israeli War Since 1948.* Chicago, IL: Capstone Global Library, 2012.

Wolfson, Ron. *Relational Judaism: Using the Power of Relationships to Transform the Jewish Community.* Woodstock, VT: Jewish Lights Publishing, 2013.

Wood, David. "My Place in the Sun," in *Interpreting Nature: The Emerging Field of Environmental Hermeneutics,* Forrest Clingerman, Brian Treanor, Martin Drenthen, and David Utsler, eds. Bronx, NY: Fordham University Press, 2014.

Wortsman, Peter. "Introduction," in Johann Reuchlin, *Recommendation Whether to Confiscate, Destroy, and Burn All Jewish Books,* Peter Wortsman, tr. and ed. Mahwah, NJ: Paulist Press, 2000.

Wrede, William. *Paul,* tr. E. Lummis. London, England: Green & Hull, 1907.

Wright, J. H. *God's People in God's Land: Family, Land and Property in the Old Testament.* Carlisle, UK: Paternoster Press, 1997.

Wright, Nicholas T. *Paul for Everyone: Romans.* Louisville, KY: Westminster John Knox Press, 2004.

Wright, Christopher J. H. *The God I Don't Understand: Reflections on Tough Questions of Faith.* Grand Rapids, MI: Zondervan Publishing, 2008.

Wylen, Stephen M. *Settings of Silver: An Introduction to Judaism.* Mahwah, NJ: Paulist Press, 2000.
Wyman, David S. *The Abandonment of the Jews: America and the Holocaust, 1941–1945.* New York: The New Press, 1998.
Wynbrandt, James. *A Brief History of Saudi Arabia.* New York: Infobase Publishing, 2004.
Wyschogrod, Michael. *Abraham's Promise.* Grand Rapids, MI: Wm. B. Eerdmans Publishing Co., 2004.
Yaakov Ein. The Ethical and Inspirational Teachings of the Talmud. New York: Jason Aronson, 1999.
Yehoshua, A. B. "Who Is a Jew?" in *Contemplate 3,* 2005–2006.
Ye'or, Bat. *Islam and Dhimmitude: Where Civilizations Collide.* Cranbury, NJ: Associated University Presses, 2002.
Yitzhak, Ronen. *Abdullah Al-Tall, Arab Legion Officer: Arab Nationalism and Opposition to the Hashemite Regime.* Eastbourne, UK: Sussex Academic Press, 2012.
Younan, Munib. *Witnessing for Peace: In Jerusalem and the World.* Minneapolis, MN: Augsburg Fortress Press, 2003.
Young, Brad H. *Paul the Jewish Theologian.* Peabody, MA: Hendrickson Publishing, 1997.
Youngblood, Ronald. *The Book of Genesis: An Introductory Commentary.* Grand Rapids, MI: Baker Book House, 1991.
Zakim, Leonard P. *Confronting Anti-semitism: A Practical Guide.* Hoboken, NJ: KTAV Publishing House, 2000.
Zander, Walter. *Israel and the Holy Places of Christendom.* London: Weidenfeld & Nicolson, 1991.
Zaslow, David. *Jesus: First-Century Rabbi.* Brewster, MA: Paraclete Press, 2014.
Zeitlin, Irving M. *The Historical Muhammad.* Cambridge, UK: Polity Press, 2007.
Zephyr, Alexander. *State of Israel: Its Friends and Enemies: Prophetic Future.* Bloomington, IN: iUniverse, 2013.
Zetterholm, Karin Hedner. *Jewish Interpretation of the Bible: Ancient and Contemporary.* Minneapolis, MN: Augsburg Fortress Press, 2012.
Zick, Andreas. "Anti-Semitism," in *Encyclopedia of Group Processes and Intergroup Relations,* John M. Levine and Michael A. Hogg, eds. Thousand Oaks, CA: SAGE Publications, Inc., 2010.
Zucker, David J., and Moshe Reiss. *The Matriarchs of Genesis: Seven Women, Five Views.* Eugene, OR: Wipf and Stock Publishers, 2015.
_____*The Torah: An Introduction for Christians and Jews.* Mahwah, NJ: Paulist Press, 2005.
Zuckerman, Bruce, and Zev Garber. *The Impact of the Holocaust in America.* West Lafayette, IN: Purdue University Press, 2008.
Zweig, Ferdynand. *Israel: The Sword and the Harp: The Mystique of Violence and the Mystique of Redemption; Controversial Themes in Israeli Society.* Cranbury, NJ: Associated University Presses, 1969.

GENERAL INDEX

GOLDEN key PRESS

Featuring the Informative, Inspiring Books of
Dr. John D. Garr

Our Lost Legacy: Restoring Christianity's Hebrew Foundations is a provocative, inspiring primer on the Jewish roots of the Christian faith. This volume presents selected essays in which Dr. John D. Garr urges the church to recover its Hebrew heritage. These pages call Christians back to the Bible, to the roots of faith and understanding of their Hebrew Lord.

240 pages, ISBN 0-96782797-2-2.

God and Women: Woman in God's Image and Likeness is a comprehensive, scholarly examination of the way in which God created woman in order to mirror the divine image and likeness. These pages will take you back to the beginning when God created male and female and then made them one, coequal, consubstantial, and complementary.

320 pages, ISBN 978-0-9794514-4-7.

Coequal and Counterbalanced: God's Blueprint for Women and Men is an in-depth analysis of God's creation of humanity with a focus on the coequality of male and female that makes it possible for men and women to live counterbalanced and complementary lives of loving mutuality and respect. These pages will give you new insight about female and male relationships.

368 pages, ISBN 978-0-9794514-9-2.

Feminine by Design: The God-Fashioned Woman is an exhaustive study of the manner in which God designed woman in the beginning of time with all the unique qualities, characteristics, preferences, and predilections that made the woman uniquely feminine and provided the means by which every woman can achieve self-fulfillment.

368 pages, ISBN 978-0-9794514-5-4.

Blessings for Family and Friends provides you with solid information about God's blessing system and with demonstrations and examples of blessings that you can pronounce over your family and friends for all occasions. This is a spectacular gift book that you will want to keep for yourself. Amazing blessings await you in this inspiring book.

160 pages, ISBN 978-0-9794514-3-0.

The Hem of His Garment: Touching the Power in God's Word discusses the context of the woman who was healed when she touched the hem of Jesus' garment. You will simply be amazed at the great impact that the ancient Jewish tradition of attaching fringes to the four corners of their mantles had upon the lives of biblical people, including this woman.

160 pages, ISBN 0-96782797-0-6.

Living Emblems: Ancient Symbols of Faith will help you understand the biblical symbols that were designed by God and by his people Israel. Each emblem is full of rich insight that points to the person and work of the Messiah, Jesus. Recognizing these spiritual truths is a profound means of underscoring the truth of Christianity's Jewish connection.

160 pages, ISBN 096782797-1-4.

God's Lamp, Man's Light: Mysteries of the Menorah is a masterful analysis of the menorah, the only biblical symbol that has the distinction of being designed by God himself. As you read this book, you will be amazed at the wealth of insight that has been hidden from the historical church because of its separation from Judaism and things Jewish.

160 pages, ISBN 0-9678279-4-9.

Family Worship: Making Your Home a House of God is a provocative look at the modern home that offers clear answers for families in crisis and for those who want to restore their families to biblical foundations. Reading this book will be a life-changing experience for you and for your family as you learn to adopt a biblical family lifestyle by doing what Bible teaches about family.

240 pages, ISBN 978-0-9794514-7-8.

Bless You! Restoring the Power of Biblical Blessing is a systematic, comprehensive study of the biblically Hebraic concept of blessing and the impact that it has had in the lives of believers from ancient times until today. This powerful dynamic of biblical faith can now be experienced in every Christian home. As you read this, you will recover a key part of the faith of Jesus and the apostles.

160 pages, ISBN 096782797-7-3.

Passover: The Festival of Redemption helps Christians understand the biblical festival that is part of their heritage, celebrating the Exodus and Calvary. With this exciting resource, you can celebrate Passover just as Jesus and the disciples did at the Last Supper. And you can remember the Lord's death as he commanded at the time when he died.

160 pages, ISBN 978-0-9794514-6-1.

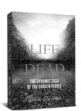

Life from the Dead: The Dynamic Saga of the Chosen People examines the sweep of history to discover the amazing divine protection that has been upon the children of Abraham in order to preserve them through constant threat of extinction and to establish them as the people of God. This volume demonstrates unequivocally the resurrection power of God in everyday life.

380 pages, ISBN 978-1-940685-20-5.

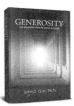

Generosity: The Righteous Path to Divine Blessing is a study of the Hebraic foundations of biblical giving with a view to understanding why believers should tithe and give of their means. It is only through the Hebraic model of generosity that people can find the amazing blessings that God has promised to those who obey him and his precepts for living.

304 pages, ISBN 978-1-940685-20-5.

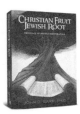

Christian Fruit: Jewish Root: Theology of Hebraic Restoration is an in-depth study of the foundational principles of Christian faith which reveals the Jewish roots of each principle from the Hebrew Scriptures and from the teachings of Second Temple Judaism. This volume provides solid academic insight into the biblical foundations of the Christian faith.

416 pages, ISBN 978-1-940685-27-4.

Golden Key Press
P.O. Box 421218
Atlanta, Georgia 30342, U.S.A.
www.GoldenKeyPress.org

P.O. Box 421218
Atlanta, Georgia 30342, U.S.A.
www.GoldenKeyPress.org